P9-ARH-481

INTERNATIONAL
TERRORISM AND
POLITICAL CRIMES

Ghandi and Mahmoud Bassiouni
Birla House—India
March 18, 1939

Conference on Terrorism and Political Crimes,
3d., Syracuse, Sicily, 1973.

INTERNATIONAL TERRORISM AND POLITICAL CRIMES

Edited By

M. CHERIF BASSIOUNI,

LL.B., J.D., LL.M., J.S.D.

Professor of Law

De Paul University

Chicago, Illinois

CHARLES C THOMAS · PUBLISHER

Springfield · Illinois · U.S.A.

341.77
C7482

Published and Distributed Throughout the World by
CHARLES C THOMAS • PUBLISHER
BANNERSTONE HOUSE
301-327 East Lawrence Avenue, Springfield, Illinois, U.S.A.

This book is protected by copyright. No part of it may be reproduced in any manner without written permission from the publisher.

© 1975, by CHARLES C THOMAS • PUBLISHER
ISBN 0-398-03257-2 cloth 0-398-03296-3 paper
Library of Congress Catalog Card Number: 74 12120

With THOMAS BOOKS *careful attention is given to all details of manufacturing and design. It is the Publisher's desire to present books that are satisfactory as to their physical qualities and artistic possibilities and appropriate for their particular use.* THOMAS BOOKS *will be true to those laws of quality that assure a good name and good will.*

Printed in the United States of America
N-1

Library of Congress Cataloging in Publication Data

Conference on Terrorism and Political Crimes, 3d,
    Siracuse, Sicily, 1973.
    International terrorism and political crimes.

    "Sponsored by the International Institute for
Advanced Criminal Sciences."
    Bibliography: p.
    1. International offenses.   2. Terrorism.
3. Political crimes and offenses. I. Bassiouni, M.
Cherif, 1936-   ed. II. International Institute for
Advanced Criminal Sciences. III. Title.
LAW   341.77   74-12120
ISBN 0-398-03257-2
ISBN 0-398-03296-3 (pbk.)

TO

MAHMOUD BASSIOUNI

IN MEMORIAM

Born in Assiut, Egypt in 1868 he died in 1944 after serving with rare distinction in many important positions. His career began as a practicing lawyer specializing in Criminal Law, but he soon became an activist politician. In 1919 he led upper Egypt in the first Egyptian revolt against Britain's occupation of his country since that colonial régime was established in 1881. He was arrested and tried by a British High Military Tribunal and charged with 14 counts of assorted crimes against the British crown and its domination of Egypt; each count carried the death penalty. The Military tribunal found him guilty and sentenced him to death. On appeal to the Privy Council the conviction was reversed on the grounds that no witness had testified against him in open court concerning any of the charges. Nonetheless in 1922 he was exiled temporarily to the Western desert in the Maharick Camp because of his continued peaceful militance against British domination. In 1923, the Egyptian independence movement, spearheaded by the Wafd party under the leadership of Saad Zagloul, had succeeded in its efforts, and Egypt became Nominally, an independent state. Egypt's first constitution was adopted and Mahmoud Bassiouni was one of its drafters. He was then elected to the first senate in Egypt's history, and thereafter reelected until his death in 1944. He served as Vice President of the Senate from 1923 to 1936, and thereafter as its President.

A distinguished lawyer, he was elected President of the Bar Association four consecutive times and served the profession in that capacity for over 17 years until his death. A popular leader, who epitomized the highest calling of the legal profession throughout his life, he was a symbol of personal courage and in-

v

N.C. WESLEYAN COLLEGE LIBRARY 70427

tegrity. Always dedicated to peace and human rights, he counted among his friends such other activist pacifists as Ghandi.

A hero to his people, a terrorist to their oppressors, he never engaged in violence, but was an apostle of peaceful resistance. To this man, my grandfather, whose inspiration has lead me to the same commitment, I dedicate this modest effort, which in part highlights the dilemma of peaceful evolution and violent revolution. To the late Mahmoud Bassiouni, only the observance of the Rule of Law and the preservation of human rights could mediate between human enmities, and thus right and not might was the only alternative to violence.

PREFACE

THE CONTRIBUTIONS TO THIS VOLUME came primarily from papers presented at the III International Symposium sponsored by the International Institute for Advanced Criminal Sciences, (Siracuse-Italy). The Symposium which was organized and chaired by this writer benefited from the participation of several world renown experts whose names follow:

PARTICIPANTS IN THE CONFERENCE ON TERRORISM AND POLITICAL CRIMES (JUNE 4-16, 1973)

ANTONIO PECORARO ALBANI
Professor of Criminal Law
The University of Naples
Naples, Italy

M. CHERIF BASSIOUNI
Secretary-General
International Penal Law Association
Professor of Law
DePaul University
Chicago, Illinois, USA

RICHARD R. BAXTER
Professor of Law
Harvard University
Cambridge, Massachusetts, USA

IMRE BEKES
Associate Professor of Criminal Law
The University of Budapest
Budapest, Hungary

ANTONIO BERISTAIN
Professor of Criminal Law
The University of San Sebastian
San Sebastian, Spain

PIERRE BOUZAT
President
International Penal Law Association
Dean Emeritus and Professor
of Criminal Law
The University of Rennes
Rennes, France

J. Y. DAUTRICOURT
President
Criminal Court of Brussels
Brussels, Belgium

BART B. DeSCHUTTER
Professor of International Law
Director of Graduate International
Law Studies
The Free University of Brussels
Brussels, Belgium

BLANCA MARIN-DIAZ
Judge, Trial Court
San Luis, Argentina

YORAM DINSTEIN
Professor of International Law
The University of Tel Aviv
Tel Aviv, Israel

NICHOLAS KITTRIE
Professor of Law
American University
College of Law
Washington, D.C., USA

RICARDO ABARCA LANDERO
Section Chief
Ministry of Foreign Affairs
Mexico City, Mexico

ANDREW LEE
Dean and Professor of Criminal Law
Soochow University
Taiwan, Republic of China

GEORGE LeVASSEUR
Professor of Criminal Law
The University of Paris
Paris, France

SALLY MALLISON
Research Associate
George Washington University
Washington, D.C., USA

W. T. MALLISON, JR.
Professor of Law
Director of International Legal
Studies
George Washington University
Washington, D.C., USA

STEPHEN MARKS
Attorney at Law
Rene Cassin Institute of Human
Rights
Strasbourg, France

MARIO MIELE
Professor of International Law
The University of Macerata
Marcerata, Italy

JOHN F. MURPHY
Professor of Law
The University of Kansas
Lawrence, Kansas, USA

FRANK C. NEWMAN
Professor of Law
The University of California
Berkeley, California, USA

PAUL O'HIGGINS
Professor of Law
Christ College
Cambridge University
Cambridge, England

BRUCE PALMER
Attorney at Law
United States Treasury Department
Washington, D.C., U.S.A.

PIERO PARADISO
Professor of Criminology
The University of Messina
Messina, Italy

FRANCO SALOMONE
Il Tempo di Roma
Rome, Italy

MARINO BARBERO SANTOS
Professor of Criminal Law
The University of Valladolid
Valladolid, Spain

GALAL SARWAT
Professor of Criminal Law
The University of Alexandria
Alexandria, Egypt

G. O. SEGOND
Legal Advisor
Canton of Geneva
Geneva, Switzerland

ALAN SEWELL
Assistant Professor of Psychology
DePaul University
Chicago, Illinois, USA

GEORGE SLIWOWSKI
Professor of Criminal Law
The University of Tarun
Tarun, Poland

ALFONSO M. STILE
Associate Professor of Criminal Law
The University of Urbino
Urbino, Italy

JACOB SUNDBERG
Professor of Jurisprudence
The University of Stockholm
Stockholm, Sweden

JIRI TOMAN
Director of Research
Henry-Dunant Institute
Geneva, Switzerland

OTTO TRIFFTERER
Professor of Criminal Law
The University of Giesen
Giesen, Germany

KAREL VASAK
Secretary-General
Rene Cassin Institute of Human
Rights
Strasbourg, France

MICHEL VEUTHEY
Legal Advisor
International Commission of
The Red Cross
Geneva, Switzerland

THEO VOGLER
Professor of Criminal Law
The University of Berlin
Berlin, Germany

BOGDAN ZLATARIC
Dean Emeritus
Professor of Criminal Law
The University of Zagreb
Zagreb, Yugoslavia

L. KOS-RABCEWICZ-ZUBKOWSKI
Professor of Criminology
The University of Ottawa
Ottawa, Canada

The Conferees discussed various questions relating to terrorism from June 4 to June 16, 1972, often for up to eight hours a day. This was one of the most intense and productive international conferences to have ever been held on the subject. One of the interesting features of this conference was the interaction of penalists, publicists and social scientists from twenty-two different countries who represented all political ideologies and juridical trends. The debates were serious explorations of geniunely different points of view, but they were always friendly and in a cooperative spirit. These concerned and responsible scholars pursued their work in a realistic sense which enabled them to reach substantial conclusions. The conferees colloborated in small working groups to present certain conclusions and recommendations which were then drafted into a "Final Document," and follows this Preface. This document contains the ideas discussed at the conference as well as specific recommendations which deserve the careful attention of scholars, decision makers and all persons interested in a rational regulation of this coercive process. Considering the diversity of the group which contributed to this document, it attests to the very real possibility of scholarly cooperation in the development of International Criminal Law. This writer is grateful to all Conferees for the privilege of having worked with them and for being part of their efforts.

In addition to the conference papers all relevant reaties and documents have appended where appropriate and additional contributions were added to complement and enhance this book.

ALONA E. EVANS, (Ph.D.)
Professor of Law and Political Science
Wellesley College
Wellesley, Massachusetts, U.S.A.

LEWIS HOFFACKER
Ambassador, Special Assistant to the
Secretary of State for International
Control of Terrorism
Department of State
Washington, D.C., U.S.A.

JOHN HUBBARD, (M.D.)
Director, The Aberrant Behavior
Center
Dallas, Texas, U.S.A.

LUIS KUTNER
Attorney at Law
Chairman, International Commission
on Due Process of Law
Chicago, Illinois, U.S.A.

KATHLEEN LAHEY
Instructor in Law
Osgood Hall
York University
Toronto, Canada

SLOAN T. LETMAN
Assistant Professor of Sociology
Loyola University
Chicago, Illinois, U.S.A.

JAMES MURPHY
Attorney at Law
Chicago, Illinois, U.S.A.

JOHN NOVOGRAD
Attorney at Law
New York, N.Y., U.S.A.

LEWIS SANG
Attorney at Law
Chicago, Illinois, U.S.A.

NINA STRICKLER, (Ph.D.)
Instructor in Philosophy
DePaul University
Chicago, Illinois, U.S.A.

Lewis Sang and Kathleen Lahey graciously assisted me in some of the editorial tasks involved in the preparation of this book.

M. C. Bassiouni

FINAL DOCUMENT: CONCLUSIONS AND RECOMMENDATIONS*

I. GENERAL PART

1. The problem of the prevention and suppression of "terrorism" arises in part because there is no clear understanding of the causes leading to conduct constituting "terrorism." The International Community has been unable to arrive at a universally accepted definition of "terrorism" and has so far failed to control such activity.

2. Acts commonly referred to as "terrorism" are often done under the claim that they are intended to uphold human rights, but paradoxically, they also usually violate human rights by endangering the personal safety, fundamental freedoms and property of persons uninvolved in the original violation allegedly sought to be redressed. Acts of terror, both governmental and private, are prohibited by many international human rights documents presently or soon expected to be in force, including the United Nations Charter, the Universal Declaration of Human Rights, the International Covenant on Economic, Social and Cultural Rights, the International Covenant on Civil and Political Rights, the Convention on the Prevention and Punishment of the Crime of Genocide, the International Convention on the Elimination of All Forms of Racial Discrimination, the European Convention for the Protection of Human Rights and Fundamental Freedoms, the American Convention on Human

---

*This document embodies the various ideas, positions, conclusions and recommendations of the Conference participants. It contains the contributions of all conferees and was drafted by Professor M. C. Bassiouni with assistance from Professors George Levasseur (Paris), Bogdan Zlataric (Zagreb), Jacob Sundberg (Stockholm), John Murphy (Kansas) and Mr. Stephen Marks (Strasbourg) which is gratefully acknowledged.

Rights, the Nuremberg principles and the 1949 Geneva Conventions.

3. These texts are admirable statements of international law, but by themselves do not assure that human rights will be protected in the absence of implementation and enforcement. It must therefore be recognized that failure to implement and enforce human rights breeds terror. It is therefore acknowledged that whenever states engage in serious and repeated violations of fundamental human rights, especially those involving strategies of violence and terror, this is likely to breed individual terrorism.

4. The Universal Declaration of Human Rights reminds us that "it is essential, if man is not to be compelled to have recourse, as a last resort, to rebellion against tyranny and oppression, that human rights should be protected by the rule of law." We must, however, distinguish between legitimate rebellion and indiscriminate terror tactics. The resort to violence by individuals or groups engaging in wars of national liberation is lawful whenever it remains within the confines of international law which recognize such activities. It is when acts of violence are committed indiscriminately, disproportionately and contain an international element or are against internationally protected targets that such acts become terrorism.

5. Article 30 of the Universal Declaration of Human Rights specifies that "[n]othing in this Declaration may be interpreted as implying for any State, group or person any right to engage in any activity or to perform any act aimed at the destruction of any of the rights and freedoms set forth herein." This provision and its equivalent in Article 5 of both the International Covenant on Economic, Social and Cultural Rights and the International Covenant on Civil and Political Rights, Article 17 of the [European] Convention for the Protection of Human Rights and Fundamental Freedoms and Article 29 (a) of the American Convention on Human Rights amount to a condemnation of both individual and state terrorism. Consequently, there can be no contextual excep-

tions drawn between individual actors or state agents who engage in conduct defined as "terrorism." The law must apply equally to all.

6. Recognizing that no one group of scholars can exhaustively study all forms of terror violence, the focus of this Conference and the subject of its proposals and recommendations relate essentially to individual forms of international terrorism.

7. The methodology pursued has been to define certain conduct containing an "international element" or directed against "internationally protected targets" in order to place certain targets and arenas outside the scope of "strategies of terror violence." The proposed doctrine of "internationally protected targets" is intended to neutralize such objectives and unequivocally prohibit the use of certain coercive conduct against them. In so doing, this removes these targets from the purview of any conflict, insuring thereby to some extent a reduction in the level of applied violence.

8. Acts committed by agents of a state, which fall within the definition of terrorism as stated below, subject such persons to the same criminal responsibility as other individuals without the benefit of the act of state doctrine, the defense of obedience to superior orders and international immunities of otherwise applicable.

9. After defining terrorism and discussing its elements and application, certain proposals are made in the "Special Part." These include, *inter alia:* 1) to require states to prosecute persons who violate these proscriptions, or 2) in the alternative, to extradite such persons, or 3) in the alternative, in the event an international criminal court exists, to surrender such persons thereto, 4) to vest all states with universal jurisdiction to prosecute such offenders; 5) to hold states responsible for failure to undertake such obligations whenever they induce, encourage or harbor such persons. In view of the need for worldwide cooperation in this area, a multilateral treaty on terrorism is recommended as well as the creation of an International Criminal Court.

10. DEFINITION OF TERRORISM

Individual or collective coercive conduct employing strategies of terror violence which contain an international element or are directed against an internationally protected target and whose aim is to produce a power-oriented outcome. Such conduct contains an international element when:

1) the perpetrator and victim are citizens of different states or
2) the conduct is performed in whole or in part in more than one state.

Internationally protected targets are:

1) innocent civilians;
2) duly accredited diplomats and personnel of international organizations acting within the scope of their functions;
3) international civil aviation;
4) the mail and other means of international communications; and
5) members of nonbelligerent armed forces.

A power oriented-outcome is: an outcome which is aimed at changing or preserving the political, social or economic structures or policies of a given state or territory by means of coercive strategies.

II. SPECIAL PART

The following are specific areas which, because of their importance, are dealt with explicitly.

1. Terrorism and the Role of the Mass Media

1. The problem of sensational press reports concerning terrorism, which encourage and promote future terrorism, suggests that the mass media has the responsibility of exercising restraint in this regard.
2. Recognizing the basic human rights to free speech and freedom of information, and condemning any attempts at censorship, it is nonetheless necessary that the mass media establish guidelines and procedures for reports on terrorism and violence.

3. Consideration should be given by the mass media to the establishment of a press council or council of editors, representing all forms of mass media, which would meet periodically to regulate this problem. (Such a procedure is presently employed in certain countries.)

2. Terrorism in Armed Conflicts

1. The customary law of armed conflicts and the Geneva Conventions of 1949 prohibit acts of terrorism.
2. Because of the limited scope of the IVth Geneva Convention for the Protection of Civilian Populations, particularly concerning protected persons in the territory of the parties to a conflict and in occupied territories, it is necessary to enlarge the application of the convention and to extend the prohibition against acts of terrorism so as to protect all civilian populations.
3. Regarding conflicts not of an international character, though the Geneva Conventions do prohibit in Article 3 several forms of terrorism, improvements are necessary in the substance and implementation of rules on such conflicts.
4. For these reasons the recent efforts of the 1971 and 1972 Conferences of Governmental Experts for the Reaffirmation and Development of Humanitarian Law are commended.
5. Furthermore, the Draft Additional Protocol to Article 3, which prohibits acts of terrorism in noninternational conflicts, is recommended for adoption at the next Diplomatic Conference of 1974, and for ratification by all states.
6. It is also recommended that governments and other interested organizations take all necessary and appropriate measures for the dissemination of information on the humanitarian law of armed conflict.

3. Terrorism and Wars of National Liberation

1. Self-determination is a right recognized by international law.
2. The exercise of this right may result, *inter alia,* in:
    1) the political independence of a people, or
    2) various forms of political association.

3. When the right of self-determination results in various forms of political association, every group is entitled to the preservation of its ethnic and cultural identity.

4. Recognizing that in many instances the right of self-determination is not implemented and, as a result, various groups have resorted to the use of force in order to exercise this right, we recommend that present international procedures for conflict resolution be improved and that the existing machinery of negotiation, inquiry, mediation, conciliation, arbitration and the advisory and contentious jurisdiction of the International Court of Justice, including the jurisdiction to decide cases *ex aequo et bono,* be more fully utilized.

5. In the event of the use of violence, all parties to the conflict are obligated to confine the use of violence so as to avoid injury to uninvolved states and their nationals.

6. At all times, the parties to the conflict must apply international humanitarian law, specifically the four Geneva Conventions of 1949, the Genocide Convention of 1948, the Hague codification of the customary rules of war and the Nuremberg principles. Recognizing that there is disagreement as to the definition of "peoples," "minorities," and "ethnic groups," and as to the methods of implementing the right of self-determination, we, therefore, recommend that the United Nations establish a special committee for the study of this problem and make appropriate recommendations.

4. Aircraft Hijacking

1. International civil aviation is a vital link between nations and peoples of the world and consequently it is of paramount importance that its activities be unimpaired.

2. International civil aviation must be considered neutral with respect to all types of conflicts.

3. International recognition of this principle is manifested in the 1963 Tokyo Convention, the 1970 Hague Convention and the 1971 Montreal Convention.

4. All signatory states are urged to ratify these conventions and are called upon to enforce their provisions.

5. Nonsignatory States are urged to accede to these conventions at the earliest opportunity.
6. An international conference should be convened with the view to propose a multilateral convention on implementing existing conventions such as: established principles of State responsibility and other appropriate sanctions against States who, by their consistent conduct, encourage violations and refuse to take any measures to cooperate in the world community's effort to prevent unlawful seizures of aircrafts and other crimes against international civil aviation.

5. Kidnapping of Diplomatic Personnel and Other Persons

1. The frequency of kidnappings in some countries has reached an alarming level.
2. Such conduct threatens international diplomacy, economic stability and relations, in some cases the sovereignty and territorial integrity of states and, in all cases, it destroys or threatens the life and physical integrity of individuals.
3. In order to protect diplomats and personnel of international organizations within the scope of their functions, civilians uninvolved in a conflict situation and members of the armed forces, public agents and officials of uninvolved states, such persons must be deemed "protected targets" and attacks upon them must be prohibited.
4. Whenever such acts fall within the definition of terrorism as stated above they are to be considered international crimes.
5. All persons who engage in such prohibited conduct are to be held responsible whether they are acting in their individual capacity or as agents of a state.
6. States who encourage, entice, induce or protect individuals who engage in such conduct are to be held responsible under international law principles of state responsibility.
7. We recommend that appropriate sanctions be established in the form of a multilateral convention imposing upon States the obligation to extradite or effectively prosecute and punish the perpetrators of such acts.

8. We also recommend that States take immediate steps including, *inter alia*, convening an international conference to determine appropriate collective action against States who by their consistent conduct, encourage or condone such acts and refuse to take any measures to cooperate in the world community's effort to prevent and suppress them.

6. Creation of an International Criminal Court

1. The proposal to create such a court reaffirms a lengthy history on the subject, support for which has been expressed by distinguished jurists since the end of World War I, and was manifested in the 1937 Convention on the Prevention and Punishment of Terrorism and the two draft conventions elaborated by United Nations Committees in 1951 and 1953.

2. It is recommended once again that such a court be established with jurisdiction over international crimes and in particular over acts falling within the definition of terrorism.

3. A draft statute for such court should be elaborated at the earliest opportunity, taking into consideration several existing proposals and in particular the proposed 1953 United Nations draft. Such a statute should also include questions of enforcement and sanctions.

4. The court should exercise its jurisdiction over persons and corporate entities but not over states, since questions involving states are within the jurisdiction of the International Court of Justice.

5. The proposed International Criminal Court could be created by the United Nations or be an organ thereof, as in the case of the International Court of Justice, or be independently created and operate as an autonomous international body. The realization of such a proposal could be by virtue of:
   a) a single multilateral treaty-statute;
   b) multilateral treaties on this and other subjects;
   c) bilateral treaties;
   d) amending protocols to existing international conventions;
   e) unilateral declarations;

f) enactment of national legislation; or,

g) voluntary submission to the jurisdiction of such Court or any other special arrangement.

7. Jurisdiction and Extradition

1. Insofar as it has been established that terrorism is an international crime, any such offender should be effectively prosecuted and punished or extradited to a requesting state. This position embodies the maxim *aut dedere aut iudicare*.

2. Extradition to a requesting state should be granted in the absence of prosecution by the requested state unless an international criminal court is created with jurisdiction over such matters, in which case the accused should be surrendered to the court's jurisdiction.

3. All states should be vested with universal jurisdiction with respect to crimes of terrorism.

4. Whenever a state other than the state in which the act of terrorism was committed seeks to prosecute a terrorist, a reasonable number of observers from interested states and international organizations should be allowed to see the evidence and attend all proceedings.

5. Whenever extradition is contemplated the ideological motives of the accused should not be the sole basis for the granting of asylum or for denying the extradition request.

6. Whenever an act of terrorism as defined herein is committed, or whenever other international crimes, i.e. crimes against humanity, grave breaches of the Geneva Conventions, or serious violation of fundamental human rights are committed, extradition should be granted regardless of the ideological motives of the actor.

7. In all other cases in which the political offense exception shall apply, the judge or other person making the decision must, *inter alia*, weigh the harm committed against the values sought to be preserved by the actor and the means employed in relationship to the goal pursued in light of the proportionality theory.

8. In the event of multiple extradition requests for the same

offender, priority should be given to the requesting state relying on territorial jurisdiction in its request, followed by the
state relying on the theory of protecting fundamental national
interests.

9. The rights of the individual in extradition proceedings must
always be upheld and he or she should not be precluded from
raising any defenses available under extradition law and
other relevant aspects of national and international law.

10. Extradition should not be granted when the individual
sought is to be tried by an exceptional tribunal or under a
procedure patently violative of fundamental human rights.
In such cases, however, the requested state must, prosecute the
accused.

11. To avoid that requesting states resort to means other than
extradition to secure a person, extradition procedures should
be expedited but without sacrificing the protections afforded
to the individuals. Furthermore, to ensure against unlawful
seizure of persons, requested states who do not wish to extradite such an offender must prosecute them without unnecessary delay.

12. In order to ensure adequate administration of justice, judges,
public officials and lawyers should be familiar with international criminal law and comparative law and those public
officials directly involved should be specialists in the subject
matter. Furthermore, it is recommended that special educational programs be established in legal institutions and other
institutions of learning in the subject of international criminal law.

8. Treatment of Political Offenders and Nondelinquent Detainees

1. Among the aims of Criminal Law are deterence, prevention
and the resocialization of offenders, but these can seldom be
achieved with respect to ideologically motivated offenders. It
is therefore recommended that studies be undertaken concerning such offenders and that programs suited to them during imprisonment and the use of alternative measures of in-

capacitation or social defense oriented programs be developed.
2. Consideration should be given to the establishment of a uniform standard of penalties imposed on terrorists in different countries in order to eliminate significant disparities.
3. All offenders must be treated without discrimination and in accordance with international human rights protections, as enunciated in the Universal Declaration of Human Rights, the International Covenant for the Protection of Civil and Political Rights and, specifically, the United Nations Standard Minimum Rules for the Treatment of Offenders.
4. Political offenders and nondelinquent detainees are persons deprived of their liberty without having been accused, prosecuted or convicted of penal offenses arising out of national or international law. Such persons should not be treated by lesser standards than other offenders and should at least benefit from the protections and standards stated in paragraph 3 above.

9. Terrorism and Human Rights

1. Legitimate resistance to oppression and tyranny is an internationally recognized right as a "last resort" when political and juridical avenues of redress have been exhausted. This does not justify, however, indiscriminate, disproportionate and unlawful use of violence or terrorism as defined in paragraph 10. Such matters must be adjudicated preferably by an international body taking into account all factors underlying such acts for purposes of mitigation and aggravation.
2. While international human rights law is fully consistent with the vigorous prosecution of terrorism (as defined herein), international controls must, however, observe, *inter alia,* the following guidelines:
   a) Norms of international human rights law must not be infringed;
   b) Norms of international human rights law such as minimum standards of fairness and justice must be observed and references should be made to specific provisions in human rights conventions;

c) Accused terrorists like all other offenders should be treated at all times in accordance with human rights standards;

d) Condemnation of terrorism should not give rise to over-reaction, which becomes the basis for infringement of the human rights of other persons; and,

e) The condemnation of terror and terrorism must be evenhanded and apply to all of its forms and manifestations.

10. Education and Information

1. The general and special parts of this document indicate the need for general and specific information and education in various areas concerning the causes, prevention, control and suppression of terrorism.

2. It is therefore recommended that the United Nations and its specialized agencies and policy makers in the informational and educational fields develop programs to increase public knowledge in the areas discussed in this document. It is particularly recommended that human rights, international criminal law and conflict resolution become the subjects of universal attention.

3. A special recommendation is made to all institutions of legal learning to provide in their curricula courses on human rights, international criminal law and conflict resolution.

4. Furthermore, scholars and experts in these fields and related disciplines should meet frequently to discuss and clarify international legal norms and disseminate their findings to the general public through all available means.

CONTENTS

Page

Dedication v

Preface vii

Final Document: Conclusions and Recommendations xi

CHAPTER I
PERSPECTIVES ON THE ORIGINS AND CAUSES OF TERRORISM

Section

1. THE ORIGINS AND FUNDAMENTAL CAUSES OF TERRORISM 5

2. POLITICAL CRIME: A PSYCHOLOGIST'S PERSPECTIVE
   Alan F. Sewell 11

3. A GLIMMER OF HOPE: A PSYCHIATRIC PERSPECTIVE
   David G. Hubbard 27

4. SOME SOCIOLOGICAL ASPECTS OF TERROR-VIOLENCE IN A
   COLONIAL SETTING *Sloan T. Letman* 33

5. TERRORISM AND THE MASS MEDIA *Franco Salomone* 43

6. ANTI-HISTORY AND TERRORISM: A PHILOSOPHICAL DIMENSION
   Nina Strickler 47

7. A PHILOSOPHICAL PERSPECTIVE ON REBELLION *Luis Kutner* .. 51

CHAPTER II
WARS OF NATIONAL LIBERATION

1. THE CONCEPT OF PUBLIC PURPOSE TERROR IN INTERNATIONAL
   LAW: DOCTRINES AND SANCTIONS TO REDUCE THE DESTRUCTION
   OF HUMAN AND MATERIAL VALUES *W. T. Mallison Jr.* and
   S. V. Mallison 67

2. A SURVEY OF INTERNATIONAL HUMANITARIAN LAW IN
   NONINTERNATIONAL ARMED CONFLICTS: 1949-1974
   Michel Veuthey 86

3. INTERNAL STRIFE, SELF-DETERMINATION AND WORLD ORDER
   John C. Novogrod 98
4. THE GENEVA CONVENTIONS OF 1949 AND WARS OF NATIONAL
   LIBERATION *R. R. Baxter* 120
5. TERRORISM AND THE REGULATION OF ARMED CONFLICTS
   Jiri Toman 133
6. TERRORISM AND WARS OF LIBERATION: AN ISRAELI
   PERSPECTIVE OF THE ARAB-ISRAELI CONFLICT *Yoram Dinstein*. 155
7. AN INTERNATIONAL LAW APPRAISAL OF THE JURIDICAL
   CHARACTERISTICS OF THE RESISTANCE OF THE PEOPLE OF
   PALESTINE: THE STRUGGLE FOR HUMAN RIGHTS
   W. T. Mallison, Jr. and S. V. Mallison 173
8. CONTROL OF TERRORISM THROUGH A BROADER INTERPRE-
   TATION OF ARTICLE 3 OF THE FOUR GENEVA CONVENTIONS
   OF 1949 *Kathleen A. Lahey and Lewis M. Sang* 191

Appendix A 201
Appendix B 204
Appendix C 205
Appendix D 207
Appendix E 209
Appendix F 213

CHAPTER III
HIJACKING

1. AIRCRAFT HIJACKING: WHAT IS BEING DONE *Alona E. Evans*. 219
2. INTERNATIONAL SUPPRESSION OF HIJACKING *Andrew Lee* ... 248

Appendix G 257
Appendix H 267
Appendix I 274

CHAPTER IV
KIDNAPPING

1. THE ROLE OF INTERNATIONAL LAW IN THE PREVENTION OF
   TERRORIST KIDNAPPING OF DIPLOMATIC PERSONNEL

James Murphy 285

Appendix J 314
Appendix K 317
Appendix L 320
Appendix M 321
Appendix N 326

2. UNLAWFUL SEIZURE OF PERSONS BY STATES *Paul O'Higgins* .. 336

3. UNLAWFUL SEIZURES OF PERSONS BY STATES AS ALTERNATIVES
TO EXTRADITION *M. Cherif Bassiouni* 343

Appendix O 369

CHAPTER V
JURISDICTION AND EXTRADITION

1. PROBLEMS OF JURISDICTION IN THE INTERNATIOAL CONTROL
AND REPRESSION OF TERRORISM *Bart DeSchutter* 377

2. PERSPECTIVES ON EXTRADITION AND TERRORISM *Theo Vogler* . 391

3. THE POLITICAL OFFENSE EXCEPTION IN EXTRADITION LAW AND
PRACTICE *M. Cherif Bassiouni* 398

4. THINKING THE UNTHINKABLE OR THE CASE OF DR. TSIRONIS
Jacob W. F. Sundberg 448

Appendix P 460

CHAPTER VI
INTERNATIONAL CONTROL OF TERRORISM

1. AN HISTORICAL INTRODUCTION TO INTERNATIONAL LEGAL
CONTROL OF TERRORISM 467

2. HISTORY OF INTERNATIONAL TERRORISM AND ITS LEGAL
CONTROL *Bogdan Zlataric* 474

3. METHODOLOGICAL OPTIONS FOR INTERNATIONAL LEGAL
CONTROL OF TERRORISM *M. Cherif Bassiouni* 485

4. UNITED NATIONS PROPOSALS ON THE CONTROL AND REPRESSION
   OF TERRORISM *John F. Murphy* 493

5. CODIFICATION OF TERRORISM AS AN INTERNATIONAL CRIME
   Bruce Palmer 507

6. THE CREATION OF AN INTERNATIONAL CRIMINAL COURT
   L. Kos-Rabcewicz Zubkowski 519

7. THE U.S. GOVERNMENT RESPONSE TO TERRORISM: A GLOBAL
   APPROACH *Lewis Hoffacker* 537

Appendix Q 546
Appendix R 557
Appendix S 564
Selected Bibliography 582
Index 595

INTERNATIONAL
TERRORISM AND
POLITICAL CRIMES

CHAPTER I

PERSPECTIVES ON THE ORIGINS AND CAUSES OF TERRORISM

THE ORIGINS AND FUNDAMENTAL CAUSES OF INTERNATIONAL TERRORISM

A UNITED NATIONS STUDY ON:

"Measures to prevent international terrorism which endangers or takes innocent human lives or jeopardizes fundamental freedoms, and study of the underlying causes of those forms of terrorism and acts of violence which lie in misery, frustration, grievance and despair and which cause some people to sacrifice human lives, including their own, in an attempt to effect radical changes."*

THE NATURE OF INTERNATIONAL TERRORISM

THE ELABORATION OF A PRECISE definition of international terrorism is a task which may eventually devolve on the General Assembly or on some other body. For the purpose, however, of preparing a report dealing with the origins and underlying causes of international terrorism, it is necessary to formulate, at least in broad outline, a concept of the area to be dealt with.

The present agenda item deals only with *international* terrorism. It thus excludes activities that are the internal affairs of individual States. The acts of Governments within their own territories in respect of their own citizens have already been extensively dealt with in the work of the United Nations, in particular in that on human rights. To come within the scope of the subjects, the interests of more than one State must be involved, as, for example, when the perpetrator or the victim is a foreigner in the country where the act is done, or the perpetrator has fled to another country.

Study prepared by the United Nations Secretariat in accordance with the decision taken by the Sixth Committee at its 1314th meeting, on 27 September 1972.

The ordinary meaning of the word *terrorism* has undergone an evolution since it first came into use at the end of the eighteenth century, and has been differently interpreted according to the different types of acts which were uppermost at the time in the minds of those discussing the subject. While at first it applied mainly to those acts and policies of Governments which were designed to spread terror among a population for the purpose of ensuring its submission to and conformity with the will of those Governments, it now seems to be mainly applied to actions by individuals, or groups of individuals.

Terrorism, as shown by the derivation of the word, involves the infliction of terror. This is not always done to the immediate victims, who may be destroyed without warning, but the act must be such as to spread terror or alarm among a given population, or among broad groups of people. The act is necessarily a conspicuously violent one, which is often intended to focus public attention and to coerce a State into a particular action. One of the most effective means towards that aim is to endanger, threaten or take innocent human lives and to jeopardize fundamental freedoms.

At various times during the previous work on the subject at the international level, discussion was restricted to terrorist acts with political motives. Yet it is now found that quite similar acts, spreading similar terror or alarm among the population, are done for ordinary criminal motives, such as extortion of large sums. It seems difficult to delimit a legal topic on the basis of motives, which often lie hidden deep in the minds of men. Both political and nonpolitical acts constitute current problems. From the standpoint of the effect on the innocent, there is no reason to limit international discussion to terrorist acts with political aims, while leaving aside very similar acts with ordinary criminal aims.

The subject of international terrorism has, as the Secretary-General has already emphasized, nothing to do with the question of when the use of force is legitimate in international life. On that question the provisions of the Charter, general international law, and the declarations and resolutions of the United Nations organs, in particular those of the General Assembly relating to national liberation movements, are not and cannot be affected. But even when the use of force is legally and morally justified, there are some means, as in every form of human conflict, which must not be used; the legitimacy of a cause does not in itself legitimize the use of certain forms of violence, especially against the innocent. This has long been recognized even in the customary law of war.

International terrorism has also a different character from revolutionary mass movements, which are directly aimed at, and capable of, effecting radical changes in society, involving changes of conduct and attitude on the part of large numbers of people. The terrorist act, on the other hand, even if its main purpose is to draw attention to a political cause or situation, has as its immediate aim something comparatively limited, although important, such as the acquisition of funds, the liberation of prisoners, the spread of general terror, the demonstration of the impotence of Government authorities, or the provocation of ill-judged measures of repression which will alienate public opinion. Thus the terrorist act usually lacks any immediate possibility of achieving its proclaimed ultimate purpose.

ORIGINS AND UNDERLYING CAUSES
OF TERRORISM

The causation of human action has as yet been most incompletely explained by modern psychology, genetics, sociology and related disciplines. In particular, in the field of use of violence by individuals, barely a beginning has been made in identifying underlying conditions and correlating them with particular acts; and such correlations, even if established, do not explain why only a few at most of those exposed to those conditions become criminals. The discussion of the causes of terrorism is thus apt to give rise to disagreement. This is all the more so since certain terrorist acts may be viewed by some as serious crimes, while to others they are acts of patroitism or heroism. The following remarks are made in compliance with the request of the Sixth Committee, but cannot aspire to be either complete or universally convincing, nor has any attempt been made to deal with any specific historical or current situations with which terrorism has been associated.

Man is one of the few species that frequently uses violence against its own kind. He has done so since the dawn of history. In the past, periods in which violence has been especially conspicuous have been those of rapid social change. During the years of the existence of the United Nations, when in most parts of the world, and in both the developed and the developing countries, the patterns of society are changing with almost unprecedented speed, violence has been frequent.

The interlinked growth of technology and growth of population have tended to create new hopes, expectations and needs in many social groups. These new attitudes mark a departure from the resignation and passivity with which most men in the past accepted the ills of life. The United Nations Charter is the voice of the aspirations of mankind when it contemplates the establishment of a world in which aggression and the threat or use of force in international relations would be effectively outlawed, friendly relations would exist among nations on the basis of respect for the principles of equal rights and self-determination of peoples, international disputes would be settled justly by peaceful means, and international cooperation would solve international economic and social problems and promote respect for human rights and fundamental freedoms for all.

The period of the existence of the United Nations, however, has shown very incomplete and uneven progress towards these goals. While major wars involving the great Powers have not occurred, force has often been resorted to, and has inflicted suffering and exile upon peoples. While progress has been made against colonialism and racism; those evils have not yet been completely eliminated. Even where political independence has been established, in many cases much remains to be done in assisting the populations to attain the minimum level necessary for decent conditions of life. Few advances have been made towards the peaceful settlement of some major international disputes, which are too often left to fester and poison international relations. Among groups where economic and social progress has been relatively slow, conditions have been unfavourable to the exercise of and the respect for human rights and fundamental freedoms.

The lack or slowness of advance towards these goals has contributed toward the "misery, frustration, grievance and despair" which, while not themselves causes of terrorism, are psychological conditions or states of being which sometimes lead, directly or indirectly, to the commission of acts of violence. While in the United Nations context it is perhaps appropriate to give special attention to the international factors that contribute to violence, there are also many situations in individual nations which may give rise to the grievance of a particular group or person, leading to acts having international repercussions. Purely personal circumstances can also often have the same result. There are also cases in which there is no genuine grievance at all, and a violent crime affecting more than one country seems to have been committed from mere cupidity, or a desire to escape criminal prosecution. The General Assembly, however, in stressing "misery, frustration, grievance and despair," seems to have singled out for special attention those situations which have the common characteristic of calling for redress.

Why is it that the violence resulting from these circumstances takes with increasing frequency the form of international terrorism, threatening, endangering or killing innocent victims? As the peoples of the world grow more interdependent the solution of many problems no longer hangs on any local ruler or government, but on actions and decisions taken thousands of miles away. Men think their ills have been produced by some vast impersonal force, which is deaf to their pleas for justice or impotent to find solutions, rather than by other men, striving for similar although opposed ends and bound to them by the claims of a common humanity. Modern communications and the growth of the public information media have transformed local incidents into world events, especially when the incidents have an international character. A terrorist act focuses world attention upon the terrorist and upon any cause he may claim to represent. In these circumstances, some such acts—which, as has already been said, cannot possibly by themselves effect radical social changes— are really acts of communication. They are intended to show the world that the determination and devotion of the terrorists are sufficient to compensate in the long run for their apparent inferiority in strength; that their cause is more holy to them than life itself, must be taken seriously, and is worthy of support; and that neither their foe nor the world at large is able to prevent their success in their purpose, or ensure punishment of their deeds and those of their associates.

Other such acts, however, seem to be more the result of blind fanaticism, or of the adoption of an extremist ideology which subordinates morality and all other human values to a single aim. In either case, the result is the same; modern life and modern weapons bring more and more strangers and foreigners within the reach of the terrorist, and he uses them as instruments for his purpose. As violence breeds violence, so terrorism begets counter-terrorism, which in turn leads to more terrorism in an ever-increasing spiral.

The modern aircraft—which is perhaps the most vulnerable of all the high and complex developments of technology, which contains assemblages of people from many countries, and which if brought under the terrorists' control, offers a speedy and safe means of reaching a distant asylum abroad—is often a factor in modern forms of international terrorism. The many problems of protecting aircraft without destroying the speed and convenience of air travel, or imposing unacceptable procedures upon air travellers, have not yet been completely solved.

It thus appears that the "misery, frustration, grievance and despair" which lead to terrorism have many roots in international and national political, economic and social situations affecting the terrorist, as well as in his personal circumstances. The precise chain of causation of particular acts cannot be traced with scientific exactitude. Nevertheless, the General Assembly may wish to identify types of situations which, if a remedy could be found to bring them more into accord with justice, will cease to contribute to the spreading terrorism which has shocked the world.

POLITICAL CRIME:
A PSYCHOLOGIST'S PERSPECTIVE

ALAN F. SEWELL

L AWYERS MAY OR MAY NOT AGREE that the term crime is subject to a variety of interpretations. In a simplistic legal sense, a crime is simply a violation of certain laws which are in the criminal codes of a given jurisdiction. Following this line of argument, criminal behavior in one jurisdiction may not be criminal behavior in another; and this amounts to an extension of cultural relativism to the law and its processes.

When pressed, lawyers frequently resort to a *social values* definition of crime. The essential ingredient of such a definition is an assertion that society establishes what is and what is not permissible, what goals should and should not be sought, what means may and may not be employed. When suitably codified, these values become the wellsprings of law and sometimes the law itself. Crime thereby achieves legal definition, presumably on the basis of negative social values consensually deplored by society.

The *social values* approach to a definition of crime provokes a number of difficulties. The primary difficulty concerns the identification of the society which provides the values to be codified. In a pluralistic society, it seems inevitable that certain behaviors deplored by the majority will attain the status of *crime,* whether or not minorities within the society regard these behaviors as reprehensible; indeed, history has noted many examples in which the mere existence of a minority is regarded as criminal.

A second difficulty lies in the possibility that the social values upon which laws are based may either have been incorrectly understood by the lawmakers or they may have changed since the time of the lawmaking. Certainly every criminal code contains exam-

11

ples of laws which are no longer enforced because they have out-lived their usefulness.

Certain other difficulties stemming from a *social values* defini-tion of crime could easily be demonstrated by those more con-cerned with legal theory. Despite such difficulties, this approach to a definition has a long history, and, if only in default of a more satisfactory approach, seems likely to continue. It is clearly prefer-able to an absolutist approach, wherein criminality is defined on an authoritarian basis.

The two difficulties noted here—potential tyranny of the major-ity and potential irrelevance of the law—are particularly acute be-cause of law's inherent conservatism. Laws, although sometimes difficult to enact, tend to be extraordinarily difficult to modify or repeal. The sources of this conservatism are of special interest to the psychologist, and in particular to the psychologist concerned with the structures and operations of society. One source of con-servatism seems to be almost biological in nature, or at least to have biological analogs: the first obligation of any organism, in-cluding a society, is to perpetuate itself. To the extent that laws embody the values of a society, changes in those laws imply changes in the values which typify the society and must lead to changes in the society itself.

The second source of law's conservatism is very closely related to the first; indeed, it constitutes one of the major ways in which social values are maintained. Laws, which are presumably based upon consensual values, establish norms of behavior, and to the extent that behavior of individuals conforms to these norms, the legitimacy of the law is upheld. That is, laws not only encodify social values; they also tend to shape behavior into patterns which reinforce those values. Although a given law may originally have been arbitrarily imposed, adherence to it can easily become *natural.* In such a way, a law which has long ceased to accommo-date social value can continue to maintain that value.

If the problem of defining *crime* seems both difficult and cir-cular, in no aspect of criminal law is the difficulty more acute than in defining *political crime.* The ostensibly distinctive feature of the political crime is that it constitutes a violation of the political values of a society. But *political values* are even more resistant to delineation than *social values*. Are political values different from social values? There are some who might argue that any violation of social values is an attack upon the social system and, hence, a simultaneous violation of political values; in such a view, any crime is a political crime.

Probably the most common definition of political crime concerns actions intended to disrupt or destroy the integrity of a governmental system. At least two subdivisions of political crime seem immediately appropriate: those directed against a system governing the offender, and those directed against an external system. The first of these might be termed "internal political crime;" and the second, "external political crime." In a more popular terminology, the second of these would be referred to as "international political crime." The "internal political crime" would involve violations of political values presumably endorsed by the offender's society, while the "international political crime" would involve violations of either supra-national political values or values of a foreign political system.

Those acquainted with international law will certainly be familiar with the numerous historical and current attempts to define political crime.[1] Most of these have adopted very limited objectives, typically in the form of identifying and condemning such highly specific offenses as assassination of a head of state and piracy. The list of such attempts is far longer than the list of adoption of international agreements stemming from the attempts. The core of the problem appears to be an inability to agree that all behaviors intended to harm a foreign political system are internationally opprobrious; most states are quite willing to overlook the disruption of a competitive state. It would seem that as long as states pursue competitive programs and policies, international agreement on political crime is unlikely.

---

[1] A survey of some historical attempts to deal with varieties of international political crimes was recently provided by John Dugard, Professor of Law, University of the Witwatersrand, Johannesburg, South Africa. Delivered at the 67th Annual Meeting of the American Society of International Law, Washington, D.C., April 12, 1973, Prof. Dugard's paper was titled "Toward the Definition of International Terrorism." 1973 *Proceedings of The American Society of International Law.* See also Bassiouni, *intra* note 8.

TOWARD A BEHAVIORAL DEFINITION
OF POLITICAL CRIME

There appears to be a general tendency to consider political crime as an uncomplicated, unitary act. In actual practice, however, it seems virtually impossible for this to be the case; the political crime seems necessarily to be complex—to combine elements of common crime with political intent. Even such an apparently simple political offense as espionage, for example, which by definition is intended against a state, will typically include such typically common crime elements as burglary or theft.

But the political crimes which most trouble contemporary society are far more complex, even in the legal sense. These offenses are terrorism, assassination, kidnapping, skyjacking, and a variety of other activities which are reported almost daily in newspapers throughout the world. The notable characteristic of all these activities, apart from the social unrest they create, is that each prominently includes a major element of common crime. Assassination is, of course, murder, an offense condemned by all societies. Kidnapping is a common crime in itself. The problem which must be dealt with is that of determining in precisely which cases the common crime becomes a complex political crime.

This problem may be exemplified by reference to a Draft Convention for the Prevention and Punishment of Certain Acts of International Terrorism submitted to the General Assembly of the United Nations by the United States in September, 1972.[2] Although intentionally limited in scope, this Draft Convention does undertake to define at least one variety of political crime: international terrorism, which is defined to include homicide, serious assaults, kidnapping, and participation in such offenses. At least by implication, a political crime is such an act when it has "international significance," and "international significance" is scrupulously defined as being involved if the act:

---

[2]The full text occurs in 67 *Department of State Bulletin*, 431, October 16; 1972. See also *Appendix R*, p. 557.

"(a) is committed or takes effect outside the territory of a State
of which the alleged offender is a national; and

(b) is committed or takes effect:

    (i) outside the territory of the State against which the act
is directed, or

    (ii) within the territory of the State against which the act is
directed and the alleged offender knows or has reason
to know that a person against whom the act is directed
is not a national of that State; and

(c) is committed neither by or against a member of the Armed
Forces of a State in the course of military hostilities; and

(d) is intended to damage the interests of or obtain concessions
from a State or an international organization."[3]

Hence the killing of a citizen of Switzerland by a citizen of the
United States within the boundaries of Italy is at least potentially
an act of "international significance"—a political crime. Clearly
much more must be known of the specifics of the incident before
such a determination can be made. Various interesting possibilities
can be imagined.

1. The offender and his victim are both diplomats, and preceding the offense, national insults were exchanged between the
participants, stemming from disagreement on an international
trade protocol.

2. The victim was a diplomat, and the offender acted in the
course of a robbery attempt.

3. The victim was attempting a robbery, and the offender was
a diplomat in process of being the robber's victim.

4. The offender and his victim were both diplomats, and the
act occurred in the course of an argument centering on an *affaire
de coeur.*

5. The offender and the victim were both businessmen secretly
conducting trade negotiations on behalf of their governments; the
act stemmed from a disagreement about the negotiations.

6. The offender and victim were patrons of an art exhibition;
the offender became incensed by what he considered a national in-

---

[3]*Ibid.,* Article 1.

sult rendered by the victim.

Such a list of imaginary circumstances could continue indefinitely. The important point to be made is that details of these circumstances *must* be known before the suitability of a political characterization of the offense can be decided. And the critical element of the circumstances is the offender's *intention*. According to the Draft Convention[4] the act must be "intended to damage the interests of or obtain concessions from a State. . ."

> While it is generally true that a crime is committed only when the physical element, the *actus reus,* of the crime and the mental element, the *mens rea,* of the crime occur simultaneously, . . . the argument . . . misconstrues the meaning of *mens rea* and confuses legal *intention* with the behaviorally relevant but legally unimportant concept of *motive*.[5]

And again: ". . . the law presumes that a man intends those consequences which represent the very purpose for which an act is done or are known to be substantially certain to result."[6] In the terms of the Draft Convention, an argument, whether plausible or not, could be made that in each of the hypothetical situations noted above, damage to the interests of a State is a foreseeable consequence of the offense, although the severity of the damage is clearly greater in some cases than in others. Hence, in one way or another, any of these situations *could* be construed as a *political crime*.

Yet common sense clearly argues that not all are; and, indeed, perhaps none is. The final determining element is obviously not legal *intent* but behavioral purpose or *motive*.

Undoubtedly the distinction between intent and motive is clearest in the case of the offense known as skyjacking. The *actus*

---

[4]*Ibid.*
[5]The quotation is abstracted from a paper title "Complex Political Crime: The Legal Viability of the Grand Nueremberg Defense in the United States" by Paul Jeffrey Brantingham, Assistant Professor of Criminology, The Florida State University, Talahassee, Florida. The paper was delivered at the First Interamerican Congress of the American Society of Criminology and the Interamerican Association of Criminology, Caracas, Venezuela, November, 1972. Brautingham's paper makes a clear distinction between the legal concept of "intent" and the behavioral concept of "motivation." See also Bassiouni, *Criminal Law and Its Processes,* 62 (1969).
[6]*Ibid.*

reus of this offense is the simple seizure of an aircraft and its subsequent diversion to a new destination. The common crime here, at least to the layman, is misappropriation of property; on a number of occasions this act has been compounded by physical harm to passengers, crew members or persons in the area of the aircraft. At least three conventions have been concluded to prohibit various aspects of skyjacking.[7]

To the extent that national boundaries are crossed in the course of the offense, skyjacking is at least an international crime. But the question to be considered here is whether skyjacking is a *political* crime. Following the line of argument recommended by the Draft Convention previously noted, the offense can be characterized as political if the offender's intention was to damage the interests of a State or to obtain concessions from a State. It would appear that if the aircraft happens to be the property of the State, then the State's interests are indeed harmed; and concessions in the form of ransoms have indeed been demanded by skyjackers. Even when the aircraft is not state owned, it could well be argued that the interests of the state are harmed because of commercial disruptions or interference with interests established by included freight or mail or by virtue of state subsidies. Hence it would seem quite possible to view any skyjacking as a political crime. The same argument could be made for those skyjackings which do not transgress state boundaries; these would constitute "internal political crimes."

The seriousness with which a government may view protection of its interests against skyjacking can be seen in recent United States regulations concerning aircraft security. These measures, which include examination of carry-on baggage, screening of passengers with metal detection devices, and, in some circumstances, personal searches, are expected to cost approximately $400 million

---

[7] All three were sponsored by the International Civil Aviation Organization: the Tokyo Convention of 1963 (Convention on Offences and Certain Other Acts Committed on Board Aircraft, 2 *International Legal Materials*, 1042, 1963) ; the Hague Convention of 1970 (Convention for the Suppression of Unlawful Seizure of Aircraft, 10 *International Legal Materials*, 133, 1971) ; Montreal Convention of 1971 (Convention for the Suppression of Unlawful Acts Against the Safety of Civil Aviation, 10 *International Legal Materials*, 1151, 1971). See also Appendices G, H, I to Chapter III.

during their first year of application—an amount greater than the annual budgets of some nations! This first-year expense is probably also greater than the value of property lost in all skyjacking to date. These countermeasures have evidently been totally successful to date in the United States, but then the world-wide incidence of skyjacking seems to have simultaneously decreased. The consequences of such countermeasures will be considered later in this paper.

The extent and cost of anti-skyjacking measures in the United States must lend credence to a conjecture that the United States harbors great numbers of political criminals. But an alternate hypothesis is available: that these measures constitute a reaction or perhaps over-reaction which indicates the *perceived* magnitude of the threat. Skyjacking serves as an enlightening example of behavior which is certainly inherently criminal and which has been subjected to the criminalization process; but it has additionally been subjected to a process of *political criminalization,* both in the public consciousness and by virtue of the extraordinary countermeasures it has provoked. Whether or not skyjacking or any other form of putative political crime is indeed political crime cannot be established within the confines of the concept of intention; a concept of behavioral motivation must be entered. Thus, while every political crime is a crime, not every crime is a political crime.

It is sound psychological theory to regard all behavior as value-directed. That is, behavior expresses values held by the behaver. And each behavior is at least potentially analyzable in terms of the values it expresses. Defensive and protective behavior, for example, is indicative of a high positive value upon the protected object. Aggressive behavior indicates a high negative value upon the object of attack. Indeed, true political crime is aggressive behavior toward a negatively valued political system.

It is also sound psychological theory to expect to find value consistency; that is, over time an individual's behavior should consistently reflect the same values. Hence it is possible to learn an individual's values by observing his behavior over time. Patterns of value expressions thus determined will reveal the individual's value orientation.

While there are, of course, a great many ways in which values and value orientations can be classified, the social psychologist's preference would be for a schema reflecting variations in the social and personal qualities of values. In such a schema it is possible to imagine a value continuum: at one end of the continuum would be totally personal value orientations, while at the other end would be totally social value orientations. Most human behavior is adaptive or adapted; that is, while the behavior itself is a personal event, the behaver does consider the demands of his social milieu. For example, an individual who observes a religious prohibition against certain foods satisfies a social demand while simultaneously satisfying a personal (biological) requirement in his choice of alternate comestibles. Such an individual can be said to have a personal-social value orientation, an integrated value orientation.

On the other hand, it is possible to imagine residents of the same social milieu who do not observe the prohibition, and it is thereupon reasonable to inquire into the causes of their behavior: that is, to establish their motivations. To determine motivation in this case, the inquiry must focus upon two questions: (1) Is this behavior consistent over time? (2) Is this behavior socially performed or solitary? The important characteristic of these two questions is that both can be objectively answered; neither requires subjective analysis.

The various combinations of these two factors lead to rather different motivational inferences:

1. The inconsistently performed violation by a solitary offender constitutes eccentric or abnormal behavior and implies an eccentric or abnormal personality.

2. Inconsistently performed violations by a social grouping also appears abnormal, but in any event it would seem to be irrelevant to the group's purpose or organizational principle; otherwise an inconsistent pattern would not be manifested.

3. A consistent pattern of violations by a solitary individual seems to imply a purpose (because of the consistency), but a highly individual purpose.

4. A consistent pattern of violations by a group clearly implies

that the violation is central to the group's purpose or organizational principle.

Clearly four quite distinct motivational bases can exist simply on the evidence provided by the offender's behavior. To determine the specific motivation in a given case, it is necessary to consider the values expressed by the behavior itself. Returning to the concept of a value continuum, the critical question can now be asked: To what extent does the behavior express social values, as opposed to personal values?

Patterns of inconsistent behavior cannot really reflect social values, since social values are by definition consensual and, hence, consistent. While consistent violations of a given set of social values may represent socialized opposition to those values, inconsistent violations cannot support a similar inference. That is, these inconsistent patterns better reflect idiosyncratic values than social values.

When such thinking is applied to the problem of defining political crime, a new and, hopefully, helpful theoretical framework is available. In this framework, the *actus reus* does not establish the politicality or nonpoliticality of the offense—and it is useful to note here again that the *actus reus* definition is that which has been typically applied or implied in attempts at international agreements; the offender's motivation is the crucial definitional factor. According to this proposed theoretical framework, at least three relatively clear varieties of putative political offenders can be determined:

1. The *psychopathological offender,* whose inconsistent behavior reflects idiosyncratic values. To the extent that political crime represents opposition of social value systems, this offender's behavior cannot be politically motivated.

2. The *common criminal,* whose behavior is consistent but does not imply values in conflict with those of his society; this offender's deviation from social values is in the realm of means, not ends. Hence, this offender's behavior also cannot be politically motivated.

3. The *ideologically motivated offender* is the true political criminal. His behavior demonstrates a consistent opposition of the values of another society to those of the society in which the

offense is committed. His motivation is indeed to harm the political system of one society in furtherance of the political system of another society.[8]

APPLICATION OF THE BEHAVIORAL DEFINITION

The utility of this proposed definitional classification of political crime can, perhaps, best be demonstrated by its application to skyjacking. While, as noted earlier, countermeasures intended to prevent skyjacking imply a political characterization to this offense, the only psychological study of the skyjacker has reached far different conclusions. Employing a psychoanalytic framework in his analysis, the American psychiatrist Hubbard appears to have concluded that all skyjackers are disturbed personalities.[9] Since political consequences of the behavior of a disturbed personality can only be accidental, such an offender cannot be identified as a true political criminal, and his offense cannot truly constitute a political crime.

While the offenders studied by Dr. Hubbard do all appear to be of the type identified here as psychopathological offenders, his conclusion seems to be properly restricted to only that variety; that is, Dr. Hubbard apparently did not include other varieties of skyjackers in his study. But do these other conceptual varieties actually exist? There is sufficient evidence, even in popular press accounts of skyjacking incidents, to indicate that they do, indeed, exist: that the behavioral definition is both conceptually and existentially valid.

The skyjacking committed by a *psychopathological offender* will bear the perpetrator's distinctive marks: the event will have all the characteristics of an impulsive act, poorly conceived and clumsily executed. During the act the offender's behavior will seem bizarre and poorly controlled. Despite possible verbalizations which may appear to be ideological, the ideology will be bizarre

---

[8]The author is grateful to Professor M. C. Bassiouni for the terminology of "ideological motivation" and for his guidance through the legal problems of this concept, presented in "Ideologically Motivated Offenses and the Political Offenses Exception in Extradition: A Proposed Juridical Standard for an Unruly Problem," 19 *DePaul Law Review*, 217-269 (1970).

[9]D. G. Hubbard, *The Skyjacker, His Flights of Fantasy* (New York, Macmillan, 1971).

and typically unacceptable to any organized group associated with such an ideological position. The offender's history will not indicate any consistent attachment to an ideological position; indeed, more often than not it will reveal frequent ideological shifts. In short, the values expressed by the offender's behavior are idiosyncratic, unsocial rather than antisocial in that they do not conform to the values accepted by any large social group. As a rule, the psychopathological offender is a solitary, primarily because he cannot find others to subscribe to his values; occasionally a small group of similarly disturbed persons will cooperate in a skyjacking, but again the fundamental problem is an impossibility of reaching consensual values in a larger group. Typical of such offenders are the cases reported by Dr. Hubbard,[10] and it seems likely that most of the skyjackings which have occurred in the United States were perpetrated by this type of offender.

There have been, however, a number of skyjackings which appear to have been the work of *common criminals*. Such incidents also bear striking behavioral characteristics. They are more likely to be successful because the offender is not a disturbed personality —at least not in the sense of the psychopathological offender. The conception or plan of the offense is clearer, and its execution is rational. The offender's background will give little evidence of bizarre behavior—although criminality may appear in the offender's history. The offender will possess the skills and instruments necessary to successful execution of his plan; his objective, after all, is to succeed in the execution of a crime for profit, and not to commit suicide. Whereas the psychopathological offender may demand ransom and/or transportation to an ideologically different State, the common criminal is less interested in ideology than in profit: hence the ransom demanded will be more nearly rational, and his chosen destination will provide escape rather than ideological comfort.

A further important consideration is that the success of the common criminal's offense crucially depends upon his ability to evade capture. This largely means that he must be able to "melt into" a society: his behavior and the values expressed by that behavior must be consonant with those of the society into which he makes

10*Ibid.*

his escape. The psychopathological offender, because of his bizarre values, cannot "melt into" any society; he will attempt to escape into a society which advocates values *different* from those of the society in which the offense was committed. But the common criminal will seek to escape into the same society or into a society professing similar values. Further, the common criminal, unlike the psychopathological offender, is reality-oriented; he will not attempt a skyjacking if the risk of capture is excessive; the psychopathological offender pays little heed to such risks. Few skyjackings appear to have been committed by common criminals.

Finally, the only skyjackings which have truly been political crimes have been those executed by *ideologically motivated offenders*. Ideology and the ideological consequences of the offense are the determinative characteristics of these offenses. It will be important for the offender to identify the ideological bases of his behavior and, more often than not, to identify himself with an ideological social group, and to denounce the ideology of the social group against which the offense is committed. The offender's background will typically provide evidence of consistent and long-held ideological commitment.

The act itself may or may not provide evidence of careful planning and skillful execution, depending, perhaps, upon the degree of fanaticism and desperation involved. For the process which yields the ideologically motivated offender—a process of hypersocialization, as opposed to the psychopathic offender's hypo-socialization and the common criminal's normo-socialization—is that which produces fanatics: individuals who have so completely adopted the values of a given society or political system that they have come to identify with it. Just as the psychopathological offender's values are idiosyncratic because he cannot identify with a society, so the ideologically motivated offender has no nonsocial, no personal values because he has surrendered his individuality to the social system. If the psychopathological offender is a "rebel without a cause," then the ideologically motivated offender is a rebel with a cause and for a cause.

A substantial number of skyjackings, international skyjackings in particular, have been the work of ideologically motivated offenders. On the basis of the descriptive criteria given herein it is quite easy to identify and classify these individual occurrences of skyjacking. Is the same true of other varieties of putative political crimes? The answer is an emphatic affirmative; instances of assassination and kidnapping can as easily be classified.

ADVANTAGES OF A BEHAVIORAL DEFINITION

Laws which attempt to regulate human conduct have two general purposes: to prevent by *fiat* unacceptable behavior, and to provide for the disposition of those who violate social dicta. That is, laws theoretically provide for deterrence and for retribution. Laws which attempt to regulate political conduct must consider the dual nature of most acts which may be classed as political crimes: as noted earlier, these acts include a criminal component and a political component. If political freedom is indeed to be cherished, then laws and legal processes should concern themselves with the criminal aspects of such crimes and seek to avoid sanctions against political behaviors.

For example, homicide must be regarded as homicide and nothing more, regardless of whether it occurred at the whim of a madman or in the course of a common crime or as a product of ideological inspiration. Legal systems are currently eminently capable of law's fact-finding mission, the verification of the *actus reus*. But appropriate disposition of the offender cannot be attained within legal systems which limit their concern to the establishment of legal *intent;* the appropriate disposition must inevitably be concerned with the offender's motivation. This is most clear in the case of the "external political crime," wherein the possibility of extradition poses clear choices. The decision in the case of an offense committed by a psychopathological offender is clear enough; inasmuch as his offense was nonpolitical in nature, although it may have had serious political consequences, the offender's political rights will not be jeopardized by extradition to the jurisdiction in which the offense occurred. The same is true of the offense committed by the common criminal. However, the same act committed by an ideologically motivated offender merits special consideration; he ought not to be subject to extradition insofar as his offense was truly political in nature, yet he must be made subject to the penalties of the law for the common crime elements of his act.

The definitions suggested herein would appear to be capable of providing a reasonably objective test of the politicality of a given offense. Applying the facts and circumstances of a given offense against the standards of such a test would permit clear determination of the political or nonpolitical nature of the offense. The next step, obviously, is the establishment of processes and mechanisms capable of impartially rendering such determinations in order to punish without repressing political impulses which can motivate crime.

NEED FOR AN INTERNATIONAL TRIBUNAL

Because the basic motivation of any organism or system is to preserve itself, it is clearly unrealistic to expect that any national judicial system, underwritten by national social and political values, can remain forever unbiased in its treatment of the true political criminal. It seems more reasonable to expect that such a system would be inclined to treat the ideologically motivated offender more harshly than other perpetrators of similar offenses; hence, the political criminal would be held culpable not only for the criminal aspects of his behavior but for the political aspects as well.

What must be universally condemned is criminal behavior, not political behavior. And the political criminal must be expected to find himself internationally accountable for his crime but not for his politics. Disposition of political criminals must be assigned to a body which will not be swayed by the special political considerations of the case. The need is for the establishment of an international tribunal, the responsibilities of which would be twofold: to determine, upon the basis of some standard as that proposed herein, the degree of criminality and politicality in a given offense; and to establish disposition appropriate to the preceding determination. The ideologically motivated offender ought not to be subject to extradition, and the extradition decision ought not to depend, as it does now, upon the political considerations of the state of asylum.

N.C. WESLEYAN COLLEGE LIBRARY

70417

His offense should be subject to uniform penalties dependent solely upon the criminality of his act, and legal sanctions should be internationally enforced. Any offender could claim the benefits of the political offense exception to extradition, regardless of the nature of the offense, and he and the international community would know that while the right to political activism is maintained, it cannot be exercised in the absence of accountability. The burden of proof for the applicability of the political offenses exception to extradition should rest upon the claimant; the claim could be documented, for example, by demonstration of membership in a recognized or avowed political organization.

Certainly great difficulties stand in the way of establishment of such an international tribunal—difficulties which are themselves primarily of a political nature. Nevertheless, the historical failures of international attempts to prohibit specified acts of putative politicality appear to require a new and more realistic approach to the increasing problems of international crimes and terrorism. A reasonable first stage in such an approach would be a recognition that while all political crimes are crimes, not all crimes are political crimes. This will require replacement of the timid concept of intent by a concept of objectively determinable motivation.

A GLIMMER OF HOPE:
A PSYCHIATRIC PERSPECTIVE

DAVID G. HUBBARD

NOT ALL ACTS OF TERRORISM involve aircraft, but all skyjackings involve terrorism.* If terrorism can be defined as a violent or potentially violent act committed upon unknown others proceeding about their civilian affairs by persons who intend to control their victims and/or population (government/industry) through duress and threats of destruction, then all skyjackers are terrorists.

Our study** included individual, carefully performed psychiatric interviews of fifty-two American and Canadian skyjackers out of about one hundred sixty. These studies, backed by a nearly equal number of studies of Black Panthers and F.L.Q. members, demonstrate the probability that terrorism is a more controllable phenomenon than is currently believed possible.

Our studies began with skyjackers. Certain consistent similarities emerged and it shortly became evident that crew behavior also had certain similarities and illogics and were also studied. These crew studies threw into sharp focus those consistent attitudes, and predictable responses, characteristic of airline managements and governmental leaders who were *behind* the crews.

At the onset, and even half way through our study project, it appeared reasonable to believe the skyjackers of South America, the Middle East and Far East had little in common with those from the United States. Then three facts emerged:

---

*Ed.'s note: Not all skyjackings involve terrorism since some are committed for personal profit or by psychopathological persons. See Sewell, Sec. 2, p. 20-21.

**Ed.'s note: The author is relying on his noted book, *The Skyjacker, His Flights and Fantasy* (1971).

1. Skyjackers raised in Yugoslavia, Scotland, Guatemala and Cuba were not significantly different from those raised in Savannah, Ottawa or Seattle. Being black, white or Latin did not alter the picture, either.
2. Psychiatric information about offenders from places like Leningrad, Athens and Beirut began to filter in. The reports were filled with details such as flight fantasies, delusional cancers and the need to "speak-to-the-world-through-the-media-to-show-all-Arabs-don't-wear-black-hats." Similarities regarding modes, threats, ultimatums, response to force and reason rounded out the sharp picture.
3. Common societal responses to the crime, regardless of ethnic base or governmental forms, had amazing similarities the world around.

These similarities make it probable but not proven that the deep human factors involved in terrorism/skyjacking do not vary from state to state or ideology to ideology. It is probable that the offenders who are kooks, wherever they act, have more in common with each other than they have with the society to which they ostensibly belong. Moreover, governments and bureaucrats, whatever their ideology, also have more in common with each other than they hold in common with the offenders that originate *or* are sheltered in their country. The logical but startling conclusion is that human beings are human and act like it, and their governmental agencies act like it, too.

It also became evident that crew behavior, corporate attitudes and governmental policies were little more than the instinctive *paralytic response* seen in most animals when confronted with a frightening unknown. Paralysis is a normal first response to fear and a second response is irrational application of force. Both responses stem from fear and the fear from ignorance and neither response is valid in order to satisfy the needs of society.

It is the author's personal conviction that society has responded hysterically to terrorism just as it has responded hysterically to skyjackers. Much of this hysteria results from exaggerated attitudes of self-importance among national leaders, as well as from operational defects in the authoritarian model and ignorance of cause and effect relationship.

Society conducts its affairs through authoritarian models in which an organized body of law is vested in the hands of national leaders. Resultant national and international policies are conducted according to the personal lights of those leaders and are accepted in good or bad humor by the majority of the population. Those opposing these policies can be divided into reasonably humanistic minorities employing methods short of terrorism and a tiny fragment of the population who create those acts of terrorism which shatter the authoritarian model.

The skyjacker-terrorist has a high capacity to challenge the authoritarian model. This challenge inevitably brings this previously unimportant individual or group into direct personal conflict with national leaders. The total bureaucracy is thus instantly flanked by the willingness of international leaders to involve themselves with the management of these affairs and this basic social defect guarantees the success of terrorism.

Quite apart from the recognized conceit of heads of nations, there is another basic reason for this weakness: bureaucracy is not devised to handle emergencies. Quite the contrary, a bureaucracy, with its limited pace, rules, regulations and red tape, is devised to slow down the impact of societal concerns and to reduce them from the level of personal urgencies into more mundane events. This becomes a fixed state of mind among bureaucrats which, when confronted by the desperate words and actions of terrorists, is quite incapable of any action other than paralysis on the part of the bureaucrat. His job is in jeopardy should untoward events develop as a consequence of positive action on his part. In most nations the only member of the ruling clique with the necessary power for individual decision/action is the head of the national state, which is an expression of ignorance of cause and effect and requires correction.

There are many drawbacks to this state of affairs. National leaders have no expertise in the understanding of the complex motivations or of the emotions of those individuals who have brought themselves to a high enough level of desperation to be able to perform the acts required for terrorism. The political skill of the leaders rests on their knowledge of the majority and minority who accept their authority and who are willing to deal with the leaders through the bureaucracy. At the same moment the pride of these national leaders and their aides is involved, as are the leaders' personal political and publicity needs. These facts appear to be true of all governments.

Serious students of these phenomena must recognize that terrorism is not the weapon of any sizeable fragment of any society. If it were, the number of terrorists acts would be ten thousand to one-hundred thousand times greater than those which do occur. A wave of letter bombs does not require the activities of a large number of people. More likely than not, a maximum of two men can produce explosions simultaneously in Paris, Rome, London, Sydney, Montreal, Hong Kong, New York and every other major city on the globe. If one were to argue terrorism as the declared policy of a government, one would then be obligated to explain why most airlines are still in business. From information available to us in our studies it is obvious that any air carrier in the world, whether it be privately owned or merely a reflection of state ownership, could have been put completely out of action through careful planning and dispersal of less than one hundred men. Appraisal of this potential forces one to the conclusion that if governments or quasi-governmental groups are involved at all, it is only for the secondary purpose of harrassment and embarrassment.

Careful analysis of the terrorist acts which involved aircraft from Europe to Arab countries in the year 1973 raises the probability that not even quasi-governmental prior participation is reflected in these events. It is far more likely that governments and quasi-governments simply tolerate the presence of such groups and capitalize on the short-term political gains to be had when such events occur. Studies which would demonstrate the emotional instability, political unreliability and basic opposition of the offenders to all forms of authority including the one which shelters them would quickly demonstrate that every existing government has more in common with every other existing government including one's enemies than it has with these offenders. Copied precedents, passed off as reasoned decision by government, constitute one of the major reasons for such tolerance. When following precedent, a government is often completely unaware of doing so and is as devoid of valid reason for its conduct as is the offender himself.

A case in point is the recent retention of an Arab who skyjacked in order to utilize the world press to demonstrate the fact that "all Arabs do not wear black hats." This man had broken Libyan law and wounded the pride of his national leaders. Without question he would have been punished if returned; however, the *host* found him to be a "poor, drunken, and disturbed boy who will be our guest for awhile." The same government did not question's military craft's penetrating the borders of an adjoining nation to divert the course of a commercial aircraft in the belief that "individuals associated with skyjacking were on board." In both of these actions, the *host* government only *followed and reinforced previous precedent.* Complex rationalization was employed while so doing, but this did not conceal the administrative ignorance involved (this comment is not an attack on Libya, Israel, Cuba or Algeria, none of whom set the original precedents in this matter. The original ignorance was manifest by U.S. armed and diplomatic forces in Western Europe in the late 1940's).

In an attempt to create an image of themselves as intellectual leaders the commonest error of administrators is to categorize offenders. Such groupings as "emotionally disturbed," "fleeting felons," and "political activists" are created as superficial attempts to give the appearance of knowledge on the part of the government involved. Such explanations fail to explain the inference to be drawn from such spurious systems. There are several million emotionally disturbed persons; why do only a handful of them elect to participate in these activities? There are several million fleeing felons; why do only a handful elect themselves? There are several million political activists; why do only a handful of them make the same election? The real questions are 1) what do these tiny handfuls of men have in common, and 2) are they all responding to facts they understand to be common defects to all governments and all national leaders regardless of political orientation.

Thorough, objective and nonpolitical study of the offenders *can* answer both of these questions. Findings in such studies would provide an objective data base upon which rational government action could be based as opposed to current nationalistic fervor, publicity needs of politicians and career needs of administrators.

These crimes must be *down-graded* in importance such that no national leader either during or after the event can be involved in its outcome. At the same time these crimes must be *upgraded* in importance sufficiently to be scientifically and impartially studied and the results of these studies made available to the administrators responsible for their prevention and management. Such administrators, mindful of the facts of such crimes, would be less blinded by nationalistic poses or short term goals.

Thus, society requires an international chain of administrators empowered to act in emergency and educated in the special requirements of such actions as determined by appropriate studies of the offenders. The development of such a group will be slow and long range, but it is feasible, even though many time-honored precedents which currently dominate our selection of diplomatic goals, judicial procedures, legislative actions, administrative procedures, news media techniques, aircraft insurance, police methods, corporate attitudes, crew attitudes, public notions about hostages, and scientific thought would be set aside. Such changes would not announce the millenium nor require a Utopia. They represent small adjustments of existing institutions, to be employed in specific emergencies, based upon knowledge rather than ignorance and fear. Appropriate diplomacy, punishment, prevention and control must be based upon the offenders.

Learned scholars argued for centuries as to the number of angels which could reside upon the head of a pin. If they could have captured and studied a few, the argument would have been quickly settled. We could negotiate or legislate into eternity about terrorists, but the fact is we have already captured quite a few of them. All that remains is to study them and apply the findings.

SOME SOCIOLOGICAL ASPECTS OF TERROR-VIOLENCE IN A COLONIAL SETTING

SLOAN T. LETMAN*

INTRODUCTION

THE PARADOX OF TERROR-VIOLENCE is that no society can tolerate it but to some extent all societies may perpetuate it and
this is particularly true in a colonial context. This chapter will,
therefore, focus on the relationship between colonialism and
terrorism as a manifestation of alienation of the colonized.

Colonization seems to give rise to two types of terrorism:
organized and individual. Organized terrorism is to some degree
understood as a military strategy while isolated individual acts of
terror violence are generally characterized as senseless crimes. To
some extent, therefore, organized group terror violence is more
readily acceptable than the same species of conduct when committed randomly by individuals who are not part of an organized
group. This latter observation may not necessarily be a valid
characterization of individual terrorism because it is behavior
proceeding from the same circumstances giving rise to what has
been legitimized as guerrilla warfare.

VIOLENCE BREEDING ALIENATION

There are four types of alienation: economic, political, cultural and military. There are also four models of behavior to
which these observations apply and whose understanding is
crucial to appreciate the causes of terrorism.

---

*The author wishes to acknowledge the assistance received from Professor Bassiouni
and to express his appreciation for it.

33

At the outset it must be stated that all forms of alienation are interactive; each is both a cause and a consequence for the other and they operate in such a way so as to reinforce each other in a spiraling process which must inevitably escalate until it erupts in violence. Thus the inescapable resort to terror violence as a liberating and cleansing phenomena through which the processes of colonial oppression are eradicated.

Economic Alienation

The type of economic alienation which engenders violent behavior on the part of an outgroup is best described in Frantz Fanon's *Wretched of the Earth*. In this colonial model, the outgroup is an important, but dependent, component of the ingroup's economic system. The colonies were originally exploited as a source of raw materials, which were turned into manufactured goods and distributed in the European market. In later stages of development, the colonies became a market for those consumer goods manufactured by the mother country.[1]

According to the Marxist model of alienated labor, it was theoretically possible for the worker to eradicate his alienation from his own labor-commodity (and the result of his own labor, the product-commodity) by seizing control of production and therefore of his own labor.[2]

But as Fanon suggests, there is an added wrinkle in the colonial situation which is racially based, because "the cause is the consequence; you are rich because you are white, you are white because you are rich."[3] Consequently, while it may be possible to cross economic barriers, it is not possible to cross racial barriers and therefore race solidifies class into caste and caste strengthens racism.

---

[1] Frantz Fanon, *The Wretched of the Earth* (1968), p. 65. Colonial economic alienation can also operate within a single country as Carmichael and Hamilton have shown in *Black Power: The Politics of Liberation in America*.
[2] Easton and Guddat, *Writings of the Young Marx on Philosophy and Society* (1967), p. 289.
[3] Fanon, *Supra* Note 1, p. 40.

Political Alienation

Political alienation can, through laws and political systems, explicitly exclude certain groups. Slavery and the apartheid system in South Africa are obvious examples of *de jure* political alienation. There are also situations in which certain groups see themselves as *nations* but are not recognized as political units either by the society which claims them as part thereof or for that matter by the international legal order. The Bantus in South Africa and the Palestinians are examples of both categories.

De facto political alienation is probably the most common form of all four types of alienation and its manifestations can be found in many societies. This type of denial of human rights is, if not totally conscious, at least a matter of choice on the part of the settler. According to Hannah Arendt economic deprivation, however, runs into a political alienation in that they are "a political, not a natural phenomenon, and the result of violence and violation, rather than scarcity."[4] This position has a liberating value on the alienated group because it opens to the native the possibility of political change, even though oppression by economic scarcity inhibits human potential and curbs political activism.

Cultural Alienation

Almost all groups possess cultural patterns peculiar to themselves, and they suffer mild forms of cultural alienation as a result of social interaction with other groups. This could be considered a normal process of acculturation if it were a conscious and deliberate choice which is not the cause in the colonial context. In that respect cultural alienation is usually a consequence of political and economic alienation rather than its cause.

In that context and particularly with respect to colonized black Africans, Carmichael and Hamilton state that "the groups which have access to the necessary resources and the ability to effect change benefit politically and economically from the con-

[4]H. Arendt, *On Revolution* (1965), p. 57.

tinued subordinate status of the black community."[5] When members of a certain group consistently have the lowest paying jobs, token political representation, no capital, and no control over institutions, they begin to "question and doubt whether they, their family, and their group really deserve no more respect from the larger society than they receive."[6] This cultural alienation is the inevitable product of economic and political alienation but conversely once it is achieved, serves to fuel the ideological premises supporting all other forms of alienation.

Military Alienation

There are two separate military worlds—one for the colonial powers and another for the colonized. The colonial powers have the military wherewithal, while the colonized cannot match it in any terms except perhaps by having more human power. It is obvious, however that human power cannot be a match to fire power and therefore guerrilla warfare developed as a feasible strategy.

Guerrilla strategy, however, typically includes terror violence as a tactic designed to produce a psychological conditioning of civilian population to attain political or para-military outcomes. Thus to that extent, terrorism becomes the only contextual means to achieve or accelerate the inevitable end. Alienation thus breeds violence but not necessarily in all people. It can be seen to produce four different models of behavior in the colonized but inevitably these models reinforce tendencies to violence.

Behavioral Models

These four behavior models among natives are "passing," "zombi," "revolutionary violence," and "isolated terrorism." The interraction between these models is based on the observation

---

[5]Carmicahel and Hamilton, *Black Power: The Politics of Liberation in America* (1967), p. 22.

[6]K. Clark, *Dark Ghetto* (1965), p. 63.

Clark was actually speaking of personal indignities rather than political and economic conditions, but we feel these are even more at the root of the indignity than are personal experiences.

that individuals go from one to another usually in order of violent ascendence.

The Passing Model

The Passing Model is a passing solution to alienation because it involves the attempt of the outgroup to assimilate and acculturate itself with the ingroup. It is premised on the acceptance of acculturation and tolerance of alienation.

This alienation from self, group and cultural heritage is manifested by conformity and conformism to the norms of ingroup but it can also work in reverse, namely, through the cultural co-optation of the outgroup by transferring it into a conforming ingroup. This has been the case of some conditioned black Africans which developed into an acculturated European group.[7] In essence, the outgroup's problem was solved as Fanon would see it: you are rich because you are white, therefore, you became rich by becoming white.

The Zombi Model

The Zombi Model takes its name from Fanon's description of native cultures which solve the dilemma by setting up a superstructure of myth and magic which replaces the dominance of the ingroup:

> By terrifying me, it integrates me in the traditions and history of my district or of my tribe, and at the same time, it reassures me, it gives me status, as if it were an identification paper. . . . Believe me, the zombies are more terrifying than the settlers; and in consequence the problem is no longer that of keeping oneself right with the colonial world and its barbed-wire entanglements but of considering three times before urinating, spitting, or going out into the night.[8]

This solution has the value of integrating the native into his own culture and therefore contains no element of alienation from self or group; but it also severs the native from resistance to colonialism. The Bantus of South Africa are the White's dominance response to the natives awakening. It is the zombi model par excellence.

---

[7] Carmichael and Hamilton, *Supra*, note 5, p. 29.
[8] Fanon, *Supra*, note 1, p. 55-56.

The Revolutionary Violence Model

For Fanon, the native's only realistic response to colonialism occurs when the native finally realizes that his minimum demands are intransigent maximum demands.[9] In other words, when the demand is that "the last shall be first."[10] In which case, the only solution is the violent dismantling of the existing structure. The syllogism is reversed: "You are rich because you are *not* white, you are *not* white because you are rich," and thus, "the last shall be first."

This solution solves the dilemma of alienation in that the native will no longer be alienated from self or group because "decolonization unifies the people by the radical decision to remove from it its heterogeneity, and by unifying it on a national, sometimes a racial, basis."[11] Simultaneously, the native is no longer alienated from the white man's world because he has made a conscious effort to enter that world but on his own hard carved terms. Thus revolutionaly violence liberates not only the native but the oppressor from the inhumane role of colonizer. It emancipates the native but also frees the oppressor.

The Uncoordinated Terrorism Model

The fourth model centers on uncoordinated acts of individual violence which develop because alienation has intensified into a form of anomie.[12]

In the other three solutions, the native is steadied by some sense of values and norms. In the first model, it was the values of the settler; in the second, it was a superstructure of myth and magic; and in the third, it was maximal demand.

If, however, the native is unable to develop a sense of values commonly shared by any group, he becomes consumed by hatred for the settler's world, or by hatred for his own culture. At this juncture behavior may tend to become violent but disoriented.

---

[9]*Ibid.*, p. 58.
[10]*Ibid.*, p. 46.
[11]*Ibid.*, p. 38.
[12]Emile Durkheim, who developed the modern theory of anomie, does not believe anomie is typical of poor peoples.

This model, therefore, springs from the native's double sense of alienation from the settler's world and from his own world, to that individual lashing out in indiscriminate violence. Misdirected as such violence may appear, it is a form of release as well as a way of calling attention to the dilemma he is in. The settler therefore, focuses attention on the individual native and through him on the native community.

ALIENATION AND A MODEL OF SOCIAL INTERACTION

Alienation and anomie, as cause of violence and terrorism is in effect a form (model) of social interaction.

This model is based on the mutual relationship of two societies, which for the purposes of this article, are presumed to be between a dominant Western society and a Third World non-aligned developing society.

In this model, socially meaningful interaction takes place between individuals and groups and through it as a certain medium of communication is established. Usually because the settler group has control of such a medium, it is first to convey to the native group its values which are invariably presented with a sense of the superiority of the settler's society over the native community. The native community which in turn communicates its values to the settlers has only limited recourse and does so from a position of inferiority.

The normative relationship for the settler society is that "in the colonial context, the settler only ends his work of breaking in the native when the latter admits loudly and intelligently the supremacy of the white man's values."[13]

Thus the communication impact of the settler community over the natives far overshadows the impact the native community has on the settlers and consequently on that type of mixed society.

As a result of this unequal social interaction, the Third World community is more apt to have its social processes radically altered or even totally uprooted. Indigenous *religious* practices

---

[13]Fanon, *Supra* note 1, p. 43.

and beliefs may be replaced by the settler's version thereof and the *political* structure may lose much of its tribalism or family orientation in favor of structures duplicating those of the settler group in its indigenous context. Similarly the community *economy,* which may have been dependent on agriculture or on village units, may begin to take on some of the characteristics of the settler society even though the community itself may have little inclination in that direction. The native community is then made to develop an awareness of its own inadequacies as a perceived contrast to the settler's society. Thus the dynamic process of society-culture-personality is stymied. This is so because that process consists of the intersecting components of social and cultural values, and the personality of its members.

All human groups are motion, involved in a process of shifting from one social system to another, and invariably such process entails a changing of values and individual personality.

This transitional process involves a transition from gemeinschaft (community) to gesselschaft (society) and whenever it evolves on a continuum, it is nonviolent.

In the colonial setting, however, the transition does not occur on a continuum but as the result of a social dichotomy. If the native opts for the "passing" model, he forsakes the stage of gemeinschaft altogether and admits to the supremacy of the dominant society's values. If the native opts for the "zombi" model he does the reverse and makes any transition wholly irrelevant because it never leads to the stage of gessellshcaft but revolves at best around that of gemeinschaft. If the native follows the maximal course and demands that "the last shall be first," he carries the values of gemeinschaft into the stage of gessellschaft. He attempts to make society through force but without rejecting his own community; in other words, he proceeds along the basis of a positive uprooting process in which the community is radically altered but without rejection of origin. This then avoids dichotomy and presents a harmonized transition which when it is inspected is thrust forward by violence.

This then creates a dynamic balance between aggressive and integrative roles. The aggressive roles correspond roughly to *con-*

flict and *competition,* while the integrative roles correspond to *cooperation, acculturation,* and *assimilation.*

This balance of integrative and aggressive drives remains a static dichotomy until the latter overweighs the former. In other words, there exists a total confrontation of values which reduces the dominance of the settler values to the maximal demands of the natives.

Thus Fanon's vision of revolutionary violence solves the dichotomy to a limited extent because the native relates in an integrative manner his own group but in an aggressive manner to the settler's. However, the success of this solution depends on the submergence of the individual personality in the group and the dominance of revolutionary violence over all other forms of group behavior. Nonetheless the dichotomy still exists in that the native continues to act aggressively toward the settler, while integratively toward his community but in this case it becomes a positive factor. Uncoordinated violence epitomizes aggression among natives and toward the settler which can become a negative factor in attaining gemeinschaft within gessellschaft.

As a result and for many reasons, the native group may develop self-hatred along with increased hatred for the settler society and the ultimate society sought to be created. This then is likely to generate spiraling violence without positive outcomes.

Under these circumstances, terror violence, though self-destructive and seemingly senseless, can at least serve as an attention-getting device or a polarization strategy which could become integrative of the community. In this case, the development becomes positive and leads to another stage in the creation of society.

Colonization is a caste, not a class system, and consequently there are several mobility limitations placed on the native. The native who attempts to "pass for white" or at least "act white" is confronting the most obvious mobility limitation—his race. His aim is to move vertically into society, even if he must reject horizontal mobility within his native community.

The native who opts for the superstructure of myth opts out status in the white society entirely, in favor of horizontal and vertical mobility within the confines of his own culture. On the other hand, the native who opts for Fanon's revolutionary violence based on maximal demands is not concerned at all about individual status because he has made the decision to move vertically into society but as an integral part of his community. Vertical mobility is, therefore, important only in the context of the entire community moving upward. This approach rejects individual terror violence because individual status is not at stake nor theoretically is the quest for leadership based on a personality cult. Thus only that type of violence which has a community purpose will be tolerated by the group.

CONCLUSION

Colonial alienation breeds liberating violence. It is an almost indispensable factor in the emancipation process without which neither the native feels cleansed nor the settler freed from the stigma of colonialism. It is not however, wholly indiscriminate or senseless violence, it is a strategy of terror-violence which may occur randomly, but which is invariably linked to a goal and is part of a policy. It is to that extent antithetical to haphazard or even systematic individual violence because there is in these instances no legitimizing end to be served. That end is not only liberation from colonialism but the creation of a new society after liberation. That type of terror violence thus serves a dual purpose, one with respect to ending colonialism and the other with respect to forging the bonds of the new society. To some extent it is a form of violence which is based on a nexus between the means employed and a well defined objective whose value-oriented goal is the accelerating attainment of the perceived goal.

TERRORISM
AND THE MASS MEDIA*

FRANCO SALOMONE

THE MASS MEDIA HAS FROM time to time been charged with fostering or subtly encouraging terrorism because of its *sensationalistic* approach to the coverage of violent events. As a consequence, suggestions have been made to place some limitations or restrictions on the media as a means of controlling terrorism.

These two questions of the relationship of terrorism and the media, and placing restrictions of the media as a means of controlling terrorism, are the object of this presentation.

The spread of terrorism compels us to no less than a reexamination of the assumptions which we have heretofore taken for granted in dealing with this problem which requires radical solutions since it appears that it cannot be dealt with in conventional terms.

Probably the most significant question for the media and particularly the printed media (which follows in time of coverage radio and television) is the issue of *sensationalism*. Major daily newspapers cannot avoid responding sensationally to sensational news because the role of such dailies is to serve as a vehicle for news and information. But all too often, as Marshall McLuhan puts it, the medium is confused with the message. In our view, it is not the coverage which is sensational as much as the news. There is however no question that the manner in which it is presented, by way of headlines, pictures and captions, is intended to

---

*This article is a summary of Mr. Salomone's presentation at the conference and was prepared by the editor.

have a vivid effect on the reader. There are several points which merit consideration in this respect. The first is that the printed media, particularly with respect to acts of violence and terror, invariably reaches the public after the audio-visual media and consequently it has less of a shock impact on the readership which is likely to have already heard the news. The perpetrators of such acts rely less on printed coverage for publicity because it is slower and reaches a smaller audience. From the terrorist's point of view it is also less effective even though headlines and banners may have a sensationalistic flavor as some would see it. Nevertheless the printed media (in countries where the press is free) will usually take positions which may endorse or condemn the action which has taken place. In the case of my newspaper, (ILTEMPO di Roma) we have a policy of opposing acts of terror-violence and our coverage of such acts is intended to reveal to what extent such acts violate public order and victimize others, particularly innocent persons. While it must be admitted that acts of terror-violence are a psychological strategy designed to have its effect on the general public through media coverage and other forms of publicity, it is not equally true that such coverage fosters or encourages violence by the mere conveying of facts and information. Certainly editorial positions and columns which represent a given point of view give to the events they relate to an ideological coloring but its impact is not known. Nevertheless a general impression which is commonly accepted is that the public, in all countries where acts of terror-violence have taken place, is shocked by such acts and overwhelmingly condemns them. Certainly mass media communication has had something to do with this general attitude which is from my point of view a healthy one. Considering, however, that the perpetrators of acts of terror-violence take into account the revulsion of the general public to such acts, then if their intended purpose is to generate sympathy for their cause, the outcome is usually the opposite. It is advanced however that terrorists do not seek sympathy or support, but publicity, and also they seek to polarize people in order for their radicalization program to become effective. This opinion may indeed be valid and in this case the perpetrators of terror-violence seek the media for itself rather than for the position which it takes. In other words the terror strategy relies on the very communication rather than what is being communicated. It is precisely this observation which leads to the most important question at stake: freedom of communication. The question of whether or not to place limitations or restrictions on freedom of communication and information as a means of controlling terrorism depends on the values attributed to freedom of information and communication and the perceived need to restrict it in order to accomplish a more socially imperative value, presumably that of depriving terrorist of dissemination news of their actions. While this appears to be a difficult question it is not so if one considers its components. On the one hand freedom of information and communication has become a right established in international human rights law, and in the constitution and national laws of almost all countries in the world. It is fought for where it does not exist in fact or where it is curtailed and it is strenuously defended whenever and wherever it is attacked, particularly in the free world. It is considered by the standards and values of almost all people in the world as a main tenet of democracy and freedom. Its existence is deemed almost essential to the exercise of democratic control over public entities, governments, public servants, private institutions, and as a means of highlighting social issues and focusing on social needs. All these social values and others embodied in freedom of information and communication do not however mean that this right is immune from legal and ethical limitations as indeed it is not. The questions then are what type of controls, how much of it and in what manner are they to apply? To decide these questions, we must have some empirical data to indicate among other things the degree to which any restrictions on the mass media are likely to have a beneficial effect on the control of terrorism. There is no data on this point and therefore it is difficult to propose any plan on the basis of untested if not uncertain assumptions. To the extent, however, that there is a general impression that some connection exists between certain acts of terrorism and a certain type of mass media coverage it is necessary to consider what should be done about it. This assumption, however, is predicated on the fact that the individual motivation of persons who engage in actual terror-violence differ. According to Professor Bassiouni there are three categories: the psycho-pathological, the common criminal, and the ideologically motivated. It appears that as to all three categories it is possible to develop a media policy which could eliminate an inducing factor from the individual's decision to engage in terror-violence. To do so, however, requires more knowledge than we now have as to such motivations and a great deal of speculation as to the deterrence assumptions we are relying on to hope that we can by any means of restricting media coverage help prevent acts of terrorism. Assuming that some benefit may derive from, for example, temporarily withholding certain facts from general publication or such other idea, then it is best developed through a mass media council which would develop its own standards and enforce them through the profession. This would safeguard the independence of the profession and its freedom from governmental intervention while leaving to its experts the task of determining what to do and how to do it. Such voluntary restraints should be reached through cooperation between the profession, competent governmental agencies and public interest groups. The objective of such a policy would be to devise those means which are compatible with the principle of freedom of information and communication and which are most likely to attain certain results in the effort against terrorism. The media mindful of its responsibilities to the public should cooperate in such an effort but understandably it is first interested in finding out the basis upon which such cooperation is to be undertaken in order to protect its first duty, that of freedom of information and communication.

ANTI-HISTORY AND TERRORISM: A PHILOSOPHICAL DIMENSION

Nina Strickler

THE PRACTICAL INTERESTS of international law and the severe repercussions of terrorism at an international level largely preclude the development of philosophical perspectives on the subject. Some significant work has been done in the area of ideology and terror by Hannah Arendt. In *On Revolution* she discusses the relationship as one which developed during the French Revolution. She also contends that

> to the extent that the greatest event in every revolution is the act of foundation, the spirit of revolution contains two elements which to us seem irreconcilable and even contradictory. The act of founding the new body politic, of devising the new form of government involves the grave concern with the stability and durability of the new structure; the experience, on the other hand, which those who are engaged in this grave business are bound to have is the exhilarating awareness of the human capacity of beginning, the high spirits which have always attended the birth of something new on earth.[1]

This insight lays the foundation for a philosophical discussion of terrorism and anti-history. It illustrates the role of ideology in the revolutionary spirit as well. For behind every revolutionary act, individual or collective, there is a fundamental view of the rights of man. While the passing of generations naturally selects and reinforces certain of these fundamental views in a more or less subtle interaction, the contradiction that Hannah Arendt finds in all revolt reveals the difficulties of selection of views from a rejected tradition and the alternative of making a single selection into something absolute.

---

[1]Hannah Arendt, *On Revolution* (New York, 1963), p. 225.

In face of this contradiction, the creation of a new order is shown clearly to evolve from established values as they are selected, made essential and threatened. Terrorism appears to intervene by destroying the tradition, forcing the selection of rights that remain to be pronounced and finally defending the exercise of those rights.

In the Marxian tradition, the contradiction between the destruction of the past and the creation of the future in the present is represented historically by two classes, however that polarity may vary.

The proletariat is seen as the agency which is not only revolutionary in thought but in action as well. Everything depends on a fundamental decision not just to understand the world, but to change it. In the 19th and 20th centuries, this decision to change the world countered a philosophical tradition of seeking reason in history in which revolution was merely an affair of reason and will. Reason is materialized by way of those classes by which history is delivered. Reason is a class reason and proletariat *praxis* is the vehicle of an effective universality which shows man's creative force in history. It further reveals the contingencies of law. Traditional truths and established principles of human nature are not merely historical products, revealing a duality between formal legality and moral authority.

Since the goal of revolution is the act of foundation or creation, the present is a state of contradiction and something merely to be tolerated. Acts of terror can act to "purge" the present of history, eradicate the contradiction and allow the new humanity to arise without limitation or bias. However, the process of "purging" the present is a process of eliminating values, a devaluation. Men could now condemn one another to death because they did not see the future the same way.

The fundamental contradiction of a present faced with creating a future anew and conserving the "eternal laws" of society appears in each attempt to construct theories of revolutions or analyses of their ideological foundations. The Marxian tradition, an historical tradition in which events arise "in a context" seems to undermine the pretense to reevaluate society and create entirely new structures. Man is either the spectator or interpreter of a closed history or the material of an active one. Proletariat *Praxis* introduces the element of construction rather than knowledge as an end in itself. So the world is not merely an object of contemplation but something to be transformed.

The International Covenant on Economic, Social and Cultural Rights and the International Covenant on Civil and Political Rights, and the Convention for the protection of Human Rights and Fundamental Freedoms of the American Convention on Human Rights condemn both individual and state terrorism. Legitimate resistance to oppression and tyranny is an internationally recognized right as a "last resort" when political and juridical avenues of redress have been exhausted. Ideology functions not merely to define the fundamental human rights in the absence of "eternal laws," but it also functions to define the threat and expose the meaning of the "last resort." For reaction against every threat at once infringes and defends a human right. A rationale which secures a compelling state interest or international interest places in balance the relative value of the right asserted or sought. The standard of fundamental human rights formulated in the *Covenant* and the *Convention* are rather simple ones and meet those standards which are attributable to reasonable men who seek constraint of terror. But this standard is for those who "interpret" a "closed history." The standard is another convention, the enemy of the future and the virtual object of terror. Philosophically, the opposition to history buries the possibilities of legitimate resistance or redress as long as the terrorist rejects the avenues of redress at the outset. Terrorism repudiates those norms and conventions which have incurred historical injustice.

Thus terrorism begins in negation. The metaphysical model varies, but philosophical nihilism is fundamentally exhibited, appearing in the history of revolutionary movements as consistently as the duality of past and future. In the language of the Russian revolutionary Bielinsky, "the annihilation of the past is the procreation of the future."[2] The present is merely an interference between the destruction of the past and the creation of the future.

---

[2]Maurice Merleau-Ponty, *Humanism and Terror* (Boston: 1947), p. 129.

It is the contradiction which terrorism finally consumes in a simultaneous act of sacrifice (of the present insofar as it is a remnant of the past) and murder.

Devoid of history, the new creators thus take on a god-like quality. The new man, successful in having "overcome" the past in a Nietzschean "transvaluation of values" will be, in strictly philosophical language, both the essential and the existential, a traditional definition of God. The dynamic death-wish in terrorism exhibits the knowledge in Nietzsche's terms that *being* is merely a continual *has been*, a thing that lives by denying and destroying and contradicting itself. The terrorist has nothing to lose. Similarly, the revolutionary Bielinski claims that the individual cannot accept history as it is. He must destroy reality, not collaborate with it, in order to affirm his own existence. Negation is my god, as reality formerly was. My heroes are the destroyers of the past. . . ."[3] Renouncing the past completely, the revolutionary believes the human personality can be reconstructed. He could thus augment Nietzsche's requirement that the new humanity be one which has overcome history in the accomplishment of a transvaluation of values, a new genesis of norms. Precisely because it is an institution of another set of norms, however, the renouncement becomes an act of faith and the personal solution to the injustice perceived as historical product simply consists in endowing negation with the intransigence and passion of faith in the form of a new conservatism. This is the paradox of anti-history and social change, and it is a paradox which illustrates part of the difficulties faced by International Congresses attempting to effect practical international controls by selecting among traditions those norms which supplant no "fundamental rights" but rather lend validity and sanction to the expectations of the reasonable man.

---

[3]*Ibid.*

A PHILOSOPHICAL PERSPECTIVE ON REBELLION*

Luis Kutner

Liberty is a boisterous sea. Timid men prefer the dead calm of despotism.
*Rebellion to tyrants is obedience to God.***

FOR SOME 3,500 YEARS, man has been at war nine hours out of every ten. During the past twenty years, mankind has survived 379 armed conflicts. Beginning with the American and French Revolutions, the dominant characteristic of the contemporary world has been revolution. The Soviet, Chinese and other contemporary revolutions are extensions of what may be regarded as a revolutionary tradition. The purpose of these revolutions is not merely to replace one authority with another, but to change the underlying social system.[1] The underlying ideology of these revolutions encompasses such universal values that revolution in one country challenges the *status quo* elsewhere and posits a change in the international system.[2] Clearly, revolution or acts of rebellion in one state involve questions of international law such as intervention or nonintervention by other states or by the international community, the right of national self-determination, the rights of de jure

---

*Reprinted with permission of Valparaiso Law Review, Vol. 7, 1972. Excerpts from "Due Process of Rebellion."

**From a letter which is of great significance in the history of the freedom of the press. Publisher Woodfall was prosecuted for seditious libel; the jury brought in a verdit of "guilty of printing and publishing only." After a second trial, Woodfall was freed on payment of costs. J. Bartlett, *Familiar Quotations*, 13th ed. 1002b (1965).

[1]H. Arendt, *On Revolution*, 1961.

[2]M. Kaplan, and N. Katzenbach ed., *Revolution In World Politics* (1962) p. 5-10.

and de facto governments, and the rights of individuals who have committed—or are affected by—acts of rebellion or revolution.

The focus of this work is upon the international protection of the rights of both active and passive participants in revolutionary action. The basis for such international protection lies in the recognition of the right to rebel under certain circumstances and upon a consideration of the international consequences of revolution.

THE ORIGIN OF THE CONCEPT OF
LEGITIMATE REBELLION

Political writers from antiquity have stressed the need for obedience to law and the horrors of anarchy. However, private action to overthrow a tyrant has been considered justified. In the republican city-state of Greece, the tyrant was a usurper; thus, it was considered as honorable for a citizen to stake his life in an attempt to remove the usurper as it was for him to sacrifice his life to repel the invader. Though at first "tyranny" referred to the method by which the tyrant came to power, the term later came to refer to the nature of the rule.[3] To Plato, the distinguishing characteristic of the tyrant is his egocentric and licentious disregard of the welfare of the people he rules. In Plato's view, the mechanical test of legality or constitutionality is not the fundamental issue; what is more important is the ruler himself and the nature of his rule. Similarly, Aristotle regarded tyranny as a perversion of monarchy in which the leader exercises irresponsible rule over subjects against their will, with a view to his own private interests rather than the interests of the persons ruled. Tyranny is marked by the arbitrary and irresponsible power of a single individual. Neither Plato nor Aristotle seriously considered arguments for tyrannicide or resistance of the tyrant; these considerations were developed by later writers.

Cicero and the Stoic philosophers stressed the importance of natural law, derived from right reason, in binding the common-

---

[3]O. Jaszi, and J. Lewis, *Against the Tyrant* 4 (1957). For a systems analysis *see* N. Leites, and C. Wolf, *Rebellion and Authority, An Analytic Essay on Insurgent Conflicts* (1970).

wealth. Although opposed to the dissolution of the Roman Republic, Cicero justified the assassination of Julius Ceasar under the natural law.[4] Seneca, who saw the depths to which political degeneration could descend under the tyranny of Nero, recommended tyrannicide as the only cure.[5] Although the Roman jurists recognized that what pleases the prince has the force of law, they also developed the doctrine that even imperial power is subject to law's control. The sharp distinction between the lawful ruler, who seeks first his own ends, was fundamental in both Greek and Roman political thought.

Early Christians, following Paul, adhered to the belief that government is made necessary by the depravity of man and insisted upon the Christian duty of obedience to the ruler, who was considered to be God's instrument for repressing evil. Such commandments as "[t]he powers that be are ordained by God" and the injunction to "submit yourselves to every ordinance of man for the Lord's sake" were the guidelines for early believers.[6] Augustine stressed that the authority of all rulers is derived from God and hence is subject to obedience. Though recognizing that one who kills another in obedience to God's direct command is not guilty of sinful murder, the direction of Augustine's writing upholds the divine right of kings. According to Augustine and Gregory the Great, God sends good kings as well as bad, and those who murmur against the rulers murmur against God.[7] However, one early church father, Isidor of Seville, distinguished between kings and tyrants and urged that the title "king" belongs to him who governs rightly and is lost to those who govern unrighteously. Pope Nicholas I stressed that obedience is required to him who is truly a king.

Medieval thinkers were particularly concerned with the problem of resistance to authority. Though the king's rule was acknowledged to be absolute, it was still subject to the law. To Bracton, this meant that the king may not alter or abolish the law. He must not change the traditional form of government; his judgments of right

[4]O. Jaszi, and J. Lewis, *Against the Tyrant* 9 (1957), p. 9.
[5]*Ibid.,* p. 10-11.
[6]*Romans* 13:1-5; I *Peter* 2:13-14.
[7]O. Jaszi, and J. Lewis, *Against the Tyrant* (1957), pp. 13-15.

must follow the rules laid down by custom; and he cannot take the property of his subjects (except as penalty for crime) without their consent.[8] Other scholars stressed adherence to the ethical and rational principles derived from natural law. Divine law was also held to limit the king. The king derives authority from the community and acts on the community's behalf. Any check on his authority can only come through private resistance by individuals or groups. Within this context, the tyrant can be differentiated from the king. The tyrant bases his authority not on law, but on force. While the king assumes a likeness of divinity, the tyrant takes on the likeness of the devil.[9] Wycliff, however, believed that the tyrant must be obeyed, with punishment to the ruler coming in the hereafter. Aquinas and Occam asserted the right to disobey those commands which were either contrary to fundamental law or outside the scope of the ruler's legitimate authority. Strong currents of medieval thought supported the view that the king who misuses his power may be resisted forcefully. The idea of contractual obligations between king and subject was first explicitly expressed by Manegold of Lautenbach.[10] Though Aquinas regarded sedition as a moral sin, he did not consider it seditious to resist a tyrant. Rather, it is the tyrant who, in violating the law, commits sedition. But Aquinas, citing ancient and hence inapplicable precedents,[11] opposed private action against a tyrant who has a legitimate title to rule, urging, instead appeal to higher authority. Some writers sought an institutional check by appeal to the Pope. Marsiglio of Padua urged the establishment of an independent agency of the people to discipline the ruler.

Clearly, while the doctrine of tyrannicide was not predominant in medieval thought, it was consistent with the main tendencies of medieval political theory. The king, as protector of the common good, is bound by the principles of nature which objectively define this common good. The resister of the law-defying tyrant acts not for the protection of his own private values, but for protection of

---

[8]*Ibid.*, p. 19.
[9]*Ibid.*
[10]*Ibid.*, p. 31.
[11]*Ibid.*, pp. 20-27.

the entire community. Tyrannicide and resistance function as an institutionalized check upon the ruler. Though ultimate authority stems from God, immediate authority comes from the common will of the community. No one denied that a private person may resist and take the life of a tyrant without title; the problem arose with regard to the right of a private person in relation to a titled ruler who becomes a tyrant by abuse of power.

In the early modern period, characterized by the centralized authority of the kings, the trend was toward absolution. Though Luther had contempt for the dignity of princes, he denounced resistance. Calvin was also opposed to the resistance of authority, but followers such as John Knox urged resistance where religious belief was threatened. John Knox condoned Protestant resistance to Mary Tudor and Mary Stuart.[12] Resistance was also condoned when the French persecuted the Huguenots. Thus, the development of Protestant thought ranged from a theory of passive obedience to theoretical support for the right and duty of resistance. The growth of the resistance theory was basically a response to the political situation in Scotland and France. Those who supported resistance relied upon the earlier medieval body of thought.

Two significant 16th century humanists who justified rebellion were John Buchanan and Etienne de la Boetie. Buchanan, in defending the deposition of Mary Stuart, argued in his *DeJuri Regni and Seotos* that the authority of kings is established by the consent of the people, resting on a social contract which encompasses the king's acceptance of the rule of law.[13] The law, like the king's authority, is derived from the community; thus, those who confer authority on the king can limit that authority as well as punish kings who exceed that authority. When the king dissolves the bonds of authority, no obedience is owed to him. Under these circumstances, a rebellion is justified and a private person may kill the law-defying king. La Boetie's *Discourse on Voluntary Servitude* departed from Aristotelian and medieval conventions by digging at the roots of tyranny. He found psychological reasons for the roots of

---

[12]*Ibid.,* pp. 48-49. *See* Kenyon, *A Hectic Revolution, The New York Review of Books* (Jan. 4), pp. 27-29.
[13]O. Jaszi, and J. Lewis, *Against the Tyrant* (1957), pp. 53-56.

tyranny in the fact that custom gradually wears away man's natural love of liberty and leads to his submission to servitude. Tyranny, then, is supported by a hierarchy of those who benefit from the tyrant. La Boetie's cure for tyranny lay in passive resistance, the refusal of the subjects to consent and obey.[14]

Two Jesuit writers who justified tyrannicide were Suarez and Mariana. Mariana's *De Regis Institutione,* published in 1599, included a bitter denunciation of tyranny, urging that the people from whom a king derives power may overthrow him. According to Mariana, there is no question that a usurper—a person who assumes authority without a valid title—may be killed by anyone since he is a public enemy. Where, however, a rightful king abuses his authority his power must be tolerated more patiently. If the king destroys the commonwealth, plunders private fortunes, or holds the laws and religion in contempt, a representative body must warn him. If the king refuses to heed the warning, this body can depose him and there exists a justification for his death. If the ruler prevents the convening of a public assembly, this in itself is conclusive evidence of his tyranny, and the king can be overthrown. Before taking any action, however, the liberator should first consult "learned and grave men."[15] Mariana's book was burned in France. Mariana's views departed from those of Suarez and the traditional Jesuit and Catholic approach in that Mariana was not concerned with the right of the Pope to absolve subjects from their allegiance, thus tending to be more secular and conventional. In France, the Jesuits were denounced as disturbers of the public peace, while in England, Presbyterians, as well as Jesuits, were similarly denounced.[16]

During the 17th and 18th centuries, the concept of the social contract was formulated in English thought by Hobbes and Locke. To Hobbes, the sovereignty of the state is based upon the social contract, which ends the war of one-against-all in the state of nature. Authority is considered necessary for individual security. An individual may not breach his contractual obligations—especially

---

[14]*Ibid.,* pp. 56-57.

[15]*Ibid.,* pp. 68-71.

[16]*Ibid.*

the obligation to obey the sovereign—unless the state threatens to take his life. Thus, a prisoner condemned to death has the natural right to attempt an escape.[17] Locke, however, perceived the individual as having certain rights in the state of nature which are retained subsequent to the formation of the social contract. Where these rights are infringed, as by the denial of property, a right to rebel exists.[18] The right of rebellion is based upon a two-party relationship between the people and their government. Locke's concept influenced the framers of the Declaration of Independence who justified the revolt of the American colonies.[19]

The defense of the right of tyrannicide and of rebellion throughout the 17th century was essentially conservative in that the object was to destroy an improper innovation and restore former values to the community, not to clear the way for new social organization. The justification for tyrannicide and rebellion was the vindication of commonly shared and well-rooted values. In the 17th century, the issue arose within the context of conflict between emerging absolutist monarchs and the older traditions. At first, many thinkers considered enlightened absolutism as derived from the divine right to eliminate feudal anarchy and religious wars. Subsequently, there was an emerging awareness that the new absolutism leads to the development of tyrannical traits and oppression. However, the feeling developed that the mere killing of the king does not solve the problem of a tyrannical system. The community must not only resist, but also establish new constitutional institutions. Within this context, Locke conceived that a tyrannical system causes authority to revert back to the community, thus giving the people the right to revolt. The American colonists were clearly the heirs of this tradition. To Jefferson, resistance against tyranny is not merely justified but at times posi-

---

[17]Hobbes, *Leviathan* in Barker, ed., *Social Contract* (1952), pp. 107-109.
[18]Locke, "Second Treatise on Civil Government" in Barker, ed., *Social Contract* (1952), pp. 100-104.
[19]Stern, *John Locke and the Declaration of Independence*, 15 *Clev.-Mar. L. Rev.*, 186 (1966).

tively essential to the maintenance of human liberty.[20] But, as with Locke, mere resistance to a tyrant is not considered adequate; this, the participants in the American Revolution deliberately constructed a constitution based on a theory of representative government with checks and balances to restrain power. The concept of separation of powers was considered fundamental to the protection of freedom.[21]

The French Revolution, like the American, emphasized the symbol of the tyrant. Particularly, the Jacobins and the leftwing revolutionaries believed themselves to be the successors of the old Romans who had fought for the liberty of the Republic. The debate concerning the execution of Louis XVI centered upon the symbol of the tyrant. Merely killing the tyrant was an insufficient measure. Tom Paine declared: "Execute the king but not the man!"[22] Thus, by the end of the 18th century, thinking turned away from theories of tyrannicide and individual resistance and toward theories of revolution. Under the new theories of revolution, the use of force by the entire community is the avenue through which people can eliminate unbearable abuses. By so doing, the people can increase individual and social happiness by crushing the whole corrupt regime. The people can also create a new and better constitution in which representative government, separation of powers, and the definition of inalienable human rights serve as institutional checks against the very possibility of tyranny.[23]

In the 19th century, new concepts of tyranny emerged. Bentham, who rejected natural law concepts, defined tyranny in terms of degrees of unhappiness. When, according to his hedonistic calculus, the amount of unhappiness exceeds the amount of happiness,

---

[20]Jefferson, in reacting to Shay's Rebellion, stated:

God forbid that we should ever be twenty years without such a rebellion. . . . What country can preserve its liberties, if their rulers are not warned from time to time that the people preserve the spirit of resistance? The tree of liberty must be refreshed from time to time with the blood of patriots and tyrants. It is its natural nature.

II Malone, *Jefferson and His Time* (1951), xvii, pp. 165-167.

[21]O. Jaszi, and J. Lewis, *Against the Tyrant* (1957), pp. 104-105.

[22]*Ibid.,* p. 110.

[23]*Ibid.*

one has the right to resist authority and to rebel. While Bentham believed that representative government effectively serves to harmonize the self-interest of the rules with the self-interest of the ruled, he feared that the unenlightened masses can themselves become tyrannical. The true tyranny of human ignorance, stupidity and superstitution is, of course, invisible. An anarchist such as Tolstoy condemns the entire social structure as immoral since it is founded on force. To Marx, tyranny is derived from the laws of economic evolution and the class structure. Many of Marx's followers opposed acts of individual violence and revolt, believed rather in the laws of economic determinism.

The old tradition of tyrannicide was retained in Italy where liberal writers protested against the petty tyrants who emerged during the struggle for freedom and unity. The Italian tradition furnished the motivating force for other revolutionary movements. During the French Revolution, the doctrine of tyrannicide was espoused by Babeoufism and also by Blanqui, who, in 1824, sought to seize power through revolt of an armed minority and thus establish the dictatorship of the proletariat. Between 1837 and 1870, the Blanquists participated in 13 uprisings. Interestingly, Blanqui's concepts were later revived by Lenin. Nineteenth century anarchists such as Bakunin and Kropotkin regarded both the political and economic systems then existing as tyrannous, thereby justifying individual revolts. A similar tradition of putschism existed in central Europe. In contrast, the responsible leaders of Marxism repudiated putschism. For example, Lenin conceived the role of the intellectual as including a duty to expose the tyranny of the prevailing system—not only as it pertains to the proletariat, but as it affects all classes.[24]

With the advent of the German resistance to Nazism, there developed a new social concept of revolt. To groups of German Catholics and Protestants, the bestiality of the Nazi regime created a moral obligation to organize conspiracies for revolt which culminated in plots to assassinate Hitler. Theologians such as Max

---

[24]*See* V. Lenin, *State and Revolution* (1916). The Marxist position is summarized in S. Hook, *Marx and the Marxists: The Ambiguous Legacy* (1951).

Pribilla[25] and Otto Dibelius[26] reiterated the traditional doctrines as to the right of resistance and revolt when the state exceeds the bounds of morality.

The dictatorships of the 20th century represent the emergency of a new and systematic form of tyranny, differing from the 18th century absolute monarchies and the Napoleonic Empires. In some ways, the tyrannies of these recent dictatorships are similar to the tyrannies of the city-states of antiquity and the Renaissance. The similarities include (1) personal rule unbounded by law; (2) military despotism based on private armies; (3) continuous ventures into dangerous diplomatic situations with the risk of war; (4) luxury and ostentation typifying the life style of the dictator and his "gang"; (5) bounteous remuneration for the obedient servants of the system; (6) intimidation of the people; and, (7) suppression which leaves no possibility for the expression of opinions contrary to the dictatorship for the organization of popular forces to effectuate change. The depravity of the moral structure is the element common to both the old tyranny and the new totalitarianism. The modern tyrannies, however, making use of contemporary technology, exhibit a higher degree of moral depravity. Nevertheless, there have arisen a number of dictatorial regimes which may be regarded as more enlightened, such as that of Kemal Ataturk in Turkey. The new tyranny differs from the old only by espousing a doctrine such as Fascism or Communism. The general aim is to make total the annihilation of the individual personality. There are, however, significant differences between tyrannies, e.g. between Fascism and Bolshevism. The latter has not engaged in some of the excesses of systematic murder characteristic of the former.[27]

---

[25]Pribilla, *An den Grenzen der Staats gewalt,* 142 Stimmen der Zeit, Monatsschrift fur das Geistesleben der Gegenwart (1948) p. 410.

[26]O. Jaszi, and J. Lewis, *Against the Tyrant* (1957) p. 203. Delebius, however, takes a lukewarm position, contending that the resister would involve himself in guilt. Pribilla is more outspoken in justifying rebellion to Nazism.

[27]*Ibid.,* ch. xix. However, there were many parallels between Stalin's and Hitler's totalitarianism. *See* H. Arendt, *The Origins of Totalitarianism* (1952). Significantly, Fidel Castro, in his famous defense speech at the Moncada Trial in Santiago De Cuba in 1953 made reference to the classical arguments regarding the resistance to tryranny in justifying his revolt against Batista. F. Castro, *History Will Absolve Me* (1969).

Colonialism is still another context wherein revolt against authority has found justification. Gandhi, beginning in the 1920's, led organized campaigns of passive resistance to disobedience against what he and the Indian Congress Party regarded as the imposition of immoral rule by Britain in India. Influenced by Thoreau and Tolstoy, as well as by Hindu tradition, Gandhi based his resistance on principles of nonviolence as governed by *Satyagraha* and *Ahinsa* to effect a change in the heart and mind of the oppressor. These methods, with modification, were applied in Africa and in the civil rights struggle in the United States. Although unsuccessful, the late Albert Luthuli led a series of civil disobedience campaigns against the system of apartheid in South Africa.[28]

Many of the colonial revolutions such as those in Palestine, Indonesia, Cyprus, Indochina and Algeria were of a violent nature. A system of guerrilla warfare and terrorism was employed to expel the colonial power. The struggle for national independence in Asia and Africa is being stimulated by ideologies of nationalism and popular sovereignty. These philosophies, originally imported from the West, have achieved universal application.[29]

Clearly, the justification for rebellion and revolution is derived from a tradition of political thought having roots in antiquity. This tradition was adapted to Christian principles by medieval theologians and further refined in the course of the Reformation and the struggle for popular sovereignty in the 16th and 17th centuries. The principles were transformed in the 19th and 20th centuries in order to promote the overthrow of institutions deemed tyrannous and the establishment of constitutional systems based on popular freedom conducive to the development of human dignity. The rise of totalitarianism in the 20th century has created situations wherein revolt may become morally obligatory. The struggle for independence by oppressed people has also created situations in which rebellion is justified.

---

[28]M. Sibley, *The Quiet Battle* (Anchor ed. 1963), pp. 236-287.
[29]*See* M. Kaplan, and N. Katzenbach, ed., *The Revolution in World Politics* (1962).

FORMS OF REBELLION

Power is defined as the capacity of a group or an individual to modify the conduct of other individuals. The organized and sanctioned power in a society is designated as "authority," having the capacity to make binding decisions for the community.[30] This capacity is the function of popular consent—active or passive acceptance by the population. This consent is frequently related to the objectives pursued by an elite on behalf of the community. Sometimes this consent is granted when the elite is regarded as legitimatized by moral or metaphysical considerations. Where these sources of consent are absent, the elite engaged in pursuing social objectives must rely on force exercised by armies, police units and other instruments of coercion. Hence, authority is a balance of force and consent with respect to a set of social objectives. Though an element of force is needed, consent is also needed for the functioning of social institutions. The seizure of power is the seizure of a balance of coercion and consent which involves not only the capture of the instruments of force in society but also the winning of a certain degree of popular acceptance. The objectives of the elite must conform to changes in society. Where values and social expectations change, the structure of authority undergoes crises, of which revolution is the most extreme form. Revolution involves the termination of state authority and presupposes the collapse of both consensus and organized force. Once the instruments of force disintegrate simultaneously with, or as a result of, popular rebellion, revolution is likely. The revolutionary seizure of power involves the destruction of the old power base and the establishment of a new one. There need not be a mass rebellion. The key to success is massive alienation from the old government. The strategy for revolution was well developed by the Bolsheviks and subsequently by Mao Tse Tung.

While revolution involves the complete disintegration of state institutions, the coup d'etat involves the seizure of these institutions with the new authority evolving from the old. The loyalties of the

---

[30]The discussion in this section is based generally upon A. Janos, *The Seizure of Power and Popular Consent* (1964).

effective power instruments of the state are transferred from one group or individual to another, with a gap being created between formal and effective power in society. Subsequently, the holders of formal power are forced to withdraw or be eliminated. Often, the existing heads of state are coerced to sanction their own demise by signing a document or by submitting to a vote of confidence extorted behind closed doors. The process may not be sudden or dramatic, and it is often even orderly. One type of coup d'etat is the palace revolution in which a small group of conspirators removes one of its number by arrest or assassination. A palace revolution occurred when Mussolini was deposed in 1943 as a result of a conspiracy involving King Victor Emmanuel, the members of the Fascist Grand Council and a number of high ranking military officers. Another recent palace revolution occurred in Soviet Russia, leading to the ascendency of Khrushchev and subsequently of Brezhnev and Kosygin. Another type of coup is characterized by conspirators who, while unable to gain control of the state apparatus, nonetheless represent important factions within society, such as the army, which factions enable them to move in response to popular dissatisfaction. The crucial element in this form of coup is the threat of civil conflict which may be regarded as a greater evil than the ascendency of the political opponent. The coup does not develop suddenly, but involves extensive plotting. An alternative approach lies in infiltration, which is the placement of trusted individuals in strategic positions in an attempt to change the loyalties and goals of established organizations. This approach is used by the Communists of Eastern Europe.

In contrast to a revolution in which popular support is achieved first, followed by the seizure of the state apparatus, a coup entails first the seizure of authority and then the gaining of popular consent. The participation of the military alone is insufficient for gaining popular support. An aura of legitimacy, such as the inclusion of cabinet ministers and members of parliament, is needed. An attempt is usually made to coerce approval from political leaders. Parliamentary institutions may be taken over by rigging the elections.

Putschism is the term applied to a crude and unsuccessful attempt to seize power. Such an attempt, as was undertaken by Blanqui, was criticized by the Bolsheviks who eschewed the mere occupation of the chancery and stressed the importance of acting only when conditions favoring a seizure of power were present. Nevertheless, the sudden putsch has been attempted in countless instances and romanticized by some writers. A comic example is Hitler's beer hall putsch in Munich. Sometimes an attempt is made to capture one instrumentality, such as the effort by Chilean Nazis in 1938 to take over the radio station.

Until World War II, the popular image of revolutions was closely connected with barricades, urban masses and stormy politics. The success of the partisans in Europe and the victory of guerrilla movements in Asia have popularized terrorism and mobile guerrilla warfare. Though there have been a number of successful campaigns, there have also been some failures. The success of guerrilla warfare lies in combining military techniques with the establishment of base areas of popular support in the mobilization and creation of revolutionary authority, as was well perceived by Mao. The authority of the state cannot be seized by military power alone. Putsches often result in failure because they emphasize the destructive and ignore the constructive aspects of the seizure of power.

The forms of rebellion which have been undertaken have had international consequences. The international community and the states which comprise it must determine whether intervention is to be undertaken to determine the course of a particular revolutionary situation. Questions arise involving recognition of a change of government, the status of insurgents and the rights of individuals who have been affected by acts of rebellion or who are or have been rebels.

CHAPTER II

WARS OF NATIONAL LIBERATION

SECTION 1

THE CONCEPT OF PUBLIC PURPOSE TERROR IN INTERNATIONAL LAW: DOCTRINES AND SANCTIONS TO REDUCE THE DESTRUCTION OF HUMAN AND MATERIAL VALUES*

W. T. MALLISON, JR. AND S. V. MALLISON

From your perspective or mine the creative opportunity is to achieve a self-system larger than the primary ego; larger than the ego components of family, friends, profession, or nation; and inclusive of mankind.[1]

INTRODUCTION

"TERROR" AND "TERRORISM" are not words which refer to a well-defined and clearly identified set of factual events. Neither do the words have any widely accepted meaning in legal doctrine. "Terror" and "terrorism," consequently, do not refer to a unitary concept in either fact or law.

As considered here, terror is the systematic use of extreme violence and threats of violence in order to achieve public or political objectives. Such public purpose or ideologically motivated terror is conducted by governments, groups of diverse characteristics, and individuals. While it is conceded that the control of such terror conducted by governments and nongovernmental groups may be different in some detailed features, the present analysis focuses upon common sanctions applicable to

---

*This article was reprinted with permission in 18 *Howard L. J.* 1 (1974). and appended to *Hearing Before the Subcommittee on International Organizations and Movements of the Committee on Foreign Affairs,* H.R. (April 4, 1974).
[1]Introduction to McDougal, and Feliciano, *Law and Minimum World Public Order* (1961) xxiv.

both. Acts of terrorism which are designed to promote the private gain or profit of common criminals as well as terrorism by the mentally ill are beyond the scope of the present paper. This analysis is designed to deal with the basic problems which arise in the reduction of public purpose terror through the use of international law. Doctrines concerning terror, like other ones of international law, are not ends in themselves. Affirmatively, they are means to achieve values, and negatively, they may be used to prevent the destruction of basic values including life itself. The ideal long-range objectives which are postulated here may be briefly stated as the elimination of acts of terror and their destructive consequences. Initial objectives, which may be more rapidly achieved, may be specified as the substantial reduction of the destruction of human and material values resulting from terrorism. Such an approach must permit identification of the basic causes of terror as well as consideration of some of the more relevant doctrines and sanctions.

In spite of the diversity of participants, objectives, and methods of operation involved in the activities connected with public purpose terrorism, some preliminary conclusions may be made with a degree of assurance. One is that the nongovernmental groups and individuals frequently are convinced that they have no effective alternative to acts of terror to achieve their ends and to protest and dissent from a state of affairs that commonly excludes the terrorists, as well as the peoples they claim to represent, from the minimal sharing of values including the physical protection and human rights accorded to others as a matter of course. These individuals and small groups have employed terror as a desperate attempt to communicate demands for respect and other basic values.[2] Governments frequently have alternative courses of action available to them but have, nevertheless, often responded

---

[2]Terror as a method of communication is considered in the study prepared by the United Nations Secretariat entitled "Measures to Prevent International Terrorism Which Endangers or Takes Innocent Human Lives or Jeopardizes Fundamental Freedoms," and "Study of the Underlying Causes of Those Forms of Terrorism and Acts of Violence Which Lie in Misery, Frustration, Grievance and Despair and Which Cause Some People to Sacrifice Human Lives, Including Their Own, in an Attempt to Effect Radical Changes," A/C.6/418 (Nov. 2, 1972).

with massive military measures which cause a further escalation of the terror. The labels such as "war," "hostilities," "reprisals," and "self-defense," among others, which are often attached to such activities do not, unfortunately, reduce the quantum of violence. The more effective alternatives available to the governments include honoring their existing basic legal obligations under the United Nations Charter and the Geneva Conventions of 1949 for the Protection of War Victims.

It should be obvious that many of the causes of terrorism arising out of basic injustices and the deprivation of elementary human rights are most efficiently eliminated by humanitarian means including political accommodation and compromise. Many governments, however, have preferred to use military means including aerial bombing with civilians as the principal victims. There is considerable historic evidence that no governmental attempt to suppress terrorism has been successful in the absence of a political program designed to eradicate the causes. President Magsaysay used land reform measures to defeat the Huk rebellion in the Philippine Republic, and the British Government in post World War II Malaya created a political and economic situation where the population voluntarily supported the Government and opposed the guerrillas.[3]

Diverse Concepts of Terror

If there is to be effective juridical control of terrorism, the perspective in which the problem is viewed is of considerable importance. There are those who are only willing to examine "the top of the iceberg" rather than seeking to get at the basic causes. They are eager to give a public relations impression of decisiveness and efficiency by treating the symptoms of terrorism, but they make no inquiry concerning its causes.

The Limited Concept of Nongovernmental Terror

The United States Government offered a draft resolution on terrorism to the United Nations General Assembly on September

---

[3]Consideration of political measures to defeat guerrilla terrorism appears in R. Thompson, *Defeating Communist Insurgency* (1966). The author was directly involved in the guerrilla war in Malaya.

26, 1972.[4] Although it recognizes the existence of governmental terrorism by referring in the preamble to the duty of states to refrain from participating in or assisting acts of terror in other states, it focuses attention upon group or individual terrorism and places much emphasis upon the detection and prevention of aircraft hijacking. The Resolution does not take into account the basic differences between political hijackings and criminal ones carried out for private purposes. Both are obviously undesirable and if both are to be prevented, an elementary first step would be to take into account the different purposes involved. However, the draft resolution was written upon the premise that such individual and group terrorism could be minimized, or eliminated, by the application of sufficient governmental power without regard to the causes of such terrorism. The fifth draft paragraph was an important one, and its wording stated that the General Assembly:

> *Strongly recommends* that member governments establish procedures for the exchange of information and data on the plans, activities and movements of terrorists, in order to strengthen the capability of governments to prevent and suppress acts of international terrorism and to prosecute and punish those perpetrating such acts.[5]

The U.S. Government has such arrangements in effect now with other governments which prefer to focus attention on nongovernmental terrorism, and this recommendation, if effectuated, would merely increase the number of governments involved in exchanging information. Nothing in the resolution is designed to restrict governmental terrorism directed at individuals, groups, or peoples.

The draft resolution, which was not accepted by the General Assembly, was accompanied by a draft convention for the prevention and punishment of "certain acts" of international terrorism.[6] This draft convention purports to deal only with what are regarded as the most serious acts of nongovernmental terrorism, those involving unlawful killing, serious bodily harm, or kid-

---

[4]U.S. Dept. of State Bulletin 433, Oct. 16, 1972, p. 67.
[5]*Ibid.*, p. 434.
[6]*Ibid.*, p. 431.

napping. Each of the following four conditions must exist before the convention would apply to these acts. First, the act must be committed or take effect outside the territory of a state of which the offender is a national. This is apparently designed to leave domestic terrorism to municipal law. Second, the act must be committed or take effect outside the territory against which the act is directed. Thus the convention does not cover conflicts taking place within a particular state and directed against it. The "territory" of a state is subsequently defined in broad terms to include all territory under the administration (including, of course, military occupation) of a state. Third, the act does not cover terror committed either by or against a member of the regular armed forces of a state "in the course of military hostilities." The assumption may be that other international agreements including the Geneva Conventions of 1949 for the Protection of War Victims deal with regular armed forces. The provision, however, can amount to an ignominious retreat from the principles of the major *Nuremberg Trial* where acts of terror were not excused because committed by or against regular armed forces. In addition, limitation of the exclusion to regulars is not consistent with article 4A (2) of the Geneva Prisoners of War Convention which accords organized resistance movements who meet the same criteria as regulars the same juridical status. Fourth, the act must be intended to damage "the interests" of a state or to "obtain concessions" from it. The draft convention does not distinguish between a state acting consistently with international law and one acting in flagrant violation of it in terms of the "concessions" involved. The draft has been accompanied with disclaimers that a definition of terrorism is intended.[7] Its clearest feature, however, is a narrow definition which excludes any acts by governments as well as any acts which are not directed against governments. Although it is advertised as a serious measure to control terrorism, it strains at the gnat of group and individual terrorism while swallowing the camel of governmental terrorism. Even if it is

---

[7]See Professor John N. Moore (Counselor on International Law in the U.S. Dept. of State), "Towards Legal Restraints on International Terrorism." 1973 *Proceedings of the American Society of International Law*. Professor Moore also downgrades the importance of the causes of terror.

rationalized as merely a first step to the solution of the problem, it is inadequate to that modest task.

The Comprehensive Concept of Terror

The inadequacy of the fragmentary and superficial approach which has just been considered in dealing with such a serious and complex problem is apparent. Fortunately, the United Nations General Assembly has taken a different approach. An item on terrorism was included in the agenda of the 27th General Assembly of the United Nations at the request of the Secretary General. The Sixth Committee (Legal) asked the Secretariat to prepare a study on the subject and this was presented to the General Assembly on November 2, 1972.[8] Because of the short time available, it was necessarily a preliminary survey. It, nevertheless, deals with some of the relevant fundamentals.

The study refers to the stated purposes of the United Nations set forth in article 1 of the Charter that:

> [F]riendly relations would exist among nations on the basis of respect for the principles of equal rights and self-determination of peoples, international disputes would be settled justly by peaceful means, and international cooperation would solve international economic and social problems and promote respect for human rights and fundamental freedoms for all. . . .[9]

It then points out that:

> The lack or slowness of advance towards these goals has contributed toward the "misery, frustration, grievance and despair" which, while not themselves causes of terrorism, are psychological conditions or states of being which sometimes lead, directly or indirectly, to the commission of acts of violence.[10]

The Resolution stressed the importance of achieving "a just and peaceful solution to the underlying causes" of terrorism. Its fourth paragraph states that the General Assembly:

> *Condemns* the continuation of repressive and terrorist acts by colonial racist and alien regimes in denying peoples their legitimate

---

[8]The study prepared by the United Nations Secretariat, *Supra* note 2.
[9]*Ibid.*, p. 8.
[10]*Ibid.*

rights to self-determination and independence and other human rights and fundamental freedoms.[11]

Other provisions of the Resolution request states to terminate the oppressive regimes which lead to acts of terrorism. At the outset of the 27th General Assembly, the U.S. Government and the Government of Israel demonstrated considerable interest in the subject of terrorism, but both voted against the General Assembly resolution of December 18, 1972 which was adopted by more than the two-thirds vote required for important questions.[12]

This General Assembly Resolution should be considered in the context of the U.N. Charter's prohibition of discrimination. Article 56 of the Charter requires each member state to take action to implement the provisions of article 55. Article 55 (c) states that the United Nations shall promote:

> universal respect for, and observance of, human rights and fundamental freedoms for all without distinction as to race, sex, language or religion.

This fundamental Charter obligation is as applicable to the avoidance of discriminatory concepts of terrorism as it is to other fields. It is clear that no act of terror should be excused because of the identity of the terrorist; and it is equally essential that no act of terror be excused because of the identity of the victim. Thus, terrorism directed at Asians and Africans must be as effectively reduced as terrorism directed against Europeans and North Americans. The protection of diplomats and members of other elite groups may be most effectively achieved along with the protection of members of the mass. It is an elementary practical reality that preferred groups or individuals, according to a discriminatory value orientation, are not likely to be immunized from terror unless the less favored are immunized along with them. The result of terrorism is to deprive its victims, whoever they are, of their most basic human rights.

---

[11]U.S. Dept. of State Bulletin 94, Jan. 22, 1973, p. 68.
[12]*Ibid.*, p. 93.

A Double or Single Standard of Law in Appraising Acts of Terrorism?

The killings at the Munich Olympic Games in September, 1972 were a tragedy for all of the victims without regard to their national or religious identification. While nothing could or should justify these grim events, it is essential to examine all of the relevant factors which were involved. The immediate causes were first, the attempt of a group of Palestinians, acting without authority from the people whom they claimed to represent, to kidnap Israeli athletes who were to be held as hostages to obtain the release of Palestinians held in prison in Israel; and second, the decision of German Government officials, acting with the advice of Israeli police officers flown in for the occasion, to ambush the kidnappers and engage in a shoot-out at the Munich Airport. This relatively recent example of terrorism is another event in the long history of the Zionist-Palestinian conflict. In time it came long after the start of the Zionist terror[13] which is best known through the massacres of Palestinian villagers at Deir

---

[13]The Zionist terror is a useful example of institutionalized, and since 1948, governmentalized terror because it is so thoroughly documented. Among the more important primary sources are: U. Avner, *Memoirs of an Assassin: Confessions of a Stern Gang Killer* (1959); M. Begin, *The Revolt: Story of the Irgun* (1964); G. Frank, *The Deed: The Assassination in Cairo During World War II of Lord Moyne* (1963); N. Lorch, *The Edge of the Sword* (1969); M. Mardor, *Haganah* (1964).

Pro-Zionist scholarly accounts of Zionist history with reports on the terror include C. Sykes, *Cross Roads to Israel* (1965) and Y. Bauer, *From Diplomacy to Resistance: A History of Jewish Palestine* 1939-1945 (1970).

The most recently declassified and published U.S. Government reports concerning the Zionist terror appear in *Foreign Relations of the United States*, vol. 5, 1947, "The Near East and Africa" 1971. See the page references in the index heading, Terrorism in Palestine, p. 1368. Earlier volumes in the same series report the earlier events of the terror.

It should not be supposed that there were no Jewish victims. The steamer *Patria* loaded with Jewish refugees was blown up by the Hagana (the predecessor of the Israeli Army) in 1940 with the resulting killing or drowning of hundreds. See Y. Baur, *op. cit.*, pp. 108-109.

The Jewish opposition to the Zionist terror is expressed historically in the writings of Achad Ha'am (the pen name of the Jewish humanitarian, Asher Ginsberg) and contemporaneously by Professor Israel Shahak, the president of the Israel League of Human and Civil Rights, as well as by anti-Zionist religious leaders.

Yassin in 1948 and at Kafr Kassem in 1956. From a factual standpoint, Munich was the reaction of some Palestinians to the Zionist conquest of Palestine and the expulsion of the Palestinians. If cause and effect are to be considered, it is closely related to the refusal of the Government if Israel for a period of a quarter of a century to accord the Palestinian people either repatriation or compensation.[14]

One of the few voices of reason raised in the emotionalism in the United States following Munich was that of Rabbi Elmer Berger, the president of American Jewish Alternatives to Zionism. In an article entitled "Requiem to Reason," written shortly after the Israeli Air Force "retaliation" bombings of Palestinian refugee camps in Lebanon and Syria, Rabbi Berger stated:

> The United Nations Security Council met on September 10, in this atmosphere of sustained public hysteria and escalating fighting. The United States insisted upon including in any resolution the "cause" of Israeli retaliation. But it could reach back into memory no farther than Munich. It is unsportsmanlike to recall Deir Yassin, Kibya, Es-Samu. It is out of bounds to remember Israeli continuing defiance of all United Nations resolutions calling for the Palestinians to have a choice between repatriation and compensation. It is unfair to remind anyone that Israel has "annexed" Jerusalem, contrary to every consensus of world opinion. . . .
>
> Playing the game with these rules, acting as both participant and umpire, the United States vetoed a resolution which called simply for "the parties concerned to cease immediately all military operations and exercise the greatest restraint in the interests of international peace and security. . . ."[15]

The type of factual clarification and relevant context just quoted is an indispensable first step to a meaningful legal analysis. After the facts are ascertained dispassionately and in relevant historical context, recourse may be had to the applicable legal principles. Among such principles is the primacy of the national state in the international law decision-making and enforcement processes. Its corollary is the responsibility of the state and its officials

---

[14]United Nations General Assembly Resolution 194, U.N. Doc. A/810, Dec. 11, 1948, repeated annually, specifies repatriation or compensation of the refugees.
[15]Published as a part of Report No. 16, Sept. 1972, of American Jewish Alternatives to Zionism, 133 E. 73rd St., Suite 404, New York, New York 10021.

under law. In a pragmatic sense, the doctrines and principles of international law, including the United Nations Charter, are those common norms which states have agreed to enforce upon themselves and other states.[16] It is highly desirable that individuals and groups claiming to represent peoples who have been denied basic rights under international law adhere zealously to that law even when the governments of states depart from the international law which they have established. It is, however, probably not realistic to expect them to do so in these circumstances.

Ambassador Malik of the Soviet Union made a statement in the Security Council after the United States cast its veto of September 10, 1972:

> [T]he Soviet delegation, . . . has stressed the inadmissibility of putting on the same footing, from the point of view of international law and responsibility, acts of terror committed by private groups of persons who do not represent States but only themselves and acts of aggression organized, planned and sanctioned by the Government of a State. . . .[17]

The distinctive merit of his statement is that it was based upon the well-established doctrine of governmental responsibility under law. The Government of Israel agreed to the same legal principle a few months later in a somewhat different factual context. In a paper entitled "Accessories to Terror: The Responsibility of Arab Governments for the Organization of Terrorist Activities,"[18] submitted to the Secretary-General of the United Nations, the Government of Israel made the argument that the Arab governments had full responsibility for terrorist activities which they support or condone. If this is so, it follows, *a fortiori,* that a government which conducts terrorist activities directly is even more responsible under law.

---

[16]The statements of basic principles are widely reflected in the leading authorities. A traditional authority, Lauterpacht, ed., *Oppenheim's International Law* (2 vols.; 1952 and 1955), is concerned exclusively with the role and responsibility of the national state. A contemporary authority, McDougal, and Associates, *Studies in World Public Order* (1960) emphasizes the state while recognizing the existence of other subjects of law.

[17]Provisional Verbatim Record of the Security Council, S/PV.1662, Sept. 10, 1972, p. 46.

[18]U.N. Doc. A/C.6/L872, Nov. 20, 1972.

Ambassador Bush of the United States attempted to justify the United States veto in, *inter alia,* the following words:

> We do not countenance violations of international law; we do not countenance terrorist acts. We seek and support a world in which athletes need not fear assassins and passengers on aeroplanes need not fear hijacking or assassination. We seek a just and lasting peace in the Middle East. We shall continue to work towards those ends.[19]

While there should be no prejudice against athletes or aircraft passengers, it is clear that a broader conception which includes all innocent victims of all kinds of terror is needed if the U.S. Government is serious in its professed desire to reduce international terrorism. It is difficult upon the basis of the record to avoid the conclusion that this government practices a double standard concerning this problem.

Another example of the governmental double standard of law is provided by the case of the Libyan airliner which was shot down over the Sinai on February 21, 1972. The definitive condemnation on legal grounds of the destruction of a civilian airliner with attendant loss of life has been provided by the governments of Israel and the United States following the shooting down of an Israeli airliner which inadvertently over-flew Bulgarian air space on July 27, 1955. Both governments, in bitter diplomatic protests to the Bulgarian Government and in remarkably similar legal arguments presented to the International Court of Justice, denounced the Bulgarian action as in violation of the applicable principles of international law as well as elementary considerations of humanity.[20] In the words of the Government of Israel, the airliner was "callously clawed out of the sky and destroyed" by Bulgarian fighter aircraft.[21]

It is now known that the French pilot of the Libyan aircraft had inadvertently strayed over the Israeli occupied Sinai and had almost succeeded in returning to the Suez Canal and the safety of Egyptian controlled air space when Phantom jets shot it down

---

[19]Provisional Verbatim Record of the Security Council, *Supra* note 17, p. 32.
[20,9]Whiteman, *Digest of International Law,* U.S. Dept. of State, 326-340 (1968).
[21]*Ibid.,* p. 329.

on the explicit orders of the Israeli chief of staff.[22] In striking contrast to its reaction to the Bulgarian incident, the United States Government reacted to the destruction of the Libyan aircraft and the loss of life of about one hundred persons by sending *pro forma* expressions of regret to Tripoli and Cairo, and it has made no protest to the Government of Israel even though an American was among the victims. It is interesting to consider the probable reaction of the U.S. Government had the facts been reversed and an Israeli civil airliner strayed into Egyptian or Libyan air space with the same results.

Individuals and groups who attempt to achieve political objectives through terror should recognize that governmental success in using terrorism provides no assurance that others will be equally successful. It is obvious that there is a tremendous disparity in the military power of governments in comparison with individuals and groups. Such realities must be stressed along with appeals on other grounds to use peaceful procedures. It should be recognized, however, that since counsels of elementary morality have been so ineffective with some governments,[23] there is little cause to believe that they will be effective with desperate individuals and groups. Such individuals and groups have been so systematically excluded from the existing distribution of values, that they have little or nothing to lose by resorting to terror. Some nongovernmental terrorists appear to be eager to demonstrate that, having previously lost everything else, they are now

---

[22]Factual description and reprints of press accounts and commentary appear in Libyan Embassy in London, *Slaughter in the Skies: The Last Flight of LN 114* (undated).

[23]The tremendous governmental terror capability, ranging from mass bombing to assassinations to letter-bombs is one of the factors which encourages governmental terrorism as a method of operation. The following example is only one of many which illustrate its futility:

> Consider it. You go to your office one morning. You open your mail and a bomb explodes in your face. Mightn't you think seriously of changing your job? If you are Palestinian, probably not. . . .
> That was last year. Today, Bassam — scarred, mutilated, wearing dark glasses — is back in his office among the handouts, the coffee cups and the posters. As before, he is dispensing information, not organizing terror.

G. Young, "Despair Keeps Movement Alive for Palestinians," The Washington Post, May 17, 1973, p. F2, cols. 1-2.

quite ready to lose their lives as well.

The hard fact is that a flow of accurate information is more dangerous to some governments than a counter-terror. The emphasis of the Israeli secret forces on killing Palestinian diplomatic and informational personnel is not adequately known. See, "Attacks on Palestinians, Middle East Int'l" [London] (Feb. 1973), p. 20. The operations of Israeli secret forces in Norway in the summer of 1973 have been exposed to some extent as the result of the murder of Ahmed Bouchike. See Time, Aug. 6, 1973, pp 31-32.

THE ENFORCEMENT OF EXISTING LAW AS SANCTIONS TO REDUCE TERROR BY GOVERNMENTS, GROUPS, AND INDIVIDUALS

While it is easy to agree with the verbal position that terror is a bad thing, it is somewhat more difficult to formulate a concept which is adequate to cover the factual aspects of terror and it is considerably more difficult to take concrete steps to reduce and then to eliminate it. The purpose of the present section is to examine existing international law, the enforcement of which would constitute a significant first step toward this ultimate objective. There is, unfortunately, a good deal of overlapping between terror and war or hostilities. A serious effort to reduce international terrorism may be assisted by reference to the laws of war.

Hague Convention IV of 1907 and its Annexed Regulations[24] were written upon the assumption that certain minimum standards of law must be maintained even in a wartime situation. A provision of the Regulations states:

> Family honour and rights, the lives of persons, and private property, as well as religious convictions and practice, must be respected.[25]

It is apparent that the values protected by the quoted provision are inconsistent with the use of terror. The same value orientation appears in the famous De Martens clause in the preamble to

---

[24]36 Stat. 2277; Treaty Series No. 539.
[25]Art. 46(1).

Hague Convention IV:

> Until a more complete code of the laws of war has been issued, the High Contracting Parties deem it expedient to declare that, in cases not included in the Regulations adopted by them, the inhabitants and the belligerents remain under the protection and the rule of the principles of the law of nations, as they result from the usages established among civilized peoples, from the laws of humanity, and from the dictates of the public conscience.

One of the most significant features of the major *Nuremberg Trial* conducted before the International Military Tribunal is that government officers who acted in an official capacity and pursuant to superior orders, nevertheless, were held to be criminally responsible for acts committed in violation of international law. The principles involved in that trial have been approved by the U.N. General Assembly[26] and formulated by the International Law Commission in the following terms. Principle III provides:

> The fact that a person who committed an act which constitutes a crime under international law acted as Head of State or responsible Government official does not relieve him from responsibility under international law.

Principle IV provides:

> The fact that a person acted pursuant to order of his Government or of a superior does not relieve him from responsibility under international law, provided a moral choice was in fact possible to him.[27]

The evidence before the International Military Tribunal at Nuremberg established far beyond any reasonable doubt the existence of systematic terror which was planned and executed by governmental authorities. These acts of extreme violence included, but were not limited to, murder, enslavement, and deportation of civilian populations. The Nuremberg Principles reflect universal international law and they should accordingly be applied to the officials of all governments without exception with the same vigor used where German officials were the defendants. Justice Jackson, the chief prosecutor for the United States, recog-

---

[26]1 U.N. GAOR 1144 (1946); G.A. Res. 95(I); U.N. Doc. A/236 (1946).
[27]The principles are printed in 45 *Am. J. Int'l L. Supp. Off. Docs* 125 (1951).

nized in his opening address that the law applied to Germans was also the standard applicable to Americans and others:

> We must never forget that the record on which we judge these defendants today is the record on which history will judge us tomorrow.[28]

The four Geneva Conventions of 1949 for the Protection of War Victims[29] were written in the shadow of the Second World War. The governments represented at the Conference which wrote the Conventions had had considerable experience with the Nazi, the Fascist, and the Japanese militarist terror as conducted during the Second World War. The Civilians Convention was particularly designed to change the law which was previously in effect by providing new and effective protections for civilians. Among the common articles which appear in all four of the Conventions, article 3 covers armed conflicts which are not of an international character and which were previously unregulated by international law. The provisions of article 3 are designed to prevent terror by all parties to such domestic conflicts by specifically prohibiting, *inter alia,* "violence to life and person, in particular murder of all kinds, mutilation, cruel treatment and torture" as well as "outrages upon personal dignity, in particular humilating and degrading treatment." Those provisions were flagrantly violated during the civil war in East Pakistan (now Bangladesh) as they have been elsewhere.

Article 33 of the Civilians Convention appears in a section which applies comprehensively to civilian persons within the territories of the parties to the conflict and also to occupied territories. It states, *inter alia:* "Collective penalties and likewise all measures of intimidation or of terrorism are prohibited." The prohibited penalties are adequately illustrated by the "neighborhood punishments" used in Israeli occupied territories.

While a comprehensive evaluation of aerial bombardment under international law is beyond the scope of the present paper, some basic factors will be considered briefly. If the quantum of the destruction of human values is employed as the test, the

[28]2 Trial of the Major War Criminals before the I.M.T. 98:101 (1947).
[29]6 U.S. Treaties & Other Int'l Agrees, at 3114, 3217, 3316, & 3516 (1956); Treaties & Int'l Agrees. Series Nos. 3362, 3363, 3364, and 3365.

aerial bombardment of civilians as an instrument of national policy causes much greater terror than the efforts of the nongovernmental terrorists. In addition, if the governments involved should terminate aerial attacks upon civilians, they would clearly be in a better position to induce desperate resistance groups and individuals to terminate acts of terror which involve far less destruction of human values.

Throughout the Second World War, the United States used approximately two million tons of aerial bombs. Thus far in the war in South-East Asia and including the bombing of Cambodia, the United States has used more than seven million tons of bombs. The existence of the much advertised "smart" (that is, target-seeking) bombs makes the use of saturation bombing of densely populated areas substantially more dubious on legal and moral grounds than it was before the invention of such bombs. Even from a narrow military viewpoint, the availability of the "smart" bomb to attack military targets renders it unnecessary to conduct an aerial bombing that results in large civilian casualties.

Other provisions of the Civilians Convention have received inadequate attention. For example, article 49 (6) provides: "The Occupying Power shall not deport or transfer parts of its own civilian population into the territory it occupies." The negotiating history of this provision shows that it was adopted in reaction to the notorious Nazi practice of removing the "inferior" indigenous population and transferring racial "Aryans" or Germans into the territory.[30] It is a prohibition upon "creating facts" in occupied territory by the establishment of colonies comprised of the occupant's nationals. The Government of Israel has systematically violated this provision and also article 49 (1) which prohibits individual or mass "forcible transfers" and "deportations" of civilians from occupied territory.[31] It must be doubted that acts of terrorism by a few of the victims of these governmental violations of law can be prevented effectively without an attempt to enforce international law upon governments as well.

---

[30] 4 Pictet, ed., I.C.R.C. Commentary 283 (1958).

[31] See M. Mehdi, "Israeli Settlements in the Occupied Territories, Middle East Int'l" [London] 21 (Jan. 1973; J. Cooley, "Israelis Put Down Roots in Arab Soil," Christian Science Monitor (May 30, 1973), p. 7, cols. 1-6.

The common article 1 of each of the 1949 Conventions provides in full: "The High Contracting Parties undertake to respect and to ensure respect for the present Convention in all circumstances." The International Committee of the Red Cross *Commentary* on the Civilians Convention states: "[I]t is clear that article 1 is no mere empty form of words but has been deliberately invested with imperative force."[32] This obligation to ensure the respect of the other parties is directed particularly to the great powers and is based upon the assumption that they will also respect it themselves. When the legal obligations to respect and ensure respect are honored, the great powers will then have the moral stature to seek to reduce and eliminate group and individual acts of terrorism.

WHERE DO WE GO FROM HERE?

Ambassador Charles W. Yost, shortly after the Munich killings, wrote about the terror in plain words:

> What indeed of aerial bombing? When the Nazis bombed Warsaw or Rotterdam or Coventry, we called it "terror bombing," but when we bomb North or South Vietnam we call it "protective reaction." Yet we are killing incomparably more people, including more wholly innocent civilians, than the Palestinian terrorists have killed in all these years. Understandable as they may be, can we justly exclude from the definition of terrorism the Israeli retaliatory raids against Palestinian camps in Lebanon and Syria last week, which surely killed many wholly innocent people and which probably helped create a new crop of terrorists among their relatives and friends? Was that either humane or wise?
>
> The fact is, of course, that there is a vast amount of hypocrisy on the subject of political terrorism. We all righteously condemn it—except when we ourselves or friends of ours are engaging in it. Then we ignore it or gloss it over or attach to it tags like "liberation" or "defense of free world" or "national honor" to make it seem something other than what it is.[33]

It should be added that there may be racist implications in the U.S. Government's double-standard concept of terrorism: the

---

[32]4 Pictet, ed., I.C.R.C. Commentary 17 (1958).

[33]"Forms and Masks of Terrorism," Christian Science Monitor, (September 14, 1972), p. 20, col. 5.

Vietnamese, and other South-East Asians, along with the Palestinians, and other South-West Asians as well as North Africans, are functionally the present-day North American Indians. They may be killed with impunity and without suggestion of guilt. The same treatment applied to European settlers or their descendants, such as the white Rhodesians or the Zionists in Palestine, would be regarded as genocide.

The existing double standard of morality and law which Ambassador Yost has described promotes terror. It reinforces the conviction of the nongovernmental terrorists that they and the dispossessed and oppressed peoples they claim to represent cannot achieve justice through peaceful procedures. It is predicated upon the acceptance of a self-system inconsistent with the humanitarian recommendation of Professor Lasswell quoted at the beginning of this paper. This recommendation of a system embracing humanity is also the most practical prescription for survival in a world of weapons of mass destruction.

The double standard is also based upon the totalitarian assumption that of all the human institutions designed to serve mankind, only the state and its government officials are above the law.

More than half a century ago, Professor Leon Duguit wrote:

> Any system of public law can be vital only so far as it is based on a given sanction to the following rules: First, the holders of power cannot do certain things; second, there are certain things they must do.[34]

The words, when written, referred to the law of a national state, but they must be equally applicable to international law if it is law rather than a facade to conceal decisions made on power considerations alone. The comprehensive single standard and nondiscriminatory conception of terrorism which is recommended provides the constructive alternative which can, if it is used, bring about a significant reduction, and even the elimination, of politicilly motivated terrorism. First, it prohibits the "holders of power" from using terror in its many governmental manifestations. This includes, *inter alia*, the placing of effective community restraints upon acts of terror or "retaliation" conducted pursuant

---

[34]*Law in the Modern State* 26 (Laski transl., 1919).

to unilateral and open-ended governmental concepts of "self-defense" which are without support in either the U.N. Charter or in customary international law.[35] Second, it requires the "holders of power" to use the peaceful procedures of diplomacy and political compromise in situations where their opponents have an objective which is contrary to their own. In short, it imposes the obligation to use peaceful procedures upon the powerful as well as the weak.

The acceptance or rejection of these prohibitions and obligations by governments will have a decisive impact in determining whether we will live in an environment where acts of terror or peaceful procedures will have a predominant role.

---

[35]The legal limitations upon self-defense are set forth in Mallison, "Limited Naval Blockade or Quarantine-Interdiction: National and Collective Defense Claims Valid Under International Law" 31 *Geo. Wash. L. Rev.*, 335 (1962).

SECTION 2

A SURVEY OF INTERNATIONAL HUMANITARIAN LAW IN NONINTERNATIONAL ARMED CONFLICTS: 1949-1974*

MICHEL VEUTHEY

U NTIL 1949, INTERNATIONAL HUMANITARIAN law was applicable only in international wars between States.

The Diplomatic Conference, in Geneva, 1949, after long debates,[1] accepted that a common article, containing some fundamental humanitarian principles, would apply "in the case of armed conflict not of an international character." This Article 3 common to the four Geneva Conventions of August 12, 1949, qualified by a delegate to the Diplomatic Conference as the "mini-Convention,"[2] was most certainly a big step forward in the codification of international humanitarian law. The faithful application of these provisions would allow the avoidance of the gravest violations, such as murders, torture, inhuman treatment. Thereafter efforts were made to complement this article.

Four years after the adoption of Article 3 common to the four Geneva Conventions of 1949, the ICRC convened at Geneva, in 1953, a "Commission of experts for the examination of assistance

---

*See also by the same author, "Some Problems of Humanitarian Law in Non-international Conflicts and Guerilla Conflicts," in Vol. I, Bassiouni and Nanda, *A Treatise On International Criminal Law* (1973), p. 422-52.

[1]See *Final Record of the Diplomatic Conference of Geneva of 1949*, Vol. II B, pp. 9-15, 34-35, 40-48, 75-79, 82-84, 90, 93-95, 97-102, 325-339.

See also, a compilation on the work of this Diplomatic Conference on this subject. F. Siordet, *The Geneva Conventions and Civil War* (Geneva, ICRC, 1950).

[2]Pictet, J. S. (ed.), *Commentary, III, Geneva Convention relative to the treatment of Prisoners of War* (Geneva, 1960), p. 34.

to political detainees";[3] in 1955, a "Commission of experts for the study of the question of the application of humanitarian principles in the event of internal disturbances";[4] and, in 1962, a "Commission of experts for the study of the question of aid to the victims of internal conflicts."[5]

Along with these conferences of experts, the International Conferences of the Red Cross were seized with this problem which they had been dealt with already since 1912:[6] in 1963, the Centenary Congress, convened at Geneva, took note of the report of the Commission of experts of 1962, and requested the ICRC to continue its action with a view to extending the humanitarian aid of the Red Cross to victims of noninternational conflicts.[7] The XXth International Conference, convened at Vienna in 1965, confirmed the Resolution of 1963, stressing the insufficiency of the protection of prisoners and detainees.[8] In 1969, at Istanbul, the XXIst Conference adopted two resolutions, the first on the necessity to devote particular attention to this problem in the development work of humanitarian law,[9] the second considering that "combatants and members of resistance movements who participate in noninternational armed conflicts and who conform

---

[3]ICRC, *Commission of experts for the examination of the question of assistance to political detainees* (Geneva, June 1943).

[4]ICRC, *Commission of experts for the study of the question of the application of humanitarian principles in the event of internal disturbances* (Geneva, October, 1955).

[5]ICRC. *Commission of experts for the study of the question of aid to the victims of internal conflicts* (Geneva, October 1962).

[6]At the IXth International Conference of the Red Cross, convened at Washington in 1912, a question about civil war was posed by a delegate of the American Red Cross, who presented a report on the subject of the role of the Red Cross in case of civil war or of insurgency, and containing a draft from the International Convention. The Conference broke up without having discussed the matter, but it should be remembered the thought of a representative of the Imperial Russian Government who felt that the Red Cross Societies would not have any duties to fill towards insurgent groups or revolutionaries, since they are considered by law in his country only as criminals.

[7]Council of Delegates, Centenary Congress, Geneva, 1963, Resolution No. IX, *International Red Cross Handbook* 11 ed. (Geneva, 1971), pp. 457-458, referred to as *Handbook*.

[8]Resolution No. XXXI, in *Handbook*, p. 458.

[9]Resolution No. XVII, in *Handbook*, p. 458.

to the provisions of Article 4 of the Third Geneva Convention of August 21, 1949 should when captured be protected against any inhumanity and brutality and receive treatment similar to that which that Convention lays down for prisoners of war."[10]

In 1965, at Vienna,[11] and in 1969, at Istanbul,[12] the ICRC presented reports on the problem of noninternational armed conflicts.

In 1970, the ICRC consulted a series of experts, among whom were experts in guerrilla and counter-guerrilla warfare, on noninternational armed conflicts and guerrilla warfare.[13] The report on these consultations should permit clarifying the complexity of the matter, likewise that of some guidelines.[14]

In 1971, for the first session of the Conference of Government Experts,[15] the ICRC submitted two documents on this problem: a general one on noninternational armed conflicts,[16] the other on the particular problems posed by guerrilla warfare. [17] These two documents did not require a draft regulation, but general remarks as well as suggestions of particular legal instruments to be discussed by the government experts.

The first session stressed the necessity, for the majority of experts, to define the meaning of "noninternational armed conflict"[18] and elaborated on a draft Additional Protocol to Article 3[19] on the basis of a "Canadian Draft Protocol to the Geneva Conventions of 1949 relative to Conflicts not International in

---

[10]Resolution No. XVIII, in *Handbook*, pp. 458-459.

[11]Protection of Victims of Noninternational Conflicts (D 6/1). Report submitted by the ICRC.

[12]Protection of Victims of Noninternational Conflicts (D.S. 5 a-b.)
  — Reaffirmation and Development of the Laws and Customs Applicable in Armed Conflicts (D.S. 4 a, b, c.)

[13]ICRC, *Preliminary Report on the Consultation of Experts concerning Noninternational Conflict and Guerrilla Warfare* (Geneva, July, 1970, D1153).

[14]*Ibid.*, Introduction, p. 1.

[15]Conference of Government Experts on the Reaffirmation and Development of International Humanitarian Law Applicable in Armed Conflicts.
  — first session, Geneva, 24 May — 12 June 1971;
  — second session, Geneva, 3 May — 3 June 1972.

[16]ICRC, *Protection of Victims of Noninternational Armed Conflicts* (CE/5b, Geneva, 1971).

[17]ICRC, *Rules Applicable in Guerrilla Warfare* (CE/6b Geneva, 1971).

Character."[20]

A Norwegian proposal of a unique international instrument applicable to all armed conflicts[21] was also presented but did not receive the approval of the majority of experts.[22]

In 1972, at the second session of the same Conference of Government experts, the ICRC presented three texts:

—a "Draft Additional Protocol to Article 3 Common to the Four Geneva Conventions of August 12, 1949";[23]

—"Regulations Concerning Special Cases of Armed Conflicts not of an International Character";[24]

—a "Declaration of fundamental rights of the individual in time of internal disturbances or public emergency."[25]

These three texts should have enlarged the scope of humanitarian application in covering lesser situations than the classic level of civil war.

The second session of the Conference of Government Experts discussed for a long time, article by article, this Draft Additional Protocol and a Drafting Committee formulated many variations of each article.

The draft of "Regulations Concerning Special Cases of Armed

---

[18]ICRC, *Report on the Work of the Conference*, "Definition of Noninternational Armed Conflicts," (Geneva, 1971) par. 129-191, ch. II.

[19]*Ibid.*, "The Content of A Possible Protocol," paras. 219 to 278.

[20]*Ibid.*, CE/Plen. 2 bis "Canadian Draft Protocol to the Geneva Conventions of 1949 relative to Conflicts not International in Character, p. 57.

[21]*Ibid.*, (CE/COM II/1), p. 61.

[22]*Ibid.*, para. 134.

[23]ICRC, *Conference of Government Experts on the Reaffirmation and Development of International Humanitarian Law Applicable in Armed Conflicts*, I, Basic Texts (Geneva, January 1972), pp. 35-45, "Draft Additional Protocol to Article 3 Common to the Four Geneva Conventions of August 12, 1949."

[24]*Ibid.*, p. 45. This Annex, "Regulations Concerning Special Cases of Armed Conflicts not of an International Character" proposed the application of the four Geneva Conventions of 1949 and of the Additional Protocol in two situations:

1. When the party opposing the authorities in power has a government which exercises effective power, by means of its administration and adequately organized armed forces, over a part of the territory.

2. When the armed forces of other States take a direct part in the hostilities.

[25]Already submitted in 1971, in Document V (*supra* note 16) the first session was not able to discuss this Declaration. ICRC, *Report on the Work of the Conference* (Geneva, 1972), paras. 2.564 to 2.570.

Conflicts not of an International Character" anticipated the application of the four Geneva Conventions and the Protocol applicable in international armed conflicts in two situations: first, when the insurgent party controls a part of the territory and effectively exercises public power; secondly when one or more third States give assistance to one or more Parties to the conflict under the form of armed forces taking direct part in the hostilities.

The experts rejected this draft, some considering it as an "attempt to revive the idea of recognition of belligerency which had now fallen into oblivion,"[26] others expressing the fear that, for the international qualification of a conflict, the utilization of the criterion of an outside military aide would constitute an indirect justification of the interference of a third State in another State.[27]

With regard to the declaration on internal disturbances, it was referred to the Diplomatic Conference.[28]

After this Conference of Government Experts, the ICRC, at the request of several experts, convened at Geneva a "Consultative Group of Government Experts," bringing together the Chairmen, Vice-Chairmen and Rapporteurs of the Conference who were chosen, during the course of two sessions, in January and March 1973), to try to reduce the still existing divergences.[29] The result of these deliberations was to lead the ICRC to present (also relying on the basis of the important work of the Secretary-General of the United Nations on the topic of "respect for human rights in armed conflicts" in 1969,[30] 1970,[31] 1971[32] and 1972[33]) a "Draft Protocol Additional to the Geneva Conventions of August 12, 1949, and Relating to the Protection of Victims of Noninter-

---

[26]ICRC, *Report on the work of the Conference* (Geneva 1972), para. 2.340.

[27]*Ibid.*, para. 2.343.

[28]*Ibid.*, para. 2.567.

[29]See e.g. the Press Release 1147, of January 16, 1973 "Government Experts Meeting at ICRC."

[30]*Report of the Secretary-General (A/7720, 20 November 1969)*, see, *inter alia*, the paragraphs 104 to 108 and 168 to 177.

[31]*Report of the Secretary-General (A/8052, 18 September 1970)*.

[32]*Report of the Secretary-General (A/8370, 2 September 1971)*.

[33]*Report of the Secretary-General (A/8781, 20 September 1972)*.

national Armed Conflicts."[34]

Beginning with the *Preamble* of this draft Protocol of 1973, was the reaffirmation of the values of Article 3 and of the international instruments of law as well as the renewal of the "Martens Clause." These diverse provisions should, all reinforce the humanitarian rules applicable in certain types of noninternational armed conflicts, allow other situations, notably lesser than the level fixed by the first article of this draft, not to be left outside of the scope of humanitarian law.

Article 1 ("Material field of application") comprises three paragraphs: the first giving a definition of armed conflicts ("between armed forces or other organized armed groups under responsible command"); the second paragraph excludes riots, isolated and sporadic acts of violence, and "other acts of a similar nature," and risks giving a pretext too easy for excluding the benefit of humanitarian law (and perhaps not only these resolutions of the Protocol) in some guerrilla warfare situations; the third paragraph partially enables mitigating which expresses the autonomy of the application of Article 3.

Article 2 ("Personal field of application), in its first paragraph, takes up the principle of nondiscrimination of the benefit of the humanitarian provisions just as stated by Article 3, extended—which does not anticipate Article 3—to combatants. The second paragraph, envisaging a prolonged protection of persons deprived of liberty even after the end of a conflict until their liberation, allows assuring a humanitarian protection that the after-effects of a number of contemporary conflicts have made apparent as necessary and possible.[35]

Article 3 of the Protocol, relating to the legal status of the parties to the conflict, takes up and extends[36] the rule contained in the last paragraph of Article 3 of the Geneva Conventions of

---

[34]International Committee of the Red Cross, *Draft Additional Protocols to the Geneva Conventions* of August 12, 1949 (Geneva, June 1973), pp. 33 to 46.

[35]After the end of the Greek civil war in 1948, the ICRC was authorized to go on with its visits to political detainees, which was done until the end of 1970.

[36]Article 3 common to the four Geneva Convention of 1949 speaks only of the legal status of the parties to the conflict; Article 3 of the Protocol mentions further the legal status of the territories on which they exercise authority.

1949. It lays out in effect that "The legal status of the parties to the conflict or that of the territories on which they exercise authority shall not be affected by the application of the provisions of the present Protocol, or by all or part of the provisions of the Geneva Conventions of August 12, 1949, and of the Additional Protocol relating to the protection of victims of international armed conflicts brought into force in accordance with Article 38 or by the conclusion of any agreement provided for in the Geneva Conventions and their Additional Protocols."[37]

It is interesting to remark that this article, which is reinforced by the following provision (*Article 4,* entitled "Nonintervention") expressly reserving the sovereignty of States, is taken up *mutatis mutandis* in the Protocol relating to the victims of international armed conflict:[38] these articles mark somehow the unique character of humanitarian law, as independent as possible from legal and political military confrontations.

As for *Article 5* ("Rights and duties of the parties to the conflict"), it explains,[39] in the context of noninternational armed conflict, the principle of the equality of the belligerents.[40] The sense of this article does not indeed authorize reprisals, prohibited elsewhere,[41] but as well, having in mind the disproportion of means, the imbalance which often exists between parties to a noninternational conflict, asking all parties to the conflict to respect the humanitarian rules to the best of their ability.

Part II, on the "Humane Treatment of Persons in the Power

---

[37]Author's emphasis of this excerpted quote.

[38]Draft Protocol Additional to the Geneva Conventions of August 12, 1949, and relating to the Protection of Victims of International Armed Conflicts, Article 4 (Legal status of the Parties to the conflict):

The application of the Conventions and of the present Protocol, as well as the conclusion of the agreements therein provided, shall not affect the legal status of the Parties to the conflict or that of the territories over which they exercise authority.

[39]Article 3 of the Conventions of 1949 stipulates simply that "each Party to the conflict shall be bound to apply, as a minimum, the following provisions: . . ."

[40]See H. Meyrowitz's, *Le principe de l'égalité des belligérants devant le droit de la guerre* (Paris, 1970).

[41]Articles 8, para. 4, for the "persons whose liberty has been restricted," and 19, for the wounded, the sick, and the shipwrecked, medical personnel medical units and means of medical transport, as well as 26, for the civilian population.

of the Parties to the Conflict," contains in Articles 6, 7 and 8 some fundamental rules on humanitarian treatment granted to persons not or no longer participating directly in the hostilities. These provisions are certainly a very welcome extension. They mention the prohibition of acts of terrorism in the form of violence against persons *hors de combat*,[42] in foreseeing the possibility of liberating and sending back to the adverse party the captured combatants.[43] Articles 9 and 10 of the same Part explain the "legal guarantees" mentioned in Article 3 of the Conventions of 1949,[44] noting again the general principles but also introducing new provisions limiting the death penalty. This last limitation is particularly desirable if we want to avoid the repetition of reprisals with a view towards stopping these executions.[45]

Part III, on the "Wounded, Sick and Shipwrecked Persons," elaborates on a certain number of rules for their respect and protection. Beyond certain general provisions,[46] this Part introduces some rules of which contemporary conflicts have shown the tragic necessity: Article 16 ("General protection of medical duties") aspires to avoid the repetition of penal persecutions or imprisonments exercised against persons who have carried out activities of a medical nature.[47] The application of Article 17, which demands the respect and the protection of units and means of medical transport, as that of Article 18 on the distinctive emblem and of Article 19 prohibiting reprisals, must be so much the more

---

[42]Article 6, para. 2, letter (c).

[43]Article 7, paragraph 2.

[44]Article 9 ("Principles of penal law") forbids collective penalties, retroactivity, and reaffirms the principle of *ne bis in idem* as well as the presumption of innocence.

Article 10 ("Penal prosecutions") takes up again the principle of fundamental judiciary guarantees, the right of appeal, certain limitations on the death penalty, the extenuating circumstances for having respected the Protocol, the possibility of an amnesty at the end of hostilities.

[45]Such as the execution of three French prisoners by the ALN in Algeria, in May 1958 (ICRC, *Rapport d'activité,* 1958, p. 10).

[46]Articles 11 ("Definitions"), 12 ("Protection and care"), 13 ("Search and evacuation"), 14 ("Role of the civilian population"), and 15 ("Medical and religious personnel").

[47]Such methods have as well been seen in international armed conflicts, as in the fight against the Resistance Movements during the Second World War.

absolute that the means at the disposition of the two parties would well be different: one side may have hospitals, the other only clandestine dispensaries, sometimes underground, to escape detection; one side may have latest medical transports, the other simple stretchers. This imbalance should not be injurious with respect to the wounded and sick and to the extent that the observation of rules protecting the wounded and sick are observed, they bring a similar humanitarian advantage to the two parties.

Part IV ("Methods and Means of Combat") is completely new: for the first time,[48] conventional international rules would limit the means and methods of combat of the adversaries in a noninternational armed conflict. The resolutions proposed are for the most part reprises of the Hague Regulations of 1907.

Part V ("Civilian population") takes up, in an almost uniform way, the provisions of the Draft Protocol relating to international armed conflicts. It consists of rules appearing necessary, such as the prohibition of methods intended to spread terror among the civilian population,[50] the prohibition of means and methods which strike indiscriminately the civilian population and combatants,[51] the prohibition of attacking, destroying or rendering useless objects indispensable to the survival of the civilian population,[52] of attacking or destroying works containing dangerous forces such as dykes,[53] the prohibition of—along with exceptions—the forced displacement of civilian population.[54]

Part VI ("Relief.") The dispatching of relief should be im-

---

[48]If we accept the *Draft Rules for the Limitation of the Dangers incurred by the Civilian Population in Time of War"* drawn up by the ICRC in 1957, which should assure equal protection of the civilian population as much as in international armed conflicts as noninternational, but which are not accepted by the States.

[49]With the exception of Article 25 ("Definition") which does not take up again the fourth paragraph of Article 45 of the Draft Protocol relating to international armed conflicts according to which:

> In case of doubt as to whether any person is a civilian, he or she shall be presumed to be so.

[50]Article 26 ("Protection of the civilian population.") paragraph 1.

[51]Article 26, paragraph 3.

[52]Article 27 ("Protection of objects indispensable to the survival of the civilian population").

[53]Article 28 ("Protection of works and installations containing dangerous forces").

[54]Article 29 ("Prohibition of forced movement of civilians").

proved, taking into account recent experiences, when the civilian population is insufficiently supplied. This could bring particular difficulties; such as procuring the supplies because the territorial control could resemble a leopard skin; or politics since parties which are not recognized hesitate to allow the dispatching of relief—even strictly humanitarian—to the adversary which does not want to recognize its existence. Article 3 ("Legal status of the parties to the conflict") permits the dispatching of relief without compromising the respective positions of the parties on the political and legal plan.

Part VII ("Execution of the present Protocol") first of all it puts the parties to the conflict themselves under their proper responsibilities to assure the respect of the Protocol (thus, the Articles 36 on the "Measures for execution" or 37 "Dissemination"). This Part also allows in Article 38, by the conclusion of special agreements, putting in force some more provisions of humanitarian law. Taking into account practice, Article 38 anticipates not only the procedure of special agreement between parties but also unilateral declarations addressed either to the depository State of the Conventions of 1949, or to the ICRC. Finally Article 39 anticipates, for the assistance in the observance of the Protocol, the appeal to an organism such as the ICRC which would also be able to offer its services.

This draft Protocol was submitted in November 1973 to the XXIInd International Conference of the Red Cross convened in Teheran.

The delegates present at this Conference—who represented National Red Cross Societies (Red Crescent, Red Lion and Sun) but also the States Parties to the Geneva Conventions of 1949— issued a certain number of propositions on this Draft Protocol.[55]

These propositions had only a preliminary character, since this draft had to be discussed—and eventually adopted—by the *Diplomatic Conference on the Reaffirmation and the Development of International Humanitarian Law Applicable in Armed Conflicts.*

---

[55]See ICRC, *Report on the Study by the XXIInd International Conference of the Red Cross of the Draft Additional Protocols to the Geneva Conventions of August 12, 1949* (Geneva, January 1974) Chapter III, paras. 70 to 87.

Called together by Switzerland, the Depository State of the Geneva Conventions, this Conference held the first session at Geneva, from February 20, to March 29, 1974.

A second session, lasting three months, is to be convened at Geneva from February 3, 1974.

This first session, which brought together 126 States—the exact double of the Diplomatic Conference of 1949—could not arrive at, in a substantial manner, the examination of this Draft Protocol relating to the protection of the victims of noninternational armed conflicts: the Conference could only set the problems of procedure (participation, nomination of officers, etc., agenda) , at the same time starting the discussion of other articles of the Draft Additional Protocol to the Geneva Convention of August 12, 1949 relating to the Protection of the Victims of International Armed Conflicts. Thus, the first article of this Draft Protocol I defines the scope of application of the Protocol and of the Geneva Conventions of 1949.

An amendment (CDDH/I/71) to the draft of Article 1 was adopted by 70 votes to 22 with 12 abstentions asking the inclusion in international conflicts of the "armed conflicts in which peoples are fighting against colonial and alien occupation and racist regimes in the exercise of their right of self-determination, as enshrined in the Charter of the United Nations and the Declaration of Principles of International Law concerning Friendly Relations and Cooperation among States in accordance with the Charter of the United Nations."

The will of a number of States to qualify as international conflicts armed struggles for self-determination played an important role for delaying the examination of Draft Protocol II, in addition to the time devoted to the discussion of Draft Protocol I.

Nevertheless, there remains a number of written amendments that had already been laid down on articles of Draft Protocol II, and that, with reservations on the definite formulation of the scope of application of Draft Protocol II, Articles 23 and 25, on the protection and definition of the civilian population had been discussed in depth and approved.

It is proper to stress the importance of these provisions, which contain only slight differences from the corresponding provisions adopted in the Draft Protocol I: which fills in fact a wide gap in humanitarian law than the codification of The Hague Convention of 1907 and the Geneva Conventions of 1949.

We must hope that the adoption of these essential provisions will increase the chances of the adoption of the Draft Protocol Relating to the Protection of Victims of Noninternational Armed Conflicts. This does not compromise the sovereignty of the States, or limit their legal or material possibilities of re-establishing internal order or resist foreign interventions. It permits the respect by all the parties to the conflict of fundamental humanitarian principles in very troubled and touchy, but also, unfortunately, very frequent situations. After years of work by experts and by the ICRC, it is now up to the international community to take up its responsibilities in the effort of completing the humanitarian codification in all kinds of armed conflicts.

INTERNAL STRIFE, SELF-DETERMINATION, AND WORLD ORDER*

JOHN C. NOVOGROD

INTRODUCTION: INTERNAL STRIFE AS AN INTERNATIONAL EVENT[1]

IN OUR TROUBLED WORLD it is becoming increasingly apparent that internal strife[2] must be viewed as "a pervasive and dangerous characteristic of international life."[3] Understandably, the two opposing systems of public order and the resulting bipolarization of the world community[4] have generated pressures which have made the powerful nations vitally concerned with the outcome of civic strife in smaller states. The crucial nature of the ideological confrontation between the two power blocs has made this a fact of international life. For, although the causes of civil strife most often are found in the political and social structure of the disrupted state,[5] the outcome of that strife very frequently has a profound in-

---

*Reprinted with permission of the JAG Journal. For an expanded and detailed treatment of the subject, see "Civil Strife and Indirect Aggression," in Vol. I, Bassiouni and Nanda, *A Treatise on International Criminal Law* (1973), p. 198-238.

[1]*Cf.* Moore, *International Law and Some Current Illusions* (1924), p. 37. "I have often remarked that International wars will cease when civil wars end."

[2]In this chapter "internal strife" and "civil strife" will be used synonymously and interchangeably as all-inclusive terms for genuine, internal "attempts to change by violence, or threat of violence, a government's policies, rules, or organization." Eckstein, "Toward the Theoretical Study of Internal War," in Eckstein (ed.), *Internal War: Problems and Approaches* (1964) p. 1.

[3]Falk, "The Internaational Regulation of Internal Violence in the Developing Countries, *A.S.I.L. Proc.* 58, 60 (1966).

[4]*See, eg,* Herz, *International Politics in the Atomic Age* (1959) pp. 76-95.

[5]Kaplan, "Intervention in Internal War. Some Systematic Sources," in Rosenau, ed., *Inernational Aspects of Civil Strife* (1964) p. 92..

fluence on the allocation of power in the world community.[6] In effect, then, the pressures of the contemporary bipolarized world community have magnified the importance of every foreign internal power struggle in the eyes of the major protagonists of the world's power process.[7] Because of the commonly shared reluctance to risk the horrors of nuclear warfare, today's Great Power confrontations are rarely direct; presently, the confrontations are manifested in the civil strife of a third state, especially in civil strife heavily imbued with ideological overtones.[8] Indeed, as one observer of international affairs has written:

> Violent encounter of major rivals in world affairs has always been primarily a matter of warfare *between* states; now suddenly it is participation in warfare *within* states.[9]

Most commentators seem to agree that the frequency of internal strife appears to be increasing in recent years.[10] The advent of the newer states into international society and the process of social and economic development which they are undergoing have increased the probability that instances of domestic violence will yet become more numerous. It has been observed that

> [w]ithout a constitutional tradition of peaceful change some form of violence is virtually inevitable. In the underdeveloped areas the alternates, broadly speaking, are not constitutional change or violent change, but gradual change throughout a succession of reform coups d'etat or tumultuous change through revolutionary wars or revolutionary coups d'etat.[11]

The great likelihood of internal strife in the emerging nations increases the potential arenas for Great Power confrontations

---

[6]*Cf.* McDougal, "The Impact of International Law Upon National Law: A Policy-Oriented Perspective," in McDougal, and Associates, *Studies in World Public Order* (1960) p. 165. To a large degree, states are like individuals in their readiness to perceive danger to their security. *See, eg,* Brown, *War and the Psychological Conditions of Peace* (1942) .

[7]*Cf.* Calvocoressi, *World Order and New States* (1962) p. 101.

[8]*See* MacPherson, "Revolution and Ideology in the Late Twentieth Century," in Friedrich ed., *Revolution* (1966) pp. 139-158.

[9]Falk, "Janus Tormented: The International Law of Internal War," in Rosenau, *supra* note 5, p. 185.

[10]Rosenau, "Introduction," in Rosenau, *supra* note 5 p. 5.

[11]Huntington, "Patterns of Violence in International Politics," in Huntington, ed., *Changing Patterns of Military Politics* (1962), p. 34.

through participation in such conflicts. Thus, the possibility of larger and more destructive conflicts erupting from this participation in the civil strife of smaller states is eminently real. This chapter will re-examine the law regulating external participation in internal strife with a view to assessing its contemporary viability.

It is unfortunately no simple task to review the international law of third-party involvement in civil strife. The literature in this area of the law is contradictory and, in addition, abounds with normative ambiguity, shifting references, and illogic. One means, however, to effect the needed clarification of the law is to guide one's analysis by the values to be promoted by the legal doctrine chosen. It is submitted that the present task of examining and assessing the law regulating external participation in internal strife self-determination and world order. In this chapter "self-determination" will be used to mean the genuine self-direction of a territorial community in establishing its own internal public order, no matter what form that public order may take, nor policies it may pursue. The term "world order," rather than connoting an international system, will be employed to mean the maximum promotion of peaceful relations between states and the minimum resort to international violence.

Ideally, then, the law regulating external participation in internal strife should have the effect of allowing the will of a people to express itself in the form of a freely chosen government (even if by violence) and, at the same time, permit legitimate governments to exercise their lawful authority in suppressing threats to their existence which are manifested in armed insurrections. Additionally, the formulation of the law should have the effect of reducing the instances of Great Power confrontations through participation in the civil strife of third states.

It is a commonly accepted proposition that all states have a duty of nonintervention in the internal affairs of other states.[12] The basis for this duty is that all sovereign states are equal and must do noth-

---

[12]*See, e.g.,* Art. 15 of the Charter of the Organization of American States (1948), T.I.A.S. 2361: "No State or group of States has the right to intervene directly or indirectly, for any reason whatsoever, in the internal or external affairs of any other State."

ing in derogation of the sovereignty of a sister state.[13] "The most basic principle of international law," writes one commentator, "is the equal claim to integrity of all states, regardless of their political or social ideology. Without such an assumption, it is impossible to maintain even a minimum of universal international order."[14]

Although the problems of the international regulation of external participation in the internal affairs of foreign states have inspired efforts toward clarification by numerous legal scholars, there is, lamentably, little agreement on what the term "intervention" and its corollary "nonintervention" really mean.[15] Indeed, as Professor Fenwick has expressed quite sharply:

> Of all the terms in general use in international law none is more challenging than that of "intervention." Scarcely any two writers are to be found who define this term in the same way or who classify the same situations under it.[16]

Some writers take the position that intervention is limited to the interference by one state in the internal affairs of another against its will; others apply the term only when one state participates in the civil strife of another state; still other observers apply the term to any involvement of one state, whether or not requested, in the internal affairs of another. In order to avoid the semantic difficulties inherent in the use of the word "intervention," this article will employ the word "interference" as an all-inclusive term to denote the unlawful intrusion into the internal affairs of a foreign state.[17]

It is assumed throughout this study that unsolicited or dictatorial involvement by one state in the internal matters of another

---

[13]U.N. Charter, Art 2(1); Charter of the Organization of American States, Art. 6, *supra* note 12; Convention on the Rights and Duties of States in the Event of Civil Strife, Art. 4 (Montevideo, 1933), T.S. 881. *See also* Henkin, "Force Intervention, and Neutrality in Contemporary International Law, (1963) *Proc. A.S.I.L.* pp. 147, 156.

[14]Friedmann, Intervention, Civil War and the Role of International Law, *A.S.I.L. Proc.* (1965) p. 67.

[15]*See* Grob, *The Relativity of War and Peace* (1949) p. 227, for perhaps the best expression of this conclusion.

[16]Fenwick, "Intervention: Individual and Collective," 39 *A.J.I.L.* 645 (1945).

[17]*See* Hull, and Novogrod, *Law and Vietnam* (1968) pp. 1-3, for a fuller discussion of the problems arising from the use of the word "intervention."

state is unlawful and must be characterized as interference. The relevant issue, however, in light of the fundamental community policy of fostering self-determination and world order, is whether *requested* aid from one state to the *de jure* government of another during civil strife should also be branded as unlawful. This article will analyze the three major positions espoused by international jurists on this issue which have been denominated "the classical doctrine," "the 'merits of the cause' position," and "the absolute neutrality principle."

THE CLASSICAL DOCTRINE

In analyzing the ascending intensities of internal stife, general international law traditionally speaks in terms of rebellion, insurgency, and belligerency.[18] Rebellion is said to exist when it remains certain that the domestic police force of the state will still be able to induce "the seditious party to respect the municipal legal order."[19] To phrase it differently, rebellion is considered no more than a sporadic and short-lived challenge to the incumbent government. A state of insurgency, however, exists when the internal conflict has reached a state of war in the material, but not in the legal sense.[20] The exact legal content of this term is not altogether clear and some prominent jurist have defined it only negatively. For example, it is said that the difference between war in the material sense (insurgency) and war in the legal sense (belligerency) is that "belligerency is a relation giving rise to definite rights and obligations while insurgency does not."[21] A state of belligerency, in the context of civil strife, occurs when a state of war in the legal sense exists and is declarative of a state of war between, in essence,

---

[18]*But see* Padelford, "International Law and the Spanish Civil War," 31 *A.J.I.L.*, 226, 227 (1937) who speaks also of insurrection, revolution, and civil war.

[19]Kotzsch, *The Concept of War in Contemporary History and International Law* (1956), p. 230.

[20]Thomas, and Thomas, *Non-Intervention: The Law and Its Import in the Americas* (1956), p. 216; Hershey, *The Essentials of International Public Law and Organization* (1929), p. 202. *See also The Three Friends,* 166 *U.S. 1,* 33-66 (1877).

[21]Lauterpacht, *Recognition in International Law* (1947), p. 270 Insurgency, as distinguished from organized crime, is opposed by the troops of the state instead of the police. *See* Weisse, *Droit International Appliqué Aux Guerres Civiles* (1898), p. 1.

two quasi-international bodies within the confines of a single jurid-ical entity.[22]

What are the rights and obligations attendant to each stage of civil strife under traditional international law? At the outset, it must be made clear that the outbreak of a rebellion or of other sporadic instances of resistance to the *de jure* government does not in any way alter the relationship that the troubled state enjoys with others. Rebellions or other cases of minor resistance to the incumbent's authority are considered a police problem at most and those in revolt are deemed traitors and may be treated as criminals.[23] During rebellion there is no dispute that assistance may be given to the legitimate government upon request, but, contrarily, none may be rendered to the rebels.[24] This normative framework should be deemed consistent with the stated policy goals of fostering self-determination and world order. There certainly can be no denigration of the right of self-determination in assisting the legitimate government during rebellion since the actions of isolated groups of criminals can scarcely be character-ized as the manifestation of the will of the people. World order is promoted because the established government has been aided in reasserting its lawful authority over the dissident elements in its society, thus eliminating the possibility of a Great Power con-frontation in its domestic strife.

Upon analysis it is not surprising that even when the revolt becomes somewhat more sustained in time and place and is or-ganized under responsible leaders, the resulting insurgency still does not affect the rule that the established government may be as-sisted[25] but the insurgents may not.[26] The rationale appears to be

---

[22]Lauterpacht, ed., *II Oppenheim, International Law* (7th ed. 1952), pp. 659-660; O'Rourke, "*Recognition of Belligerency and the Spanish War,* 31 *A.J.I.L.,* 398, 403 (1937).

[23]*See* Wehberg, *"La Guerre Civile et le Droit International,"* 63 *Hague Recueil des Cours,* 7, 41 (1938).

[24]*See* note 26, *infra.*

[25]The list of authorities supporting this proposition is impressive. *See, e.g.,* Thomas, and Thomas, *supra* note 20 218: Garner, "Questions of International Law *in the Spanish Civil War,"* 31 *A.J.I.L.,* 66, 68 (1937); Hull *and Novogrod, supra* note 17 pp. 75-96; Fawcett, "Intervention in International Law," 103 *Hague Recueil des Cours,* 343, 365-66 (1961); Baty, *The Canons of International Law 100* (1930); Rou-

that insurgency is an intermediate stage between a state of internal tranquillity and all-out war[27] and thus does not affect the state's juridical status as a member of the world community.[28] The duty of noninterference, of course, remains obligatory on outside states. The question of neutrality does not arise because "neutrality is a status which is created only when war in a legal sense exists,"[29] that is, after the belligerency of the insurgents has been recognized. Therefore, if an outside state should recognize a state of insurgency, it has done nothing more than to recognize the *fact* of insurrection; "the recognition of insurgency does not create any special status for the parties concerned."[30]

It must be noted in passing, however, that while a declaration of insurgency creates no new status under international law, it does, nevertheless, confer upon the insurgents some new rights relative to the conduct of the warfare itself. After a declaration of in-

gier, *Les Guerres Civiles et le Droit des Gens (1903); Alford,* "The Legality of American Military Involvement in Viet Nam: A Broader Perspective," 75 *Yale L.J.* 1109-1116 (1966); Moore, "The Lawfulness of Military Assistance to the Republic of Viet-Nam," 61 *A.J.I.L.,* 31 (1967); Von Glahn, *Law Among Nations* (1965) 83; Baxter, Legality of American Action: The War in Vietnam, *The Times,* (London, Sept. 5, 1967); Higgins, *The Development of International Law Through the Political Organs of the United Nations* (1963) 210-11; Lauterpacht, "The Contemporary Practice of the United Kingdom in the Field of International Law — Survey and Comment" 7 *I.C.L.Q.* 92, 102-104 (1958); Kotzsch, *supra* note 19 pp. 230-33; Kelsen, *Recent Trends in the Law of the United Nations,* (1951) p. 934; Borchard, "Neutrality and Civil Wars," 31 *A.J.I.L.* 304, 306 (1937); O'Rourke, *supra* note 22 p. 410; Padelford, *International Law and Diplomacy in the Spanish Civil Strife* (1939) 4; Woolsey, *International Law* 43 5th ed. (1897). *Cf.* McDougal, and Feliciano, *Law and Minimum World Public Order* (1961), 194 n. 164.

[26]The United Nations has repeatedly condemned assistance to rebel forces during rebellion and insurgency. *See, e.g.,* Resolution 380 (V), U.N. Gen. Ass. Off. Rec., 5th Sess., Supp. No. 20, 13 (A/1775) (1950); Draft Code of Offenses Against the Peace and Security of Mankind, Arts. 2 (4), 2 (5), and 2 (6), U.N. Gen. Ass. Off. Rec., 9th Sess., Supp. No. 9 at 11 (A/2693 (1954); Resolution 2131 (XX), U.N. Gen. Ass. Off. Rec., 20th Sess., Supp. No. 14, p. 11 (A/6014) (1965). *See also* Kelsen, *supra* note 25, p. 935.

[27]Chen, and Green, *"The International Law of Recognition,"* 398 (1951); Hershey, *supra* note 20, pp. 200-203.

[28]*Garner, supra* note 25, p. 67.

[29]*Ibid.*

[30]Chen, and Green, *supra* note 27, p. 399. *But see, e.g.* Powers, "Insurgency and the Law of Nations," 16 *J.A.G.J.,* 55, 65 (May 1962), who calls for the creation of a special international status of insurgency.

surgency, the members of the insurgent forces may no longer be considered murderers, pirates, or criminals, but henceforth must be treated as soldiers under the protection of the internationally recognized laws of war.[31] Furthermore, there is a substantial body of opinion holding that insurgents have a limited right of war. Under this theory the exercise of war rights by the insurgents within their own lands and their own territorial seas is considered an unquestionable right.[32] For example, the insurgents, consistent with this view, have the right to make a "reasonable effort . . . within the territorial waters appurtenant to an area under their control to prevent military aid from reaching their foes. . . ."[33] Concomitantly, it is settled that when the established government declares a state of insurgency, it no longer can be held liable for damage done by insurgent forces so long as it continues to make diligent efforts to suppress the insurrection.[34]

It bears reiteration at this point that, even when recognized by the legitimate government of foreign states, a state of insurgency confers no new rights with respect to the lawfulness of outside assistance to the parties involved. Under traditional norms, the legitimate government may continue to receive foreign assistance but the insurgents, as during a state of undeclared insurgency, may not.[35]

Implicit in the permissibility of assistance to the lawful government during rebellion and insurgency is the understanding that

[31]Under the Geneva Convention of 1949 the minimum standards of humanitarian treatment under the laws of warfare are made applicable to "conflicts not of an international character" whether or not insurgency is recognized. *See, e.g.* Art. 3 of the Geneva Convention Relative to the Treatment of Prisoners of War (1949), T.I.A.S. 3364.

[32]*See* Chen, and Green, *supra* note 27, pp. 401-07 and the authorities cited therein.

[33]III Hyde, *International Law Chiefly as Interpreted and Applied by the United States*, 2186 (1945). After a state of insurgency has been declared, outside states generally recognize the validity of the insurgents' legislative acts. *See, e.g.* Banco de Bilbao v. Rey, 2 K.B. 176 (1938); Lauterpacht, *supra* note 21, p. 273.

[34]Padelford, *supra* note 25, p. 197; Powers, *supra* note 30, p. 58; II Hyde, *supra* note 33, pp. 980-84.

[35]*See, e.g.* The Convention on Duties and Rights of States in the Event of Civil Strife (1928), Art. 1(3), which calls upon its signatories to "forbid the traffic in arms and war material, except when intended for the Government, while the belligerency of the rebels has not been recognized. . . ." IV Hudson, *International Legislation*, 2416 (1928-29).

such aid is based on the express or tacit consent of the strife-torn state.[36] Without the requisite consent of the incumbent government, any assistance thrust upon it would be unwarranted interference in its internal affairs. But a request for assistance must be scrutinized with care in order to determine

> the extent to which the request for help was prompted by pressure from the assisting state. If no such pressure is found, the foreign nation may extend the demanded support. But should such pressure exist, it would serve to invalidate the invitation, for, in effect, the request would be an infringement on the target-state's sovereignty.[37]

It is clear that both unrequested assistance or assistance flowing from coerced request make a mockery of the complementary rights of political independence and self-determination.[38]

Equally significant in assessing the lawfulness of assistance to the legitimate government is the determination that the faction aided is indeed the legitimate governmnt. There is little dispute with the proposition that it is within the sovereignty of a state to request aid.[39] However, as Professor Wright has made clear, ". . . sovereignty belongs to the *state* and not to the *government* . . ."[40] Hence, it is a matter of major importance for the assisting state to establish that the legitimate government still enjoys such a status, for, "only if the incumbent government is still considered the representative of the state will assistance to it be lawful."[41] Professor Wright believes that to meet this test the government must be "in firm possession of the territory of a state."[42] This proposition has generally been rejected as too rigid. Rather, it is widely accepted that

> so long as the revolution has not been fully successful and so long as the lawful government, however adversely affected by the fortunes of

---

[36]Fawcett, *supra* note 25, pp. 366-67; Kelsen, *supra* note 25. For the distinction between "state" and "government" and its relevance in a civil war context, *see* text accompanying notes 40-44, *infra*.

[37]Hull, and Novogrod, *supra* note 17, p. 87.

[38]Nor, if one state forces a government upon another state, is the former permitted to assist the later. *See* Baty, *supra* note 25, p. 101.

[39]*See* Baxter, *supra* note 25.

[40]Wright, "International Law and Civil Strife," *A.S.I.L. Proc.* (1959) 145, 148.

[41]Hull, and Novogrod, *supra* note 17, p. 87. *See also* Bluntschli, *Le Droit International Codifié*, 272 (1874).

[42]Wright, "United States Intervention in the Lebanon," 53 *A.J.I.L.* 112, 120 (1959).

the civil war, remains within national territory and asserts its authority, it is presumed to represent the state as a whole.[43]

There is a presumption, therefore, in favor of the incumbent government. Hence, under general international law the *de jure* government alone must be regarded as the representative of the state until it has been definitely supplanted.[44]

But, while general international law permits foreign assistance to the established government during insurgency, it, nevertheless, imposes no duty to do so in absence of a treaty.[45] Thus, in the case of an insurgency where there is no treaty obligation to aid the incumbent government, the choice of whether or not to do so is clearly political and hence free from all international prescriptions.

Consistent with the norm that rebels must not be given assistance, however, international law does impose several affirmative duties upon foreign states both prior to and during rebellion and insurgency. The foreign state, for example, has the duty to police its frontiers to insure that its territory shall not be used as a base of operations against the legitimate government of the troubled state;[46] it may not, of course, organize hostile, revolutionary forces and send them into other states;[47] it may not conduct or participate in terrorist activities directed against the political independence or territorial integrity of another state.[48] Not only is the outside state prohibited from engaging in the above activities, but it also has the duty to exercise "due diligence" to prevent the use of its territory by private groups or individuals for hostile acts against other states. The "responsibility of the state in such cases," writes one commen-

---

[43]Lauterpacht, "Recognition of Governments: I," in *Essays on International Law* 242 (Col. L. Rev. ed. 1965).

[44]Lauterpacht, *supra* note 21, p. 233; Baty, *supra* note 25, p. 206.

[45]Thomas, and Thomas, *supra* note 20, p. 218; Garner, *supra* note 25, p. 68; Fawcett, *supra* note, 25, p. 366.

[46]*See, generally,* Garcia-Mora, "International Law and the Law of Hostile Military Expeditions," 27 *Fordham L. Rev,* 308 (1958/59); Lauterpacht, "Revolutionary Activities by Private Persons Against Foreign States, 22 *A.J.I.L.* 103, 21 (1928).

[47]Curtis, "The Law of Hostile Military Expeditions as Applied by the United States, 8 *A.J.I.L.* 34 (1941); Rights and Duties of Foreign Powers as Regards the Established and Recognized Governments in Case of Insurrection, Art. 2(3) (1900) in Scott, *Resolution of the Institute of International Law,* 157 (1916).

[48]*See* Convention for the Prevention and Punishment of Terrorism, Art. I (Geneva, 1937) in VII Hudson, *supra* note 35, p. 862.

tator, "is measured by the degree of 'due diligence' which it shows in carrying out its general obligation . . ."[49] Whether the failure to exercise due diligence is a result of hostile intent or is merely a case of ineptitude, it must nevertheless be regarded as unlawful interference in the affairs of the aggrieved state.[50]

When a state of belligerency is recognized, however, an entirely new set of prescriptions applies. Belligerency, as explained above, is descriptive of a legal state of war within the boundaries of a single state. Scholars are in complete agreement on the requisite conditions to be met before a state of belligerency may be declared. Lauterpacht has enumerated them as follows:

> First, there must exist within the State an armed conflict of a general (as distinguished from a purely local) character; secondly, the insurgents must occupy and administer a substantial portion of national territory; thirdly, they must conduct the hostilities in accordance with the rules of war and through organized armed forces acting under a responsible authority; fourthly, there must exist circumstances which make it necessary for outside States to define their attitude by means of recognition of belligerency.[51]

When an outside state declares a state of belligerency,[52] it automatically imposes upon itself all the rights and duties of a neutral state.[53] "It loses the right which it had during the period of insurgency to assist the legitimate government," Professor Garner has pointed out, "and henceforth must treat both belligerents alike."[54] After belligerency has been declared, if the foreign state assists the government, it will amount to a violation of the laws of neutrality just as during insurgency assistance to the revolutionaries would have constituted a violation of the general rule that no assistance may be given to the latter. However, as in the case of war

---

[49]Fenwick, *International Law*, (1952) p. 301.

[50]Thomas and Thomas, *supra* note 20, p. 217.

[51]Lauterpacht, *supra* note 21, p. 176, See also McNair, "The Law Relating to the Civil War in Spain," 53 *Law Q. Rev.* 471, 477-32 (1937); Beale, "The Recognition of the Cuban Belligerency," 9 *Harv. L. Rev.* 406, 407 (1896).

[52]Outside states usually declare a state of belligerency by a formal proclamation of neutrality, See, generally, Padelford, *supra* note 25.

[53]Jessup, *A Modern Law of Nations*. (1956) p. 53; Kelsen, *Principles of International Law*, (1952) 291; Thomas and Thomas, Non intervention and the Spanish Civil War, *Proceedings of the American Society of International Law*, 2, 3-4 (1967).

[54]Garner, *supra* note 25, p. 69.

between two sovereign states, after a state of belligerency has been declared, an outside state may lawfully choose to change its status from a neutral to that of a cobelligerent with one of the two factions.[55]

Recognition of belligerency bestows upon the insurgents (now one of two belligerent parties within the state) all the rights of warfare that a sovereign state possesses without actually having such a status.[56] They have the "right to obtain loans on the credit of the state; their ship's have a right to enter ports of the recognizing state; they may maintain the right of visit and search at sea, confiscate goods and maintain blockades."[57] Additionally, the laws of warfare are binding on both belligerent parties.[58] Most importantly, however, as a belligerent party the insurgents may lawfully be assisted by a foreign state which may enter the conflict as a cobelligerent. The lifting of the prohibition against aid to the insurgents affords a tremendous boost to their effort to overthrow the incumbent government. This, when combined with the acquisition of the full ambit of the rights of warfare, furthers the people's drive toward self-determination by placing the insurgents on a level of equality with the exising government.

Since the recognition of belligerency by a foreign state at once enhances the international personality of the insurgents and deprives the legitimate government of the exclusive right of assistance it had therefore possessed, the premature recognition of the belligerent status of the insurgents is universally regarded as an unfriendly act toward the *de jure* government.[59] Until the prerequisites for a recognition of belligerency exist, it is the duty of the foreign state to do nothing that would redound to the benefit of

---

[55]See Oppenheim, *supra* note 22, p. 660; Von Glahn, *supra* note 25, p. 83, 84; I Phillimore, *Commentaries Upon International Law*, (1866), p. 510.

[56]A recognition of the belligerent status of the rebels is not equivalent to their recognition as the de facto government of the state. See Garner, *supra* note 25 p. 70.

[57]Thomas and Thomas, *supra* note 20, p. 219. See also Walker, "Recognition of Belligerency and Grant of Belligerent Rights," 23 *Transactions of Grotius Society* 177 (1938).

[58]The reason for this is simply that a recognition of belligerency is declarative of a legal state of war in which the laws of warfare automatically become binding. See Hershey, *supra* note 20, p. 203.

[59]See, e.g. Oppenheim, *supra* note 22, p. 249, Higgins, *supra* note 25, p. 138; Schwarzenberg, *A Manual of International Law* (5th ed. 1967), p. 76.

the insurgents. The premature recognition of belligerency patently falls within this prescribed category of actions favoring the insurgents.

On the other hand, the refusal to recognize the belligerent status of the insurgent forces when all the requisite conditions are fulfilled is, in this author's view, equally an act of interference in the internal affairs of a sovereign state and a denial of the right of self-determination. Admittedly, this view is controversial. Although in principle the recognition of belligerency is judicial in nature since it involves the application of legal criteria to factual evidence, the majority of scholars and the practice of states regard the act as solely political or legislative.[60] But this position—which must be regarded as somewhat conservative when viewed in the light of the stated policy goal of self-determination—is not without its critics.[61] The element of political discretion reserved to the recognizing state may too often be used to frustrate a legitimate and genuine expression of the will of a people,[62] It is therefore submitted that the better view is that the insurgents' right to recognition as belligerents is a legal one, and one that will directly promote the goal of self-determination espoused by this study.

During insurgency, when the insurgents have not yet shown themselves to be an expression of the will of the people, the ends of world order are served by permitting assistance to the *de jure* government in its attempt to reassert its lawful authority. However, once the conditions of belligerency are fulfilled—conditions which serve as workable indicia of the degree to which the insurrection is popularly supported[63]—the ends of self-determina-

---

[60]See, e.g., Garner, "Recognition of Belligergency," 32 *A.J.I.L.*, 106, 112 (1938); O'Rourke, *supra* note 22, pp. 401-02, especially nn. 13-15. For a complete list of authorities supporting this position see Lauterpacht (who is among its critics), *supra* note 21, pp. 240-41.

[61]Hull & Novogrod, *supra* note 17, p. 85; Lauterpacht, *supra* note 21, pp. 186-93; Higgins, *supra* note 25, pp. 136-37.

[62]See Friedmann, *supra* note 14, p. 71.

[63]Cf. Lauterpacht, op. cit. *supra* note 25, p. 104; McDougal C Feliciano, *supra* note 25. Professor Wright, however, believes that to further self-determination "the critical line is not recognition of belligerency, but the uncertainty of the outcome." Wright, *supra* note 42, p. 122. For a critique of Wright's position, see Landsberg, "The United States in Vietnam: A Case Study in the Law of Intervention, 50 *Calif. L. Rev.*, 515, 525 (1966).

tion are fulfilled by insuring the legal right to recognition of the belligerent status of the insurgents. The *de jure* government would thus lose its exclusive right to assistance and, in addition, the insurgents would lawfully exercise the full rights of warfare.

THE "MERITS OF THE CAUSE" POSITION

This position, conceived by Vattel and perhaps the oldest of the attempts to regulate external participation in internal strife, forbids assistance to either side during all stages of the conflict, but provides that once the efforts of outside states toward mediation prove fruitless, they may "take the merits of the cause into consideration, and assist the party which they shall judge to have right on its side . . ."[64] Just as in the traditional position, the assistance must be requested. This doctrine is unacceptable in that it places "the assisting state in a position of passing judgment on matters beyond its capabilities . . ."[65] Since, even at the early stages of the conflict, the choice of the faction to be assisted is entirely in the discretion of the foreign state, the rebels could, under this theory, be aided during rebellion or insurgency which would amount to a violation of the sovereignty of the target-state and is therefore destructive of world order. In short, world order could be disrupted in that foreign states could help rebel factions at whim merely by proclaiming the justness of the revolutionary cause. For these reasons, the "merits of the cause" position cannot be supported.

THE ABSOLUTE NEUTRALITY PRINCIPLE

Utilizing a broad conception of self-determination, proponents of this position argue that there is no legal basis whatsoever for one state to render assistance to the *de jure* government of another state during time of civil strife. "Since international law recognizes the right of revolution," Professor Wright has argued, "it cannot permit other states to intervene to prevent it."[66] Perhaps the fullest ex-

---

[64]Vattel, *The Law of Nations*, 427 (Chitty ed. 1853). One gets a hint of this position in Frabight, "The Algerian War of Independence," *Proceedings of the American Society of International Law, 18* (1967).

[65]See Hull & Novogrod, *supra* note 17, p. 94; Haleck, International Law 73 (1861).

[66]Wright, "Subversive Intervention," 54 *A.J.I.L.* 521, 529 (1960). See also Weisse, *supra* note 21, p. 86.

position of this principle has been given by Hall:

> As interventions, in so far as they purport to be made in compliance with an invitation, are independent of the reasons or pretexts which have already been discussed, it must be assumed that they are either based on simple friendship or upon a sentiment of justice. If intervention on the ground of mere friendship were allowed, it would be idle to speak seriously of the rights of independence. Supposing the intervention to be directed against the existing government, independence is violated by an attempt to prevent the regular organ of the state from managing the state affairs in its own ways. Supposing it on the other hand to be directed against the rebels, the fact that it has been necessary to call in foreign help is enough to show that the issue of the conflict would without it be uncertain, and consequently that there is doubt as to which side would ultimately establish itself as the legal representative of the state. If, again, the intervention is based upon an opinion as to the merits of the question at issue, the intervening state takes upon itself to pass judgment in a matter which, having nothing to do with the relations of states, must be regarded as being for legal purposes beyond the range of its vision.[67]

It is submitted that this position, at least if taken at face value, is unnecessarily restrictive and not in accord with the demands of either minimum world order or contemporary state practice. If anything, external involvement in intrastate conflict is the practice in today's world arena[68] and practicable and acceptable norms must be devised in order to regulate such blatant involvement in the affairs of foreign states. Since the absolute neutrality principle is unrealistic and misguided, outside states do not accept such a norm, and legitimate governments in need of assistance consider it as nothing less than a limitation on their sovereignty.[69]

Furthermore, there is reason to question the very premise of the position. As Professor Moore has stated so succinctly:

> The judgment that self-determination requires that neither the recognized government nor insurgents can ever be aided disarmingly conceals the naive assumption that whatever takes place within the confines of a territorial entity is pursuant to genuine self-determination of

---

[67]Hall, *International Law* (6th ed. 1909) p. 287. For the same view, see Lawrence, The Principles of International Law 134-35 (6th ed. 1915); I Hyde, *supra* note 33, p. 253; Brownlie, *International Law and the Use of Force by States* (1963), p. 323.
[68]See text accompanying notes 8, 9, *supra.*
[69]See Spain's argument to this effect in Padelford, *supra* note 25, pp. 133, 137-38.

peoples and that outside "intervention" is necessarily destructive of self-determination.[70]

The proponents of the absolute neutrality principle appear to view self-determination as an open-ended concept which roughly amounts to a Darwinian survival of the fittest within national boundaries.[71] To contend that any civil disorder of any magnitude is a manifestation of self-determination is patently absurd.[72] The essential task is to determine the dividing line between civil strife which is basically criminal and that which is an expression of the will of the people.

It is this particular task that the classical doctrine performs so much better than the "merits of the cause" position or the absolute neutrality principle. Despite the problems and ambiguities inherent in the classical view,[73] the four criteria for determining whether a state of belligerency exists do furnish an acceptable measuring rod by which decisionmakers of outside states may judge whether or not a particular intrastate conflict is a manifestation of self-determination.[74] The classical view is, at least, the sole theory which attempts to regulate external participation in civil strife which at once allows the incumbent government to exercise the sovereignty inherent in statehood by accepting assistance during intrastate conflict and furthers self-determination by terminating that exclusive right to assistance when a state of belligerency has been declared.[75] Concededly, there have been many instances when states have not

---

[70]Moore, *supra* note 25, p. 30.

[71]See Moore "International Law and the United States Role in Vietnam: A Reply," 76 Yale L.J. 1051, 1081 (1967). Eagleton, "Self-Determination in the United Nations," 47 *A.J.I.L.* 88, 93 (1953) also decries the reckless application of the concept of self-determination.

[72]Even Brownlie, an advocate of the absolute neutrality principle, realizes the absurdity of a total proscription of the de jure government's right to assistance. Brownlie, *supra* note 67, p. 324.

[73]For a discussion, see Hull & Novogrod, *supra* note 17, pp. 77-84. Among the problems are the meaning of "general armed conflict," the meaning of "occupy and administer," and whether the insurgents must actually in practice obey the laws of warfare or simply be prepared to obey them.

[74]See text accompanying note 63, *supra*.

[75]Cf. McDougal & Feliciano, *supra* note 25.

in good faith applied the doctrine.[76] In fact, some states flaunt their determination not to be bound by its norms.[77] The problem, however, does not lie with the theory, but rather with the unwillingness of the assisting state to live up to the law.[78]

Nevertheless, the classical view has some serious weaknesses. Most importantly, since outside states are free to become a co-belligerent with the faction of their choice after belligerency exists, the likelihood of Great Power confrontation in that strife is very real.[79] Although such a confrontation may have been avoided up to that point by literal adherence to the norm that only the *de jure* government may be assisted during rebellion and insurgency, the permission to enter the conflict as a co-belligerent will bring about a situation where Great Powers may suddenly find themselves facing each other from opposite sides of what once was purely internal strife.

A second deficiency in the classical view is that a declaration of belligerency fails to encourage self-determination to a sufficient degree. Instead of merely allowing the rebels to receive aid along with the legitimate government (in addition to the exercise of the full rights of warfare), the ends of self-determination would be much better served if aid to neither side could be furnished after belligerency. Adherence to this prescription would have the dual effect of not only allowing the will of the people to express itself free from all outside influence, but would also preclude Great Power confrontations in intrastate conflict after belligerency has been declared.

---

[76]This statement is particularly applicable to the conduct of states during the Spanish Civil War where the insurgents were aided from the beginning and belligerency never was declared although all the conditions were satisfied.

[77]See e.g. the official Soviet manual of international law which explicitly legitimizes support for wars of national liberation. Academy of Sciences of the U.S.S.R., Institute of State and Law, International Law 402 (n.d.).

[78]See, letter from Professors Thomas and Thomas to Roger H. Hull quoted in Hull & Novogrod, *supra* note 17, p. 83 n. 59.

[79]Many jurists have warned of this danger. See, e.g., Wright, op. cit. supra note 42, p. 122; Friedmann, *supra* note 11, p. 73; Falk, *supra* note 9, p. 207.

INTERNAL STRIFE AND THE UNITED NATIONS CHARTER

The question must be answered whether the Charter of the United Nations has affected the customary international law of external participation in civil strife. The Charter does not specifically refer to civil strife, but Article 2(4), the cornerstone of that document's attempt to delimit the use of force,[80] is most certainly applicable:

> All Members shall refrain in their international relations from the threat or use of force against the territorial integrity or political independence of any State, or in any other manner, inconsistent with the Purposes of the United Nations.

Even in view of this general proscription of the use of force across state lines, assistance that is *requested* during a rebellion or insurgency by the *de jure* government "could hardly be deemed violative of the 'territorial integrity or political independence' of the requesting state."[81] The contention that "Article 2(4) does not forbid the threat or use of force simpliciter,"[82] but only force which is directed *against* the territorial integrity or political independence of another state is most persuasive. Since it is within the sovereignty of a state to request aid, elementary logic compels the conclusion that solicited assistance does not fall within the category of action proscribed by Article 2 (4). Furthermore, to deny the right of assistance to the *de jure* government during a state of rebellion and insurgency overlooks the true nature of the assistance given. As Professor Kelsen has pointed out:

> Since the participation of a state in a civil war within another state on the side of the legitimate government is legally possible only with the express or tacit consent of this state, the enforcement action of the assisting state is, in the last analysis, an action of the assisted state, because authorized by its government.[83]

---

[80]For an excellent discussion of the lawfulness of the use of force short of war, see Harlow, "The Legal Use of Force . . . Short of War," 92 U.S. Naval Institute Proceedings 88, (Nov. 1966).

[81]Hull & Novogrod, *supra* note 17, p. 93. See also, Landsberg, *supra* note 63, p. 523; Fawcett, *supra* note 25, p. 366.

[82]Stone, *Aggression and World Order* (1958), p. 95.

[83]Kelsen, *supra* note 25, p. 934.

Nor does the Charter appear to proscribe the right of becoming a co-belligerent with either the *de jure* government or the insurgents after belligerency has been declared. In the context of civil strife, belligerency is descriptive of a legal state of warfare between two quasi-international bodies in one juridical entity. Both factions bodies in one juridical entity. Both factions may then request aid pursuant to the right of individual self-defense,[84] and Article 2(4) would not be violated if the assistance has been requested.[85]

Recently, it has been contended that Article 39 may prevent outside assistance to the *de jure* government during civil strife. The argument is that "the United Nations is authorized to intervene where civil strife threatens international peace, as the United Nations did in the Congo, in accord with Article 39 of the Charter—but individual states are not permitted to intervene unilaterally."[86] Not only does this position ignore the argument that the assisting state's action is really an action of the assisted state and, therefore, not a violation of Article 2(4), but also relies for its support solely on the highly technical rule of construction *expressio unius est exclusio alterius*. In short, there appears to be no provision in the Charter that would have the effect of prohibiting assistance from a foreign nation to the *de jure* government of strife-torn state during rebellion and insurgency, or the rendering of assistance to either party as a co-belligerent.

It should be pointed out that there is close to universal agree-

---

[84]Cf. Art. 51 of the U.N. Charter which reads in part: "Nothing in the present Charter shall impair the inherent right of individual or collective self-defense if an armed attack occurs against a Member of the United Nations, until the Security Council has taken measures necessary to maintain international peace and security." In an international war between two states, a third state may only employ force in the aid of the party exercising self-defense. See Kunz, "Individual and Collective Self-Defense in Article 51 of the Charter of the United Nations, 41 *A.J.I.L.*, 872, 877 (1947). In the context of civil strife which has reached the state of belligerency, however, this prescription is inapplicable because, in effect, both belligerents are exericising self-defense.

[85]See text accompanying notes 81, 82, *supra*.

[86]Lawyers Committee on American Policy Toward Vietnam, Memorandum of Law, 111Cong. Rec. 24011, 24013 (daily ed. Sep. 23, 1965). Art. 39 provides:

"The Security Council shall determine the existence of any threat to the peace, breach of the peace, or act of aggression and shall make recommendations, or decide what measures shall be taken in accordance with Article 41 and 42, to maintain or restore international peace and security."

ment among all scholars (regardless of their position on the issue of lawfulness of assistance to the *de jure* government during purely internal strife) that if the rebels are furnished with outside arms, money, "volunteers," etc., the incumbent government may then be assisted no matter what intensity the intrastate conflict has reached.[87] The classical doctrine, which presupposes a purely internal conflict, becomes inapplicable as soon as there is external participation on the side of the rebels. Generally, outside assistance to the rebels is considered an armed attack against the incumbent government[88] permitting assistance to it to be characterized as an exercise of collective self-defense pursuant to Article 51 of the United Nations Charter.[89]

CONCLUSION

The fact that the contemporary practice of states reveals that one government will readily assist the government of an allied nation during civil strife requires no new emphasis. Although there has been considerable bloc erosion over the last ten years, it is still for the most part axiomatic that states within the respective power blocs request and receive aid from each other. It would appear unrealistic, as the absolute neutrality principle would require, to forbid, at any stage of the strife, *all* such aid from one state to a *de jure* government of the same bloc. On the other hand, the right to enter the conflict as a co-belligerent after belligerency has been declared, as the classical view would permit, is destructive of world order in that Great Power confrontations could very likely take place with one power supporting the insurgents and another power aiding the legitimate government. It is submitted that a better rule to foster both self-determination and world order would be a merger of the best aspects of the classical doctrine and the absolute

---

[87]Even Hyde, *supra* note 33, p. 248, and Wright, *supra* note 42, p. 123 agree with this principle.

[88]See Brownlie, *supra* note 67, pp. 279, 373; Kelsen, *Collective Security Under International Law* (1954) 88. For the rationale behind this legal conclusion, see Pompe, *Aggressive War: An International Crime* (1953) p. 53.

[89]Hull & Novogrod, *supra* note 17, pp. 113-22, 135; Moore, *supra* note 25, pp. 7-13. Contra: Falk, "International Law and the United States Role in the Viet Nam War," 75 *Yale L.J.* 122, 1137 (1966).

neutrality principle, *i.e.* during rebellion and insurgency assistance may be afforded to the *de jure* government, but not to the rebels, and, after belligerency has been declared, assistance may be given to neither faction and an outside state must assume the role of a neutral.

The proposed norm, like the classical doctrine, would allow external participation in civil strife on the side of the *de jure* government but would not require it. Therefore, although this formulation would appear to limit the right of revolution to the powerful, it would not negate such a right[90] since oppressive regimes need not be assisted and, in any case, assistance must be terminated when a state of belligerency has been declared. If states are determined to assist friendly governments, it surely is wiser to regulate that assistance by commonly accepted norms rather than bluntly to proscribe all such assistance.[91] Literal adherence to the full scope of the absolute neutrality principle, therefore, is as unacceptable to those states who have blatantly indicated their intention to help revolutionary movements as it is to those states desirous of promoting *both* self-determination and the rule of law in the world community. To be sure, it would be more than naive to expect full compliance on the part of all states with the rule that no assistance may be given to the rebels. However, there is good reason to foresee stricter adherence to the proposed doctrine which allows some participation in intrastate conflict at various stages than to the absolute neutrality principle which prohibits assistance to either faction at any time during the strife.[92]

At present, however, the classical view appears to be representative of the practice of states and opinion of the majority of jurists. Despite its imperfections, it is nevertheless preferable to both the

---

[90]Padelford goes so far as to contend that international law actually favors the rebels by providing ascending levels of protection through a declaration of insurgency followed by a declaration of belligerency. Padelford, *supra* note 18 p. 228.

[91]It has been suggested, however, that as a minimum, tactical support to either side should be proscribed in order to attempt to contain civil strife within reasonable bounds. See Farer, *"Intervention in Civil Wars: A Modest Proposal,"* 67 Col L Rev, 266, 275-77 (1967).

[92]The lack of complete adherence to a norm does not derogate from its continued authority and binding effect. *See* "Case of The Prometheus," 2 *Hong Kong L.R.,* 207, 225 (1906).

"merits of the cause" position and the absolute neutrality principle. On the other hand, the norm proposed in this article must be considered *de lege ferenda* at best,[93] but one which hopefully will become more and more accepted. Until that time the classical doctrine, combined with greater respect for international law and greater restraint on the part of all states, will have to suffice.

---

[93]Cf. Falk, *Legal Order in a Violent World* (1968), pp. 99-323.

THE GENEVA CONVENTIONS OF 1949 AND WARS OF NATIONAL LIBERATION

R. R. Baxter

T HE LAW OF WAR, whether the humanitarian international law of the Geneva Conventions of 1949 or the combat law of the Hague Regulations, reflects a reconciliation of three conflicting types of forces: political, military, and humanitarian. It should therefore not surprise us that the enthusiasm which has been shown for a new legal concept of "wars of national liberation" springs from the politics of the Middle East and of Africa, that it is designed to strengthen the military position of certain types of forces, and that its supporters speak in terms of greater protection for the victims of certain types of war.

The discussions that have taken place in recent years in the General Assembly of the United Nations, in the two Conferences of Government Experts on the Humanitarian Law of War and in other bodies make it clear that wars of national liberation are thought of in two ways. The first is the waging of hostilities by freedom fighters struggling for liberation and self-determination in territories under colonial domination. The second is resistance activities conducted against unlawful foreign occupation. The two types of conflicts present quite different problems and must be discussed separately.

Before turning to a wider consideration of these two forms of hostilities, something must be said about the legal background against which consideration of wars of national liberation is taking place. The core of the international humanitarian law of war is the Geneva Conventions for the Protection of War Victims of 1949, to which over 130 States and other political entities are now parties. The four Conventions, dealing with the wounded and sick on land and at sea, prisoners of war, and civilians, apply, with the exception of one article appearing in all four Conventions, to international armed conflicts, conflicts between two or more High Contracting Parties. That one exception is article 3, which extends its protection to the victims of noninternational armed conflicts or, put more simply, civil wars. It thus follows that the range of protection given to war victims in international armed conflicts under the 400-odd articles of the Conventions is substantially wider than that given to the victims of internal armed conflicts, to which apply only the miniconvention of article 3. Perhaps the most significant difference in treatment is that prisoners taken in international armed conflicts, if they meet certain requirements, are treated as prisoners of war protected under a special régime, whereas prisoners taken in noninternational armed conflicts may be tried and convicted as criminals under municipal law.

Let us consider first the war of national liberation as an anticolonialist war. Numerous resolutions adopted by the General Assembly have called for the application of the Geneva Conventions of 1949 in their entirety and for the holding of captured freedom fighters as prisoners of war in Southern Africa, notably in Angola, Mozambique, Guinea (Bissau) and Sao Tomé (all Portuguese colonies), South Africa Namibia, and Southern Rhodesia. The view is widely entertained that these are international armed conflicts to which the Geneva Conventions of 1949 should apply. This characterization of the armed conflicts in these areas is based on the principle that a right of self-determination has been recognized by the United Nations Charter; by the Declaration on the Granting of Independence to Colonial Countries and Peoples, adopted by the General Assembly in 1960; by the Declaration of Principles of International Law Concerning Friendly Relations and Cooperation among States in Accordance with the Charter of the United Nations, adopted by the General Assembly at its 25th anniversary session in 1970; and by other international instruments. It follows from the existence of such a right that, in the language of the Declaration on Friendly Relations;

The territory of a colony or other Non-Self-Governing Territory has, under the Charter, a status separate and distinct from the territory of the State administering it and such separate and distinct status under the Charter shall exist until the people of the colony or Non-Self-Governing Territory have exercised their right of self-determination. . . .

If these colonies and non-self-governing territories are independent political entities, then the colonial power or the power denying a territory its right to self-determination engages in an international armed conflict when it attempts to suppress the independence movement. Of course, from the perspective of Portugal or Southern Rhodesia, or South Africa, the conflict is being carried on in the territory of those states and is therefore insurrection in violation of the municipal law of those countries. The most that could be expected would be the application of article 3 of the Geneva Conventions of 1949. The crucial issue is thus whether the combatants captured by those colonial regimes should be treated as criminals violating the law promulgated by the colonial power or should be held as prisoners of war, sheltered by the Geneva Conventions and not subject to trial under municipal law.

The right of self-determination can, however, mean different things in different contexts. It is all very well to speak of anticolonialist struggles in Africa, but does a similar right of self-determination exist in the metropolitan territory of other countries? Was Biafra exercising a right to self-determination during the tragic Nigerian civil war? Was Bangladesh in its revolt against Pakistan asserting a right guaranteed to it under the Charter? States which have had experience with secessionist movements, such as Nigeria, Pakistan, and Indonesia—to name only three less developed countries—react with some surprise and resentment to the suggestion that they have been guilty of a violation of the Charter and they should have applied the whole of the international law of war in their relations with those rebelling against their authority. It is quite clear that one man's war of national liberation can be another man's war of national secession. And it would be a great pity if legitimate resentment against the remaining vestiges of colonialism in Southern Africa should be allowed to distort the whole of the law of war, applicable in all quarters of the world. The core of the problem is that we know where the right of self-determination begins but we have no shared understanding of how far the concept takes us.

As indicated, the assertion has frequently been made that in wars of national liberation against colonialist régimes the Geneva Conventions of 1949 ought to be applied. Portugal, Southern Rhodesia, and South Africa are all parties to the conventions, but the liberation movements are not and, as will be shown, cannot be parties to the conventions. As the conventions apply only as between the high contracting parties, they cannot by their terms apply to wars of national liberation.

The four conventions of 1949 are open to accession by "any power." There is no reason to suppose that this term refers to anything other than a state. The corresponding article of the two Geneva Conventions of 1929 refers to "any country," while the authoritative commentaries on the conventions of 1949 drafted by the International Committee of the Red Cross notes that the invitation to accede is directed to "states." A liberation movement does not fall within the scope of any of these terms, which appear to be interchangeable.

The same considerations apply to the third paragraph of common article 2, which provides that:

> Although one of the Powers in conflict may not be a party to the present Convention, the Powers who are parties thereto shall remain bound by it in their mutual relations. They shall furthermore be bound by the Convention in relation to the said Power, if the latter accepts and applies the provisions thereof.

This provision was intended to hold open the possibility that a state that is not a high contracting party might, through its conduct in conformity with the conventions, bring them into force in conflict with an undoubted high contracting party. The latter is bound only for so long as its adversary actually does apply the provisions of the convention. But again the difficulty is that a liberation movement is not a power in the sense of being a state.

It will be remembered that Algeria in 1960, during its conflict with France, attempted to deposit an instrument of accession to the Geneva Conventions of 1949. The Swiss Federal Council declared that so far as States which had not recognized Algeria were concerned, the accession was "without juridical relevance." It is submitted that this is the correct view. Those states that had recognized national liberation movements as states would be required to apply the conventions in conflicts with such liberation movements. Correspondingly, those states that had not recognized a national liberation movement would not be required to do so. The question would then be how Portugal or South Africa would look on a purported accession by a government speaking for Mozambique or Namibia. If Portugal refused to recognize the validity of an accession, the accession itself would be an empty gesture. The problem is compounded, moreover, by uncertainties about what group is entitled to speak for a non-self-governing territory. Peculiarly enough, in the one case in which there is a widely recognized body entitled to speak for a non-self-governing territory—the United Nations Council for Namibia—the Council has made no effort to make Namibia a party to the four conventions of 1949. That simple step would be welcome progress.

Various provisions of the Geneva Prisoners of War Conventions of 1949 make it clear that the powers which may become high contracting parties must have the attributes of statehood. Under article 102 a prisoner of war must be tried under the same law and by the same courts as members of the armed forces of the detaining power. Hence the power that detains must have a national system of law and courts. Article 87 asks that the detaining power take into account that a prisoner of war "not being a national of the detaining power, is not bound to it by any duty of allegiance." Hence the liberation movement must have created a nationality law. And one might go on with further implicit requirements of the conventions which could not be met by national liberation movements that had not yet moved to separate statehood recognized by other states.

The law of belligerent occupation laid down in the Hague Regulations of 1907 and in Part III of the Geneva Civilians Convention are simply not applicable to a civil war. Is the national liberation movement in belligerent occupation of the territory it wrests from the control of the authorities in power, or is the colonial power in belligerent occupation of that part of the territory over which it retains control and thus subject to the restraints imposed by that body of law? It is very difficult to conceive that a colonial power could be persuaded to look upon the situation in that latter way.

Aside from these legal difficulties, it is doubtful that national liberation movements would, as a matter of fact, be in a position to discharge the obligations incumbent upon a high contracting party under the roughly 400 articles of the conventions. The national liberation movement would probably lack the material means which would permit it to comply with the Prisoners of War Convention as regards prisoners taken from the forces of colonial power. The conventions were drafted with an eye to what states might be expected to do, not what national liberation movements might be expected to do.

To deny that the international law of war can apply to conflicts between colonial powers and national liberation movements is not to leave members of such movements entirely at the mercy of the enemy. Article 3 of the Conventions does apply, and the parties are also exhorted by the article to bring into force all or parts of the full conventions. And the proposals made by the International Committee of the Red Cross with respect to a Protocol on Non-International Armed Conflicts to the Geneva Conventions of 1949 would provide a much more extensive protection to those who are either nonparticipants or combatants in internal conflicts, including struggles for self-determination waged against colonialist administrations. More modest aims may ultimately do more for populations of colonies and non-self-governing territories than attempts to make the whole of the law of war applicable.

The other major form of the war of national liberation is fought against what seems to be regarded as an unlawful occupation. The General Assembly has not been content to speak of those who fight in anti-colonialist wars. In its resolution 2674 (XXV) on "respect for human rights in armed conflicts," it called for prisoner of war treatment for "participants in resistance movements and freedom-fighters in southern Africa and territories under colonial and alien domination and foreign occupation, struggling for their liberation and self-determination." "Alien domination and foreign occupation" is directed to Israel's occupation of territory of several Arab states. Israel has been reproached in a number of General Assembly and Security Council resolutions for its failure to recognize the applicability of the Geneva Civilians Convention of 1949 and for its practices in the occupied areas.

If the central difficulty about anticolonialist wars has been whether they are internal or international armed conflicts, there is no such problem about unlawful occupation of territory by a foreign state, for here by definition the conflict is an international one, governed by the entirety of the Geneva Conventions of 1949, provided that the participants are parties to the conventions. Either one of two possible assumptions must underlie the characterization of the occupation of the territory of one state by the armed forces of another as unlawful. One is that all occupations of enemy territory are unlawful, even if the occupant is acting in the exercise of its inherent right of individual or collective self-defense under article 51 of the United Nations Charter and is occupying some of the territory of its adversary as a defensive measure. The other is that only certain occupations are unlawful —namely when the occupant has resorted to the use of force in violation of article 2, paragraph 4, of the charter. Although the justification for treating hostilities against Israel as a war of national liberation has not been fully articulated, it would seem that the occupation is taken to be one in violation of the charter, notably article 2, paragraph 4. If that is so, the implication is that one body of law applies to an unlawful belligerent occupation and another to lawful belligerent occupation.

Such a theory would be a good deal easier to apply if there were any means of determining when an occupation is unlawful and when it is lawful. The central function of the Security Council is not to determine the legality of a resort to force but to bring an end to the various forms of actual or potential disturbances to the peace that are referred to in articles 33, 34, and 39 of the United Nations Charter. This is not to say that the Security Council does not from time to time indicate which party to a dispute has an obligation to cease the use of force or to withdraw, but it is not always clear in such cases whether a state is called upon to desist from a certain course of conduct because it is unlawful or because it is not conducive to the reestablishment of peace. The Security Council may, moreover, not be seized of a breach of the peace at all, as was the case with the conflict in Vietnam. The General Assembly similarly does not perform the function of determining the legality of various resorts to the use of force. Even if either organ of the United Nations were to pronounce itself on the legality of a particular resort to the use of force, its views would be entitled to great weight but would nevertheless be somewhat suspect as reflecting a political appraisal of the situation rather than a judicial determination of the merits of the matter in accordance with international law.

This being the case, there will generally be no authoritative third party determination of the legality of a resort to force or of a consequential occupation of territory. Each party to the conflict will pronounce itself upon the question according to that basic principle that "international law creates rights for me and duties for you." Translated into the terminology of war, "the wars that I fight are just wars; the wars that you fight are dirty aggressive imperialistic wars in violation of the charter."

If there is to be a double standard for the law of war—one for wars of national liberation fought against the unlawful use of force by an adversary and one for wars of national subjugation fought in violation of international law—then there will be no authoritative means of determining which standard is applicable to each belligerent. We are in the presence of a revival of the notion of the just war and of the principle that the justice of the war affects the *ius in bello*.

The law of war as presently conceived and codified makes no distinction between one belligerent and the other according to the legality of the resort to force by each. The *ius in bello* incorporated in the Geneva Conventions of 1949, the Hague Regulations, the Geneva Protocol of 1925, and the Hague Cultural Property Convention of 1954 is based upon the principle that the law relating to the conduct of warfare and the protection of war victims will be neutral and that there will be an equality of treatment of the participants in a conflict.

Particular emphasis is currently being placed on the principle that the law for the protection of war victims is a wartime application of human rights law. If the purpose of the law is the protection of the human person, then all persons in particular categories of war victims, whether prisoners of war or wounded and sick or civilians, must be treated alike on a nondiscriminatory basis. There cannot be one body of law for the protection of prisoners of war taken by the side that is fighting a just war and another body of law for prisoners taken by the side that has resorted illegally to the use of force.

One of the most powerful inducements to compliance with the law of war is that both sides equally participate in its benefits and its burdens. A belligerent is encouraged to comply with the law because it hopes that this will encourage its adversary to do the same. To the extent that the law of war imposes burdens, each belligerent knows that in legal, if not in factual terms its burdens are no more onerous than those borne by its enemy.

Were belligerents to be left to assess the legality of their conduct under the charter, each would be firmly persuaded of the legality of its conduct and would consider that human beings associated with its adversary should be given a standard of protection inferior to that demanded for a belligerent's own people. Each will respond to what it conceives to be a violation of the law by its adversary by some form of reprisals or retaliation against that adversary, and so the protection of human rights will escalate downward in a series of retaliatory measures. An instructive example is furnished by the destruction of much of the law of the sea under the pressure of reprisals and counterreprisals taken against such allegedly unlawful conduct as the sowing of mines, unrestricted submarine warfare and the arming of merchant ships. This same process can occur in land warfare. Inequality in treatment and the denial of mutuality and reciprocity in the application of legal rules is ultimately destructive of law. The sufferers are the war victims who already bear the burdens of conflict.

If the concern of those who speak of a war of national liberation against foreign occupation is with the position of those who participate in resistance activities, a closer examination of the Geneva Convention of 1949 ought to put any fears to rest. The conventions were drafted by men who were acutely conscious of the resistance activities of World War II and of the part which they had played in the victory over the Axis. Members of "organized resistance movements, belonging to a party to the conflict and operating in or outside their own territory, even if this territory is occupied" are accorded prisoner of war status if they meet the other conditions specified in article 4 of the Geneva Prisoners of War Convention of 1949. The provisions of the Geneva Civilians Conventions which deal with the repression of acts hostile to the occupant by the inhabitants of the occupied area took account of the grim lessons of World War II. The balancing of the inevitable resistance activities of the local population against the needs of the belligerent occupant had already been accomplished at the Geneva Conference of 1949. Resistance activities were not invented by the Arabs who have fought against the occupation of territory by Israel.

What really seems to be at stake in the agitation for a special legal status for wars of national liberation, whether seen as anticolonialist wars or as wars against unlawful foreign occupation, is combatant status and treatment upon capture as prisoners of war for those who fight in such a war. One who is resisting foreign domination should, it would seem, be accorded an immunity from local law; he would, if captured, be held as a prisoner of war, who is not held to any duty of allegiance to the detaining power. It would seem that liberation movements would be called upon to do the same with respect to prisoners that they might take from the armed forces of the authorities in power. Whether they would have the material means to comply with the Geneva Prisoners of War Convention of 1949 is another question. It is also open to question whether the authorities in power, representing either a colonial regime or a state in belligerent occupation of territory could be persuaded to accord an immunity from local law to members of resistance movements.

But something more is at stake. What seems to be implicit in the thinking of the advocates of wars of national liberation is that there should be a special status for members of resistance or liberation movements who fight as guerrillas or in some other covert manner.

Under the existing law, a member of a militia or a volunteer crops, to use the language of the Geneva Conventions of 1949, including a member of an organized resistance movement, must meet four requirements if he is to be treated as a prisoner of war. He must fulfill all of the following conditions of Article 4 of the conventions:

(a) that of being commanded by a person responsible for his subordinates;
(b) that of having a fixed distinctive sign recognizable at a distance;
(c) that of carrying arms openly;
(d) that of conducting their operations in accordance with the laws and customs of war.

Of these requirements, (a) can readily be complied with by irregulars, members of resistance movements, and guerrillas. For forces which rely on surprise, stealth, and concealment, (b) and (c) are difficult, and (d), conformity with the law of war, may be difficult or impossible for forces lacking facilities for the detention of prisoners of war taken by them.

At the two Conferences of Government Experts on the Humanitarian Law of War convened by the International Committee of the Red Cross, proposals were made in a Protocol on International Armed Conflicts that members of militias and volunteer crops, including resistance or independence movements, who would be entitled to prisoner of war status, should be more broadly defined than in the Geneva Conventions of 1949. Particular emphasis was placed on the notion of the openness of their activities as a governing condition for prisoner of war treatment. That criterion of openness was, in the proposal made by the International Committee of the Red Cross at the Second Conference, to be satisfied through a requirement

> that in their operations they show their combatant status by openly displaying their weapons or that they distinguish themselves from the civilian population either by wearing a distinctive sign or by any other means. . . .

The proposal was rejected because it would be too easy for participants in such movements to move at will from civilian to combatant status, the degree of disclosure of combatant status was not sufficiently high and a criterion of "any other means" was too imprecise. In short, the proposal would make it too easy for combatants to disguise themselves as civilians and slip from one status to another in a manner conducive to concealment, stealth and surprise.

The maintenance of the distinction between combatants and noncombatant civilians is vital to the law of war. A combatant is required to declare himself in order to maintain the presumption that those not so declaring themselves are peaceful civilians who are entitled to immunity from attack and to the other safeguards of the law of war. If combatants disguise themselves as civilians, then civilians become suspect. Military considerations will demand that more forceful measures be taken against them: that they be interned; that all men of military age be rounded up if there has been a *levée en masse;* that suspicious civilians be fired upon; or that civilians be more widely attacked on the ground that disguised combatants are intermingled with those who take no active part in the hostilities. Guerrilla activity and resistance activities by persons passing themselves off as civilians can readily change the presumption that a person not in uniform is a peaceful nonparticipant to a presumption that such an individual is or may be a combatant. To the extent that the line between peaceful civilians and combatants is blurred and a combatant can disguise himself, the protection of the fundamental human rights of peaceful civilians is imperiled. To maintain strict standards for irregulars and guerrillas is thus conducive to the amelioration of the conditions of warfare and the immunity of the civilian population.

The support for special law for wars of national liberation may be only a passing phase, responsive to the practices of Israel and of those states in Southern Africa that deny their nationals the right of self-determination. At the moment, the reasons adduced for laws applicable to wars of national liberation are more political than humanitarian. If separate bodies of law are created for the just and for the unjust, for those who fight lawful wars and for those who fight unlawful wars, the whole fragile fabric of the humanitarian law of war can be brought tumbling down. It would be ironic if wars fought for the protection of human rights should lead to the degradation of human rights in war.

TERRORISM AND THE REGULATION OF ARMED CONFLICTS

JIRI TOMAN

INTRODUCTION

THE INTERNATIONAL NORMS which limit *the use of force in international* relations are explicit. The threat or use of force is prohibited by international law. This rule in particular is mentioned in the Charter of the United Nations, Article 2, paragraph 4: "All Members shall refrain in their relations from the threat or use of force against the territorial integrity or political independence of any state, or in any other manner inconsistent with the Purposes of the United Nations." Accordingly, we may distinguish three categories in which force may be employed under the provisions of:

a) collective security—Article 1 al. 1, Chapter VII of the Charter;

b) self-defense expressed in Article 51 of the Charter;

c) interpretation of the Article 2, paragraph 4 and Article 1 of the Charter.

mentioned in Article 1 and, *inter alia,* for the realization of "the consistent with the Purposes of the United Nations," which means that force may be used whenever it is consistent with the purposes mentioned in Artilce 1 and, *inter alia,* for the realization of "the principle of equal rights and self-determination of peoples" (Article 1, paragraph 2). In this context the use of force by national liberation movement in order to exercise their right of self-determination is a permissible use of force under international law.

The existence of law in human society eliminates the use of

individual force except in cases of self-defense. All other uses of force and "private wars" are governed by the criminal law of the jurisdiction which deals with the individual problem.[1] But, nevertheless, the use of force by individuals exists. It exists when the jurisdiction or national authorities are unable to assure the application of justice and when the society itself creates the conditions which authorize the use of force. What are the criteria which authorize individuals or groups of individuals to use the force against the establishment?

The Preamble of the Universal Declaration of Human Rights, interpreting the provisions of the Charter, recognizes that "it is essential, if man is not to be compelled to have recourse, as a last resort, to rebellion against tyranny and oppression, that human rights be protected by the rule of law." Herbert Marcuse, called the "apostle of the youth in revolt," said that "the criteria is what is proper to promote life, what is serving the development of capacities, of the good luck and the peace of men."[2] Individual use of violence may manifest itself in individual acts or through political tensions, from internal disturbances to the civil war, at which point recognition of a belligerency may bring the law of war into play. Terrorism is only one of the forms and methods of fighting within the framework of violence.[3] Use of individual violence when authorized, however, does not mean the use of indiscriminate violence, because justification of the cause cannot justify such acts. Frantz Fanon, known as a theoretician of violence said: "brutalité pure, totale, si elle n' est pas immediatement combattue entraine immanquablement la défaite du mouvement au bout de quelques semaines."[4] In the following pages we shall study this

---

[1]"Individuals must not be permitted to do that which the magistrate can do in the name of the State, in order that there may be no occasion for rising a greater disturbance," H. Grotius citing Julius Paulus—*see* Hugo Grotius, *De Jure Belli ac Pacis*, The Classic of International Law, Carnegie Endowment (Oceana Publ., 1964), p. 91.

[2]*See* the discussion with Friedrich Hacker published in Friedrich Hacker, *Aggression, violence dans le monde moderne* (Calmann-Levy, 1972), p. 352.

[3]Very often the confusion of term violence and terrorism is made; for example, the declaration of Jamil M. Broody, representative of Saudi Arabia in the Sixth Committee of the U. N. General Assembly, who considers the terms violence and terrorism as synonymous (GA/L/1564, 9. 11. 1972,) p. 6.

[4]Frantz Fanon, *De la Violence*, p. 93-94.

relationship between terrorism and the rules of law of war by considering the following two cases: 1) international armed conflicts (as defined in the Article 2, common to the Geneva Conventions); and, 2) non international armed conflicts (Article 3, common to the Geneva Conventions).

PROHIBITION OF TERRORIST MEASURES AND ACTS AGAINST INNOCENT CIVILIANS

E. Vattel, speaking on the ravaging and burning of countries, towns and villages posed the following question: "But what nation will proceed to such extremities, merely for the sake of punishing the hostile sovereign? It is but indirectly that he will feel the punishment; and how great the cruelty, to ruin innocent people in order to reach him."[6] J. K. Bluntschli, differing with Bynkershoek and Heffter, does not recognize the soldiers right "de disposer arbitrairement du sort des habitants paisibles du territoire enemis."[7] In one of the first attempts to codify the law of war, Francis Lieber prohibits assassination without judgment (Article 148) and assures the protection of hostages (Article 55) and of civilian population (Article 4 and 47), The Oxford Manual, adopted by the Institute of International Law in Oxford on September 9, 1880, considers reprisals as "an exception to the general rule of equity, that an innocent person ought not to suffer for the guilty" (Article 84). The International Peace Conference of 1899, during the discussion on the collective penalties, touched on the problem of soldier responsibility: "il faut que la repression s' exerçant sur la collectivité ait pour fondement la responsabilité tout au moins passive de cette collectivité."[8]

---

[5]"Du point de vue strictement juridique un veritable droit de l' humanité s' est créé en vertu dequel la personne humaine, son intégrité, sa dignité, sont défendues au nom d' un principe moral qui s' élève bien au-délà des limites du droit national et de la politique. Comment peut-il s' harmoniser avec les systèmes juridiques existants et s' insérer dans la jurisprudence? C' est une question d'ordre secondaire. En premier lieu, il importe que soit sauvegardé dans tous les cas, un minimum d' humanité." (Max Huber: La Pensee et l' Action de la Croix Rouge, (Geneve, 1954), p. 290.

[6]E. de Vattel, *The Law of Nations or Principles of the Law of Nature*, (edition by J. Chitty, London, 1834), p. 367 Book III, Chap. IX. Par. 167.

[7]J. K. Bluntschli, *Le droit international codifié* (Paris, 1870), par. 568.

[8]Report of the Sub-Committee of the second Commission, prepared by H. Rolin.

The principle of Hague Law, according to which belligerents do not have an unlimited choice of means to harm the enemy, leads to three restrictions which exclude terrorism from the regular forms of fighting. These restrictions are the following:

> *ratione personae:* "Belligerent will leave noncombatants outside the area of operations and will refrain from attacking them deliberately."
>
> *ratione loci:* "Attacks are only legitimate when directed against military objectives, that is to say whose total or partial destruction would constitute a definite military advantage."
>
> *ratione conditionis:* "Weapons and methods of warfare likely to cause excessive suffering are prohibited."[9]

Terrorism appears also in the Rules of Air Warfare prepared by the Committee of Jurists designated by the Washington Conference in 1922. According to Article 22, "Any aerial bombardment for the purpose of terrorizing the civilian population or destroying or damaging private property without military character or injuring noncombatants, is forbidden." We find the similar formulation in Article 4 of the Draft Convention for the protection of civilian population against new arms of war, adopted by the International Law Association in 1938.[10]

Article 27 of the IVth Geneva Convention relative to the protection of civilian persons in time of war of August 12, 1949 declares: "Protected persons are entitled, in all circumstances, to respect for their persons, their honour, their family rights, their religion, convictions and practices and their manners and customs. They shall at all times be humanely treated, and shall be protected especially against all acts of violence or threats thereof and against insults and public curiosity. This article reflects the idea that all persons should be treated in accord with basic human rights. But terrorist acts are expressly prohibited by Article 33: "No protected person may be punished for an offense he or she has not personally

---

[9]Jean Pictet, The Principles of International Humanitarian Law (ICRC, Geneva 1966), p. 52.

[10]ILA, Report of the 40th Conference held in Amsterdam, 1938, pp. 41-54.

committed. Collective penalties and likewise all measures of intimidation or of terrorism are prohibited. . . . . pillage is prohibited
. . . . .reprisals against protected persons and their property are prohibited."

Reprisals directed at certain acts and to obtain reparation may have the effect of creating a situation of terror and was clearly prohibited in the same article "excluant toute interprétation tendant à admettre l' existence de la reserve tacite des nécessités militaires."[11] Reprisals are also prohibited in other articles, i.e. Article 46 of the First Geneva Convention and Article 47 of the Second Geneva Convention prohibit the reprisals against wounded, sick, shipwrecked personnel, protected buildings, protected ships and protected material. Article 13 of the Third Geneva Convention assures humane treatment to the prisoners of war and protects them against "all acts of violence and intimidation" and prohibits reprisals against them.[12]

The Tokyo Project for the protection of civilians in the time of war, adopted by the XVth International Conference of the Red Cross in 1934, prohibits the taking of hostages in the Article 4, which concerns enemy civilians who are on the territory of one of the belligerents. Enemy civilians in the occupied territory are covered by Article 19(a), "au cas ou, a titre exceptionnel, il paraît indispensible à l' Etat occupant de prendre des otages, ceux-ci devront toujours être traités avec humanité. Ils devront sous aucun prétexte être mis à mort ou soumis à des chatiments corporels." The experience of two world wars led the Diplomatic Conference of 1949 to include into the Geneva Conventions the formal prohibition of this practice. So, as mentioned in the article of M. C. Pilloud, the positive law has been put in complete harmony with the principles of natural law prohibiting the punishment of in-

---

[11]Commentaire de la IVème Convention de Genève, publié sous la direction de Jean S. Pictet (Genève, 1956), p. 246, hereinafter referred to as *Commentary*.

[12]The ICRC rose against the reprisal measures concerning particularly the prisoners of war appeal, which has been addressed to the belligerents in 1916 and in the Convention 1929, Article 2, alinea 3. In the beginning of the Second World War, the ICRC obtained assurance that the Geneva Conventions of 1929 will be applicable by analogy on the enemy civilians interned on the territory of the belligerent. This does not concern the civilians in the occupied territory.

nocents in the place of the guilty.[13]

In general, collective punishment which is one form of terrorizing innocent people in time of war, is prohibited by the Geneva Convention of 1929 Relative to the Treatment of Prisoners of War (Article 46) and by the Third German Convention of 1949 (Articles 87). And as we pointed out, Article 33 of the IVth Geneva Convention Relative to the Protection of Civilian Persons in Time of War of 1949 contains the same prohibition.

The Draft Rules for the Limitation of the Dangers incurred by Civilian Population in Time of War, which was adopted by the XIXth International Conference of the Red Cross in 1957, has to be applied equally to international and internal conflicts. The first paragraph of the Article 6 states that "[a]ttacks directed against the civilian population, as such whether with the object of terrorizing it or for any other reason, are prohibited." The experts invited in 1954 by the ICRC to discuss the problem of the protection of the civilian population considered that the intent to terrorize a population is difficult to prove, because such attacks when they took place, in the majority of cases, can also be considered connected to operations against military objectives. On the request of the National Societies of the Red Cross, terrorism was discussed because of its psychological interest to the population and is underscored by the Commentary to this draft which expresses reprobation toward terrorism, by maintaining that acts directed against the civilian population without other motives.[14]

Finally we must mention the resolution of the General Assembly of the United Nations 2444 (XXIII) of December 19, 1968, on Respect for Human Rights in Armed Conflicts, which states:

    a) That the right of the parties to a conflict to adopt means of injuring the enemy is not unlimited;

    b) That it is prohibited to launch attacks against the civilian population as such;

    c) That distinction must be made at all times between persons taking part in the hostilities and members of the civilian

---

[13]Claude Pilloud, "La Question des otages et les Conventions de Genève" Revue International de la Croix-Rouge, (1950), p. 17.

[14]Draft Rules for the limitation of the Dangers incurred by the civilian population in the time of war (ICRC, Geneva, 1956).

population to the effect that the latter be spared as much as possible.

The new Draft Protocol Additional to the Geneva Conventions of August 12, 1949, relating to the protection of victims of international armed conflicts, submitted to governments as the proposal for the next Diplomatic Conference in 1974, has prohibited, in Article 46 "methods intended to spread terror among the civilian population." Article 65 of the same Protocol outlawed several acts which may be terrorist and are directed against the civilian population and the civil property in the hands of one of the Parties to the conflict.

Some authors prefer to examine the acts of terrorism already in the "established categories, like sabotage, the protection of the civilian population, combatants statute, etc. . ."[15] This cannot justify the exclusion of the general and independent prohibition of the different forms under other categories. We consider that this is also the conclusion at which we may arrive from the recent conferences of the governmental experts in 1971 and 1972 in Geneva.

THE POSITION OF PERSONS WHO HAVE COMMITTED ACTS OF "TERRORISM"

Consider two situations: persons who have committed the acts of violence in armed conflict and the situation of persons who have committed the acts of terrorism outside the context of armed conflicts.

As concerns the first category, the fact that they have committed during acts of violence fighting enemy combatants does not deprive them of the rights under the Geneva Conventions. We agree with the characteristic given by the Commentary to the Geneva Convention, that the Article 13 of the First and of the Second Geneva Convention has exclusively theoretical value. On the contrary, Article 4 of the Third Geneva Convention has a constitutive character. So, ". . .tout blessé ou malade quel qu'il soit —fût-il un franctireur ou même un criminel—doit être respecté et

---

[15]*See* Michel Veuthey, Régles et Principles de droit humanitaire applicable dans la guerrilla, Revue Belge de droit international, No. 2, 1971, p. 528; he mentioned also the view of experts consulted by the ICRC. See also Veuthey, Section 2, *supra.*

traité avec humanité, comme il doit recevoir les soins que requiert son état . . . L' Article 13 ne saurait donc en aucune façon autoriser un belligérant à ne pas respecter un blessé ou à ne pas lui octroyer les soins nécessaires, alors même que cet homme ne relèverait pas d' une des catégories que mentionne l' article."[16] This concerns also the terrorists.

The persons who have committed the acts of violence during armed conflict and in the territory of the belligerents are also protected according the Third Geneva Convention if they enter into one of the categories mentioned in the Article 4 of that Convention. As members of the resistance movements or guerilla, they must respect 5 requirements which are mentioned in this article:

1) belong to a Party to the conflict;[17]
2) being commanded by a person responsible for his subordinates;
3) having a fixed distinctive sign recognizable at a distance;
4) carrying arms openly;
5) conducting their operations in accordance with the laws and and customs of war.[18]

These conditions concern the movement as a whole and individual violations of these rules does not deprive its members of their protection. Those who violate these principles are responsible for this violence.[19] On the contrary, if the movement itself does not respect these conditions, any member of this movement,

---

[16]Pictet *Commentary to the First Convention* (1952), p. 159-60.

[17]"It is essential that there should be a *de facto* relationship between the resistance organization and the party to international law which is in a state of war." Pictet (Commentary to the Third Geneva Convention (1956), p. 57.

[18]The new Draft Protocol Additional to the Geneva Conventions of August 12, 1949, and relating to the protection of victims of international armed conflicts maintains these conditions in Article 42, paragraph 1:
a) belong to a Party to the conflict, even if the Party is represented by a government or an authority not recognized by the Detaining Power;
b) are under command responsibile to a Party,
c) they distinguish themselves from the civilian population in military operations;
d) they conduct their military operations in accordance with the Convention and Protocol.

[19]This principle is mentioned in the new Draft Protocol Additional to the Geneva Convention of August 12, 1949, 42, alinea 2.

even if he personally respects the rules does not receive the benefits of privileged treatment.

As concerns terrorists, we have to mention in particular the condition under Article 4(a) (2) (d). This condition concerns not only the resistance movement, but also the regular armed forces of every state, and the liberation movements. They are obliged to respect the laws and customs of war and when they do not, they commit war crimes and are tried for those crimes.

This condition was recently mentioned in relation with others of Article 4, by the Federal Court of Malaysia in the case Mohammed Ali: "It seems to us clear beyond doubt that under International Law a member of the armed forces of a Party to the conflict who, out of uniform and in civilian clothing, sets off explosives in the territory of the other Party to the conflict, in a nonmilitary building in which civilians are doing work unconnected with any war effort. He forfeits his right on capture to be treated as a prisoner of war."[20]

As we said before, the fundamental principles of the law of war exclude the terrorist activities. This prohibition is based on the lack of distinction between legitimate and illegitimate attacks.

Often, terrorist acts are committed in countries which are not engaged in the conflict between belligerents and some individuals or groups who transfer the fight on the territory of the third, neutral states. It is natural that the neutral country has reason to apply the Geneva Conventions on these cases, because any such acts violate the neutral territory. Such acts are tried by the municipal courts as a common crime and only international provisions which applies in such cases are the norms of international law of human rights procuring the fundamental judicial guarantees.[21]

Persons who do not enter into the categories mentioned in Article 4 of the Geneva Convention Relative to the Treatment of Prisoners of War of August 12, 1949 may benefit from the other provisions of the Geneva Conventions which may apply to them or of the other dispositions of the laws and customs of war. If any pro-

---

[20][1968] 3 All. E. R. 493 (B.C.)

[21]*See* the judgment of the Geschworenengericht des Kantons Zürich, Urteil, Geschw. 6, Case Abu-El Heiga Mohamed, Yousef Ibrahim Tawfik and Dahbor Amena, December 22, 1969.

tection is not accorded by the Geneva Conventions, the person is protected by the general provision of Articles 63, 62, 142, 158 of the Geneva Conventions respectively, which oblige the Parties to the conflict to respect in all circumstances "the principles of the law of nations, as they result from the usages established among civilized peoples, from the laws of humanity and the dictates of the public conscience."

Thus, persons who are not treated as prisoners of war, may enter into the category of the protection of wounded, sick or shipwrecked. They may be protected also according to the provisions of the IVth Geneva Convention as civilians who enter into the categories of Article 4 of this Convention. This article assures the protection of persons "who, at a given moment and in any manner whatsoever, find themselves, in case of conflict or occupation, in the hands of a Party to the conflict of Occupying Power of which they are not nationals." With some limitations defined already in the Article 4,[22] the Geneva Convention for the protection of civilian persons in time of war (1949) imposes some supplementary restrictions on a person who "is definitely suspected of or engaged in activities hostile to the security of the State." During the discussions at the Geneva Diplomatic Conference in 1949, it appears necessary to limit the rights accorded to protected persons in relation to the spies, saboteurs, irregular combatants, particularly as to their freedom of the communication with exterior.[23] Because these provisions may lead to the exaggeration and false qualifications of these persons, these provisions must be interpreted restrictively and "de simple soupçons ne devraient jamais pouvoir entrainer l' application de cette disposition."[24] This provision is also applicable in the case of terrorists who come into this category. But this article points out that "in each case, such persons shall nevertheless be

[22]The Article 4 is applicable only to the "aliens in the territory of a Party to the conflict" and to protected persons in occupied territories. It does not cover the enemy aliens in nonoccupied enemy territories. This 3rd category may be important for guerrilleros and terrorists.

[23]Colonel Du Pasquier from Switzerland made a comment on this article and affirmed that the protection accorded by the Convention could not favour the subversive activities of the fifth colon (Actes de la Conférence diplomatique de Genève de 1949, Tome II, Section A), p. 779.

[24]Pictet, *Commentary* (1952), p. 65.

treated with humanity, and in case of trial, shall not be deprived of the right of fair and regular trial prescribed by the present Convention," i.e. the Articles 64 to 76 and 126.[25]

If a person does not come under one of these categories, he cannot benefit from this special privileged position and is treated according the laws and customs of war (See Articles 63, 62, 142 and 158 of the Geneva Conventions) and according to the municipal law of the belligerents.

But the fact that the privileged situation is guaranteed to the person does not protect him from judicial prosecution for the acts they commit. He benefits only from the judicial guarantees of the Conventions or from the human rights norms.

Several terrorist acts, because of their material element, are punished as war crimes or crimes against humanity. Contracting Parties to the Geneva Conventions are obliged to assure the repression of the grave breaches of the Conventions in the following forms:

—promulgate special legislation;
—search the person accused of the violation of the Conventions;
—try this person;
—transmit him to judgment to another state.[26]

WARS OF NATIONAL LIBERATION

The Charter of the United Nations gives the liberation movement fighting for self-determination the possibility of recourse to the force for the realization of these Purposes of the United Nations. This interpretation of the provisions of the Charter was particulary confirmed by the resolution of the General Assembly 1514 (XV) of December 14, 1960 and by the most recent resolu-

[25]Article 68 allows the death penalties to be imposed only in the cases where the person is guilty of espionage, of serious acts of sabotage against the military installations of the occupying power of intentional offenses which have caused the death of one or more persons. The death penalty may not be pronounced "unless the attention of the court has been particularly called to the fact, that since the accused is not a national of the occupying power, he is not bound to it by any duty of allegiance" or when the accused is under eighteen years of age at the time of the offense.

[26]1st Geneva Convention: Article 49-50; 2nd Geneva Convention: Articles 50-51; 3rd Geneva Convention: Articles 129-130; 4th Geneva Convention: Articles 146-147.

tion 2625 (XXV) "Declaration on Principles of International Law Concerning Friendly Relations and Cooperation among States in accordance with the Charter of the United Nations." The last document defines the "principle of equal rights and self-determination of peoples" as "all peoples have the right freely to determine, without external interference, their political status and to pursue their economic, social and cultural development, and every State has the duty to respect this right in accordance with the provisions of the Charter." This definition is broad enough to authorize every person under foreign domination to realize this right and to take affairs into his own hands.[27]

This declaration interpreted the right of self-determination as confering to these movements of the colonies or other Non-Self Governing Territories the "status separate and distinct from the territory of the State administrating it . . . until the people of the colony or Non-Self Governing territory have exercised their rights of self-determination. . . ."

The opponents of this interpretation must be conscious of the fact that by conferring to the liberation movement and their fight international status, they assure that these movements will be obliged to respect the laws and customs of war or respect the Geneva Conventions.[28]

Some authors raise the question of whether it is possible to confer a particular status to some conflicts on the basis of their causes. It seems to us that these conflicts are materially international because we cannot accept the fiction of the municipal law of some colonialist countries on the identity and unity of the territory. We think that the objective factors of these movements give them international statute and their conflicts international character. This right is applicable in all cases: the fight of the Angola against Portugal, of Bangladesh against Pakistan, of Biarh against Nigeria, etc.

---

[27]"When a people from good reasons takes up arms against an oppressor, it is but an act of justice and generosity, to assist the brave men in the defense of their liberties," E. de Vattel, Book II, Chapter IV, par. 56.

[28]*See* Georges Abi-Saab, "Wars of National Liberation and the Laws of War," *Annales d' Etudes Internationales*, (1972), p. 93.

GUERRILLA WARFARE AND TERRORISM

Guerrilla warfare and terrorism are the particular methods and forms of fighting which may be used as well in the internal conflict as in the international one. Both are characteristic by the diversity of means they are using. Guerrilla warfare, is, in our point of view a more general method of fighting which may use the terrorism as one of the means.[29]

General Baufre characterized terrorism as "minor form" of the guerrilla. Nevertheless, we would prefer to make a distinction between the two forms. The difference which we see being in the following points:

1) Guerrilla warfare is a more organized form of fighting than terrorism, which is the act of disorganized individuals. Thus, organization is one of the characteristics of the guerrilla and one of the conditions for the protection of guerrilleras, but not a fundamental characteristic of the terrorist acts.

2) Guerillas and partisans attack particular military objectives and utilize a method of fighting which is only quantitatively distinct from the armed conflict. Terrorism does not distinguish between its objectives, attacking indiscriminately the military and civilians. Where in fighting the fright and surprise is normal for the soldiers who are prepared for it, an attack on civilians provokes unexpected stupefaction. Guerrilla warfare does not aim to provoke fear, but only to weaken the enemy.

3) Guerrilla warfare concentrated on belligerents, on enemies and on the civilian population is a means to make the movement strong.

The use of terrorist methods by guerrillas deprive the movement of the privileged status which is conferred to guerrilla warfare by the Geneva Convention (Article 4, (A) (2) (d) of the Third Geneva

---

[29]*See* F. Kalshoven, "The position of the guerrilla fighters under the Law of War, *Revue de droit penal militaire et de droit de la guerre*, Vol. XI, No. 2, (1972) pp. 58-91.

Convention).[30] Individual guerrillas will be tried for the acts violating the laws and customs of war, but will not confer on the guerrilla movement the protection which is accorded by the Conventions.

The experts who defended, in the recent conferences of governmental experts, the terrorist methods of fighting as an "only means of combat" of guerrillas run into the majority view.[31] Naturally, we must not forget the difficulty of the determination of the military objective, as pointed out by Fritz Kalshoven. According to him "the precise definition of the notion" "military objective" is a problem for which no final solution has not yet been found, it seems hard to deny that certain key decision makers among the population can justifiably be considered as military objectives in any kind of warfare, let alone in guerrilla warfare.[32]

REGULATION OF CONFLICTS NOT OF AN INTERNATIONAL CHARACTER

As in the international conflict, terrorist acts may appear in internal conflicts and in internal disturbances.

Article 3 to the Geneva Conventions did not define what the expression "conflict not of an international character" means. The restrictive tendencies appeared during the Diplomatic Conference in 1949 where several delegations were afraid that this article would cover forms of anarchy, rebellion or banditism. The Commentary to the Geneva Conventions qualifies positively the failure of the attempts to define this conflict because the Article 3 "doit avoir un champ d' application aussi vaste que possible."[33]

Article 3 cannot be inconvenient to the States because it guarantees only a minimum of humanity, which does not change in any way the military position of the Parties and gives no advantage to anyone. This article demands only respect of some fundamental

---

[30]*See* Bindschedler-Robert, *in* "Problems of the law of armed conflicts," in Vol. I, Bassiouni and Nanda, *A Treatise on International Criminal Law* (1973) p. 295-315.
[31]*See* "Reaffirmation and Development of the Laws and Customs Applicable in Armed Conflicts," submitted by the International Committee of the Red Cross to the XXIst International Conference of the Red Cross, held at Istanbul in September, 1969.
[32]F. Kalshoven, *supra* note 29, p. 60.
[33]Commentary to the Geneva Conventions, Vol. IV, pp. 41-42.

rules which must be recognized by everybody and are a minimum of the human right requirements in all countries. Shall we find a government which will publicly refuse these rules? Will it pretend that the abandonment of wounded and sick is legal and just? That the torture, mutilation, etc. are correct as well as the killing of hostages? It will very probably not declare it publicly in front of world public opinion even if these are the normal domestic practices of some states!

Until now no definition of the term "noninternational armed conflict" was given. A committee of experts in 1962 qualified these conflicts in the following way: ". . .if hostile action against a lawful government assumed a collective character and a minimum of organization. The duration of the conflict, the number and leadership of rebel groups, their installation or action in the parts of the territory, the degree of insecurity, the existence of victims, the means adopted by the lawful Government to re-establish order, all have to be taken into account."[34]

ICRC defined these conflicts in its report presented to the International Conference of the Red Cross in Istanbul in 1969 as an "armed conflict in which armed forces are engaged in hostilities."[35] The noninternational armed conflict must be distinguished from the political tensions and internal disturbances on the one side and from the international armed conflicts on the other side. The recent conferences of experts held in Geneva in 1971 and 1972, established several criterias according to the opinions of the experts.[36] These criterias are based on the objective considerations, i.e. on the factual situation and also on the subjective approach, i.e. on the appreciation of the government on the territory of which the conflicts arise.[37] The Draft Protocol Additional

[34]Reaffirmation and Development of the Laws and Customs Applicable in Armed Conflicts, submitted by the ICRC to the XXIst International Conference of the Red Cross, held in Istanbul, September, 1969, pp. 99-100.

[35]Protection of Victims of Noninternational Conflict, Report submitted to the XXIst International Conference of the Red Cross (ICRC, Geneva, 1969), p. 4.

[36]Conference of the Governmental Experts, 1972, Report, Vol. I, pp. 70-71.

[37]The combination of the objective and subjective criterias was submitted by the experts of Romania. We do not agree with this position, which seems to us to be also in contradiction with the generally accepted theory of the declaratory character of the recognition in all socialist countries. *See* Conference of Governmental Experts, 1972, Report, Vol. II, p. 33.

to Geneva Conventions of August 12, 1949, and relating to the protection of victims of noninternational armed conflicts, which will be submitted to the Diplomatic Conference in 1974, defined these conflicts in Article 1:

Article 1—Material Field of Application

1. The present Protocol shall apply to all armed conflicts not covered by Article 2, common to the Geneva Convention of August 12, 1949, taking place between armed forces or other organized groups under responsible command.
2. The present Protocol shall not apply to situations of internal disturbances and tensions, *inter alia,* riots, isolated and sporadic acts of violence and other acts of a similar nature.
3. The foregoing provisions do not modify the conditions governing the application of Article 3 common to the Geneva Conventions of August 12, 1949.

This article excludes the protection of some individual terrorists and submits the regulation of the situation exclusively to the municipal law of the State. But let us turn first to the fundamental provision, the only one which concerns the noninternational armed conflict, and look at what is said in this provision concerning terrorist acts committed in the time of internal conflict. Article 3 assures the protection to the wounded and sick and to other persons not making active parts in the hostilities, including members of the armed forces who have laid down their arms. The article prescribes the human treatment for these persons without any distinction. It prohibits at any time and in any place some acts, which may be committed also for the reasons of terrorizing these persons. We may conclude, that as regard these categories of persons covered by Article 3, following acts are prohibited:

a) violence to life and person, in particular murder of all kinds, mutilation, cruel treatment and torture;
b) taking of hostages;
c) outrages upon personal dignity, in particular humiliating and degrading treatment;
d) the passing of sentences and the carrying out of executions

without previous judgment pronounced by a regularly constituted court, affording all the judicial guarantees which are recognized as indispensable by civilized peoples.

From the strictly legal point of view, only the Contracting Parties are obliged to respect this provision, because only these Parties have ratified the Conventions. They may discharge themselves of this obligation only by the denunciation of the Conventions. The insurgents who are not bound legally are bound morally to respect the minimum of humanity in the fight. But in case that they refuse to respect these provisions, the Contracting Party which continues to respect them there is not handicapped from the military point of view by this minimum of humane treatment, and obtains better moral credit. The rebels not respecting the Article 3, on the contrary, lose moral credit in the eyes of the public and are categorized merely as rebels.

The recent Conferences of Governmental Experts held in Geneva in 1971 and 1972, introduced definitions for acts of terrorism. According to the Reactional Committee of the last Conference in 1972, the draft contained the following Article 5:

The following acts are prohibited:

a) the taking of hostages;
b) acts of terrorism, consisting of acts of violence directed intentionally and indiscriminately against civilians taking no active part in the hostilities;
c) reprisals against persons/noncombatants and combatants rendered *hors de combat*/and objects indispensable to their survival;
d) pillage
e) all other offenses against the persons.[38]

So the future provisions have been enriched by the definition of terrorist acts and prohibition of reprisals. Unfortunately, the last version of the Draft Protocol abandoned this definition of terrorist acts and is referring only to the "acts of terrorism under the form of the acts of violence" directed against the protected persons (Article 6 of the Draft Protocol).

---

[38]Conference of Government Experts, 1972, Report, Vol. I, p. 75.

What is the role of the Red Cross when internal disturbances do not attain the level of noninternational armed conflict? The Xth International Conference of the Red Cross in 1921 formulated the following principles in its resolution XIV:

(1) The Red Cross, which stands apart from all political and social distinctions, and from differences of creed, race, class or nation, affirms its rights and duty of affording relief in case of civil war and social and revolutionary disturbances.

The Red Cross recognizes that all victims of civil wars or of such disturbances are without any exception whatsoever, entitled to relief, in conformity with the general principles of the Red Cross.

According to the Statutes of the International Committee of the Red Cross, the special role of the ICRC shall be, *inter alia,* "to take action in its capacity as a neutral institution, especially in case of war, civil war or internal strife; to endeavor to ensure at all times that the military and civilian victims of such conflicts and of their direct results receive protection and assistance, and to serve, in humanitarian matters, as an intermediary between the parties;" (Article 4, paragraph d) .

Advocating the application of Human Rights in these conflicts, but being conscious also of the time necessary to assure the most consequent application of these rights, the ICRC proposed in the last conferences of governmental experts the Draft of the Declaration of fundamental rights of the human being in the period of internal disturbances and public danger,[39] before the most complete regimentation is applicable to them. This Declaration contains the following principles:

Dans le cas où ùn danger public ou des troubles intérieurs présentent un certain caractère de gravité ou de durée et comportent des *actes de violence,* l' état d'exception étant ou non proclamé par les authorités au pouvoir, *les droits fondamentaux suivants seront respectés en toutes circonstances,* sans aucune discrimination:

1. Nul ne peut être soumis à la torture, ni à des peines ou traitements inhumains ou dégradants;

---

[39]Conference of Government Experts, Documents of the ICRC, Vol. V (Geneva, 1947).

2. Nul ne peut être puni pour une infraction qu'il n'a pas commise;

3. Nul ne peut être condamné pour une action ou une omission qui, au moment où elle a au lieu, ne constituait pas une infraction d'après le droit national ou international;

4. Sont interdites les condamnations prononcées et les exécutions effectuées sans jugement préalable, rendu par tribunal règulièrement constitúe, assorti des garanties judiciaires reconnues comme indispensable par les peuples civilisés.

5. Toute personne privée de liberté en raison des événements bénéficiera en tout temps d'un traitement humain conformément aux Règles minima pour le traitement des détenus, établies par l'Organisation des Nations Unies.
   Lorsque les garanties constitutionnelles auront été suspendues, et en particulier lorsque ces personnes seront détenues an raison des événements pour une durée indéterminée et sans être inculpées ou déférées à un tribunal, une institution humanitaire impartiale, telle que la CICR, sera authorisée à visiter ces dernières.

6. Les peines collectives, les prises d'otages, les measures de représailles envers les personnes et leurs biens sont interdites.

7. Les blessés et les malades seront recueillis et soignés en toutes circonstances.
   Les Sociétés nationales de la Croix-Rouge seront authorisées, en tout temps, à exercer leur activité secourable envers les victimes de ces situations de troubles intérieurs.

8. Un organisme humanitaire impartial, tel que le CICR, pourre, en tout temps, offrir aux authorités au pouvoir ses services en faveur de toutes les victimes.
   Ni cette offre, ni son acceptation n'aur ot d'effet sur la condition juridique des personnes impliquées dans des situations de troubles intérieurs.

The Second Conference of Governmental Experts in 1972 preferred to abandon this question in the field of human rights while leaving the study of this problem within the framework of the Red Cross.

TERRORISM IN TIME OF PEACE AND
THE ROLE OF THE RED CROSS

If terrorism is prohibited in time of war, clearly it must be prohibited in time of peace. The different external forms of terrorism and their prohibition are expressed not only in the conscience of peoples, but also in the legislation of all countries of the world. We may affirm that the prohibition of the terrorism is a part not only of the minimum standard respected by States, but also of general principles of law.

The Red Cross acts not only in time of war, but also in time of peace.[40] It's obligation is to act everywhere that man suffers. It assists impartially, neutrally and by universal and immediate means.

Concerning the victims of terrorism, it is not necessary to review the literature to expose the fundamental approach of the Red Cross. The respect for each human being, for his life and for his property is the basis of the idea which has inspired the Red Cross movement all around the world. The Red Cross must also help terrorists when they are wounded and have laid their arms.

The Red Cross must adapt itself to the new forms of fighting: "Car une institution crée pour tenter d' assurer la protection de victimes de la violence des hommes est prisonnière de sa vocation et de son image. Elle ne peut se dérober à un appel sans mettre en cause sa raison d'être et doit constamment d'adapter à des circonstances indépendantes de sa volonté, intervenir dans des catastrophes qu' il n'é tait pas en son pouvoir de conjurer et risquer ainsi son existence pour assurer ce minimum d' humanite'."[41]

During its 88th Session in Geneva in 1970, the Executive Committee of the League of Red Cross Societies adopted the resolution deploring the hijacking of airplanes and disapproving inhuman practices. It has invited the National Red Cross Societies "où des avions détournés ont atterri et où les passagers et l' équipage sont retenue, à prendre toute mesure pour leur apporter secours et réconfort jusqu' au moment où ils recouvrerant leur liberté et à se

---

[40]Pilloud, *supra* note 13.
[41]Jacques Freymond, *Face à la guerre totale: une politique humanitaire "globale,"* (1973), p. 16.

mettre en contact avec les Sociétés des pays auxquels appartiennent les passages afin de pouvoir renseigner et rassurer leurs familles."

The IXth Inter-American Conference of the Red Cross, held at Managua as from 1st to 5th December 1970, has adopted the resolution which is consistent "avec inquietude le renouvellment d' actes de violence et la persistance de troubles dans de nombreuses pays du monde."

In 1970, the IXth Inter American Conference of the Red Cross adopted the following resolution:

La Croix-Rouge, Facteur De Paix

I. La IXème Conférence interaméricaine de la Croix-Rouge ESTIME que, sans préjudice ause préceptes établis dans l'article 3 des Conventions de Genève du 12 août 1949, lorsque, sur le territoire de n'importe quel pays, des troubles de caractère social, politique, religieux ou autre ayant des effets sanglants se produisent —sous la forme notamments de guérillas urbaines ou rurales — ainsi que des enlèvements individuels ou collectifs perpétrés dans l'air, sur terre ou sur mer, et toutes les fois qu'il y a des victimes quelles qu'elles soient, *tant les autorités que les rebelles sont tenus de respecter en elles les droits imprescriptibles de tout être humain.* A cet effet, la Croix-Rouge nationale ou la Comité international de la Croix-Rouge, par l'intermédiaire de ses délégués, exhortera les parties au conflit à observer et respecter les droits de l' homme.

"II. La IXème Conférence interaméricaine de la Croix-Rouge ESTIME que lorsque se produisent des événements semblables à ceux auxquels l'article susmentionné fait allusion, *la Croix-Rouge nationale ou le CICR, par l' intermédiaire de ses délégués, doit si possible être présente sur les lieux pour apporter à toutes les victimes, sans aucune discrimination quelconque, l'assistance humanitaire rapide et efficace dont elles ont besoin;* elle doit être en mesure, en cas d'enlèvement, d'offrir et de prêter son aids à la (ou les) personne (s) enlevées (s) ainsi qu'à sa (ou leur) famille pour les soutenir de toutes les façons possibles et même pour servir d'intermédiaire en vue de sa (ou leur) libération, en observant le secret et la discrition exigés par le cas.

"III. La IXème Conférence interaméricaine de la Croix-Rouge ESTIME que dans le cas précis d'*enlèvements* sur mer ou dans l'air, la Croix-Rouge nationale ou le CICR, par l'intermédiarie de ses délégués, doit offrir sa médiation et apporter son aide aux passagers des vaisseaux (ou des appareils) enlevés et informer leurs familles de leur état, par l'intermédiaire de leurs Croix-Rouges respectives.

"IV. La IXème Conference interaméricains ESTIME que la Croix-Rouge nationale ou le CICR, par l'intermédiaire de ses délégués, peut et doit *visiter les prisonniers faits à la suite des événements indiqués ci-dessus,* leur apportant toute l'aide nécessaire et réclamant de leurs ravisseurs ou de leurs détenteurs le traitement humanitaire auquel ils ont droit et les privilèges accordés à leur état par les traités internationaux.

"V. La IXème Conférence interaméricaine ESTIME que le rôle de la Croix-Rouge en faveur des victimes des événements indiqués ci-dessus ne doit jamais être considéré comme uns atteinte à la souveraineté des Etats ou à la libre détermination des peuples, ni comme une intervention partiale favorisant l'une quelconque des parties au conflict; dans ces cas comme dans dans tous ceux où la Croix-Rouge est appelée à intervenir, son action est strictement *humanitaire et absolument neutre.*

"VI. *La IXème Conférence intaraméricaine ESTIME qu'afin que la Croix-Rouge soit un véritable facteur de paix en face de la recrudescence de la violence dans le monde entier,* le Comité international de la Croix-Rouge doit tenir compte de toutes les considérations présentes et autres tendant à ce but en vue de trouver les moyens adéquats et les instruments juridiques permettant d'attirer l'attention des Etats sur l'envergure et l'importance de sa mission humanitaire."

SECTION 6

TERRORISM AND WAR OF LIBERATION: AN ISRAELI PERSPECTIVE OF THE ARAB-ISRAELI CONFLICT

YORAM DINSTEIN

T HE ISSUES OF TERRORISM AND WARS of liberation are frequently intertwined in the vast political and journalistic literature pertaining to the Arab-Israeli conflict. But in fact—and certainly in law—these are disparate subjects that have little in common. Wars of liberation are wars the object of which is attaining political independence. Terrorism is a method of operation that can and does take place both in wartime and in peacetime, by, as well as against "freedom fighters." The determination of the legality of a war—any war—in no way resolves the legality of the means employed in its course. By way of illustration, the use of poisonous gases is prohibited in inter-State wars, even when the war is waged legally within the compass of collective security.[1] Terrorism, too, must be analyzed on its own merits, irrespective of the lawfulness of wars of liberation. As for wars of liberation, they must be examined against the silhouettes of two other intricate concepts, namely, self-determination and *bellum justum*. Our enquiry will therefore have to consist of several parts.

Another subdivision is called for inasmuch as this is an Israeli perspective of the legal situation. Not "the" Israeli, but "an" Israeli perspective; Israeli nevertheless. We must first look for the legal norms and then apply them to the special case of the Middle East conflict. All too often the impression is created that the Arab-Israeli conflict is impervious to the radiation of general rules that are valid elsewhere. It is time for Arabs and Jews alike to take the world as it is.

[1]See Sorensen, *Manual of Public International Law*, pp. 810-811.

155

WARS OF LIBERATION

Self-Determination

There is much entrenched resistance to the idea that the right of self-determination has become an integral part of positive international law.[2] That resistance I do not share. Whereas a generation ago self-determination was merely a clarion-call or a desired goal, it has presently acquired the lineaments of *lex lata*. This is only an example of the recent development of human rights. While self-determination is a right that devolves not on the corporate entity of states but on human beings, it is not an individual human right in the sense that every person can exercise by himself. Rather, it is a collective human right bestowed collectively upon whole peoples[3] to enable them to freely determine their own political status.

There is no objective and binding definition of the term *people* and consequently the first step in considering the right is to determine the collective self. The existence of a people usually signifies more than a few individuals, but there is no hard and fast rule as to the minimum size of a people. Large numbers by themselves do not settle the matter either. When thousands of human beings gather together temporarily, i.e., to watch a football match or join together in a prolonged fight for a cause, i.e., to support the women's liberation movement, they do not thereby turn themselves into a people. A people is an ethnic group, which must share some common historical links. Yet how profound these ethnic links should be and what their connection with a common territory, language or religion should be is disputable. As the Megarian paradox of the bald man[4] demonstrates, it is easier to identify a bald man when you see one than to tell at what precise point he becomes bald. The concept of *people* like baldness, is, to

---

[2]See e.g. Green, "Self-Determination and Settlement of the Arab-Israeli Conflict," 65 *A.J.I.L.*, *Proceedings*, 40-48 (1971).

[3]See Dinstein, "Human Rights: The Quest for Concretization," 1 *Israel Yearbook on Human Rights*, 13-15 (1971).

[4]i.e., would you say that a man is bald if he has only one hair? If how about two hairs, three, four, etc? Then where do you draw the line? See Kneale and Kneale, *The Development of Logic* (1962), p. 114.

a degree, a subjective state of mind rather than an objective description of a physical state of things. One may say that ethnicity is determined more by ethos than by genealogy. And it is primarily for the group itself to decide whether or not it regards itself as a people and the requirements necessary for membership in the group. There is no room for a *Diktat* from the outside in this respect: you cannot decree that somebody else's people will cease to be, nor can you gatecrash and force another people to admit you to the fold.

Peoples may live in dependent territories—colonies, trust areas, protectorates and the like—dominated by foreign states, but the right to self-determination as a human right is nevertheless still applicable. It also applies to peoples within the framework of an independent state. The right of self-determination is, therefore, granted to all peoples, not only in Asia and Africa, but also in Wales and in the Ukraine. Furthermore, the right is accorded regardless of socio-economic conditions; people that sit by the fleshpots and enjoys the wealth of the land are still entitled to self-determination.[5]

Peoplehood is not to be confused with nationhood. Nationhood is a question of nationality, of belonging to a State. All the citizens of a State form a nation, and in actuality the terms "nation" and "State" are interchangeable. But in one State and one nation there can be several peoples, large and small. One people may be dispersed across the borders of many States, constituting majority in one and minorities in others, or majorities in several States perhaps minorities in various States. In all instances, the people as a whole and every segment of it in any given State—has the right of self-determination.

Self-determination means that the people have the right to determine their own political fate. This does not necessarily entail political independence. Independence i.e. statehood is a right, or an option, of every people; it is not a duty. A people forming a minority in a certain State may freely opt to continue to live as a minority within the political ambit of that State. If such be its

---

[5]See Dinstein, "The International Human Rights of Soviet Jewry," 2 *Israel Yearbook on Human Rights*, 194, 209 (1972).

will, it is of course entitled to the collective human right of every ethnic minority to enjoy its cultural heritage. This last right is endorsed by customary international law and incorporated in Article 27 of the 1966 International Covenant on Civil and Political Rights.[7] On the other hand, if an ethnic minority—located in a well defined territorial region[8]—is dissatisfied with life under the umbrage of another people, it may exercise its right to self-determination by seceding from an existing state, e.g. Bangladesh and opting for independence.

The decision to secede—like all other options of self-determination—must evidently be made by the people as a whole, and not by private individuals with messianic complexes who know what is better for their fellow-men. The right of self-determination is a right of the people. The people's will must be expressed, in one way or another, by the people and not for the people.

What happens if a people chooses to break away from an existing state and the latter attempts to block the secession movement? This can be done through multifarious means of suasion, but it can also be done by force. If both sides use force, we are confronted with a civil war. If you wish to dub it a war of liberation, fine. But in that case, we must bear in mind that, to remain legal, a war of liberation must remain a civil war. Current international law is indifferent to the occurrence of domestic revolutions though it outlaws inter-State wars. Wars of liberation can avoid the stigma of international (in contradistinction to internal-constitutional) illegality only if and when they are domestic in essence. We should also realize that when an armed revolt breaks out, whether in a dependent territory against a metropolitan government or in the home territory of a state that has no colonies, the rebels are not necessarily exercising their right of self-determination. Not every brigand and common criminal, who happens to belong to a distinct ethnic minority, is automatically a "freedom fighter." "Freedom fighters" are only those who fight

[6]Such a State is usually called "multinational." But what is actually meant is that the (one) nation comprises several peoples.

[7]*United Nations Jurdical Yearbook*, 178, 186 (1966).

[8]When a people is dispersed all over the country, the possibility of secession scarcely exists. See Dinstein, *supra* note 5 p. 209.

for freedom *i.e.* independence, on behalf of a people with a right to self-determination, in the course of a civil war of liberation.

Bellum Justum

We live in an era in which war between states is illegal—indeed, criminal—under positive international law. The illegality of war is practically the cornerstone of modern international law. It took two cataclysmic world wars within the span of one generation for mankind to grasp the elementary truth of the use of force, or else the days of *homo sapiens* on this planet may be numbered. The crux of the contemporary *jus ad bellum* is that war between states is forbidden for any reason—good, bad or indifferent. War has been outlawed irrespective of its merits. It is illegal even if waged with the best intentions. Only counter-war—that is, response to an armed attack by way of (collective or individual) self-defense and collective security—is still permissible under the Charter of the United Nations.[9]

Admittedly, voices have been heard in recent years in support of a thesis by which certain wars—*i.e.* wars of liberation—become legal when they are just. This distinction between good wars and bad wars may sound like a roar of the wave of the future, but in reality it is an echo of the remote past. Most of the "fathers of international law" adhered to the concept, whose roots can be traced through the writings of the theologians and the canonists to the Roman *Jus Fetiale,* that war is only lawful if it is a just war *(bellum justum)*[10] War could be considered "just" only if it met certain conditions precedent, particularly if it had a just cause *(justa causa).* Spelling out the just causes proved, of course, a major undertaking. Was the propagation of the faith or the recovery of property a just cause for war? Many jurists thought so. Moreover, in the absence of a superior authority in a position to weigh the evidence and sift the justness of a cause in an impartial way, some international lawyers (mainly Vitoria) reached the

---

[9]See Dinstein, "The Legal Issues of 'Para-War' and Peace in the Middle East," 44 *St. John's Law Review, 466,* 467-468 (1970).

[10]See von Elbe, "The Evolution of the Concept of the Just War in International Law,' 33 *A.J.I.L.,* 665-688 (1939).

conclusion that war could be regarded by both sides as subjective-
ly just. Others (principally Gentili) went a step further and contended that war could be considered even objectively as just on
both sides. Not surprisingly, this led the *bellum justum* doctrine
to a dead end. Instead of keeping aggressors in check, it spurred
them on to action in the name of unfathomable justice. By the
close of the eighteenth century, the doctrine practically disappeared from the international legal scene, and its impact on the
subsequent evolution of the *jus ad bellum* is somewhat controversial. Kunz, who denies the existence of such impact, states
categorically that "[t]he concept of *bellum legale* replaced the
concept of *bellum justum*."[11] Even if a link between the two concepts is asserted, if *bellum legale* is construed as a sort of *bellum
justum positivum*,[12] we must not forget that the *justa causa* is
now laid down peremptorily in the Charter of the United Nations, and is limited to self-defense or collective security. Only
counter-wars can, consequently, vindicate a *bellum justum positivum*. Wars of liberation are not different from other wars. Their
cause may be morally just (or may at least look that way to those
who champion it), but it is not a *justa causa* in the legal sense
of the term. If this were not so, the prohibition of war would have
become a semantic exercise; the propriety of resort to force would
have been a matter of sheer dialectics. In Scheuner's words, wars
between states, having been excluded from the front door, would
reappear through the back door.[13] That would relegate the
Charter to mere chatter and make a mockery of international law.

The Middle East Conflict

In Palestine there are and have been for a long time chiefly
two peoples: Arabs and Jews. It is the irony of fate that the respective positions of both are exceedingly similar in at least three
ways. First, there are more Jews outside than inside Palestine and
there are more Arabs outside than inside Palestine. Second, it is
very difficult to answer the question: "Who is a Jew?" Is he a

---

[11]Kunz, "Bellum Justum and Bellum Legale," 45 *A.J.I.L.*, 528, 532 (1951).
[12]See Kelsen, *Principles of International Law* (1st ed., 1952) pp. 34-35.
[13]Private correspondence. Letter of September 30, 1972.

person who professes Judaism as a religion? Is he an offspring of the original twelve tribes? Is he a person who speaks Hebrew? All these are indubitably faulty criteria.[14] By the same token, it is very difficult to answer the question: "Who is an Arab?" Is he a person who professes Islam as a religion? Is he an offspring of the original desert tribes of (Saudi) Arabia? Is he a person who speaks Arabic? None of these criteria is plausible.[15]

Third, there are many (especially Arabs) who deny that Jews in Palestine belong to a Jewish (as distinct from an Israeli) people. Again, there are many (especially Jews) who deny that Arabs in Palestine belong to an Arab (as distinct from a Jordanian) people.

It is the tragedy that Arabs and Jews apply to each other arbitrary yardsticks about what constitutes a people, refusing to concede one another's determination of self as sufficient or conclusive. There is no prospect of peace in the Middle East until both sides realize that neither lives in a vacuum and that both are entitled to self-determination. There is a Jewish people (or a part of the Jewish people) in Palestine, and there is an Arab people (or a part of the Arab people) in Palestine. Each must be free to determine its political fate. Neither can dictate to the other its decision. Since both have claims over the same country, and since both want to proceed along separate paths, the only solution is partition of Palestine.

Such partition was resolved by the General Assembly of the United Nations on 29 November 1947. The original partition scheme floundered, however, on the rock of Arab opposition. The Arabs, within and without Palestine, rejected every compromise formula and initiated war. Originally (from 30 November 1947 to 14 May 1948) this was a civil war in Palestine, and as such in large measure beyond the reach of international law. But with

---

[14]For recent decisions of the Supreme Court of Israel, which however are more helpful in clarifying the issues than in laying the questions to rest, see the *Shalit* and *Tamarin Cases* excerpted in English in 2 *Israel Yearbook on Human Rights*, 317-333 (1972).

[15]Historically, a distinction has been made between "pure Arabs" and "self-styled Arabs" (*musta 'riba*), namely, local inhabitants assimilated by the conquering Arabs. See *The Cambridge History of Islam* (1970) p. 60.

the establishment of the state of Israel on 15 May 1948, and the invasion of Palestine by the regular armies of the neighbouring Arab states on that day, the war assumed an international character and became illegal on the part of those states who commenced an armed attack. Following the Arab defeat, the war ended with a different partition of Palestine, sanctioned in the Armistice Agreements of 1949. The 1949 partition diverged from the one envisaged by the United Nations not only in demarcation of boundaries, but also—and more conspicuously—in that only one independent state came into existence in Palestine. The Arab state was never launched into political orbit, not because Israel objected (it did not), but because the Palestinian Arabs themselves preferred to forego the option of independence. Having been thwarted in the attempt to destroy Israel, they acted on an all-or-nothing impulse and cast their lot with Jordan (on the west bank) and Egypt (in the Gaza Strip).

The Six-Day War changed that situation and yet the change must not be overstated or misconstrued. There are still two peoples in Palestine and both are still entitled to self-determination. I take it for granted that the ultimate peace treaty, which some day will end the hostilities, will further revise the partition borders to Israel's benefit. But barring an unforeseen development, e.g. the Palestinian Arabs choosing to join hands with Isreal, another partition will occur. Whether the Palestinian Arabs will then elect to establish their own independent state or prefer to return to the embrace of Jordan is for the Palestinian Arabs—and nobody else—to decide. Until a peace treaty is concluded, however, Israel will continue its belligerent occupation of the Arab lands, and will do so by right under international law. The Six-Day War which, as President Sadat has recently had occasion to point out, now enters its sixth year and is not yet over. The war is, and was, not between Israel and the Palestinian Arabs, but between Israel, on the one hand, and Egypt, Jordan and Syria, on the other. It is, and was, an international war, and these three Arab States are the ones responsible for its violation of international law.[16] It is not, and never was, a war of liberation in any

---

[16]Dinstein, *supra* note 9, p. 470.

credible meaning of the term.

To the extent that Palestinian Arabs are waging guerrilla warfare against Israel in the course of this war, they do not and cannot modify the nature of the war. The only question raised by the participation of Palestinian guerrillas in the war is whether they are entitled to the status of lawful combatants. The Geneva Convention of 1949,[17] reaffirming a basic tenet of the Hague Regulations of 1899 and 1907,[18] explicitly imposes four cumulative requirements on all privileged combatants. They must (a) be commanded by a person responsible for his subordinates; (b) have a fixed distinctive sign recognizable at a distance; (c) carry arms openly; and (d) conduct their operations in accordance with the laws and customs of war. Another, implicit, requirement can be deduced from the text of the Geneva Conventions. In 1969, an Israeli Military Court in the west bank ruled that Palestinian guerrilleros outlawed in Arab countries do not belong to any party to the Middle East conflict and on that ground are not entitled to the status of privileged combatants.[19] This decision has been criticized by Schwarzenberger,[20] though (as pointed out by Nurick and Barrett) it has long been recognized as "a fundamental premise" that privileged combatants must "serve a political entity which is a state."[21] Even if the Palestinian guerrillas should rightfully be treated as lawful combatants, provided they meet the other, incontrovertible, prerequisites, they are combatants in a war between Israel and independent Arab countries. There is no war between Israel and the nonexisting Arab state of Palestine. And if the Palestinian Arabs genuinely wish to create

---

[17]Article 13 of the First and Second Geneva Conventions and Article the Third. 1 *Kitvei Amana* (Israel Treaty Series) (No. 30) 393, 429, 455.

[18]Scott, ed., *The Hague Conventions and Declarations of 1899 and 1907*, (1915) p. 107.

[19]*The Military Prosecutor v. Kassem, et al.* (1969), *Law and Courts in Israel-Held Areas*, 17, 25-27 (Institute for Legislative Research a Comparative Law, 1970). See Meron, "Some Legal Aspects of Arab Terrorists' Claims to Privileged Combatancy," in Shoham, ed., *Of Law and Man*, 225, 233-240 (1971).

[20]Schwarzenberger, "Human Rights and Guerrilla Warfare," 1 *Israel Yearbook on Human Rights*, 246, 249-252 (1971).

[21]Nurick and Barrett, "Legality of Guerrilla Forces under the Laws of War," 40 *A.J.I.L.* 563, 567 (1946).

such a state, what they need is not a war of liberation but a peace of liberation. Peace with Israel will enable the Palestinian Arabs to determine their destiny again.

TERRORISM

The Law

Terrorism can be defined in many ways, but, in my opinion, it is the use of violence with an emphasis on the three a's: assassination, assault and arson with a view to inspiring terror for political ends. Terrorism must not be confused with guerrilla warfare because terrorism is not circumscribed to wartime and guerrilleros who obey the laws of war (*inter alia* by refraining from attacks against civilian objects) have nothing in common with terrorists; they are simply irregular troops.

Terrorism as a *modus operandi* is not a phenomenon unique to the Middle East conflict. King Alexander of Yugoslavia and the French Foreign Minister Barthou were killed in 1934 long before the world became aware of the Palestine question. These days one hears constantly about Croates in Sweden, Tupamaros in Uruguay and anarchists in Italy, to name but a few groups of fanatics in existence, and we must not fall prey to a fallacious equation between terrorists and Palestinian Arabs. The problem of terrorism is now a global menace. Considering the fact that one world war has already been triggered by an act of terrorism (the assassination of the Archduke Francis Ferdinand by Serbians at Sarajevo on 28 June 1914), the stakes for mankind are mortal.

The terrorist has replaced the pirate as the *hostis humani generis par excellence*. The terrorist is even more dangerous than the pirate of old, because he is backed up by organized movements and an ideology. Terrorists confront the world with a modern version of the assassins of the Old Man of the Mountain and Murder Inc. on an international scale. Their ideology is particularly obnoxious since to the terrorist the end justifies not only the means, but also the irrelevant whim or caprice of the group.

It is important that terrorists do not always act against targets in the country where their base of operations is located. Frequently, terrorism is an item of export. That is to say, the terrorists find a haven in one state, and emerge to strike in and at another state when an opportunity presents itself. The starting point of any serious discussion of the problem in the light of international law should therefore be the general principle, proclaimed by the International Court of Justice in 1949 in the *Corfu Channel Case*, that every state is under an obligation "not to allow knowingly its territory to be used contrary to the rights of other States."[22] The most important rule based on this general principle is that no state may allow the use of its territory for the organization of armed bands or saboteur gangs bent on fomenting rebellion or sowing terror in another country. Obviously, such activities may take place because the local government is unaware of what is happening or unable to forestall terrorists' designs. Just as a government cannot always prevent underground activities against itself, it is not invariably capable of foiling conspiracies against another government. But the local government incurs an obligation to exercise due diligence, i.e. to take all reasonable measures called for by the circumstances, to prevent the organization of hostile activities against a foreign country on its territory.[23]

Hence, it is necessary to subsume terrorist attacks under three distinct headings, depending on the relationship between the terrorist group in question and the local government. Each category is founded on a different factual pattern, each creates its own legal problems, and each deserves a separate solution.

The first case is that of local governmental resistance against terrorists. This is the usual situation where the terrorists pose a threat to life and limb in the home state. Government resistance, however, is also required where other countries are in the line of fire. Such resistance is usually proposed by drafters of conventions in this field, for instance the abortive Geneva Convention of 1937 for the Prevention and Punishment of Terrorism.[24] At this junc-

---

[22] *Corfu Channel Case (Merits)*, [1949] *I.C.J. Reports*, 4, 22.
[23] See Fenwick, *International Law* (4th ed., 1965), p. 360.
[24] 7 Hudson, *International Legislation*, 862, 865 (1941).

ture there is no binding international treaty of general application for the suppression of terrorism. Each country must combat terrorism on its own, which results in an unsatisfactory situation where terrorism is carried across political frontiers. A concerted action, therefore, is indispensable for the mutual protection of all States. American attempts to stir the General Assembly of the United Nations into action have culminated in a fiasco. Unfortunately, the present atmosphere in the United Nations is not conducive to a strong stand against terrorism. If any document on the subject emanates from that body in the near future, it is likely to reflect the lowest possible common denominator in terms of potential acceptance. I would rather see, however, a good treaty with fewer contracting parties than a bad one with a full roster of signatories.

What would be a good treaty? I think that several essential elements are prescribed by the exigencies of the situation:

1. A definition of terrorism as an international crime is vital.
2. The basic principle should be *aut punire aut dedere:* prosecute the offender or extradite him.
3. For the purpose of prosecution the principle of universality should be applied to establish the jurisdiction of each and every state, regardless of the location of the crime and the nationality of the offender (or his victim).
4. The state most directly affected by the perpetration of the crime ought to be recognized as the one with a prior claim for prosecuting the offender. Should the offender be present in another country, it will be bound to extradite him upon request.
5. The Convention must be regarded as a multilateral extradition treaty. Extradition must not be contingent on the inclusion of the crime in any list of extraditable offences in any other legal instrument (treaty or domestic law).
6. Terrorism must be considered a common crime for the purpose of extradition, so that the general rule against the extradition of political offenders will be inapplicable.

I submit that all these points are rooted in the practice of states. Inasmuch as the last one is also the most controversial, a few observations may be appropriate. In many countries terrorism, although still viewed as an internal rather than an international offense, is excluded from the ambit of political crimes as far as extradition is concerned. The leading case is a Swiss decision of 1928 in the *Pavan Case*.[25] Here an Italian, who had killed a fascist intelligence agent in Paris, escaped to Switzerland. The Swiss judges rejected the contention that extradition should be denied owing to the political nature of the crime. The Court ruled that, in order to substantiate the political nature of the offense, a direct link must be established between the death of the Italian agent in Paris and the undermining of the fascist regime in Rome.[26] The Court proceeded to say that an individual act of personal terrorism committed abroad can in no way be regarded as a part of an overall anti-fascist campaign.[27]

Another interesting decision was handed down in Germany in 1933 in the *Fabijan Case*.[28] Here Italy demanded the extradition of a person who had escaped to Germany after being convicted of manslaughter of a policeman. The offence was committed when the policeman sought to arrest Fabijan following an incident in which he had thrown stones at an Italian police station in the Tyrol. At the time, the Tyrol was an occupied territory and the German Supreme Court ruled that extradition must be granted. The judgement stated that the mere fact that the offense had been committed out of a political motive against an officer of an occupying power does not taint the act with political colouring.[29] For a crime to be political in nature, it has to be committed against the central political authority and not against an individual organ of the state.[30]

Attacks against the central political authority of a state are not necessarily immune from extradition either. The *attentat* clause, according to which an attempt against the life of a foreign

---

[25]*In Re Pavan*, [1923] Ann. Dig. 347 (No. 239).
[26]*Ibid.*, p. 511.
[27]*Ibid.*
[28]*In re Fabijan*, [1933-1934] *Annual Digest*, 360.
[29]*Ibid.*, p. 368.
[30]*Ibid.*, p. 367.

head of state is not deemed to be a political crime, is now a common feature of many extradition treaties[31] and domestic laws.[32] Besides, in many countries it is settled law that anarchists, being the enemies of all governments and not just one specific regime, are to be denied the status of political offenders for extradition purposes.[33]

When terrorism is stigmatized as an international crime, however, it will automatically be excluded from the range of application of the general rule relating to the nonextradition of political offenders. There is ample authority for the proposition that all crimes under international law are subject to extradition irrespective of their political nature.[34] That is certainly the *lex lata* with regard to war crimes[35] and crimes against humanity.[36] Once a *delictum juris gentium,* terrorism will certainly be drawn into the vortex of extradition.

At the other end of the spectrum is the second case of terrorists who act with the local government, which directs its activities against another state or within another state's territory. These terrorists may be looked upon as the long arm of the local government since in reality, they are officially licensed to kill and their activity entails full governmental responsibility. As Friedmann stated almost two decades ago:

> where it can be shown that an individual committed an act of terrorism on the instructions and with the direct support of a foreign government, the latter should clearly be held responsible.[37]

---

[31]See e.g. "European Convention on Extradition," 17 *Kitvei Am* 87, 90 (1957). Montevideo Convention on Extradition," 1933, 28 *A.J.I.L., Supp.,* 65, 66 (1934),
[32]Beginning with the Belgian law of 1856, enacted after an attempt against the life of Napoleon III. See Deere, "Political Offense the Law and Practice of Extradition," 27 *A.J.I.L.,* 247, 252 (1933).
[33]See *In re Meunier,* [1894] 2 *Q.B.* 415, 419 (1894).
[34]See Bassiouni, "Ideologically Motivated Offenses and the Political Offense Exception in Extradition—A Proposed Juridical Standards and Unruly Problems," 19 *De Paul Law Review* 217, 241 (1969).
[35]See Lauterpacht, "The Law of Nations and the Punishment of War Crimes" 21 *B.Y.B.I.L.,* 58, 91 (1944). Morgenstern, "Asylum for War Criminals, Quislings and Traitors," 25 *B.Y.B.I.L.,* 382, (1948).
[36]See *In re Bohne,* 62 *A.J.I.L.,* 784, (1968).
[37]Friedmann, "Some Impacts of Social Organization on International Law" 50 *A.J.I.L.,* 475, 494 (1956).

A state cannot wash its hands of acts which are in the final analysis its own. The imputation of an act to a state depends not on nomenclature but on substance. Whenever a State sanctions an act performed by an individual, the act becomes an act of state. The terrorist, in other words, is an organ of the state.

When an act of terrorism is perpetrated by an organ of one state against another, this is an armed attack within the meaning of Article 51 of the Charter of the United Nations, and the victim state is entitled to self-defense. The term "armed attack" is not confined to an all-out invasion of one country by another because small scale armed attacks are still armed attacks.[38] The victim state may exercise the various options of self-defense, which include reprisals and in certain circumstances war as a counteraction.[39]

In between the two extreme cases, of governmental resistance to the terrorists and governmental complicity with them, is the third case of governmental indifference. The local government may simply be unable or unwilling to fight the terrorists. In the absence of connivance, there is no direct state responsibility for terrorist strikes against another state and if the central government is too weak to exercise due dilligence against the terrorists, its responsibility for the abuse of its territory as their base of operations may be nominal. Still, that does not mean that the victim state must sit idly by, absorbing devastating blows and sustaining itself with the noble thought that no independent state is to blame for the turn of events. The terrorist raids continue to be armed attacks, which permit response by way of self-defense even if conducted from, and not by, another state. This is an extraordinary case, which demands and must receive an extraordinary legal solution. Self-defense is permitted inside the territory of another state directed against the terrorists rather than the ineffective local government. I have elaborated elsewhere[40] this mode of self-defense, which I call execution. Others prefer the appellation necessity. Either way the leading precedent is to

---

[38]See Dinstein, "A Survey of Self-Defense in International Law," in Vol. I Bassiouni, and Nanda, ed., *Treatise on International Criminal Law*, (1973) 273, 277.
[39]*Ibid.*, pp. 278-279, 281-282.
[40]*Ibid.*, pp 279-281.

be found in the famous *Caroline* incident.[41] In 1837, during a rebellion in Canada, the steamboat "Caroline" was used for transporting supplies from the American bank of the Niagara River to a rebel-held island. The federal government in Washington was unable to stop this activity since the Canadian insurgents benefited from the militant support of public opinion in the state of New York. When British protests proved of no avail, a British unit crossed the American border and destroyed the vessel with some loss of lives. Originally, the incident brought the United States and Great Britain to the brink of war, but ultimately Washington was persuaded that under the exceptional circumstances the British had no other choice. This is still the law today.

The Middle East Conflict

Some Palestinian Arab groups are continuously and increasingly resorting to indiscriminate terrorism, without any scrupulous method of operations. In political terms, the only net result is that more bad blood has been created between Arabs and Jews, and they have been driven farther apart. By no stretch of the imagination can a credible scenario be unfolded in which the protagonists will get closer to the solution of the Middle East conflict as a result of terrorist activities. In time, no doubt, this plain truth will dawn on Arab leadership but meanwhile many innocent bystanders will have lost their lives in vain.

Legally, we must apply the three-pronged approach to an analysis of the phenomenon of Arab terrorism. Most Arab countries have been prepared to aid and abet the terrorists in a flagrant way. These countries have become fully and directly responsible under international law for the consequences of the support extended to the terrorists. Insofar as the terrorist attacks can be classified as armed attacks (surely the cases in the Munich and Lod Airport incidents), the states which can be considered accessories to the crimes open themselves to counter-attacks by way of self-defense. When an Arab country ratifies the acts of the terrorist, the terrorists become its organs and the acts turn into acts of state. Israel, and any other injured state, may regard that

---

[41] See Jennings, "The Caroline and McLeod Cases," 32 *A.J.I.L.*, 82 (1933).

Arab country as the alter ego of the terrorist group. Reprisals and even war, as a measure of counter-force in self-defense, are the price of folly.

As for the Arab states, which merely tolerate the presence of the terrorists on their territory without supporting their cause they also run a risk. The traffic of violence can move in a two-way street. Just as armed attacks may spring from the local territory without being directed by the government, counter-attacks in self-defense may end up in that territory without being directed at the government. When the terrorists have the run of the land, an impotent government must not complain if the victims resort to self-help and execution ensues. *A fortiori*, it must not interfere in the course of execution. As the judgment of the Nuremberg Military Tribunal in the *Ministries Case* proclaimed, "there can be no self-defense against self-defense."[42] A government that is unable to repel terrorists must not try to display unwanted prowess when the victims implement the law.

There is no problem with those Arab states that fight the terrorists. Wherever the terrorists are caught, they should either be prosecuted or extradited. As pointed out above, terrorists do not usually benefit from the rule precluding the extradition of political offenders. Yet, extradition usually hinges on the pre-existence of a treaty, and prosecution is contingent on the availability of criminal jurisdiction under international law. This is why the absence of an international convention for the suppression of terrorism is acutely felt.

Occasionally, statements are made to the effect that the Arab terrorists should be excused in view of the continuing state of belligerency between Israel and the Arab states; *à la guerre comme à la guerre*. But not even the laws of war countenance terrorism. These laws are predicated on the fundamental distinction between combatants and non-combatants. Indiscriminate terrorist attacks against civilians, by any means whatever, are prohibited. Terrorization is simply not a legitimate objective of warfare.[43] Even if the Palestinian Arabs belong to a party to the

---

[42]*Trials of War Criminals before the Nuremberg Military Tribunal* (NMT) *14*:329. The phrase is actually borrowed from Wharton.

[43]See Schwarzenberger, *The Law of Armed Conflict*, (1968) p. 112.

Middle East conflict, they are supposed to conduct their operations in accordance with the laws and customs of war. They are expected to abandon terrorism and comply with the *jus in bellum*.

AN INTERNATIONAL LAW APPRAISAL OF THE JURIDICAL CHARACTERISTICS OF THE RESISTANCE OF THE PEOPLE OF PALESTINE: THE STRUGGLE FOR HUMAN RIGHTS*

W. T. MALLISON, JR. AND S. V. MALLISON

THE JURIDICAL STATUS OF THE PALESTINIAN MILITARY RESISTANCE

AMONG THE ASPECTS of a resistance movement which are affected by international law is the military one. It is necessary, therefore, to evaluate the juridical status of the Palestinian military resistance under the criteria of the international law of war.

Organized Resistance

A lawful resistance movement must be comprised of individuals who are privileged combatants under the international law of war. According to that law, a privileged combatant is one who is entitled to the benefits and protection of prisoner of war (P.O.W.) status if he is captured. Attention should, therefore, be directed to that part of international law which identifies these individuals. The applicable international agreement is the Geneva Prisoners of War Convention of 1949,[1] and all of the states which have participated in the recurring Arab-Israeli hostilities are parties to it. The P.O.W. Convention provides that it "shall apply to all cases of declared war or of any other armed conflict" which may

---

Reprinted with permission of The Journal for Palestine Studies.
[1]U.N. Treaty Series 135, 6 U.S. Treaties & Other Int'l Agreements 3316, p. 75 Treaties & Other Int'l Acts Series No. 3364.

arise, "even if the state of war is not recognized by one" of the parties to the Convention. It is clear beyond any doubt that the Convention applies to armed forces involved in the Arab-Israeli hostilities whether these hostilities are regarded as "war" or "armed conflict." It is an established principle of international law that a ceasefire or an armistice does not terminate a war or conflict.[2]

Article 4A (2) of the P.O.W. Convention, after specifying that members of regular armed forces are privileged combatants and are therefore entitled to P.O.W. status if captured, deals with the status of "organized resistance movements." It provides that the following persons are also privileged combatants who are entitled to P.O.W. status if captured:

> Members of other militias and members of other volunteer corps, including those of *organized resistance movements,* belonging to a Party to the conflict and *operating in or outside their own territory, even if this territory is occupied,* provided that such militias or volunteer corps, including such organized resistance movements, fulfil the following conditions:
>
>   (a) that of being commanded by a person responsible for his subordinates;
>   (b) that of having a fixed distinctive sign recognizable at a distance;
>   (c) that of carrying arms openly;
>   (d) that of conducting their operations in accordance with the laws and customs of war.[3]

The requirement of "belonging to a Party to the conflict" does not mean the subordination of the resistance movement to a state which is a party to the conflict or the dependence of such a movement upon such a state. The authoritative official commentary of the International Committee of the Red Cross on this provision of the P.O.W. Convention emphasizes that an informal or *de facto* relationship between the resistance movement and the state party to the conflict is sufficient. The commentary provides:

> It [the requirement] may find expression merely by tacit agreement if the operations are such as to indicate clearly for which side the resistance organization is fighting.[4]

---

[2] 2 Oppenheim-Lauterpacht, *International Law* (7th ed. 1952) pp. 544-547.
[3] The emphasis is added to the quotation.
[4] Pictet, commentary on The III Geneva Convention relative to the treatment of prisoners of war (1960) p. 57.

The relationship between the Allied Armies in Europe and the French Forces of the Interior provides an example of such an informal relationship. A similar relationship existed between Marshall Tito's partisan forces and the Allied Armies. This provision of the P.O.W. Convention was designed merely to codify the requirement of an informal relationship which developed in customary international law during World War II. It is apparent that a similar relationship has existed for some time between the organized Palestinian guerrilla forces and a number of the Arab government armies.

The negotiating history of this article of the Convention makes it clear that there was no intention to impose a higher standard upon guerrilla forces than that applied to regular armed forces. The requirements set forth as (a) through (d) above are designed to apply to guerrilla fighters the same basic criteria which are applicable to regular armed forces. The organized character of units of the Palestinian guerrilla forces, including the fact that they are "commanded by a person responsible for his subordinates," is well known. Even the Government of Israel has recognized their status and Ambassador Tekoah of Israel has referred to "the organized military character" of the Palestinian guerrillas in statements made to the United Nations Security Council. The contemporary uniforms of regular armed forces are designed to provide effective camouflage, and guerrillas may, consequently, wear a similar uniform with "a fixed distinctive sign" which may, for example, consist of a particular type of cap or headgear. In the same way, guerrilla forces may carry weapons such as automatic pistols and hand grenades attached to belts under coats and comply with the requirement of "carrying arms openly." With respect to the requirement concerning complying with "the laws and customs of war," it should be recognized that guerrillas have the same obligations as regular armed forces.

The most innovative or "law-making" feature of article 4 is that the "organized resistance movements" are given a legal right to conduct their guerrilla activities even if their own territory is occupied by the enemy. Such forces are entitled as a matter of law to conduct operations "in or outside their own territory," without regard to the question of whether or not the military occupant is adhering to the international law of war including the Geneva Civilians Convention of 1949.[5] This absolute right to military resistance stands in striking contrast with earlier international law which undertook to prohibit resistance movements by postulating a "duty of allegiance" owed by the inhabitants of occupied territory to military occupants. The experience of the Second World War, which was carefully taken into account in writing both the Prisoner of War Convention and the Civilians Convention, indicated clearly that it was impossible to separate resistance forces from the civilian population. Article 68 of the Civilians Convention also emphasizes this change in the preexisting law by laying it down flatly that a civilian protected person in the occupied territory "is not a national of the occupying power" and "is not bound to it by any duty of allegiance." Since civilians who are not participating in the resistance have no duty of allegiance to the military occupant, it is clear, *a fortiori,* that organized guerrilla forces who comprise the military resistance have no such duty to the occupying power, without regard to whether or not the occupant adheres to its obligations under the Civilians Convention.

It should be emphasized in summary that the P.O.W. Convention gives to organized resistance forces exactly the same status as privileged combatants under international law which it accords to regular armed forces.

Unorganized Resistance

Article 4A (2) of the P.O.W. Convention does not specifically deal with the juridical status of unorganized resistance forces. The Report of Committee II at the Geneva Diplomatic Conference of 1949 made it clear, however, that participating nations at that Conference did not, in specifically according P.O.W. status to captured members of organized resistance movements, attempt to restrict or deny basic international law protections to guerrilla-type resistance undertaken by inhabitants of occupied territories against an occupant's violations of international law limitations

---

[5]75 U.N. Treaty Series 287, p. 75. 6 U.S. Treaties & Other Int'l Agreements 3516, p. 6. Treaties & Other Int'l Acts Series No. 3365.

on his authority. The Report states that the Danish Delegation

> asked that the Summary Record should mention that no objection
> had been raised, during the discussion in the Special Committee,
> against his view that Article (4) [of the P.O.W. Convention] could
> not be interpreted in such a way as to deprive persons not covered by
> the provisions of Article (4), of their human rights or of their right of
> self-defence against illegal acts. . . .

The outcome of this authoritative interpretation of the work of the 1949 Conference which adopted the P.O.W. Convention is that unorganized resistance may be lawfully conducted by the civilian population, providing that the military occupant commits "illegal acts" in violation of the Geneva Civilians Convention of 1949 and other applicable provisions of law. The unorganized resistance fighters must be accorded status as privileged combatants, even if they do not meet all of the requirements which are specified for organized resistance forces in article 4 of the P.O.W. Convention. If such unorganized resistance fighters or guerrilla forces are not accorded the benefits of P.O.W. status under the P.O.W. Convention, the Civilians Convention requires that they must be classified as "protected persons" who are entitled to a large number of procedural and substantive protections including all of the elements of a fair trial.

Thus the legality of the acts of unorganized resistance fighters is dependent on the occupying power's failure to act in accordance with international law. The principal law on this subject is contained in the Geneva Civilians Convention. This Convention, it must be recalled, was written in the shadow of the Second World War when the overwhelming majority of states in the world community were determined to prevent a repetition of the terrible acts carried out under the Nazi occupations in Europe and the Japanese occupations in Asia. The State of Israel and all of the Arab States which have been involved in the recurring hostilities with Israel are parties to the Geneva Civilians Convention and there is no question but that it is applicable, at least in territories occupied since 1967. Even the United States Government has taken the position that the Civilians Convention applies to and limits the actions of the Government of Israel. Ambassador Yost stated this in the U.N. Security Council on July 1, 1969 and added that the U.S. Government has "so informed the Government of Israel on numerous occasions since July, 1967."[6] Since international law is not self-enforcing, it is regretable that the U.S. Government did not follow its words with actions designed to implement them.

For an appraisal of the Government of Israel's role in the more recently occupied territories since the 1967 hostilities, several reports of United Nations investigations (made without the cooperation of the Government of Israel) and the resolutions of various organs of the United Nations are available.[7] A recent example is the United Nations Human Rights Commission resolution of March 23, 1972.[8] It states, in part, that the Human Rights Commission is:

> Gravely concerned with all acts and policies that affect the status or the character of those occupied territories and the basic rights of the inhabitants thereof, such as:
>
> (a) The declared intention to annex certain parts of the occupied Arab territories,
>
> (b) The establishment of Israeli settlements on those territories and the transfer of parts of its civilian population into the occupied territories,
>
> (c) The evacuation, transfer, deportation and expulsion of the inhabitants of occupied territories,
>
> (d) The destruction and demolition of villages, quarters and houses and the confiscation and expropriation of property,
>
> (e) The denial of the right of the refugees and displaced persons to return to their homes,
>
> (f) Collective punishment and ill-treatment of prisoners and detainees,
>
> (g) Administrative detention and holding prisoners incommunicado.

Each of the above quoted portions of the Commission's Resolution deals with an express violation of one or more pro-

---

[6] 61 U.S. Dep't State Bull, 76, 77, July 28, 1969.

[7] These resolutions from 1967 through 1971, are collected in F. A. Sayegh, and S. A. Soukkary, eds., *Palestine: Concordance of United Nations Resolutions 1967-1971* (1971).

[8] U.N. Hum. Rts. Comm. 28th Sess., 1161st Meeting; U.N. Press Release HR/812.

visions of the Geneva Civilians Convention of 1949. It follows that, in view of the illegal character of the Israeli military occupation, there is ample authority in international law for the Palestinians to conduct unorganized military resistance. This legal authority is further strengthened by the U.N. General Assembly Resolution of December 6, 1971, considered in Section IV A below, which recognizes the legality of the fight for basic rights of the people of Palestine and of specified African peoples.

THE JURIDICAL STATUS OF THE PALESTINIAN POLITICAL-LEGAL RESISTANCE

In appraising both military and political-legal resistance, it must be recognized that there are many close relationships between the two and that it would be inaccurate to attempt to draw a rigid distinction between them. It is generally recognized that military resistance has significant political-legal impacts. It is not as widely recognized, but it is equally true, that political-legal resistance has significant military impacts. It is difficult to see how military resistance can be a significant factor unless it is connected with a viable entity and an accompanying political institution. If status in law can be obtained for the entity and the institution, the entire resistance is strengthened.

The Subjects of International Law: Public Bodies

It is well known that the subjects of international law are no longer limited to national states. Among the subjects of international law, international public bodies or organizations are of particular importance. One definition of a public body is that it is a nonterritorial government. Although particular public bodies may be, in effect, governments-in-exile, this is not a necessary characteristic of public bodies as a group. In general, the group comprises entities established for public purposes which, like states, are subjects of international law. A memorandum of the Secretary-General of the United Nations has described the current situation as follows: "Practice has abandoned the doctrine that

States are the exclusive subjects of international rights and duties."[9]

Public bodies are usually constituted or created as subjects of international law through the explicit multilateral agreement of states, that is, through conventional law. Such bodies may, on occasion, be constituted by necessary implication drawn from an appraisal of their substantive powers. The United Nations, in spite of its preeminent position as the principal general function public body, is not explicitly constituted as a public body by its Charter. The International Court of Justice in the *United Nations Reparation Case*,[10] however, determined that the United Nations has juridical status as a subject of international law by necessary implication from the substantive powers which are granted to it by the Charter. It would have been unsound to allow the substantive grants of power to be frustrated through the failure to find the necessary ancillary juridical status. The Court found the United Nations to be a "subject of international law and [a public body] capable of possessing international rights and duties. . . ." The present significance of the case is that it illustrates the empirical analysis which must be made in an inquiry concerning status as a public body-subject of international law. Professor Hersh Lauterpacht has provided these succinct criteria:

> In each particular case the question whether a person or a body is a subject of international law must be answered in a pragmatic manner by reference to actual experience and to the reason of the law as distinguished from a preconceived notion as to who can be subjects of international law.[11]

These empirical tests must be employed in determining the public body status of the Palestine Liberation Organization.

The Palestine Liberation Organization as a Public Body in International Law

Palestinian leaders have recognized that even the most elementary and well established human and political rights are not

---

[9]Memo. of Sec. Gen. U.N., Survey of Int'l Law in Relation to the Work of Codification of the Int'l Law Comm., A/cn.4/1/Rev. 1, p. 19 (Feb. 10, 1949).
[10][1949] I.C.J. 174, (1949).
[11]International Law and Human Rights 12 (1950).

self-fulfilling and that there is a practical need for a public institution to achieve such rights. The Palestine Liberation Organization was established in 1964 with the assistance of other Arab
groups and through the multilateral authority of the League of
Arab States as a public body to represent and act for the people
of Palestine.[12] The League of Arab States has recognized its
public and representative capacities from its establishment to the
present. The overwhelming majority of the Arab States recognize
it in the same capacities. It maintains offices in a number of Arab
States and these offices and the Palestinian officials who serve in
them are accorded diplomatic status and privileges.

Some states outside of the Arab world also recognize the
public body status and the representative capacity of the P.L.O.
It is particularly important that one of the great powers which
is a permanent member of the United Nations Security Council,
the People's Republic of China, is one of these states and that it
has extended recognition since 1965.

The United Nations has accorded unofficial observer status to
the P.L.O. and its delegation in New York City works with the
delegations of states in seeking Palestinian objectives. The preeminent objectives are to achieve first the recognition and then
the implementation of the rights of the Palestinians and of other
oppressed peoples. By working with states and with other peoples
for common goals, the P.L.O. has demonstrated the universal
characteristics of its own goals. Through the P.L.O., the Palestinian people have an institution of their own to speak and act for
them in national and international affairs. Its character as a
public body provides the indispensable juridical status to achieve
their political and legal objectives.

The Recognition of the People of Palestine
by the United Nations

Until 1969, the United Nations referred to the Palestinians as
"refugees" and dealt with them in that capacity. There is no
doubt, as a factual matter, that many Palestinians have been
refugees since the establishment of the State of Israel as a Zionist

---

[12]The Palestinian National Covenant (1964).

State. The Palestinians, nevertheless, have insisted upon the maintenance of their status as a people. On December 10, 1969, in a resolution adopted by more than the two-thirds majority required by the Charter for important questions, the General Assembly of the United Nations stated that:

> *Recognizing* that the problem of the Palestine Arab refugees has arisen from the denial of their inalienable rights under the Charter of the United Nations and the Universal Declaration of Human Rights, [the General Assembly of the United Nations is]
> *Gravely concerned* that the denial of their rights has been aggravated by the reported acts of collective punishment, arbitrary detention, curfews, destruction of homes and property, deportation and other repressive acts against the refugees and other inhabitants of the occupied territories, [and it] . . .
> . *Reaffirms* the inalienable rights of the people of Palestine.[13]

Thus the General Assembly of the United Nations, the same organ which adopted the ill-fated Palestine Partition Resolution of 1947, has recognized that the Palestinians are a people under international law and that they are entitled to the same inalienable rights as other peoples.

Articles 55 and 56 of the U.N. Charter require all member states to promote and to take action to achieve

> universal respect for, and observance of, human rights and fundamental freedoms for all without distinction as to race, sex, language or religion.

The individuals comprising the people of Palestine are Palestinians of Moslem, Christian, or Jewish religious identification consistent with the quoted nondiscriminatory requirements of the United Nations Charter as well as with the Palestinian objectives of democracy and secularism.[14] The people of Palestine, as recognized by the U.N. General Assembly, comprise a distinct nationality entity which, for the time being, exists without a national state.

This recognition of the Palestinian people as a national entity provides a firm juridical foundation upon which the Palestinian people under the leadership of the Palestine Liberation Organiza-

---

[13]U.N. Gen. Ass. Res. 2535 B.
[14]Yusif Sayegh, Towards Peace in Palestine (Beirut, 1970).

tion can effectuate the same rights which have been achieved by other peoples under the United Nations Charter. This recognition of the Palestinians as a people is equally as important as the establishment of the P.L.O. as a public body.

It is well known that the Government of Israel does not recognize the status of the Palestinians as a national entity. The consistent Zionist-Israel position is reflected in the official statement of Mr. Galili, the minister of information of the Government of Israel, in 1969: "We do not consider the Arabs of the land an ethnic group nor a people with a distinct nationalistic character."[15] International law, as manifested by the December 10, 1969 Resolution of the General Assembly, has rejected this position.

The People of Palestine Contrasted with "the Jewish People"

A better insight into the characteristics of the people of Palestine may be obtained by a comparison with "the Jewish people," as it is termed in Zionist-Israel public law. The latter is the alleged transnational nationality entity which is claimed by the Zionist Organization and the State of Israel to comprise their constituency.[16] The "Jewish people" concept is a Zionist-Israel legislative one which emphasizes "Jewish" nationalism and the claimed juridical obligations of all Jews to the State of Israel. It is a discriminatory concept as it is applied both in the international arena and in Israeli municipal law. It is internationally discriminatory because it seeks to impose membership in "the Jewish people," with accompanying duties to the State of Israel, upon Jews outside of Israel without regard to their voluntary assent or their established nationality status. It is equally discriminatory in Israeli municipal law because membership in "the Jewish people" is the basis upon which "Jewish people" nationals of the State of Israel are given preferential treatment as opposed to the treatment accorded to Christians and Moslems.

---

[15]Quoted by Prof. Jacob Talmon of the Hebrew University of Jerusalem in An Open Letter to Y. Galili, 15 Arab World No. 9, p. 3 (1969). Prof. Talmon strongly criticizes the quoted words.

[16]Mallison, "The Zionist-Israel Juridical Claims to Constitute "The Jewish People" Nationality Entity and to Confer Membership in It: Appraisal in Public International Law," 32 *Geo. Wash. Law Rev.*, 983 (964).

The Israeli Law of Return[17] provides a brief but adequate illustration of the discriminatory characteristics of the "Jewish people" concept. Under its terms, a member of "the Jewish people" who is born anywhere in the world has a right to immigrate to Israel where he automatically becomes an Israeli citizen upon arrival. Under the same law, a Palestinian Moslem or Christian who was born in the country, or who is the child of a person born in the country, has no right to return to it. As a practical necessity in interpreting the Law of Return, the Zionist juridical meaning of the terms "Jew" and "the Jewish people" is one of the most important subjects of litigation in the Israel Supreme Court. Among the well-known cases which have defined these terms are the *Brother Daniel Case* and the more recent *Shalit Case*. While the Zionists accept this type of litigation as necessary to maintain the "Jewish" character of the State of Israel, it is highly offensive to anti-Zionist Jews who recall that Nazi Germany used similar juridical criteria in defining the terms "Aryan" and "German."

The Government of Israel, in a manner reminiscent of George Orwell's *The Animal Farm,* treats some Jews as "more equal" than others. Although they are within the "Jewish people" concept, it is well known that Sephardic and Oriental Jews are second class "Jewish" nationals within the State of Israel. It is less well known that Israeli anti-Zionist Jews are increasingly discriminated against as Jewish dissent within the State of Israel becomes more articulate and viable.[18] These Jews in Israel are regarded as "traitors" to Zionism and its "Jewish people" concept, as are anti-Zionist Jews living outside of Israel.

The objective of obtaining international law recognition of "the Jewish people" was accorded the highest priority by Dr. Chaim Weizmann, the long-time president of the Zionist Organi-

---

[17]Israel Laws (authorized transl.) 114 (1950, as amended) p. 4.
[18]See, as illustrative of the Jewish dissent, the publications of the Israel League of Human Rights (Prof. Israel Shahak of the Hebrew University of Jerusalem, Chairman) and the strong criticisms of the continuing military occupation by Dean Ammon Rubinstein of the Tel Aviv University Law Faculty summarized in Israeli Concern Grows Over Occupation Stand, The Washington Post, April 10, 1972 at A 14, cols. 1-6.

zation/Jewish Agency and the first president of the State of Israel.[19] He believed that such recognition would provide a secure juridical foundation for the establishment of the State of Israel as a Zionist state. He failed to achieve this in the Balfour Declaration of 1917 because of the inclusion of the two safeguard clauses which protected the rights of the Moslem and Christian Palestinians as well as the rights of anti-Zionist Jews. It is significant that these safeguards were placed in the Declaration over the strong objections of the Zionist negotiators and at the insistence of Edwin Montagu who was the only Jewish member of the British Cabinet which issued the Declaration.[20] The objective was also frustrated in the League of Nations Mandate for Palestine of 1922. The Mandate included both of the safeguard clauses from the Declaration and, in addition, provided for Palestinian nationality on a nondiscriminatory secular basis and did not provide for a "Jewish people" nationality. In the same way, the U.N. General Assembly Palestine Partition Resolution of 1947, in spite of its basic fallacies, did not provide for a recognition of the Zionist claimed "Jewish people" entity. If it had done so, it is obvious that such a provision would have violated articles 55 and 56 of the Charter.

Failure to obtain complete enforcement of the safeguard clauses and other legal restrictions placed upon the Zionists in the Balfour Declaration, the Palestine Mandate, and the Partition Resolution permitted the establishment of the Zionist state as a factual reality even though it was in violation of the governing principles of international law. Nevertheless, these safeguards and restrictions did prevent the juridical recognition of the "Jewish people" concept in international law. Dr. Weizmann well understood that the lack of such recognition endangers the Zionist nature of the State of Israel and makes that State far more vulnerable to future international action to change its character.

Since the establishment of the State of Israel, its government has consistently attempted to obtain international law recognition

---

[19]Mallison, *supra* note 16.
[20]Mallison, "The Balfour Declaration: An Appraisal in International Law" in Abu-Lughod, ed., *The Transformation of Palestine* (1971), p. 61.

of "the Jewish people" in a variety of ways. For example, the *Eichmann Case*[21] was based on the claimed jurisdictional authority of "crimes against the Jewish people." This immoral claim is based upon the conception that crimes against Jews, including mass murder, are crimes against "the Jewish people" rather than against the common humanity of all.

It is significant that the U.S. Department of State in a letter of April 20, 1964 addressed to Rabbi Elmer Berger,[22] the leading American anti-Zionist Jew, agreed with his position that the U.S. Government does not have authority under the First Amendment to the Constitution to assent to the "Jewish people" concept. The official letter, after stating that it "does not recognize a legal-political relationship based upon the religious identification of American Jews" between them and the State of Israel, continued: "Accordingly, it should be clear that the Department of State does not regard 'the Jewish people' concept as a concept of international law." The Zionist frustration over their continuing failure to obtain recognition of 'the Jewish people' was indicated by strong protests including an unsuccessful attempt to have the Department of State withdraw its letter to Rabbi Berger.

THE FUNCTION OF JURIDICAL STATUS IN THE EFFECTUATION OF PALESTINIAN POLITICAL-LEGAL RIGHTS THROUGH THE UNITED NATIONS AND INTERNATIONAL LAW

The recognition of the Palestinians as a people and of the Palestine Liberation Organization as a public body, while of great importance, are not ends in themselves. The crucial test of their long-range significance exists in the ability to employ them in a functional manner to effectuate Palestinian rights. The effectuation of such rights in international law requires both their specific recognition and their practical implementation. It should not be assumed that either of these elements can be accomplished quickly or easily.

---

[21]36 Int'l Law Reps., 5, 277 (1963).

[22]The letter appears in *supra* note 16 at 1074 and in 8 Whiteman, *Digest of International Law*, 35 (1967).

The Recognition of the Rights of the People Under
The United Nations Charter

The factual characteristics of the people of Palestine as a national entity entitle them to inclusion among the peoples who are accorded rights as such under the U.N. Charter. It is, nevertheless, an essential step to the practical implementation of these rights to have them specifically and officially recognized by the United Nations rather than relying upon their recognition by implication from the provisions of the Charter.

On December 8, 1970, the General Assembly of the United Nations, by more than the two-thirds vote required for important questions, decided that the people of Palestine are entitled to self-determination:

> *Bearing in mind* the principle of equal rights and self-determination of peoples enshrined in Articles 1 and 55 of the Charter of the United Nations and more recently reaffirmed in the Declaration on Principles of International Law Concerning Friendly Relations and Co-operation Among Nations, [the United Nations General Assembly]
> *Recognizes* that the people of Palestine are entitled to equal rights and self-determination, in accordance with the Charter of the United Nations.[23]

It is thereby made clear that among the rights of the Palestinians is the preeminent right to self-determination. Specialists in legal theory will, of course, produce arguments and counter-arguments as to whether resolutions of the General Assembly enacted by the two-thirds majority required for important questions are international law in themselves or merely evidence of a world community consensus as to the existence of international law. Whichever argument is accepted, it is evident that the people of Palestine now have the legal right to their national state.

It is well established in international law that a successful revolution thereby becomes a legal revolution. It is significant that the General Assembly of the United Nations, after careful

---

[23]U.N. Gen. Ass. Res. 2672 C. The Palestinian right to self-determination, along with that of the peoples of southern Africa, was mentioned in connection with the condemnation of governments which deny the right in U.N. Gen. Ass. Res. 2649 (30 November 1970).

consideration, has decided that some revolutions which are as yet unwon are legal revolutions because of their consistency with the basic principles of the United Nations. On December 6, 1971 the General Assembly, again by the more than two-thirds majority required for important questions (and again against the consistent opposition of the Governments of Israel and the United States) decided that it:

> *Confirms* the legality of the people's struggle for self-determination and liberation from colonial and foreign domination and alien subjugation, notably in southern Africa and in particular that of the peoples of Zimbabwe, Namibia, Angola, Mozambique and Guinea (Bissau), as well as the Palestinian people, by all means consistent with the Charter of the United Nations;
>
> *Affirms* man's basic human right to fight for the self-determination of his people under colonial and foreign domination;
>
> *Calls upon* all States dedicated to the ideals of freedom and peace to give all their political, moral and material assistance to peoples struggling for liberation, self-determination and independence against colonial and alien domination.[24]

The Palestinian people's resistance and "struggle for self-determination and liberation," along with that of the specified African peoples, is thereby accorded a legal status in international law. In addition, the right to fight for self-determination is declared to be a "basic human right." This right may be most constructively interpreted as embracing a wide variety of methods including the implementation of the Palestinian rights through political-legal techniques. It is significant that the resolution calls upon states which are committed to the ideals of freedom and peace to provide both moral and material assistance. Such assistance, consequently, may not be interpreted as illegal acts of intervention.

In summary, these resolutions of the General Assembly provide the recognition of Palestinian rights and the basis in legal authority to take steps toward implementation.

---

[24]U.N. Gen. Ass. Res. 2787.

The Practical Implementation of the International Law
Rights of the People of Palestine

As outlined in the introduction to this paper, a workable conception of international law requires not only the formulation of legal principles based upon justice, but also their effectuation. In this respect, international law, as the organized decision-making function of mankind, operates very much in the same way that an individual operates in taking the steps from ideas to words to actions. The words set forth in international law principles remain empty and misleading slogans unless they are recognized as applicable to particular entities and then practically implemented.

In seeking to improve enforcement and sanctions, the question "is there a sanction?" is not very helpful since either a "yes" or a "no" answer is usually incomplete and inaccurate. The most relevant questions, it is submitted, are these: (1) What is the present effectiveness or ineffectiveness of enforcement? (2) How may present enforcement processes be improved? (3) What additional enforcement processess are available both in the short-range and in the long-range? (4) Which comprehensive sanctioning processes are most likely to assure enforcement of the legal rights involved with the least cost in terms of destruction of human and material values? Whether or not effective sanctioning processes can be applied to achieve the recognized rights of the people of Palestine is not a sterile academic question. It is the most practical question which can be asked on the subject and its importance far transcends the specialized knowledge and competence of international lawyers. While international lawyers may and should provide creative help, the question as to whether or not the recognized rights of the people of Palestine will be implemented will be answered by all of the peoples, governments, and individuals who seek peace based upon justice under international law. To have a strong and effective sanctioning process it is imperative to have the consistent support of an informed, concerned, and active public opinion.

There is wisdom in the ancient Arab saying that a journey of a thousand miles must start with a single step. Some of the first steps have now been taken in the General Assembly of the United Nations. These resolutions are not only for the benefit of the Palestinians and other oppressed peoples, but they constitute important steps toward restoring the integrity and credibility of the United Nations and the legal principles which its Charter embodies.

CONTROL OF TERRORISM THROUGH A BROADER INTERPRETATION OF ARTICLE 3 OF THE FOUR GENEVA CONVENTIONS OF 1949

KATHLEEN A. LAHEY AND LEWIS M. SANG

INTRODUCTION

WHILE MOST SOLUTIONS to terrorism have tried to regulate the acts which cause terror and violence, the real solution lies in regulating the causes of these acts. By examining the circumstances out of which these acts arise, it will become clear that the international community has an interest in regulating terrorism and that some form of international control is, therefore, necessary.

We propose the following three-pronged solution to terrorism, which is designed to contain and minimize acts of terror arising out of conflicts of a noninternational nature and to protect the international community's interest in preserving minimum world public order: 1) a broader application of article 3 of the four Geneva Conventions of 1949 to include groups which can be identified as the nucleus of a future insurgency or rebellion; 2) adoption of minimum standards for the treatment of prisoners of noninternational conflicts; and 3) adoption of the doctrine of protected targets in order to immunize innocent civilians, international civil aviation, diplomats and the mails and other forms of international communications.*

---

*Ed's Note: This proposal is made in reliance on the conclusions reached in the *Final Document of the Syracuse Conference* p.p. XI et Seq.

PROPOSED SCOPE OF APPLICATION
OF ARTICLE 3

Article 3 of the four Geneva Conventions of 1949 governs the treatment of prisoners and civilians by the parties to noninternational conflicts.[1] Current application of article 3 is to conflicts which fulfill the requirements for classification as a belligerency, which in effect exludes most types of conflicts out of which acts of terrorism arise. According to classical international law, the elements of a belligerency are a civil war must be in progress along with a state of general hostilities; *de facto* authority over persons within a determinate portion of the national territory; and armed forces which act under the direction of an organized authority and are prepared to observe the ordinary laws of war.[2]

---

[1]Article 3 provides in its entirety:

In the case of armed conflict not of an international character occurring in the territory of one of the High Contracting Parties, each Party to the conflict shall be bound to apply, as a minimum, the following provisions:

(1) Persons taking no active part in the hostilities, including members of armed forces who have laid down their arms and those placed *hors de combat* by sickness, wounds, detention, or any other cause, shall in all circumstances be treated humanely, without any adverse distinction founded on race, colour, religion or faith, sex, birth or wealth, or any other similar criteria.

To this end the following acts are and shall remain prohibited at any time and in any place whatsoever with respect to the above-mentioned persons:

   (a) violence to life and person, in particular murder of all kinds, mutilation, cruel treatment and torture;
   (b) taking of hostages;
   (c) outrages upon personal dignity, in particular humiliating and degrading treatment;
   (d) the passing of sentences and the carrying out of executions without previous judgment pronounced by a regularly constituted court, affording all the judicial guarantees which are recognized as indispensable by civilized peoples.

(2) The wounded and sick shall be collected and cared for.

An impartial humanitarian body, such as the International Committee of the Red Cross, may offer its services to the Parties to the conflict.

The Parties to the conflict should further endeavor to bring into force, by means of special agreements, all or part of the other provisions of the present Convention.

The application of the preceding provisions shall not affect the legal status of the Parties to the conflict.

[2]II Oppenheim (Lauterpacht), *International Law*, 249 (1955).

To deny participants in an armed conflict the protection of article 3 for failure to meet these three requirements defeats the entire purpose of article 3. Any opposition group engaged in an armed conflict which meets these requirements is better off claiming prisoner of war status under article 4 of the III Geneva Convention Relative to the Treatment of Prisoners of War of 1949,[3] than hoping for article 3 protection. It is inconceivable that the same degree of organization need be present in order to invoke the protection of article 3 as is needed to gain prisoner of war status under article 4. The unreasonableness of this position is further demonstrated by an obvious contradiction in policy toward combatants in noninternational armed conflicts by the International Conference of the Red Cross.

The Twenty-first International Conference of the Red Cross at Instanbul declared:

> . . . combatants . . . who conform to the provisions of article 4 of the Third Geneva Convention of August 12, 1949, should, when captured, be protected against any inhumanity and brutality and receive treatment similar to that which that Convention lays down for prisoners of war.[4]

Jean S. Pictet, however, stated that the language of article 4, which defines "protected persons," encompasses every possible case of a person in the hands of the enemy and suggests that combatants in noninternational armed conflicts are to be accorded prisoner of war status:

> In short, all the particular cases we have just been considering confirm a general principle which is embodied in all four Geneva Conventions of 1949. Every person in enemy hands must have some status under international law; he is either a prisoner of war and, as such, covered by the Third Convention, a civilian covered by the Fourth Convention, or again, a member of the medical personnel of the armed forces who is covered by the First Convention. *There is no* intermedi-

---

[3]Article 4 states that there are four conditions with which combatants not belonging to the armed forces of a party to a conflict must comply in order to claim prisoner of war status: 1) the combatants must be commanded by a person responsible for his subordinates; 2) they must have a fixed distinctive sign recognizable at a distance; 3) they must carry their arms openly; and 4) they must conduct their operations in accordance with the laws and customs of war.

[4]Resolution XVIII, "Status of Combatants in Noninternational Armed Conflicts."

ate status; nobody in enemy hands can be outside the law. We feel that this is a satisfactory solution—not only satisfying to the mind, but also, and above all, satisfactory from the humanitarian point of view.[5]

Clearly this contradiction must be resolved and the human rights of those no longer in combat must be protected. To illustrate as clearly as possible the point at which we would mandate application of article 3, the following three hypothetical fact situations will be analyzed.

EXAMPLE 1: If one man acting on his own without any political or ideological motivations shoots and kills another man, this act of violence is murder and falls within the domestic jurisdiction of the country in which the act was committed. The international community has no interest in this act.

EXAMPLE 2: If one man conspires with another man to shoot a government official in order to overthrow the government of a country and in furtherance of the conspiracy they kill the official, the act is murder but there is an international interest which derives from the threatened overthrow of a government which disrupts or could disrupt world public order.

The crucial issue in example two, however, is whether the international interest in protecting world public order is of a degree sufficient to warrant the interposition of international regulation over domestic law. It is clear that if international regulation were applied at this stage there would be no real need for domestic criminal laws or even the preservation of the doctrine of sovereignty. But the doctrine of sovereignty is at present the accepted jurisdictional foundation of the nations of the world and cannot be aborgated. The international interest in this example does not outweigh the interest of the sovereign and thus international regulation would be inappropriate.

EXAMPLE 3: If a group of men and women conspire to overthrow the government and these people are politically affiliated or ideologically aligned, the murder of a government official in furtherance of that conspiracy again confronts the international community's interest in protecting minimum world public order.

---

[5]Pictet, Commentary III *Geneva Convention of August 12, 1949 Relative to the Treatment of Prisoners of War of 1949,* (1956), p. 51.

The difficulty here, however, is the conflict between the concepts of sovereignty and self-determination. If the facts show that the group of men and women in this example form the nucleus of a future insurgency or rebellion, then that group theoretically should be entitled to exercise the right of self-determination against the existing government. If the international community tries to regulate the conflict, the doctrine of sovereignty must in part be invaded. Since the degree of organization and civilian support and sympathy are greater for a group of this size than for a conspiracy of two, the issue of whether the international interest should outweigh the interest of the state is, therefore more clearly developed.

The international community does not recognize a group fighting against an existing state until that group receives recognition and assistance from other states, thus implicitly inducing increased violence. These nations give help in the form of arms, money and material to the group even though such conduct may amount to illegal third party intervention, serves to intensify the international community's interest in the conflict.

The question therefore is whether the international community should protect its interest in preserving minimum world public order where a group is the nucleus of a future insurgency or rebellion, by expanding the protections of international law.

The key to international action in this case is to find a form of regulation which respects the doctrine of sovereignty and the right of self-determination while at the same time protecting the interest of the international community. James E. Bond suggests that international sanctions should be derived by examining the nature of the human right to be protected and not the level of the conflict.[6] Following this reasoning, the international community can best protect its interest by protecting the human rights of all the participants involved in the conflict.

Implementation of the protection of the human rights of the participants in incipient insurgencies or rebellions need not come from new laws, because the language of article 3 of the four

---

[6]Bond, "Internal Conflict and Article Three of the Geneva Conventions," 48 *Denver L. J.*, 263, 274 (1971).

Geneva Conventions of 1949 is satisfactory. Article 3, however, was originally intended to apply only to noninternational armed conflicts which rose to the level of a belligerency.[7] Jean Pictet in his "Commentary" claims that these criteria are "useful as a means of distinguishing a genuine armed conflict from a mere act of banditry or an unorganized and short-lived insurrection." We submit that there are noninternational conflicts which are serious enough to merit regulation but which do not rise to the level demanded by the delegates to the Geneva Conventions. Left unregulated, conflicts which do not meet the requirements of classical belligerency are a threat to world public order.

By extending the scope of application of article 3 and thus prohibiting execution, mutilation, torture, humiliating treatment and the taking of hostages and guaranteeing due process during detention, participants in incipient insurgencies or belliegerencies will feel less jeopardy in engaging in acts of violence *in the territory of the conflict* because they will know that once captured treatment usually accorded dissidents will be tempered by the humanitarian rules of article 3. And certainly if the rebels adhere to the dictates of article 3, the existing government cannot claim

---

[7]The proposed amendments to article 3 were:
1. That the Party in revolt against the *de jure* Government possesses an organized military force, an authority responsible for its acts, acting within a determinate territory and having the means of respecting and ensuring respect for the Convention.
2. That the legal Government is obliged to have recourse to the regular military forces against insurgents organized as military and in possession of a part of the national territory.
3. (a) That the *de jure* Government has recognized the insurgents as belligerents; or
   (b) That it has claimed for itself the rights of a belligerent; or
   (c) That the dispute has been admitted to the agenda of the Security Council or the General Assembly of the United Nations as being a threat to international peace, a breach of the peace, or an act of aggression.
4. (a) That the insurgents have an organization purporting to have the characteristics of a State.
   (b) That the insurgent civil authority exercises *de facto* authority over persons with a determinate portion of the national territory.
   (c) That the armed forces act under the direction of an organized authority and are prepared to observe the ordinary laws of war.
   (d) That the insurgent civil authority agrees to be bound by the provisions of the Convention.

that "it is *entitled* to make use of torture and other inhuman acts prohibited by the Convention, as a means of combating its enemies," because "[i]t is not possible to talk of 'terrorism,' 'anarchy' or 'disorders' in the case of rebels who complied with humanitarian principles."[8] (emphasis added)

The operative effect of such an application of article 3 is that persons no longer taking part in the conflict are protected by the provisions of article 3. No protection is given those who are physically engaged in combat. But those participants will know that if captured they will be treated humanely, thereby providing an incentive for the group to come under the protection of article 3 to avoid criminal penalties and possible execution for treason.[9]

The crux of the issue posed is whether the international interest in maintaining minimum world public order should at some point supercede the doctrine of sovereignty. Applying the proposed application of article 3 to example 3, we see that the conduct of the group would be insulated from reprisals by the existing government. International law would in effect supercede domestic law to the extent of the provisions in article 3 and pierce the doctrine of sovereignty by requiring that captured members of the group be held for the duration of the conflict and that certain minimum standards of treatment of prisoners as set out in article 3 be observed.[9] The same would hold true for captured government soldiers held by the group. The international community would, therefore, regulate the conflict by making it more advantageous to be in the regulated group than to go it alone, while at the same time helping to humanize the conflict through a broader application of article 3.[10]

---

[8]Pictet, *supra* Note 5, p. 31.

[9]Lauterpacht and McDougal agree that treason trials should be delayed pending the outcome of the conflict in order to preserve the principle of humanity upon which the Geneva Conventions are grounded even in the event that article 3 is not applied. Oppenheim (Lauterpacht), *supra* note 2, p. 211; McDougal, and Feliciano, *Law and Minimum World Public Order* (1961), p. 538.

[10]It should be emphasized also that the application of article 3 clearly is not intended to and does not affect the legal status of the party to whom it is applied. In its expanded scope of application, article 3 still cannot be used to affect the legal status of the parties, rather, article 3 should be viewed only as providing for minimum standards of humanitarian treatment of prisoners of the conflict.

We recommend, therefore, that article 3 be expanded to include within its protection legitimate liberation movements and by so doing the international community will make a humanitarian compromise between the conflicting doctrines of sovereignty on the one hand and the right of self-determination on the other. A by-product of this recommendation is that those actors, who in the past have been responsible for creating terror and violence, will be induced to act more responsibly and humanely if they expect to be guaranteed by the international community fair treatment once captured.

MINIMUM STANDARDS

Article 3 states that prisoners of war and persons not actively engaged in noninternational armed conflict must receive minimum standards of treatment. We submit that although the Geneva Convention standards embodied in article 3 apply to political prisoners, the United Nations minimum standards for the treatment of common criminals[11] are incorporated therein because of the humanitarian nature of the United Nations standards.

Comprehensive minimum standards will further encourage an opposition group to come within the ambit of article 3 in order to guarantee its members uniform treatment if captured. The opposition participants, on the other hand, by treating captured government soldiers in a humane way, avoid characterization as terrorists, thereby shifting the burden to the existing government to treat its captured prisoners in an equally humane way.

In addition, section 1 (d) of article 3 of the four Genevan Conventions of 1949 should be amended to provide for the return of all prisoners of conflict at the end of the hostilities in order to strengthen the provision in section 1 (a) that detained combatants not be executed by their captors.

CURRENT DEVELOPMENTS

The alternative to broadening the dimensions of article 3 is seen in the International Committee of the Red Cross Draft Protocol Additional to Geneva Conventions of August 12, 1949,

---

[11]A/6/1/Corr 1 22 August 1956.

and Relating to the Protection of Victims of Noninternational Armed Conflicts, submitted June 1973.[12] This draft applies to all armed conflicts not covered by article 2 common to the Geneva Conventions of August 12, 1949, but excludes "situations of internal disturbances and tensions, *inter alia,* riots, isolated and sporadic acts of violence and other acts of a similar nature." The draft further recites that it does not "modify the conditions governing" the application of article 3. Thus, the new draft protocol is in essence an expanded version of article 3 under another title, which resolves within its articles many of the problems that were pointed out earlier in this paper.

The draft expands the fundamental guarantees of article 3 to include in its category of prohibited acts: acts of terrorism, slavery and slave-trade, pillage and threats of all prohibited acts. In addition, articles 7 and 8 list minimum standards of treatment of enemy soldiers and persons captured and articles 9 and 10 state minimum standards of judicial treatment which guarantee the dignity of man by insuring him minimum human rights, including the granting of amnesty at the end of the hostilities.

It is clear that the draft protocol is designed to fill the gaps intrinsic in article 3 and its adoption would resolve many of the questions which currently arise concerning the treatment of victims of noninternational armed conflicts.

PROTECTED TARGETS

The protected targets theory[13] is both an independent theory relating to the overall problem of terrorism and an effective adjunct to the proposition that the scope of application of article 3 be expanded. This theory provides that certain targets be protected from all forms of terrorism. These targets are innocent civilians, duly accredited diplomatic and international personnel acting within their legitimate functions, international civil aviation and the mails and other means of international communications, which are protected from attack inside or outside the terri-

---

[12]*See* Appendix E.
[13]*See* Final Statement of the III International Symposium on Terrorism and Political Crime, p. XI but see in particular pp. XIII - XVI.

tory of the conflict. If one of these targets is attacked, the terrorist will be subject to extradition to the country of the conflict or tried in the country of capture or tried by an international criminal court.

If the terrorist comes within the proposed requirements for article 3 protection, however, any attack on another participant to the conflict in the arena of the conflict which results in his capture will be treated in accordance with the minimum standards of treatment of prisoners of conflicts. The distinction between these two offenses is that the offender in the first instance would be tried as a common criminal and would not be eligible to receive the benefits of the protection of article 3 or the minimum standards of treatment. By acting within the territorial limits of the arena of the conflict, however, the terrorist is entitled to treatment according to the minimum standards. In effect, this part of the proposal further encourages that the violence arising out of a conflict be confined to the arena of that conflict.

CONCLUSION

The problem of terrorism is caused by a certain level of conflict, and in examining the causes of that conflict, a reasonable solution for restricting violence can be found. This solution draws on existing international law and advocates the extension of the humanitarian policy behind it to noninternational conflicts. Part of the solution is also a new proposal which is aimed at overt acts of violence and designed to bring the responsible actors to justice. The adoption of this solution would extend greater protection to the individual's minimum human rights and inhibit future acts of terrorism. The United Nations, states, international lawyers and scholars should examine this proposal in light of the continuing interest in the protection of human rights.

APPENDIX A

Declaration on Principles of International Law Concerning
Friendly Relations and Cooperation Among States in Accordance
with the Charter of the United Nations, Approved by the
General Assembly in Resolution 2625 (XXV) of 24 October 1970

O̲N̲ O̲C̲T̲O̲B̲E̲R̲ 24, 1970, the General Assembly, by resolution
2625 (XXV), approved a Declaration based on the work of
the Special Committee on Principles of International Law concerning Friendly Relations and Cooperation among States, which
had met from 1963 to 1970. In the preamble to this resolution, the
General Assembly declared itself to be "deeply convinced" that
the adoption of the Declaration "would contribute to the
strengthening of world peace and constitute a landmark in the
development of international law and of relations among States,
in promoting the rule of law among nations and particularly the
universal application of the principles embodied in the Charter."
The Declaration contains a provision concerning terrorism, included in the section entitled "The principle that States shall refrain in their international relations from the threat or use of
force against the territorial integrity or political independence of
any State, or in any other manner inconsistent with the purposes
of the United Nations." Another provision concerning terrorism
appears in the section entitled "The principle concerning the
duty not to intervene in matters within the domestic jurisdiction
of any State, in accordance with the Charter." The following are
applicable excerpts:

The General Assembly,

. . .

1. *Solemnly proclaims* the following principles:

*The principle that States shall refrain in their international
relations from the threat or use of force against the territorial in-*

tegrity or political independence of any State, or in any other manner inconsistent with the purposes of the United Nations,

. . .

Every State has the duty to refrain from organizing instigating, assisting or participating in acts of civil strife or terrorist acts in another State or acquiescing in organized activities within its territory directed towards the commission of such acts, when the acts referred to in the present paragraph involve a threat or use of force.

. . .

Nothing in the foregoing paragraph shall be construed as enlarging or diminishing in any way the scope of the provisions of the Charter concerning cases in which the use of force is lawful.

. . .

The principle concerning the duty not to intervene in matters within the domestic jurisdiction of any State in accordance with the Charter:

. . .

No State may use or encourage the use of economic, political or any other type of measures to coerce another State in order to obtain from it the subordination of the exercise of its sovereign rights and to secure from it advantages of any kind. Also, no State shall organize, assist, foment, finance, incite or tolerate subversive, terrorist or armed activities directed towards the violent overthrow of the régime of another State, or interfere in civil strife in another State.

. . .

Nothing in the foregoing paragraphs shall be construed as affecting the relevant provisions of the Charter relating to the maintenance of international peace and security.

2. *Declares that:*

In their interpretation and application the above principles are interrelated and each principle should be construed in the context of the other principles.

---

[1]*General Assembly Official Records: Twenty-third Session, Annexes,* agenda item 87, A/BUR/171, para. 4 and A/7250, para. 10.

. . .

3. *Declares further* that:

The principles of the Charter which are embodied in this Declaration constitute basic principles of international law, and consequently appeals to all States to be guided by these principles in their international conduct and to develop their mutual relations on the basis of the strict observance of these principles.

APPENDIX B

Declaration on the Strengthening of International Security, Incorporated in General Assembly Resolution 2734 (XXV) of 16 December 1970

IN THIS DECLARATION, the General Assembly, recalling, *inter alia*, "the determination of the peoples of the United Nations, as proclaimed by the Charter, to save succeeding generations from the scourge of war, and to this end to live together in peace with one another as good neighbours and to unite their strength to maintain international peace and security,"

> *Solemnly reaffirms* that every State has the duty to refrain from the threat or use of force against the territorial integrity and political independence of any other State, and that the territory of a State shall not be the object of military occupation resulting from the use of force in contravention of the provisions of the Charter, that the territory of a State shall not be the object of acquisition by another State resulting from the threat or use of force, that no territorial acquisition resulting from the threat or use of force shall be recognized as legal and that every State has the duty to refrain from organizing, instigating, assisting or participating in acts of civil strife or terrorist acts in another State.

APPENDIX C

Report of the Special Committee on the Question of Defining
Aggression Established Pursuant to General Assembly
Resolution 2330 (XXII) of 18 December 1967

THE REPORT OF THE Special Committee on the Question of Defining Aggression on the work of its 1972 session reproduces some draft definitions submitted to the Committee which deal with terrorism. Operative paragraph 2C of the draft definition submitted by the Union of Soviet Socialist Republics reads as follows:[1]

> C. The use by a State of armed force by sending armed bands, mercenaries, terrorists or saboteurs to the territory of another State and engagement in other forms of subversive activity involving the use of armed force with the aim of promoting an internal upheaval in another State or a reversal of policy in favour of the aggressor shall be considered an act of indirect aggression.

Operative paragraph 7 of the draft definition submitted by Colombia, Cyprus, Ecuador, Ghana, Guyana, Haiti, Iraq, Madagascar, Mexico, Spain, Uganda, Uruguay and Yugoslavia reads as follows:[2]

> 7. When a State is a victim in its own territory of subversive and/or terrorist acts by irregular, volunteer or armed bands organized or supported by another State, it may take all reasonable and adequate steps to safeguard its existence and its institutions, without having recourse to the right of individual or collective self-defence against the other State under Article 51 of the Charter.

According to operative paragraph IV of the draft definition submitted by Australia, Canada, Italy, Japan, the United King-

---

[1]Report of the Special Committee on the Question of Defining Aggression, 31 January-3 March 1972, *General Assembly Official Records, Twenty-seventh Session, Supplement No. 19* (A/8719), p. 8.
[2]*Ibid.*, p. 10.

dom of Great Britain and Northern Ireland and the United States of America,

> The uses of force which may constitute aggression include . . . a use of force by a State. . . . By such means as. . . . (7) Organizing, supporting or directing violent civil strife or acts of terrorism in another State. . . .[3]

---

[3]*Ibid.*, pp. 11 and 12.

APPENDIX D

Draft Code of Offences Against the Peace and Security of Mankind, Prepared by the International Law Commission at Its Sixth Session, in 1954

IN ITS RESOLUTION 177 (II) of November 21, 1947 on the formulation of the principles recognized in the Charter of the Nuremburg Tribunal and in the judgement of the Tribunal, the General Assembly entrusted the International Law Commission with the task of preparing a draft code of offences against the peace and security of mankind. The draft code,[1] prepared in 1954 by the International Law Commission in pursuance of that resolution, deals with terrorism in article 2, paragraph 6, under which "the undertaking or encouragement by the authorities of a State of terrorist activity in another State, or the toleration by the authorities of a State of organized activities calculated to carry out terrorist acts in another State" is declared to be an offence against the peace and security of mankind, and therefore, according to article 1, a crime "under international law." In the commentary on this article, the International Law Commission, after recalling that "Article 1 of the Convention for the Prevention and Punishment of Terrorism of November 16, 1937 contained a prohibition of the encouragement by a State of terrorist activities directed against another State," went on to observe that "the offence defined in this paragraph can be committed only by the authorities of a State. A criminal responsibility of private individuals under international law may, however, arise under the provisions of paragraph (12) of the present article [covering conspiracy, direct incitement, attempted offences and complicity]."

It should be noted that, at the time of the preparation of the draft code, the Secretariat submitted to the International Law

---

[1]*Yearbook of the International Law Commission,* 1951, vol. II, p. 134 and 1954, vol. II, p. 150.

Commission a Memorandum, part III of which, concerning the various international offences which should be included in the code, contains the following paragraphs under the heading "Acts of terrorism affecting international relations":[2]

> Under the Code it should be a punishable act to incite, encourage or tolerate activities designed to spread terror among the population in the territory of another State. These activities might take the form either of attempts' on the life of persons charged with public functions or holding public positions or against public property or the crimes which create a common danger and imperil the lives of any part of the population.
>
> The problem for all practical purposes is to find a formula applicable to the serious offences dealt with in the Convention for the Prevention and Punishment of Terrorism, which was opened for signature at Geneva on 16 November 1937 under the auspices of the League of Nations.
>
> . . .
>
> It might be possible to adopt some broader formulas covering all offences directed against the security of one State which involve either action or wilful encouragement or tolerance on the part of another State.
>
> . . .

It may be well to recall that, in its resolution 1186 (XII) of December 11, 1957, the General Assembly decided to transmit the text of the draft Code to Member States for comment, and to defer consideration of the question until such time as it again took up the question of defining aggression. The attention of Member States was drawn to the draft Code when, at its twenty-third session (1968), the General Assembly again took up the question of defining aggression. However, the General Committee decided that it was not desirable at that stage, prior to the completion of the Assembly's consideration of the question of defining aggression, for the draft Code to be included in the agenda of the General Assembly, and that it should be taken up at a later session when further progress had been made in arriving at a generally agreed definition of aggression.[1]

---

[2]*Yearbook of the International Law Commission,* 1950, vol. II, p. 340; document A/CN. 4/29, p. 157, 159.

APPENDIX E

DRAFT ADDITIONAL PROTOCOL TO THE GENEVA CONVENTIONS OF AUGUST 12, 1949, AND RELATING TO THE PROTECTION OF VICTIMS OF NONINTERNATIONAL ARMED CONFLICTS

Humane Treatment of Persons in the Power of the Parties to the Conflict

Article 6.—Fundamental Guarantees

1. All persons who do not take a direct part or who have ceased to take a part in hostilities, whether or not their liberty has been restricted, are entitled to respect for their person, their honour and their religious convictions and practices. They shall in all circumstances be treated humanely, without any adverse distinction.

2. The following acts against the persons referred to in paragraph 1 are and shall remain prohibited at any time and in any place whatsoever:

    (a) violence to life and person, in particular murder of all kinds, mutilation, cruel treatment and torture;

    (b) taking of hostages;

    (c) acts of terrorism in the form of acts of violence committed against those persons;

    (d) outrages upon personal dignity, in particular humiliating and degrading treatment;

    (e) slavery and the slave-trade in all their forms;

    (f) pillage;

    (g) threats to commit any of the foregoing acts.

3. Women shall be the object of special respect and shall be protected in particular against rape, enforced prostitution, and any other form of indecent assault.

Article 7.—*Safeguard of an Enemy* Hors de Combat

1. In accordance with Article 6, it is forbidden to kill, injure, ill-treat or torture an adversary *hors de combat*. An adversary *hors de combat* is one who, having laid down his arms, no longer has any means of defence or has surrendered. These conditions are considered to have been fulfilled, in particular, in the case of an adversary who:

   (a) is unable to express himself, or
   (b) has surrendered or has clearly expressed an intention to surrender
   (c) and abstains from any hostile act and does not attempt to escape.

2. If a party to the conflict decides to send back to the adverse party those combatants it has captured, it must ensure that they are in a fit state to make the journey without any danger to their safety.

Article 8.—*Persons Whose Liberty Has Been Restricted*

1. All persons whose liberty has been restricted by capture or arrest for reasons in relation to the armed conflict, shall, whether they are interned or detained, be treated humanely, in accordance with Article 6.

2. In addition, the parties to the conflict shall respect at least the following provisions:

   (a) the wounded and sick shall be treated in accordance with Article 12;
   (b) the persons referred to in paragraph 1 shall be accommodated in buildings or quarters which afford reasonable safeguards as regards hygiene and health and provide efficient protection against the rigours of the climate and the dangers of the armed conflict;
   (c) they shall be provided with adequate supplies of drinking water and with food rations sufficient to keep them in good health; they shall be permitted to secure or to be provided with adequate clothing;
   (d) women shall be held in quarters separated from men's

quarters. They shall be under the immediate supervision of women. This does not apply to those cases where members of the same family are in the same place of internment.

3. The parties to the conflict shall also respect the following provisions within the limits of their capabilities:

(a) the persons referred to in paragraph 1 shall be allowed to receive individual or collective relief;

(b) they shall be allowed to practise their religion and receive spiritual assistance from chaplains and other persons performing similar functions;

(c) they shall be allowed to send and receive letters and cards. The parties to the conflict may limit the number of such letters if they deem it necessary;

(d) places of internment and detention shall not be set up close to the combat zone. The persons referred to in paragraph 1 shall be evacuated when the places where they are interned or detained become particularly exposed to dangers arising out of the armed conflict, if their evacuation can be carried out in adequate conditions of safety.

4. Measures of reprisals against the persons referred to in paragraph 1 are prohibited.

5. Subject to temporary and exceptional measures, the parties to the conflict shall endeavour to facilitate visits to the persons referred to in paragraph 1 by an impartial humanitarian body such as the International Committee of the Red Cross.

Article 9.—*Principles of Penal Law*

1. No one may be punished for an offence which he or she has not personally committed; collective penalties are prohibited.

2. No one may be punished on account of any act or omission contrary to a duty to act which was not an offence at the time when it was committed.

3. No one shall be liable to be prosecuted or punished for an offence for which he has already been finally acquitted or convicted.

4. No one shall be held guilty of an offence except under those

provisions of law which were in force at the time when the offence was committed.

5. Everyone charged with an offence is presumed innocent until proved guilty according to law.

Article 10.—Penal Prosecutions

1. No sentence shall be passed or penalty inflicted upon a person found guilty of an offence in relation to the armed conflict without previous judgment pronounced by a court offering the guarantees of independence and impartiality which are generally recognized as essential, in accordance with a procedure affording the accused the necessary rights and means of defence.

2. Everyone shall have the right of appeal against any sentence pronounced upon him. He shall be fully informed of his right to appeal and of the time limit within which he may do so.

3. The death penalty pronounced on any person found guilty of an offence in relation to the armed conflict shall not be carried out until the hostilities have ceased.

4. The death penalty shall not be pronounced for an offence in relation to the armed conflict committed by persons below eighteen years of age and shall not be carried out on pregnant women.

5. In case of prosecutions carried out against a person only by reason of his having taken part in hostilities, the court, when deciding upon the sentence, shall take into consideration, to the greatest possible extent, the fact that the accused respected the provisions of the present Protocol.

6. At the end of hostilities, the authorities in power shall endeavour to grant amnesty to as many as possible of those who have participated in the armed conflict, in particular those whose liberty has been restricted for reasons in relation to the armed conflict, whether they are interned or detained.

APPENDIX F

UNITED NATIONS GENERAL ASSEMBLY RESOLUTION 3103 (XXVII)*

Basic Principles of the Legal States of the Combatants Struggling Against Colonial and Alien Domination and Racist Regimes

The Geneva Assembly

Recalling that the Charter of the United Nations reaffirms faith in the dignity and worth of the human person,

Recalling resolution 2444 (XXIII) of 19 December 1968 in which the General Assembly, *inter alia,* recognized the need for applying the basic humanitarian principles in all armed conflicts,

Recognizing further the importance of respecting the 1907 Hague Conventions,[1] the 1925 Geneva Protocol,[2] the Geneva Conventions of 1949,[3] and other universally recognized norms of modern international law for the protection of human rights in armed conflicts,

Reaffirming that the continuation of colonialism in all its forms and manifestations, as it was noted in General Assembly resolution 2621 (XXV) of 12 October 1970, is a crime and that colonial peoples have the inherent right to struggle by all necessary means at their disposal against colonial Powers and alien domination in exercise of their right of self-determination recognized in the Charter of the United Nations and the Declaration on Principles of International Law concerning Friendly Relations and Cooperation among States in accordance with the Charter of the United Nations,[4]

*Adopted by a vote of 83 to 13, 19 abstentions, at the 2197th Meeting, Dec. 12, 1973.
[1]Carnegie Endowment for International Peace, *The House Conventions and Declarations of 1899 and 1907* (New York, Oxford University Press, 1915).
[2]League of Nations, *Treaty Series,* vol. XCIV, No. 2133, p. 65.
[3]United Nations, *Treaty Series,* vol. 75, Nos. 970-73.
[4]General Assembly resolution 2625 (XXV).

Stressing that the policy of *apartheid* and racial oppression has been condemned by all countries and peoples, and that the pursuing of such a policy has been recognized as an international crime,

Reaffirming the declarations made in General Assembly resolutions 2548 (XXIV) of 11 December 1969 and 2703 (XXV) of 14 December 1971 that the practice of using mercenaries against national liberation movements in the colonial territories constitutes a criminal act,

Recalling numerous appeals of the General Assembly to the colonial Powers and those occupying foreign territories as well as to the racist régimes set forth, *inter alia,* in resolutions 2383 (XXIII) of 7 November 1968, 2508 (XXIV) of 21 November 1969, 2547 (XXIV) of 11 December 1969, 2652 (XXV) of 3 December 1970, 2678 (XXV) of 9 December 1970, 2707 (XXV) of 14 December 1970, 2795 (XXVI), 2796 (XXVI) of 10 December 1971 and 2871 (XXVI) of 20 December 1971, to ensure the application to the fighters for freedom and self-determination of the provisions of the Geneva Convention relative to the Treatment of Prisoners of War, of 12 August 1949, and the Geneva Convention relative to the Protection of Civilian Persons in Time of war, of 12 August 1949,

Deeply concerned at the fact that, despite numerous appeals of the General Assembly, the compliance with the provisions of the said Conventions has not yet been ensured,

Noting that the treatment of the combatants struggling against colonial and alien domination and racist régimes captured prisoners still remains inhuman,

Recalling its resolutions 2674 (XXV) of 9 December 1970 and 2852 (XXVI) of 20 December 1971, which pointed out the need for the elaboration of additional international instruments and norms envisaging, *inter alia,* the increase of the protection of persons struggling for freedom against colonial and alien domination and racist régimes,

Solemnly proclaims the following basic principles of the legal status of the combatants struggling against colonial and alien domination and racist régimes without prejudice to their elaboration in future within the framework of the development of international law applying to the protection of human rights in armed conflicts:

1. The struggle of peoples under colonial, alien domination and racist régimes for the implementation of their right to self-determination and independence is legitimate and in full accordance with the principles of international law;

2. Any attempt to suppress the struggle against colonial and alien domination and racist régimes are [*sic.*] incompatible with the Charter of the United Nations, the Declaration on Principles of International Law concerning Friendly Relations and Co-operation among States in accordance with the Charter of the United Nations: the Universal Declaration of Human Rights, the Declaration on the Granting of Independence to Colonial Countries and Peoples and constitutes a threat to international peace and security;

3. The armed conflicts involving the struggle of peoples against colonial and alien domination and racist régimes are to be regarded as international armed conflicts in the sense of the 1949 Geneva Convention and the legal status envisaged to apply to the combatants in the 1949 Geneva Conventions and other international instruments are to apply to the persons engaged in armed struggle against colonial and alien domination and racist régimes;

4. The combatants struggling against colonial and alien domination and racist régimes captured prisoners are to be accorded the status of prisoners of war and their treatment of them should be in accordance with the provisions of the Geneva Convention relative to the Treatment of Prisoners of War of 12 August 1949;

5. The use of mercenaries by colonial and racist régimes against the national liberation movements struggling for their freedom and independence from the yoke of colonialism domination is considered to be a criminal act and the mercenaries should accordingly be punished as criminals;

6. The violation of the legal status of the combatants struggling against colonial and alien domination and racist régimes in the course of armed conflicts entails full responsibility in accordance with the norms of international law.

CHAPTER III

HIJACKING

AIRCRAFT HIJACKING:
WHAT IS BEING DONE*

ALONA E. EVANS

THE CONTEMPORARY SCENE

Incidence of Aircraft Hijacking

SIXTY-SIX AIRCRAFT of United States or foreign registration were hijacked from January 1, 1961 through 1968; 277 aircraft of U.S. or foreign registration were hijacked from January 1, 1969 through 1972; nine aircraft of foreign registration, and none of U.S. registration, were hijacked in the first eight months of 1973. Inherent in these figures is an evolution in the nature of the offense and an intensification of rigor in the national and international response to the offense, as well as the emergence of certain legal and political problems as yet unresolved. At the same time, the dramatic decline in hijacking between January and August 31, 1973 should be greeted with caution, not euphoria, lest there be a regression to the condition of national and international complacency about aircraft hijacking which obtained up to 1968.

In considering the incidence of aircraft hijacking, it must be observed that the available statistics are not entirely satisfactory because many reports of hijackings are sketchy at best and because compilers differ in their interpretations of particular incidents, even where the facts are adequately established. For example, there would be little doubt that if an aircraft on a scheduled flight from New York to Chicago is hijacked to Havana, this is a successful hijacking. If this same flight were hijacked to Miami, and the

---

*Reprinted with permission of the *American Journal of International Law* where this article appeared in a slightly different form in Vol. 67 p. 641-671 (1973).

hijacker were apprehended on landing, would this be a successful hijacking? What about the situation where an individual on boarding an aircraft threatens to hijack it and is apprehended before take-off, or where he makes the threat in the airport boarding area and is then apprehended? For the purpose of the present survey of recent developments respecting aircraft hijacking at the national and international levels, the incidents will be classified into five categories: successful international, successful domestic, unsuccessful international, unsuccessful domestic, and attempts.[1] As used here, a successful international hijacking is defined as one in which an aircraft is diverted to a foreign destination from its scheduled domestic or foreign destination, e.g. an aircraft scheduled to fly from New York to Miami which is hijacked to Havana or an aircraft scheduled to fly from Rome to Athens which is hijacked to Damascus. A successful domestic hijacking is defined as one in which an aircraft is diverted from its scheduled destination to a different destination within the same country, e.g. an aircraft scheduled to fly from Philadelphia to New York which is hijacked to Lake Jackson, Texas. The categories of unsuccessful international or domestic hijackings include the relatively few episodes in which an effort to seize control of an aircraft in flight was thwarted and the aircraft either continued to its scheduled destination or returned to the point of previous departure. Statistics on international and domestic hijackings in the United States used here are reliable; those on international hijackings abroad are quite reliable; but the statistics on domestic hijackings abroad are incomplete. The fifth category, "attempts," comprehends unsuccessful efforts to seize control of aircraft not yet in flight, a situation distinguishable from threats or from banter with stewardesses or ticket agents about side trips to Cuba and similar follies,[2] enunciated before boarding. Attempts will be considered

---

[1]The Federal Aviation Administration uses the following categories: "successful," where "hijacker controls flight and reaches destination or objective;" "unsuccessful" where "hijacker attempts to take control of flight but fails;" and "incomplete" where "hijacker is apprehended or killed during hijacking or as a result of 'hot pursuit'." Federal Aviation Administration, Office of Air Transportation, Hijacking Statistics, May 1, 1973.

[2]When a passenger was asked whether he had checked his luggage and he replied,

here only incidentally, as information about these acts in the
United States is incomplete, and there is very little available
about the incidence of such acts abroad.

The record from January 1, 1961 through 1972 shows that
there have been 343 successful and unsuccessful international and
domestic hijackings worldwide. If attempted hijackings of aircraft in the United States and abroad are added, there have been
396 endangered flights during this period. The record for the first
eight months of 1973 shows that there were five attempts on aircraft in the United States, eight succesful international and
domestic hijackings abroad, and one unsuccessful domestic hijacking, which, with two attempts abroad, brought the total of
endangered flights to 16 in this period.[3] The United States has
been the principal victim of aircraft hijacking during the twelve-
year period. There were 157 successful or unsuccessful hijackings
of aircraft of U.S. registration. Successful hijackings included 91
flights of U.S. aircraft diverted from this country to foreign desti-

---

"I don't need any bags to highjack the plane," the carrier was held to have acted
reasonably in refusing to allow him to board the aircraft. Wolfer v Northeast Airlines, Inc., 12 Av. Rept. 17, 186 (Small Claims Count (Dade Co., Fla.), (1971). A
comparable statement resulted in a conviction under 49 U.S.C. §1472(m). Taylor v.
United States, 358 F. Supp. 384 (S.D. Fla. 1973).

[3]Statistics based upon compilations by Department of Justice, Federal Aviation
Administration, International Federation of Air Line Pilots Associations, and re-
ports in Boston Herald American, Chicago Tribune, New York Times, Wall Street
Journal.

Successful and Unsuccessful Worldwide Hijackings

Year	International	Domestic	Total
1961	6	4	10
1962	1	2	3
1963	1	0	1
1964	1	1	2
1965	0	5	5
1966	2	2	4
1967	5	1	6
1968	28	7	35
1969	75	13	88
1970	60	23	83
1971	29	19	48
1972	28	30	58
	236	107	343

nations, 11 flights scheduled between foreign destinations which were diverted to different foreign destinations, and 14 domestic flights. There were 40 unsuccessful hijackings of U.S. domestic flights, and one of an international flight.[4] Two hundred and seven aircraft registered in 60 other states were successfully or unsuccessfully hijacked from January 1961 through August 1973, Colombia with 25 hijacked aircraft being the principal victim among these states.[5] One hunderd and thirty-four of these in-

[4]

Successful and Unsuccessful Hijackings: United States

Year	International	Domestic	Total
1961	2	2	4
1962	1	1	2
1963	0	0	0
1964	1	0	1
1965	0	4	4
1966	0	0	0
1967	1	0	1
1968	17	3	20
1969	31	6	37
1970	15	8	23
1971	12	11	23
1972	11	19	30
	91	54	145

[5]Other states which have had 5 or more hijackings: Argentina 8, Brazil 10, Canada, 5, Cuba 5, Czechoslovakia 6, Ecuador 5, Egypt 7, Ethiopia 5, Greece 5, Japan 5, Mexico 10, Poland 7, Soviet Russia 8, Venezuela 7.

[6]

Successful and Unsuccessful Hijackings: Other Countries

Year	International	Domestic	Total
1961	4	2	6
1962	0	1	1
1963	1	0	1
1964	0	1	1
1965	0	1	1
1966	2	2	4
1967	4	1	5
1968	11	4	15
1969	44	7	51
1970	45	15	60
1971	17	8	25
1972	17	11	28
1973 (8/31)	7	2	5
	153	54	207

stances were international hijackings; 35 were domestic. There were 19 unsuccessful international hijackings abroad and 20 unsuccessful domestic hijackings of aircraft of foreign registration.[6] Cuba has been the state of first landing or of ultimate destination for 149 hijacked flights. Forty-five other states and four other areas have also provided planned or fortuitous destinations for hijackers.[7] In at least four instances, hijacked aircraft have been refused landing in the state of first choice and had to find another destination.[8]

The Changing Character of Aircraft Hijacking

The statistics, however reliable or vagarious they may be, only crudely delineate the scope of aircraft hijacking. They show a marked increase in incidents from 1968 through 1972 and a marked decline in 1973. But underlying these raw data are some significant changes in the character of the offense and in the motivation of the offenders. Where the acts had been committed almost entirely for what may be described as "personal" or "private" objectives—by the fugitive from justice, the military deserter, the disgruntled spouse, the forlorn adolescent, the escapee from an oppressive society, the real or alleged political offender, the homesick political refugee, the mentally deranged person— from 1968 on, hijacking evolved into the weapon, or the platform,

---

[7]Aden, Albania, Algeria, Argentina, Austria, Bahamas, Bulgaria, Canada, Chile, China, Costa Rica, Cuba, Curacao, Denmark, East Berlin, Egypt, El Salvador, Falkland Islands, Federal Republic of Germany, Greece, Honduras, India, Iraq, Israel, Italy, Jamaica, Jordan, Kuwait, Lebanon, Libya, Malawi, Morocco, North Korea, North Vietnam, Pakistan, Saudi Arabia, South Vietnam, Spain, Sudan, Syria, Trinidad, Turkey, United Kingdom, United States, Uruguay, Venezuela, West Berlin, Yugoslavia, Zaire.

[8]Albania refused to allow an Algerian aircraft to land. It went on to Yugoslavia. N.Y. Times, Sept. 1, 1970, 58:3 (All references to N.Y. Times are to the city ed.). Haiti refused landing to a Dominican Republic aircraft which then returned to the Dominican Republic. Chicago Tribune, Jan. 27, 1971. El Salvador refused to allow a Colombian aircraft to land. In a hedge-hopping trip, including five intermediate stops to refuel, the flight finally ended in Buenos Aires. N.Y. Times, June 2, 1973, 12:3. A Japanese aircraft was refused landing by Iraq, Bahrein, Kuwait, Abu Dhabi, and Saudi Arabia. N.Y. Times, July 24, 1973, 1:1.

of persons acting for "public" or political reasons.[9] Political "fronts" consisting of terrorist or guerrilla groups or factions and radical political elements have made hijacking the vehicle for the extortion of money or the release of prisoners or for publicity for their causes. The group commonly known as the Popular Front for the Liberation of Palestine (PFLP) initiated the use of hijacking for blackmail with the diversion of an aircraft of Israeli registration to Algeria in July 1968. After forty day's detention, twelve Israeli passengers and crewmembers and the aircraft were released by Algeria in exchange for the release of sixteen members of Al Fatah and other Arab guerrilla groups held by Israel.[10] That incident was followed over the next four and one half years by some 16 successful and unsuccessful political hijackings by the PFLP. These had their counterpart in 19 other successful or attempted political hijackings by such groups or factions as the Eritrean Liberation Front, the Japan Red Army, the Kashmiri National Liberation Front, the People's Revolutionary Army, Ustasha, the Armed Liberation Front, and the Thai Black September as well as by Iranian Communists and Philippine Maoists.[11]

---

[9]There have been several instances of hijacking apparently for the purpose of political kidnapping. The most serious in its international ramifications was the kidnapping in 1967 of the late Moise Tshombé, sometime premier of the Congo Republic (Kinshasa) (now Zaire), from Spain to Algeria. Held in prison in Algeria, pending his surrender to the Congo Republic on extradition charges, Tshombé died in prison in 1969. *Bull. of the International Commission of Jurists*, 28-29, No. 32 (Dec. 1967); N.Y. Times, July 1, 1969, 18:3. The hijackings to Cuba of two aircraft of U.S. registration in 1968 may have involved the kidnapping of Cuban or former Cuban nationals. N.Y. Times, March 13, 1968; 1:7; July 1, 1968, 16:6.

[10]N.Y. Times, Sept. 1, 1968, 1:7; Sept. 4, 2:6; Sept. 18, 6:1.

[11]Eritrean Liberation Front, N.Y. Times, Sept. 14, 1969, 16:4 (also involved in three other incidents between 1969 and 1972); Jewish Defense League, *See* United States v. Hershkovitz, 70 CR 741 (E.D.N.Y. 1971) (not published): Japan Red Army, N.Y. Times, March 31, 1970, 1:3; Afro-American Freedom Fighters, Sunday Herald Traveler (Boston), May 3, 1970, 42:6; Kashmiri National Liberation Front, N.Y. Times, Feb. 1, 1971, 6:6; Jordanian Liberation Front, Chicago Tribune, Feb. 20, 1972; Black Revolutionary Army, Herald Traveler (Boston), March 9, 1972, 13:3; Black Panthers, N.Y. Times, June 4, 1972, 1:8; People's Revolutionary Army, Chicago Tribune, Aug. 16, 1972; Organization of Unity of South Yemen, N.Y. Times, Aug. 23, 1972, 2:4; Ustasha, N.Y. Times, Sept. 16, 1972, 1:7; Armed Liberation Front, Chicago Tribune, Nov. 9, 1972; Thai Black September, N.Y. Times, March 29, 1973, 19:2; Punto Cero, N.Y. Times, May 20, 1973, 14:3; Sons of Occupied Territory, N.Y. Times, July 24, 1973, 1:1. Iranian Communist Party, Sunday Herald Traveler (Boston), Oct. 11, 1970, 4:4; Philippine Maoists, N.Y. Times, March 31, 1971, 16:5.

That political hijackings by the PFLP or their associates have been successful is quite evident from the record, for commencing with the 1968 episode they have been able to obtain the release of some 78 of their followers of whom 16, convicted of terrorist acts, including murder, assault, and willful destruction of aircraft and related ground facilities, were imprisoned in Greece, Switzerland, and the Federal Republic of Germany.[12] The same kind of ploy apparently brought the release of four Nicaraguan guerrillas in exchange for the lives of four American nationals who were passengers on board a hijacked aircraft of Costa Rican registration in 1970; however, these hijackers were not reported to have represented a political faction.[13] Three members of Ustasha, a Croatian terrorist organization, forced the Swedish government in September 1972 to release six Croats from prison who had been convicted in the murder of the Yugoslav Ambassador to Sweden.[14] In November 1972, members of the Armed Liberation Front, reported to be a left-wing Mexican political faction, forced the release of six prisoners in partial exchange for the release of 29 passengers held on board an aircraft of Mexican registration before hijacking the aircraft to Cuba.[15]

At the same time, an account of the successes must be balanced by the failures. Twice in 1972, Turkish guerrillas hijacked Turkish aircraft to Bulgaria and threatened to destroy the planes and all on board, if prisoners in Turkey were not released. The Turkish government refused to comply in each instance, and the hijackers surrendered to Bulgarian authorities without further action.[16] The most recent attempt at this form of blackmail occurred on May 18, 1973, when four members of a Venezuelan guerrilla group calling themselves Punto Cero hijacked an aircraft of Venezuelan registration to Mexico. There they threatened to blow up the aircraft with all on board unless some 79 prisoners

---

[12]N.Y. Times, July 23, 1970, 1:6; *ibid.*, Oct. 30, 1972, 1:1.
[13]Chicago Tribune, Oct. 22, 1970.
[14]*Cited, supra* note 11.
[15]*Cited, supra* note 11.
[16]N.Y. Times, May 5, 1972, 2:4; Oct. 24, 1972, 9:1. On Oct. 9, 1970, alleged representatives of the Iranian Communist Party hijacked an Iranian aircraft to Baghdad where they held it for eight hours, demanding the release of 21 political prisoners. When their demands were not met, they surrendered to Iraqi police. *Cited supra* note 11.

in Venezuela were released. The Venezuelan government refused the demand. The aircraft was then permitted by Mexico to go to Cuba with all aboard, but accompanied by an official of the Secretaría de Gobernación.[17]

Hijacking for the purpose of extorting money from the carrier is another conspicuous development since 1968.[18] The United States experienced a veritable epidemic of such incidents in 1972, after one in 1970, and three in 1971. None of the 22 incidents in the three year period appeared to have been motivated by political considerations.[19] Hijackers demanded sums of money ranging from $50,000 to $2,000,000, and in one instance the demand included fifteen pounds of gold (then valued at about $8,000).[20] In eight instances the extortionists asked for parachutes and bailed out of the hijacked aircraft; seven were subsequently captured with their loot. In four instances, the extortionists successfully hijacked the aircraft to foreign destination.[21] In 18 of

[17]N.Y. Times, May 20, 1973, 14:3; May 21, 11:1. The Japanese Deputy Minister of Transport served as a substitute for 99 passengers on a Japanese aircraft hijacked to North Korea in 1970. N.Y. Times, April 4, 1970, 1:4.

[18]From time to time, there have been hijackings for the purpose of robbing the passengers and crew or robberies have been incidental to the objective of diverting the aircraft to an unscheduled destination. Philippines, N.Y. Times, Nov. 7, 1968, 3:1 (robbery was apparent motive for hijacking); United States, Herald Traveler (Boston), Nov. 5, 1968, 44:3 ($405 returned by Cuba), N.Y. Times, March 6, 1969, 76:4 ($1,750 returned by Cuba), Chicago Today, Jan. 9, 1972, 7:1 ($333 returned by Cuba). An aircraft of U.S. registration was hijacked to Cuba for the purpose of kidnapping an individual for $290,000 ransom. N.Y. Times, April 9, 1972, 32:3. A Nepalese aircraft was hijacked to India apparently for the theft of $400,000 belonging to the Central Bank of Nepal which was being carried thereon. Herald American (Boston), June 12, 1973, 2:7.

[19]The first reported hijacking of a U.S. aircraft for extortion occurred on June 4, 1970, when Arther G. Barkley forced a Trans World Airlines Boeing 727, en route from Phoenix to St. Louis, to fly to Washington, D.C., where he demanded $1,000,-000. Authorities delivered $100,750 to him. In the melee incident to his capture, the hijacker shot the pilot and was wounded himself. N.Y. Times, June 5, 1970, 1:4. The three incidents in 1971 were initiated on November 24 when "D. B. Cooper" parachuted out of an aircraft over Oregon with $200,000. He has not been heard from since. The other two occurred on Dec. 24 and Dec. 26. N.Y. Times, Nov. 26, 1971, 1:4; Dec. 25, 1:4; Chicago Tribune, Dec. 27, 1971.

[20]N.Y. Times, Aug. 19, 1972, 1:6.

[21]N.Y. Times, May 6, 1972, 1:1 (hijacker bailed out over Honduras; returned voluntarily; money found in Honduras and returned); June 4, 1972, 1:8 (hijackers received asylum in Algeria, money returned by Algeria); Aug. 1, 1972, 1:4 (hijackers received asylum in Algeria; money returned by Algeria); Nov. 12, 1972, 1:1 (hijackers received asylum in Cuba, money not returned by Cuba).

these 22 hijackings for extortion, the hijackers surrendered, were overcome, captured, or killed. The money has been recovered in 20 of the 22 instances.

Extortion was also the principal motive for 12 successful or unsuccessful international or domestic hijackings or attempts on aircraft of foreign registration between May 1971 and May 1973.[22] The PFLP, Ustasha, and the Armed Liberation Front engineered three of these hijackings, but only the PFLP was successful in the effort, retaining custody of the $5,000,000 which it extorted from Lufthansa in February 1972.[23]

Violence has been a conspicuous factor in aircraft hijacking during the past four and one half years. Some 147 persons—passengers, crew, ground personnel, police, and hijackers—have been killed or injured in the United States and abroad in the course of efforts by security personnel on board aircraft or police or other authorities on the ground to thwart a hijacking or to apprehend the hijacker. If the deaths of passengers and crew in aircraft which have been destroyed by midair explosions or which have crashed apparently in the course of a hijacking are added to this record as well as the casualties resulting from attacks upon airports and related facilities, as in the Lod Airport incident on May 30, 1972, or from efforts to take hostages, as in the massacre of the 11 Israeli Olympic athletes in Munich on September 5, 1972, then these figures would be very much higher.[24]

Another aspect of the trend to violence has been the deliberate destruction of hijacked aircraft where there has been a slow or negative response to threats of political extortion. The PFLP blew up four aircraft of U.S., Swiss, and United Kingdom registration in one week in September 1970, in order to emphasize their determination to obtain the release of their followers held in

---

[22]Australia, May 1971; Canada, Nov. 1971; Federal Republic of Germany, Feb. 1972; Indonesia, April 1972; Ecuador, May 1972; Rhodesia, May 1972; Brazil, May 1972; Sweden, Sept. 1972; Italy, Oct. 1972; Japan, Nov. 1972; Mexico, Nov. 1972; Colombia, May 1973.

[23]N.Y. Times, Feb. 26, 1972, 1:8.

[24]N.Y. Times, Feb. 22, 1970, 1:4 (explosion on Swiss aircraft); *ibid.*, May 31, 1972, 1:8 (Lod Airport). A Soviet aircraft is reported to have crashed with all aboard during an attempted hijacking in May 1973. Chicago Tribune, June 9, 1973.

prison in various countries and to dramatize their cause.[25] On similar reasoning, two Indian nationals describing themselves as members of the Kashmiri National Liberation Front destroyed an Indian aircraft which they had hijacked to Pakistan when the Indian government refused to comply with their demand for the release of Kashmiri political prisoners. It is not clear why a Japanese Boeing 747 was hijacked, detained for three days at Dubai, and subsequently blown up at Benghazi.[26]

The data above suggest something of the evolution of aircraft hijacking during the past four and one half years from an act committed primarily for personal reasons into a weapon of terrorist or guerrilla groups, which has been accompanied by an increase in violence affecting all parties concerned. It may be asked whether the response of states acting singly or in concert has kept pace with these developments.

CHANGING RESPONSES TO AIRCRAFT HIJACKING

"Response" seems to have characterized the attitude of the United States and other states to the development of the contemporary offense of aircraft hijacking. If there were enough incidents, enough violence, enough private indignation, as witness the boycott instituted by the International Federation of Air Line Pilots Associations (IFALPA) on June 19, 1972, then something drastic would be done at the state level, and even at the international level, as witness the rapid conclusion and acceptance of the 1970 Convention for the Suppression of Unlawful Seizure of Aircraft (Hague Convention).[27] Consider U.S. response to aircraft hijacking over the past twelve years. Five successful international and domestic hijackings of aircraft of U.S. registration between May 1 and August 9, 1961, led an aroused Congress to amend the 1958 Federal Aviation Act, creating, *inter alia,* the offense of "air-

---

[25]For a discussion of the negotiations during this incident, *see,* J. W. F. Sundberg, *"La Guerre contre l'aviation civile internationale," 52 Rev. De Droit Pénal Et De Criminologie,* (1971-1972), No. 3-4 (Dec. 1971-Jan. 1972), 419, 422-25 (hereinafter cited R.D.P.C.)

[26]Christian Science Monitor, Feb. 17, 1971, 3:1. N.Y. Times, July 21, 1973, 1:1; July 25, 1:3.

[27]22 UST 1641; TIAS 7192; 65 AJIL 440 (1971); 10 ILM 133 (1971).

craft piracy" which was made punishable by penalties ranging from a minimum of 20 years imprisonment to death.[28] The increasing incidence of hijacking beginning in 1968 led to new measures designed to combat this burgeoning menace. The Civil Aeronautics Board authorized carriers to deny transportation to any person who refused to permit a search of his person or luggage.[29] Signs in English and Spanish appeared at airport ticket counters and boarding areas warning that hijacking and the carrying of concealed weapons on board aircraft were federal offenses and putting travelers on notice that they were liable to search. Electronic surveillance was instituted by some carriers in 1969. Airport personnel were instructed in the use of a "behavioral profile" or compilation of psychological characteristics devised by the Federal Aviation Administration as a way of identifying potential hijackers.[30] The PFLP's massive attack on international civil aviation between July and September 1970, which included the destruction of two aircraft of U.S. registration, led to the establishment of the "sky marshal" program which placed federal officers on duty in aircraft on long distance flights and in many airports.[31] These measures of deterrence had positive results as there was an appreciable decrease in the number of successful international and domestic hijackings of U.S. aircraft in 1970 and 1971. Nevertheless, the voluntary nature of the security program as well as a certain casualness on the part of airports and carriers permitted hijackers to continue to accomplish their objectives.[32] Indeed,

---

[28]75 Stat. 466 (1961); 49 U.S.C. §1472(i).

[29]CAB Local and Joint Passenger Rules Tariff No. PR-5, CAB No. 117, at 9 (1968).

[30]The nature of the profile is highly confidential. For a general discussion of the subject, see United States v. Lopez, 328 F. Supp. 1077, 1086-87 (E.D.N.Y. 1971).

[31]N.Y. Times, Sept. 12, 1970, 11:5; Sept, 22, 1:2. The presence of marshals on board aircraft did not provide an effective deterrent, possibly because of concern for the dangers in a shootout in flight. N.Y. Times, Oct. 26, 1971, 10:3.

[32]Eastern Airlines was reported to have installed electronic surveillance on Oct. 15, 1969; it was not apparently in use at Newark Airport on Feb. 10, 1970, when an Eastern aircraft was hijacked to Cuba. N.Y. Times, Feb. 17, 1970, 69:6. On Oct. 9, 1971, a hijacker who fitted the profile forced his way on board an aircraft with weapon in hand. *Ibid.*, Oct. 10, 1971, 73:1. On May 5, 1972, a hijacker, who fitted the profile and was searched before boarding, hijacked an aircraft to Honduras, having concealed a weapon in a book. Metal detecting devices were reported as not operating at the boarding gates at the local airport. *Ibid.*, May 17, 1972, 15:2.

there was a certain Kafkaesque quality about a 1972 hijacking in Reno, Nevada, which was accomplished by a man who approached the aircraft from across the field, wearing a ski mask, riding a bicycle, and carrying a rifle on the handlebars. This plane was hijacked to Vancouver, thence to Seattle where the hijacker was ultimately captured.[33]

The rash of hijackings *cum* extortion, with and without parachute accompaniment, together with IFALPA's threat of a policy of resort to self-help manifested in its boycott of international civil aviation in June 1972, led the Federal Aviation Administration to remove the sky marshals from duty on aircraft entirely to duty in airports and to allocate $3,500,000 for electronic detection devices. After two aircraft belonging to Pacific Southwest Airlines were hijacked within two days of each other in July 1972, a presidential directive ordered security inspection of all passengers and cabin luggage on East and West Coast commuter lines.[34] Two hijackings to Cuba within a period of twelve days in the late autumn of 1972, in which one airline employee was killed, five other persons injured, and $2,000,000 extorted from one of the two carriers involved, resulted in the adoption of the present program of 100 percent screening of boarding passengers and mandatory inspection of cabin luggage which became effective on January 5, 1973.[35] All airports were also ordered to provide armed guards at all boarding gates after February 6, 1973.[36] Air-

---

[33]N.Y. Times, Aug. 19, 1972, 1:6; Aug, 20, 24:1. He was convicted on a charge of aircraft hijacking and sentenced to 30 years imprisonment. Department of Justice, Criminal Division, Hijacking Statistics, May 1973.

[34]White House *Press Release,* July 7, 1972. *See also,* 37 Fed. Reg. 5689 (Mar. 18, 1972).

[35]N.Y. Times, Dec. 6, 1972, 77:1. This screening includes visitors accompanying or meeting passengers; some carriers and airports, however, refuse to allow visitors in the boarding areas.

[36]37 Fed. Reg., 25934 (Dec. 16, 1972), 14 C.F.R. §§107.1, 107.4. The deadline was extended by court order to Feb. 16. Wall Street Journal, Feb. 6, 1973. The Airport Operators Council International unsuccessfully sought a preliminary injunction to restrain the enforcement of this order on Feb. 16. Airport Operators Council International v. Shaffer, 354 F.Supp. 79 (D.D.C. 1973). The evolution of these security measures is summarized in a speech of May 18, 1973, by Lt. Gen. Benjamin O. Davis, Jr., Asst. Secretary of Transportation for Environment, Safety, and Consumer Affairs. Department of Transportation News, 28-DOT-73.

ports and carriers which have failed to meet these security requirements have been subject to civil fines and the attendant unwel-
come publicity.[37] The United States probably now has the strict-
est security measures for deterrence and control of hijacking of
any country. It should be observed, however, that other countries
engaged in major air transport also subject passengers to search.[38]
Some states, e.g. Israel and Ethiopia, have for a number of years
made a practice of stationing security guards on their aircraft.
That ground security controls have not been strictly observed or
even instituted in some states is evident, however, in a number of
instances of hijacking of aircraft by force of arms or in such
episodes as the Lod Airport massacre.[39]

A number of factors have contributed to the slowness of state
response to the need for vigorous measures to control aircraft hijacking and to the somewhat haphazard character of that response.
There is an obvious quantitative factor to be reckoned with in
any assessment of the incidence of aircraft hijacking. For example,
in 1971 the world's scheduled airlines had the following international and domestic traffic record:

Passengers carried	325,000,000
Passengers kilometers flown	402,000,000,000 km.
Freight-tons flown	11,000,000,000 km.
Mail-tons flown	2,440,000,000 km.[40]

Worldwide in 1971, there were 48 successful international and

[37]Four airports which failed to inform the Federal Aviation Administration by Jan.
6, 1973 about their plans for providing armed guards were fined $1000 a day until
they supplied the necessary data. N.Y. Times, Jan. 10, 1973, 81:6. Two carriers which
allowed a U.S. Senator to board their aircraft without submitting to electronic surveillance or a search of his hand luggage were fined $500 each. Newsweek, May 7,
1973. An airport which allowed two gates to be opened and unguarded and otherwise failed to carry out the security plan which it had filed with the Federal Aviation Administration was fined $1000. Wall Street Journal, June 6, 1973, 32:2.
[38]The International Civil Aviation Organization adopted Resolution A17-10 at the
Extraordinary Assembly, June 1970, recommending certain security measures of a
general nature. 9 ILM 1278, 1281-83 (1970).
[39]*E.g.* N.Y. Times, May 10, 1972, 1:1 (seizure of Belgian aircraft en route from
Vienna to Tel Aviv).
[40]*The State of the Air Transport Industry. 1972, Annual Report* by Knut Hammar-
skjöld, Director General, International Air Transport Association, for the 28th
Annual General Meeting, London, Sept. 25-27, 1972, at 8.

domestic hijackings of aircraft which carried some 2343 passengers and crew. In 1972 U.S. scheduled carriers made 5,046,438 revenue aircraft departures, logging 2,375,876,000 revenue miles.[41] In this same year, there were 30 successful international and domestic hijackings of flights originating in the United States. Adding 20 attempted hijackings to this figure, the total of endangered flights originating in the United States came to 50. It must be concluded that the risk factor is not impressive.

Another consideration is the economic factor. The air transport industry, whether privately or publicly owned and operated, is not marked by spectacular returns on the investment. The Director General of he International Air Transport Association in his Annual Report for 1972 described 1971 as a year of "generally unsatisfactory performance," noting that scheduled traffic on a worldwide basis increased by only half the rate of growth in 1970 and by only one third the rate of growth of the preceding five years.[42] The vice president of Southern Airways, the carrier which was the last victim of a hijacking from the United States in 1972, commenting on the loss of $2,000,000 extorted by the three hijackers before the aircraft was forced to make a final foray to Cuba, said that the $2,000,000 ". . . if not returned, will exceed our profit for 1972, and this is the first time in 4 or 5 years that we have been in a profitable position."[43] It may be added that as of August 31, 1973, Cuba had not returned the carrier's money. If the air transport industry is not markedly profitable, it follows that the economic factor will weigh heavily in regard to reaction to hijacking. A carrier's foothold in a given geographical area

[41]*Annual Report 1972*, Air Transport Assoc. of America 24 (1973).

[42]P. 4, *supra* note 40.

[43]*The Administration's Emergency Anti-Hijacking Regulations, Hearings on S. 39, before the Subcomm on Aviation of the Senate Comm. on Commerce*, 93rd Cong., 1st Sess., ser. 93-1, at 29 (1973) (hereinafter cited as *Hearings*). The three hijackers who were wanted on various criminal charges seemed uncertain as to their destination, forcing the aircraft, a DC 9, to fly to Jackson, Miss., Detroit, Cleveland, Toronto, Lexington, Ky., Chattanooga, Havana, Orlando, Fla., and back to Havana. The caper lasted for 29 hours in the course of which the hijackers threatened to destroy the Atomic Energy Commission's installation at Oak Ridge, Tenn., by crashing the aircraft into it. The FBI shot out the tires as the aircraft left Orlando, which action contributed to a hair-raising landing in Havana. N.Y. Times, Nov. 12, 1972, 1:1; Herald Traveler (Boston), Nov. 14, 1972, 1:3.

might be too valuable a franchise to be jeopardized by demanding rigorous response by the carrier's state of registration to occasional hijackings in the area.[44]

The political factor must also be considered in an analysis of state response to the incidence of hijacking. In the United States, for example, the federal government has been reluctant for historical reasons of federal-state relations to assert criminal jurisdiction over air transport. Theft of an aircraft in interstate commerce only became a federal offense in 1945,[45] while commission of an act of violence in a U.S. aircraft flying over the high seas became a federal offense in 1952.[46] The Nixon Administration's policy of "shared responsibility" between the federal government and state and local governments affected the proposed legislation for the implementation of the 1970 Hague Convention, and the 1971 Convention for the Suppression of Unlawful Acts against the Safety of Civil Aviation (Montreal Convention).[47] This legislation passed both Houses of Congress at the end of the session in 1972 but lost in Conference Committee because of failure to resolve the issue of whether airport security measures should be the responsibility of the federal government, as the Senate preferred, or be ". . . shared by the Federal Government, the airlines, the airports, and local law-enforcement personnel," as the House, following the Administration view, preferred.[48] The Senate's 1972 proposal including the provision for a federal air transportation security program was reintroduced in the Senate on January 3, 1973 and received its approval on February 21.[49] This bill was sent to the House Committee on Interstate and Foreign Commerce on February 22 where it remained, as of August 31, 1973.

In retrospect, the international reaction to the menace of air-

[44]*E.G.*, Lufthansa's payment of $5,000,000 to the PFLP in South Yemen in February 1972. *Cited supra* note 23.

[45]18 U.S.C. §2312. *See*, McBoyle v. United States, 1930 *Av. Rept.* 99; 1931 *Av. Rept.* 27.

[46]66 Stat. 589 (1952); 18 U.S.C. §7(5). *See*, United States v. Cordova, 89 F.Supp. 298 (E.D.N.Y. 1950).

[47]TIAS 7570; 66 *A.J.I.L.* 455 (1972); 10 *I.L.M.* 1151 (1971).

[48]*Hearings, supra* note 43 at 77 U.S. H.R. Conf. Rep. No. 92-1599, 92nd Cong., 2nd Sess. (1972).

[49]S. 39, 93rd Cong., 1st Sess. (1973).

craft hijacking seems to have been as deliberate as that of the United States. Until 1969 when hijackings abroad exceeded those originating in the United States, the offense at times seemed to be treated as a peculiar manifestation of the strained relations obtaining between the United States and Cuba.[50] The PFLP's hijacking spree in September 1970, however, created a sense of urgency about the need for international measures to control the offense which resulted in the speedy conclusion of the Hague Convention in December and its entry into force a year after these incidents. The absence of this sense of urgency had been evident in the six years which elapsed before the 1963 Convention on Offenses and Certain Other Acts Committed on Board Aircraft (Tokyo Convention) went into force,[51] and, to some extent, it may explain the 15 months which passed between the conclusion of the 1971 Montreal Convention and its coming into force.

The political factor comprehends the condition of relations between states, but it also involves another matter of great complexity, one which thrusts to basic beliefs about human rights and self-determination of peoples. This is the problem of political motive: nationals of Eastern European states seeking political asylum in Austria, Denmark, or the Federal Republic of Germany; the PFLP acting on behalf of Palestinian refugees and displaced persons; Eritreans seeking independence from Ethiopia; Angolans seeking independence from Portugal. A person seeking political asylum may act with violence, as happened, for example, in 1972 when ten Czech nationals killed the pilot and wounded the copilot in the course of hijacking an aircraft to the Federal Republic of Germany,[52] although violence has occurred rather infrequently in this context. On the other hand, the members of

---

[50]Comparison of hijackings originating in U.S. and abroad:

Year	United States	Abroad
1968	20	15
1969	37	51
1970	23	60
1971	23	25
1972	28	28

[51]20 UST 2941; TIAS 6768; 58 *A.J.I.L.* 566 (1964).
[52]N.Y. Times, June 9, 1972, 2:4.

the political "fronts" have adopted violence as a method of action; moreover, their numerous victims are usually travelers in no way associated with the cause allegedly so advanced. In the situation involving an individual's search for political asylum, the asylum state has a hard decision to make about the disposition of the hijacker, particularly if such a state is a party to the Hague Convention and/or the 1951 Convention Relating to the Status of Refugees.[53] It is, however, an internal decision with international ramifications. In the second situation, given the present climate of international opinion, "wars of national liberation" serve as an excuse for, as well as the genuine rationale of political hijackings, and reaction in the form of condemnation or prosecution of the perpetrators is inhibited in many states by official sympathy for the cause of liberation or by a realistic appreciation of the presence in the country of supporters of self-styled political fronts. This dilemma of motive was clearly posed in 1972 in the UN General Assembly's consideration of measures to prevent international terrorism.[54] As far as aircraft hijacking is concerned, as well as with regard to attacks upon internationally protected persons and acts of terrorism generally, the political motive is an aspect of the political factor which is basic to any analysis of deterrence or methods of control of these offenses.

HIJACKING LAWS AND THEIR ENFORCEMENT

The United States and 21 other nations have specific laws dealing with aircraft hijacking.[55] A number of other countries consider that the provisions of their penal codes are sufficiently

---

[53]189 UNTS 150; modified by the 1967 Protocol, 19 UST 6223, TIAS 6577.

[54]*See* UN General Assembly, "Measures to Prevent International Terrorism," A/C.6/418 (Nov. 2, 1972). *See also,* UN General Assembly, Secretariat, Compilation of Relevant Views Expressed in the Course of the General Debate at the General Assembly, A/C.6/L.867, Nov. 8, 1972/Corr. 1/Corr. 2; Summary of records of the 24 meetings of the Sixth Committee on the terrorism issue, A/C.6/SR.1355-1390 (Nov. 14, 1972-Dec. 15, 1972).

[55]Argentina, Australia, Brazil, Canada, Cuba, Federal Republic of Germany, France, Israel, Japan, Lesotho, Mexico, Netherlands, Norway, Portugal, Rwanda, South Africa, Soviet Union, Spain, Sweden, Switzerland, and United Kingdom.

comprehensive to permit them to prosecute hijackers.[56] But it is one thing to enact laws and another to enforce them. The United States record shows that 75 hijackers have been taken into custody since 1961. Fifty-six of these persons were arrested following domestic hijackings; 19 returned to the United States, either voluntarily or by deportation, following successful international hijackings. In 65 criminal proceedings, 48 hijackers were convicted. Seven hijackers, including two accomplices to the offense, have been acquitted, three on a plea of insanity or of lack of responsibility at the time of the offense. Seven persons have been found incompetent to stand trial. Federal charges were dismissed in 10 cases. Fifteen hijackers have been committed to state mental institutions. In addition to aircraft piracy, hijackers have also been charged in the United States with such offenses as kidnapping, interference with flight crew, assault, and carrying weapons illegally aboard aircraft;[57] their convictions on lesser charges have often resulted from plea bargaining.

Given the variety of charges on which hijackers have been convicted and the variety of judges and juries which have heard these cases, it is not surprising that variety has marked the sentences handed down in these cases. The death penalty has not been sought by the Department of Justice in any hijacking case;[58] however, the trend in sentencing has been toward increasing severity, especially since the beginning of 1972. Four persons have been sentenced to life imprisonment on conviction of aircraft piracy and a fifth, on conviction of aiding and abetting aircraft piracy. Thirty-five persons have been sentenced to 10 or more

---

[56]It has been pointed out with respect to Austria, for example, that the acts listed in Art. 1 of the Hague Convention are comprehended in §98 of the Penal Code and that universal jurisdiction (Art. 4(2) Hague Convention) has always been recognized in Austria. R. Grassberger, *Prise de position de l'Autriche*, in R.D.P.C., 350, *cited supra* note 25. For an analysis of selected laws concerning hijacking, *see* the series of articles comprising a study entitled, "Attentats contre la navigation aérienne," in R.D.P.C., *See also*, the brief accounts of relevant legislation in *Enquête de la commission diplomatique*, Rev. Générale de l'air et de l'espace, 34th year (1971), no. 3, at 327-37. (hereinafter cited as R.G.A.E.)

[57]Based upon Federal Aviation Administration, Office of Air Transportation Security, Legal Status of Hijackers—Summarization (1 May 1973).

[58]*Hearings, supra* note 43 at 112.

years of imprisonment on federal, or occasionally state, charges arising out of hijackings. Eight juveniles have been sentenced under the Youth Corrections Act (18 U.S.C. §5032).

Data regarding the prosecution and sentencing of persons charged with aircraft hijacking in countries other than the United States are not readily available. However, some indication of the scope of efforts at this method of control of the offense follows. It may be estimated that some 537 persons have actively participated in the hijacking, internationally or domestically, of aircraft registered in states other than the United States since 1961. Some 97 persons have been arrested in the state of first landing or in their own state where the hijacking was domestic. Twenty-four hijackers have been killed by police or security agents, and four have committed suicide. Forty-one persons have been returned to the state of departure from their foreign destinations, 38 by deportation, one by extradition (Cuba to Mexico in 1961), and two voluntarily. Extradition has been denied in seven instances and is pending in one.[59]

Criminal proceedings against persons accused of hijacking and related offenses have resulted in convictions in 25 states and one

---

[59]Extradition of hijackers has been denied by Yugoslavia to Algeria, Denmark to Poland (2), Federal Republic of Germany to Czechoslovakia, Cuba to Mexico (2), and North Korea to Japan. In the case of P. and A. Brazinskas who hijacked a Soviet aircraft on Oct. 15, 1970 from the Soviet Union to Turkey, killing one crew member and wounding another in the course of the flight, a superior court ordered the release of the hijackers on the political offense defense. The Supreme Court of Turkey reversed this decision on March 9, 1971, on the ground that hijacking was a criminal act, hence that extradition could be granted. The final decision as to surrender of the accused was at the discretion of the government. N.Y. Times, Oct. 15, 1970, 1:5; Nov. 22, 24:1; March 9, 1971, 15:3. Where an Algerian aircraft was hijacked to Yugoslavia, after being refused landing in Albania on Aug. 31, 1970, the court of first instance at Dubrovnik concluded that extradition would be in order. The Supreme Court reversed apparently on defendants' argument that the hijacking was a continuous act, part of which took place in Yugoslavia, hence that the Yugoslav court had jurisdiction to try the offenders. The trial court gave them suspended sentences. T. Vasiljevic, *Mesures à l'égard de la piraterie aérienne en Yougoslavie (état actuel)*, in R.D.P.C., 463-66, *cited supra* note 25. Apparently, the hijackers returned to Algeria where they were prosecuted, convicted, and sentenced to 6 to 12 years imprisonment.

acquittal.[60] Five persons have been committed to mental institutions. Sentences have varied as much as the charges in these cases. The death penalty was exacted in three instances (USSR 2, Philippines 1) and life imprisonment in four (Canada, Egypt, Israel 2).[61] Other severe sentences have ranged from 25 years (Poland) down to ten years (Egypt). A successful domestic hijacking in Argentina brought the perpetrator a six year sentence; a successful international hijacking of an aircraft of U.S. registration from Mexico to Argentina resulted in sentences of five and three years, respectively, for the two hijackers, one of whom was a U.S. national and the other, a Guatemalan national.[62] In general, sentences have ranged between two and seven years with some as low as eight months.[63]

---

[60]Number of hijackers convicted (international and domestic hijackings only): Algeria 3, Argentina 3, Austria 3, Brazil 4, Bulgaria 8, Canada 2, Denmark 1, Egypt 3, Federal Republic of Germany 13, France 5, German Democratic Republic 1, Greece 1, Israel 2, Italy 1, Lebanon 1, Mexico 1, Philippines 1, Poland 3, Spain 1, Sweden 1, Switzerland 3, Turkey 2, USSR 6, Uruguay 1, Yugoslavia 3.

[61]Following the first successful international hijacking of a Canadian aircraft, the hijacker, who forced the aircraft to return to Canada after a foray into the United States, was convicted and sentenced in April 1972 to life imprisonment on four charges involving hijackings, 14 years on extortion, and 10 years on illegal possession of firearms and explosives. It was noted in the local press that he would be eligible for parole in 1979. Calgary (Alberta) Herald, April 12, 1972, 1:5, April 13, 4:1.

[62]Re Jurado Albornoz, 143 Revista Argentina La Ley 3 (Sept. 8, 1971); Re Jackson and Sanchez Archila, Fed. Court, La Plata, Dec. 15, 1971 (unpub. decision).

[63]E.G., An Austrian court sentenced two Polish hijackers, R. Zelotucho and W. Szymankiewicz, to two years and two years and three months, respectively, in March 1970 after they pleaded guilty to charges of blackmail, inhibiting personal freedom, and illegal possession of firearms. Frankfurter Allgemeine Zeitung, March 12, 1970, at 9. In the first case arising under the new hijacking law in the Federal Republic of Germany, two Czech hijackers, A. Lerch and K. Dolezel, were sentenced to seven years on July 31, 1972. Die Welt, Aug. 1, 1972, at 1. Christian Belon who hijacked a United States aircraft to Lebanon in January 1970, was sentenced to nine months imprisonment by Lebanon on Oct. 30, 1970. Upon his return to France, he was prosecuted in the same factual situation on a charge of illegal possession of firearms. He was sentenced to eight months on Feb. 1, 1971. *See,* note by M. de Juglart and E. du Pontavice, La Semaine, Juridique, 46th year, no. 7, item 16994 (Feb. 16, 1972). Rafael Minichiello who hijacked a Trans World Airlines aircraft from Los Angeles to Rome on Oct. 31, 1969, and who was characterized at his trial as a "romantic pirate," was sentenced Nov. 11, 1970 to seven and one half years on charges of kidnapping, violence to a public official, and illegal possession of firearms, and fined $580. The Court of Appeals of Rome reduced the sentence to three and

As a method of control of aircraft hijacking, the obvious defect of prosecution is the necessity of obtaining custody of the accused, for *in absentia* proceedings, where legally acceptable, are hardly a substitute. A total of 198 persons have been actively involved in the hijacking of aircraft in or from the United States between May 1, 1961 and August 31, 1973. One hundred and twenty-seven of these hijackers are at large abroad, and one is presumably still at large in the United States. Of the estimated 537 persons who have hijacked aircraft registered in states other than the United States between July 3, 1961 and August 31, 1973, at a guess, some 400 are still at large. As suggested earlier, aircraft hijackers act for a variety of motives: private political views, membership of political fronts, family difficulties, psychological aberrations, and escape from criminal proceedings or from prison. Many of the hijackers at large are fleeing from criminal charges, as in the last two successful international hijackings of U.S. aircraft, both to Cuba. The hijacking of October 29, 1972, was done by four men who were wanted for armed robbery including the murders of a bank manager and a policeman and who subsequently killed an airline ticket agent and wounded another airline employee in the course of the hijacking.[64] The second hijacking, which took place on November 10, 1972, involved three men, two of them fleeing from charges of rape and one escaping from prison.[65] These persons are appropriate subjects for extradition within the terms of the 1904 Extradition Treaty with Cuba (33 *Stat.* 2265). The 60 states bound by the Hague Convention, assuming that they have observed the requirements of Articles 2 and 4, now have the alternative under Article 7 of extradition or submission of the hijacker "without exception whatsoever" to prosecution in accordance with their own legal procedures. Such prosecution, whether resulting in conviction or acquittal, does not obviate the subsequent grant of political asylum to a hijacker. Nor does such prose-

---

one half years which combined with his 18 months in jail before and during trial and a two-year general amnesty decree enabled him to be released on May 1, 1971. *See*, M. Pisani, *"Le déroutement d'avions et la loi italienne T.F.,"* R.D.P.C., 391 *supra* note 25.

[64]N.Y. Times, Oct. 30, 1972, 1:2.

[65]*Ibid.*, Nov. 12, 1972, 1:1.

cution violate the commitments of states party to the Convention or the Protocol Relating to the Status of Refugees. There is little justification for the "hijack haven" in the contemporary development of international penal law, to which national and international efforts to control aircraft hijacking have contributed appreciably.

SOME LEGAL PROBLEMS OF HIJACKING: UNITED STATES EXPERIENCE

The enforcement of the United States hijacking law and the regulations implementing it has produced a number of challenges in federal and state courts. The legality of the use of the Federal Aviation Administration's psychological profile as a means of distinguishing potential hijackers, of submission to electronic surveillance, and of the search of person and luggage, has been widely questioned, especially where a search has resulted in the prosecution of the would-be traveler on a charge unrelated to aircraft hijacking, usually the illegal possession of narcotics. The trend of the decisional law seems to be in support of the use of these security measures. Carrier liability under Article 17 of the Warsaw Convention[66] as modified by the Montreal (IATA) Agreement for personal injuries sustained during a hijacking has been upheld.[67] In *Pan American World Airways, Inc. v. The Aetna Casualty and Surety Co.,*[68] the issue was whether the loss of the carrier's Boeing 747, destroyed by hijackers in Cairo on September 6, 1970, and amounting to $24,288,759, would be covered by the all-risk insurers or by the war-risk insurers. The District Court for the Southern District of New York held that the all-risk insurers were liable for plaintiff's entire loss on the theory that the destruction of the aircraft arose out of an improvised action by members of the Popular Front for the Liberation of Palestine rather than a war, rebellion, or other warlike conduct directed by a "military . . . or usurped power."[69]

---

[66]49 Stat. 300; 137 LNTS 11.
[67]Husserl v. Swiss Air Transport Co., Ltd., 351 F.Supp. 702 (S.D.N.Y. 1972), affd. per curiam, 485 F.2d 1240 (2d Cir. 1973).
[68]71 Civ. 1118 (S.D.N.Y. 1973).
[69]*Ibid.,* pp. 89-94.

AIRCRAFT HIJACKING: WHAT IS TO BE DONE?

As the foregoing discussion suggests, much has been done by some states unilaterally and by a number of states in concerted efforts through multilateral conventions to bring the international offense of aircraft hijacking under control. That much remains to be done is a conclusion which is by no means disproved by the marked worldwide decline in the incidence of hijacking during the first eight months of 1973. Indeed, this decline could presage a return to the condition of complacency which obtained before 1968. That this tendency is surfacing in the United States was evidenced by a report in June to the effect that the Federal Aviation Administration was considering the relaxation of its 100 percent security screening program in response to an increasing number of travelers' complaints, ranging from pleas of personal inconvenience to charges of unconstitutionality.[70] The report may have been a trial balloon, however, for soon thereafter, following a meeting of the security officers of some 20 scheduled airlines and security representatives of the Federal Aviation Administration, the chairman of the Air Transport Association announced that the 100 percent security screening program would continue.[71] It was also indicated that efforts were being made by airlines to develop new electronic devices which would facilitate the search program, presumably with a minimum of inconvenience to all.[72]

Inconvenience, expense, infringement of individual rights (all accruing to the traveler) are among factors inhibiting deterrence of hijacking through strict preboarding security programs at the national level. At the international level, other considerations such as the utility of hijacking as a method of exacerbating relations between states, deference to acts sought to be legitimized by

---

[70]Wall Street Journal, June 6, 1973, 32:1: Christian Science Monitor, June 8, 1973, 1:1. The report received unfavorable editorial response in such papers as the N.Y. Times, June 10, 1973, §4, 14:2; Wall Street Journal, June 8, 1973; Herald Advertiser (Boston), June 13, 1973, 46:1; Chicago Tribune, June 9, 1973.

[71]Air Transport Association, *Press Release* No. 49, June 19, 1973. The F.A.A. has affirmed this statement. N.Y. Times, Aug. 11, 1973, 38:1.

[72]In a full page advertisement in the N.Y. Times, Trans World Airlines announced a new x-ray device which could inspect luggage as rapidly as the magnetometer inspected the passenger. June 28, 1973, at 15.

the label of "wars of national liberation," commitment to the concept of right to political asylum, all inhibit the development of international legislation looking to the control of hijacking. There are three conventions which deal with this offense: The Tokyo Convention, which binds 64 states, emphasizes the facilitation of the resumption of a hijacked flight. The Hague Convention, which binds 60 states, is punitive in focus, directing states to extradite offenders or to submit them to prosecution. The Montreal Convention, which binds 40 states, is concerned with such acts as sabotage of aircraft and attacks upon air navigational facilities and also directs states party to extradite offenders or to submit them to prosecution.[73] Only Tokyo has wide support, if 64 states can be so regarded. Of the three principal states which have acquired the reputation of being "hijack havens" because hijackers can remain in them with impunity, if not with approbation, *i.e.* Cuba, Algeria, and Libya, only Libya is bound by any of these conventions (Tokyo Convention).

The next stage in the development of the antihijacking treaty network has been seen as a multilateral convention designed to enforce the other three. The United States and Canada have been strong proponents of such a "sanctions convention" and drafted one in April 1971, which was not acted upon by the International Civil Aviation Organization (ICAO). A meeting of the Special Subcommittee of the ICAO Legal Committee was convened in Washington in September 1972, under a sense of urgency sparked by the IFALPA boycott of June and reinforced by the massacre of the Israeli athletes at Munich on September 5, for the purpose of considering such a sanctions convention.[74] The Subcommittee prepared some draft articles providing, *inter alia,* for a commission of experts to hear complaints against states that detained aircraft or failed to prosecute or extradite hijackers. The punitive features of the draft, which were proposed by the United States, Canada, the Netherlands, and the United Kingdom, provided that where a state had been found to have threatened the safety of civil

---

[73]ICAO figures as to current ratifications and accessions to the conventions from Department of State Treaty Division (as of August 31, 1973).

[74]*ICAO Special Subcommittee Meets at Washington,* 67 Dept. State Bull. 357 (1972).

aviation by such conduct and refused to remove the threat as recommended by the commission of experts, its rights under the 1944 Convention on International Civil Aviation (Chicago Convention) and the 1944 International Air Services Transit Agreement[75] as well as bilateral air services agreements would be suspended.[76] At best, the meeting afforded an opportunity for airing diverse views on the subject for consideration by the Legal Committee.

The meeting in January 1973 of the ICAO Legal Committee resulted in some indication of the scope and limits of any prospective sanctions convention and in several proposals for future consideration. Members agreed in principle that a sanctions convention should have no binding effect with respect to nontreaty states, although recommendations could be made to such states respecting conduct regarded as violative of the convention. If the Chicago Convention were to be amended by an instrument comprising the sanctions provisions, members agreed that such instrument could provide that sanctions be taken against states party to it by organs other than those of the United Nations and in cases other than those covered by the Chicago Convention.[77]

In regard to specific proposals for some kinds of international enforcement measures, there was a division between those states that favored an independent sanctions convention and those that preferred to amend the Chicago Convention for this purpose. The delegates of Denmark, Finland, Norway, and Sweden submitted a proposal (Nordic proposal) providing that a contracting state which considered that another state had detained aircraft and the persons on board, or had not taken measures to assure control of the aircraft to its commander, or had failed to take a violator into custody, or to extradite him or submit such person to prosecution could request that the ICAO Council be convened to deal with the complaint. The Council could inquire into the factual situation or, if authorized, could appoint a commission of experts to do so. If the Council found that the complaint was

---

[75]61 Stat. 1180, 15 UNTS 295; 59 Stat. 1693; 84 UNTS 389.

[76]67 Dept. State Bull. 357, 361-64 (1972). ICAO. Report, Special Subcommittee on the Council Resolution of 19 June 1972, LC/SC CR (1972)-Report 15/9 /72.

[77]ICAO, Secretariat Note, LC/Working Draft No. 833. Rev., 22/1/73, at 3.

valid, it could recommend that the state concerned ". . . take appropriate measures to remedy the situation."[78] If the offending state did not comply with the recommendation or if the Council failed to arrive at a decision on the complaint, any state party to this convention could request the Secretary-General of ICAO to convene a conference of the other states party, including the state concerned, which would be authorized to ". . . take appropriate measures to remedy the situation."[79] The President of the ICAO Council could offer good offices or invite the states party to suggest other remedies.

The Nordic proposal represented an obvious compromise, reflecting aspects of the September draft, which left all sanctions to be determined by ICAO organs on an *ad hoc* basis. The proceeding would involve "all deliberate speed;" but on the other hand, it could be argued that any proceeding would be an improvement over the current situation and that the Nordic proposal was realistic for the times.

The Soviet Union suggested another form of sanction (which it had also raised at the September meeting), *i.e.* that the Hague Convention be amended to make extradition to the state of registration of a hijacked aircraft mandatory except where the offender was a national of the state having custody of him.[80] This proposal was hardly realistic in the light of the firm commitment of many states to right of political asylum and the common provision in extradition conventions making an exception for political offenses.[81]

The alternative thrust in dealing with the problem of enforcement was to amend the Chicago Convention, thereby reaching its membership of 125 states which are bound by a commitment to abide by this Convention and its amendments or suffer the conse-

---

[78]ICAO, Proposal by the Delegations of Denmark, Finland, Norway, and Sweden, LC/Working Draft No. 831. Rev. 24/1/73, at 3.

[79]*Ibid.*

[80]ICAO, Draft Protocol to the Convention for the Suppression of Unlawful Seizure of Aircraft Signed at The Hague on 16 December 1970, LC/Working Draft No. 826, 9/1/73.

[81]*See,* for example, Art. 129, Constitution of USSR (1936). *See also,* Art. 83, Criminal Code of the RSFSR, in H.J. Berman, Soviet Criminal Law and Procedure, 184 (1966).

quences. The United Kingdom-Swiss proposal suggested a new chapter in the Chicago Convention which would comprehend the offenses listed in Article 1 of the Hague and of the Montreal Conventions and the commitment to facilitate resumption of interrupted flight provided in Article 11 of the Tokyo Convention. France submitted that the text of the Hague Convention should be incorporated into the Chicago Convention.[82] Both of these proposals would face the necessity of approval by two thirds of the states parties to the Chicago Convention, which would amount to a substantially greater number of states than were bound by any one of the three hijacking conventions. The meeting concluded with the recommendation that the United Kingdom-Swiss and French proposals be considered at an extraordinary session of the ICAO Assembly to be held in the summer of 1973 and that the Nordic and USSR proposals be submitted to a diplomatic conference to be held at the same time.[83]

There are alternatives to sanctions against hijack havens based upon multilateral conventions or amendments to the Chicago Convention. Bilateral agreements such as those which the United States and Canada have with Cuba could be used more widely to deter hijackers by eliminating specific havens, assuming that such agreements would be enforced by the parties. The 1973 agreement between the United States and Cuba, it may be noted, contained an exception for ". . . persons . . . being sought for strictly political reasons . . . [who] were in real and imminent danger of death without a viable alternative for leaving the country, provided there was no financial extortion or physical injury to the members of the crew, passengers, or other persons in connection with the hijacking."[84]

---

[82]United Kingdom-Swiss Proposal, LC/Working Draft No. 829; French Proposal, LC/Working Draft No. 821, 17/1/73.

[83]ICAO, Proposal by the Austrian Delegation, LC/Working Draft No. 839, 27/1/73. The two meetings were scheduled to be held in Rome from Aug. 28 through Sept. 21, 1973, 28 ICAO Bull. 13 (April 1973).

[84]"Memorandum of Understanding on the Hijacking of Aircraft and Vessels," Dept. State *Press Release* No. 35, at 2 (Feb. 15, 1973); TIAS 7579; 67 AJIL 619 (1973); 12 ILM 370 (1973). This is an interesting example of an international agreement between two states which do not have diplomatic relations. The agreement reflects

Another method of control is by unilateral state action, although this one would only be available to a country with massive air transport, and it could backfire readily. For example, the U.S. Antihijacking Act of 1973, now before Congress, contains a provision for the suspension of air services between the United States and any state which the President has found to be ". . . acting in a manner inconsistent with" the Hague Convention or to be serving ". . . as a base of operations or training or as a sanctuary which arms, aids or abets in any way terrorist organizations which knowingly use the illegal seizure of aircraft or the threat thereof as an instrument of policy . . ."[85] Moreover, this Act would require that any state maintaining air services with the United States would have to conform to the security measures described in Resolution A17-10 of the 17th Assembly of ICAO, or to such measures as might subsequently be established under the Chicago Convention, or face the imposition of conditions upon its air services to this country or suspension thereof.[86]

That control of aircraft hijacking is a public responsibility would seem self-evident. But where states have failed to act or have procrastinated in adopting adequate repressive measures, IFALPA has demonstrated that private pressure group tactics may supply the incentive to activity. The worldwide 24-hour boycott of civil air transportation on June 19, 1972, was prompted by a record of 34 successful international and domestic hijackings from January 1, 1972, through the first week in June. The boycott was directed against those countries which had failed to implement the three hijacking conventions, related UN resolutions, or which did not extradite or punish hijackers and saboteurs. A specific demand was directed to Algeria to extradite or punish the two hi-

---

the Cuban hijacking law, Ley No. 1226, Sept. 16, 1969, 8 ILM 1175 (1969). The Soviet Union is reported to have a bilateral agreement with Afghanistan providing for mandatory extradition of hijackers. ICAO, Report, Special Subcommittee on the Council Resolution of 19 June 1972, at 33, LC/SC CR (1972) Report, 15/9/72.

[85]S. 39, 93rd Cong., 1st Sess. (1973) at 4-5.

[86]*Ibid.,* 5-7. This provision and the provision regarding hijack havens were also included in S. 2280, 92nd Cong., 2nd Sess. (1972) which failed to receive approval of a Conference Committee in 1972. *See,* Report of Senate Comm. on Commerce on S. 2280, S. Rep. No. 92-1012, 92nd Cong., 2nd Sess. (1972).

jackers of a U.S. aircraft hijacked to that country on June 3.[87] Essentially, IFALPA was urging speedy attention to a sanctions convention.[88] According to reports, the boycott was more extensive and more effective in its impact on international air transportation than could have been anticipated. Service was substantially curtailed in most of Europe, in several Middle Eastern and African states, in much of Latin America, and in Canada.[89] In the United States the Air Transport Association obtained a temporary restraining order from the Court of Appeals for the District of Columbia Circuit, prohibiting the Air Line Pilots Association from participating in the strike; however, the pilots of some carriers did join.[90]

In the last analysis, what is to be done depends upon the willingness of states, acting singly and in concert, to build upon what has been done. The three hijacking conventions are the first stage in the development of an international regime for the control of aircraft hijacking. They should be as widely accepted as the Chicago Convention; the United Nations should make vigorous efforts to urge their acceptance. The next stage should be a convention establishing minimum specific standards for airport security screening programs. After that, should come a sanctions convention and in tandem with it should be plans for the establishment of an international system for the prosecution and punishment of hijackers as well as other violators of international penal laws. In the perspective of time, the efforts to control hijacking have had more success than might have been expected for a matter which is fraught with complex national and international political considerations. It remains to be seen whether the momentum of the past four years will be sustained to the point of completing the international legal network of controls over aircraft hijacking.

---

[87]IFALPA, *Press Release* 2/5/2 CCJ/NMM, June 8, 1972.

[88]IFALPA, *Press Release,* Joint Statement by IFALPA and ITF, June 19, 1972.

[89]N.Y. Times June 20, 1972, 20:2; June 21, 20:4.

[90]*Ibid., June* 19, 1972, 1:8. On appeal, the order was upheld by the Supreme Court.

——— **SECTION 2** ———

INTERNATIONAL SUPPRESSION OF HIJACKING

ANDREW LEE

DURING THE PAST FIVE YEARS, 180 attempts to forcibly seize aircraft have jeopardized the lives of over 9,500 passengers on planes from 70 countries and have rendered no state immune from unlawful seizures of its aircraft. Late in 1968 there was a sudden increase in the number of hijackings. During that year, 27 aircrafts carrying 1,490 passengers were diverted from their scheduled routes by threat or force.[1] During 1969 to 1970, the number of hijacking incidents reached 89 and involved 4,519 passengers. In 1971 there was no decrease in the frequency.

Within the 10 months during 1970 to 1972, 49 persons were killed or wounded in the course of attempted hijackings.[2] Forty-seven lives were lost in a 1970 sabotage incident.[3] Sixty million dollars worth of property damage was suffered in 1970 alone due to destruction of aircrafts.[4] The losses occasioned by diversion of aircraft and crew from commercial service were staggering, and the terror imposed on innocent passengers was, by any measure, intolerable.

In recent years civil aviation has faced increased risks from intentional acts of hijacking and sabotage. These acts not only threaten direct personal injury to passengers and crew, but also, by interrupting communications, changing flight paths and altering landing destinations, strip from the air traveler many of the carefully developed safeguards of the air transport intrastructure.

---

[1]Evans, "Aircraft Hijacking: Its Cause and Cure," 63 *A.J.I.L.*, 695, 698 (1969).
[2]Unofficial Statistics, Department of State, Washington, D.C.
[3]Unofficial Statistics, Department of State, Washington, D.C.
[4]D. Hubbard, *The Skyjacker*, (1970), p. 221.

Hijacking cases are easily categorized as robbery, extortion, guerrilla warfare and escape cases. The great majority of cases belong to the last category,[5] although in the United States seven hijacking incidents were motivated by extortion between January and October of 1972.

Attempts to eliminate hijacking have been frustrated by the attitude of intransigent and irresponsible governments, unwilling to take effective action against and even welcoming hijackers landing in their territory.[6] It is essential not to let up on the effort to force recognition that hijackers, regardless of claimed political motives, offend against the international air transport system as well as against national safety and property interests, and above all a recognition by all nations that to punish such offenders is in their best interests.[7] There can be little doubt that hijacking is a fully developed international offense which can only be controlled by concerted action by states acting both unilaterally and jointly.

It was not until September 11, 1970, after the Palestine Liberation Front's terrorist attacks upon international air transport[8] that the United States undertook a crash program of training skymarshals for duty on board aircraft and in airports. Their usefulness has begun to show, for in the first six months of the current year (January-July, 1972) they have reportedly thwarted four out of five attempted hi-jackings.[9] It is true that although there were still eleven successful hijackings of American aircraft originating in the United States during the same period, the skymarshals program, together with the use of electronic searches, is apparently contributing to a decline in the rate of successful hijacking of aircraft from the U.S.[10]

---

[5]N. Y. Times, June 5, 1970, Col. 2, 38.

[6]Convention, Art. 8.

[7]In February 1972, the U. S. Congress passed an Act imposing a mandatory death penalty on hijackers. However, four months later, the Supreme Court ruled that "the imposition and carrying out of the death in these cases constitutes cruel and unusual punishment in violation of the Eighth and Fourteenth Amendments." See Furman v. Georgia, 408 U.S. 845 (1972).

[8]The Air Transport Report: ". . . . .electronic detection devices have led to the arrest of 273 persons on charges of hijacking, smuggling, and relating offenses, within a sixteen month period." N. Y. Times, June 19, 1971 Col. 8, P. 54.

[9]N. Y. Times, Sept. 12, 1970, Col. 5, P. 11; Sept. 22, Col. 2, P. 1.

[10]Christian Science Monitor, June 15, 1971, Col. 4, P. 8.

The airlines should be encouraged to develop screening procedures which would keep potential hijackers from boarding their aircraft. Preboarding controls should be strengthened by the use of more screening profiles, and use of weapons detection devices should be increased. More international conferences by experts on detection devices and policy coordination should be called.

A convention highlighting the responsibility to the international community of each state to join in the international effort to protect civil aviation would mark a juridical breakthrough and would contribute to the effective prevention of hijacking by providing a practical incentive and rationale for states to act against hijackers seeking their political sympathy.[11]

In the initial stage of drafting The Hague Convention, the United States argued for a mandatory extradition provision.[12] This proposal ran squarely up against the international traditions of political asylum. A compromise was eventually reached in recognition of the asylum tradition by requiring prosecution for the hijacking and leaving extradition optional.[13] It is to be hoped that severe penalties for hijacking would limit refugee hijackings. The incidence of this type of hijacking depends on a number of factors but increasingly severe sentences in states of landing, generated by system interests, are likely to cause such hijackers to look carefully for alternative methods of escape.[14]

A state which does not wish to prosecute or extradite a hijacker might be willing to enforce the criminal judgment rendered against him in another state. The European Convention on the International Validity of Criminal Judgments, concluded by the Council of Europe on May 28, 1970,[15] suggests this direction and has, moreover, far reaching implications for the establishment of a a common system of criminal law within the European community.

Because of its novelty, hijacking *per se* is not a municipal offense in many states; accordingly, the offender must be tried in

[11]37 *J of AIRL. & Com.* p. 190 (1971).

[12]ICAO, LC/SC. SA WD 7 (1969) Also: Report of ICAO Legal Sub-Committee on Unlawful Seizure (1969).

[13]Art. 7, Convention for the Suppression of Unlawful Seizure of Aircraft.

[4]Rein "A Government Perspective" 37 *J. of AIRL. & Com.* 190 (1971).

[15]European T. S. No. 70, (1970).

these jurisdictions for a collateral offense, such as assault, intimidation, kidnapping or theft, etc.[16] If it is unknown over which state a hijacking occurred, or if the offense took place over the high seas, the municipal laws of any particular country would not provide a basis for jurisdiction. The crime therefore could go unpunished.[17] In the United States, for instance, until a series of hijackings caused Congress to amend the Federal Aviation Act in 1961, prosecution was primarily for transporting stolen property in interstate commerce, kidnapping or obstructing commerce by threats or violence.[18]

It is known that recently the Chinese Civil Aeronautics Administration has proposed to submit, through the Ministry of Communication, to the Executive Yuan a draft amending the present Civil Aviation Law and that two new articles are included in the draft:

(1) Article 85:

A person who, by force or threat thereof, or by other unlawful means, seizes an aircraft shall be punished with death, imprisonment for life. An attempt to perform such an act is punishable.

(2) Article 86:

A person who, by force or threat thereof, or by other unlawful means, endangers the safety of an aircraft in flight and air navigation facilities shall be punished with imprisonment for not more than five years, detention, or a fine of not more than 5,000 Yuan and not less than 1,000 Yuan. If the aircraft and its facilities are, as a result, damaged, the offender shall be punished with imprisonment for not less than one year and not more than five years; if the offense results in serious bodily injury to others shall be punished with imprisonment for not less than three years and not more than ten years, and if death results from such an offence the offender shall be punished with death,

---

[16]Mendelsohn "In Flight Crime, The International and Domestic Picture Under the Tokyo Convention," 53 *Va. L. Rev.* 509 (1967).

[17]See Mendelsohn, *supra* note 16, p. 513.

[18]U.S.C., 1201 (1966). Also see United States v. Healy 276 U.S. 75 (1964).

imprisonment for life, or imprisonment for not less than ten years.

The first international legal effort related to hijacking supported welfare and safety interests. The Tokyo Convention of 1963 required signatory states to return hijacked aircraft to the control of their commanders and to facilitate passengers' return to their scheduled destinations. It also established a basis for national jurisdiction over crimes committed aboard aircraft in international airspace.[19]

However, the Tokyo Convention deals with ordinary criminal offences committed on board aircraft. It has a wide scope of application, which includes criminal offenses committed among passengers, such as theft committed on board aircraft of other passengers' properties; it is not limited to the punishment of hijacking. Moreover, the Tokyo Convention does not expressly specify that hijacking is an international crime; it does not provide for compulsory extradition either. Thus, on September 23, 1971, the member states of the ICAO convened again in Montreal, Canada and concluded the Convention for the Suppression of Unlawful Acts Against Safety of Civil Aviation. Article 1 of the Convention sets out the definitions and the necessary elements of the various unlawful acts endangering the safety of civil aviation. Article 3 stipulates that the contracting parties agree to impose severe punishment on the commission of such acts; it also confers jurisdiction over such acts on the domestic law of the contracting states. Above all, article 8 makes crimes endangering the safety of civil aviation extraditable offenses which can be invoked by the contracting states under any extradition treaty existing between the contracting states; and in the absence of an extradition treaty, the contracting states may request extradition on the basis of this convention. The convention further stipulates that if a contracting state refuses to extradite the criminal suspect, it must put him on trial in its own court. If the convention can muster the joint support of all nations, hijackers would not be able to evade the sanction imposed by the various states and hijacking would thus be effectively re-

---

[19]Convention on Offenses and Certain Other Acts Committed on Board Aircraft, Sept. 14, 1963 (1969).

sympathetic to the concept of an international criminal court to strained; if so, it would certainly be a remarkable improvement in the antihijacking effort. According to the information released in Washington, D. C. by UPI on November 1, 1972, when the Montreal Convention for the Suppression of Unlawful Acts Against the Safety of Civil Aviation, was signed, the President of the United States issued a statement which read:

> The government has recently set up an action committee for the suppression of terrorism to ensure full governmental support in the areas of intelligence gathering and coordination in attack on any terrorism.

In fact, it is not sufficient to place the offense of hijacking under national jurisdiction. It should be rather placed under the jurisdiction of an International Criminal Court which would take jurisdiction over such international crimes as hijacking, terrorism and kidnapping of foreign diplomatic personnel.[20]

An international criminal court might well be the catalyst for the emerging international system of criminal law. States must come to grip with the fact that international standards must be applied if antihijacking efforts are to be effective. So long as the power of application rests with national sovereignty, the international community must exert effective pressure against member states to ensure action.

It is true in a way that prosecution of hijackers becomes more complex when the defense of political motive is invoked by the accused. But while the traditional asylum for political motivation should be granted, still the offense for hijacking could be prosecuted and sentenced. Even if the hijacker is genuinely seeking political asylum, he should attempt to find other means of escape before any question of political asylum is considered, and he should suffer a punishment for the hijacking.

This is a far different matter from a freedom seeker who swims to Hongkong at the risk of his own life. The upsurge of hijackings involving political elements has recently recreated an atmosphere

---

[20]League of Nations Document, C. 548, M. 385. See also: United Nations Committee on International Criminal Jurisdiction, Draft Statute for an International Criminal Court, U.N. Doc. No. A/AC 48/4 (1951).

deal with hijackers along the lines of the 1937 Convention.[21] While a draft resolution calling for the setting up of an international criminal court for hijackers failed to be adopted at the 54th, I.L.A. Session on August 24, 1970,[22] two weeks later Operation Abu Thalaat prompted the former Secretary-General of the United Nations to suggest that "all governments pledge themselves to extradite hijackers, irrespective of the nationality or political affiliation, and bring them before an agreed international tribunal."[23]

Most experts agree that in so far as the suppression of hijackings and aircraft terrorism are concerned, we are on the start of a long road, but bringing the hijackers to an international criminal court for justice seems to be the best way of minimizing the hijacking evils.

It is regrettable that both the 1970 Hague Convention for the Suppression of Unlawful Seizure of Aircraft and the 1971 Montreal Convention for the Suppression of Unlawful Acts Against the Safety of Civil Aviation did not provide any status or immunity from jurisdiction for the benefit of the passengers and crew in the state to which the aircraft has been hijacked. This is urgently needed, particularly in the event of an unlawful seizure of an aircraft.[24] Persons disembarking from a hijacked aircraft are sometimes searched and detained, frequently for purely political reasons, but they may also be arrested and subsequently prosecuted for any offense which they allegedly committed in a state to which they had no intention of returning and where they were brought against their will.[25] The 54th Conference of International Law Association, which met at The Hague in 1970, adopted a resolution to be submitted to ICAO and other appropriate organizations

---

[21]Sundberg, Relazione, 17 *Transporti Aerei 5,* 20 (1970).

[22]While there were intense debates among state representatives over the hijacking matter before the 55th session held in N. Y. in July 1972, there was no resolution whatsoever.

[23]Address by U Thant, United Nations 25th Anniversary Program New York City, Sept. 14, 1970, Press Release SC/SM/1333.

[24]R. H. Mankiewicz, "The 1970 Hague Convention." 37 *J. of AIRL. & Comm.,* 208 (1971)Referring to *Annuaire Francais De Droit International,* 524, involving the seizure of passenger's luggage, it was suggested that this rule should be embedded in a general convention relating to facilitation of air transport.

[25]1970 Revue Francais de Droit Aerien 377.

calling attention to the well established rule in customary international law that grants a degree of immunity from local jurisdiction to ships, their crew, passengers and cargo entering a foreign port in distress; this principle should be applicable to distressed aircraft. Unfortunately, in terms of the protection of human rights, these two conventions did not act upon the suggestion.[26]

All responsible governments should consider it a matter of imperative and urgent duty to ratify and implement the conventions as soon as possible. In the ROC, the Legislative Yuan, after having read the two Conventions three times, have resolved to ratify them.

The Hague Convention clearly acknowledged that the actions of states against hijackers were in part in pursuit of their own police responsibilities and in part in pursuit of their responsibilities to the ICAO. By imposing these responsibilities without exception, the Convention acknowledged that the interest in the international aviation system is sufficient for states to disregard the political issue of furthering their own international interests. Thence, under the circumstances, the members of the international community should be permitted to consider a joint action against the state in violation, including suspension of commercial air services.[27] Only a joint international enforcement of obligation could ably maintain such international systems which become necessary and increasingly important in an interdependent world community.

However, conventions are not necessarily adequate to cope with steady growth in the frequency and seriousness of hijackings, if they lack universality. Though jurists advocate varying approaches, nearly all agree that unless a proposal gains universality, control measures can never be expected to be effective in con-

---

[26]ICAO Doc. SA 19.

[27]Regarding hijacking, the Cuban Government for many years adopted an uncooperative attitude and it even welcomed the landing of hijackers in its territory with a view to granting them asylum and freedom. However, recently (November 11, 1972) three American hijackers, who asked for 10 million dollars ransom for the return of the hijacked Southern Airlines jet, were arrested by the police right after the plane landed at Cuban airport. And more importantly, in February 1973, Cuba has concluded agreements with the U.S. and Canada respectively setting out detailed rules regarding prevention and punishment of hijacking.

trolling hijacking. The most vexing feature of aircraft hijacking is the paucity of unanimity among the affected nations in finding programatic methods for its control.

The ICAO, a United Nations related group with representatives from 124 states should draft a convention permitting sanctions against nations that cooperate with hijackers. Law abiding states should abstain from flying to defaulting countries' airports, and the airlines of defaulting countries should be denied landing rights in law abiding states. The time has come for severe countermeasures to this menace which reflects the mounting world-wide abhorrence of acts of criminal violence inflicting on the innocent, both travelers and the crew that serve them.

The Cabinet of the Republic of China on March 2, 1973, approved the draft of a revised Aviation Law calling for death penalty to hijackers.

The highlights of the revised law include the following:

—Hijacking of airplanes shall be punishable by death, life imprisonment or imprisonment of not less than 20 years.

—Interference with aviation by means of violence or threat shall be punished by death, life imprisonment or a prison detention or a fine of NT$15,000.

—Damage to airplanes and airport facilities occasioned in the aforesaid act shall be punishable by a prison term of not less than five years.

—In case of death or injury due to the aforesaid cause, hijackers shall be punished by death, life imprisonment or a prison term of not less than 10 years.

—Riding airplanes with concealed weapons or other items that may endanger the airplanes shall be punishable by a prison term of upward to one year, detention or a fine of NT $6,000.

—Owners of airplanes shall be held responsible for damages in case of accidents resulting in the loss of life or property.

—Foreign aircraft, either piloted or unmanned, shall not be permitted to enter the airspace of the Republic of China without prior consent of the Ministry of Foreign Affairs.

The draft law will be sent to the Legislative Yuan for deliberations shortly.

APPENDIX G

Convention on Offences and Certain Other Acts Committed on Board Aircraft, Done at Tokyo on 14 September 1963[1]

THE STATES Parties to this Convention
HAVE AGREED as follows:

Chapter I—Scope of the Convention

Article 1

1. This Convention shall apply in respect of:

   (a) offenses against penal law;

   (b) act which, whether or not they are offenses, may or do jeop-

---

[1]Entered into force on 4 December 1969; ratified or acceded to by: Argentina, Australia, Barbados, Belgium, Brazil, Burundi, Canada, Chad, Cyprus, Denmark, Dominican Republic, Ecuador, Fiji, Finland, France, Gabon, Federal Republic of Germany, Greece, Guatemala, Hungary, Iceland, Israel, Italy, Ivory Coast, Japan, Kenya, Lesotho, Libyan Arab Republic, Luxembourg, Madagascar, Mali, Mexico, Netherlands, Niger, Nigeria, Norway, Panama, Paraguay, Philippines, Poland, Portugal, Republic of China,* Republic of Korea, Kwanda, Saudi Arabia, Senegal, Sierra Leone, Singapore, South Africa, Spain, Sweden, Switzerland, Thailand, Togo, Trinidad and Tobago, United Kingdom of Great Britain and Northern Ireland, United States of America, Upper Volta, Yugoslavia, Zambia.

*According to information received from the depositary, the Convention was signed and ratified by the "Republic of China" on December 16, 1970 and July 27, 1972 respectively. In this connexion, it will be recalled that, by its resolution 2758 (XXVI) of October 25, 1971, the General Assembly decided:

> . . . to restore all its rights to the People's Republic of China and to recognize the representatives of its Government as the only legitimate representatives of China to the United Nations, and to expel forthwith the representatives of Chiang Kai-shek from the place which they unlawfully occupy at the United Nations and in all organizations related to it.

By a note dated September 25, 1972, addressed to the Secretary-General, the Minister for Foreign Affairs of the People's Republic of China, stated *inter alia* that:

> As from October 1, 1949, the day of the founding of the People's Republic of China, the Chiang Kai-shek clique has no right at all to represent China. Its signature and ratification of, or accussion to, any multilateral treaties by usurping the name "China" are all illegal and null and void. My Government will study these multilateral treaties before making a decision in the light of the circumstances as to whether or not they should be acceded to.

ardize the safety of the aircraft or of persons or property therein or which jeopardize good order and discipline on board.

2. Except as provided in chapter III, this Convention shall apply in respect of offenses committed or acts by a person on board any aircraft registered in a Contracting State, while that aircraft is in flight or on the surface of the high seas or of any other area outside the territory of any State.

3. For the purposes of this Convention, an aircraft is considered to be in flight from the moment when power is applied for the purpose of take-off until the moment when the landing run ends.

4. This Convention shall not apply to aricraft used in military, customs or police services.

Article 2

Without prejudice to the provisions of Article 4 and except when the safety of the aircraft or of persons or property on board so requires, no provision of this Convention shall be interpreted as authorizing or requiring any action in respect of offenses against penal laws of a political nature or those based on racial or religious discrimination.

Chapter II—Jurisdiction

Article 3

1. The State of registration of the aircraft is competent to exercise jurisdiction over offenses and acts committed on board.

2. Each Contracting State shall take such measures as may be necessary to establish its jurisdiction as the State of registration over offenses committed on board aircraft registered in such State.

3. This Convention does not exclude any criminal jurisdiction exercised in accordance with national law.

Article 4

A Contracting State which is not the State of registration may not interfere with an aircraft in flight in order to exercise its criminal jurisdiction over an offense committed on board except in the following cases:

(a) the offense has effect on the territory of such State;
(b) the offense has been committed by or against a national or permanent resident of such State;
(c) the offense is against the security of such State;
(d) the offense consists of a breach of any rules or regulations relating to the flight or manoeuvre of aircraft in force in such State;
(e) the exercise of jurisdiction is necessary to ensure the observance of any obligation of such State under a multilateral international agreement.

Chapter III—Powers of the Aircraft Commander
Article 5

1. The provisions of this Chapter shall not apply to offences and acts committed or about to be committed by a person on board an aircraft in flight in the airspace of the State of registration or over the high seas or any other area outside the territory of any State unless the last point of take-off or the next point of intended landing is situated in a State other than that of registration, or the aircraft subsequently flies in the airspace of a State other than that of registration with such person still on board.

2. Notwithstanding the provisions of Article 1, paragraph 3, an aircraft shall for the purposes of this Chapter, be considered to be in flight at any time from the moment when all its external doors are closed following embarkation until the moment when any such door is opened for disembarkation. In the case of a forced landing, the provisions of this Chapter shall continue to apply with respect to offenses and acts committed on board until competent authorities of a State take over the responsibility for the aircraft and for the persons and property on board.

Article 6

1. The aircraft commander may, when he has reasonable grounds to believe that a person has committed, or is about to commit, on board the aircraft, an offense or act contemplated in Article 1, paragraph 1, impose upon such person reasonable measures including restraint which are necessary:

(a) to protect the safety of the aircraft, or of persons or property therein, or

(b) to maintain good order and discipline on board; or

(c) to enable him to deliver such person to competent authorities or to disembark him in accordance with the provisions of this Chapter.

2. The aircraft commander may require or authorize the assistance of other crew members and may request or authorize, but not require, the assistance of passengers to restrain any person whom he is entitled to restrain. Any crew member or passenger may also take reasonable preventive measures without such authorization when he has reasonable grounds to believe that such action is immediately necessary to protect the safety of the aircraft, or of persons or property therein.

Article 7

1. Measures of restraint imposed upon a person in accordance with article 6 shall not be continued beyond any point at which the aircraft lands unless:

(a) such point is in the territory of a non-Contracting State and its authorities refuse to permit disembarkation of that person or those measures have been imposed in accordance with Article 6, paragraph 1 (c) in order to enable his delivery to competent authorities;

(b) the aircraft makes a forced landing and the aircraft commander is unable to deliver that person to competent authorities; or

(c) that person agrees to onward carriage under restraint.

2. The aircraft commander shall as soon as practicable, and if possible before landing in the territory of a State with a person on board who has been placed under restraint in accordance with the provisions of Article 6, notify the authorities of such State of the fact that a person on board is under restraint and of the reasons for such restraint.

Article 8

1. The aircraft commander may, in so far as it is necessary for the purpose of subparagraph (a) or (b) of paragraph 1 of Article 6, disembark in the territory of the State in which the aircraft lands

any person who he has reasonable grounds to believe has committed, or is about to commit, on board the aircraft an act contemplated in Article 1, paragraph 1(b).

2. The aircraft commander shall report to the authorities of the State in which he disembarks any person pursuant to this Article, the fact of, and the reasons for, such disembarkation.

Article 9

1. The aircraft commander may deliver to the competent authorities of any Contracting State in the territory of which the aircraft lands any person who he has reasonable grounds to believe has committed on board the aircraft an act which in his opinion, is a serious offense according to the penal law of the State of registration of the aircraft.

2. The aircraft commander shall as soon as practicable and if possible before landing in the territory of a Contracting State with a person on board whom the aircraft commander intends to deliver in accordance with the preceding paragraph, notify the authorities of such State of his intention to deliver such person and the reasons therefor.

3. The aircraft commander shall furnish the authorities to whom any suspected offender is delivered in accordance with the provisions of this Article with evidence and information which, under the law of the State of registration of the aircraft, are lawfully in his possession.

Article 10

For actions taken in accordance with this Convention, neither the aircraft commander, any other member of the crew, any passenger, the owner or operator of the aircraft, nor the person on whose behalf the flight was performed shall be held responsible in any proceeding on account of the treatment undergone by the person against whom the actions were taken.

Chapter IV—Unlawful Seizure of Aircraft
Article 11

1. When a person on board has unlawfully committed by force or threat thereof an act of interference, seizure, or other wrongful

exercise of control of an aircraft in flight or when such an act is about to be committed, Contracting States shall take all appropriate measures to restore control of the aircraft to its lawful commander or to preserve his control of the aircraft.

2. In the case contemplated in the preceding paragraph, the Contracting State in which the aircraft lands shall permit its passengers and crew to continue their journey as soon as practicable, and shall return the aircraft and its cargo to the persons lawfully entitled to possession.

Chapter V—Powers and Duties of States
Article 12

Any Contracting State shall allow the commander of an aircraft registered in another Contracting State to disembark any person pursuant to Article 8, paragraph 1.

Article 13

1. Any Contracting State shall take delivery of any person whom the aircraft commander delivers pursuant to Article 9, paragraph 1.

2. Upon being satisfied that the circumstances so warrant, any Contracting State shall take custody or other measures to ensure the presence of any person suspected of an act contemplated in Article 11, paragraph 1 and of any person of whom it has taken delivery. The custody and other measures shall be as provided in the law of that State but may only be continued for such time as is reasonably necessary to enable any criminal or extradition proceedings to be instituted.

3. Any person in custody pursuant to the previous paragraph shall be assisted in communicating immediately with the nearest appropriate representative of the State of which he is a national.

4. Any Contracting State, to which a person is delivered pursuant to Article 9, paragraph 1, or in whose territory an aircraft lands following the commission of an act contemplated in Article 11, paragraph 1, shall immediately make a preliminary inquiry into the facts.

5. When a State, pursuant to this Article, has taken a person into custody, it shall immediately notify the State of registration of the

aircraft and the State of nationality of the detained person and if it considers it advisable, any other interested State of the fact that such person is in custody and of the circumstances which warrant his detention. The State which makes the preliminary inquiry contemplated in paragraph 4 of this Article shall promptly report its findings to the said States and shall indicate whether it intends to exercise jurisdiction.

Article 14

1. When any person has been disembarked in accordance with Article 8, paragraph 1, or delivered in accordance with Article 9, paragraph 1, or has disembarked after committing an act contemplated in Article 11, paragraph 1, and when such person cannot or does not desire to continue his journey and the State of landing refuses to admit him, that State may, if the person in question is not a national or permanent resident of that State, return him to the territory of the State of which he is a national or permanent resident or to the territory of the State in which be began his journey by air.

2. Neither disembarkation, nor delivery, nor the taking of custody or other measures contemplated in Article 13, paragraph 2, nor return of the person concerned, shall be considered as admission to the territory of the Contracting State concerned for the purpose of its law relating to entry or admission of persons and nothing in this Convention shall affect the law of a Contracting State relating to the expulsion of persons from its territory.

Article 15

1. Without prejudice to Article 14, any person who has been disembarked in accordance with Article 8, paragraph 1, or delivered in accordance with Article 9, paragraph 1, or has disembarked after committing an act contemplated in Article 11, paragraph 1, and who desires to continue his journey shall be at liberty as soon as practicable to proceed to any destination of his choice unless his presence is required by the law of the State of landing for the purpose of extradition or criminal proceedings.

2. Without prejudice to its law as to entry and admission to, and

extradition and expulsion from its territory, a Contracting State in whose territory a person has been disembarked in accordance with Article 8, paragraph 1, or delivered in accordance with Article 9, paragraph 1 or has disembarked and is suspected of having committed an act contemplated in Article 11, paragraph 1, shall accord to such person treatment which is no less favourable for his protection and security than that accorded to nationals of such Contracting State in like circumstances.

Chapter VI—Other Provisions
Article 16

1. Offenses committed on aircraft registered in a Contracting State shall be treated, for the purpose of extradition, as if they had been committed not only in the place in which they have occurred but also in the territory of the State of registration of the aircraft.
2. Without prejudice to the provisions of the preceding paragraph, nothing in this Convention shall be deemed to create an obligation to grant extradition.

Article 17

In taking any measures for investigation or arrest or otherwise exercising jurisdiction in connection with any offense committed on board an aircraft the Contracting States shall pay due regard to the safety and other interests of air navigation and shall so act as to avoid unnecessary delay of the aircraft, passengers, crew or cargo.

Article 18

If Contracting States establish joint air transport operating organizations or international operating agencies, which operate aircraft not registered in any one State those States shall, according to the circumstances of the case, designate the State among them which, for the purposes of this Convention, shall be considered as the State of registration and shall give notice thereof to the International Civil Aviation Organization which shall communicate the notice to all States Parties to this Convention.

Chapter VII—Final Clauses
Article 19

Until the date on which this Convention comes into force in accordance with the provision of Article 21, it shall remain open for signature on behalf of any State which at that date is a Member of the United Nations or of any of specialized agencies.

Article 20

1. This Convention shall be subject to ratification by the signatory States in accordance with their constitutional procedures.
2. The instruments of ratification shall be deposited with the International Civil Aviation Organization.

Article 21

1. As soon as twelve of the signatory States have deposited their instruments of ratification of this Convention, it shall come into force between them on the ninetieth day after the date of the deposit of the twelfth instrument of ratification. It shall come into force for each State ratifying thereafter on the ninetieth day after the deposit of its instrument of ratification.
2. As soon as this Convention comes into force, it shall be registered with the Secretary-General of the United Nations by the International Civil Aviation Organization.

Article 22

1. This Convention shall, after it has come into force, be open for accession by any State Member of the United Nations or of any of the specialized agencies.
2. The accession of a State shall be effected by the deposit of an instrument of accession with the International Civil Aviation Organization and shall take effect on the ninetieth day after the date of such deposit.

Article 23

1. Any Contracting State may denounce this Convention by notification addressed to the International Civil Aviation Organization.
2. Denunciation shall take effect six months after the date of re-

ceipt by the International Civil Aviation Organization of the notification of denunciation.

Article 24

1. Any dispute between two or more Contracting States concerning the interpretation or application of this Convention which cannot be settled through negotiation, shall, at the request of one of them, be submitted to arbitration. If within six months from the date of the request for arbitration the Parties are unable to agree on the organization of the arbitration, any one of those Parties may refer the dispute to the International Court of Justice by request in conformity with the Statute of the Court.

2. Each State may at the time of signature or ratification of this Convention or accession thereto, declare that it does not consider itself bound by the preceding paragraph. The other Contracting States shall be bound by the preceding paragraph with respect to any Contracting State having made such a reservation.

3. Any Contracting State having made a reservation in accordance with the preceding paragraph may at any time withdraw this reservation by notification to the International Civil Aviation Organization.

Article 25

Except as provided in Article 24 no reservation may be made to this Convention.

Article 26

The International Civil Aviation Organization shall give notice to all States Members of the United Nations or of any of the specialized agencies:

(a) of any signature of this Convention and the date thereof;

(b) of the deposit of any instrument of ratification or accession and the date thereof;

(c) of the date on which this Convention comes into force in accordance with Article 21, paragraph 1;

(d) of the receipt of any notification of denunciation and the date thereof; and

(e) of the receipt of any declaration or notification made under Article 24 and the date thereof.

APPENDIX H

Convention for the Suppression of Unlawful Seizure of Aircraft
Signed at The Hague on 16 December 1970[1]

PREAMBLE

THE STATES PARTIES TO THIS CONVENTION

CONSIDERING that unlawful acts of seizure or exercise of control of aircraft in flight jeopardize the safety of persons and property, seriously affect the operation of air services, and undermine the confidence of the peoples of the world in the safety of civil aviation;

CONSIDERING that the occurrence of such acts is a matter of grave concern;

CONSIDERING that, for the purpose of deterring such acts, there is an urgent need to provide appropriate measures for punishment of offenders;

HAVE AGREED AS FOLLOWS:

Article 1

Any person who on board an aircraft in flight:

(a) unlawfully, by force or threat thereof, or by any other form of intimidation, seizes, or exercises control of, that aircraft, or attempts to perform any such act, or

---

[1]Entered into force on 14 October 1971; ratified or acceded to by: Argentina, Brazil, Bulgaria, the Byelorussian Soviet Socialist Republic, Canada, Chad, Chile, Costa Rica, Cyprus, Czechoslovakia, Dahomey, Ecuador, Fiji, Finland, France, Gabon, the German Democratic Republic, Hungary, Iran, Iraq, Izrael, Japan, Jordan, Mali, Mexico, Mongolia, the Niger, Norway, Panama, Paraguay, Poland, Republic of China, Romania, South Africa, Sweden, Switzerland, Trinidad and Tobago, the Ukrainian Soviet Socialist Republic, the Union of Soviet Socialist Republics, the United Kingdom of Great Britain and Northern Ireland, the United States of America, Uganda.

(b) is an accomplice of a person who performs or attempts to perform any such act

commits an offense (hereinafter referred to as "the offense").

Article 2

Each Contracting State undertakes to make the offense punishable by severe penalties.

Article 3

1. For the purposes of this Convention, an aircraft is considered to be in flight at any time from the moment when all its external doors are closed following embarkation until the moment when any such door is opened for disembarkation. In the case of a forced landing, the flight shall be deemed to continue until the competent authorities take over the responsibility for the aircraft and for persons and property on board.

2. This Convention shall not apply to aircraft used in military, customs or police services.

3. This Convention shall apply only if the place of take-off or the place of actual landing of the aircraft on board which the offense is committed is situated outside the territory of the State of registration of that aircraft; it shall be immaterial whether the aircraft is engaged in an international or domestic flight.

4. In the cases mentioned in Article 5, this Convention shall not apply if the place of take-off and the place of actual landing of the aircraft on board which the offense is committed are situated within the territory of the same State where that State is one of those referred to in that Article.

5. Notwithstanding paragraphs 3 and 4 of this Article, Articles 6, 7, 8 and 10 shall apply whatever the place of take-off or the place of actual landing of the aircraft, if the offender or the alleged offender is found in the territory of a State other than the State of registration of that aircraft.

Article 4

1. Each Contracting State shall take such measures as may be necessary to establish its jurisdiction over the offense and any other

act of violence against passengers or crew committed by the alleged offender in connection with the offense, in the following cases:

(a) when the offense is committed on board an aircraft registered in that State;

(b) when the aircraft on board which the offense is committed lands in its territory with the alleged offender still on board;

(c) when the offense is committed on board an aircraft leased without crew to a lessee who has his principal place of business or, if the lessee has no such place of business, his permanent residence, in that State.

2. Each Contracting State shall likewise take such measures as may be necessary to establish its jurisdiction over the offense in the case where the alleged offender is present in its territory and it does not extradite him pursuant to Article 8 to any of the States mentioned in paragraph 1 of this Article.

3. This Convention does not exclude any criminal jurisdiction exercised in accordance with national law.

Article 5

The Contracting States which establish joint air transport operating organizations or international operating agencies, which operate aircraft which are subject to joint or international registration shall, by appropriate means, designate for each aircraft the State among them which shall exercise the jurisdiction and have the attributes of the State of registration for the purpose of this Convention and shall give notice thereof to the International Civil Aviation Organization which shall communicate the notice to all States Parties to this Convention.

Article 6

1. Upon being satisfied that the circumstances so warrant, any Contracting State in the territory of which the offender or the alleged offender is present, shall take him into custody or take other measures to ensure his presence. The custody and other measures shall be as provided in the law of the State but may only be continued for such time as is necessary to enable any criminal or extradition proceedings to be instituted.

2. Such State shall immediately make a preliminary inquiry into the facts.

3. Any person in custody pursuant to paragraph 1 of this Article shall be assisted in communicating immediately with the nearest appropriate representative of the State of which he is a national.

4. When a State, pursuant to this Article, has taken a person into custody, it shall immediately notify the State of registration of the aircraft, the State mentioned in Article 4, paragraph 1 *(c)*, the State of nationality of the detained person and, if it considers it advisable, any other interested States of the fact that such person is in custody and of the circumstances which warrant his detention. The State which makes the preliminary inquiry contemplated in paragraph 2 of this Article shall promptly report its findings to the said States and shall indicate whether it intends to exercise jurisdiction.

Article 7

The Contracting State in the territory of which the alleged offender is found shall, if it does not extradite him, be obliged, without exception whatsoever and whether or not the offense was committed in its territory, to submit the case to its competent authorities for the purpose of prosecution. Those authorities shall take their decision in the same manner as in the case of any ordinary offense of a serious nature under the law of that State.

Article 8

1. The offense shall be deemed to be included as an extraditable offense in any extradition treaty existing between Contracting States. Contracting States undertake to include the offense as an extraditable offense in every extradition treaty to be concluded between them.

2. If a Contracting State which makes extradition conditional on the existence of a treaty receives a request for extradition from another Contracting State with which it has no extradition treaty, it may at its option consider this Convention as the legal basis for extradition in respect of the offense. Extradition shall be subject to the other conditions provided by the law of the requested State.

3. Contracting States which do not make extradition conditional

on the existence of a treaty shall recognize the offense as an extraditable offense between themselves subject to the conditions provided by the law of the requested State.

4. The offense shall be treated, for the purpose of extradition between Contracting States, as if it had been committed not only in the place in which it occurred but also in the territories of the States required to establish their jurisdiction in accordance with Article 4, paragraph 1.

Article 9

1. When any of the acts mentioned in Article 1 *(a)* has occurred or is about to occur, Contracting States shall take all appropriate measures to restore control of the aircraft to its lawful commander or to preserve his control of the aircraft.

2. In the cases contemplated by the preceding paragraph, any Contracting State in which the aircraft or its passengers or crew are present shall facilitate the continuation of the journey of the passengers and crew as soon as practicable, and shall without delay return the aircraft and its cargo to the persons lawfully entitled to possession.

Article 10

1. Contracting States shall afford one another the greatest measure of assistance in connection with criminal proceedings brought in respect of the offense and other acts mentioned in Article 4. The law of the State requested shall apply in all cases.

2. The provisions of paragraph 1 of this Article shall not affect obligations under any other treaty, bilateral or multilateral, which governs or will govern, in whole or in part, mutual assistancse in criminal matters.

Article 11

Each Contracting State shall in accordance with its national law report to the Council of the International Civil Aviation Organization as promptly as possible any relevant information in its possession concerning:

(a) the circumstances of the offense;

(b) the action taken pursuant to Article 9;

(c) the measures taken in relation to the offender or the alleged offender, and, in particular, the results of any extradition proceedings or other legal proceedings.

Article 12

1. Any dispute between two or more Contracting States concerning the interpretation or application of this Convention which cannot be settled through negotiation, shall, at the request of one of them, be submitted to arbitration. If within six months from the date of the request for arbitration the Parties are unable to agree on the organization of the arbitration, any one of those Parties may refer the dispute to the International Court of Justice by request in conformity with the Statute of the Court.

2. Each State may at the time of signature or ratification of this Convention or accession thereto, declare that it does not consider itself bound by the preceding paragraph. The other Contracting States shall not be bound by the preceding paragraph with respect to any Contracting State having made such a reservation.

3. Any Contracting State having made a reservation in accordance with the preceding paragraph may at any time withdraw this reservation by notification to the Depositary Governments.

Article 13

1. This Convention shall be open for signature at The Hague on December 16, 1970, by States participating in the International Conference on Air Law held at The Hague from December 1 to 16, 1970 (hereinafter referred to as The Hague Conference). After December 31, 1970, the Convention shall be open to all States for signature in Moscos, London and Washington. Any State which does not sign this Convention before its entry into force in accordance with paragraph of this Article may accede to it at any time.

2. This Convention shall be subject to ratification by the signatory States. Instruments of ratification and instruments of accession shall be deposited with the Governments of the Union of Soviet Socialist Republics, the United Kingdom of Great Britain and Northern Ireland, and the United States of America, which are

hereby designated the Depositary Governments.

3. This Convention shall enter into force thirty days following the date of the deposit of instruments of ratification by ten States signatory to this Convention which participated in The Hague Conference.

4. For other States, this Convention shall enter into force on the date of entry into force of this Convention in accordance with paragraph 3 of this Article, or thirty days following the date of deposit of their instruments of ratification or accession, whichever is later.

5. The Depositary Governments shall promptly inform all signatory and acceding States of the date of each signature, the date of deposit of each instrument of ratification or accession, the date of entry into force of this Convention, the other notices.

6. As soon as this Convention comes into force, it shall be registered by the Depositary Governments pursuant to Article 102 of the Charter of the United Nations and pursuant to Article 83 of the Convention on International Civil Aviation (Chicago, 1944).

Article 14

1. Any Contracting State may denounce this Convention by written notification to the Depositary Governments.

2. Denunciation shall take effect six months following the date on which notification is received by the Depositary Governments.

APPENDIX I

Convention for the Suppression of Unlawful Acts Against the
Safety of Civil Aviation, Signed at Montreal on
23 September 1971[1]

THE STATES PARTIES TO THIS CONVENTION
CONSIDERING that unlawful acts against the safety of civil
aviation jeopardize the safety of persons and property, seriously affect the operation of air services, and undermine the confidence of
the peoples of the world in the safety of civil aviation;

CONSIDERING that the occurrence of such acts is a matter of
grave concern;

CONSIDERING that, for the purpose of deterring such acts,
there is an urgent need to provide appropriate measures for
punishment of offenders;

HAVE AGREED AS FOLLOWS:

Article 1

1. Any person commits an offence if he unlawfully and intentionally;

    (a) performs an act of violence against a person on board an air-
craft in flight if that act is likely to endanger the safety of
that aircraft; or

    (b) destroys an aircraft in service or causes damage to such an
aircraft which renders it incapable of flight or which is likely
to endanger its safety in flight; or

    (c) places or causes to be placed on an aircraft in service, by any
means whatsoever, a device or substance which is likely to
destroy that aircraft, or to cause damage to it which renders
it incapable of flight, or to cause damage to it which is likely

---

[1]Not yet entered into force; ratified or acceded to by: Brazil, Canada, Chad,
Israel, Luxembourg, Mali, the Niger, Panama, South Africa, Trinidad and Tobago,
Yugoslavia.

to endanger its safety in flight; or

(d) destroys or damages air navigation facilities or interferes with their operation, if any such act is likely to endanger the safety of aircraft in flight; or

(e) communicates information which he knows to be false, thereby endangering the safety of an aircraft in flight.

2. Any person also commits an offense if he:

(a) attempts to commit any of the offenses mentioned in paragraph 1 of this Article; or

(b) is an accomplice of a person who commits or attempts to commit any such offense.

Article 2

For the purposes of this Convention:

(a) an aircraft is considered to be in flight at any time from the moment when all its external doors are closed following embarkation until the moment when the door is opened for disembarkation; in the case of a forced landing, the flight shall be deemed to continue until the competent authorities take over the responsibility for the aircraft and for persons and property on board;

(b) an aircraft is considered to be in service from the beginning of the preflight preparation of the aircraft by ground personnel or by the crew for a specific flight until twenty-four hours after any landing; the period of service shall, in any event, extend for the entire period during which the aircraft is in flight as defined in paragraph *(a)* of this Article.

Article 3

Each Contracting State undertakes to make the offenses mentioned in Article 1 punishable by severe penalties.

Article 4

1. This Convention shall not apply to aircraft used in military, customs or police services.

2. In the cases contemplated in subparagraphs (a), (b), (c), and (e) of paragraph 1 of Article 1, this Convention shall apply, ir-

respective of whether the aircraft is engaged in an international or domestic flight, only if:

    (a) the place of take-off or landing, actual or intended, of the aircraft is situated outside the territory of the State of registration of that aircraft; or

    (b) the offense is committed in the territory of a State other than the State of registration of the aircraft.

3. Notwithstanding paragraph 2 of this Article, in the cases contemplated in subparagraphs (a), (b), (c) and (e) of paragraph 1 of Article 1, this Convention shall also apply if the offender or the alleged offender is found in the territory of a State other than the State of registration of the aircraft.

4. With respect to the States mentioned in Article 9 and in the cases mentioned in subparagraph (a), (b), (c) and (e) of paragraph 1 of Article 1, this Convention shall not apply if the places referred to in subparagraph (a) of paragraph 2 of this Article are situated within the territory of the same State where that State is one of those referred to in Article 9, unless the offense is committed or the offender or alleged offender is found in the territory of a State other than that State.

5. In the cases contemplated in subparagraph (d) of paragraph 1 of Article 1, this Convention shall apply only if the air navigation facilities are used in international air navigation.

6. The provisions of paragraphs 2, 3, 4 and 5 of this Article shall also apply in the cases contemplated in paragraph 2 of Article 1.

Article 5

1. Each Contracting State shall take such measures as may be necessary to establish its jurisdiction over the offenses in the following cases:

    (a) when the offense is committed in the territory of the State;

    (b) when the offense is committed against or on board an aircraft registered in that State;

    (c) when the aircraft on board which the offense is committed lands in its territory with the alleged offender still on board;

    (d) when the offense is committed against or on board an aircraft leased without crew to a lessee who has his principal place of business or, if the lessee has no such place of business, his permanent residence, in that State.

2. Each Contracting State shall likewise take such measures as may be necessary to establish its jurisdiction over the offenses mentioned in Article 1, paragraph 1 (a), (b) and (c), and in Article 1, paragraph 2, in so far as that paragraph relates to those offenses, in the case where the alleged offender is present in its territory and it does not extradite him pursuant to Article 8 to any of the States mentioned in paragraph 1 of this Article.

3. This Convention does not exclude any criminal jurisdiction exercised in accordance with national law.

Article 6

1. Upon being satisfied that the circumstances so warrant, any Contracting State in the territory of which the offender or the alleged offender is present, shall take him into custody or take other measures to ensure his presence. The custody and other measures shall be as provided in the law of that State but may only be continued for such time as is necessary to enable any criminal or extradition proceedings to be instituted.

2. Such State shall immediately make a preliminary inquiry into the facts.

3. Any person in custody pursuant to paragraph 1 of this Article shall be assisted in communicating immediately with the nearest appropriate representative of the State of which he is a national.

4. When a State, pursuant to this Article, has taken a person into custody, it shall immediately notify the States mentioned in Article 5, paragraph 1, the State of nationally of the detained person and, if it considers it advisable, any other interested States of the fact that such person is in custody and of circumstances which warrant his detention. The State which makes the preliminary inquiry contemplated in paragraph 2 of this Article shall promptly report its findings to the said States and shall indicate whether it intends to exercise jurisdiction.

Article 7

The Contracting State in the territory of which the alleged offender is found shall, if it does not extradite him, be obliged, without exception whatsoever and whether or not the offense was committed in its territory, to submit the case to its competent authorities for the purpose of prosecution. Those authorities shall take their decision in the same manner as in the case of any ordinary offense of a serious nature under the law of that State.

Article 8

1. The offenses shall be deemed to be included as extraditable offenses in any extradition treaty existing between Contracting States. Contracting States undertake to include the offenses as extraditable offenses in every extradition treaty to be concluded between them.

2. If a Contracting State which makes extradition conditional on the existence of a treaty receives a request for extradition from another Contracting State with which it has no extradition treaty, it may at its option consider this Convention as the legal basis for extradition in respect of the offenses. Extradition shall be subject to the other conditions provided by the law of the requested State.

3. Contracting States which do not make extradition conditional on the existence of a treaty shall recognize the offenses as extraditable offenses between themselves subject to the conditions provided by the law of the requested State.

4. Each of the offenses shall be treated, for the purpose of extradition between Contracting States, as if it had been committed not only in the place in which it occurred but also in the territories of the States required to establish their jurisdiction in accordance with Article 5, paragraph 1 (b), (c) and (d).

Article 9

The Contracting States which establish joint air transport operating organizations or international operating agencies, which operate aircraft which are subject to joint or international registration shall, by appropriate means, designate for each aircraft the State among them which shall exercise the jurisdiction and have the attributes of the State of registration for the purpose of this Convention and shall give notice thereof to the International Civil Aviation Organization which shall communicate the notice to all States Parties to this Convention.

Article 10

1. Contracting States shall, in accordance with international and national law, endeavor to take all practicable measures for the purpose of preventing the offenses mentioned in Article 1.
2. When, due to the commission of one of the offenses mentioned in Article 1, a flight has been delayed or interrupted, any Contracting State in whose territory the aircraft or passengers or crew are present shall facilitate the continuation of the journey of the passengers and crew as soon as practicable, and shall without delay return the aircraft and its cargo to the persons lawfully entitled to possession.

Article 11

1. Contracting States shall afford one another the greatest measure of assistance in connection with criminal proceedings brought in respect of the offenses. The law of the State requested shall apply in all cases.
2. The provisions of paragraph 1 of this Article shall not affect obligations under any other treaty, bilateral or multilateral, which governs or will govern, in whole or in part, mutual assistance in criminal matters.

Article 12

Any Contracting State having reason to believe that one of the offenses mentioned in Article 1 will be committed shall, in accordance with its national law, furnish any relevant information in its possession to those States which it believes would be the States mentioned in Article 5, paragraph 1.

Article 13

Each Contracting State shall in accordance with its national law report to the Council of the International Civil Aviation Organization as promptly as possible any relevant information in its possession concerning:
  (a) the circumstances of the offense;
  (b) the action taken pursuant to Article 10, paragraph 2;

(c) the measures taken in relation to the offender or the alleged offender and, in particular, the results of any extradition proceedings or other legal proceedings.

Article 14

1. Any dispute between two or more Contracting States concerning the interpretation or application of this Convention which cannot be settled through negotiation, shall, at the request of one of them, be submitted to arbitration. If within six months from the date of the request for arbitration the Parties are unable to agree on the organization of the arbitration, any one of those Parties may refer the dispute to the International Court of Justice by request in conformity with the Statute of the Court.

2. Each State may at the time of signature or ratification of this Convention or accession thereto, declare that it does not consider itself bound by the preceding paragraph. The other Contracting States shall not be bound by the preceding paragraph with respect to any Contracting State having made such a reservation.

3. Any Contracting State having made a reservation in accordance with the preceding paragraph may at any time withdraw this reservation by notification to the Depositary Governments.

Article 15

1. This Convention shall be open for signature at Montreal on September 23, 1971, by States participating in the International Conference on Air Law held at Montreal from September 8 to 23, 1971 (hereinafter referred to as the Montreal Conference). After October 10, 1971, the Convention shall be open to all States for signature in Moscow, London and Washington. Any State which does not sign this Convention before its entry into force in accordance with paragraph 3 of this Article may accede to it at any time.

2. This Convention shall be subject to ratification by the signatory States. Instruments of ratification and instruments of accession shall be deposited with the Governments of the Union of Soviet Socialist Republics, the United Kingdom of Great Britain and Northern Ireland, and the United States of America, which are hereby designated the Depositary Governments.

3. This Convention shall enter into force thirty days following the date of the deposit of instruments of ratification by ten States signatory to this Convention which participated in the Montreal Conference.

4. For other States, this Convention shall enter into force on the date of entry into force of this Convention in accordance with paragraph 3 of this Article, or thirty days following the date of deposit of their instruments of ratification or accession, whichever is later.

5. The Depositary Governments shall promptly inform all signatory and acceding States of the date of each signature, the date of deposit of each instrument of ratification or accession, the date of entry into force of this Convention, and other notices.

6. As soon as this Convention comes into force, it shall be registered by the Depositary Government pursuant to Article 102 of the Charter of the United Nations, and pursuant to Article 83 of the Convention on International Civil Aviation (Chicago, 1944).

Article 16

1. Any Contracting State may denounce this Convention by written notification to the Depositary Governments.

2. Denunciation shall take effect six months following the date on which notification is received by the Depositary Governments.

CHAPTER IV

KIDNAPPING

THE ROLE OF INTERNATIONAL LAW IN THE PREVENTION OF TERRORIST KIDNAPPING OF DIPLOMATIC PERSONNEL

JAMES MURPHY

Guadalajara, Mexico, May 5—United States Consul General Terrence G. Leonhardy, 58, was seized last night by four pistol-armed youths who police said threatened to kill him unless Mexican authorities free 30 political prisoners and fly them to Cuba.[1]

THIS SCENE, REPEATED NUMEROUS times in the recent past, was one of the latest in a growing series of terrorist kidnappings which have caused increasing international concern for the safety of the diplomatic community. In fact, rising world-wide alarm over the integrity of the diplomatic process has been responsible for a number of proposals on how to effectively deal with the situation, probably the most notable of which is the International Law Commission's Draft Articles on the prevention of crimes against diplomats.

In this section not only the International Law Commission's Draft Articles but also the work of the United Nations Ad Hoc Committee on International Terrorism, as well as many other proposed solutions for the problem of diplomatic kidnapping will be considered. Because of the diplomats' *special* standing in international law, a cursory examination of the historical development of diplomatic privileges and immunities will be given. This will include the various theories offered to support the claim of diplomatic immunity such as extraterritoriality, functional necessity,

---

[1]Chicago Tribune, May 6, 1973, p. 3.

etc. In this respect consideration will also be given to the various types of persons to whom the concept of immunity has been extended.

Instances where possible abuses of the concept of immunity may occur will also be discussed. This is important since this is often the type of defense the terrorists offer for their actions—that the victim (or the victim's country) was not entitled to diplomatic immunity through its dealing with the régime in question. There are, of course, a number of traditional ways of dealing with violation of diplomatic privilege and these will also be covered. Finally, the solutions themselves will be analyzed with due consideration given to each, including a proposal which this writer feels would effectively aid in decreasing the terrorist kidnappings —by creating a special class of "internationally protected persons." Of course, there are problems inherent in all the solutions, including this one, and they will be discussed at the proper place.

The recent concern over the safety of diplomatic personnel has somewhat overshadowed the historical role of the diplomat in international law. For the diplomat, or the "king's representatives," as they were called long ago, can be traced back to 3000 B.C. and the oldest recorded negotiations between the kings of Lagash and Umma.[2] In 423 B.C., Thucydides tells of recorded diplomatic practices, such as a guarantee of safe conduct through the receiving state.[3] And in the fifth century B.C., Herodutus records the tale of the murder of Persian diplomats by the Athenians and Spartans. Later, when two Spartans offered themselves as atonement, Xerxes, the son of King Darius, stated he would not behave like the Spartans who "had broken the law which all the world holds sacred."[4] Later, during Rome's ascendency, its ambassadors were likewise accorded special treatment.

The Bible also contains references to the importance of diplomats. There is, for instance, the story of how King David waged a war because another power had mistreated his ambassadors.[5] Much later, Grotius, a noted chronicler of international law,

---

[2]R. N. Swift, *International Law: Current and Classic,* (1969). p. 416.
[3]*Ibid.*
[4]*Ibid.* p. 417.
[5]D. B. Michaels, *International Privileges and Immunities* (1971), p. 7.

stated that it was one of the laws of the nations that "first ambassadors are to be admitted; and then that they are not to have violence offered them."[6]

Much of the early rules, however, concerned only special envoys or ambassadors, resulting in only a temporary duty of protection owed by the receiving state. It was not until 1450 A.D. in Milano that the first permanent representation of a country at a foreign capital was established.[7] Permanent diplomatic missions were established in Europe on a large scale by the Treaty of Westphalia in 1648 which ended the Hundred Years War.[8] Thus arose the special duties of protection which the receiving state owed the representatives of the sending country. It was now left to individual states to pass national legislation implementing these principles. One of the first to act was England with the passage by Parliament of the historic Act of Anne in 1708.[9] This introduced the practice of formally protecting or exempting the diplomat from much legal action in the host country, and acted as a standard for similar laws enacted by other nations.[10]

It was not until 1815, in a Europe ravaged by the Napoleonic wars, that the first International Convention on the status of diplomatic agents was held in Vienna.[11] This was really the first modern effort to classify the rights and duties of diplomatic personnel. From this period until the end of World War I the concept of privileges was limited to those diplomats representing one state or another. After the first World War, however, the idea of diplomatic privileges was expanded to include personnel of international organizations, such as those belonging to the newly created League of Nations.[12]

This forms a basis for understanding the developments in

---

[6]Swift, *supra* note 2, p. 418.

[7]G. von Glahn, *Law Among Nations* (1970), p. 375.

[8]*Ibid.* p. 376.

[9]7 Anne, Chapter XII, 1709. Also appears in, U.N., Laws and Regulations Regarding Diplomatic and Consular Privileges and Immunities," ST/LEG./Ser. B7 (1958).

[10]C. E. Wilson, *Diplomatic Privileges and Immunities* (1967), p. 2.

[11]P. Cahier, and L. T. Lee, *Vienna Convention On Diplomatic and Consular Relations* (1969), p. 1.

[12]K. Ahluwalia, *The Legal Status, Privileges and Immunities of the United Nations and Certain Other International Organizations* (1971).

1961, at a time when the world was divided between John Kennedy and Nikita Khrushchev. In a special conference called to deal with the problem of diplomatic privileges and immunities, held appropriately at Vienna, where the first conference in 1815 had been held, the United Nations issued a Convention on Diplomatic Relations. Officially calling itself the United Nations Conference on Diplomatic Intercourse and Immunities, it convened from March 2 through April 14, 1961.[13] The finished product was the Vienna Convention on Diplomatic Relations which formally comprised 53 articles along with numerous other annexes, optional protocols, and resolutions. Articles 29 through 41 of the final act are of greatest immediate interest since they are the ones primarily relating to the personal privileges and immunities of diplomatic agents. Of particular interest is Article 29 which reads:

> The person of a diplomatic agent shall be inviolable. He shall not be liable to any form of arrest or detention. The receiving state shall treat him with due respect and shall take *all appropriate* steps to prevent any attack on his person, freedom or dignity.[14]

This position was one widely recognized already and was accepted without change from the International Law Commission's draft proposal—Article 27.[15] In this respect the report of the United States Delegation to the Conference indicates that at least that delegation interpreted these articles in general (29-41), and Article 29 in particular, to "accord generally with accepted principles of international law and practice."[16] That this accurately reflected the United States position even before the Vienna Conference is evident from remarks made by Secretary of State Cordell Hull back on November 27, 1935, when he promised that the U.S. had "no intention of departing from its obligation under international law"[17] in regard to the matter of diplomatic

---

[13]U.N., Vienna Convention On Diplomatic Relations—Official Records," A/Conf. 20/14/Add. 1 (1962).
[14]*Ibid.*, 85.
[15]*Ibid.*, p. 5.
[16]U. S. Department of State, Report of the Delegation of the United States of America on the United Nations Conference on Diplomatic Intercourse and Immunities, Vienna, Austria, March 2-April 14, 1961, State Pub. No. 7289, (1962), p. 15.
[17]P. E. Corbett, *Law In Diplomacy* (1959), p. 25.

privileges and immunities.

Obviously, as laws become more comprehensive in regulating diplomatic relations and conduct, the importance of the diplomat himself is being underscored. It should be noted here that there are a number of reasons advanced by students of international law to justify the initial granting of diplomatic privileges and immunities. Or, simply put, why diplomats are given such special treatment.

There are a number of theories behind the granting of diplomatic privileges and immunities. For a proper perspective it will suffice here merely to mention the three major theories. These theories basically are (1) personal representation, a theory which originally viewed the diplomat as the king's representative and now as the personal representative and embodiment of his country and thus the receiving state owes the diplomat a high degree of protection; (2) extraterritoriality, in which the diplomat is viewed as still being a part of his country and thus beyond the jurisdiction of the receiving state; and, (3) functional necessity, considered the prevalent theory today, based on the belief that since the diplomatic functions are necessary, adequate grants of privileges and immunities should be made to ensure proper achievement of diplomatic ends.[18]

While some may disagree with the assessment of functional necessity as currently the dominant theory for diplomatic privileges and immunities, a number of prominent scholars in international law still attribute great importance to the role of the diplomat. One writer has flatly stated that "diplomatic missions are indispensable."[19] Of course a number of important functions can be attributed to the diplomat. For instance, a specific and important task of the diplomatic mission is the protection and aid which the embassy offers to nationals of that country abroad.[20] In fact, that is considered by many as one of the diplomat's primary objectives abroad.[21] What it all boils down to is that most scholars

[18]Michaels, *supra* note 5 pp. 47-48.

[19]Corbett, *supra* note 17, pp. 23-24.

[20]F. S. Dunn, *The Protection of Nationals: A Study In the Application of International Law* (1932), pp. 12-13.

[21]W. M. Franklin, *Protection of Foreign Interests* (1969), p. 2.

feel the diplomat is important because of the "practical value of diplomatic missions in the necessary intercourse of governments."[22]

While the United Nations has not explicitly adhered to a particular theory as justification for the existence of diplomatic privileges and immunities, it states in the Vienna Convention on Diplomatic Relations that "the purpose of such privileges and immunities is not to benefit individuals but to ensure the efficient performance of the functions of diplomatic missions. . . ."[23] Or, as the later International Law Commission's Draft Articles on the prevention of crimes against diplomats stated, "the entitlement to special protection referred to . . . must be for or because of the performance of official functions."[24] It would thus seem that international organizations adhere to the functional theory.

Regardless of the particular theory behind the privileges and immunities accorded today's diplomat, there is an almost world wide acceptance of the International Law Commission's statement that the receiving state is under a special duty to take "all appropriate steps" to protect the diplomatic person, premises, etc.[25] Thus, when violence is visited upon a diplomat it can be said that the act has "shattered the ancient protocols of international relations."[26]

With the recent wave of terrorist attacks it is apparent that the grant of diplomatic privileges and immunities by the receiving state does not really have a deterrent effect on urban guerrillas. It is sadly true that "diplomatic immunity may protect a diplomat from parking tickets, but not necessarily from a murderous band of guerrillas."[27] In fact, it is often precisely because the host country is understood as being under an obligation to protect foreign diplomats that anti-regime terrorists strike. Yet, the real problem

---

[22]P. E. Corbett, *Law and Society In the Relations of States* (1951), p. 207.

[23]U.N., Vienna Convention, *supra* note 13 p. 62.

[24]Int'l. L. Comm'n., "Draft Articles On the Prevention and Punishment of Crimes Against Diplomatic Agents and Other Internationally Protected Persons," 11 *Int'l. Legal Mat.—Curr. Doc.* 981 (1972).

[25]C. W. Jenks, *International Immunities,* (1961). pp. 47-48.

[26]68 Life, June 26, 1970, p. 81.

[27]96 Senior Scholastic, April 27, 1970, p. 15.

is, in what better way can international law be utilized to aid in solving this dilemma?

Diplomatic immunity carries with it a responsibility also. As the class of persons entitled to diplomatic immunity grew, so did the potential for abuse. Not only did we have the question of diplomatic immunity but different rights and duties attached to other classes or divisions of the sending country's representatives. Consuls,[28] for instance, are usually distinguished from and ranked lower than ambassadors. Oftentimes consuls will not be entitled to all the diplomatic privileges and immunities accorded ambassadors.[29] Not only that but the host country usually has a different set of regulations or national legislation concerning consuls or ambassadors or envoys, etc.[30]

The United States government itself recognizes the following classes of people as being entitled to all or some of the diplomatic privileges and immunities: "Ambassadors, Envoys Extraordinary, Ministers Plenipotentiary, Ministers Resident, Commissioners, Charges d'Affaires, Counselors, Agents, Attaches and Secretaries of Embassies and Legations."[31] As a result of all the different classes entitled to diplomatic privileges and immunities, there was not only the Vienna Convention on Diplomatic Relations, but also the Vienna Convention on Consuler Relations and the Convention on Special Missions.[32] And, as was mentioned earlier, this is not the limit of grants of privileges and immunities, for with the growth of international organizations, a whole new class was formed. This resulted in The Convention on the Representation of States in their relations with International Organizations; the Convention on the Privileges and Immunities of the United Nations; and, the Convention on the Privileges and Immunities

---

[28]H. Blix, *The Rights of Diplomatic Missions and Consulates To Communicate With Authorities of the Host Country*, (1964), p. 40.

[29]I. Stewart, *Consular Privileges and Immunities*, (1968), p. 14.

[30]W. A. McKean, "The Consular Privileges and Immunities Act of 1971," 5 *New Zealand U.L. Rev.*, 184 (1972).

[31]4 Hackworth, *Digest of International Law*, 393-394 (1942).

[32]Int'l. L. Comm'n., "Question of the Protection and Inviolability of Diplomatic Agents and Other Persons Entitled to Special Protection Under International Law," 11 *Int'l. Legal Mat.—Corr. Doc.*, 494 (1972).

of the Specialized Agencies.[33] With the creation of this large a group of persons entitled to diplomatic privileges and immunities, abuse of the privilege can, and often does, occur.

Abuse, of course, could take many forms. It might be an "intelligence agent" assigned as a staffer in some embassy to "spy" on certain of the host country's operations. Obviously, exceeding the allowable boundaries of the privileges and immunities can take just about any form imaginable. As one member of the International Law Commission indicated in the commentary on the recent ILC Draft Articles on the prevention of crimes against diplomats, there is an "obligation incumbent upon all persons entitled to special protection not to interfere in the internal affairs of the host or receiving state and, in particular, not to interfere directly or indirectly in insurrectionist movements."[34]

When abuse of the diplomatic privileges takes a traditional form, such as spying or blatant disregard of the host country's laws, there are certain options open to the host country. Among these are requests made to the offender's country for his recall, outright expulsion and possibly even arrest and prosecution when the diplomat's offense is excessive and flagrant. Since much has already been written about these remedies for diplomatic abuse, they will here be considered only briefly.

Recall procedures may be instituted by either host country or the offending diplomat's own government. Usually, it is initiated by a formal complaint lodged by the host country which usually results in the recall of the person charged with the violation. Expulsion is also available to the host country, especially if an important factor is time and the formal procedures of recall are foreseen as being too lengthy. Or it might be used when either the sending country or the diplomat himself proves uncooperative. Expulsion is usually resorted to in situations where the diplomat has become involved politically in the host country's internal affairs, as compared to recall which usually follows repeated minor infractions. A third solution available to the host country is the arrest and prosecution of the diplomat. This rather drastic

---

[33]*Ibid.*
[34]*Int'l. L. Comm'n., supra* note 24, p. 980.

course of action is usually taken in major criminal cases where the offense is a felony. For instance, in a relatively recent case in the United States where the charge was espionage, the diplomat in question was sentenced to fifteen years imprisonment.[35]

Obviously, the limitations listed above on diplomatic immunity are those available to a host country. But it must be remembered that other situations may arise where the receiving state would have no desire to utilize any of these procedures. As the member of the International Law Commission noted, part of the diplomat's obligation was "in particular not to interfere directly or indirectly in insurrectionist movement."[36] Certainly, if the diplomatic agent is aiding the host state in combatting an insurrectionist or self-determinist movement, his recall will not be requested. And this is precisely where problems arise!

The situation where the diplomat has exceeded the acceptable limits of his duties under international law but has done so with the consent and probably at the request of the receiving state is important because it is here that the inapplicability of the traditional solutions can be seen. Recent examples of this might be the work of some United States Ambassadors in South Viet Nam, such as Ellsworth Bunker's role in supervising some of the pacification programs aimed at the insurrectionist Viet Cong by the Republic of Viet Nam. Also notable are certain U.S. programs offered to existing governments which are often used by such governments to further entrench themselves in power. For instance, one victim of terrorists was Dan A. Mitrione, a United States AID official specializing in police training.[37] While there is no attempt here to justify the brutal coldblooded murder of Mr. Mitrione, the question might be asked whether he actually came within the scope of diplomatic privileges and immunities. And what if he or some other officials were training police in repressive measures to be used to violate the fundamental human rights guaranteed by the United Nations Charter? Another possible example is the diplomatic agents the United States allegedly sent

---

[35]United States v. Coplon & Gubitchev, 84 F.S., 915 (1950).

[36]Int'l. L. Comm'n., *supra* note 24, p. 980.

[37]63 U. S. Dep't. State Bull. 246 August 31, 1970.

to King Hussein to help advise him on activities directed against the Palestinian refugees.[38]

Since the traditional methods of dealing with an abuse of diplomatic rights were initiated usually at the request of the receiving state, the difficulties in the above situations are obvious. In cases like the above, the receiving state is highly unlikely to request recall when the diplomatic agent is engaging in activities either requested or sanctioned by that country. Thus terrorist attacks against diplomatic agents have often been justified as the only available means to both halt activities which the agent is directing against the guerrillas and to apply pressure on the government of the host country for some political concession. And to the terrorist, kidnapping the diplomat is the easiest and most dramatic way to achieve this.

Obviously, then the traditional methods of dealing with diplomatic abuse are really available only to governments in power and not any other groups, regardless of how affected they may be by the diplomatic abuses. But why kidnapping rather than some other means of protest? Kidnapping, political and otherwise, while never before used to the extent it currently is, certainly is not a new tactic. At one time or other, most nations have used it, even the United States. During the U.S. Civil War, for example, the Confederacy had sent two of its ablest diplomats to Europe to try to obtain recognition for the South. The two diplomats, James M. Mason and John Slidell, boarded a British ship, the Trent, in Havana. The North was aware of their presence and a Union warship halted the Trent on its way to England on November 6, 1861. After the Confederate diplomats were removed, the British ship was allowed to continue. And even though the Southerners were released early in 1862, because of the Union's violation of international law in stopping the Trent, the time gained, allowing the North to strengthen itself, was invaluable.[39]

---

[38]I would like to mention that there is no intention here of implying the U. S. is the only country which might be considered to have breached diplomatic privilege. It could just as easily be French diplomats in Algeria or Indochina, the Russians anywhere in Eastern Europe, the Chinese in Asia, and so on. The actual identity of the participants should not obscure the problem of how to limit such abuses.

[39]T. A. Bailey, *A Diplomatic History of the American People,* (1964), pp. 327-331.

Kidnapping has also been utilized when one country fails to persuade another country to extradite a fugitive.[40] Or perhaps one country does not even bother to start the extradition proceedings but just "snatches" its fugitive from the territory of another country. The Israelis and their pursuit of Nazi war criminals are good examples of this. Of particular interest is the Israeli "snatch" of Adolph Eichmann from South America. There are, of course, many reasons why a state would refuse to grant extradition, and this is particularly true in cases of ideological difference. Thus, the state wishing the return of the fugitive, for whatever reason, often considers kidnapping a solution in lieu of extradition.[41]

While this shows a prior resort to political kidnapping, by no means does it explain the systematic use of diplomatic kidnapping and harassment of the last half decade. At least one writer has attributed the sudden rise of diplomatic kidnapping as well as urban terrorism in general to the fact that this type of tactic has replaced the prior jungle-type guerrilla warfare popularized by Cuba's Che Guevara in the early sixties.[42]

The start of the recent rise in terrorist attacks directed at diplomatic agents can be seen in the January, 1968, machine-gun murders of two United States military attaches in Guatemala[43] and the later kidnapping attempt on the U.S. Ambassador to Guatemala, John Gordon Mein. When Mein tried to escape the kidnappers' ambush he was murdered.[44] In the years following this the kidnappings have increased both in frequency and in the number of diplomatic hostages, although the specific instances are far too numerous to be identified individually.[45]

There have been a number of solutions proposed to alleviate the current kidnapping problem. So far, unfortunately, most of the solutions have attacked the problem from a limited viewpoint

[40]M. H. Cardozo, "When Extradition Fails, Is Abduction the Solution," 55 *A.J.I.L.* 127-130 (1961). See also O. Higgins pp. 314-320 and Bassiouni, pp. 343-373.

[41]T. H. Sponsler, "International Kidnapping," 5 *Int'l. Lawyer*, 27-28, (1970).

[42]R. O'Mara, "Snatching the Diplomats," *Nation*, 21 (May 4, 1970), pp. 518-519.

[43]J. Means, "Political Kidnappings and Terrorism," 5 *North Am. Rev.* 16 (Winter, 1970).

[44]*Ibid.*

[45]For an indication of the frequency of terrorist incidents affecting U. S. personnel see Appendix I pp. 28-30.

resulting in relatively ineffective stopgap measures. The solutions that will now be explored are essentially of this kind.

Obviously, the more traditional ideas concerning diplomatic privileges and immunities have done nothing to thwart the kidnappers. Traditionally, diplomats could rely on international custom and the host country's laws to protect them from hostile acts. Yet neither of these proved adequate safeguards for the U.S. and Belgium diplomats murdered in the Sudan in March, 1973. Some of this disregard can be blamed on a "less than full acceptance of a system which stems from European cultures and traditions."[46] A system which, it must be remembered, provided the traditional reason for diplomatic "immunity."

Other traditional restraints such as "courtesy," a country's sense of "civic virtue" or "enlightened public policy" are meaningless to those groups which have nothing really to lose by not adhering to them.[47] Certainly these types of restraints are not strong enough to make the terrorists pay heed. And holding the host state "strictly accountable" for the injury to diplomats (a traditional alternative) [48] usually plays right into the terrorists' hands, particularly when one of the kidnappers' major purposes is to harm the relations between the countries in the hope of discrediting the government they are trying to overthrow.[49] Basically it is because of the very nature of these traditional restraints that the terrorist has been so spectacularly successful; "by setting aside both legality and ethical norms, the revolutionary antagonist gains a large advantage."[50] It is with the failure of the traditional restraints in mind that the new proposed solutions should be analyzed.

A major proposal, and certainly an important one from the standpoint of international law, is the "diplomatic" solution. One writer has defined it as "envisaging a multilateral pact, which

---

[46]Wilson, *supra* note 10 p. 61.

[47]J. Eayrs, *Diplomacy and Its Discontents* (1971), p. 9.

[48]Wilson, *supra* note 5 p. 54.

[49]U. S. News & World Report, 22 (August 24, 1970), pp. 22-23.

[50]National Review, 22 (June 30, 1970), p. 658.

would deny asylum to both kidnappers and any released prisoners."[51]

Latin America, the scene of a great number of kidnappings, has been the first to propose joint action on this specific subject. The Organization of American States (OAS) on February 2, 1971 approved a convention that both condemned and classified certain acts of terrorism against foreign officials as international crime.[52] Six member Republics, unfortunately, did not sign the pact because they felt it did not go far enough in defining and classifying terrorism.[53] In reality the OAS accomplished about as much as realistically possible in view of the number of countries with strong traditional beliefs in the principle of political asylum.

In the past, problems such as political asylum, a country's traditional right to determine whether the crime committed by an individual now within its borders is an extraditable offense and the issue of whether such offense was a "political" or "common" crime have frustrated any attempts at permanent international agreement. Since many nations consider asylum one of their most important privileges, a few aspects of it are worth mentioning.

The OAS drafting committee, for instance, met strong resistance to anything individual members felt would be a restriction on the right to asylum. Of couse, Latin America has an especially strong tradition of asylum. Any person committing a crime in connection with a political goal has almost always been able to gain asylum, regardless of the cruelty of his act.[54]

However, there are even now a number of restrictions on the right of asylum. Often there are official distinctions between what are called "common" and "political" crimes. If the crime was committed for political purposes or was politically motivated, then extradition would probably be refused. On the other hand, if it was a "common" crime the state harboring the fugitive had a

---

[51]I. Stechel, "Terrorist Kidnapping of Diplomatic Personnel," 5 *Cornell Int'l. L.J.* 210 (1972).

[52]Bulletin 64, U. S. Dept State Bull, Feb. 22, 1971, p. 231.

[53]*Ibid.*

[54]C. N. Ronning, *Diplomatic Asylum: Legal Norms and Political Reality in Latin American Relations* (1965), pp. 184-186.

traditional duty to extradite the offender.[55] The plea of political murder, for example, has been eliminated through treaties in many countries as well as by the historic "Belgian Attentat Clause of 1856"[56] which was adopted and expanded throughout Europe.

Most exceptions to the right of asylum are couched in general terms such as "international crimes" which include "crimes against peace, war crimes, and crimes against humanity."[57] All of these crimes "by their very nature affect the world community as a whole and, as such, despite their political connections, they are excluded from the 'political offense' exception (to extradition)."[58] This obviously is very general, still leaving it to the individual country to determine the offense. And, even now, many nations still consider some "crimes against peace" as being purely political.[59] The obvious tactic here, as many writers have noted, is to seriously limit the types of crimes to which political motives can be attributed.[60] Even now many people consider political murder justifiable,[61] although presumably not all would extend such justification to the murder of a diplomat or other protected person under international law. One international legal scholar suggests the following principle as a base: "The principle that should underlie this whole area of extradition law (political offense) is the necessity for excluding from the category of political offenses, crimes that cause unnecessary suffering and useless destruction of human lives."[62]

In the past when extradition problems had arisen they would usually be settled in the courts of the country within which the fugitive had taken refuge. In a 1941 Palatine case the court refused to consider any plea that the crime was political, stating "we

[55]E. Collins, Jr., *International Law In A Changing World*, (1970), pp. 215-216.

[56]M. G. Najar, "The Right of Asylum In International Law: Its Status and Prospects, 17 *St. Louis L.J.* 31 (1972).

[57]*Ibid.*, p. 36.

[58]*Ibid.*

[59]M. R. Garcia-Mora, "The Crimes Against Peace," 34 *Fordham L. Rev.*, 2 (1965).

[60]*Ibid.*, pp. 20-22.

[61]M. R. Garcia-Mora, "The Present Status of Politics in the Law of Extradition and Asylum," 14 *U. Pittsburgh L. Rev.*, 305 (1953).

[62]M. R. Garcia-Mora, "Crimes Against Humanity and the Principle of Nonextradition of Political Offenders," 62 *Mich. L. Rev.*, 960 (1964).

know of nothing in the criminal law of this country or of England that creates a special offense called political murder."[63] Or, as a French Court stated, "the offense does not derive its political character from the motive of the offender but from the nature of the rights injured."[64] The French view is somewhat different from the so-called "political incidence" test applied by England.

Other cases which have considered the political offense exception have held that the "offense to be political must be directed against the state, its constitution, or the country's constitutional condition;"[65] or have cautioned against the idea that the courts will allow ordinary crimes to be excused as political crimes,[66] or, as did a Swiss Federal court, widen it to exclude escape from the state, e.g. as from an "iron curtain" country.[67]

On July 2, 1968, a British Court decided to extradite James Earl Ray for the murder of Dr. Martin Luther King, even though Ray's defense was that the offense was a political crime and non-extraditable. The decisive argument was made by the barrister representing the United States who said: "A lone murder of a politician, still less of a political figure, cannot satisfy the definition of an offense of political character."[68] Obviously, asylum and the related issue of extradition must be taken into consideration before any meaningful international solution could be achieved.

Certainly asylum posed a very real problem for the OAS when it first met in 1970 to consider the issue of diplomatic kidnapping. The United States recognized the dilemma and, in a statement by its chief representative to the OAS, John Jove, stated that it did not wish to stifle expressions of discontent with authoritarian governments but wanted to condemn only those acts which "violate all concepts of diplomatic relations between status, all prin-

---

[63]"Yourssef Said Abu Dourrah v. Attorney General," *Law Rep Palestine, 8:*43 (1941). Also cited in M. C. Bassiouni, "Ideologically Motivated Offenses and the Political Offense Exception In Extradition—A Proposed Judicial Standard For An Unruly Problem, 19 *DePaul L. Rev.,* 248 (1969).

[64]Giovanni Gatti, *Ann. Dig.* 145 (1947). Also cited *Ibid.,* p. 251.

[65]In Re Castioni, *QB, 1:*149 (1891). Also cited in Najar, *supra* note 56, p. 34.

[66]Ex Parte Kolczynski, 1 *Q.B.,* 450 (1955).

[67]In Re Kavic, *I.L.R.,* 372 (1952).

[68]M. D. Szabo, "Political Crimes: A Historical Perspective," 2 *Denver J. Int'l. L. & Pol.,* 21 (1972).

ciples of civilized behavior and of human decency and compassion."[69] These sentiments were echoed by then U. S. Secretary of State Rogers on January 27, 1971, when he stated before a special session of the OAS that while he had no desire to undermine the tradition of asylum, nevertheless "we all agree that, regardless of motive, they [the diplomatic kidnappings] should be treated as common crimes and not political offenses. . . ."[70] Yet in view of the objections of many countries the OAS decided to leave to the individual state the responsibility for determining how best to deal with each specific situation.

The OAS Convention as drafted was a somewhat ambiguous and loosely worded structure. In spite of this and the fact that not all members of the OAS ratified the Convention it was left open for signature by all other nations. The United States, for one, quickly sent the Convention to the Senate for confirmation. A message from President Nixon accompanying it called the Convention "a significant contribution to international law" and went on to state "it represents an important first step in the development of effective moral and legal deterrents to crimes against diplomats. . . ."[71]

In terms of international significance, the most important parts of the OAS Convention are Articles Two and Six. Article Two states:

> For the purposes of this convention, kidnapping, murder, and other assaults against the life or personal integrity of those persons to whom the state has the duty to give special protections according to international law, as well as extortion in connection with those crimes, shall be considered common crimes of international significance, regardless of motive.[72]

Article Six then reassures many of the Latin American nations alarmed over Article Two by stating:

> None of the provisions of this convention shall be interpreted so as to impair the right of asylum.[73]

---

[69]62 U. S. Dept. State Bull 661 May 25, 1970.
[70]Dept. State Bull., *supra* note 52, p. 229.
[71]65 U. S. Dept. State Bull 28 July 5, 1971.
[72]Dept. State Bull., *supra* note 52, p. 231.
[73]*Ibid.*, p. 232.

Despite these reassurances and the fact that the OAS Convention was open for signature by all members of the world community for a long period of time, it has become apparent, as the legal adviser for the U. S. State Department once remarked, that many nations prefer to develop another convention in the broader U.N. forum, based on the work and comments of a wider group of states.[74] Because of this apparent preference and the pressing need for some solution, the third part of United Nations General Assembly Resolution 2780 (xxvi) of December 3, 1971 requested the International Law Commission to study the question of protection of diplomats with a view to submitting draft articles on the subject. The International Law Commission Draft Convention was eventually completed and submitted, with commission members' comments, to the U.N. General Assembly on July 22, 1972.

The comments themselves are interesting since they show the concern expressed by the members of the International Law Commission in the consideration of a number of problem areas during the compiling of the "Draft Articles." Questions of purpose, scope, application, jurisdiction and penalties, as well as the usual conflict between asylum and extradition were raised by various members. For instance, early in its deliberations the Commission decided to limit the special protection required of the receiving States only to those cases where the incident occurs "for or because of the performance of [the victim's] official functions."[75]

Other points advocated by the Commission were that no time limit should be set within which prosecution would have to be brought;[76] and that any penalty meted out should be harsh because they should "take into account the importance of the world interests that are impaired by these attacks."[77] Concerning the trial itself, the I.L.C. theorized "that no obligations is created . . . to punish or conduct a trial. The obligation of the State where

[74]J. R. Stevenson, "International Law and the Export of Terrorism," 11 *Record Ass'n. B. City N.Y.*, 721-722 (1972).

[75]Int'l. L. Comm'n., *supra* note 24, p. 979. For the full text of the final draft please see Appendix J pp. 31-34.

[76]*Ibid.*, p. 995.

[77]*Ibid.* p. 986.

the alleged offender is present will have been fulfilled once it has submitted the case to its competent authorities, which will, in most States, be judicial in character, for the purpose of prosecution."[78] Yet, in this regard, the Commission also pragmatically advocated "a legal basis for extradition of alleged offenders in a variety of situations so that the State in which the alleged offender is present will be afforded a real rather than an illusory choice."[79]

The Draft Articles (as they appear in Appendix B) were circulated to members of the U.N. for their comments and opinions. These comments, as did the comments of the Commission, focused on a variety of controversial areas. Even the importance of the articles themselves was an issue. States such as France, which held that the protection of diplomats was the sole responsibility of the receiving State,[80] or Brazil, which felt that "the persons whom such a restricted convention would cover already enjoy sufficient international protection in the field of law,"[81] disputed the current need for such a convention. Yet other members, such as Canada, calling the convention "highly desirable,"[82] and Belgium, calling for the "widest possible agreement,"[83] indicated their desire for the passage of such a convention.

There were two areas dealing with jurisdiction and prosecution which appeared to be of the greatest importance to members. Belgium, for instance, felt that the offense was of such a nature that the offenders could be "tried by the competent authorities of any State on whose territory they are found, unless extradition proceedings have been started against them."[84] Likewise, Japan felt that the State in which the offenders took refuge must be obliged to either extradite or prosecute them;[85] and the U.S.S.R. indicated that if the State did not extradite them, then it must

---

[78]*Ibid.* p. 990.

[79]*Ibid.* p. 990.

[80]U.N., Comments of Member States on the Question of the Protection and Inviolability of Diplomatic Agents and Other Persons Entitled to Special Protection Under International Law . . ., p. 191 A/8710/Add. 1 (1972).

[81]*Ibid.*, p. 7.

[82]*Ibid.*, p. 8.

[83]*Ibid.*, p. 5.

[84]*Ibid.*

[85]*Ibid.*, p. 28.

begin prosecution "irrespective of the place where the offense was committed."[86]

Allied with this requirement of prosecution or extradition is the previously discussed "political offense" exception to many extradition treaties. A number of countries such as the U.S.[87] and Yugoslavia[88] called for the disallowance of any claim that such a crime was a "political offense." Canada referred to one of its recent treaties which limited the political offense exception. Canada felt that specifically refusing such a claim in connection with an offense against a diplomat "has the advantage of allowing the State concerned to grant political asylum [in general], while at the same time excluding from the class of political offenses proper, those indirect and specially grave political offenses whose victims are innocent foreigners, and whose effects go far beyond the framework of domestic politics and threaten international relations as a whole."[89] Should such an act occur it would ideally be met with world wide censure.

Although the I. L. C proposals were submitted to the 27th U.N. General Assembly in 1972, the U.N. itself has yet to officially act on a final elaboration of a draft convention dealing specifically with the protection of diplomats.

The United Nations, while not adopting the International Law Commission's draft articles, did pass a resolution dealing with the manifestations of "international terrorism." U.N. General Assembly Resolution 3034 (xxvii) expressed concern with the spread of "international terrorism" and urged the formation of an Ad Hoc Committee to study the problem.

At the time of its passage there was a split among U.N. members over the wording of the resolution. Ambassador Bush of the United States expressed his country's disapproval with the version as passed because it dealt "almost exclusively with causes. One searches in vain throughout the operative paragraphs of that resolution for the word 'measures,' for any hint of action to meet this threat. The resolution establishes a committee but it adopts no

[86]*Ibid.*, p. 41.
[87]*Ibid.*, p. 46.
[88]*Ibid.*, p. 47.
[89]*Ibid.*, p. 11.

time limit for its work. I can easily see that sort of committee spending an entire year discussing its terms of reference, because there are no terms of reference."[90] These sentiments are echoed by Finland who advocates taking some meaningful steps toward the immediate punishment of terrorist acts as well as analyzing its causes because "it would not be just to leave the fundamental freedom of the innocent to expect protection until the causes of terrorism have been removed. . . ."[91]

A contrary position, and one which is exemplified by the U.N. Resolution as passed, is taken by those countries who feel that any hastily-enacted measure to combat international terrorism would be utilized to stifle legitimate expressions of discontent. The U.S.S.R., for example, declared: "It is unacceptable to give a broad interpretation to the term 'international terrorism' and to extend it to cover national liberation movements, acts committed in resisting an aggressor in territories occupied by the latter, and action by workers to secure their rights against the rule of exploiters."[92] Or, as Sweden stated, "It does not doubt that acts of violence described as 'international terrorism' may in many cases have their root causes in 'misery, frustration, grievance and despair.' "[93] The belief of these countries was that the growing acts of terrorism, including diplomatic kidnapping, are merely reflections of existing injustices and until these conditions are changed there can be no truly effective international legal measures to curb these acts.

Obviously, in view of the divergent views expressed above, the establishment of a comprehensive international convention covering all aspects of international terrorism would involve a difficult and time-consuming process. Probably more practicable would be an approach similar to that taken by the Organization of American States and the International Law Commission; that

---

[90]68 U. S. Dept. State Bull, 88 Jan. 22, 1973.

[91]U. N. Observations of States Submitted In Accordance With G.A. Res. 3034 (XXVII) 7, A/AC./60/1/Add. 1 (June, 1973).

[92]*Ibid.*, p. 28.

[93]U. N., Analytical Study Prepared by the Sec'y.-Gen'l. of Observations of States Submitted in Accordance with G.A. Res. 3034 (XXVII) p. 16, A/AC./60/2 (June, 1973).

is, deal with the types of terrorist acts in separate conventions, as in this case one covering the protection of diplomats.

Even by providing separate conventions to deal with different terrorist acts, it is quite apparent that the major drawback to any type of diplomatic solution is the need for an international accord. And, as has just been shown, this remains a very real obstacle. In fact, not even all agree that the problem is an urgent one or that an international agreement would be the best way to solve it. Many people, for instance, "think kidnapping a relatively benign way to deal with revolutions."[94] After all (or so their thinking goes), better for the victim to be a single diplomat rather than a large number of innocent people.

Of course, as the comments by U.N. members indicated, there are many who feel that the repression of the official government is often to blame for terrorism occurring in a country. From the terrorist's point of view, it is highly appropriate to use the diplomatic personnel of unfriendly foreign powers to gain their demands. And even though the diplomat may not intend to be pro-government there is not very much he can do about it. "He cannot consistently with protocol, hobnob with the opposition. . . . He gets only one side of the story, often the losing side."[95]

That the terrorist has little use for the norm expected by most western countries in regards to diplomatic immunity is obvious. In the terrorist's view, the kidnapping of diplomats, like the robbery of banks, attacks on military targets and bombing of buildings is all part of the same struggle to achieve their political ends.[96] To one writer the kidnappings are just part of the cycle of authoritarianism, repression and revolution. His standard to remove such crimes from a "political" context would be that it comprise armed action which is not related in any way to the political awareness of the masses. And without genuine social change, greater freedom and equality, he forecasts that the kidnappings will continue and even increase.[97] Or, as the terrorists

---

[94]M. M. Alves, "Greek Tragedy On A Latin Stage," 92 *Commonwealth* 312, June 26, 1970).

[95]Eayrs, *supra* note 47, p. 7.

[96]Alves, *supra* note 94.

[97]*Ibid,* p. 314.

themselves might well ask: "When government acts in a corrupt manner and against all humanity, can it expect humanity in return?"[98]

Although the "diplomatic solution" is the one which most nations feel offers the best hope for a permanent solution, a number of other measures have been proposed. For instance, Article Twenty-nine of the Vienna Convention on Diplomatic Privileges and Immunities, discussed earlier, directs the host state to take "all appropriate steps" to safeguard or protect the diplomatic agent. This has been interpreted by many nations to require an increase in security measures.

The United States, for instance, responded to the recent wave of attacks on diplomats by enacting new legislation giving the Federal government important new powers in the area. The former U. S. law, Title 18 U.S.C.A. 112, provided in part that fine or imprisonment awaited:

> whoever assaults, strikes, wounds, imprisons or offers violence to the person of a head of foreign state or foreign government, foreign minister, ambassador or other public minister in violation of the law of nations.[99]

However, it was because this law was virtually ignored and the protective duties left to the states that the new federal legislation was enacted. Jointly sponsored before Congress by the Departments of Justice and State, the new act was designed to protect both U.S. officials as well as foreign diplomats.[100] Stringent minimum penalties and comprehensive federal jurisdiction over any such offenses were stressed. During the subsequent debate over the bill, U.S. Deputy Under Secretary of State William B. Macomber stressed the importance of thwarting "militant activists and terrorists" since they seek not only to harm the diplomat and his country but also "seek to embarrass the host state, whose duty it is to protect the diplomat."[101]

The stringent penalties were justified by then U.S. Secretary

---

[98]*Ibid.*
[99]Created by Act of Congress, April 30, 1790.
[100]65 U. S. Dept. State Bull 268-270 Sept. 6, 1971.
[101]66 U. S. Dept. State Bull. 609 April 24, 1972.

of State Rogers who stated: "We're going to be as tough as we possibly can. . . . They're savages, literal savages; and we, the civilized community can't put up with it. . . . we've got to be as tough as we possibly can."[102] The strategy behind the "hard-line" approach is, of course, the prevention of future diplomatic kidnappings by minimizing the potential rewards while maximizing the risks. Yet simply relying on the fear of penalties has been faulted by a number of scholars who feel that "the concept of deterrence has an inherent bias in favor of negative sanctions that raises serious questions about its utility as a tool of foreign policy . . ."[103]

Another aspect of increased security measures is the drastic reduction in diplomatic travel, the shroud of secrecy which covers the planning of any essential trip, a much closer cooperation with the host country's security officers, and maintaining a tighter embassy guard.[104] Yet, as one top diplomat noted, "if terrorists are willing to go below the rank of ambassador in search of their victim, and if they really want to get you, they'll get you."[105] In U. S. Embassies the regulations have become so strict that one official has revealed, "we tell each other where we're going and what we're planning to do only on a 'need to know' basis."[106]

The increased security measures have extremely curtailed one of the diplomat's traditional roles; a role which former U. S. diplomat George Kennan claims is the diplomat's central function: "To serve as a sensitive, accurate, and intelligent channel of communication between one's own government and another one."[107] And, as U. S. Secretary of State Elihu B. Root once wrote, "The diplomatic agent must have full access to the accrediting state, else he cannot enter upon the performance of his . . . duty."[108] A similar view was expressed much later by an Acting Legal Adviser for the U. S. State Department when he wrote:

---

[102]68 U. S. Dept. State Bull. 380, April 2, 1973.
[103]D. A. Baldwin, "Thinking About Threats," 15 *J. Conflict Res.* 77 (March, 1971).
[104]For details of recent U. S. security measures see Appendix C, p. 35.
[105]Newsweek, 75:41 (April 6, 1970).
[106]Eayrs, *supra* note 47, p. 11.
[107]G. F. Kennan, *Memoirs 1925-1950*, (1967), p. 245.
[108]Hackworth, *supra* note 31, pp. 513-514.

"An Ambassador and his government would in all likelihood consider that he had been hampered in the performance of his duties, if, for example, the Ambassador felt obliged to restrict his movements."[109]

Not only are the increased security measures hampering the diplomat but in the present age of instant communication, jet-travel and the shrinking globe, many people are questioning the usefulness of most ambassadorial posts. One former diplomat feels that modern communications have reduced the role of the diplomat to that of "messenger boy."[110] This view is seconded by a diplomatic scholar who believes that most nations are "wildly over-represented" overseas, often only because of simple vanity. Because of this and instant communication (the "hot" lines) he feels that the diplomat "might as well stay home."[111] Absolute refusal to bargain with the kidnappers is another option often advocated. Thus, any ransom demands submitted by the kidnappers would be steadfastly rejected.[112] Many feel this way and can envision an end coming to the current wave of diplomatic kidnapping only "by refusing to pay any ransom for kidnap victims thereby convincing the kidnappers that it is an unprofitable enterprise."[113] Or, as one high ranking U. S. State Department official wrote: "To deal with the terrorists is to invite more terror groups into the field to try to gain attention (and funds) for whatever cause they desire to promote."[114]

There has been a great deal of disagreement over the merits of this refusal to bargain policy. Many feel that the results of such "hard-line" stands would be disastrous. Practically speaking, each situation should be considered on its own merits—thus reserving to the State a flexible position. Leaving the options with the individual State was also recommended by the U. S. Ambassador to

---

[109]Letter from Leonard C. Meeker, Acting Legal Ad., Dept. State, to Nathan J. Paulson, Clerk of the U.S. Ct. of App. for the D.C. Circuit, January 13, 1965.

[110]B. Teixeira, *Diplomatic Immunity* (1971). p. 15.

[111]Eayrs, *supra* note 47, pp. 7-12.

[112]U. S. News & World Report, *68:23* April 20, 1970.

[113]O'Mara, *supra* note 42, p. 519.

[114]Letter from source requesting anonymity to this writer, Sept. 21, 1973. In this regard see also Appendix M.

the Organization of American States: "Each case requires individual treatment in view of the emotional nature of some of the kidnappers and the importance of making every effort within reason to save the human lives at stake."[115] All told, there are a number of reasons for the disenchantment with the "hard-line" approach. Some may be based on humanitarian reasons, some out of sympathy for the offenders and some on the grounds that an absolute refusal would violate the duties required of the host state by Article Twenty-nine of the Vienna Convention.

A Proposal

The proposals discussed above have been, for the most part, representative of a majority of those dealing with terrorist kidnapping of diplomatic personnel. As has been clearly seen, all have their supporters and detractors, yet none seem to be clearly capable of absolutely solving the problem. This writer would now like to submit a proposal which considers the problem from both the States' (Host and Sending countries) and the offender's points of view. It is hoped that by inclusion in the framework of the decision-making process the terrorists will also realize that it is essential to all interests (including theirs) that diplomatic personnel be assured the status of "internationally protected persons."

There is an obligation, as was mentioned earlier, "incumbent upon all persons entitled to special protection not to interfere in the internal affairs of the host or receiving state and, in particular, not to interfere directly or indirectly in insurrectionist movements."[116] Previously, this duty has been only generally expressed, such as in Article Forty-One of the Vienna Convention on Diplomatic Relations. Article Forty-One reads:

1. Without prejudice to their privileges and immunities, it is the duty of all persons enjoying such privileges and immunities to respect the laws and regulations of the receiving State. They also have a duty not to interfere in the internal affairs of that State.

3. The premises of the mission must not be used in any manner incompatible with the functions of the mission as laid down in the present Convention or by other rules of general international law or by

---

[115]Letter from Ambassador Jova to this writer, Sept. 17, 1973.
[116]Int'l. L. Comm'n. *supra* note 24, p. 980.

any special agreements in force between the sending and the receiving State.[117]

Yet such nebulous and imprecise guidelines have long allowed certain members of the diplomatic community to operate in various countries as almost quasi-governmental extensions of the party in power. And such operations have often been carried out at the expense of those out of power in that country. If it is true that it is important to safeguard the traditional invioability of diplomatic personnel, then the cloak of such inviolability should be strictly applied. In this regard the protection of an international convention must be restrictively applied only to those agents actually carrying on diplomatic work.

This is certainly not a startling position since the restrictiveness of a convention dealing with diplomatic protection has been referred to by countries such as Canada, "the essential purpose of the convention would be to provide protection against crimes committed because of the victim's official status; . . . it must . . . avoid sanctioning crimes in which the special status of the victim did not enter into consideration."[118] and Great Britain, "the justification . . . lies in the internationally recognized status of diplomats and other protected persons, and it may be open to criticism if it applied to offenses which had no connection with that status."[119]

It is felt here that the creation of a very restrictive or narrowly-defined class of "internationally protected persons" provides the best method for a lasting solution. This class would be composed primarily of diplomats such as Ambassadors, Consuls and Envoys but would also include diplomatic personnel of international organizations and members of special missions. The further one widens the class, the greater the chance of disagreement, so in the interest of achieving the widest possible adherence the class should be as restrictive as possible.

Accompanying the creation of a limited class of "protected persons" would be corresponding limitation on the legitimate

---

[117]U. N., Vienna Convention, *supra* note 13, p. 87.
[118]U. N., Comments of Member States, *supra* note 80, p. 9.
[119]*Ibid.,* p. 43.

activities this class may engage in. This, of course, entails the development of criteria upon which to base this limitation. Criteria would include activities such as interfering in movements of national liberation or in the internal politics of the host State. A set of guidelines by which to judge the conduct of those internationally protected persons could easily be drafted by a group such as the International Law Commission. However, suggestions should be solicited from representatives of some of the major revolutionary movements active in the world today. Asking these groups for their comments is one of the simplest and most feasible ways of arriving at a solution that will convince most terrorists there is an overriding international reason why diplomats should not be considered mere pawns in political power plays. Once this has been achieved, should a diplomat engage in or commit one of these "forbidden offenses" he would lose his "protected status" and become, in effect, fair game for the terrorists.

Obviously there are some immediately visible problem areas. Questions will arise such as who makes the determination that an activity engaged in would be considered "forbidden;" or that such an offense has actually been committed by the protected person; or whether that person has actually lost his protected status? And, of course, how are these questions solved? At this point a brief illustration might be helpful.

Assume that a diplomat is accredited to a country ruled by an unpopular monarchy. While he is there, at the request of the host state and with the consent of his own government, he engages in activities designed to weaken the anti-monarchial movement in the country. This could easily be considered a violation of his duties as an "internationally protected person." As a result, while the host State might still owe him all due care in its protection, an act directed against him would not be considered an international crime. In this example, let us assume further that this diplomat is kidnapped by revolutionaries and held in exchange for the release of political prisoners and safe conduct to another country. The monarchy complies and the rebels are allowed to escape to

---

[120]Appendix K. Information obtained from U.S. Dept. State, Bureau Pub. Affairs, Release No. 94, May, 1973.

another country where the diplomat is released. This brings us to the third consideration.

The State which now harbors the revolutionaries would be bound to do one of three things under the plan which this writer advocates. First, the State could extradite the fugitives to the country where the offense is committed. Second, the State could prosecute the fugitives in their own courts under the terms of this proposal. Third, the State could also turn them over to an international tribunal like the International Court of Justice for proceedings there under the proposal. Should the first option be taken, most countries have extradition proceedings in the form of trials at which time the revolutionaries could raise as justification for their act the violations by the protected person. This would result in the subsequent loss of the diplomat's protected status thus making their offense a "political crime" and, as such, not an extraditable offense. It would then, of course, be a factual matter to determine whether or not this did occur. This procedure would also be relatively similar in the second and third instances. But it should be clear that under such an international agreement the State is required to take some course of action. It is not allowed, for example, to merely grant asylum on political grounds. The actual success of this approach will not be able to be measured without the submission of a few of the kidnapping cases to the courts mentioned above.

This proposal, it is felt, is probably the most feasible means of achieving any type of international accord on such a sensitive question. The desired result is, of course, a decrease in the terrorist kidnapping of diplomats. Recent steps taken in international law have included a regional agreement by the Organization of American States, the submission to the United Nations by the International Law Commission of their draft articles dealing with the problems, and the creation by the U.N. of a special ad hoc committee to deal with international terrorism in general, both crimes and causes. And yet despite these actions diplomatic kidnappings continue. The proposed solutions have obviously failed in the extremely important area of universality of agreement. Because of this, it is respectfully submitted that the proposal outlined above may succeed where the others have failed—in uniting the international community behind one agreement, and as such, one set of rules. By thus exhibiting a united world community the kidnappers potential rewards would be minimized, the risks would be greatly enhanced, and the desired deterrent effect achieved positively. And while this proposal might not always yield the desired results, this writer feels it offers the most promising framework and acceptable opportunity for adoption of a realistic international agreement.

APPENDIX J

INDIVIDUAL OPINIONS OF INTERNATIONAL EXPERTS ON THE PROBLEM OF KIDNAPPING OF DIPLOMATS

WHILE ENGAGED IN RESEARCH for the preceding article, this writer sent out a number of questionnaires to leading authorities—both at the United States Department of State and those representing various countries or organizations at the United Nations. The questionnaires sought to determine what these individuals thought was the best way to deal with the problem and listed most of the solutions cited in the article above. Even though not all questionnaires were returned and, of those returned, a number requested anonymity, many responses are quite interesting. For that reason this appendix will break down the responses into categories quoting the more interesting ones.

With one exception, all of the responses received agreed that terrorist kidnapping was a problem for international law. Yet even the one exception, the Yugoslavian mission to the U.N., did not dismiss international law. Its representative added: "Strictly speaking, it is not a problem for international law, it is a problem for the normal maintenance of international relations. . . . (in this respect) international law therefore can deal with it."

There was a much greater divergence of opinion on the question which dealt with which proposal they felt offered the best hope of solution. The proposal which everyone supported was "an international agreement to condemn any terrorist activity against diplomats and promise penalties or extradition regardless of what country the terrorists flee to." This would, in effect, make it a truly international crime to kidnap or assault a diplomat. Other proposals supported to lesser degrees were: To completely refuse any dealings with the terrorists, 30%; That countries affected should agree among themselves not to deal with the terrorists, 20%; to increase security measures, 50%; and, to deal with the kidnappings on individual basis, 20%.

As to whether or not a solution can truly be found through international law there were only a few who thought that it could not. The Yugoslavian representative repeated his refusal to place a great deal of faith in international law and stated: "The international law can only indicate and prescribe ways of dealing with terrorism; the real solution depends on strict implementation of these by states."

Also State Department Ambassador at Large, U. Alexis Johnson, now heading the U.S. Mission to the SALT talks in Geneva, indicated his belief that international law could not provide a truly viable solution to the problem.

Of course, there were other reservations expressed, even though these people thought that international law could provide a solution. For instance, a high-ranking State Department official who shall remain unidentified wrote that international law can provide a solution "up to a point. Law can provide solutions where the 'client' is willing. It is not yet clear that a sufficiently broad political will exists."

Mr. John Jova, the U.S. Ambassador to the Organization of American States wrote, international law could help "only partly." Part of this help would come "by creating a climate of conscience regarding the special status (protected persons) of diplomats or representatives of states." Mr. Morris Rothenberg, the Deputy Director of the State Department's United Nations Political Affairs division also expressed a reservation. He wrote that international law can only "provide an important element in a solution." His concept of international law "encompasses the idea of international cooperation going beyond the establishment of legal norms." Mr. Rothenberg feels "the basic problem is to separate this issue from sensitive political questions which greatly complicate chances for dealing with criminal actions." Or as another State Department Deputy Assistant Secretary wrote: "International law can provide a solution if all the national members of the international community accept the problem as one which should be met frontally through a general agreement to define and act against this sort of terrorism."

Not all responses received however were equivocal on the solution which international law would provide. To give an example, the Venezuelan mission to the U.N. stated that international law did indeed provide the best hope for solution because the recent terrorism falls directly within its very special competence.

The responses indicated above are a very representative sampling of the answers received to this writer's questionnaire.

APPENDIX K

CHRONOLOGY OF SIGNIFICANT TERRORIST INCIDENTS INVOLVING U.S. FOREIGN SERVICE PERSONNEL

Date	*Country*	*Incident/Synopsis*
Nov. '63	Venezuela	Deputy Chief, U.S. Military Mission kidnapped by FALN, released after 6 days.
Oct. '64	Venezuela	Deputy Chief, U.S. Air Mission, kidnapped by FALN. Released after 3 days.
June '65	Argentina	U.S. Consul Temple Wanamaker shot and seriously wounded by unknown assailant.
Jan. '68	Guatemala	Two U.S. military attaches killed.
Aug. '68	Guatemala	Ambassador John Gordon Mein killed during kidnap attempt.
July '69	Japan	Secretary Rogers and Ambassador Meyer attacked at Tokyo International Airport by knife-wielding assailant. Neither injured.
Mar. '70	Guatemala	US Labor Attache Sean Holley kidnapped and exchanged for 4 political prisoners by Guatemalan Government.
Mar. '70	Dom. Rep.	U.S. Air Attache, Lt. Col. Crowley kidnapped, ransomed for 20 political prisoners by Government of Dominican Republic
Apr. '70	Brazil	U.S. Consul, Curtis C. Cutter, escapes kidnapping attempt.
Apr. '70	Ethiopia	Jack Fry, Peace Corps, kidnapped from train. Released 5 days later.
June '70	Jordan	Morris Draper, Chief, Political Section, held 22 hours by PFLP. Release negotiated by Jordanian Government.
June '70	Jordan	Several Americans, including a Foreign

317

		Service Officer, held hostage by Fedayeen in Amman. Subsequently released unharmed.
June '70	Jordan	Major Robert Perry, Assistant DAO, murdered by Fedayeen at his home.
June '70	Jordan	Fedayeen entered homes of American personnel in Amman, searched, looted, and raped two U.S. wives.
July '70	Uruguay	USAID Public Safety Advisor Daniel Mitrione kidnapped in Montevideo, subsequently murdered when ransom not provided. AID Advisor Dr. Fly kidnapped a few days later, held until release in Feb. 1971.
Aug. '70	Uruguay	USAID Public Safety Officer Spann held by Tupamaros in Montevideo while his car was used in bank robbery. Subsequently released unharmed.
Sept. '70	Jordan	USIS Cultural Affairs Officer John Stewart held at PLA one day. Interrogated. No ransom demand.
Sept. '70	Jordan	USDAO Sgt. Graham held 8 days, interrogated. No ransom demand by PLA.
Nov. '70	Iran	Ambassador MacArthur evaded kidnap attempt. At least one shot fired at Ambassador and hand axe hurled through rear window of his limousine. No injuries.
Feb. '71	Turkey	Five U.S. Airmen kidnapped, later released unharmed.
Sept. '71	Cambodia	Bicycle bomb directed at Ambassador Swank's car while en route to Embassy. Bomb did not detonate.
Sept. '71	Cambodia	Two Embassy personnel (one MSG) killed, 10 others wounded by explosive devices thrown onto softball field by terrorists.
Mar. '72	Turkey	Three NATO technicians kidnapped, killed when Turkish Government refused ransom demands.

Sept. '72   Cambodia   Charge Thomas Enders subjected to bomb attack while enroute to Embassy in car. Occupants of car unhurt, although car seriously damaged, bystanders killed.

Jan. '73   Haiti   Ambassador Knox kidnapped on road to his residence, held approximately 18 hours with Consul Ward Christensen for release of Haitian political prisoners. Released unharmed after ransom.

Mar. '73   Sudan   Ambassador Cleo Noel, Jr. and Charge d'-Affaires George Moore along with Belgian Charge d'Affaires Guy Eid were seized and later killed when ransom demands were not completely met by Sudanese.

May, '73   Mexico   Consul General Terrence Leonhardy kidnapped and later released when Mexican Government agreed to release prisoners, pay a ransom and give the group a safe conduct out of the country.

Editor's Note:

Lest the impression be given that this is strictly an American problem, the following countries (to name a few) also have had diplomatic personnel subjected to terrorist attacks, particularly kidnapping. In alphabetical order, they are:

Austria	Malawi
Belgium	Paraguay
Brazil	Russia
Britain	Saudi Arabia
Canada	South Africa
Ghana	Switzerland
Iraq	Syria
Israel	Turkey
Japan	West Germany
	Zaire

And it might be noted these attacks occurred all over the world: South America, North America, Europe, the Middle East, and Asia.

APPENDIX L

PROTECTION OF US DIPLOMATIC PERSONNEL

U.S. Measures: On September 25, 1972 President Nixon established a 10-member Cabinet Committee to Combat Terrorism. This committee, headed by Secretary of State Rogers, mobilizes and coordinates the capabilities of the relevant Federal Government agencies in the campaign to protect US and foreign diplomats against terrorism.

Since the March 2 murders at Khartoum of Ambassador Cleo Noel and Deputy Chief of Mission G. Curtis Moore by Black September guerrillas the Department of State has requested additional funds from the Congress for the strengthening of protective security measures abroad. These include:

—Routine protective measures for the security of U.S. Embassy personnel (e.g. follow-on cars, training of local police, radio equipment).

—Development of contingency plans for swift response to terrorist attacks against U.S. missions.

—Assignment of additional Security Officers to missions in vulnerable areas.

—Additional U.S. Marine protection at our posts abroad.

—Additional armored cars for high-risk posts.

—Expanded use of closed-circuit TV.

—Strengthening cooperation with other concerned nations to develop improved intelligence-sharing, technological and identification techniques.

APPENDIX M

Convention to Prevent and Punish the Acts of Terrorism Taking the Form of Crimes Against Persons and Related Extortion That Are of International Significance, Signed at Washington February 2, 1971[1]

WHEREAS:

THE DEFENSE OF FREEDOM and justice and respect for the fundamental rights of the individual that are recognized by the American Declaration of the Rights and Duties of Man and the Universal Declaration of Human Rights are primary duties of States;

The General Assembly of the Organization, in resolution 4, of June 30, 1970, strongly condemned acts of terrorism, especially the kidnapping of persons and extortion in connection with that crime, which it declared to be serious common crimes;

Criminal acts against persons entitled to special protection under international law are occurring frequently, and those acts are of international significance because of the consequences that may flow from them for relations among States;

It is advisable to adopt general standards that will progressively develop international law as regards cooperation in the prevention and punishment of such acts; and

In the application of those standards the institution of asylum should be maintained and, likewise the principle of nonintervention should not be impaired,

THE MEMBER STATES OF THE ORGANIZATION OF AMERICAN STATES HAVE AGREED UPON THE FOLLOWING ARTICLES:

---

[1]Not entered into force; signed by Colombia, Costa Rica, the Dominican Republic, El Salvador, Honduras, Jamaica, Mexico, Nicaragua, Panama, Trinidad and Tobago, United States of America, Uruguay, Venezuela.

321

Article 1

The Contracting States undertake to cooperate among themselves by taking all the measures that they may consider effective, under their own laws and especially those established in this convention, to prevent and punish acts of terrorism, especially kidnapping, murder, and other assaults against the life or physical integrity of those persons to whom the State has the duty according to international law to give special protection, as well as extortion in connection with those crimes.

Article 2

For the purposes of this Convention, kidnapping, murder and other assaults against the life or personal integrity of those persons to whom the State has the duty to give special protection according to international law, as well as extortion in connection with those crimes, shall be considered common crimes of international significance, regardless of motive.

Article 3

Persons who have been charged or convicted for any of the crimes referred to in Article 2 of this Convention shall be subject to extradition under the provisions of the extradition treaties in force between the parties or, in the case of States that do not make extradition dependent on the existence of a treaty, in accordance with their own laws.

In any case, it is the exclusive responsibility of the State under whose jurisdiction or protection such persons are located to determine the nature of the acts and decide whether the standards of this Convention are applicable.

Article 4

Any person deprived of his freedom through the application of this Convention shall enjoy the legal guarantees of due process.

Article 5

When extradition requested for one of the crimes specified in Article 2 is not in order because the person sought is a national of the requested State, or because of some other legal or constitutional impediment, that State is obliged to submit the case to its competent authorities for prosecution, as if the act had been committed in its territory. The decision of these authorities shall be communicated to the State that requested extradition. In such proceedings, the obligation established in Article 4 shall be respected.

Article 6

None of the provisions of this Convention shall be interpreted so as to impair the right of asylum.

Article 7

The Contracting States undertake to include the crimes referred to in Article 2 of this Convention among the punishable acts giving rise to extradition in any treaty on the subject to which they agree among themselves in the future. The Contracting States that do not subject extradition to the existence of a treaty with the requesting State shall consider the crimes referred to in Article 2 of this Convention as crimes giving rise to extradition, according to the conditions established by the laws of the requested State.

Article 8

To cooperate in prevention and punishing the crimes contemplated in Article 2 of this Convention, the Contracting States accept the following obligations:

(a) To take all measures within their power, and in conformity with their own laws, to prevent and impede the preparation in their respective territories of the crimes mentioned in Article 2 that are to be carried out in the territory of another Contracting State.

(b) To exchange information and consider effective administrative measures for the purpose of protecting the persons to whom Article 2 of this Convention refers.

(c) To guarantee to every person deprived of his freedom through the application of this Convention every right to defend himself.

(d) To endeavour to have the criminal acts contemplated in this Convention included in their penal laws, if not already so included.

(e) To comply most expeditiously with the requests for extradition concerning the criminal acts contemplated in this Convention.

Article 9

This Convention shall remain open for signature by the member States of the Organization of American States, as well as by any other State that is a Member of the United Nations or any of its specialized agencies, or any State that is a party to the Statute of the International Court of Justice, or any other State that may be invited by the General Assembly of the Organization of American States to sign it.

Article 10

This Convention shall be ratified by the signatory States in accordance with their respective constitutional procedures.

Article 11

The original instrument of this Convention, the English, French, Portuguese, and Spanish texts of which are equally authentic, shall be deposited in the General Secretarist of the Organization of American States, which shall send certified copies to the signatory Governments for purposes of ratification. The instruments of ratification shall be deposited in the General Secretariat of the Organization of American States, which shall notify the signatory Governments of such deposit.

Article 12

This Convention shall enter into force among the States that ratify it when they deposit their respective instruments of ratification.

Article 13

This Convention shall remain in force indefinitely, but any of the Contracting States may denounce it. The denunciation shall be transmitted to the General Secretariat of the Organization of American States, which shall notify the other Contracting States thereof. One year following the denunciation, the Convention shall cease to be in force for the denouncing State, but shall continue to be in force for the other Contracting States.

APPENDIX N

RESOLUTION ADOPTED BY THE GENERAL ASSEMBLY

Convention on the Prevention and Punishment of Crimes Against Internationally Protected Persons, Including Diplomatic Agents*

The General Assembly,

Considering that the codification and progressive development of international law contributes to the implementation of the purposes and principles set forth in Articles 1 and 2 of the Charter of the United Nations,

Recalling that in response to the request made in General Assembly resolution 2780 (XXVI) of December 3, 1971, the International Law Commission, at its twenty-fourth session, studied the question of the protection and inviolability of diplomatic agents and other persons entitled to special protection under international law and prepared draft articles[1] on the prevention and punishment of crimes against such persons,

Having considered the draft articles and also the comments and observations thereon submitted by States, specialized agencies and other intergovernmental organizations[2] in response to the invitation extended by the General Assembly in its resolution 2926 (XXVII) of November 28, 1972.

Convinced of the importance of securing international agreement on appropriate and effective measures for the prevention and punishment of crimes against diplomatic agents and other internationally protected persons in view of the serious threat to the

---

*Resolution adopted by the General Assembly A/RES/3166 (XXVIII) February 5, 1974.
[1]*Official Records of the General Assembly, Twenty-seventh Session, Supplement No. 10* (A/8710/Rev.1), chap. III, sect. B.
[2]A/9127 and Add.1.

326

maintenance and promotion of friendly relations and cooperation among States created by the commission of such crimes,

Having elaborated for that purpose the provisions contained in the Convention annexed hereto,

1. *Adopts* the Convention on the Prevention and Punishment of Crimes against Internationally Protected Persons, including Diplomatic Agents, annexed to the present resolution;

2. *Reemphasizes* the great importance of the rules of international law concerning the inviolability of and special protection to be afforded to internationally protected persons and the obligations of States in relation thereto;

3. *Considers* that the annexed Convention will enable States to carry out their obligations more effectively;

4. *Recognizes also* that the provisions of the annexed Convention could not in any way prejudice the exercise of the legitimate right to self-determination and independence, in accordance with the purposes and principles of the Charter of the United Nations and the Declaration on Principles of International Law concerning Friendly Relations and Cooperation among States in accordance with the Charter of the United Nations,[3] by peoples struggling against colonialism, alien domination, foreign occupation, racial discrimination and *apartheid;*

5. *Invites* States to become parties to the annexed Convention;

6. *Decides* that the present resolution, whose provisions are related to the annexed Convention, shall always be published together with it.

2202 plenary meeting
14 December 1973

The States Parties to this Convention,

Having in mind the purposes and principles of the Charter of the United Nations concerning the maintenance of international peace and the promotion of friendly relations and cooperation among States,

Considering that crimes against diplomatic agents and other internationally protected persons jeopardizing the safety of these

---

[3]See General Assembly resolution 2625 (XXV), annex.

persons create a serious threat to the maintenance of normal international relations which are necessary for cooperation among States,

Believing that the commission of such crimes is a matter of grave concern to the international community,

Convinced that there is an urgent need to adopt appropriate and effective measures for the prevention and punishment of such crimes,

Have agreed as follows:

Article 1

For the purposes of this Convention:

1. "internationally protected person" means:
   (a) a Head of State, including any member of a collegial body performing the functions of a Head of State under the constitution of the State concerned, a Head of Government or a Minister for Foreign Affairs, whenever any such person is in a foreign State, as well as members of his family who accompany him;
   (b) any representative or official of a State or any official or other agent of an international organization of an intergovernmental character who, at the time when and in the place where a crime against him, his official premises, his private accommodation or his means of transport is committed, is entitled pursuant to international law to special protection from any attack on his person, freedom or dignity, as well as members of his family forming part of his household;

2. "alleged offender" means a person as to whom there is sufficient evidence to determine *prima facie* that he has committed or participated in one or more of the crimes set forth in article 2.

Article 2

1. The intentional commission of:
   (a) a murder, kidnapping or other attack upon the person or liberty of an internationally protected person;

   (b) a violent attack upon the official premises, the private accommodation or the means of transport of an internationally protected person likely to endanger his person or liberty;

   (c) a threat to commit any such attack;

   (d) an attempt to commit any such attack; and

   (e) an act constituting participation as an accomplice in any such attack shall be made by each State Party a crime under its internal law.

2. Each State Party shall make these crimes punishable by appropriate penalties which take into acount their grave nature.

3. Paragraphs 1 and 2 of this article in no way derogate from the obligations of States Parties under international law to take all appropriate measures to prevent other attacks on the person, freedom or dignity of an internationally protected person.

Article 3

1. Each State Party shall take such measures as may be necessary to establish its jurisdiction over the crimes set forth in article 2 in the following cases:

   (a) when the crime is committed in the territory of that State or on board a ship or aircraft registered in that State;

   (b) when the alleged offender is a national of that State;

   (c) when the crime is committed against an internationally protected person as defined in article 1 who enjoys his status as such by virtue of functions which he exercises on behalf of that State.

2. Each State Party shall likewise take such measures as may be necessary to establish its jurisdiction over these crimes in cases where the alleged offender is present in its territory and it does not extradite him pursuant to article 8 to any of the States mentioned in paragraph 1 of this article.

3. This Convention does not exclude any criminal jurisdiction exercised in accordance with internal law.

Article 4

States Parties shall cooperate in the prevention of the crimes set forth in article 2, particularly by:

(a) taking all practicable measures to prevent preparations in their respective territories for the commission of those crimes within or outside their territories;

(b) exchanging information and coordinating the taking of administrative and other measures as appropriate to prevent the commission of those crimes.

Article 5

1. The State Party in which any of the crimes set forth in article 2 has been committed shall, if it has reason to believe that an alleged offender has fled from its territory, communicate to all other States concerned, directly or through the Secretary-General of the United Nations, all the pertinent facts regarding the crime committed and all available information regarding the identity of the alleged offender.

2. Whenever any of the crimes set forth in article 2 has been committed against an internationally protected person, any State Party which has information concernining the victim and the circumstances of the crime shall endeavour to transmit it, under the conditions provided for in its internal law, fully and promptly to the State Party on whose behalf he was exercising his functions.

Article 6

1. Upon being satisfied that the circumstances so warrant, the State Party in whose territory the alleged offender is present shall take the appropriate measures under its internal law so as to ensure his presence for the purpose of prosecution or extradition. Such measures shall be notified without delay directly or through the Secretary-General of the United Nations to:

(a) the State where the crime was committed;

(b) the State or States of which the alleged offender is a national or, if he is a stateless person, in whose territory he permanently resides;

(c) the State or States of which the internationally protected person concerned is a national or on whose behalf he was exercising his functions;

(d) all other States concerned; and

(e) the international organization of which the internationally protected person concerned is an official or an agent.

2. Any person regarding whom the measures referred to in paragraph 1 of this article are being taken shall be entitled:

(a) to communicate without delay with the nearest appropriate representative of the State of which he is a national or which is otherwise entitled to protect his rights or, if he is a stateless person, which he requests and which is willing to protect his rights; and

(b) to be visited by a representative of that State.

Article 7

The State Party in whose territory the alleged offender is present shall, if it does not extradite him, submit, without exception whatsoever and without undue delay, the case to its competent authorities for the purpose of prosecution, through proceedings in accordance with the laws of the State.

Article 8

1. To the extent that the crimes set forth in article 2 are not listed as extraditable offenses in any extradition treaty existing between States Parties, they shall be deemed to be included as such therein. States Parties undertake to include those crimes as extraditable offenses in every future extradition treaty to be concluded between them.

2. If a State Party which makes extradition conditional on the existence of a treaty receives a request for extradition from another State Party with which it has no extradition treaty, it may, if it decided to extradite, consider this Convention as the legal basis for extradition in respect of those crimes. Ex-

tradition shall be subject to the procedural provisions and the other conditions of the law of the requested State.

3. State Parties which do not make extradition conditional on the existence of a treaty shall recognize those crimes as extraditionable offenses between themselves subject to the procedural provisions and the other conditions of the law of the requested State.

4. Each of the crimes shall be treated, for the purpose of extradition between States Parties, as if it had been committed not only in the place in which it occurred but also in the territories of the States required to establish their jurisdiction in accordance with paragraph 1 of article 3.

Article 9

Any person regarding whom proceedings are being carried out in connection with any of the crimes set forth in article 2 shall be guaranteed fair treatment at all stages of the proceedings.

Article 10

1. State Parties shall afford one another the greatest measure of assistance in connection with criminal proceedings brought in respect of the crimes set forth in article 2, including the supply of all evidence at their disposal necessary for the proceedings.

2. The provisions of paragraph 1 of this article shall not affect obligations concerning mutual judicial assistance embodied in any other treaty.

Article 11

The State Party where an alleged offender is prosecuted shall communicate the final outcome of the proceedings to the Secretary-General of the United Nations, who shall transmit the information to the other States Parties.

Article 12

The provisions of this Convention shall not affect the application of the Treaties on Asylum, in force at the date of the adoption of this Convention, as between the States which are parties to those Treaties; but a State Party to this Convention may not invoke those Treaties with respect to another State Party to this Convention which is not a party to those Treaties.

Article 13

1. Any dispute between two or more States Parties concerning the interpretation or application of this Convention which is not settled by negotiation shall, at the request of one of them, be submitted to arbitration. If within six months from the date of the request for arbitration the parties are unable to agree on the organization of the arbitration, any one of those parties may refer the dispute to the International Court of Justice by request in conformity with the Statute of the Court.

2. Each State Party may at the time of signature or ratification of this Convention or accession thereto declare that it does not consider itself bound by paragraph 1 of this article. The other States Parties shall not be bound by paragraph 1 of this article with respect to any State Party which has made such a reservation.

3. Any State Party which has made a reservation in accordance with paragraph 2 of this article may at any time withdraw that reservation by notification to the Secretary-General of the United Nations.

Article 14

This Convention shall be open for signature by all States, until December 31, 1974 at United Nations Headquarters in New York.

Article 15

This Convention is subject to ratification. The instruments of ratification shall be deposited with the Secretary-General of the United Nations.

Article 16

This Convention shall remain open for accession by any State. The instruments of accession shall be deposited with the Secretary-General of the United Nations.

Article 17

1. This Convention shall enter into force on the thirtieth day following the date of deposit of the twenty-second instrument of ratification or accession with the Secretary-General of the United Nations.
2. For each State ratifying or acceding to the Convention after the deposit of the twenty-second instrument of ratification or accession, the Convention shall enter into force on the thirtieth day after deposit by such State of its instrument of ratification or accession.

Article 18

1. Any State Party may denounce this Convention by written notification to the Secretary-General of the United Nations.
2. Denunciation shall take effect six months following the date on which notification is received by the Secretary-General of the United Nations.

Article 19

The Secretary-General of the United Nations shall inform all States, *inter alia:*
   (a) of signatures to this Convention, of the deposit of instruments of ratification or accession in accordance with articles 14, 15 and 16 and of notifications made under article 18;
   (b) of the date on which this Convention will enter into force in accordance with article 17.

Article 20

The original of this Convention, of which the Chinese, English, French, Russian and Spanish texts are equally authentic, shall be deposited with the Secretary-General of the United Nations, who shall send certified copies thereof to all States.

IN WITNESS WHEREOF the undersigned, being duly authorized thereto by their respective Governments, have signed this Convention, opened for signature at New York on December 14, 1973.

UNLAWFUL SEIZURE OF PERSONS BY STATES

PAUL O'HIGGINS

O NE OF THE MOST DISTURBING FEATURES of modern times is the willingness of states to resort to unlawful means in order to recover custody of individuals who are regarded as politically obnoxious. There are all too many such modern examples, many of them involving officials of democratic and apparently civilized states. To cite a few examples at random (to give a complete catalogue would make very depressing reading) the seizure by South African police of Anderson Ganyile, a Pondo political leader, in Basutoland and his return to South Africa and trial there; the extraordinary series of kidnappings by South Korean agents of politically suspect Korean students in Europe, especially in the Federal Republic of Germany in 1967; the arrest by French agents in the territory of the German Federal Republic of Colonel Argoud; the kidnapping of Ben Barka in France by Moroccan agents, etc. Resort to illegality as a means of recovering custody of the politically subversive has a very long history, not least of all in the practice of the United Kingdom. In 1536 Catholic Imperial agents secured the person of the translator of the Bible into English at Antwerp where he, William Tyndale, had taken refuge; this was followed ironically by the seizure in 1569, also at Antwerp, of Dr. John Story, an English protestant, whose religious views were equally unacceptable to the latest British monarch.

We thus see that political motivation all too often provokes states into lawlessness in order to recover possession of political opponents. On the other hand it would be misleading to suggest that this was the sole motivation for the use of unlawful means to recover fugitives abroad; the motive may equally well be that there

336

is no other available means of obtaining the person sought, there may be no adequate extradition machinery available or where it exists it may not be applicable for technical reasons, such as the nature of the crime alleged to have been committed by the fugitive, or even because of the political exemption provisions in such extradition arrangements.

Where a state seeks the recovery of someone physically present in the territory of another state there are a variety of means whereby such persons abroad can be recovered. First of all there is the machinery of extradition where it exists; secondly there is the possibility which has occurred in British practice on a number of occasions of exercising a right given by treaty with the state where the fugitive happens to be, of sending a police officer to capture and arrest him and to bring him within the territory of the state seeking the recovery of his person. Thirdly there is the possibility of securing the wanted person's deportation from the state where he happens to be and his dispatch on a ship or aircraft destined for the state seeking his recovery. Such proceedings may or may not involve a violation of the municipal law of the state where the person happens to be. Fourthly, the state seeking custody of a person abroad may bribe or in some other way secure the unlawful (in municipal terms) cooperation of local officials to detain and transfer the wanted person to the custody of agents of the state concerned. This happened when Israeli officials handed Dr. Soblem over to FBI agents in 1963 and when Mexican officials handed over Dr. Sobell to American agents in 1955. A fifth method resorted to in British practice is for British consular officials in the country where the wanted person happens to be to obtain custody of the passports of the individuals concerned. This they are legally entitled to do because passports are the property of the Crown and not of the individual holders thereof. The effect of being without a passport in a country abroad is usually that the host country then asks the British subjects concerned to leave, and all too often in practice the only direction in which they are free to travel is homeward. Put another way, since other countries may be unwilling to admit them without a passport the only country which they can enter after leaving the host country is the United

Kingdom. There are other methods, but the most important in practice, as illustrated by the Eichmann case, is the seizure by agents of the state concerned of the person it wants in the territory of another state. It is to this problem that I will principally direct my attention. I want to consider it under three main heads:

A. The legal effects of a seizure abroad of a fugitive for the puposes of the municipal law of the state concerned;

B. The effect of the seizure upon the international rights and obligations of the host and seizing state;

C. The consideration of some proposals to remedy the situation.

My first question is what effect the unlawful seizure has upon the competence of the municipal courts, in municipal law, of the state responsible for the seizure. Are they competent in municipal law?

In certain countries, unlike the U.K. and Republic of Ireland, where treaties become part of the law of the land, a seizure abroad in violation of a treaty may mean that municipal courts lack competence to try the person seized.

Where the seizure abroad is a violation only of customary international law, the position is a curious one. The District Court of Jerusalem had to consider this question in the Eichmann case.[1] The Court said:

> It is an established rule of law that a person being tried for an offense against the laws of a state may not oppose his trial by reason of the illegality of his arrest or the means whereby he was brought within the jurisdiction of the state. The courts in England, the United States and Israel have constantly held that the circumstances of the arrest and the mode of bringing the accused into the territory of the state have no relevance to his trial, and they have constantly refused in all instances to enter upon an examination of these circumstances.
>
> "This principle was first established in *Ex parte Susannah Scott* (1829) . . ."

It is a curiosity of the history of the law of nations that this case has played a decisive role in the development of the doctrine applied in later courts of the USA, France, Palestine, Israel, etc. that seizure abroad of a fugitive in violation of customary international law is no bar in municipal law to his trial in the courts of the state responsible for the seizure.

---

[1] 36 *I.L.R.*, 5 (1961); 36 *I.L.R.*, 277 (1962).

Ex parte Scott[2] is too slight an authority upon which to base so fundamental a doctrine. In *Ex parte Scott* no consideration seems to have been given to the question of the violation of customary international law. The court spoke only in terms of the violation of English or Belgian municipal laws. As a leading English authority, Ms. Morgenstern, has said: "It is significant that the learned judge seems to have thought only in terms of a violation of Belgian law, not of international law." The judge in deciding the case applied cases that involved violations only of English municipal laws.

Had the question put to the court been whether the seizure was a violation of the law of nations the Court might have reached a different conclusion. The early nineteenth century was still sufficiently close to the eighteenth century for the principle "The Law of Nations is part of the Law of England" to be applied, as it was applied in other areas in the eighteenth century, so as to bar the judisdiction of English municipal Courts. As it happened, however, the court in *Ex parte Scott* never reached the question: What effect has an arrest in violation of the law of nations or the jurisdiction of municipal courts to try the arrested person. The Court never decided this question but it has been relied upon in the jurisprudence of very many countries as though it had. Yet curiously in another area, namely the competence of English courts to entertain proceeding for the record of penalties for the violation of customs laws, it had already been held that an arrest which was unlawful in municipal law was a barrier to the competence of such courts. The courts denied competence following an unlawful arrest for two very significant reasons:

1.) Any other rule would encourage public officials to abuse their power and violate the law; and
2.) Because foreigners were involved, the Court should behave with the utmost propriety.

If one is to understand the true significance of *Ex parte Scott* one must first of all insist that it did not decide anything concerning the effort of an arrest in violation of international customary law on the competence of municipal courts to try the arrested person.

---

[2]109 *Eng, Rep.*, 166 (K.B. 1829).

Secondly one must understand something about the British system of public law, or if you prefer, the British lack of a system of public law. This means that there is no constitutional guarantee of fundamental rights or of due process which can be invoked to invalidate the actions of the police. There is little in the way of an exclusionary rule of evidence in respect of evidence unlawfully obtained. Further, in the field of police activity there has never been any code of police powers giving them legal authority to do all the things expected of the police. In consequence the police have constantly, in order to effectively prevent crime, detect and arrest criminals and bring them to trial, had to resort to unauthorized practices. Sometimes these practices although not expressly authorized by law have not involved the violation of any legal right. Sometimes these practices have not only not been authorized by law but have involved a violation of a legal right. At first, dealing with practices not violating a legal right, the courts in the eighteenth century said they were unlawful because a public officer, a policeman, may only act when he has been given authority by law to act. Later the courts relaxed this rule. In the second kind of practice English courts, realizing that the police needed such power in order to do their job, ignored the violation of law and even on occasion said it was justifiable in the interests of the efficient administration of justice.

Even in the early nineteenth century, in the absence of extradition treaties, there was cooperation between the officials of states in the arrest of fugitives from justice. Even without the cooperation of foreign police, English policemen often arrested British subjects abroad in the early nineteenth century. It was just such a practice that the court had to consider in *Ex parte Scott* and since the court considered only the illegality of the arrest under municipal law, it chose, as one would expect, to turn a blind eye to such illegality.

In only one English case has the effect of a violation of customary international law upon the competence of English courts been considered. That was in *R. v. Garrett* (1917) in which it was said that such violation could be pleaded in an English court, although it was not stated what the result would be. One judge applied *Ex parte Scott* to the facts of the case because there was no violation of international law involved.

One may summarize English jurisprudence which has been so relied on, but one would submit that a mistaken understanding of this jurisprudence has been relied upon, for in not a single English case was there an actual violation of customary international law. Only in one English case, *R v. Garrett* was the effect of a violation of international law considered, and in that case the Court suggested if the facts had involved such a violation that the question of competence could have been argued.

I come to my second general question—what does international law say about the competence of municipal courts to try a person seized abroad in violation of international law? The answer seems clear—national courts do not have competence in such circumstances. How do we bridge the apparent conflict between the lack of competence under international and the apparent competence under municipal law, based as we have seen on a line of decision in many countries relying on *Ex parte Scott?* My third question is how do we remedy the situation?

Perhaps in those European countries party to the European Convention on Human Rights and Fundamental freedoms we have unwittingly remedied the situation. Article 5(1) of the Convention says that everyone has the right to liberty of the person subject to certain exceptions, principally after "lawful detention . . . after conviction by a *competent Court.*" If competence was determined by international law rather than municipal law, then there is an enforceable right not to be determined on conviction by a court lacking competence, as where the accused was seized abroad in violation of international law.

If the Convention does not have this effect one must plead for the overthrow of municipal decisions based on a mistaken view of the significance of *Ex parte Scott.*

One must seek the following reforms:

1) Extradition law making it quite explicit that the surrender may take place only in the conditions provided for in such law;

2) The adoption of an exclusionary rule relating to the person of an accused, anologous to the exclusion of illegally ob-

tained evidence in some systems, that an accused whose apprehension involved a violation of international law cannot be tried by the municipal courts of the arresting State.

We have talked a good deal here in Siracuse about the problem of political terrorism against states and others. It is my plea that we should also concern ourselves with the lawless activities of states directed against individuals, often individuals who are the political opponents of the states concerned. Deep ideological differences are equally the cause of political terrorism and of state lawlessness against its opponents.

UNLAWFUL SEIZURES OF PERSONS BY STATES AS ALTERNATIVES TO EXTRADITION*

M. CHERIF BASSIOUNI

EXTRADITION IS A LEGAL DEVICE whereby a state requests from another the surrender of a person accused or convicted of a crime.[1] It is one of the modes of cooperation in penal matters between states. One rationale for extradition is that all states have an obligation to cooperate in the suppression of criminality and must, therefore, surrender to each other accused and fugitive offenders. This rationale is based on the maxim *aut dedere aut iudicare*.[2] Extradition law and practice have been slow to recognize the rights of those persons who are the objects of its proceedings. In fact, the whole process of extradition is considered as a relationship between states in which the individual has no rights other than those conferred on him or her by the requested and requesting states. This situation permits the violation of human rights and only recently has been challenged.[3] The processes of extradition involve the requested and requesting states, but there are two additional participants whose interests must be considered: the individual and the world community. For the first participant, certain minimum

---

*Excerpted from 7 Vanderbilt Journal of Transnational Law (1973) and Bassiouni, *International Extradition and World Public Order*, (Sijthoff, 1974).

[1] See Bassiouni, "International Extradition in American Practice and World Public Order," 36 *Tenn. L. Rev.*, 1 (1968).

[2] See generally Wise, "Some Problems of Extradition." 15 *Wayne. L. Rev.*, 709 (1969). This maxim is also stated *aut dedere aut punire* (literally, "either surrender or punish").

[3] For the reports on extradition to the Xth International Penal Law Congress held in Rome in 1969, ad the United States report and a proposal by this writer, see 39 "*Revue Internationale de Droit Penal*" 495-518 (1959), reprinted in 15 *Wayne L. Rev.*, 733, (1969).

human rights must be protected, for the second, minimum world order must be preserved. So far, these two interests are not adequately recognized and extradition continues to be practiced as a matter solely concerning the respective states without regard for human rights and the impact of the practice on minimum world order.[4] This article deals only with one of the facets of the problems of extradition law and practice, focusing attention on human rights and world community interests in the preservation of such rights, the integrity of the international legal process and the preservation of minimum world order.

TYPOLOGY AND RATIONALE[5]

The outcome of extradition processes is the rendition of a person against his or her will by one state to another through certain legal formalities. Extradition is thus a formal legal process, but it is not always resorted to by states who are desirous of securing a person outside their jurisdiction. The means resorted to by states as alternatives to extradition are unlawful seizures and irregular rendition devices. The words "alternatives to extradition" do not mean extradition other than by treaty, although some states, such as the United States, who adhere to extradition only by treaty regard any other basis for extradition (such as reciprocity or comity) as an alternative to extradition. "Alternatives to extradition" here refers to those legal and extralegal rendition devices that do not fall within the framework of formal extradition. The outcome of any rendition device, be it extradition or any alternative thereto is the same; what is at issue, however, is not the result but the processes employed. These rendition techniques outside the framework of extradition fall into three categories: (1) the abduction and kidnapping of a person in one state by agents of another state; (2) the informal surrender of a person by agents of one state to another without formal or legal process; and (3) the use of immigration laws as a device to directly or indirectly surrender a person or place

[4]See Bassiouni, "World Public Order and Extradition: A Conceptual Evaluation," in Oehler and Potz, ed., *Aktuelle Problems des Internationalen Strafrechts* (1970).
[5]Only two types of unlawful seizures and irregular rendition devices discussed in the original article and book by the same author are discussed herein, they are "Abduction and Kidnapping" and "Informal Rendition."

him in a position in which he or she can be taken into custody by the agents of another state.

Professor Paul O'Higgins has classified these situations as follows:[6]

(1) the recovery of fugitive criminals in violation of international law—seizure in violation of customary international law or in inviolation of conventional international law;

(2) the apprehension of a fugitive criminal in the territory of state B by private individuals, nationals of state A, with the connivance of the official of state A;

(3) the apprehension of a fugitive criminal in the territory of state B by private individuals, nationals of state A, without the connivance of the official of state A;

(4) the irregular apprehension of a fugitive criminal in state B by an official of state B prior to extradition to state A;

(5) the mistaken surrender of a fugitive criminal by one state to another.

This typology is important to the determination of the existence and extent of state responsibility.

These various rendition techniques exist, in fact, because of the inappropriate application of the maxim *mala captus bene dentingtus,* by which municipal courts asset in personanam jurisdiction without inquiring into the means by which the presence of the accused was secured.[7] Aside from the flagrant violation of the individual's human rights, the practice of abduction and kidnapping affects the stability of international relations and subvert the international legal process.

Most of the devices and strategies listed above are extralegal,

---

6O'Higgins, "Unlawful Seizure and Irregular Extradition," 36 *Brit. Y. B. Int'l. L.,* 279, 280 (1960).

"Jurisdiction Following Seizure of Arrest in Violation of International Law," 28 A. J. a Foreign Country by Force or Fraud: A Comparative Study," 32 *Ind. I. J.,* 427 (1957); Scott, "Criminal Jurisdiction of a State over a Defendant Based upon Presence Secured by Force or Fraud" 37 *Minn. L. Rev.* 91 (1953). For a case cited by numerous countries as a landmark for the *mala captus bene detentus* rule see Ker v. Illinois, 119 U.S. 436 (1886). See Dickinson "Jurisdiction Following Seizure or Arrest in Violation of International Law," 28 *A.J.I.L.,* 231 (1934): Fairman, Ker v. Illinois Revisited, 41 *A.J.I.L.,* 678 (1953); Preuss, "Kidnapping of Fugitives from Justice on Foreign Territory, 29 *A.J.I.L.,* 502 (1935).

either in form, in substance, or both, but there is no deterrent or sanction to prohibit them because their utilization produces legally valid results. When states can benefit from these practices, further violations are encouraged and voluntary observance of international law, whether by states or by individuals, is eroded. Consider, for example, the attempts to control individual terrorism and the inevitable argument that arises in the context of kidnapping—why is an act characterized as terrorism if it is committed by a private person acting alone or on behalf of a political group and not as terrorism when the same act is committed by agents of a state? At this stage in the development of international law it is no longer possible to rationalize violations of international law on grounds of *raison d'etat* or to allow such violations to be perpetuated without an adequate deterrent-remedy.

The techniques stated above are extraordinary in the legal sense, since an ordinary legal process does exist, i.e. extradition. However, the recourse to these practices may well occur because of the frustration of the legitimate efforts of a requesting state following formal channels, leading one writer to ask, "When extradition fails is abduction the solution?"[8] Indeed, there are numerous examples illustrating this unfortunate dilemma. The difficulties encountered in some instances by states desirous of securing a fugitive or convicted offender—difficulties producing failure to extradite for unwarranted reasons—have caused in part the resort to these alternatives to extradition. The delays and costs involved in formal extradition proceedings are often advanced as other reasons. The proper alternative, however, is to make extradition more workable and not to subvert it by resorting to unlawful means.

Abduction and Kidnapping

This device is characterized by agents of one state, acting under color of law, unlawfully seizing a person within the jurisdiction of another state, without its consent and in violation of its sovereignty and territorial integrity. Abduction and kidnapping must be distinguished from any other formal or quasi-formal means of ren-

---

[8]Cardozo, "When Extradition Fails, Is Abduction the Solution?," 55 *A.J.I.L.*, 127 (1961).

dition and from the erroneous exercise of a formal process, as when an unauthorized public official in one state acting under color of law surrenders or causes to be surrendered a fugitive who sought refuge in that state to the agents of another state.[9]

This device involves three distinct violations: disruption of world public order; infringement of the sovereignty and territorial integrity of another state; and violation of the human rights of the individual unlawfully seized. The most dramatic causes célèbres remain the *Soblen*,[10] *Eichmann*,[11] *Argoud*,[12] *Ahlers*,[13] and *Tshom-*

---

[9]For the classic example see Savarkar Case (France v. Great Britain), Hague Court Reports (Scott) 275, 276 (Perm. Ct. Arb. 1911). Other examples may be found in unpublished materials of the Department of State, which are cited in Evans, "Acquisition of Custody over the International Fugitive Offender—Alternates to Extradition: A Survey of United States Practice," 40 *Brit. Y. B. Int'l. L.*, 77 (1966). These materials will be cited hereinafter as Dep't State Ms. File No.—together with the name of the country and the date. See e.g. Dep't State Ms. File No. 211.12 Hinojos, Efren/2 (Mexico 1936) (Governor of Chihuahua mistakenly assumed he was empowered by article IX of the Treaty of Extradition with Mexico, March 8, 1899, 31 Stat. 1818, T.S. No. 242, to extradite fugitives to the United States).

In another case, "[w]here a fugitive was removed to Canada without court order by representatives of the Canadian Government before he could appeal against the dismissal of his petition for habeas corpus in extradition proceedings, Canadian authorities return him at the request of the United States. His appeal was then heard; the grant of extradition was affirmed." Evans at 89 n. 1. See also Wentz v. United States, 244 F.2d 172 (9th Cir.), cert. denied, 355 U.S. 806 (1957) (illegal action by Mexican authorities in returning a fugitive to the United States did not oust the court of jurisdiction); People v. Pratt, 78 Cal. 345, 20 P. 731 (1889) (fugitive returned from Japan at the request of the Government of California after the Department of State refused to request extradition in the absence of a treaty; court noted that Governor's action was probably illegal, but that this did not oust the court of jurisdiction over the fugitive).

[10]For an analysis of the legal issues in the Soblen case see O'Higgins, Disguised Extradition: The Soblen Case," 27 *Modern. L. Rev.*, 521 (1964). The case has aroused considerable interest. *See Ibid.* 1 n.l. Dr. Soblen was party to the following cases: R. v. Secretary of State for Home Affairs, Ex parte Soblen, [1962] 3 All E. R. 373 (C.A.); R. v. Brixton Paison (Governor), Ex parte Soblen, [1962] 3 All E.R. 641 (C.A.); United States v. Soblen, 199 F. Supp. 11 (S.D.N.Y. 1961), aff'd, 301 F.2d 236 (2d Cir.), cert. denied, 370 U.S. 944 (1962) For a brief account of the Israeli phase of the case see "Soblen Case Summarized," 5 *The Israeli Digest*, 8 (August 1962). "Deportation" in the broadest sense comprehends exclusion and expulsion among other methods for the ouster of aliens from a country. These are hardly terms of art, depending as they do for definition upon particular national law and practice. United States ex rel. Paktorovics v. Murff, 260 F.2d 610 (2d Cir. 1958).

[11]For a discussion of Eichmann see Attorney General of Israel v. Adolf Eichmann,

be[14] cases. In these spectacular cases, the method by which each fugitive was sought and brought to trial can be characterized as exceptional, and violative of international due process of law.[15] The most recent case occurred in February 1973, when eleven persons were forcibly seized by Israeli armed forces in Lebanon and subsequently tried in Israel by a military tribunal. Seizure was justified on the grounds that the defendants belonged to an organization that caused harm or intended to cause harm to Israel; this justification apparently applied regardless where such acts actually occurred. In rejecting the arguments of the first defendant, a Turkish citizen named Faik Bulut, the military tribunal relied in part on the *Eichmann* case as valid precedent.[16] There are, of course, other cases possibly less notorious, but nonetheless equally viola-

---

36 *I. L. R.*, 5 (D. Ct. Jerusalem 1961), aff'd, 36 *I. L. R.*, 277 (Supreme Court, Israel 1962). See also Papadatos, *The Eichmann Trial* (1964); Musmanno, "The Objections in Limine to the Eichmann Trial," 35 *Temp. L. Q.*, (1961). For a discussion of Argoud see De Schutter, "Competence of the National Judiciary Power in Case the Accused has been Unlawfully Brought Within the National Frontiers," *Revue Belge De Droit International* 1:88-124 (1965). The decision in Argoud was rendered by the Cour de Suretè de l'Etat on December 28, 1963.

[12]Argoud was a leader of the military revolt against President de Gaulle during the controversy over Algeria's independence, was kidnapped from Munich in February 1963, and later sentenced to life imprisonment. West Germany protested the kidnapping. N.Y. Times, Dec. 31, 1963, at 3, col. 4 (city ed.); *Ib. a.*, Jan. 1, 1964, at 3. col. 5 (city ed.).

[13]Conrad Ahlers, one of the editors of Der Spiegel, fled to Spain after police raids on the magazine following his criticism of the state of military preparedness in West Germany. He was summarily deported from Spain to Germany at the request of German authorities. Defense Minister Strauss was subsequently dropped from the Government for his part in the affair. In October 1964, Ahler and two others were indicted for treason on the charge of publishing State secrets in the magazine. N.Y. Times, Oct. 28, 1964, at 3, col. 1; *Ibid.* Nov. 9, 1964, at 11, col. 1; id. Nov. 11, 1964, at 6, col. 3. Charges against Ahlers and the publisher of Der Spiegel dismissed by Federal Supreme Court in May 1965. N.Y. Times, May 15, 1965, at 5, col. 5.

[14]For a discussion of the Tshombe case see International Commission of Jurists, Bull. No. 32, pp. 30-31 (1967).

[15]For the text of Argentina's protest against Israel for the kidnapping of Eichmann and the Security Council's action see 15 U.N. SCOR, U.N. Doc. S/4349. See also Brennan, "International Due Process and the Law," 48 *Va. L. Rev.*, 1258, 1962).

[16]*Jerusalem Post Weekly*, August 14, 1973 p. 4; *Time Magazine*, August 20, 1973, p. 31. judgement was rendered Aug. 7, 1973 by the Military Court, LoD, Israel.

tive of international law.[17]

As stated above, the inducement for the continuation of these illegal practices is the tendency of domestic courts to consider the physical presence of the fugitive sufficient cause for jurisdiction to attach to the person notwithstanding the manner in which that physical presence was secured. The case of *Ker v. Illinois*[18] is cited by almost every court before which such a case is presented; but all too often the facts are not analogous to *Ker* and a careful reading of *Ker* would reveal that it is not always applicable. One such inappropriate application of *Ker* was in the trial mentioned above of Faik Bulut, a Turkish citizen seized by Israeli armed forces in a Palestinian refugee camp located 100 miles inside Lebanese territory. Bulut was charged with a violation of an Israeli law purporting to apply to anyone, anywhere who participates in an organization intending to cause harm to the state or its citizens. Counsel for defendant Bulut raised a jurisdictional question on the grounds that Bulut and the other defendants were seized in violation of international law and that the Israeli law could apply to him only if he had committed a crime in Israel or against Israeli citizens. The military tribunal on July 23, 1973, rejected both arguments and

---

[17]For example, Egyptian agents attempted to kidnap Mordechai Luk, an alleged double agent for Egypt and Israel, by shipping him in a trunk to Egypt. Two Egyptian diplomats were expelled from Italy in the matter. Luk returned to Israel, apparently voluntarily, where he was wanted for military desertion. N.Y. Times, Nov. 18, 1964, at 1, col. 5 (city ed.); *Ibid.*, Nov. 19, 1964, at 1 col. 2; *Ibid.* Nov. 25, 1964, at 6, col. 4. The disappearance of Professor Jesus de Galindez from New York in March 1956 has never been fully solved. It is believed that he was kidnapped by agents of the Trujillo regime, taken to the Dominican Republic and killed. See N.Y. Times, Mar.-Dec. 1956. See also 36 Dep't State Bull. 1027 (1957). The particularly vigorous campaign for the "repatriation" of defectors, conducted in the late 1950's by the Soviet Union and other Communist-bloc states, can also be closed as a form of "irregular recovery." See Evans, "Observations on the Practice of Territorial Asylum in the United States, 56 *A. J. I. L.*, 148, 151-53 (1962). Following the West Germany Government's offer of a $25,000 reward for the recovery of Martin Bormann, a Government official was reported to have pointed out that if Bormann were recovered by kidnapping, "the reward would be paid only if the country of hiding later gave its approval." N.Y. Times, Nov. 24, 1964, at 12, col. 4 (city ed.). See also McNair, "Extradition and Extraterritorial Asylum," 28 *Brit. Y. B. Int'l. L.*, 172 (1951).

[18]119 U.S. 436 (1886). See also Fairman, "Ker v. Illinois Revisited," 47 *A. J. I. L.*, 678 (1953).

cited *Eichmann* and *Ker* as authority.[19] Prescinding from the issue
of unlawful seizure, the two cases were inappropriately relied on by
the military tribunal because in *Ker,* Illinois had proper subject
matter jurisdiction since a crime had been committed there (territoriality), and in *Eichmann,* there was universal jurisdiction for
international crimes (Israel, however, had also improperly relied
on the passive personality theory on the assumption that it represented the "Jewish people"everywhere, even if it existed as a
state.). The inappropriate references to *Ker* and *Eichmann* illustrate the courts' confusion of subject matter jurisdiction with
jurisdiction over the person, and of the power to prescribe with
the power to enforce.

The United States courts have ruled inconsistently in abduction
cases, but remained fixed to the *Ker* position,[20] provided there is
valid subject matter jurisdiction. This is also the position of England as enunciated in 1829 in *Ex parte Susannah Scott.*[21] The *Ker*
principle was reaffirmed by a unanimous decision of the Supreme

[19]See note 15 supra and accompanying text.

[20]Frisbie v. Collins, 342 U.S. 519 (1952); United States v. Sobell, 142 F. Supp. 515
(S.D.N.Y. 1956), aff'd, 244 F.2d 520 (2d Cir.), cert. denied, 355 U.S. 873 (1957); Ex
parte Campbell, 1 F. Supp. 899 (S.D. Tex. 1932); United States v. Unverzagt, 299 F.
1015 (W.D. Wash. 1924), aff'd sub nom. Unverzagt v. Benn, 5 F. 2d 492 (9th Cir.),
cert. denied, 269 U.S. 566 (1925); Lawshe v. State, 121 S.W. 865 (Tex. Crim. App.
1909); Converse and Blatt Case, Foreign Rel. U.S. 606 (1918); Adsetts Case (1907),
4 G. Hackworth, *Digest of International Law* 14-15 (1945); Myers and Tunstall
Case (1862), J Moore, *A Digest of International Law,* 4:332-34 (1906); State v.
Brewster, 7 Vt. 118 (1835). For an excellent survey of United States practice see
Evans, supra note 8.

[21]109 Eng. Rep. 166 (K.B. 1829). See Mahon v. Justice, 127 U.S. 700, 708 (1888)
(Court relied on Ex parte Susannah Scott). See also O'Higgins, supra note 5. As for
the practice between England and the United States, "the case of Townsend, concerning the kidnapping of an American national from the United Kingdom by an
American police officer," is also instructive. "The Law Officers of the Crown, in an
Opinion of 1865, did not challenge the validity of the jurisdiction so acquired;
however, they did suggest that '. . . it would be proper and expedient that the attention of the Government of the United States should be called to this case,
in order that such instructions may be given to their police authorities as
may prevent the possibility of the repetition of similar proceedings.' In Blair's
case involving the forcible removal of a British subject from the United States, the
Law Officers in 1876 did not challenge the validity of jurisdiction so acquired as a
matter of law, but questioned it as a matter of policy." Evans, supra note 8, p. 90
n.2.

Court as late as 1952.[22] Many other countries have found themselves embroiled in the same application of the maxim *mala captus
bene detentus.*

Arguably, to be unlawful under international law, the abduction must be executed by public agents or other persons acting
under color of state law; they cannot be bona fide volunteers.[23] This
argument relies on the notion that international law is designed to
restrict state conduct and not to secure the integrity of a process violated by individuals acting in their private capacity. Presumably,
that would be left to national legislation. This theory was presented in the *Eichmann* case, but it was established that those
"private volunteers" were operating "with the connivance of the
Israel Government." *Eichmann* was nevertheless tried and convicted. In contrast, in the *Vincenti* case, United States Department
of Justice agents unlawfully seized a United States citizen in England, but when the English Government complained, he was released and the United States apoligized to Great Britain for the
improper seizure, stating that the agents "acted on their own initiative and without the knowledge or approval of this Government."[24]
If the rationalization that the practice is valid because committed
by private volunteers is to stand, it would mean that states would
only have to allow their agents to act as "private volunteers." and
thereby avoid the whole problem. This, however, would not square
with efforts to curb terrorism by private individuals who resort to
the same technique. The paradox is quite interesting in that states
on the one hand seek to curb terrorism (which includes kidnapping), and yet condone kidnapping when committed by their
agents or by "private volunteers" if it is to their benefit. This dual
standard is all too evident and leads only to further disregard of international law, which, after all, relies on voluntary compliance.

The question of connivance between officials may be classified
as a form of abduction, but a distinction ought to be drawn between these two techniques. Abduction occurs only when the state

---

[22]Frisbie v. Collins, 342 U.S. 519 (1952).

[23]See Cardozo, supra note 7, pp. 132-34. For a critique of this position see Dickinson,
"Jurisdiction Following Seizure of Arrest in Violation of International Law,"
28 *A. J. I. L.*, 231 (1934).

[24]Quoted in I. G. Hackworth, 1 *Digest of International Law*, 624 (1940).

of refuge or asylum is not a party to the plot; when two interested states through their agents, whether public or private, act under color of law or by official connivance, the instance should be placed in another category. This distinction is predicated on the difference between an abduction and an informal surrendering of a person by means approved by the respective states; when both states condone the method of surrender of the fugitive no violence of the territorial integrity or sovereignty of the state of refuge occurs and, consequently, there is little likelihood that the practice would lead to disruptive relations between the respective states. There remains, however a violation of the human rights of the individual, and the legal doctrine expressed in the writings of scholars remains opposed to these practices and to the application of the maxim *mala captus bene detentus.*[25] The surrender of the fugitive by means agreed to by both states is referred to as informal rendition and is discussed below.

Informal Rendition

Informal rendition occurs when the official of the state of refuge act outside the framework of a formal process or without authority to facilitate the abduction or cause the surrender of the fugitive. Informal rendition practices, however, are difficult to document since they presuppose the connivance of the two governmental agencies which would otherwise bring the matter to the attention of the judiciary.[26] The existence of such cooperative undertakings by state agents, even though violative of international due process, evidences the cooperation and friendly relations of the respective states, except when the agents of the respective states are acting on their own, without their superiors' knowledge and approval and undertake such ventures on a purely personal basis. This kind of ultra vires activity is seldom documented in legal or diplomatic records available to researchers. Frequently, however, agents of

---

[25]For citation to some of these cases, mostly from diplomatic archives, see Evans, supra note 8, pp. 90-92. See also Collier v. Vaccaro, 51 F.2d 17 (4th Cir. 1931); Ex parte Lopex, 6 F. Supp. 342 (S.D. Tex 1934); Vaccaro v. Collier, 38 F. 2d 862 (D. Md. 1930); 1 G. Hackworth, supra note 19, p. 624.

[26]See, e.g. O'Higgins, supra note 5; De Schutter, *supra* note 10. For a comparative view see 39 *Revue Internationale de Droit Penal* (1968).

neighboring states may seek to cut through red tape of formal processes and act on their own; but usually, their conduct is either known or condoned by their superiors and their actions cannot be deemed private or personal ventures.

The present position of the individual in international law and in most states very likely prevents his being able to raise the issue of the validity of such practices in domestic courts. The plea of kidnapping by connivance between officers of the Federal Bureau of Investigation and Mexican Security Police was advanced unsuccessfully in *United States v. Sobell,* a case in which the Second Circuit Court of Appeals, sustaining the jurisdiction of the district court to try Sobell on espionage charges, said:

> But it can hardly be maintained, still assuming the truth of appellant's charges, that the unlawful and unauthorized acts of the Mexican police acting in behalf of subordinate agents of the executive branch of the United States Government were any more acts of the United States than the unlawful and unauthorized acts of the emissary of the Chief Executive [in *Ker*]. We think the question presented is indistinguishable from that before the Supreme Court in Ker, and that our decision here is controlled by the case.[27]

Most informal renditions occur between neighboring states and, in particular, when the individual who is the object of these devices is a national of the state to whose agents he or she is delivered. The commonplace examples occur between the United States and Canada and the United States and Mexico.[28]

In *Ker*[29] and *Sobell,*[30] United States public agents participated in the abduction of a United States citizen in foreign countries—Peru and Mexico—with the assistance and cooperation of public agents of the two states. These facts distinguish *Ker* and *Sobell* from the pure abduction cases exemplified by *Eichmann* and others.

In the *Ker* case, a private detective from the United States, while in Peru, received duly executed extradition papers from the United States Government, conforming to the requirements of the

---

[27]United States v. Sobell, 244 F. 2d 520, 525 (2d Cir. 1957).

[28]See e.g. Evans, supra note 8.

[29]Ker v. Illinois, 119 U.S. 436 (1886).

[30]142 F. Supp. 515 (S.D.N.Y. 1956), aff'd, 244 F.2d 520 (2d Cir.), cert. denied, 355 U.S. 873 (1957).

extradition treaty between the United States and Peru. He did not use them, however, because he had no access to the proper government of Peru, which was disorganized as a result of military occupation of the capital city by Chilean forces. He secured the assistance of United States officers to force Ker aboard a United States vessel. At no time did Peru object to the proceedings. If Peru had protested, a question could have arisen whether the Chilean occupation had so deprived the Peruvian Government of dominion and control over the territory where Ker was found that it had no standing to object to police action by foreign authorities because its sovereignty and territorial integrity had not been impaired. It was just such a situation that enabled the United States Government in 1946 to have Douglas Chandler seized in Germany by United States military forces and forcibly returned to the United States for trial on charges of treason.[31] There was no state whose sovereignty was offended by the action of foreign officers on its soil.

In the *Sobell* case the abducting party in Mexico was allegedly made up originally of Mexican officers. Sobell was carried, against his will, to the border and there he was turned over to United States authorities even before crossing into United States territory. The latter authorities took him to New York, where he was tried for conspiracy to commit espionage and convicted. He lost in his efforts to obtain release on various grounds, including the claim that the extradition treaty had been violated. It seems clear that the collaboration of the Mexican police, like that of the French police in the *Savarkar Case*,[32] deprived Mexico of any basis for complaint, even if it had wanted to raise an objection. Many years before, however, the Mexicans had protested vigorously against retention by the United States of one Martinez, who was forcibly taken from Mexico to the United States by another Mexican. The latter was extradited by the United States to stand trial in Mexico for kidnapping, but the United States refused to release Martinez.[33]

---

[31]Chandler v. United States, 171 F.2d 921 (1st Cir. 1948), cert. denied, 336 U.S. 918 (1949).

[32]Savarkar Case (France v. Great Britain), Hague Court Reports (Scott) 275 (Perm. Ct. Arb. 1911) (reprinted in 5 Am. J. Int'l. L. 520 (1911) and C. Fenwick, *Cases on International Law* 420 (2d ed. 1951)).

[33]Letter from the Acting Secretary of State to the Mexican Chargé, [June 22, 1906] 2 Foreign Rel. U.S. 1121-22 (1906). See also Ex parte Lopez, 6 F. Supp. 342 (S.D. Tex. 1934); Savarkar Case, supra note 27.

The delay and formalism surrounding extradition processes as well as the exclusive dependence on the decision-making process of the requested stage arguably leave the requesting state with no choice but to seek other means to secure the return of the fugitive. The classic example when such an instance could have arisen, but did not, is the *Artukovic* case.[34] Indeed, suppose, as Professor Cardozo wrote, that headlines in United States press should state: " 'War Criminal Abducted from California Home: Spirited to Yugoslavia by Serbian Patriots.' Would we be outraged at the evident offense to our sovereignty? Or would we be glad to be rid of a fugitive who had been accused of responsibility for wartime atrocities on a massive scale under Nazi auspices? The questions are not just academic, for there lives in California one Andrija Artukovic, against whom the Yugoslavs level charges of enough murders of bishops, priests, rabbis, Serbs, Croats, Gypsies, Jews, women and children to brand him a major war criminal. Their efforts to have him formally extradited under treaty and statutory procedures have finally been frustrated by decisions of the United States courts. It would hardly be incredible if a group of Serbs, inspired by hatred, revenge, and patriotism, should try to emulate the "volunteers' who successfully contrived to move Adolph Eichmann from his refuge in Argentina to a prison in Israel."[35] Artukovic was charged with war crimes and mass murder on a genocidal scale, but his extradition was denied after almost nine years of attempts by Yugoslavia to extradite him. He was not extradited because the United States courts found that the crimes alleged were within the "political offense exception" listed in the treaty between the United States and the (former) Kingdom of Serbia, to which the new government of Yugoslavia was deemed to have succeeded. In cases involving "ideologically motivated offenders"[36] wanted more frequently than other fugitives), under treaty-imposed political offense exceptions, extradition is denied without recourse; the resort to one of the alternatives discussed in this article therefore becomes likely.

[34]United States v. Artukovic, 170 F. Supp. 383 (S.D. Cal. 1959).

[35]Cardozo, *supra* note 7, p. 127.

[36]See Bassiouni, "Ideologically Motivated Offenses and the Political Offenses Exception in Extradition—A Proposed Juridical Standard for an Unruly Problem," 19 *De Paul L. Rev.*, 217 (1969).

UNLAWFUL SEIZURES, STATE RESPONSIBILITY AND INTERNATIONAL PROTECTION OF HUMAN RIGHTS

The Validity of Mala Captus Bene Detentus

The importance of distinguishing among the types of unlawful seizures and irregular methods of rendition discussed above is to ascertain the existence and extent of state responsibility. It is useful prior to a discussion of the subject of state responsibility to consider the premise on which these alternatives to extradition rely, namely the maxim *mala captus bene dentenus*. The application of this Roman law maxim by municipal courts in the past 100 years has been inconsistent with other Roman law maxims. The improper application results from the judicial disregard of two higher principles.

The first of these is procedural: *nunquam decurritur ad extraordinarium sed ubi deficit ordinarium,* or never resort to the extraordinary until the ordinary fails. Thus, valid resort to *mala captus bene detentus,* an extraordinary process must be preceded by an exhaustion of all ordinary procedures available and cannot be permitted as a surrogate procedure while existing ordinary channels are ignored. So long as the formal processes of extradition are available unlawful seizure and irregular rendition are improper.

The same principle of exhaustion of ordinary remedies is well established in international law, and was reaffirmed in the 1959 decision of the International Court of Justice in the *Interhandel Case* (Switzerland v. United States).[37] The Court held in *Interhandel* that when rights claimed by one state have been disregarded by another in violation of international law, all local remedies and means of redress must first be resorted to before recourse to the International Court of Justice is permitted. In other words, the ordinary must be exhausted before resorting to the extraordinary.

The second of the higher principles is substantive: the principle *ex injuria ius non oritur*. This principle was the Roman law's counterpart to the "exclusionary rule" developed in the United States[38]

---

[37][1959] I.C.J. 6.
[38]For a discussion of the rule and relevant cases see C. Bassiouni, *Criminal Law and its Processes*, (1969), pp. 370-376.

that certain violations of law could not ripen into lawful results. The principle was deemed under Roman law, as well as under some contemporary laws, an indispensible corollary to certain rights without which these rights would have no real significance. In Roman law, these protected rights were those interests the violation of which was considered an *injuria* (which is not to be confused with injury as understood in the common law of torts). Every *injuria* had a legal remedy apart from the general principle that no legal validity attached to consequences of an *injuria*. The author of an *injuria* had to redress in a prescribed manner the wrong committed; in addition, there could be no lawful consequences deriving from the transgression. The principle *ex-injuria ius non oritur* was not, therefore, designed to redress the wrong perpetrated against a legally protected interests which had a specific remedy, but was intended to sanction the transgression of the law itself. The "law" was meant *lato senso*, the integrity of the law and the legal process.

A threshold question arises—whether the violations that take place by virtue of the practices discussed above constitute an *injuria* in international law. The peculiarity of international law compels us to examine this question in light of the existing law of state responsibility.

State Responsibility

Before considering the applicable principles of state responsibility, it is important to bear in mind the three categories of violations which are at issue in the practices discussed in the article. These categories of violations are: (1) violation of the sovereignty, territorial integrity and the legal processes of the state in which the extralegal acts occurs; (2) violations of the human rights of the individual involved; and (3) violation of the international legal process. The law of state responsibility clearly has been applied to violations of the first category,[39] and also, in some respects, to violations of the second category;[40] but, tenuously at best to violations of

---

[39]See, e.g. Eichmann Case, *36 I.L.R.*, 5 (Supreme Court, Israel 1962): note 86 *infra*.

[40]See, e.g. Chattin Case (United States v. United Mexican States), 4 U.N.R.I.A.A. 282 (1927). For state responsibility towards aliens see Barcelona Traction, Light & Power Co., Ltd. (Belgium v. Spain), [1970] I.C.J. 3. The latest decision on Namibia (South West Africa) also stands for the proposition advanced. See Advisory Opinion on South West Africa (Namibia), [1971] I.C.J. 16.

the third category. It is the opinion of this writer that the general principles and policies of state responsibility are broad enough to encompass without doubt the three categories of violations stated above.[41] The following statement made by F. V. Garcia Amador, Special Rapporteur for the International Law Commission on the subject of state responsibility, supports this contention:

> An analysis of the traditional doctrine and practice shows that the acts or omissions which give rise to international responsibility fall into the one or other of the following two categories of wrongful acts: (a) acts which affect a State as such, i.e. those which injure the interests or rights of the State as a legal entity; and (b) acts which produce damage to the person or property of its nationals. The first category comprises the most diverse acts or omissions, some being ill-defined or even undefinable. Acts in this category include failure to comply with the terms of a treaty, whatever the nature or purpose of the treaty, failure to respect diplomatic immunities and, in general, the violation of any of the rights which are intrinsic attributes of the personality of the State—political sovereignty, territorial integrity, property rights. The second category includes acts or omissions which give rise to the "responsibility of States for damage done in their territories to the person or property of foreigners." This is the principal subject of the literature, private and official codifications and judicial decisions which treat of the responsibility of States.
>
> As will be seen hereunder, the above classification, from the traditional point of view, is more concerned with form than with substance, for it has been said that, whichever category they fall into, the acts or omissions in question have this in common: they damage interests which, in the final analysis, vest in the State exclusively. Apart from this aspect of the question, . . . the classification may become meaningless in some cases which come within the scope of both categories. An example of such a case would be the nonperformance of a treaty, where the interests of the nationals of one of the contracting States are prejudiced and the claim is based on this prejudice. [W]e shall now consider what acts or omissions are more generally regarded as giving rise to an international responsibility on the part of the State.
>
> Within the second subdivision, too, the wrongful acts capable of giving rise to responsibility on the part of the State are not all of the same character. Although in these cases the international responsibility does not originate in the act itself but rather in the conduct of

---

[41]See C. Eagleton, *The Responsibility of States in International Law* (1928); Bassiouni, "The Nationalization of the Suez Canal and the Illicit Act in International Law, 14 *De Paul L. Rev.*, 258-63 (1965).

the State in relation to the act (failure to exercise due diligence, connivance, manifest complicity, etc.), the nature of the act committed by a private person or of acts committed during internal disturbances is bound to influence the way in which the law regards the State's conduct as a source of international responsibility. Typical examples of wrongful acts which can be committed by private persons are attacks or insults against a foreign State, in the person of the head of that State, its agencies or diplomatic representatives; acts offensive to its national flag; and illegal acts—whatever their degree of seriousness may be—which cause damage to the person or property of the nationals of a foreign State. When disturbances occur in a State, the acts concerned are usually of a more serious character; in some cases, they are specifically intended to cause damage to the property or person of foreigners.

Although not exhaustive, the foregoing enumeration presents a fairly accurate picture of the acts and omissions which according to traditional doctrine and practice, give rise to international responsibility on the part of the State. In any case, it makes it possible to define the character of those acts and so to determine the type of responsibility to which they can give rise.[42]

The general statement quoted above indicates that state responsibility attaches to actions by the state through its agents for specific acts as well as for failures by state to act, presumably whenever there is a preexisting legal obligation to do so. Two essential questions, therefore, arise in the context of the statement quoted above: First, what is the connection which must be established between the state and its agents or between the agents of the state and individuals acting in their private capacity in order for state responsibility to attach? Secondly, is a state obligated merely to refrain from engaging in violative conduct, is there an obligation to prevent such conduct from occurring, or is a state an insurer of the lawful conduct of its agents?

As to the first question raised, state responsibility clearly attaches to acts committed by agents of a state or by private individuals acting for or on behalf of the state.[43] The connection that must be established between the individual (acting privately) and the state in order to impute that individual's act to the state is not very

---

[42] *Y. B. Int'l. L. Comm'n.* 173, 181, (1958) U.N. Doc. A/CN.4/Ser. A/1956/Add. 1.

[43] "A state owes at all times a duty to protect other states against injurious acts by individuals from within its jurisdiction." C. Eagleton, *supra* note 40 p. 80.

clear; customary international law does not provide us with reliable criteria. There is, however, no uncertainty in cases in which the
state, through its agents, incites, encourages or induces private individuals to undertake such actions with a view to benefit the state.
It is obvious that the less direct the connection between the state
and the individual acting privately, the more difficult it will be to
ascribe state responsibility for individual conduct even when that
conduct inures to the benefit of the state.

As to the second question raised, a policy question arises in the
context of the practices at issue, namely, whether responsibility, is
to be based only on positive conduct (when a state causes a given
act to take place) or whether it extends also to passive conduct
(when a state merely permits conduct to take place). Is there a duty
on the part of a state to prevent unlawful conduct if it has the
knowledge of impending illegalities or has the capacity to prevent
unlawful conduct from occurring; or is a state to be held responsible, even without prior knowledge of the contemplated action or
without the capacity to prevent it? The statement by Garcia
Amador on state responsibility raises an inference that states are in
some instances insurers, but in the context of alternatives to extradition that inference cannot be applied. The general statement
by Garcia Amador would seem, however, to encompass a range of
doctrines of responsibility, but neither customary nor conventional
international law has applied these doctrines to the law and practice of extradition except in cases in which a state through its
agents or private persons acting on its behalf have committed ab-
ductions. The *Eichmann* case is probably the most illustrative example of this exception. The search for state responsibility criteria
in this area leads this writer to suggest resorting to analogies with
other aspects of state responsibility. A parallel would be the regulation of armed conflicts and general principles of international criminal responsibility from which applicable rules for state and individual responsibility for violations of international extradition law
can be derived.[44] The writings of scholars, however, have never
suggested this analogy, and, to the extent that it is a novel doctrine,

---

[44]See generally C. Bassiouni, and V. Nanda, eds., *A Treatise on International Criminal Law* Vol. I pt. 4. § 2, (1973).

it requires refinement. Consider, however, the applicablity of this doctrine to problems of command responsibility and defenses such as the defense of obedience to superior orders.[45] If rules of individual responsibility would be made applicable to individual abductors, they would be considered responsible under international criminal law without benefit of the defense of obedience to superior orders; and superiors of the abducting agents would also be accountable under the command responsibility theory.

As stated above, state responsibility attaches under contemporary international law to unlawful seizures of persons committed by agents of a state or individuals acting for or on its behalf. Such responsibility attaches because an *injuria* has been perpetrated. The only established remedies are reparations and diplomatic apologies, and the return of the person seized unlawfully is not yet recognized as a required remedy, even though some courts have seen fit to require the return of the seized person. This remedial approach of denying a violation the chance to ripen into lawful outcomes is in keeping with the higher principle *ex injuria ius non oritur*. Indeed, without such a remedy the integrity of the international legal order would not be preserved.

Human Rights and State Responsibility

State responsibility hinges on the existence of an international right or duty the transgression of which would cause certain consequences requiring the attachment of a remedy and sanction. The existence of state responsibility for the second category of violations involved in the practices examined in this article—violations of human rights—depends, therefore, on the answers to these questions: What are these rights? Where do they originate? What is their binding legal effect? What sanctions apply? Who applies them? In judicial terms, these questions require analysis of the following issues: (1) the legally binding nature of human rights; (2) the self-executing nature of obligations to preserve and protect human rights; (3) the penetration of international law into municipal law; and (4) the enforcement of human rights provisions. A complete treatment of all these questions is obviously beyond the

---

[45]*Ibid.* pt. 2, § 4.4, at 450, pt. § § 1-3.

scope of this analysis, but some general observations must be made.

An initial observation focuses on the attitudes of municipal courts toward internationally protected human rights. Time and again, decisions in cases containing allegations of unlawful seizures and irregular rendition practices distinguish between violations of international law and violations of municipal law. Once this dichotomy is accepted, it is relatively simple for municipal courts considering the issue to deem themselves jurisdictionally unimpaired by violations of international law and to proceed with the case as if the violation of international law did not exist.

The rationale sustaining this dichotomy between violations of internal law and violations of international law is predicated on one interpretative approach to the doctrine of separation of powers in municipal law. Under this approach violation of international law are deemed within the prerogatives of the executive, not the judiciary, and, furthermore, municipal courts assert that they have no enforceable sanctioning powers over such violations; only the executive can deal with such questions. Governments, on the other hand, also argue that human rights are nonenforceable by municipal courts for a variety of reasons, including the following:

(1) Except as provided by treaty, there are no binding international sanctions for violations of human rights.

(2) Except as provided by treaty, there are no existing binding obligations arising out of internationally enunciated human rights that are applicable to municipal courts.

(3) Self-executing enforcement of internationally enunciated human rights would violate state sovereignty.

The validity of these assertions in the present state of international law is by no means as clear-cut as either the proponents of human rights or the proponents of state sovereignty claim. In fact, no other area of international law is as riddled with confusion between *lex lata* and *legge ferenda* as is the literature on international protection of human rights. One may even occasionally find some arguments in the nature of *legge desiderata,* which are incorrectly advanced as *lex lata.*

The observations that follow by no means purport to exhaust the arguments debated on these issues, but are intended to present a cursory view of the present state of the law and its likely immediate development.

The central issue is not whether there are human rights,[46] but whether there are rules for the protection of human rights with enough specific content to be deemed legally binding on states and to require enforcement. Thus, there is a need to identify the source of these rights, to determine whether these sources refer to a specific right with a sufficiently defined content requiring a sanction-remedy and applying to unlawful seizures and irregular rendition practices. The applicable sources of international law are: the United Nations Charter, the Universal Declaration on Human Rights, multilateral treaties, decisions of international courts, and United Nations resolutions.[47] This classification is based on the degree of applicability and binding nature of specific obligations within the meaning of internationally protected human rights.

AN APPRAISAL OF RENDITION DEVICES AS ALTERNATIVES TO EXTRADITION AND WORLD AND PUBLIC ORDER

If the premise is accepted that extradition is the only legitimate process to secure rendition of a person sought by a state other than the state in which the fugitive sought refuge, then all other means of rendition are illegitimate. The alternatives to extradition discussed in this article are all irregular and extraordinary. They range from outright criminal means (abduction) to the irregular use of legal devices available under the immigration laws of the state of refuge. What, however, are the alternatives available when the only legitimate process, i.e. extradition, fails? This is only one of the questions raised by these irregular methods; others are: Is the individual entitled to have the requesting and requested states follow exclusively a single process, i.e. extradition, in the exercise of their mutual cooperation in penal matters? Can either state insist on that single process as the exclusive means of cooperation be-

---

[46]See Bassiouni, "The Human Rights Program:" The Veneer of Civilization Thickens," 21 *De Paul L. Rev.*, 271 (1971). See also L. Sohn, and T. Buergenthal, *International Protection of Human Rights* (1973).

[47]A discussion of these sources can be found in the original version of this article which was abridged for purposes of this book.

tween them? Should international law prohibit the use of irregular devices to secure rendition? Should there be a formal alternative process to extradition? Should there be some other legal recourse or legal remedy in case extradition fails?

There is an obvious correlation between the resort to irregular methods of rendition and either the failure of the formal process extradition or the stringency of its requirements. This conclusion tends to indicate the endemic weakness of a process that relies on many legal formalities and that is shrouded with a formalism that appears to have become inherent. As stated by Professor Evans:

> Accepting the premise that the established method of recovery of the international fugitive offender is by extradition proceedings which are ordinarily governed by both treaty and statute, it may be asked whether *Eichmann, Ahlers* and similar cases are the exceptions which prove the rule. If, however, resort to methods of recovery other than extradition is a common occurrence, it may be asked whether the extradition process is failing to serve its objective of providing a state with a formal method of acquiring custody of a fugitive offender in which the interests of the asylum state, the requesting state and of the accused are procedurally protected. In other words, does the relative stringency of the extradition process make it an anachronism in an age of rapid communication? Again, approaching the issue from the broader context of that public concern with the recognition of the rights of the individual and their protection under international law which has gained increasing momentum during the past two decades, it may be asked whether the international fugitive offender has any right as against the asylum state to demand surrender only through extradition proceedings. Conversely, it may be asked whether the asylum state is under an obligation to disregard any request for surrender other than one through the formal channel of extradition and to refrain from using such legal processes as exclusion or expulsion as convenient substitutes for extradition and from condoning the use of irregular methods of recovery of fugitives by other states.
>
> The answers to these questions are not readily supplied, for each question tends to raise other questions about the scope of the territorial jurisdiction of the state, the plenary power of the state over the responsibility of the state for enforcing law and order by bringing criminals to justice, the right of the state to protect itself from becoming a haven for criminals. In the last analysis the answers must be found in information about the nature of state practice in the matter of acquiring custody over international fugitive offenders by methods other than extradition.[48]

---

[48]Evans, *supra* note 8, 78-79.

At the policy level the dilemma is characteristic: It is a conflict between two processes, one that is *means*-oriented and the other that is *result*-oriented. The choice between these divergent policies will depend on the value-oriented goals of the system of justice administered in that particular state.

To preserve minimum world order, a distinction must be drawn between irregular situations that result from the cooperative undertakings of the respectively interested states and situations in which one state resorts to a method that violates the territorial integrity, sovereignty or legal processes of another state. In both situations, the main deterrent to their use would be the recognition of a principle of legality of process that would disallow the application of *mala captus bene detentus,* and establish the primacy of a formal legal process over any irregular processes by declaring any resort to the irregular practices unlawful under international law. Such a deterrent-remedy is still not well established in international law, even though the writings of publicists continue to decry violations of human rights and international due process of law. When one state acts without the cooperation or consent of another, threats to minimum world order have three dimensions: violation of the sovereignty, territorial integrity and legal process of the state of refuge; violation of the individual's right to freedom from arbitrary arrest and detention and to international due process and fairness; and violation of the integrity of the international process.

REMEDIES FOR UNLAWFUL SEIZURES BY STATES

The sources mentioned above indicate that violations of certain specific internationally protected human rights give rise to internationally enforceable rights, and that such violations constitute *injuriae* to which state responsibility attaches and which cannot produce legitimate outcomes.

In the context of unlawful seizures and irregular rendition the first question is whether arbitrary arrest and detention falls within the category of serious violations of internationally protected human rights and can be considered an *injuria,* warranting a legal remedy. The answer seems obvious; there can be no greater internationally protected human right, after the right to life, than the right to liberty. A second question relates to the extent of a state's obligation to protect such rights. Clearly, a state cannot infringe these rights without due process of law; but does this duty of non-infringement extend to an obligation on the part of the state to insure against such violations of due process by other states? Such a proposition is not yet recognized because of the relatively recent development of the law of human rights; but if this extended duty were recognized, then the state in which the violation occurred would be aggrieved in two ways. First, its obligation to secure for the individual the right of freedom from arbitrary arrest and detention would be violated by the actions of another state. Secondly, and as a logical consequence of the individual state's obligation, all states sharing a common duty to insure the safeguard of internationally protected human rights are collectively affected by a transgression of these commonly binding obligations. Under this argument, the rights of an injured state cannot be severed from those of the individual whose international protected rights were infringed. The remedy applicable to an international *injuria* should bar the ripening of such violations into lawful outcomes. An example when a remedy applicable to an *injuria* found its expression is the *Jacob-Solomon Case*.[49] In this case a former German citizen was taken into Germany from Switzerland by force and deceit. Under a 1921 treaty between Germany and Switzerland concerning unresolved disputes, the matter was submitted to an international court of arbitration.[50] Shortly after the case was initiated, Germany admitted error and returned Jacob to Swiss authorities.

Four other cases deserve mention. The first is a 1933 case, *In re Jovis,* in which a Belgian citizen was seized by French agents and brought to trial in France. The Tribunal Correctional d'Avesnes held[51] that the defendant should be returned to Belgium because he had been seized illegally. The defendant was returned immediately to Belgium. In a 1965 issue between Italy and Switzerland,

---

[49]Settlement of the Jacob Kidnapping Case (Switzerland-Germany), in 30 *A. J. I. L.,* 23 (1936).

[50]Treaty of Arbitration and Counciliation Between the Swiss Confederation and the German Reich, Dec. 3, 1921, No. 320, *LNTS, 12*:281.

[51][1933-1939] *Ann Dig* 191 (No. 77) (Tribunal Correctional d'Avesnes, France 1933).

the *Affaire Mantovani,*[52] an unlawfully seized person was returned to Switzerland and the Italian authorities extended their apologies to the Swiss Government. A third example is the 1962 case known as *The Red Crusader,*[53] which involved Denmark and the United Kingdom. The case concerned the illegal seizure of a fishing boat captain by Denmark, which sought to prosecute him for illegally fishing in its territorial waters, and resulted in the release of the accused and his return to England. The case of Kim Dae Jung involved Japan and South Korea. In August 1973, Jung was kidnapped from a Tokyo hotel room by Korean agents claiming to act in their "personal capacity." After Japan's protest Korea agreed not to prosecute Jung and extended its apologies to Japan.[54]

These cases upheld and vindicated the principle *ex injuria non oritur,* which is also embodied in the unanimous resolution of the Security Council in the complaint of Argentina against Israel in the *Eichmann* case. The Council stated: "That acts such as that under consideration, which affect the sovereignty of another state and, therefore, cause international friction, may, if repeated, endanger peace and security. [The Council requests] the government of Israel to make appropriate reparation in accordance with the Chapter of the United Nations and the rules of International Law."[55]

Surely, Charter principles and rules of international law include international protection of human rights and proscribe the violation of those rights by the practices exemplified by the *Eichmann* case. The conclusions of this writer are:

(1) States must abide by specific human rights and norms, and in spirit fulfill the principles and purposes of the Charter and those instruments that interpret it.

(2) Unlawful and improper seizures in violation of international law mean renditions executed without benefit of a legal process insuring minimal standards of due process or in violation of specific human rights provisions; these

---

[52]In *Revue Generale de Droit International Public, 69:*761 (1965).
[53]*ILR, 35:*485 (Commission of Enquiry (Denmark-United Kingdom) 1967).
[54]Time, Nov. 12, 1973, p. 72.
[55]U.N. Doc. S/1439, June 23, 1960.

seizures violate international law; sanctions include the following:

(a) the perpetrators, their aiders and abettors and responsible superiors are to be held responsible for the international crime of kidnapping;

(b) the person who was subjected to these practices is to be returned to the state from which he or she was seized and is entitled to damages;

(c) the state in which the act occurred is entitled to reparations and apologies.

(3) The International Court of Justice should be empowered (by a special supplement to its statute) to hear petitions by states on behalf of individuals who were the object of such treatment and should have compulsory jurisdiction over these states to decide the proper sanction-remedy. The Court should also be empowered to issue writs of habeas corpus.[56]

---

[56]This proposal was made by the author to the Xth International Penal Law Congress. Bassiouni, 39 *Revue International de Droit Penal,* 518 (1968). See also L. Kutner, *World Habeas Corpus* (1962).

APPENDIX O

RELEVANT EXCERPTS FROM INTERNATIONAL HUMAN RIGHTS TREATIES ON UNLAWFUL SEIZURE OF PERSONS

1. The International Covenant on Civil and Political Rights

Article 9

1. Everyone has the right to liberty and security of person. No one shall be subjected to arbitrary arrest or detention. No one shall be deprived of his liberty except on such grounds and in accordance with such procedure as are established by law.

2. Anyone who is arrested shall be informed, at the time of arrest, of the reasons for his arrest and shall be promptly informed of any charges against him.

3. Anyone arrested or detained on a criminal charge shall be brought promptly before a judge or other officer authorized by law to exercise judicial power and shall be entitled to trial within a reasonable time or to release. It shall not be the general rule that persons awaiting trial shall be detained in custody, but release may be subject to guarantees to appear for trial, at any other stage of the judicial proceedings, and, should occasion arise, for execution of the judgment.

4. Anyone who is deprived of his liberty by arrest or detention shall be entitled to take proceedings before a court, in order that that court may decide without delay on the lawfulness of his detention and order his release if the detention is not lawful.

5. Anyone who has been the victim of unlawful arrest or detention shall have an enforceable right to compensation.

Article 12

1. Everyone lawfully within the territory of a state shall, within that territory, have the right to liberty of movement and freedom to choose his residence.

2. Everyone shall be free to leave any country, including his own.

3. The above-mentioned rights shall not be subject to any restrictions except those which are provided by law, are necessary to protect national security, public order (order public), public health or morals or the rights and freedoms of others, and are consistent with the other rights recognized in the present Covenant.

4. No one shall be arbitrarily deprived of the right to enter his own country.

Article 13

An alien lawfully in the territory of a State Party to the present Covenant may be expelled therefrom only in pursuance of a decision reached in accordance with law and shall, except where compelling reasons of national security otherwise require, be allowed to submit the reasons against his expulsion and to have his case reviewed by, and be represented for the purpose before, the competent authority or a person or persons especially designated by the competent authority.

2. The Convention Relating to the Status of Stateless Persons

Article 31

1. The Contracting States shall not expel a stateless person lawfully in their territory save on grounds of national security or public order.

2. The expulsion of such a stateless person shall be only in pursuance of a decision reached in accordance with the process of law. Except where compelling reasons of national security otherwise require, the stateless person shall be allowed to submit evidence to clear himself, and to appeal to and be represented for the purpose before competent authority or a person or persons specially designated by the competent authority.

3. The Contracting States shall allow such a stateless person a reasonable period within which to seek legal admission into another country. The Contracting States reserve the right to apply during that period such internal measures as they may deem necessary.

3. The Convention Relative to the Status of Refugees

Article 32

Expulsion

1. The Contracting States shall not expel a refugee lawfully in their territory save on grounds of national security or public order.

2. The expulsion of such a refugee shall be only in pursuance of a decision reached in accordance with due process of law. Except where compelling reasons of national security otherwise require, the refugee shall be allowed to submit evidence to clear himself, and to appeal to and be represented for the purpose before competent authority or a person or persons specially designated by the competent authority.

3. The Contracting States shall allow such a refugee a reasonable period within which to seek legal admission into another country. The Contracting States reserve the right to apply during that period such internal measures as they may deem necessary.

Article 33

Prohibition of Expulsion or Return ("Refoulement")

1. No Contracting State shall expel or return ("refouler") a refugee in any manner whatsoever to the frontiers of territories where his life or freedom would be threatened on account of his race, religion, nationality, membership of a particular social group or political opinion.

2. The benefit of the present provision may not, however, be claimed by a refugee whom there are reasonable grounds for regarding as a danger to the security of the country in which he is, or who, having been convicted by a final judgment of a particularly serious crime, constitutes a danger to the community of that country.

4. The European Convention for the Protection of Human Rights and Fundamental Freedoms

Article 5

1. Everyone has the right to liberty and security of person. No one shall be deprived of his liberty save in the following cases and in accordance with a procedure prescribed by law:

(a) the lawful detention of a person after conviction by a competent court;

(b) the lawful arrest or detention of a person for noncompliance with the lawful order of a court or in order to secure the fulfillment of any obligation prescribed by law;

(c) the lawful arrest or detention of a person effected for the purpose of bringing him before the competent legal authority on reasonable suspicion of having committed an offense or when it is reasonably considered necessary to prevent his committing an offense or fleeing after having done so;

(d) the detention of a minor by lawful order for the purpose of educational supervision or his lawful detention for the purpose of bringing him before the competent legal authority;

(e) the lawful detention of persons for the prevention of the spreading of infectious diseases, of persons of unsound mind, alcoholics or drug addicts or vagrants;

(f) the lawful arrest or detention of a person to prevent his effecting an unauthorized entry into the country or a person against whom action is being taken with a view to deportation or extradition.

2. Everyone who is arrested shall be informed promptly, in a language which he understands, of the reasons for his arrest and of any charge against him.

3. Everyone arrested or detained in accordance with the provisions of paragraph 1(c) of this Article shall be brought promptly before a judge or other officer authorized by law to exercise judicial power and shall be entitled to trial within a reasonable time or to release pending trial. Release may be conditioned by guarantees to appear [for] trial.

4. Everyone who is deprived of his liberty by arrest or detention-shall be entitled to take proceedings by which the lawfulness of his detention shall be decided speedily by a court and his release ordered if the detention is not lawful.

5. Everyone who has been the victim of arrest or detention in contravention of the provisions of this Article shall have an enforceable right to compensation.

5. The Inter-American Convention on Human Rights

Article 7

Right to Personal Liberty

1. Every person has the right to personal liberty and security.

2. No one shall be deprived of his physical liberty except for the reasons and under the conditions established beforehand by the constitution of the State Party concerned or by a law established pursuant thereto.

3. No one shall be subject to arbitrary arrest or imprisonment.

4. Anyone who is detained shall be informed of the reasons for his detention and shall be promptly notified of the charge or charges against him.

CHAPTER V

JURISDICTION AND EXTRADITION

PROBLEMS OF JURISDICTION IN THE INTERNATIONAL CONTROL AND REPRESSION OF TERRORISM

BART DeSCHUTTER

INTRODUCTION

THE LOW DEGREE OF EFFECTIVENESS of the provisions concerning penal sanctions contained in international conventions creating substantive legal norms, which amount to characterizing certain patterns of conduct as international criminal offenses, is another characteristic of this area.

The implementation of international obligations through effective enforcement of international law is in most instances exclusively or primarily the responsibility of the national authorities which have received the right or contracted the duty to exercise jurisdiction for prosecution and punishment. In practice these kind of provisions have given way to a series of striking cases of lack of action notwithstanding factual situations clearly containing the constitutive elements of an international crime.[1]

It would be erroneous to think that the absence of judiciary action constitutes proof of the nonexistence or nonacceptance by states of substantive international criminal law. The rigidity with which the domestic penal lawyer approaches the test of anti-social conduct, e.g. the necessity of clear constitutive elements of the incrimination, the competent court, the specific penalties provided for, cannot be merely transplanted into the international law area. The absence of a supranational structure providing the international community with a complete mechanism in which

---

[1]e.g. The genocides in Burundi and Ruanda, the repeated breaches of international legal rules by both parties in the Middle East situation.

the criminal process can take place, including investigation, trial and execution of judgment requires a different approach in the law-making and law-applying process. To define terrorism or certain of its forms as a crime under international law would constitute a major step forward, even in the absence of workable means of enforcement.[2]

Legal action of redress on behalf of the international community after the commission of a serious breach of international law, is only one of the means—if not the last and worst—to control the behavior of potential terrorists. The attempt to control the phenomenon called "terrorism" has undergone a radical shift in orientation, marked by the 27th session of the General Assembly. Put on the agenda by the Secretary-General under the label

> Measures to prevent terrorism and other forms of violence which endanger to take innocent human lives or jeopardize fundamental freedoms.[3]

the emphasis shifted towards

> study of the underlying causes of those forms of terrorism and acts of violence which lie in misery, frustration, grievance and despair and which cause some people to sacrifice human lives, including their own, in an attempt to effect radical changes.[4]

Transplanting into the international crime area of the criminological theories of decriminalization by emphasizing the search for causes and the possibilities of their elimination does not seem to have received a warm response in certain groups of states. The attitude of most of the third world countries is felt by the western countries to be a maneuver to icebox legislative action, diminish-

---

[2]Many attempts have been made to define the nation of international terrorism. Among the agreed constitutive elements are the indiscriminate use of force on an excessive scale; the resulting mass fear; the innocent character of the victim. G. Schwarbenberger, "Terrorists, Hijackers, Guerrileros and Mercenaries," 24 *Current legal problem*, 257, (1971) p. 258; Intervention de Délégué belge à la 6e Commission au sujet du point 92 de l'ordre du jour de la 27e sess. de l'Ass. Gén. in, Min. Aff. Etrang., Recueil de points de vue Belges sur la politique internationale (72) 23, p. 8; A. Sotille, "Le terrorisme international," 65 *Rec. Cours. Acad. D. Int.*, (1938) 92, p. 100.

[3]Note made by the Secretary General, *U.N. Gen. Ass. Doc.* A/8791; A/8791/Add. 1 and corr. 1.

[4]U.N. Gen. Ass. Doc. A/C.6/413.

ing the chances for a universal ban on terrorism in a single convention.

Official inquiry into the causes of terroristic behavior has no valid relationship to the development of feasible enforcement measures.* Enforcement measures aimed at controlling skyjacking were formulated without analyzing its underlying causes. The International Law Commission is sufficiently alarmed by the kidnapping and murdering of diplomats not to wait until a study has been made of the motives for these desperate acts.

It is unlikely that the very roots of terrorism will ever be agreed upon. Every effort must be made to avoid reducing the issue to a political question. The anti-terrorist convention, hijacking and kidnapping prove to the extent that penal sanctions remain necessary, that the study of the measures to be taken can be conducted simultaneously with the study of the causes.

It is unlikely that the very roots of terrorism can ever be eliminated even if identified. Punishment has to remain an element of deterrence and can achieve that effect. However, the substantive incriminating rules are equally necessary to give other methods of enforcement their optimal effect. The reactions of international political bodies, public opinion, press action and even moral judgments are important. Even in the absence of court action, international criminal law can have a certain effect, and bring about complaint behavior. The implementation of enforcement measures to repress breaches is important but not fundamental.

REPRESSION OF TERRORISM

Repression of international crimes can be handled through international courts or national courts. Terrorism, a crime of an international nature, theoretically requires judicial action by an organization of an international nature. We deal with a *hostis humani generis,* who endangers the universal social and political stability, the international public order and the superior interests of humanity. The acts of terrorism are usually performed in abnormal circumstances and are intended to alarm and horrify

---

*Ed's Note: This very point is much debated and the present U.N. position is contrary to that of the author. See *supra* note 4 cited by this author and e.g Chapter I of this book.

certain responsible leaders or groups (subjective element), thus creating a situation of collective danger (objective element).[5]

Except for cases where the act of terrorism is merely a common crime with no political or social motivation *(le terrorism crapuleaux)*, we are dealing with a crime of a *sui generis* nature, which does not fit in the frame of the philosophy and the economy of the basic national criminal law provisions. The introduction of foreign elements, e.g. nationality of author or victim does not alter this rule. The only issue is the application of international procedural provision to the extra-territorial competence of the criminal judge. Political and social terrorism belong *in se* to an international judiciary.

In addition, international prosecution is the only acceptable way to deal with terrorism perpetrated by the state and acts of a political character which are linked with situations of armed conflict but occur outside the zone of conflict. For these reasons, the only valid response to the type of international crime we are dealing with is the creation of an international criminal court.

The Necessity of Domestic Court Intervention

Nevertheless, a certain sense of reality indicates that the realization of an international criminal court is far in the future, despite valid efforts by several qualified nongovernmental organizations.[6] In the meantime it is important to ascertain whether states have jurisdiction to prescribe and enforce domestic provisions of substantive and procedural criminal law which may be useful in dealing with crimes of international terrorism.

International law is at the present stage equipped with commonly agreed principles conferring upon states jurisdiction over territorial and extraterritorial crimes. Treaties obliging or allow-

---

[5]Tran Tam, "Le terrorisme et le droit pénal international contemporain," 45 *Rev. D. int. & sc. diplom. et pol.* 11, 13, (1967).

[6]Groups of experts elaborated a *Draft convention on international crimes and a Draft statute for an International Criminal Court* during conferences held in Bellagio (It.) and Wingspread (USA) (1972) and sponsored by the Foundation International Criminal Law Conferences, *The Establishment of an International Criminal Court* (1972) p. 35.

ing states to assume such power,[7] as well as customary principles, such as the one embodied in the Lotus principal allowing states to exercise criminal jurisdiction in the absence of a prohibitive rule,[8] lead to the same conclusion: a state is allowed under international law to issue rules dealing with the conduct of terrorists, acting within or without the realms of the sovereign.

Domestic criminal law is also equipped with generally accepted theoretical justifications conferring jurisdiction. The reach of the criminal law can be determined by applying several principles.

The most evident and basic principle remains the *territorial principle*. No criminal legislation will ever know a different starting point; penal law is directed towards the safety and social equilibrium of those who agree to place themselves and remain under the protection of a given sovereign. This protection will be offered in all circumstances, without distinctions. Acts of terrorism, whether committed by nationals or aliens, fall undoubtedly within the area of competence of the sovereign. Exceptional circumstances and certain elements of the case, from the viewpoint of criminological social theory produce arguments in favor of intervention by the territorial sovereign (extradition, transmission of prosecution). If a national of A commits an act of terrorism in B against other nationals of A or against the sovereign A, a sound administration of justice might require that preference be given to the action of state A, e.g. when the presence of the author in B is purely accidental.

However, this does not in any case reverse the fundamental right of the state to deal with all violations within its territorial

---

[7]e.g. The Genocide Convention, art. 5, *UNTS*, *78*:277; The 4 Geneva Conventions of 1949, art. 49 (I), 50(II), 129 (III), 146 (IV); The 1937 Convention for the prevention and punishment of terrorism, art. 2 and 3. The Convention for the suppression of unlawful seizure of aircraft, The Hague, Dec. 1970, art. 4 The Convention for the suppression of unlawful acts against the safety of civil aviation, Montreal Sept. 1971, art. 5;

[8]The case of the *S.S. Lotus, P.C.I.J. Ser. A. No.*, 10 (1923) Hudson, 2 *World Court Rep*, 20 (1929).

reach.[9] State jurisdiction over acts of international terrorism committed on its territory has a sound theoretical basis and is universally accepted.[10]

Equally accepted is jurisdiction based on the *protective principle*. A state may deal within its sovereign limits with crimes of terrorism committed outside its boundaries, but directed against its own security or very existence.[11] From the viewpoint of the attacked state the quality of nationality of the agent does not affect the degree of immediate danger caused by the acts. Criminal law thus permits action against terrorists acting outside a given country but directed against it.

More controversial is the *personality principle*. On one hand the countries of the common law seem somewhat reluctant to taking jurisdiction solely on the basis of nationality. On the other hand, they are more reluctant to assert jurisdiction based on the passive personality theory; i.e. jurisdiction based on the nationality of the victim. However, the Anglo-Saxon criminal law seems to be willing to accept specific cases of extra-territorial competence based on the author's nationality. In addition, theoritical constructions such as the *constitutive presence doctrine* or the *theory of effect* narrow considerably the gap between Anglo Saxon and other criminal law systems.[12]

---

[9]Harvard Research In International Law, "Draft Convention on Jurisdiction With Respect To Crime," 29 *A.J.I.L.*, 435 (1935). art. 3; Consultative Assembly of the Council of Europe, "Draft European Convention on Conflicts of Jurisdiction in Criminal Matters, (1965), art. 3, Doc. 1873; American Law Institute, *Restatement of the Law, 2nd, Foreign relations law of the United States* (1965) §17, p. 45 and §20, p. 59.

[10]Convention for the suppression of unlawful seizure of aircraft, The Hague 1970, art. 4, 1a; (*ICAO Doc.* 8920) Convention for the suppression of unlawful acts against the safety of civil aviation, Montreal 1971, art. 5, 1a; (*ICAO Doc.* 8966); United States draft convention for the prevention and punishment of certain acts of international terrorism (1972) art. 4, 1a; (*U.N. Gen. Ass. Doc.* A/C.6/L.850); The concept of territoriality includes the so-called *floating territoriality*. Ships and planes carrying the distinctive marks of his nationality fall under the control and competence of the sovereign, be it not necessarily the exclusive one. (Restatement §28 and 29; Harvard draft, art. 4).

[11]Harvard Draft, art. 7; Council of Europe draft, art. 7; Restatement, §33, p. 92.

[12]Harvard Draft, art. 5; Council of Europe draft, art. 4 (including persons domiciled in the country); Restatement §30, p. 86.

Action taken because nationals have been victims of terrorists activities is more difficult to sustain on the above theory of jurisdiction. It may lead to subjective and selective prosecutions and extremist protection or control over nationals abroad. Practice shows that only few codes contain such provisions, very often subject to severe limitations.[13]

General criminal law practice shows that a domestic judge can generally assert jurisdiction over nationals accused of an act of terrorism committed outside the national territory. Jurisdiction over a terrorist whose victim abroad was a national of the state asserting jurisdiction has not received general acceptance in all major legal systems.

The principle of *universality* is widely accepted for specific grave breaches of an international character. Antisocial behavior which affects mankind may be prescribed on the basis of *judex deprehensionis*. Treaty provisions, also in the area of terrorism, bring ample proof of the general acceptance of this principle in the area we deal with.[14]

In conclusion one can argue that international as well as national criminal law is theoretically equipped to adequately punish authors of international crimes of terrorism. The question can, however, be reversed; even if nothing prevented a national court from asserting such broad jurisdiction, does anything encourage extraterritorial competence under the circumstances?

The fact that acts of international terrorism concern matters related to the universal conscience of mankind lifts them out of the usual scope of domestic criminal law. To channel these cases through national courts obviously confounds the underlying philosophy of an international crime, a rule of conduct for individuals coming out of a transnational sphere. In addition, domestic criminal law imposes upon the judge a certain number of basic principles which may be difficult to fulfill in these matters. Will there always be a sufficiently clear incrimination with precise constitutive elements? Can a civil law country think in terms

---

[13]e.g. Total application of the rule is found in the German penal code (Chap. 4,2), conditional application in the Belgian code of criminal procedure, introductory title, art. 10.4.

[14]See *infra* App. p.p. 546 and note 32.

of *nullum crimen sine lege* within its domestic court system? Aren't there enough examples of the nonreadiness of Parliaments to enact national substantive rules in the execution of treaty provision requiring the enactment of implementary legislation?[15] In addition, conflicting decisions rendered by different national courts on international crimes would constitute a serious setback in the development and harmony of international criminal law.[16]

Criminal law is built within a conceptual frame of a given organized society. If the domestic juridical institutions are to be utilized, the fight against international terrorism should be organized in order to avoid interfering with the economy and philosophy of the *droit penal commun*. If we wish to achieve maximum acceptability of national court action in the area of recognized international crimes, the traditional internal schemes must in our view be adapted so as to approach as closely as possible the goal of international repressive action.

CONVENTIONS ON TERRORISM

Specific aspects of the jurisdictional issues relevant to terrorist activities have been codified in a series of international instruments:

a) the 1937 Geneva Convention for the Prevention and Pun-

---

[15]e.g. the status of the criminal laws punishing breaches of the 4 Geneva Conventions. When, at the request of the ICRC, the Parties to the Conventions were asked to inform the Committee about the provisions of their codes relative to article 49 of Convention I, 50 of Convention II, 129 of Convention III and 146 of Convention IV, only 49 answers were received out of 120 States bound by this obligation. Among those, not all can be considered as a sufficient fullfillment of the obligation. Respect of the Geneva Conventions—Measures taken to repress violations, Reports submitted by the ICRC; XXe Int. Conf. of the Red Cross (Vienna, 1965) doc. *Conf. D.4.a/1;* XXIe Int. Conf. of the Red Cross (Istanbul 1969) doc. *Conf. D.S. 4a, b, c;* additional report (Genève 1971) D 1198—*Réimpression DS 3/3;* The Belgian Parliament failed to take adequate action since 1952, even though Belgian experts were the initiators of a model-law submitted in 1953 to the ICRC. B. De Schutter, "De Humanitaire Conventies van Genève en 18 jaar Belgische Inactiviteit," 33 *Rechtsk Wkbld,* 977-982, (1970).

[16]The Zyklon B case, 1 *Law Rep. of Trials of War criminals* (H.M.S.O.) 1947, p. 93 (death penalty for subordinate agents) vs. Honig, Criminal justice in Germany today; 5 *Ybk World Aff* (1951) 131, at 141 (5 years penalty for the manager of the same chemical plant).

ishment of Terrorism;[17] (Appendix G)

b) the 1949 Geneva Conventions on Humanitarian Law;[18]

c) the 1963 Tokyo Convention on offences and certain other acts committed on board aircraft;[19] (Appendix F)

d) the 1970 Hague Convention for the suppression of unlawful seizure of aircraft;[20] (Appendix H)

e) the 1971 Montreal Convention for the suppression of unlawful acts against the safety of civil aviation;[21] (Appendix I)

f) the 1971 Organization of American States Convention to prevent and punish the acts of terrorism taking the form of crimes against persons and related extortion that are of international significance.[22] (Appendix M)

g) the 1974 United Nations Convention on the Prevention and Punishment of Crimes Against Internationally Protected Persons Including Diplomatic Agents. (Appendix N)

In addition, some recent draft proposals are of equal importance:

a) The 1972 I.L.C. Draft articles on the prevention and punishment of crimes against diplomatic agents and other international protected person which was adopted by the General Assembly in 1974.[23] (Appendix N)

b) The United States draft convention for the prevention and punishment of certain acts of international terrorism;[24] (Appendix R) which has not been adopted.

All these texts contain specific jurisdictional provisions: The main features are:

1. An obligation is imposed upon states parties to make the acts listed *criminal offenses* within their national legislations and provide for severe penalties, corresponding to the importance

---

[17]League of Nations Doc. C. 546.M 383.1937. V.

[18]75 *UNTS* 31, 85, 135, 287; Parl. papers Misc. N°4 (1950), Cmd. 8033.

[19]ICAO Doc. 8364.

[20]*Supra,* note 10.

[21]*Supra,* note 10.

[22]Text in, *U.N. Gen. Ass. Doc.* A/C6/418 Annex V (cited as: OAS Convention)

[23]Report of the International Law Commission on the work of its 24th session, *U.N. Gen. Ass. Doc.* A/8710, p. 247; *U.N. Gen. Ass. Off. Doc. 27th sess. Suppl. N°10,* A/8710/Rev. 1. (cited as : ILC Draft).

[24]*Supra,* note 10.

of the universal interests, which are infringed upon by these attacks.[25]

2. A state must exercise jurisdiction in all cases having a *territorial* character.[26]

3. Contracting Parties assume obligations to submit those crimes to the rule of universality.[27]

4. Contracting Parties must confirm the traditional rule *aut dedere aut iudicare*.[28] States do have a duty to act in view of repressing the criminal behavior, but are allowed a choice of means. This allows the coverage of cases where the individual whose prosecution is sought but who cannot be extradited because of legal provisions preventing extradition e.g. nonextradition of nationals, or the unwillingness of another State to request or to accept extradition. No obligation to try and punish is created; the contracting party agrees only to submit the case to the competent national authority for prosecution. This authority will decide whether to prosecute, decisions to be made in good faith.[29] This formulation clearly respects the rule of separation of powers, giving the judiciary a free hand, a fundamental principle in any democratic system.

5. Some of the conventions expressly state that they do not exclude any criminal jurisdiction exercised in accordance with national law.[30] This leaves room for the active and passive personality theories, upon which some states may wish to base their jurisdiction.

6. The classification of the different jurisdiction is expressly provided for.[31] However, these provisions are limited to the situa-

[25]1937 Convention, art. 2; Hague Convention, art. 2; Montreal Convention, art. 3; OAS Convention, art. 1; US draft, art. 2; I.L.C. Draft, art. 2.2.

[26]Tokyo Convention, art. 3.1; Hague Convention, art. 4.1; Montreal convention art. 5.1; OAS convention, art. 1, I.L.C. Draft, art. 2; U.S. draft, art. 4.1.

[27]I.L.C. Draft, art. 2.2.

[28]1937 Convention, art. 9 & 10; Hague Convention, art. 4.2 and art. 7; Montreal Convention, art. 5.2. and art. 7; OAS Convention art. 5; I.L.C. Draft, art. 2 and art. 4; US Draft art. 3 and art. 4.2.

[29]U.N. Gen. Ass. Doc. 8710, p. 271 (french edit.)

[30]Tokyo Convention, art. 3.3.; Hague Conventions, art. 4.3.; Montreal Convention, art. 5.3., U.S. Draft, art. 4.3.

[31]I.L.C. Draft, art. 7, though limited to the case of several requests for extradition. See also U.S. Draft, art. 7.5.

tions of concurrent request for extradition. This rule is fundamental to the objectives of fair trial and adequate prosecution
and should, therefore, be included in the solution. It is evident
that priority must go to the territorial judge or the national
judge of the author, the *judex deprehensionis* having only a
secondary interest in the case.[32]

7. Ample provisions are made for extradition and the duty to
render all criminal assistance necessary to prevent and prosecute these crimes.[33] This may include the communication of
all available information on the crime and the author, of actions short of criminal taken against certain persons or group
in order to prevent and impede the preparation within the
territory of crimes, as well as the classical forms of assistance
(rogatory commissions, communications of criminal records,
etc.)

The various existing conventions and the drafts all make
available or impose clear obligations to make effective sufficient
ways to deal adequately with international terrorism. The lack
of state enforcement of sanctions against terrorism must be attributed to the failure to act by responsible rulers and not to gaps in
legal sanctions.

In the near future the only possible international terrorism
will be the exclusive jurisdiction of the individual sovereign
states. However, in view of the international or universal character of these crimes, an effort must be made to induce the domestic
mechanisms of enforcement to respond better to prosecutorial requirements. When municipal courts implement international
criminal law, they can be considered as *de facto* agents of the
international community. They are under a mandatory obligation to administer the universal response to acts rejected as an
unlawful conduct under international standards. This means in
the meantime ways must be sought to "internationalize" as much
as possible the administration of national justice in these cases.

---

[32]The Council of Europe draft, *supra* note 9 provides us with a well balanced network of classified competences; see art. 3.3., Art. 4.2., Art. 5.

[33]1937 Convention, art. 15 and art. 16; Hague Convention art. 10; Montreal convention, art. 11; OAS Convention, art. 8; US Draft, art. 11; I.L.C. Draft, art. 10.

In executing its treaty obligations relative to the adaptation of its national legislative provisions, a state should pay careful attention to the kind of legislative action it will take. It seems far better to elaborate special legislation in a separate law or code, instead of including sections or articles in existing penal codes, which concentrate upon the classical violations in the conduct of social relations linked to a specific organized society.

In order to avoid a repressive trend, existing law and new regulations should be grouped into one set of rules with clear and precise definitions. Linked to it should be the applicable rules as to acts of omission, acts of participation, attempts, superior orders, mitigating circumstances, etc. To provide for repressive rules on basis of one complete, easily identifiable and cohesive text also is an advantage for the realization of other steps which deviating from the classical procedures.

Reviewing the theoretical justifications for sovereign interventions in extraterritorial matters, attention has been drawn to the universality principle. However, virtually no national legislation contains provisions on *universality* of a general character, independent of specific treaty obligations. This means that without conventional norms most national judges have no jurisdiction in their capacity of *judex deprehensionis* to try aliens who committed an international crime outside their country. It must be remembered that these crimes are mostly political or assimilated political ones, leading to nonextradition and the granting of asylum.[34] An important step would, therefore, be the extension of the extraterritorial reach of national criminal legislation to the overall universality principle for grave breaches. The danger of excessive intervention in the primary competence of another sovereign can be tempered by setting strict conditions for its application.

As to the investigation and trial proceedings, a series of ideas

---

[34]e.g. The ABARCA case (1963), where Belgium refused Switzerland the extradition of a Spanish national, who had placed a bomb in an Iberia plane at Geneva Airport. The refusal was based on the political character of the act. No prosecution was possible under Belgian law, which amounted to an unpunished grave breach against the safety of civil aviation. 1 *Rev. Belge D. Int.*, 274-275, (1966); Belgium, *Anuales Parlementaires* 1963-64, June 25, 1964, p. 6.

may be launched in order to try to internationalize national legal proceeding. One measure could be the presence of an international legal observer in court. This system would be feasible only if institutionalized through governmental action. The presence of nongovernmental international watchdogs has been effective in guaranteeing the criminal a minimum standard of justice in a number of cases. In order to avoid the partiality and biased approach of some of these organizations, arbitrators of the Permanent Court of Arbitration may be called upon. The judge-observer would receive access to the file, but would not participate in the deliberation of the court. He would, however, have the right to file an *ad hoc* opinion in the case which would be published together with the decision.

It may be better to hold proceedings involving international crimes in special chambers of the domestic court or even in special domestic courts. Most of the national courts function with sections or chambers and arrive indirectly at a division of work. The creation of an independent tribunal will, of course, contain the inherent danger of the "exceptional tribunal" which is incompatible with the democratic scheme. It must be clear that such courts would have to be included in the regular judicial system, with full respect of the basic fundamental rights of the defendant. An international criminal court could be developed to parallel youth tribunals, traffic courts or family courts. Cases like the ones under consideration require a knowledge of and a feeling for international criminal law, its interpretation and elaboration, its underlying motivation, the impact of compromise between different schools of thought or ideologies and the sociological context based on aspects of international relations. The curricula of legal studies, studies in criminology and international relations should offer adequate training in the handling of such international problems. States should designate a certain number of qualified criminal judges with proven knowledge of international criminal law, international law and comparative criminal law and procedure to sit in these courts. Such judges are more likely to arrive at consistent decisions in similar factual situations.

Along the same line, a further integration between the national and the international methods of repression of terrorism would be to have specialized courts, have one or more international observers, resulting in a new type of *mixed tribunal*. Using the above mentioned specialized court as a starting point, agreements could be worked out to extend the composition of such courts to have one or more international *ad hoc* judges, who would assume the main responsibility as to the international law-finding in a specific case. Their powers, rights and duties would be comparable to those of domestic judges, and their participation in a national prosecution would assure the exact application of the international law norm.

The feasibility of these ideas depends more on the political willingness of governments more than on the possibility of overcoming legal obstacles. Two approaches are possible: 1. Considering the improbability of legislative initiative in this area, the acceptance of the international observer would be the first step toward internationalization; 2. If a state declines such an idea on the claim of sovereignty and noninterference in domestic affairs, then the idea of a specialized court should receive support. The mixed court idea is difficult to achieve and it would be preferable to try for the creation of an international criminal court, as difficult as that proposal appears.

CONCLUSION

International and national law are theoretically equipped with rules allowing repression of terrorism. In fact, existing international conventions provide the contracting parties with the necessary provisions to make the substantive law effective. However, the existing mechanisms are polarized: at the one extreme, the ideal of the international criminal court, the best answer to the transnational character of the breaches occurring through acts of terrorism and on the other extreme the unsatisfactory domestic criminal courts.

Maybe the time has come to devote more attention to intermediate solution and to the introduction of certain internationalizing elements. Some of the ones mentioned in this paper seem feasible and have an acceptable character for any sovereign concerned with the safety and security of mankind.

SECTION 2

PERSPECTIVES ON EXTRADITION AND TERRORISM

Theo Vogler

EXTRADITION IS THE TRANSFER of a person from one state to another state for prosecution, and is the oldest form of cooperation between states in the struggle against criminality. Its origins go back to the very beginnings of formal diplomacy. In what has been described as the oldest document in diplomatic history, the peace treaty between Ramses II of Egypt and the Hittite prince Hattusili III (1280 B.C.), provision was made for the return of the criminals of one party who fled and were found in the territory of the other.[1]

The law of extradition thereafter evolved through bilateral and multilateral conventions, internal extradition laws, and customary international law. Difficulty arises, however, in its application to acts of terrorism because of the lack of a specific meaning of the word terrorism.[2] One of the principles of extradition is double criminality, whose application takes two forms: (1) enumeration of crimes for which extradition is granted; or (2) elimination of crimes for which extradition is not granted.

The first condition to extradition is a showing that the crime for which the individual is sought is punishable under the laws of both states. As far as I know, no existing bilateral or multilateral extradition convention and no internal extradition law mentions terrorism as an extraditable offense.[3] Terrorism refers to certain acts which are crimes recognized as punishable acts. Terrorists'

---

[1] I. A. Shearer, *Extradition in International Law* (1971), p. 5.

[2] *See*, Tran-Tam, "Crimes of Terrorism and International Criminal Law," in Bassiouni, and Nanda *A Treatise on International Criminal Law*, (1973), Vol. I; p. 490.

[3] The Terrorism Convention of 1935 has not entered into force since its elaboration.

crimes not only threaten the life and property of individuals, but also concurrently constitute danger to the whole world and its civilization, by jeopardizing simultaneously social order, international public order and the broader interest of humanity.[4] Terrorism means an international *modus operandi* of crime characterized by terror and violence, seeking to achieve an intended goal. Thus, terrorism may be defined as acts of international crime committed by means of terror, violence, and intimidation, with the purpose of obtaining predetermined goals and purposes.[5] Viewed from the point of extradition, however, there is a difficulty in the fight against terrorism because it is necessary to overcome the terminology in order to establish a line of demarcation between terrorist acts and crimes properly called political delictum (political crimes).

The concept of a political offense,[6] as a formal limitation on the practice of extradition, is of relatively recent origin. The extradition treaties of ancient times and the Middle Ages were very largely designed to secure the surrender of political enemies rather than common criminals, while the treaties of the eighteenth century evidenced a continued interest in the surrender of political criminals and also in the return of deserting troops, who in modern times have become like political offenders both in extradition law and in practice of asylum. As late as 1834 a treaty between Austria, Prussia and Russia engaged the parties to deliver up persons guilty of high treason, armed rebellion or acts against the security of the throne or the government, and with France's introduction of the exception of political offenders into its treaties after 1834, the idea soon gained wide currency.

If the distinction of having first formalized the concepts of "political offense" and "acts connected with a political offense" must be awarded to any country, it must be to Belgium, which included these expressions in its extradition law of October 1, 1833.[7]

---

[4]See A. Sottile, "Le Terrorisme International," *Recueil des Cours de l'Academie de Droit International* (1939), p. 5.

[5]Tran-Tam, *Supra* note 2.

[6]I. A. Shearer, *Supra* note 1 p. 166.

[7]*Ibid.*, p. 167.

Since extradition was a matter largely reserved to the executive sphere of government in civil law countries until statutes in the twentieth century secured a measure of judicial control, the courts of Great Britian and the United States were the first to give detailed consideration of the implications of treaty provisions prohibiting the surrender of political offenders. While some of these decisions touch at the heart of the concept of political offenses, they nevertheless show that the foundation of a workable rule is nearly impossible.[8]

European diplomatic and judicial experience relating to the delimitation of political offenses may be regarded as having been synthesized in article 3 of the European Convention on Extradition of 1957. This article reflects the classification of political offenses preferred by Continental and Latin American writers, which distinguishes three categories of political offenses: (1) the purely political offense, which is an act directed solely against the political order; (2) the delit complexe, where the same act is directed at both the political order and private rights e.g. the "hijacking" of a privately owned aircraft for political purposes; and (3) the *delit connexe,* which is in itself not an act directed against the political order but which is closely connected with another act which is so directed e.g. fraudulently obtaining paper in order to print subversive literature.[9]

The purely political offense is a comparatively simple one. The vast majority of allegations that an offense is political fall into the second category, about which for example the Swiss courts have adopted a theory of "preponderance."[10] In a mixed common-political offense whether the political or the common elements preponderates will determine the characterization of the offense as political or extraditable.[11] A more recent refinement of this idea has been the introduction of the concept of the "relation of means and purpose," which looks to the means used in relation to the political end sought by the fugitive and categorizes the act as a crime if the means are excessive. When, for example, several

[8]*Ibid.,* p. 178.
[9]*Ibid.,* p. 181.
[10]*Ibid.,* p. 182.
[11]*e.g.* In re Pavan [1923] *Ann Dig,* 347 No. 329.

crew members of a Yugoslav passenger aircraft subdued the other crew members and brought the aircraft down in Switzerland in order to escape from Yugoslavia, it was held that the political motive and the means used could "excuse, if not justify, the injury to private property."[12] By contrast, when a fugitive murdered a fascist in Italy in December 1945, long after hostilities had ceased, he was extradited since the relation between the end sought (the suppression of fascism) and the means used was not sufficiently proportional to qualify the act as political.[13] The fugitive should have denounced his victim to the authorities because homicide, the court remarked, was not allowable to achieve a political end.

While the Swiss courts, like the British and American ones, at first saw political offenses in terms of a violent struggle for power between contending forces, they later took a more liberal view. In the first abovementioned case (Re Kavic) it was pointed out that since the rise of totalitarian states, a political character must also be attributed to offenses committed in order to escape from the constraint of a state which made all opposition and fighting for power impossible.[14] Thus, it can be seen that there is a certain unity of feeling on the subject of political offenses but a considerable diversity in the statement and application of rules.[15]

This, therefore, is the scene for perspectives on Extradition and Terrorism; on the one side an uncertain exclusion of political offenses from extradition and on the other side a more uncertain exclusion of terrorism from the uncertain exclusion of political offenses. The trend in treaties and other instruments relating to extradition is toward exclusion of terrorism and other serious offenses from the categories of the political offense exception. This occurs because terrorism is not positively defined but rather specified acts are excluded from the category of non-extraditable political offenses. This may be referred to as the doctrine of the "exception to the exception," which was developed by professor M. C. Bassiouni in his article on "Ideologically

---

[12]Re Kavic, Swiss Federal Tribunal, 19 *I.L.R.*, 371 (1952).
[13]Re Peruzov, Swiss Federal Tribunal 18 *I.L.R.*, p. 38, (1951).
[14]I. A. Shearer, *Supra* note 1, p. 183.
[15]*Ibid.*, p. 187.

motivated offenses and the political offense exception in extradition—a proposed juridical standard for an unruly problem."[16]

As it is stated in the study prepared by the Secretariat of the United Nations in accordance with the decision taken by the sixth Committee in 1972, there appear to be mainly three ways of solving this problem:

(1) By incorporating the so-called "Belgian" or "attentat" clause according to which certain acts against Heads of State or Government shall not be considered political offenses;

(2) By providing that certain specified activities or crimes other than those covered under the Belgian clause shall not constitute political offenses; or

(3) By including a clause to the effect that an offense in which the common crime predominates is not a political offense.

While all three ways seem to me to be insufficient, there is yet another difficulty. German practice since 1949 regarding the characterization of political offenses has been governed by the application of the constitutional guarantee that "the politically persecuted shall enjoy the right of asylum."[17] The approach of the West German courts is to inquire whether the fugitive is entitled to asylum as a politically persecuted person rather than to apply any principle of extradition laws. The quality of the persecution is decisive and not the quality of the act. A fugitive who can qualify as a persecuted person under the German constitution, as liberally construed by the courts, may not be extradited.[18] The constitutional protection is held to apply to persons who "in the event of their extradition would be in danger in their home countries of being persecuted for political reasons and of being subjected to risk of life and limb and restrictions of personal liberty."[19] This idea has also received recognition in paragraph 2 of article 3 of the 1957 European Convention on Extradition and

---

[16]19 *DePaul Law Review*, 217 (1969); also in Bassiouni, *International Extradition and World Public Order* (1974) Reprinted in part in Section 3 of this chapter.

[17]Constitution Art. 4, § 2 Federal Republic of Germany, 1949.

[18]I. A. Shearer, *Supra* note 1, p. 184.

[19]9 *BVerfGE*, 174; see also 3 *BGHSt* 392.

reflects the spirit of various human rights conventions.

The problem raised here is whether the extradition principle of speciality may not in fact prove to be an effective protection against the possibility of the fugitive's persecution for other than criminal reasons. But even if the fugitive may be tried for only the common offense, the conduct of the trial and the sentence imposed after conviction may demonstrate that in reality he also was being punished for the political offense.[20] The German Federal Constitutional Court has indeed expressly questioned the effectiveness of the principle of speciality in these circumstances.[21] But what assurances are there that subtle means might not be used by the requesting state after surrender to ensure that the fugitive "voluntarily chose" to waive his treaty right to return to the requested state before being prosecuted for other offenses?[22]

The question now is what to do in this situation? One proposal is to elaborate a convention which would cover certain fundamental rules but without too much detail.

Among these fundamental rules are:

(1) The basic principle of *aut dedere aut iudicare*. It is important to restate the law of extradition as well as to seek to advance it in light of new developments (transfer of proceedings, international validity of criminal judgements, and so on) ;

(2) All states should be vested with universal jurisdiction with respect to crimes of terrorism, regardless of the location of the crime and the nationality of the offender or his victim;

(3) The convention must be regarded as a multilateral extradition treaty, so that extradition is granted regardless whether the crime is mentioned in any list of extraditable offenses in any other legal instrument (treaty or domestic law) ;[23]

---

[20]I. A. Shearer, *Supra* note 1, p. 189.

[21]*Ibid.*, p. 184.

[22]*Ibid.*, p. 189.

[23]See the proposal made by Professor Bassiouni in his report to Xth Int. Penal Law Congress of Rome (1969) entitled "International Extradition: A Summary of the Contemporary American Practice and a Proposed Formula," 39 revue internationale de droit pénal 485 (1968) reprinted in 15 *Wayne L. Rev.*, 733 (1968).

(4) Terrorism must be considered a common crime for the purpose of extradition, so that the general rule against the extradition of political offenders will be unapplicable;

(5) The rights of the individual in extradition proceedings must be upheld. Extradition is not to be granted when the individual sought is to be tried by an exceptional tribunal or under a procedure violating fundamental human rights.

It must be admitted that the present unsettled state of international practice in the matter of characterization of terrorism results largely from the ideological differences that divide the world community. As Professor Bassiouni stated in his opening remarks to the III International Symposium of the International Institute of Advanced Criminal Sciences (Siracuse, Italy) : "what is terrorism for the one side, is heroism for the other." I, therefore, believe that the creation of an international court must be established on the model of the European Commission and the European Court of Human Rights. Terrorism once defined as involving specific crimes such as hijacking, kidnapping, assassination, letter bombs and other acts should be considered like other international crimes, i.e. genocide, as a crime against humanity. Both the genocide convention and the Hague convention on aircraft hijacking, adopt the position that such acts are international crimes for which there is universal jurisdiction and give the state the option to prosecute or extradite, which means that in the absence of prosecution extradition is mandatory and the political offense exception is inapplicable.

THE POLITICAL OFFENSE EXCEPTION IN EXTRADITION LAW AND PRACTICE

M. Cherif Bassiouni

HISTORICAL DEVELOPMENT AND MEANING

Historically, extradition was the means resorted to for the surrender of political offenders. These were persons guilty of crimes of *lése majesté* which included, *inter alia,* treason, attempts against the monarchy or the life of a monarch and even contemptuous behavior toward the monarch. The first known European treaty which dealt with the surrender of political offenders was entered in 1174 between England and Scotland. It was followed by a treaty in 1303 between France and Savoy. In the XVIIth century Hugo Grotius gave the practice a theoretical framework, which is still the cornerstone of classic extradition law. Until the nineteenth century extradition constituted a manifestation of cooperation between the family of nations as attested by various alliances in existence between the reigning families of Europe.

The French Revolution of 1789 and its aftermath started the transformation of what was the extraditable offense *par excellence* to what has since become the nonextraditable offense *par excellence.* In 1833 Belgium became the first country to enact a law on nonextradition of political offenders, and by the beginning of the nineteenth century almost every European treaty contained an exception for political offenses. By 1875, the practice was sufficiently established that the determination of what constituted a political offense was reached in accordance with the laws

*Excerpted from Bassiouni, *International Extradition and World Public Order* (1974) pp. 370-487. Reprinted with permission of Sijthoff Publishing Co.

of the requested state. This development gave rise to the increased role of the judiciary in the practice which except for England and Belgium (since 1833) had played no part in the process.

The political offense exception is now a standard clause in almost all extradition treaties of the world and is also specified in the municipal laws of many states.[1] Even though widely recognized, the very term "political offense" is seldom, if ever, defined in treaties or municipal legislation and judicial interpretations have been the principal source for its significance and application.[2] This may be due to the fact that whether or not a particular type of conduct falls within that category depends essentially on the facts and circumstances of the occurrence. Thus, by its very nature it eludes a precise definition which could restrict the flexibility needed to assess the facts and circumstances of each case.

As a consequence of this preeminent role played by the judiciary in defining and applying this exception, the courts of the requested state unavoidably apply national conceptions, standards and policies to an inquiry which relates, however, to a process

---

[1] Whiteman, states:

. . . Most extradition laws and treaties provide that extradition need not or shall not be granted when the acts with which the accused is charged constitute a political offense or an act connected with a political offense. Generally, a distinction is drawn between "purely" political offenses e.g. treason, sedition, and "relative" political offenses or offenses "of a political character" e.g. murder committed in the course of a rebellion, although generally both types are excepted from extradition . . .

In the case of laws and treaties which contain a list of specific offenses for which extradition shall be granted, exception of "purely" political offenses is usually considered unnecessary since such offenses may be excepted by merely not being included in the list. However, provision is often made regarding "relative" political offenses.

6 Whiteman, *Digest of International Law,* 799-800 (1968). See also Shearer, *Extradition in International Law* (1971), pp. 166-198; Bedi, *Extradition in International Law and Practice,* (1968), pp. 179-191, *Harvard Research in International Law, Draft Convention on Extradition,"* 29 *A.J.I.L.* Supp. p. 21, 107 (1935).

[2] Deere, "Political Offenses in the Law and Practice of Extradition," 27 *A.J.I.L.,* 247, 240 (1933); Garcia-Mora, "The Present Status of Political Offenses in the Law of Extradition and Asylum," 14 *U. Pitt. L. Rev.,* 371-372 (1953); Evans, "Reflections upon the Political Offense in International Practice," 57 *A.J.I.L.,* 1, 15 (1963); Garcia-Mora, "The Nature of Political Offenses: A Knotty Problem of Extradition Law," 48 *Va. L. Rev.,* 1226, 1230 (1962).

transcending the interests of that one participant.[4] As to the term, according to Oppenheim, it was unknown to international law until the French Revolution[5] and even when the European practice was to secure the surrender of political offenders the term was not employed.[6]

The history of the political offense exception is inexorably linked to the rise of eighteenth century political theories on freedom and democracy. Since then the development of this exception has been intricately linked to asylum even though prior to the eighteenth century this relationship was very tenuous. Indeed, asylum, as practiced in the Mediterranean Basin (Egypt, Mesopotamia, Greece and Rome), had little resemblance to the later European practice bearing the same nomenclature.

The introduction of the political offense exception in the practice of extradition after Belgium's legislative initiative in 1833 was aptly discussed in the case of *In re Fabijan* wherein the Supreme Court of Germany in 1933 stated:

> What the Belgian legislature understood by the term "political offense" is to be ascertained from the Belgian public and criminal law of the time when the law of 1833 was made . . . Using the term not in the legal sense but as it is understood in politics, the legislature meant essentially high treason, capital treason, acts against the external security of the state, rebellion and incitement to civil war . . . Since these acts, because they were political, were not listed among the offenses and crimes enumerated in Article I of the law and were thus not extraditable, it was not necessary to provide specifically in Article 6 that no extradition was admissible in respect of political offenses. This followed also from the so-called principle of identity of extradition and prosecution, laid down elsewhere in the law. But special mention of the matter had to be made because the legislature did not merely wish to exclude from extradition offenses against the state, but also certain connected offenses. It was considered that an offense

---

[3]*Ibid*, Garcia-Mora, "The Nature of Political Offenses: A Knotty Problem of Extradition Law," 1229.

[4]Evans, *supra* note 2, p. 17.

[5]I. Oppenheim, *International Law* (8th ed., Lauterpacht, 1955), p. 704.

[6]See Bassiouni, *International Extradition and World Public Order* (1974) notes 5-6. As late as 1834 a treaty between Austria, Prussia, and Russia called for the surrender of persons accused of high treason, armed rebellion, acts against the security of the throne or the government and acts of *lése majéste,* see 15 Martens, *Nouveau Recevil des Traités.*

against the state, especially when it took the form of an armed rising against the existing state authority, ought (in order to make the principle of nonextradition effective) to embrace other acts attending it and contributory crimes in themselves, in particular offenses against life and property, as well as offenses respecting the person and liberty of the individual. For persons committing such offenses in connection with and in furtherance of an offense against the state appeared to be not less deserving of asylum than the principal actors themselves. Looked at alone, such offenses are "ordinary offenses." By them the Belgian legislature meant such offenses as were "ordinary" crimes and were closely connected with a "political" offense . . . The term "connected offense" is clearly borrowed from Article 227 of the *Code d'Instruction Criminelle,* where it is used with reference to the joinder of several courts in one indictment. In the Law of Extradition, just as in the Code of Criminal Procedure, the term refers to a plurality of criminal acts which are connected by some common feature. It follows from this that an offense against the state in the above sense must actually exist and have taken shape. "Connection" exists if another offense, in itself an "ordinary" offense, stands in a particular relation to this "principal fact." A purely external connection—identity of time, place, occasion or person—is not alone enough; rather, what is required is a conscious and deliberate relation of cause and effect. The "ordinary" criminal act must, in fact, have been a means, method or cloak for the carrying out of the "political" offense. To this extent—and to this extent only—the political object of the criminal is relevant for the determination of the question whether his crime is a "connected" act. The antithesis of a "connected" offense is an "isolated" offense, e.g. the murder of a statesman unconnected—or at least without the connection being discerned—with any political revolt. Such "isolated" offenses are extraditable notwithstanding that the motive is political; political asylum does not extend to them.[7]

After Belgium in 1833, France and Switzerland enacted similar laws in 1834 and England followed in 1870.[8] The United States did not enact special legislation to that effect save for the provision on political asylum in Immigration Statutes,[9] but it made the exception part of its practice as of 1843.[10]

---

[7][1933-1934] *Ann Dig* 360-361-363 (No. 156) (1933-1934); and Billot, *Traité de L'extradition* (1874) 109; Shearer, Supra note 1, pp. 166-167.

[8]33-34 Vict. S. 52 S. 53 (1878).

[9]Section 213.

[10]Malloy, *Treaties* 26; also 4 Moore, *Digest of International Law* 332 (1906).

IDEOLOGICALLY MOTIVATED OFFENDERS AND POLITICAL OFFENSES[11]

To secure their institutions, societies have devised laws to punish those who seek to affect the existence or functioning of these institutions. These laws may be designed to preclude change altogether or to prevent change by certain means and are enacted to protect a given social interest which presuppose a value judgment as to the social significance of what is sought to be preserved by this type of legislation. Paradoxically, the violators of these laws are usually committed to affecting that very interest sought to be preserved and do not perceive their conduct as morally blameworthy. Indeed, the converse is almost always true. Such an offender is referred to as the ideologically motivated offender. That type of offender denies the legality of the system, the legitimacy of a given law or the social order it seeks to protect claiming adherence to a higher legitimating principle. This perception may be based on commonly understood ideals of political freedom or specific notions which may or may not reflect the common values of the ordinary reasonable person in that society or internationally recognized minimum standards of human rights. That type of violation of the law is, therefore, incidental to the ideological or political purposes of the offender and the social order that he is confronting with such conduct. In a democratic society where laws are said to embody social values and change accordingly, the element of social or moral blameworthiness will depend largely on the degree to which the violated law truly embodies prevailing social values. This is particularly true with respect to the enforcement of criminal laws, but even among such laws distinctions must be made.

Throughout the history of humankind, organized societies have characterized certain forms of behavior as offensive to their common morality. These forms of behavior have invariably included that which harmfully affects an interest commonly perceived by

---

[11]This section is based in part on Bassiouni, "Ideologically Motivated Offenses and the Political Offense Exception in Extradition—A Proposed Juridical Standard For an Unruly Problem," 19 *DePaul L Rev*, 217, 218-226 (1969).

almost every member of society irrespective of ideology. Among these have been certain acts affecting the life and physical integrity of individuals which by virtue of their consistent recognition in the legal controls of almost all social systems are referred to as "common crimes."

Every legal system also has enactments which do not enjoy the same level of recognition granted "common crimes." These offenses may lack the foundation of commonly perceived and shared values or they may simply be regulatory norms. Furthermore, certain offenses may embody ideological values which do not correspond to the commonly perceived values of almost all members of a given society, as in the case of dictatorial regimes.

Some legal doctrines would see no basis for distinguishing between these different types of legal controls on the assumption that any violation of any law is equally reprehensible as a violation of law. Other doctrines seek to distinguish between types of violations because such distinctions would, if nothing else, correspond to a greater degree of individualization of the offense which is sound criminological policy. As applied to the ideologically motivated offender, this later approach would recognize that such an offender cannot be deterred by the penalty attached to the transgressed legal mandate. But, the inquiry, however, must not be limited to an examination of the professed motivations of the actor, it must also take into account the legal norm which was transgressed in order to have some objective basis. There is a distinction between offenses which embody an ideological purpose and ideologically motivated offenders. The first applies to those legal norms designed to prohibit conduct actuated by values which conflict with those values embodied in or are represented by the law which is being violated. In this case, the violation proper becomes incidental to the competing ideological values represented on the one hand by a legal norm designed to protect an interest albeit also socially relevant, but other than that encompassed in the definition of common crimes and the opposing values of the offender. However, not every ideologically motivated offender necessarily commits an ideological offense. The two concepts must be distinguished because the nature of the offense does not depend on the motives of the actor just as nature of the offense may not confer upon the actor certain motives which were not present at the commission of the violation. The character of the offense emanates from the social interest it seeks to preserve while the characterization of the actor's conduct stems from a differing individual perception of the social interest. The ideologically motivated offender, therefore, acts in a way so as to harm the legally protected social interest in order to protect or promote another interest he perceives to be more socially redeeming.

Whenever the law, which was violated, embodies the protection of socio-political structures and the actor was moved by a commitment to differing ideological values or beliefs and harms such interests without committing a "common crime," that offense is said to be "purely political." However, if such an offense also involves the commission of a "common crime," usually a private wrong, it ceases to be a purely political offense and could then be labelled either a "relative political offense" or a "common crime."[12]

The problem lies in distinguishing between types of offenses and typology of offenders. Western European doctrine makes a classification whereby it separates relative political offenses in *delits connexes* and *delits complexes*. In both cases a common crime is committed with or without the commission of a purely political offense, but is actuated by ideological motives. This approach, however, fails to appreciate the distinction between the nature of the offense and the motives of the actor. These approaches will be discussed below, but two general observations must be borne in mind throughout the discussion of this exception:

1. The significance of value-oriented legal mandates by their very nature fluctuate in time and are relative to a given societal framework and, therefore, cannot give rise to their international recognition except when the proscribed conduct is sanctioned by the common morality of mankind, as

---

[12]This distinction between *delits complexes* and *delits connexes* was first made by Billot in his *Traité de L'Extradition* (1874), p. 104.

in the case of international crimes discussed below.[13]

2. It must, however, be recognized that every offense committed by an ideologically motivated offender is an attack
upon the law, but not every attack upon the law is to
benefit from the characterization of political offense as an
exception to extradition.

1. THE PURELY POLITICAL OFFENSE

Such an offense is usually conduct directed against the sovereign or a political subdivision thereof, and constitutes a subjective
threat to a political, religious or racial ideology or its supporting
structures or both without, however, having any of the elements
of a common crime. The conduct is labelled a crime because the
interest sought to be protected is the sovereign to be distinguished
from any private wrong. The word sovereign includes all the
tangible and intangible factors pertaining to the existence and
functioning of the state as an organization. It refers to the violation of laws designed to protect the public interest by making an
attack upon it a public wrong and are not to be confused with a
private wrong as in the case of common crimes. Such laws exist
solely because that very political entity, the state, criminalized
such conduct for its self-preservation. It is nonetheless deemed a
crime because it violates positive law, but it does not cause a
private wrong.

Treason, sedition and espionage are offenses directed against
the state itself and are, therefore, by definition, a threat to the
existence, welfare and security of that entity, and as such, they
are purely political offenses. A purely political offense, when
linked to a common crime, loses that characteristic. This is illustrated in the following case.

In 1928, Germany sought the extradition from Guatemala of
Richard Eckermann for the crime of murder. It was charged that
in 1923 Eckermann was a prominent member of a secret organization of former German officers in Germany known as the Black

---

[13]See Donnedieu de Vebres, *Introduction a L'étude du Droit Pénal International*
(1928); and Donnedieu de Vabres, *Les Principes Modernes du Droit Pénal International* (1938).

Army whose purported purpose was to protect Germany in case of attack by its neighbors and to suppress communism and bolshevism in Germany. When one Fritz Beyer tried to join the Black Army, the other members thought him to be a spy and eventually it was alleged Eckermann gave directions to a subordinate as a result of which Beyer was shot, killed and buried. The crime was not discovered until more than a year later. The subordinate and four others who took part were tried and imprisoned, but Eckermann escaped to Mexico and then to Guatemala. The case eventually came to the Supreme Court of Justice of Guatemala, Eckermann claiming that the crime was political, particularly in the context of the abnormal conditions which prevailed in Germany after World War I as a result of social, political and economic upheavels. The Guatemalan constitution provided that "extradition is prohibited for political crimes or connected common ones." In 1929, the court held that extradition should be granted. It stated:

> . . . That the fact that Eckermann formed part of a patriotic society secretly organized to cooperate in the defense of his country cannot in any way tie the character of political crimes to those committed by its members . . . Universal law qualifies as political crimes sedition, rebellion and other offenses which tend to change the form of government or the persons who compose it; but it cannot be admitted that ordering a man killed with treachery, unexpectedly and in an uninhabited place, without form of trial or authority to do it, constitutes a political crime.[14]

Prescinding from the question of what elements and what facts are needed to constitute the offense of treason, the concept of treasonous conduct gives rise to a variety of by-products which

---

[14]*In re Michard Eckermann*, [1929-1930] *Ann. Dig.*, 293, 295 (No. 189); and Garcia-Mora, *"Treason, Sedition and Espionage as Political Offenses under the Law of Extradition"* 26 *U. Pitt. L. Rev.*, 65 (1964); *In re DeBernonville*, 22 *I.L.R.* 527 (1955) holds that "treason to country is among political crimes, the author of which are not subject to extradition." *Accord, Ex parte Kolcynski*, 1 *Q.B.*, 540 (1955): "Treason is an offense of a political character." In *Chandler v. United States*, it was held *inter alia* that political offenders include persons charged with treason. 171 F. 2d 921 (1st Cir. 1948). In *In re Ockert* [1933-1934] *Ann Dig*, 268 (No. 157), it was said, "high treason, capital treason and the like are political offenses because the offense is against the state and its principal organs."

differ from country to country. As one author noted:

> Although the Soviet formulation reflects the traditional law in regarding treason as breach of allegiance to the state, it nevertheless goes amazingly far in lumping together treason, desertion and espionage, and, even more striking, in setting up escape or flight abroad as a treasonable act.[15]

Sedition in United States laws, for example, requires only a communication intended to incite a violation of public peace with intent to subvert the established form of government. The offense is complete upon the utterance and there is no necessity for any actual riot or rebellion occurring. Sedition is an insurrectionary movement tending toward treason, but wanting an overt act. It disturbs and affects the stability and tranquility of the state by means not actionable as treasonous. The distinction between treason, sedition and inciting to riot is, therefore, relative.[16]

Espionage on the other hand has a more widely recognized common denominator which is the obtaining or attempting to obtain information deemed secret or vital to the national security or defense of a given state for the benefit of another state. Unlike treason, there is no element of allegiance required on the part of the offender, hence no duty which must be breached. As with treason and sedition, it is predicated on the notion that what offends the public interest constitutes a public wrong.

Treason, sedition, espionage, peaceful dissent, freedom of expression and religion, if they do not incite to violence, are considered purely political offenses because they lack the essential elements of a common crime in that the perpetrator of the alleged offense acts merely as an instrument or agent of a political or religious thought or movement and is motivated by ideology or belief but does not cause a private harm. There is no way of defining what a purely political crime can be in a manner that

---

[15]*Ibid.*, Garcia-Mora, p. 74. Compare the Soviet Criminal Goddarts, 68-98 and 10 U.S.C. § 791-97 (1965); and U.S.C., *18*:951-69 (1965); see also, Bassiouni, "The Criminal Justice System of the U.S.S.R. and the Peoples Republic of China," 11 *Revista de Derecho Puertorriqueno*, 168 (1971); and Berman, *Soviet Criminal Law and Procedure* (1966). pp. 178-186.

[16]For sedition in United States law, see Bassiouni, *Criminal Law and Its Processes*, (1969), pp. 289-291.

would exhaust the imagination of lawmakers but a proposed definition is as follows:

> A purely political offense is one whereby the conduct of the actor manifests an exercise in freedom of thought, expression and belief (by words, symbolic acts or writings not inciting to violence), freedom of association and religious practice which are in violation of law designed to prohibit such conduct.[17]

2. THE RELATIVE POLITICAL OFFENSE

The relative political offense can be an extension of the purely political offense, when in conjunction with the latter, a common crime is also committed or when without committing a purely political offense, the offender commits a common crime prompted by ideological motives. While the purely political offense exclusively affects the public interest and causes only a public wrong, the relative political offense affects a private interest and constitutes at least in part a private wrong but done in furtherance of a political purpose. The term relative political offense is at best a descriptive label of doubtful legal accuracy because it purports to alter the nature of the crime committed depending upon the actor's motives (there are various theories on the subject which are discussed below). There is nothing that makes a given common crime political because the nature of the criminal violation and the resulting harm constitute a private wrong which, by definition, is a common crime. That the actor seeks to use the offense or its impact for ulterior political purposes does not alter the nature of the act or its resulting harm, nor does its ulterior or ultimate purpose change its character. The circumstances attending the commission of the crime and the

---

[17]Civil disorders in the United States, such as the riots of the sixties in major American cities, could be considered common crimes, relative political offenses, or purely political offenses depending upon one's ideological position. The United States government considers such acts common crimes as witnessed by the Chicago Conspiracy trial of the seven defendants accused of such crimes during the 1968 Democratic Convention in Chicago under U.S.C.A., § 231, 232 (1968), p. 18. All states have legislation which prohibits conduct such as disturbing the peace and arson which is used against rioters engaging in ideologically motivated demonstrations, e.g. See Bassiouni, *The Law of Dissent and Riots* (1971).

factors and forces which may have led the actor to such conduct render the motivation of the actor complex but not the offense. To call such crimes *delits complexes* or *delits connexes* only because the motives of the actor are taken into account even when they deserve special consideration is to confuse the nature of the crime with the motives of the actor.[18] Considerations focusing upon the offender's motives are not always accepted in all criminal justice systems. For example, United States criminal laws do not include motives as part of the elements of criminal offenses.[19] The element of intent required for all serious crimes bears upon the state of mind of the actor at the time the *actus reus* was committed. As such, *mens rea* does not contemplate the reason why the ulterior purpose or the motivating factors which brought about this state of mind.[20] Certainly motive is relevant in proving intent, but it is not an element of the crime and, therefore, has no bearing on whether or not the actor's overall conduct, the accompanying mental state and its resulting harm will be characterized a crime. It will, however, be relevant in the determination of the sentence.

The criminality of an actor is determined by what he or she did and whether he or she acted knowingly and voluntarily rather than what the ulterior purpose for the conduct aimed at. Motive is, therefore, a secondary factor in determining whether criminal intent exists except whenever a legal defense resting thereon requires its proof.[21] The significance of motive in different penal systems varies significantly, furthermore it must also be recalled that extradition is an intersystem process and, therefore, that which is significant to a given penal system may not be so with respect to another system. This therefore makes the issue of motive very complex particularly because whenever a state does not share the interest in maintaining the political ideology,

---

[18]But see *Youssef Said Abu Dourrah v. Attorney General,* 8 *Palestine Law Reports,* (1941), p. 43: "We know of nothing in the criminal law of this country or of England that creates a specific offense called political murder," also in [1941-1942] *Ann Dig,* 331 p. 336. (No. 101).

[19]See Bassiouni, *supra,* note 16, p. 62.

[20]*Ibid.* pp. 51-88.

[21]*Ibid.* pp. 134-137.

system or policies of another state, it is less likely to exhibit concern or interest in the maintenance of the internal structures and public safety of that other state. In such a case the requested state is more likely to examine the motives of the offender and find some redeeming value in such conduct and eventually deem it political in order to deny extradition. There is also another problem which generally affects all theories on the relative political offense and it deals with the technical or factual multiplicity of offenses arising out of the same criminal transaction perpetuated by the ideologically motivated offender.

Most penal systems in the world have adopted a policy of grading or dividing crimes designed to protect a given social interest into various levels of accountability. The purposes of such policy vary, but, in general, they signify that the criminality of an actor, being dependent upon what he does and how he does it, must be graded in such a manner as to have punishment fit the presupposed criminality of the actor. It is further believed that because a punishment is a deterrent, the multiplicity of offenses which relate to the same social interest by virtue of such grading will induce the potential offender to perform lesser harm whenever he engages in his intended criminal conduct. Whatever the reasons for a grading policy, one thing remains certain: too many technically different offenses cover or relate to the same social interest presumably sought to be protected.

In addition to these considerations, a given social harm by reason of its significance will invariably contain lesser or included offenses which, taken independently, are the subject of separate offenses but in the context of what was actually done, may be part of the same criminal design or transaction.

The ideologically motivated offender is not likely to commit a single or isolated criminal act. Most likely, the conduct will encompass several lesser included offenses or bear upon other nonincluded but related offenses. These multiple offenses may either arise out of a single criminal act (a bomb placed in a plane which kills ten persons and destroys the plane will produce at least eleven different crimes) or from the same criminal transaction (an elaborate scheme involving several different crimes related by the single design or scheme of the actor). These related offenses technically may be considered included offenses whenever the elements of the higher degree offense are predicated on some or all of the elements of the lesser degree offense, in which case the existence of the lesser included offense would only be technical and not real. Other offenses deemed related but not included may be committed only by reason of the actor's design or by the necessity of the scheme, such as when one crime is only a stepping stone or a means to reach the ultimate act sought to be committed. Lesser included offenses are vertically related in that the elements of the lesser are included in the higher offense. Other related offenses are at best horizontally linked but only whenever the actor's design relates them by reason of this scheme and not because of the interrelationship between the elements of the various offenses charged. This problem more than any other causes wide disparity in the application of the relative political offense in municipal laws and judicial decisions and, therefore, preclude uniform international practice.[22] Invariably, however, three factors are taken into account: (1) the degree of the political involvement of the actor in the ideology or movement on behalf of which he has acted, his personal commitment to and belief in the cause (on behalf of which he has acted), and his personal conviction that the means (the crime) are justified or necessitated by the objectives and purposes of the ideological or political cause; (2) the existence of a link between the political motive (as expressed above in (1)) and the crime committed; and (3) the proportionality or commensurateness of the means used (the crime and the manner in which it was performed) in relationship to the political purpose, goal or objective to be served. The first of these factors is wholly subjective, the second can be evaluated somewhat objectively, and the last is *sui generis*.

A dominant factor which emerges in the practice of all states recognizing the relative political offenses as falling within the purview of the political offense exception, namely that the political element must predominate over the intention to commit

---

[22]6 Whiteman, *Digest of International Law*, (1968), pp. 779-857; and I. Oppenheim, *supra,* note 5 p. 707.

the common crime and constitute the purpose for the commission of that common crime.[23]

The various theories concerning the relative political offense have emerged from the jurisprudence of the various courts determining whether or not the request is for a relative political offense. Three major theories have emerged: (A) the political-incidence theory, (B) the injured rights theory, and (C) the political-motivation theory. The European literature on the subject usually refers only to two theories, *delits complexes* and *delits connexes* but they encompass the distinctions made herein.

A. The Political-Incidence Theory—The Common Law Approach

The political-incidence theory was developed by an early English case, *In re Castioni*,[24] in which the refusal of extradition of one whose surrender had been requested by the Swiss Government for the murder of a member of the State Council of a Swiss canton held that "fugitive criminals are not to be surrendered for extradition crimes, if those crimes were incidental to and formed a part of political disturbances."[25] "Crimes otherwise extraditable, become political offenses if they were incidental to and formed part of a political disturbance."[26]

This case set up a two-fold standard which must be met for a common crime to be regarded as a relative political offense: (1) there must be a political revolt or disturbance; and (2) the act for which extradition is sought must be incidental thereto or form a part thereof.[27] The English Court stated in this case:

> The question really is, whether, upon the facts, it is clear that the man was acting as one of a number of persons engaged in acts of violence of a political character with a political object, and as part of the political movement and rising in which he was taking part.[28]

---

[23]See Belgian Extradition Law of Oct. 1, 1833, *Les Codes* 698 (31st ed. 1965); and *In re Fabijan, supra,* note 7.

[24]1 *Q.B.*, 149 (1891).

[25]*Ibid.,* p. 152.

[26]*Ibid.*

[27]Bassiouni, "International Extradition in the American Practice and World Public Order," 36 *Tenn L Rev,* 1, 17 (1968).

[28]*Supra.,* note 24, p. 159.

The *Castioni* ruling reflects the English liberal philosophy of the late nineteenth century and is a consequence of its political theories and theories of government. English and United States cases recognize the precedent of *In re Castioni* as authority.[29]

This view was confirmed in England three years after Castioni, in the case of In re Meunier[30] where a confessed anarchist was held extraditable for "in order to constitute an offense of a political character, there must be two or more parties in the state each seeking to improve the government of their own choice on the other . . . In the present case there are not . . . for the party with whom the accused is identified (ANARCHY) . . . by his own voluntary statement . . . is the enemy of all governments. Their efforts are directed primarily against the general body of citizens."[31]

Notwithstanding the validity of this position, it must be emphasized that the "political offense" concept remains essentially a flexible one. Judge Denman, in *In re Castioni,* stated: "I do not think it is necessary or desirable that we should attempt to put into language in the shape of an exhaustive definition exactly . . . every state of things which might bring a particular case within the description of an offense of a political character."[32] This opinion presaged a recent holding of the English courts in *Ex parte Kolczysnski,*[33] that mutiny by the crew of a small Polish fishing trawler was a political offense, notwithstanding the fact that it was not incident to a political uprising. This case indicates that (1) there is no absolute requirement that there be a political uprising in order for the political offense exception to be applicable, but that the only indispensable ingredient is that the acts

---

[29]*In re Ezeta*, 62 F. 2d 198 (9th Cir., 1957) rev'd on other grounds, 355 U.S. 389, 78 S.Ct. 381 2 L. Ed. 2d 356 (1958), which stated that "the general rule is that there must be an 'uprising,' and that the acts in question must be incident to it." See also, Hyde, 1 *International Law,* 573 (1922); Garcia Mora, "The Nature of Political Offenses: A Knotty Problem of Extradition Law," *supra,* note 2 p. 1240; and Deere, *supra,* note 2, p. 266.

[30]*In re Meunier,* 2 *Q.B.,* 415 (1894); see also *Re Aston,* 1 *Q.B.,* 108 (1896).

[31]*Ibid.,* p. 419.

[32]*Supra,* note 24 p. 155.

[33]16 B. 540 (1955), 21 *I.L.R.,* 240 (1954); see also, *Schtrak v. The Government of Israel,* 3 *All Eng. Rep.,* 529 (1962); see also Oppenheim, *supra,* note 6, pp. 784-785.

be politically motivated and directed towards political ends; and (2) the political offense exception legitimately can be applied with greater liberality where the demanding State is a totalitarian regime seeking the extradition of one who has opposed that regime in the cause of freedom. Indeed, these two factors are closely related, particularly because in an effectively repressive totalitarian regime, traditional political disturbances or uprisings may be unknown despite deep and widespread hostility towards the regime (the United States holds a similar position). In 1973 the House of Lords in *Cheng v. Governor of Pentonville* held that for the exception to apply in addition to the predominance of a purpose in the act it must also be directed against the opposed government.[34] In *In re Gonzalez*,[35] the United States District Court held "the issue is whether the acts of the relator should be deemed politically motivated because directed towards political ends; . . . nothing in the record suggests that the second factor is applicable as this does not appear to be a case in which the acts in question were blows struck in the cause of freedom against a repressive totalitarian régime."[36]

This approach has been followed by some Latin-American courts, even though their interpretation is often more liberal because of Western European influence and indigenous traditions towards political struggles. This position is illustrated by cases among which a case decided by the Supreme Court of Chile. Argentine had requested the extradition from Chile of Guillermo Patricio Kelly and others for murder, robbery and other offenses allegedly committed by Kelly when, during a raid on local Communist headquarters in Buenos Aires in which typewriters and other equipment were taken from the office, he shot and killed the gatekeeper. The Supreme Court of Chile, concluded that the exemption from extradition of political offenses applied only when the offense is a purely political offense or is an ordinary crime connected with a political offense. The Court held that

---

[34]2 *All Eng. Rep.*, 204 (1973).

[35]*F. Supp. 217:717*, (1963).

[36]*Ibid.*, the same position was held in *Ornelas v. Ruiz*, 161 U.S. 502, 165 at 689 (1996).

Kelly should be extradited on the murder and robbery charges, stating:

> These crimes did not occur during an attack (by Kelly) on the security of the state, such as to be considered connected to a separate political offense. They took place at a time of public tranquility during which the murder and theft were isolated acts. The ultimate objective may have been the political one of annihilating communists, but the principles of public international law which this decision accepts do not admit that an ordinary crime is converted into a political one solely because of its ultimate objective.[38]

It further stated that:

> "Political offense" does not appear to be defined in our positive legislation, nor in the international conventions and treaties previously enumerated, but generally accepted principles are in agreement that a political offense is that which is directed against the political organization of the state or against the civil rights of its citizens and that the legally protected right which the offense damages is the constitutional normality of the country affected. Also included in the concept are acts which have as their end the alteration of the established political or social orders established in the state.
>
> A majority of the authorities consider, moreover, that in order to distinguish between ordinary and political crimes, it is necessary to take into account the goals and motives of the persons charged; that is to say, to consider the objective aspect of the offense as well as its subjective one. Political and social offenses obey motives of political and collective interest and are characterized by the sense of altruism or patroitism which animates them, while ordinary criminal offenses are motivated by egotistic sentiments, more or less excusable (emotion, love, honor), or to be reproached (vengeance, hate, financial gain).
>
> In this area of nonextraditable offenses there are to be identified, *purely political* offenses, which are directed against the form and political organization of the state; improper *political offenses,* which embitter social or economic tranquility; *mixed or complex political offenses,* which damages at the same time public order and ordinary criminal law, such as the assassination of the head of state for political reasons; and *connected political offenses,* which are common crimes committed in the course of attempts against the security of the state or related to political offenses, it being necessary to examine intent to

---

[37]Garcia-Mora, *supra,* note 6, p. 378.

[38]"In the Matter of Extradition of Hector Jose Campora and others," 58 *A.J.I.L.*, 690, 694-695 (1957).

determine whether the ordinary crime is one connected, or not, to a political one."[39] [Emphasis added.]

The extension of the political-incidence test may often come from the executive rather than the judiciary.[40] This was revealed in the *Rudewitz* case in 1908 when a Russian revolutionary, a member of the Social Democratic Labor Party, was sought by the Czarist Government for the common crimes of murder, arson, burglary, robbery and larceny from the United States. The Secretary of State, subsequent to the decision of the extradition magistrate to grant the request, concluded that the offenses charged were political in nature and exercised his discretionary power in refusing to issue the surrender warrant.[41]

Another case of judicial-executive correlation in United States extradition practice is the case of *Chandler v. United States.*[42] There an American citizen was charged with treason for broadcasting hostile propaganda to the United States from Germany during World War II, thereby giving aid and comfort to the enemies of the United States. Chandler claimed that his arrest having occurred after the War while he was in Germany was a violation of his rights of asylum conferred by International Law. The United States Supreme Court held that in the absence of a treaty, a state does not violate any principle of International Law by declining to surrender a fugitive offender, but that the right

---

[39]*Ibid.*, pp. 698-694.

[40]Compare, *In re Fabijan,* supra, note 7, stating p. 367:

. . . Neither the actual attack on the policeman engaged in the lawful discharge of his duties, nor the "demonstration" of the accused and his three companions against the Carabinieri barracks, constitute a "political crime" in the strict sense of the term. Both parts of the whole act were directed, not against the central political authority, but only against individual organs of the State . . . There is no proof of a principal political crime with which the acts of the prisoner could possibly be connected. Moreover, he himself has not sought to allege the existence of any such crime, but has merely contended that he had a "political motive." However, as has been explained already, proof of political motive does not make an act a "connected" act when there is no "concrete" political act. And the case of Rudewitz, intra, note 35 and corresponding text.

[41]Letter from Secretary of State Elihu Root to Russian Ambassador Rosen, 1908, on file in Department of State, File No. 16649-9, 4 Hackworth, *Digest of International Law*, 316, pp. 49-50 (1942).

[42]*Supra,* note 14.

is that of the state (Germany) to offer asylum, not that of the fugitive to claim. It also held that since treason is a violation of allegiance, such conduct may be made (consistently with intervention of law) an offense against the United States, though the acts were committed outside its territorial jurisdiction. The court also found that the acts were political crimes for which extradition is not usually granted, and that had Germany claimed a grant of asylum to the offender it is quite possible that, in keeping with United States custom and practice Chandler would have been returned to Germany. Chandler however was in United States custody, the Court held that International Law principles were not violated by his arrest in Germany and his return to the United States and Germany did not object and therefore, there was no opportunity to see how executive discretion would have been exercised in this instance (Executive Discretion is discussed *infra,* Chapter VII).

These cases, however serve to demonstrate that it is generally within the scope of the political offense exception and in particular with respect to the relative political offense that executive discretion finds the greatest opportunity for the exercise of its determinative power to ultimately allow or deny extradition. The role of the judiciary in United States practice is definitive in finding that the exception applies, but is only conclusive in its findings that the exception is inapplicable since executive discretion can override such findings. Consistent with this policy and with the precedents discussed above, the United States decided the *Artukovic* cases.[43]

In the first of these opinions, *Karadzole v. Artukovic,*[44] the Circuit Court of Appeals affirmed a district court ruling that the crimes charged against the petitioner, whose extradition had been sought by the Government of Yugoslavia for the crimes of murder and participation in murder occurring while he served as Minister of the Interior of that country were of a political charac-

---

[43]*Ivancevic v. Artukovic,* 211 F. 2d 565 (9th Cir. 1954); *Artukovic v. Boyle,* 140 F. Supp. 245 (S.D. California, 1956); *Karadzole v. Artukovic,* 247 F. 2d 198 (9th Cir., 1957); *Karadzole v. Artukovic,* 355 U.S. 898 (1958), *United States v. Artukovic,* 170 F. Supp. 383 (1959).

[44]*Karadzole v. Artukovic,* 247 F. 2d 198 (1957).

ter within the meaning of the Treaty and that, therefore, Artukovic could not be extradited. The Yugoslav Government charged that more than 30,000 unidentified persons and over 1,200 identified persons were killed on orders of the accused in 1941 and 1942. The United States Court of Appeals, however, reversing the District Court's finding held that a valid extradition treaty existed between the United States and Yugoslavia as the successor state of Serbia with whom the extradition treaty of 1901 was in force. The District Court properly took judicial notice of the fact that various factions representing different theories of government were struggling for power during this period.

In the second opinion, *Karadzole v. Artukovic,*[45] the United States Supreme Court held, Justices Black and Douglas dissenting, that the judgment of the Court of Appeals should be vacated and remanded for hearings on the matter of the political offense. However, prior to this ruling, the Department of State representing the executive branch of government expressed its views to the court on the extradition issue that murder, even though committed solely or predominantly with the intent to destroy, in whole or in part, a national, ethnical, racial or religious group, is nonetheless murder within the meaning of the extradition treaty here involved, and is not thereby rendered an offense of a "political character within . . . the treaty . . . It does not appear on the face of the pleadings that all of the offenses . . . were necessarily connected with such struggle for power."[46]

The final judgment on that issue was in *United States v. Artukovic,*[47] where the United States Commissioner found insufficient evidence upon which to believe the accused guilty of the alleged offenses and refused extradition, holding that "the evidence presented, as well as historical facts of which I take judicial notice, proves . . . as a fact that the crimes charged in all courts of the

---

[45]355 U.S. 383 (1958).

[46]"Letter from the Legal Advisor of the Department of State to the Acting Assistant Attorney General McLean," M.S. Dept. of State, Dec. 16, 1957, file 611.6926/11-57; also "memorandum for the United States," submitted in *Karadzole v. Artukovic,* and appended to the opinion *supra,* note 44.

[47]170 F. Supp. 383 (1959).

amended complaint are political in character."[48]

The disposition of the case reflected the acceptance by the United States Commissioner of the *Castioni* standards[49] in finding that a political offense existed in fact and, therefore, that the relator was not extraditable. Since United States practice, however, does not favor the exercise of executive discretion to grant the request after its denial by the judiciary, a conflict was averted which could have arisen between these two branches had the executive department overriden the court's findings as indicated by the Department of State's views.[50] It must be noted that this case also contained a charge that the relator committed international crimes which should have precluded the court's findings of the political offense exception, but did not (see *infra*, 1-6) .

In another case, the United States Supreme Court left undisturbed the findings of the extradition magistrate but affirmed the position that relative political offenses are nonextraditable and that the best test is one of "political incidence."[51] In that case, Italy, in 1958, requested the extradition from the United States of Vincenzo Gallina who had been convicted in Italy, *in absentia,* in the court of Assizes of Caltanisetta on May 30, 1949, of the crime of robbery. After being found extraditable at the extradition hearing, Gallina applied for a writ of *habeas corpus* contending, *inter alia,* that the offense was not extraditable under the Extradition Convention of 1868 between the United States and Italy,[52] Article III, of which states that "the provisions of this treaty shall not apply to any crime or offense of a political character. . . ." The District Court rejected the contention.[53]

The United States Court of Appeals affirming held:

> Relator contends that the hearing before the Commissioner established beyond doubt that the offense for which extradition is sought were of a political character and, under Article III of the Convention

---

[48]*Ibid.,* pp. 392-393.

[49]*Supra,* note 24.

[50]See Positions of the Department of State, *supra,* note 4; and Whiteman, 6 *Digest of International Law,* 826 (1968).

[51]*Gallina v. Fraser,* 177 F. Supp. 356 (D. Conn. 1959); aff'd 278 F. 2d Cir. 1960; *cert. denied* 364 U.S. 851 (1960).

[52]U.S.T.S. 174; 15 Stat. 629; I. Malloy, *Treaties,* 966-967 (1910).

[53]*Supra,* note 48.

of 1868, nonextraditable. Counsel for relator has briefed the point extensively. According to relator, the acts to which he admitted might be ordinary crimes in an atmosphere free of any political ramifications, but because of the motivation for their commission, they must necessarily be deemed of a "political character." While the court is in general agreement with a relator's exposition of the principles of law governing the nonextraditability of political offenders who have found asylum in this country, nevertheless it is the opinion of the court that the Commissioner's decision that the specific acts ascribed to relator in the complaint of the Republic of Italy were not of a political character, whatever his other acts during the period in question might have been, is supported by the evidence in the record. . . .

The claim that what appeared to be common, ordinary crimes were so admixed with political motives and aims as to be of a political character within the meaning of the Convention of 1868 was based solely on testimony of relator himself. This testimony, to the effect that relator worked for Torrese and that Torrese took orders from Guiliano, all to advance the political aims of a Sicilian separatist movement, was contradicted by statements taken from relator's admitted accomplices after their arrest in Italy, which tended to indicate that private gain was the sole motivating factor in these robberies. There was also testimony from a Mr. Russo, a witness offered as an expert by the Republic of Italy, who had spent considerable time in Sicily during the years when a Sicilian separatist organization was active, as a member of the Office of Strategic Services, a branch of our wartime forces. Russo testified at length and unqualifiedly, both on direct and on cross-examination, that Guiliano was a bandit who had no legitimate connection with the actual separatist movement, and that Guiliano described his activities as "political" to cloak their true purpose, i.e. private gain for himself and his followers. With the evidence before the Commissioner in such posture, this court cannot say that the Commissioner's decision was not supported by competent, legal evidence. The evidence was conflicting, it is true, but it did not preponderate so heavily in relator's favor as to require a decision that his offenses were political as a matter of law.[54]

In what appears to be a contrary view in a situation equally complex and laden with political implications were the *Jimenez* cases.[55] There a former President of the Republic of Venezuela was sought from the United States for financial crimes and murder. The District Court found the murder charge to be non-

---

[54]*Supra*, note 48, p. 73.
[55]*Jimenez v. Aristeguieta*, 311 F. 2d 547 (5th Cir., 1962).

extraditable on grounds of political offense exception but found that the financial crimes were not within the exception and granted extradition. Thus establishing the precedent that where multiple charges exist and some do not fall within the political offense exception extradition shall be granted unless all charges are related or connected to the political motive and were incidental thereto. Where there is no such connection and the charges are severable, extradition can be granted on the assumption that the doctrine of specialty shall preclude the prosecution of the relator for those charges. In view of the fact that the ideologically motivated offender is a more wanted person than any other person alleged to have committed a common crime, because he struck at the very foundation of the requesting state's existence or order, it is naive to believe that the doctrine of specialty shall operate as a protective shield to the relator.

The position of the United States has been to consider the question of whether an offense is of a political character a mixed question of law and facts, but chiefly one of facts.[56] This gives, therefore, the extradition magistrate the preponderant role, leaving reviewing courts with an examination of the interpretation of the law and its proper application to the facts stated in the record.

B. The Injured Rights Theory

This theory has its basis in the French Extradition Law of March 10, 1927, and suggests that extradition cannot be granted when the circumstances show that it is sought exclusively for a political end.[57] It is not, however, the only theory followed by the French courts and is considered a supplemental theory rather than an exclusive approach. The principal theory followed in Europe is the Political Motivation Theory discussed below. The Injured Rights Theory often appears as part of the Political Motivation Theory. It has been evident in the reasoning of cases

---

[56]*Ornelas v. Ruiz, supra,* note 36; see also, *Ramos v. Diaz and Ramoz Covreta,* 178 F. Supp. 459 (S.D. Fla. 1950).

[57]See Levasseur 2 *Juris classeur de Droit International,* 405-410 (1965); this position is also in part the common law position but the latter is not limited thereto.

in France, Belgium, San Marino, Italy, Switzerland and The Federal Republic of Germany. The leading case following this theory is *In re Giovanni Gatti*[58] wherein the extradition request by the Republic of San Marino was for an attempted homicide by a member of a Communist cell. The Court granted extradition and held that: "Political offenses . . . *are* directed against the constitution of the Government and against Sovereignty . . . and disturb the distribution of powers . . . *such an offense* affects the political organization of the state. . . . The offense does not derive its political character from the motive of the offender, but from the nature of the *rights it injures.*"[59]

A second case, *In re Colman,*[60] allowed extradition upon the request of Belgium of one sought for, and already convicted *in absentia* of the Crimes of Collaboration with the enemy, carrying arms against the state and assassination: "in a country occupied by the enemy (in time of war), collaboration with the latter excludes the idea of a criminal action against the political organization of the state which characterizes the political offense."[61] In the context of the discussion of executive discretion, it is interesting to note that the offenses charged against *Colman* were not covered by the extradition treaty between France and Belgium.[62] An exchange of notes between the two governments which took

---

[58]*In re Giovanni Gatti,* [1946-1947] *Ann. Dig.,* 145 (No. 70).

[59]*Ibid.,* the Court of Appeal of Grenoble, France, further stated p. 145:
    Political offenses are those which injure the political organism, which are directed against the constitution of the Government and against sovereignty, which trouble the order established by the Fundamental laws of the state and disturb the distribution of powers. Acts which aim at overthrowing or modifying the organization of the main organs of the state, or at destroying, weakening or bringing into disrepute one of these authorities, or at exercising illegitimate pressure on the play of their mechanism or on their general direction of the state, or which aim at changing the social conditions created for individuals by the constitution in one or all of its elements, are also political offenses. In brief, what distinguishes the political crime from the common crime is the fact that the former only affects the political organization of the state, the proper rights of the state, while the latter exclusively affects rights other than those of the state.

[60]*In re Colman,* [1945-1947] *Ann. Dig.,* 139, (No. 67).

[61]*Ibid.,* p 141.

[62]*Franco-Belgian Extradition Treaty* of August 15, 1874 cited in *In re Colman, supra,* note 59.

place after the commission of the offenses set forth the terms for the exchange of such offenders considering them as falling within the scope of the treaty.[63] The court said that "the offender . . . has no right not to be surrendered though facts which were not provided for, at the time of the consummation of the offense, by the Franco-Belgian Convention to which he is not a party, as long as both French and Belgian law render criminal and punish the offenses at the time when they were committed."[64] This insistence stretches the principle of nonretroactivity of criminal laws and somewhat subverts the legislative effect of an extradition theory by its *ex post facto* amendment.

C. The Political Motivation Theory

This theory was developed by the Swiss courts which attempted to modify the political-incidence theory[65] developed by the Eng-

---

[63]A case decided by the same court nine months prior to the Colman, *supra,* note 59, decision, refusing the extradition request of Belgium for the crime of economic collaboration with the enemy, held that the exchange of notes between the countries could not be considered since it was not mentioned by the requesting government as a grounds for granting surrender. Also, that "such a convention (the notes) . . . cannot, without ratification and publication, have force of law in the meaning of Article 26 of the Constitution of the French Republic of 1946." *In re Talbot* [1945-1947] *Ann. Dig.,* 142, (No. 68).

[64]*Supra,* note 60, p. 140. For opposite holding, see *Denmark (collaberation with the enemy),* [1945-1947] *Ann. Dig.,* 146, (No. 71).

[65]The Federal Tribunal of Switzerland has stated concerning relative political offenses:

A relative political offense is one which, while having the characteristics of a common offense, acquires a political character by virture of the motive inspiring it, or the purpose for which or the circumstances in which it has been committed; in other words, it is in itself a common offence but has a predominantly political character.

In re Ficorilli, 18 I.L.R., 345 (No. 110) (1951), and *In re. Barratina,* [1938-1940] *Ann. Dig.,* 412, (No. 159).

Frequently, the term "political offense" is used to cover both "purely" political offenses and "relative" political offenses. Thus, the Belgian Court of Appeal stated in 1936:

A political offence is one which, in essence, is directed against the political regime or which, though normally constituting an ordinary crime ("crime de droit commun"), assumes the character of a political crime because the aim of the author of the crime was to injure the political regime. However, an ordinary crime committed under the influence of party passion against an adversary cannot be regarded as political unless it occurred as an episode in a civil war between combatants engaged in a violent struggle in which the constitution of the State was in issue.

lish courts. It does not look strictly to the nature of the rights injured, but it tries to correlate the ideological beliefs of the offender and the proportionate effect of his acts or offenses and the political purpose in trying to reach an equitable results which locks in the other theories.

In 1908, the Swiss Federal Tribunal stated in the case of *V. P. Wassilief*[66] that three general principles had to be met in order for an offense to be political: (1) that the offense was committed for the purpose of helping or insuring the success of a purely political purpose; (2) that there is a direct connection between the crime committed and the purpose pursued by a party to modify the political or the social organization of the state; and (3) that the political element predominates over the ordinary criminal element.

The problem of interpretation appears in the case of *In re Pavan*,[67] where the French Government requested extradition of an anti-Fascist journalist accused of the murder of an Italian Fascist. The Swiss court, rejecting the defense's plea of political offense, held that the crime "is invested with a predominantly political character only where the criminal action is immediately connected with its political object. Such connection can only be predicated where the act is in itself an effective means of attaining this object or where it is an incident in a general political struggle. . . ."[68]

The same reasoning was applied in the *Ockert* case. In 1933 the Prussian Minister of Justice requested the extradition from Switzerland of one Ockert on a charge of homicide. It appeared that Ockert, a member of the Reichsbanner, a quasimilitary organization of the Germano Social-Democratic Party, became involved in an altercation on a street in Frankfurt with certain members of the National-Socialist Party, particularly one Bleser whom he hit with his fist. Ockert then ran and when pursued by the group fired several shots at them with his pistol, two of which

---

[66]*U.S. Foreign Relations,* 1909, pp. 520-521 (Dept. State). Also, Deere, *supra,* note 2, p. 253.

[67]In Re Pavan, (1923) *Ann Dig.,* 347 (No. 239) and *In Re Peruze* 19 *I.L.R.,* 369 (1952).

[68]*Ibid,* pp. 347-349.

hit Bleser and caused his death. Ockert contended that the charge
came within article 4 of the Swiss-German Extradition Treaty
of 1874 which prohibited extradition for offenses of a political
character. The Federal Tribunal of Switzerland agreed. The
Tribunal referred to previous cases involving similar facts, particularly a case in which a Swiss Federal Court had refused extradition of a person convicted of complicity in a brawl between
members of the Fascist Party in a small Italian village and their
local antagonists on the basis that the clashes between such groups
were not mere casual disputes arising from local or personal
enmity but part of a struggle which was on such a wide scale that
it came near to being a civil war. In the instant case, the Tribunal noted that reports of the incident in German newspapers
spoke of "Marxist Murder Tactics" and "Sacrifice in the Service
of the New Reich" and concluded that the case was essentially one
of political conflict and not extraditable.[69] Relating what is called
passive resistance to political regimes and the relative political
offense, the Swiss approach in the case of *In re Kavic,*[70] linked
the nondoing of an act of opposition to the doing of an act likely

---

[69]*In re Ockert,* [1933-1934] *Ann Dig.,* 369 (No. 157). In the case referred to above,
Italy unsuccessfully sought the extradition, for attempted homicide, of one Ragni
who took part in an encounter between fascists on the one hand and Socialists,
communists, and 'Popolari' on the other, in which a number of persons were injured by shots and otherwise. *In re Ragni,* [1923-1924] *Ann. Dig.,* 286 (No. 166).

Similarly, A Swiss Federal Court refused an Italian request for the extradition of
one Camporini, former mayor of Corresio and secretary of the Social-Democratic
party, accused of shooting and fatally wounding one Tizzoni, a Fascist, during
disturbances accompanying the Italian parliamentary elections in 1924. *In re
Camporini,* [1923-1924] *Ann. Dig.,* 283 (No. 164).

The Swiss Federal Tribunal recognizing this deficiency has said in the *Kavic,
Bjelanove and Arsenijevil case,* 19 *I.L.R.,* 371 (No. 30) (1952) s . .

That restrictive interpretation . . . does not meet the intention of the law, nor
take account of recent historical developments, such as the growth of totalitarian
States . . . Those who do not wish to submit to the regime have no alternative but
to escape it by flight abroad . . . This more passive attitude for the purpose of
escaping political constraint is no less worthy of asylum than active participation
in the fight for political power used to be in what were earlier considered to be
normal circumstances . . . Recent practice has been too restrictive in making the
relative political character of an offense dependent on its commission in the framework of a fight for power.

[70]39 *I.L.R.,* 371 (1952).

to be deemed criminal.

In this case, Yugoslavia sought the extradition of the members of an airplane crew who had diverted a local flight and landed in Switzerland. They were charged with the crimes of endangering the safety of public transport and wrongful appropriation of property. The Swiss Court, in denying the extradition request, held that although the political character of the offense must outweigh common characteristics (the danger and harm to the passengers was minimal) such need not be related to a realization of political objectives or occurring within a fight for political power.[71] "That restrictive interpretation . . . does not meet the intention of the law, nor take account of . . . the growth of totalitarian states . . . those who do not wish to submit to the régime have no alternative but to escape it by flight abroad . . . this more passive attitude . . . is nonetheless worthy of asylum than active participation in the fight for political power used to be in what were . . . normal circumstances."[72]

This position is no longer valid in light of the 1963 Tokyo Convention and 1970 Hague Conventions since unlawful seizure of aircrafts became an international crime as discussed in the "exception to the exception," *(infra, 6)*.

A later case illustrating this theory is the *Ktir* case.[73] The appellant, a French national was a member of the Algerian Liberation Movement (F.L.N.). On November 14, 1960, he was responsible, with three other persons, for the murder in France of another member of the F.L.N. who was suspected by his chiefs of treason. He then fled to Switzerland. France requested his extradition. He contested that request on the ground that France was at war with F.L.N. and that the act he had committed was that of killing an enemy. He further contended that, if extradition were granted; it had to be made subject to the condition that he would not be executed, since the offenses would not be punished by capital punishment in Switzerland. The Court held that extradition must be granted for the following reasons:

---

[71] 6 Whiteman, *Digest of International Law* 371 (1968).

[72] *Supra,* note 70, p. 372.

[73] 34 *I.L.R.,* 143 (1961).

(1) Political offences included common crimes which had a predominantly political character, from their motive and factual background. However, the damage had to be proportionate to the aim sought; in the case of murder, this had to be shown to be the sole means of attaining the political aim. The offence in this case did not satisfy this requirement of proportionality.

(2) A condition that the accused would not be sentenced to death could be attached to the extradition only if the relevant treaty expressly prohibited capital punishment.

(3) The extradition should be subject to the condition that the appellant would not be prosecuted or sentenced for other activities. This was required in order to give effect to the principle of specialty contained in Article 8 of the Extradition Treaty (of July 9, 1869).

. . . .

2. According to Article 1 and 2 of the Treaty, extradition is authorized if the acts committed are punishable under both Swiss and French law; if they constitute one of the offences listed in the Convention; and if they do not constitute political offences. Political offences include offences which, although constituting acts falling under the ordinary criminal law, have a *predominantly* political character as a result of the circumstances in which they are committed, in particular as a result of the circumstances in which they are committed, in particular as a result of the motives inspiring them and the purpose sought to be achieved. Such offences, akin to relative political offences, presuppose that the act was inspired by political passion, that it was committed either in the framework of a struggle for power or for the purpose of escaping a dictatorial authority, and that it was directly and closely related to the political purpose. A further requirement is that the damage caused be proportionate to the result sought, in other words, that the interests at stake should be sufficiently important to excuse, if not to justify, the infringement of private legal rights. Where murder is concerned, such a relationship exists only if homicide is the sole means of safeguarding more important interests and attaining the political aim.[74]

Even though the case also involved an issue of exclusion for military offenses and death penalty, the court found that extradition when granted for one or more offenses charged and not for others, the Doctrine of Specialty would preclude the prosecution of the relator for such offenses but does not constitute a bar to his extradition for other offenses deemed extraditable. The position of the

---

[74]*Ibid.,* pp. 143-144.

United States is to that extent compatible with that of Switzerland and the general practice under customary international law.[75]

The contemporary position of western European states is still ambiguous as to what constitutes a relative political offense even though the 1957 European convention on extradition contains the exception in its Article 3. All fifteen member states of the Council of Europe recognized that it is a judicial question which depends essentially on the facts and circumstances of every case. Recent extradition legislation in several of the European states has yet to be applied and its jurisprudential significance remains to be established. This is the case with respect to Cyprus whose new law of 1970 has yet to be applied in the courts of that state, and also with respect to Denmark's 1967 Law and Norway's 1968 Law. The 1966 Extradition law of the Netherlands preserves the doctrine that the courts must determine the nature of the interests affected by the act and the motives of the actor. The variance in other laws is essentially as to the issue of whether the entirety of the criminal transaction is to be motivated by political purposes or only a portion thereof, and also their preponderance over all other motives.

Italy in Article 8 of its 1931 penal code requires the magistrate to determine whether the common crime was motivated in whole or in part by political motives. This was expressed in the 1934 decision of the Court of Appeals of Turin of *In re Pavelic and Kwaternik* and this position remains unchanged. This case remains a landmark because of its facts and its impact. It was based on the French government's request for the extradition of Pavelic and Kwaternik on the charge of complicity in the murder of King Alexander of Yugoslavia and the French Minister Barthou in Marseilles in October, 1934. The Italian Court of Appeals held that the offense fell within the meaning of the political offense exception embodies in Article 2 and 3 of the Treaty of May 12, 1870 between the two states and in accordance to the Italian Criminal Code which forbids extradition for political offenses. Even though extradition had been denied the authors of the *at-*

---

[75]See *supra*, note 54-55 and corresponding text.

tendant were judged in France and found guilty of common crimes. (It was after this decision that the multilateral Convention on the Prevention and Punishment of Terrorism was drafted in 1937 and proposed, *inter alia,* the creation of an international criminal court to judge such cases. Even though the convention was signed by 13 states it was never ratified by a sufficient number of states to enter into effect and is since 1973 very discussed because of contemporary efforts to draft a convention on the same subject.)

The Law of Denmark of 1947 makes the issue dependent upon the nature of interests affected. Switzerland also adheres to that position but requires in addition thereto that the political motive be predominant over the intent to commit a common crime. France adheres to its 1927 law which is vague as to its specific requirements but its jurisprudence has closely paralleled decisions in Belgium and Switzerland. Furthermore France requires the magistrate to inquire as to whether the extradition itself is sought for a political purpose. Germany also has followed closely the jurisprudence of Switzerland, France and Belgium. Sweden whose 1957 law is the broadest legislative provision in Western Europe has been liberal in its jurisprudence. Belgium which has also been liberal in its application of the exception which it was the first state to embody in its law of 1833, had amended it in 1856 with the *clause d'attentat.* This amendment was added to the 1833 law after the Belgium courts refused to extradite to France the author of the *attentat* against the life of Napoleon III. The Federal Republic of Germany has a similar clause in its law on extradition which is also embodied in Article 3.3 of the 1957 European Convention on Extradition. (The same type of provision is found in the Caracas Convention of July 18, 1911 between the Central American state; in Article 357 of the Bustamaute Code of February 20, 1923; in Article 3 of the Montivideo Convention of December 26, 1933; in Article 3 of the extradition convention of the Central American states signed in Guatemala April 12, 1934, and in Article 23 of the Montevideo Convention of March 19, 1940.)

The *clause d'attentat* is also present in several European bilateral treaties as between German, France, Belgium and Monaco. The same type of provision appears in the recent treaties of France with for example Ivory-Coast, Dahomey, Niger, Upper Volta and Mauritania. These recent treaties expand the original Belgium clause of 1856 to include all forms of assassinations, excluding such acts from the political offense exception.

The Anarchist movement of the 30's in Europe filled the anals of European extradition and in several *causes célébres* even the authors of riots were extradited without benefit of the political offense exception. This was the case with Great Britain's surrender to Italy of Rivolta and to France of Lucchesi. Italy however did not reciprocate as witness the case of Pavelic and Kwaternik (these cases have been referred to earlier in this chapter). The latest European case was *Cheng v. Governor of Pentonville* discussed above in which the House of Lords reaffirmed its earlier position but the opinion of the court and its members expressed a tightening of the hitherto liberal English position. References to the rash of terrorism taking place in Europe are a clear indication of a narrowing trend for future interpretation of the exception. In 1974 the Council of Europe will consider amending Article 3 of the European Convention on extradition to take account of the contemporary problems posed by "terrorism" and its various manifestations. This presages for all of Europe a trend for less liberal application of the exception and for specifying such exclusions as "terrorism" from the scope of the exception. The problem of defining "terrorism" will of course be the main problem but it is likely to be resolved by a listing of specific acts such as aircraft hijacking, letter bombs, etc.

A PROPOSED JURIDICAL STANDARD OF INQUIRY FOR MUNICIPAL TRIBUNALS[76]

The determination of the relationship of all offenses committed as part of a political scheme, and particularly under the relative political offense is, at first, as shown in the theories discussed above, one of motive, but further inquiry must be made into the nature of the criminal transaction. This inquiry leads to

[76]From Bassiouni, *supra,* note 11, pp. 254-257.

the following questions: (1) Were all the offenses committed part of the same (political) criminal transactions? (2) What was the number or extent of these violations? (3) How were they related in scope, time, place and social significance? (4) To what extent did the political scheme necessitate the commission of such multiple offenses? (5) Could they readily be identified as lesser included offenses, or did they appear to be related only by the actor's design?

One interesting question which could arise at this point is: What if this inquiry concluded only partially in favor of the relator? Shall the extradition judge or executive authority weigh the degree of compliance of the relator's conduct to these tests versus his noncompliance and determine its outcome by a "preponderance of compliance" test? Or shall he disqualify the relator from the benefit of the "political offense" exception because there was a single instance of noncompliance? In this case we also see the limited chances of a juridical solution in a world system wherein the ultimate relationship between political units is predicated upon a concept of co-equal sovereigns exercising all-too-often conflicting, co-equal authority. Were the alternative a vertical jurisdictional authoritative process, the issue would then be removed from the contentious or opposing co-equal horizontal authoritative process and some opportunities for direct conflict would therefore be eliminated.

The search for an objective standard gives rise to an analogy with self-defense as commonly accepted in all penal systems, wherein a person is justified in causing harm to another to insure his own safety. The primary consideration in the law of self-defense is a value-judgment based on the inherent justification of self-preservation and its overriding exonerating effect on the consequences arising out of the potential harm to be inflicted upon the aggressor. The means authorized, the use of force, is dependent upon the nature of the potential harm sought to be inflicted by the aggressor on the victim and the latter's need to prevent such harm from occurring. Hence, if fundamental human rights are seriously violated by an institutional entity or a person or persons wielding the authority of the state and acting on its behalf without lawful means of redress or remedy being made available, then the responsibility of the individual, whose conduct was necessitated by the original transgression by reason of his need to redress a continuing wrong, is justified or mitigated and, therefore, warrants a denial of extradition.

This right to ideological self-preservation or political self-defense is predicated on three categories of factors: First, *factors bearing upon the nature of the "rights" involved, which were originally violated and gave rise to the right to defend them.* These include: (a) the nature of those "rights" and their sources; (b) the extent to which those "rights" are indispensable or necessary to the survival or basic values of the people; (c) the historical and traditional existence of those "rights" and the degree of their availability and enjoyment by the people; (d) the extent of the people's reliance upon them in relation to their implantation in the social psychology as necessary, indispensable or fundamental to the way of life; (e) the duration of their abridgement and, if sporadic, their recurrence; (f) the potential or foreseeable voluntary termination of the transgression by the violating body or person; and (g) the existence or reasonable availability of a local or international remedy or legal method of redress of such wrongs. These factors, for the most part, can be ascertained objectively and tangibly by impartial and objective inquiry into their existence and their validity by the extradition magistrate or the executive authority in the exercise of his discretionary power to grant or deny extradition.

Second, *factors bearing upon the conduct of the nation-state which were seriously violative of these "fundamental rights."* These include: (a) the nature of the transgression, abridgement, violation, termination, subversion or abolition of the "right" or "rights" claimed; (b) the quantitative and qualitative evaluation of the violations; (c) the manner in which they were violated, the extent of the violation, the means used to accomplish it, the duration of the violation, and the frequency of their recurrence; (d) the avowed or implicit intentions of continuing these violations or their termination within a declared or foreseeable future; (e) whether these violations were conditioned, caused, prompted or forced by conditions of necessity, such as natural catastrophes, disasters, war, insurrection, or other factors affecting the physical and tangible existence or viability of the nation-state which would justify or mitigate such conduct; (f) any methods or means of redress, remedies or channels open or made available to the aggrieved party or group to which the relator belongs; (g) any repressive actions taken against those who claimed grievance and pursued legal channels of remedy in the prescribed manner or who challenged the offensive public conduct in a manner deemed lawful by the common standards of the ordinary times of that nation. The factors in this category also lend themselves to objective inquiry.

Third, assuming the existence and validity of the conditions of the factors in the first and second categories, *factors bearing upon the conduct of the individual who violated the positive law of the state in defense of these "Fundamental Human Rights."* These include: (a) exhaustion of all available remedies, local and international, saving risks of repression; (b) the explicit or implicit common understanding in the ordinary reasonable man (of the nation-state in question) that no redress was available in the reasonably foreseeable future and that such conduct was, if not warranted, at least excusable (exonerating or mitigating) because no other alternative existed; (c) whether the individual's conduct was proportionate or commensurate with the nature of the right or rights violated in terms of their objective significance in the common understanding of the ordinary reasonable man of the nation-state wherein the conduct took place; (d) whether the individual's conduct was related only to the original wrong in a negative or vengeful aspect or whether it was also intended to terminate it or to affect its redress and, thus, have a positive aspect to it; (e) whether the means used were limited to achieve these purposes and there was no violation committed which was not necessitated by the attainment of such goals through the least harmful manner; (f) whether the assumption of any risks created would fall on the individual perpetrator, and whether the means and tactics used would not endanger innocent persons.

This theory of ideological self-preservation is not advanced as a means to warrant or justify lawlessness, or anarchy, but is intended to relate an otherwise nebulous concept, which has been the subject of nefarious political manipulations, to the sphere of a legally or judicially manageable theory of law. While it is beyond the scope of this paper to expose and discuss the ramifications of such a proposition, this proposed theory is intended to lay a juridical framework to what could be considered a politically motivated offense, which would shield its perpetrator from the repressive powers of the state against which the violation was directed.

To discern between objective and subjective standards of evaluating the nature of the relator's conduct is not only a procedural question, but a substantive one, because it is outcome determinative of the issue of extraditability of the relator. Such a choice by national public policy is one which is largely determined by the overall political outlook of the nation-state in terms of its place in the relationship between the nation-states of the world community and the ideological political alignment of the nation-state in question. To promulgate an objective standard, however, requires the acceptance of a decision made in furtherance thereof and would eliminate opportunities for conflicts.

INTERNATIONAL CRIMES: THE EXCEPTION TO THE POLITICAL OFFENSE EXCEPTION

Offenses against the Law of Nations or *Delicti Jus Gentium* by their very nature affect the world community as a whole.[77] As such, they cannot fall within the political offense exception because, even though they may be politically connected, they are in derogation to the "laws of mankind" in general and international criminal law in particular.

The concept of crimes against "the laws of mankind" is a vague generic term intending to cover all international crimes. Such vagueness however contributes to the difficulty of having that very concept accepted as an "exception to the exception," in

[77]I Bassiouni and Nanda, *A Treatise on International Criminal Law* (1973), Part I, "The Meaning of International Criminal Law."

other words, that international crimes would be extraditable offenses which are not to benefit from the political offense exception.[78] International crimes should indeed be considered extraditable offenses without the benefit of the political offense exception but in order for this position to be accepted as a rule of international law, it must be based either on conventional international criminal law or customary international law. As of yet, there is only scant indication that it is recognized as a custom evidenced by the practice of states even though there are many scholarly writings by distinguished publicists favoring it and repeated affirmation of this position in scholarly gatherings. There is therefore a growing trend towards acceptance of this position as an essential doctrine in furtherance of the preservation of minimum world order.[79] It must however, be emphasized that a clear definition of those international crimes falling within the doctrine of the "exception to the exception" must be set forth in conventional international criminal law. Without such clear understanding of those crimes specifically encompassed within the meaning of international criminal law the rule cannot be effectively or uniformly applied and consequently such a situation would be detrimental to the goals of judicial assistance and cooperation in extradition.[80] Summarizing this problem one author noted:

> In the application of extradition treaties to the cases of persons charged with, or convicted of crimes under municipal law it may be essential, in the exercise of the generally beneficient principle that political criminals shall not be subject to extradition, to decide whether or not a crime was political. But where an offence is made by treaty a crime under international law, the principle of nonextradition of political criminals would be contrary to public policy.[81]

---

[78]See Garcia-Mora, "Crimes Against Humanity and the Principle of Nonextradition of Political Offenders," 62 *Mich L Rev*, 927 (1964); Garcia-Mora, "War Crimes and the Principle of Nonextradition of Political Offenders," 9 *Wayne L Rev*, 269 (1963); Green, "Political Offenses, War Crimes and Extradition," 11 *Int & Comp L.Q.*, 329 (1962); Neuman, "Neutral States and the Extradition of War Criminals," 45 *AJIL*, 495 (1951).

[79]E.g. McDougal and Feliciano, Law and Minimum World Public Order (1961).

[80]*Supra*, note 77 and Volume II, *Jurisdiction and Cooperation*.

[81]Johnson, "The Draft Code of Offenses Against the Peace and Security of Mankind," 4 *Int & Comp L.Q.*, 445, 456 (1955).

The concept of international crimes while encompassing two sources of offensive conduct: (1) that which offends the common morality of mankind and is recognized as offensive to mankind at large, and (2) that which my treaty has been recognized as an international crime only the latter can be recognized as falling within the "exception to the exception."

The process of positing international criminal law and attempting to codify it must be credited to the United Nations, even though certain international crimes like piracy and war crimes long predated the United Nations.

On November 21, 1947, the General Assembly established the International Law Commission as a permanent body, having for its basic objective "the promotion of the progressive development of international law and its codification."[82] In another resolution adopted on the same day, the Commission was specifically directed to:

    (a) Formulate the principles of international law recognized in the Charter of the Nuremberg Tribunal and in the judgment of the tribunal, and

    (b) Prepare a draft code of offenses against the peace and security of mankind indicating clearly the place to be accorded to the principles mentioned in sub-paragraph (a) above."[83]

In its report of 1950, the International Law Commission set forth the various principles of international law recognized in the Charter of Nuremberg and Tokyo war crime trials and in the judgment of these tribunals,[84] and in 1954 formulated the Draft Code of Offenses against the Peace and Security of Mankind.[85]

Among the considerations underlying the principles of international criminal responsibility is the belief that duties may be imposed on individuals by international law without any interposition of internal law because "crimes against international law are committed by men, not by abstract entities,"[86] and that

---

[82]G.A. Res. 174 (II) (1947).
[83]G.A. Res. 177 (II) (1947).
[84]G.A.O.R., V, Supp. 12 (A/1316), 11-14 (1950).
[85]G.A.O.R., IX, Supp. 9 (A/2693), 11-12 (1954) and Johnson, *supra*, note 81.
[86]*Trial of the Major War Criminals Before the International Military Tribunal*, Vol. I, p. 223 (1947).

only by punishing individuals guilty of an international crime independently of the law of any particular country can the peace and security of mankind be preserved. This implies that individuals have international duties which transcend national obligations of obedience imposed by individual states and places a duty upon each state to prosecute or surrender for prosecution such offenders. Put to the test this principle was not always successful. The case in point is that of Kaiser Wilhelm II and other German officials who under Article 227 and 228 of the Treaty of Versailles (1919) [87] were to be prosecuted for an "offense against international law, morality and the sanctity of treaties." The Kaiser who sought refuge in the Netherlands, was not surrendered to the Allies. The Dutch Government refused his surrender on the grounds that it had a tradition of granting asylum to the "vanquished in international conflict."[88] The refusal was on the grounds of political offense exception, and no exception there to was found applicable because the crimes charged were of an international character. It is significant to note, however, that whenever the international crime does not contain elements which could be characterized as political, such as in the case of aggression,[89] and even in the case of war crimes[90] and crimes against humanity,[91] the world community found itself cooperating in such matters as suppression of slavery and slave trade,[92] illicit traffic of narcotics,[93] counterfeiting,[94] piracy,[95] and aircraft

---

[87]For text see 13 *A.J.I.L.*, Supp. 151 (1919).

[88]For comments, see Garner, "Punishment of Offenders Against the Laws and Customs of War" 16 A.J.I.L., 70 (1931); Wright, "The Legal Liability of the Kaiser," 18 *Am. Pol. Sci. Rev.*, 121 (1919).

[89]For a summary of its development, see I Bassiouni and Nanda, *supra*, note 77, Part II, Chapter I, and Stone, *Aggression and World Order* (1958).

[90]Garcia-Mora, *supra*, note 78; see also, *Dept State Bull, 12*:160 (1945).

[91]*Ibid.*

[92]Nanda and Bassiouni, "Slavery and Slave Trade: Steps Toward Its Eradication," 12 *Santa Clara L Rev,* 423 (1972).

[93]Bassiouni, "The Internation Narcotics Control Scheme—A Proposal," 46 *St. John's L Rev,* 218 (1972).

[94]Convention for the Suppression of Counterfeiting Currency, 20 April 1920; for text see Hudson, *International Legislation, 4*:2692-705 (1931).

[95]See the 1958 Geneva Convention on the High Seas, 13 U.S.T. 2312, T.I.A.S. No. 0200 (1962) 450 U.N.T.S. 82 and Whiteman, *Digest, 4*:657 (1963).

hijacking.[96] The following is offered as a catalog of recognized international crimes, which should, therefore, constitute an exclusion from the political offense exception. They are:

1. Aggression,[97] as defined by the United Nations Charter.
2. Crimes against Humanity,[98] as defined in the formulation of the Nuremberg principles by the United Nations General Assembly[99] and the Genocide Convention.[100]
3. War Crimes,[101] as defined by the 1912 Hague Conventions,[102] and the 1949 Geneva Conventions,[103] and other

---

[96]See, *ibid.,* 1958 Geneva Convention, Article 15; the 1963 Tokyo Convention, 20 U.S.T. 2941, T.I.A.S. No. 6768 (1969), and the 1970 Hague Convention, T.I.A.S. 7192 and Whiteman, *Digest, 4:*657-659 (1963); see also:

Hirsch and Fuller, "Aircraft Piracy and Extradition," 16 *N.Y.L.E.,* 392 (1970); Evans, "Hijacking: Its Causes and Cure," 69 *A.J.I.L,* 695 (1969).

[97]See Bassiouni, "Aggression, The Crime Against Peace," in I Bassiouni and Nanda, *supra,* note 89.

[98]See Garcia-Mora, "Crimes Against Humanity and the Principle of Nonextradition of Political Offenders," *supra,* note 78; and Johnson, *supra,* note 81.

[99]*Supra,* note 83.

[100]The Convention on the Prevention and Punishment of the Crime of Genocide states: "Genocide and the other acts enumerated in Article III shall not be considered as political crimes for the purpose of extradition," it goes on to say that "The Contracting Parties pledge themselves in such cases to grant extradition in accordance with their laws and treaties in force." G.A.O.R. Res 260 at 174 (A./181) (1948). Two implications would seem to follow from this provision. The first is that under no circumstances can the parties to the Convention regard genocide as a political offense. The overriding purpose of the Convention is to punish genocide as an ordinary crime and the states cannot invoke their laws and practices to reach a different result. To this extent, one category of crimes against humanity has become an ordinary crime by the consensus of mankind. The second implication indicates that the contracting parties have assumed the explicit obligation to extradite persons accused of genocide to any government requesting their surrender. This is clearly a mandatory provision and no exception can be engrafted into its terms.

See, "Genocide as a Crime under International Law," Lemkin, 41 *A.J.I.L.,* 145 (1947); Drost, *The Crime of State: Genocide* 185-190 (1951); on Reservations to the Convention on the Prevention and Punishment of the Crime of Genocide, (1951) I.C.J. Rep 15, and Bassiouni, "Genocide, Slavery and Racial Discrimination," in I Bassiouni and Nanda, *supra,* note 77, Part V, Chapter I.

[101]See Garcia-Mora and Greene, note 78.

[102]For summary of the customary rules of warfare, see *United States Army Field Manual,* 27-10 (1956).

[103]See, Pictet, *The Geneva Conventions of August 12, 1949* (1956), *and Commentary on the Third Geneva Convention Relative to the Protection of Civilian Persons in*

rules of conduct in war and restrictions in warfare.[104]
4. Piracy.[105]
5. Hijacking.[106]
6. Slavery, White Slavery, and other forms of traffic in Women and Children.[107]
7. Counterfeiting.[108]

Time of War. Article 146 of the Third Geneva Convention states:

Each High Contracting Party shall be under the obligation to search for persons alleged to have committed, or to have ordered to be committed, such grave breaches and shall bring such persons, regardless of their nationality, before its own courts. It may also, if it prefers, and in accordance with the provisions of its own legislation, hand such persons for trial to another High Contracting Party concerned, provided such High Contracting Party has made out a prima facie case.

The same provision is found in the other three Geneva Conventions as follows: Convention for the Amelioration of the Condition of the Wounded and Sick of Armed Forces in the Field, Art. 49 (1955), 3 U.S.T. & O.I.A. 3114, 3146, T.I.A.S. No. 3362; Convention for the Amelioration of the Condition of Wounded, Sick and Shipwrecked Members of the Armed Forces at Sea, Art. 50 (1955), 3 U.S.T. & O.I.A. 3217, 3250, T.I.A.S. No. 3364. These "grave breaches" are enumerated in Article 147 of the Geneva Convention Relative to the Protection of Civilian Persons in Time of War:

Grave breaches to which the preceding Article relates shall be those involving any of the following acts, if committed against persons or property protected by the present Convention: wilful killing, torture or inhuman treatment, including biological experiments, wilfully causing great suffering or serious injury to body or health, unlawful deportation or transfer or unlawful confinement of a protected person, compelling a protected person to serve in the forces of a hostile power, or wilfully depriving a protected person of the right of fair and regular trial prescribed in the present Convention, taking of hostages and extensive destruction and appropriation of property, not justified by military necessity and carried out unlawfully and wantonly.

The other conventions also contain provisions enumerating the grave breaches which are punishable, e.g., for the wounded and Sick in the Field, see Article 50; for the Wounded, Sick and Shipwrecked at Sea, see Article 51; and for Prisoners of War, see Article 180.

[104]See I Bassiouni and Nanda, *supra*, note 77, Part III, "The Regulation of Armed Conflicts."

[105]*Supra*, note 95.

[106]*Supra*, note 96.

[107]*Supra*, note 92.

[108]Convention to Prevent and Punish the Acts of Terrorism Taking the Form of Crimes Against Persons and Related Extortions That Are of International Significance—OAS/Off. Rec./Ser. P./Doc. 68, Jan. 13, 1971; and Convention on the Prevention and Punishment of Crimes Against Internationally Protected Persons Including Diplomatic Agents. G.A. Res. A/3166 (XXVIII) Feb. 5, 1974.

8. Kidnapping of internationally protected persons.[109]
9. International Traffic in Narcotics.[110]
10. Racial Discrimination.[111]

Of all these international crimes only some have a specific requirement that extradition be granted; they are Genocide, the 1949 Geneva Conventions, the Narcotics Conventions, the Tokyo and Hague Conventions on aircraft hijacking, the Counterfeiting Convention and the Slavery Convention.[112] In all these cases, however, the obligation to extradite arises by multilateral treaty, binding only upon its signatories (subject to proper ratification) and does not constitute a self-executing obligation but must be embodied in bilateral extradition treaties. In the case of all other international crimes, the obligation to extradite arises under customary international law and general principles of international law. But these two sources are somewhat challenged by those states which like the United States and England will not recognize an obligation to extradite outside their treaties[113] as well as by other states for different reasons.[114] There is a question as to whether or not violations of minimum standards human rights have ripened into being a crime under international law, but so far there has been no such recognition either by treaty or customary international law.[115] Consequently, such violations cannot be construed, as of yet, as international crimes. Similarly, proposals covering terrorism and conscription of minors which have often been discussed at international conferences have not been adopted and, therefore, are not included in this catalog of

---

[109]October 12, 1923.

[110]See Bassiouni, *supra*, note 93.

[111]International Convention on the Elimination of All Forms of Racial Discrimination, Dec. 21, 1965, U.N. Doc. A/Conf. 3214, p. 23.

[112]See, *supra*, notes 92 to 111.

[113]See Chapter I.

[114]In the case of neutral states, for example, see, Neumann, *supra*, note 78.

[115]See Bassiouni, "The Human Rights Program: The Veneer of Civilization Thickens," 21 *DePaul L Rev*, 271 (1971). Future developments will depend largely on what the late Professor W. Friedmann wrote in his article entitled, "The Use of 'General Principles' In The Development of International Law," 47 *A.J.I.L.*, 279 (1968); See also Bin-Cheng, *General Principles of Law as Applied by International Court and Tribunals*, (1958).

international crimes. The issue of international crimes was raised in the *Artukovic* case, and the United States Court of Appeals stated:

> We now consider the question whether because the offenses are also called "war crimes" they have lost their character as "political offenses" within the meaning of the treaty. Appellant argues that "war crimes" are crimes for which extradition is to be granted within the meaning of international acts to which the United States is a party. It is argued by recent legal writers that the "barbarity and atrocity of the crimes against the law of war and crimes against humanity committed weigh so heavily upon the common crime element that the political act has practically ceased to exist and, therefore, that the extradition of the offender is the only justifiable course of action.
>
> Appellant in essence argues that by virtue of resolutions taken in 1946 and 1947 by the United Nations General Assembly as to the surrender of alleged war criminals, it is incumbent on this Court to hold that Artukovic is charged with an offense which is extraditable.
>
> We have examined the various United Nations Resolutions and their background and have concluded that they have not sufficient force of law to modify long standing judicial interpretations of similar treaty provisions. Perhaps changes should be made as to such treaties. . . .[116]

On appeal the Supreme Court vacated judgment and remanded the case to the District Court,[117] but in a clear and uncompromising decision, the District Court declined "to go into the question of extradition for so-called war crimes,"[118] and emphatically held that Artukovic's offenses were of a political character and, thus, his extradition was denied.[119] The District Court apparently saw a close connection between the common crime with which Artukovic was charged and his political activities. As noted by one author:

> A case comparable to the *Artukovic* case is that of *Jan Durcansky*, recently decided by the Buenos Aires Court of First Instance, and involving a request from the Czechoslovakian Government for the surrender of a person accused of having participated in mass murders of civilians in Czechoslovakia during the period from November, 1944 to

---

[116]*Karadzole v. Artukovic*, 247 F. 2d 193, 204-205 (9th Circ. 1957).
[117]355 U.S. 393 (1958).
[118]*United States v. Artukovic*, 150 F. Supp. 383, 392 (S.D. Cal. 1959).
[119]*Ibid.*, p. 393.

the end of the war. In refusing his extradition, the Court said that Durcansky was protected by extentive prescription according to Article 16 of the Argentine Penal Code. Though apparently the General Assembly's resolutions urging the members of the United Nations to surrender war criminals were before the Argentine court in the same manner as they were before the Court of Appeals in the *Artukovic* case, the result was still the same since, admittedly, such resolutions are too tenuous to have any legally binding force.

Apart from the countries above mentioned, it has already been seen that Great Britain and Australia have also refused to extradite war criminals upon essentially similar grounds, while Italy has based its refusal to surrender on the well established principle that a State is not required to extradite its own nationals.[120]

On other grounds, the United States refused extradition to the USSR of a Lithuanian national, to whom it had granted asylum. The relator had been convicted *in absentia* by a Russian tribunal for the mass murder of some 50,000 civilians while in command of a German punitive battalion in 1941. In rejecting the Soviet request, the Department of State vigorously asserted that "a person accused of war time mass murders might not get a trial in the

---

[120]Garcia-Mora, *supra,* note 78, pp. 290-291. The author further states:

The reluctance to extradite war criminals, almost universal among the States is excellently illustrated by the Brazilian case *In re Kahrs et al.,* involving the request for the extradition of certain Norwegian nationals accused of having been members of an organization guilty of war crimes. In denying their extradition, the Brazilian Supreme Court firmly hold that "The accused . . . are charged with genuinely political crimes. They are being prosecuted for their political ideas, such as supporting a nationalist organization or sympathizing with the ideas propogated by the same . . . There arises a question of crimes distinctly political in nature when Norwegian law punishes expressions of thought, opinion, or related matters. This decisions is quite consistent with the previous *Denmark (Collaberation with the Enemy) Case,* involving the extradition of certain Danish nationals convicted in Denmark of collaborating with the German occupation forces. In refusing their extradition, the Brazilian Supremé Court succinctly said that the crime of assisting the enemy in time of war is a political one *lato sensu* because it is a crime against the State in its supreme function, namely, its external defense and its sovereignty." The difference between these two cases and the *Artukovic* Case is radically important, for while the latter involved the commission of atrocities allegedly in the pursuit of a political end, the Brazilian cases, on the other hand, dealt with the expression of unpopular political opinion and the crime of treason, both of which have been generally regarded as purely political offenses. Thus, the reason for giving asylum to the offenders in the Brazilian cases appears fairly plain. (Page 291-292).

Soviet Union that would be considered fair according to United States standards."[121] This position is inconsistent with the "rule of noninquiry" (discussed in Chapter VII). There is no case known to this writer whose extradition was requested or granted for an international crime, other than for war crimes and crimes against humanity arising out of World War II. Similarly, there is no case where after asylum was granted a state upheld the doctrine of an "exception to the exception." Even in recent hijacking cases from Poland and Czechoslovakia to Germany the requested states, France and Germany relied on the 1963 Tokyo Convention and prosecuted the hijackers rather than surrender them.[122] Even in cases involving illicit international traffic of narcotic drugs, the request and surrender of such offenders was always on the basis of its being an extraditable offense in current treaty practice rather than in being an international crime.[123]

There is still difficulty, however, in determining what constitutes international offenses, their elements, and the factual establishment of their occurrence. There is, however, some international agreement on the notion that such offenses constitute an "exception to the exception,"[124] even though there is still no codification of international criminal law.[125]

---

[121]*N.Y. Times,* Sept. 17, 1962, p. 12, Col. 6; 2 Hyde, *International Law* (2d ed. 1945). The note of Secretary of State Lansing to the Governor of Texas explaining the refusal to extradite General Huertas to Mexico. The Department of State rejected a demand for his extradition because of the probable doubt as to the political character of the crimes charged, the lack of orderly machinery of justice by which a fair trial could be expected, and the possibility that accomplices in Mexico may take this means of obtaining the release and return of their leader. July 7, 1915, U.S. Foreign Relations, 1915, p. 834 (Dep't State, 1924).

[122]Cited in Bassiouni, *supra,* note 11, p. 219, note 5.

[123]The latest was the extradition of one August Ricord from Paraguay, charged with smuggling some two tons of heroin in the United States. The Paraguayan Supreme Court granted his extradition September 2, 1972.

[124]The late Judge Hersch Lauterpacht said in this connection that Acts which per se constitute common crimes and which are contrary to the rules of war cannot legitimately be assimilated to political offenses. See Lauterpacht, "The Prosecution and Punishment of War Crimes, 21 *Brit. Y.B. Int'l. L.,* 88 p. 91 (1944).

[125]See, however, Johnson, *supra,* note 81; and Mueller, "The United Nations Draft Code of Offenses Against the Peace and Security of Mankind: An American Evaluation" in, Mueller and Wise, ed., *International Criminal Law,* (1965), pp. 602 ff.

THE POLITICAL OFFENSE EXCEPTION AND WORLD PUBLIC ORDER: A PROPOSED INTERNATIONAL SOLUTION

The reasons for the political offense exception rest in part upon the asylum state's sense of humane treatment and belief in human rights and personal and political freedom.[126] Furthermore it is generally acknowledged that political crimes affect the demanding state's most sensitive interests, and, therefore, inspire a passionately hostile atmosphere which makes an orderly and fair trial very difficult. The asylum state also sees the political offense, unlike ordinary crimes, as a reflection of the individual's resistance to the regime of the requesting state and therefore the presence of the offender in the requested state is not usually a threat to its domestic tranquility.[127] Consequently the requested state will not be moved by ordinary criminological considerations but will be persuaded one way or another by political reasons.

The commendable humanitarian objectives of the political offense exception have unfortunately seldom been realized. The reason for this lies in the fact that in every case the definition of political offenses and the determination of whether the crimes charged by the requesting state constitute a political offense lie are made by the requested state in accordance with its public policy or political interests.

In addition courts all over the world have invariably experienced difficulty in arriving at a workable definition of what constitutes a political offense.[128] The political offense exception is a double-edged sword. While it is intended to protect individual rights and personal freedom, it imposes national standards and values on other states. More significantly however, it can, for self-serving interests, deny extradition because the presence of the fugitive in the requested state serves its political purposes.

---

[126]Garcia-Mora, *International Law and Asylum as a Human Right* (1956).

[127]See Garcia-Mora, "The Present Status of Political Offences in the Law of Extradition and Asylum," 14 *U. Pitt. L. Rev.*, 371-373-74 (1953).

[128]For the intricacies and complexities in determining the nature of a political offense, see Garcia-Mora, "The Nature of Political Offenses: A Knotty Problem of Extradition Law," 48 *Va. L. Rev.*, 1226 (1962).

The fugitive may well have committed an extraditable offense but his sudden political opposition to a foreign régime may render him so desirable to the requested state that his extradition will be denied on political offense exception grounds when in similar circumstances another fugitive may be surrendered to a friendly state.

The benefits of luring foreign defectors and offering them asylum may sometimes be commendable in terms of human rights or explainable in terms of *realpolitik* but highly explosive in terms of global strategy for minimum world order when the defector happens to have committed common crimes or international crimes to which the (political) human rights aspects is but only tenuously related. This is particularly true with respect to certain acts of terrorism.

Also at times the political refugee will be a highly placed foreign official who may have committed common crimes or international crimes, but their enormity will sometimes seem to cast his acts in a political character.[129] It would seem that humane considerations and inducements to foreign exiles, defectors, or fugitives should not overshadow concern with punishability of those who have also committed common crimes and international crimes.

The realization that such problems, few and far between as they may be, are to say that least problematic and compels the search for a new outlook to avoid the potentially detrimental effects of such problems on the preservation of minimum world order. One solution is to remove the question in its entirety from the decision-making process of the nation-states involved. This presupposes an international organ such as the International Court of Justice or a specialized branch thereto or an international criminal court which would have either exclusive or review jurisdiction over such matters. This could be accomplished

---

[129]See the *Artukovic* cases discussed above and note 116-118, where the estimates of the number of persons the relator was accused of being responsible for their death is 200,000; see also the case of Tedeekoslovak General Jan Sejna, who sought asylum in the United States in 1968 after Dubcek took over. General Sejna was accused of the death of some 10,000 persons, but he was granted asylum. See *Time* magazine, March 15, 1968, p. 27.

by a universal treaty-statute on extradition,[130] or by granting an international judicial decision-making body the exclusive jurisdiction over such cases, so as to avoid inflammatory situations which may precede a decision on the merits.

The problem of the political offense, however, goes beyond that. The definitional issue could be resolved by an international treaty-statute, but the interpretative issue remains until it can be based on certain objective criteria designed to eliminate the high degree of subjective evaluation presently undertaken by most countries particularly with respect to executive discretion in conceding or denying extradition. Admitting the difficulties in implementing such a proposal, alternatives must nonetheless be found for the serious question of insuring a fair trial to the relator faced with extradition to the jurisdiction wherein the ideologically motivated offense took place. The alternative would be to have the state of asylum or the state of which he is a national if it is not the requesting state, exercise jurisdiction over the relation and prosecute him on behalf of the jurisdiction wherein the offense took place, using the substantive laws of that jurisdiction against which the accused relator committed the alleged offense.[131] If found guilty, the offender could, depending upon the situation, be confined, if the sentence is imprisonment, either in the state where the offense was committed, or in the state where the offense was prosecuted, or in the state of which he is a national. Thus, *aut dedere aut punire* would be insured without potentially violating the human rights and right to procedural fairness of the relator and simultaneously avoiding disruptions of world public order, since there would be an alternative to pitting two or more nation-states against each other.

---

[130]This was proposed by this writer at the 1968 Freiburg International Colloquium on extradition and was submitted to the Xth International Congress on Penal Law, held in Rome in 1969; see Bassiouni, "Rapport, Etats-Unis d'Amerique" 39 *Revue Internationale de Droit Penal*, 496, pp. 516-517 (1968); and the resolution at 855; see also resolutions of the Xth International Penal Law Congress of Rome 1969 in 40 *Revue Internationale de Droit Penal*, (1969); and the International Pre-conference held in Siracuse Italy, *Pre-congresso Internazionale di Diritto Penale* (1969), Bassiouni, "Rapporto di sintezi," p. 473.

[131]For an analogy, see Jessup, "The Doctrine of *Erie Railroad v. Tomkins* Applied to International Law," 33 *A.J.I.L.*, 740 (1939).

Ideally, of course, the offender should be tried by an international criminal court and imprisoned in an international institution as in the instance of the international military tribunal at Nuremberg and the Spandau prison which stand as primary examples of the feasability of this proposal.

The attainment of world peace is dependent upon the maintenance of rules designed to safeguard world public order and to establish legal channels as alternatives to the violent means which prevail in their absence. The rule of law is not an ideological equalizer or a method of compromising opposing political doctrines, but a process of ordering and channeling conflicts through legal institutions designed for the peaceful resolution of conflicts in a judicial context. It is the gradual building of needed international legal structures, not by ideologically superimposing such structures on the nation-states, but by creating them so as to service special purposes designed to eliminate direct confrontations between states which have potential for disruption of world public order.

THINKING THE UNTHINKABLE OR THE CASE OF DR. TSIRONIS

Jacob W. F. Sundberg

INTRODUCTION

THE MAJOR RETREAT of the Europeans in Africa and the triumph of the black people are phenomena that received dramatic manifestation in the Resolution of the Heads of State in the Organization of African Unity relating to the opening up of base areas of a territory for liberation movement to be sent into neighboring states.[1] The United Nations adopted various resolutions exhorting support for people subjected to racial discrimination. The Swedish Government found in these resolutions grounds for financially assisting various liberation movements, particularly those active on Portuguese territory.[2] This doctrine of overriding legality or doctrine of self-help,[3] invoked by India in support of the Goa invasion in 1960, has led to reorientation of the Swedish foreign policy in postwar years so that a policy of confrontation succeeded the neutral and prudent policy of the 1950's, a substitution that has created overt conflict with many states.

In 1967 Swedish foreign policy became clear. The Greek coup of August 21, 1967, released a new wave of confrontation. Greece had neither a colonial past nor present, it practiced no racial discrimination and it pursued no aggressive policy against its neighbors. What it did was distrust the type of political trends that have succeeded so well in Scandinavia. Although none of the UN resolutions

---

[1]See Boutros-Ghali, "The Addis Abbeba Charter—A Commentary," 546 *International Conciliation*, 25, 32.

[2]See e.g. information supplied in J. Sundberg, *Piracy: Air and Sea*, in I Bassiouni & Nanda, *A Treatise on International Criminal Law*, (1972), p. 477 note 103.

[3]See e.g. Lillich, "Forcible Self-Help by States to Protect Human Rights, 53 *Iowa L. Rev.*, 325 sqq. (1967).

could serve as the basis for a policy of confrontation, Swedish people found inspiration to cultivate the birth of a Greek resistance movement partially directed by the dethroned Greek politician, Professor Andreas Papandreou. In the spring of 1968, the Swedish Social Democratic party decided to support the Pan-Hellenic liberation movement (PAK) and the decision was publicly announced by the Swedish Prime Minister Mr. Tage Erlander, who said that he was speaking in his capacity as Chairman of the Social Democratic Party.[4]

Mr. Papandreou was invited to direct his fight against the Greek regime from Sweden. He cooperated with Mr. Brillakis, head of the Greek Communist party to establish armed activity in Greece. During almost a year Professor Papandreou sojourned at the University of Stockholm as a visiting professor; eventually he left for Canada.

In a development parallel to this pointed and increasingly intense confrontation, the Swedish government decided to abandon its previous demands that refugees who had been given asylum in Sweden should refrain from political activity in that country.[5] Instead, it was now insisted upon that foreigners should enjoy the same freedom as the Swedes to engage in political activity in Sweden.[6]

On September 20, 1967 the Swedish Foreign Minister sent the Secretary General of the Council of Europe an application informing the European Commission of Human Rights in accordance with article 24 of the Convention on Human Rights and Fundamental Freedoms that the Greek Government had by a number of legislative and administrative measures violated certain articles of the European Convention on Human Rights. For the benefit of the general public it was declared that the Swedish government did nothing but "apply the machinery that the Council of Europe—unique among international organizations in the field of human rights—has established in order to safeguard the human rights and

---

[4]See Utrikesfråger (1968) p. 143 (published by the Ministry of Foreign Affairs in Stockholm).

[5]See Melander, Flyktingar och asyl, (thesis, Lund University), Stockholm (1972), p. 70.

[6]Kungl. Proposition (1971) No. 109, p. 4.

fundamental freedoms and which machinery Greece herself has accepted and at previous occasions used herself."[7] The Cabinet Minister Alva Myrdal was more outspoken: "Now today's regime is made to answer for its deeds before the open forum of Europe."[8] Similar applications against Greece were introduced by Denmark, Norway and the Netherlands. By the decision of January 24, 1968 the Commission declared the applications admissible.

The allegations in these applications of the use of torture in violation of article 3 and of illegal deprivation of freedom in violation of article 5 are the interesting ones in the present context. On April 3, the Commission constituted a subcommission that held a hearing on the merits of the case and heard the observations of the parties. Proceedings were carried out before this subcommission during 1968 and 1969 after which the mother commission on November 5, 1969, adopted the report of the subcommission concerning the Greek violations.[9] According to this Report "the Commission has found it established beyond doubt that torture or ill-treatment contrary to article 3 has been inflicted in a number of cases" and that "the practice followed in the deprivation of liberty in Greece on and after April 21, 1967, is contrary to article 5." The report was subsequently submitted to the committee of ministers which, in a resolution of April 15th 1970, agreed with the opinion of the commission and decided that the Government of Greece had violated articles 3 and 5 of the convention.[10]

For the western aviation industry aircraft hijackings did not become a major problem until 1969. The rising tide of discontent individuals that secured passage from the United States to Cuba by hijacking an airliner made the militant rebel movements aware of and interested in the method. The most publicity has been given to the Popular Front for the Liberation of Palestine and associated organizations when they practiced hijackings to disturb and disrupt

---

[7]Utrikesfråger (1967) p. 124.

[8]Utikesfråger (1967) p. 145.

[9]Yearbook of the European Convention on Human Rights (The Hague) (1969) p. 1-510.

[10]Yearbook of the European Convention on Human Rights, (1969) p. 511-514; compare Utikesfråger, 1970) p. 128. The quotes are taken from p. 501 and 134, respectively in the Yearbook.

air traffic to and from Israel. More hidden from Swedish eyes were many other rebel movements in Latin America, Africa and Asia, which also engaged in this type of guerrilla warfare. The Marxist militant rebel movements that dominated this field used hijackings for particular political purposes. There is today strong circumstantial evidence that these organizations cooperate internationally in conspiracies and instruction.[11]

The question arises how the new tactic combines with the idea of overriding legality that has permeated Swedish foreign policy so strongly. In the following, I will show how the case of a Greek hijacking brought to light the opposition between the new confrontation policy, here called the Papandreou Line, and municipal law. This contrast will reveal certain fundamental problems of jurisprudence.

THE CASE OF DR. TSIRONIS[12]

Vassilios Tsironis was a little Greek politician. Trained as a nurse in the Greek Army, he had been employed in the Greek prison camps after the Civil War in Greece. Influenced by what he had seen there, he had tried, with moderate success, to create a political party based on a program highly critical of the Greek establishment. His rather blunt ways brought him a reputation as a troublemaker and from time to time he visited the Greek prisons as a prisoner. During the summer of 1969 he decided to flee from Greece with his family by hijacking a domestic flight, knowing that passage on such a flight required neither passport nor permission to leave the country. On August 16, 1969, in the name of liberty and humanity, he captured an Olympic Airways airliner over the Bay of Corinth and forced it to fly to Albania. When in Al-

---

[11]At a conference in Miami on December 12, 1972, dr Manolo Reyes reported the existence of two schools for hijackers, one in Pine del Agua, Oriente, and one i Cayabas, Pinar del Rio, Cuba. Both schools, said dr Reyes, were run by the Cuban Government. He thereby made precise the allegation by James Arey that "the more organized and well-entrenched groups even offer courses at training camps to eager neophytes from other countries . . . They are all linked through contacts in Havana. The focus, at least symbolically, is all this business about groups going to Cuba to participate in the sugar harvest." The Sky Pirates, New York 1972, p. 296.

[12]An abbreviated report of this case will be found in Lowenfeld, *Aviation Law*, (1972) p. VII-34 sg. (§ 2.22).

bania, Dr. Tsironis did not know where to go. He tried Italy and France but was rejected in both countries. Knowing the Swedish engagement in the Greek politics and the Swedish relations with Professor Papandreou he then headed for Sweden with his family.

In Sweden he got a hero's welcome. To offer him conditions similar to those enjoyed by professor Papandreou was quite natural, although Professor Papandreou had left for Canada by that time. Swedish government officials made announcements along those lines. Länsarbetsnamnden stressed "the importance of giving Tsironis residence in Stockholm since he claimed to be the leader of a political party in Greece" and in the file of the State Employment Agency (AMS) it was noted: "At AMS the opinion is held that the family Tsironis is sought-after prey for the men of the junta. They are more anonymous in a big city and should be quartered in Stockholm." Dr. Tsironis was given a generous allowance and was after a while quartered with his family in Hotel Carlton in Stockholm.

On November 5, 1967, I wrote the Chief State Prosecutor inquiring why Dr. Tsironis had not been indicted for the aircraft hijacking, since it was a violation of the Swedish Penal Code. On November 12, the Chief State Prosecutor commenced an official investigation of the charge and the benevolent attitude that the Swedish authorities had toward Dr. Tsironis quickly disappeared. Dr. Tsironis seemed to be unaffected by these developments and continued to play the role of a Greek resistance politician. When he was inexplicably arrested for "hotel fraud," he resisted arrest and was also indicted for assaulting a policeman.

While the trials for these offenses took place, the hijacking investigation moved slowly because the collection of evidence was dependent upon the collaboration of the Greek régime. He was finally sentenced to three and a half years in prison for the hijacking.

POLITICAL CLIMATE

For Swedish foreign policy, having devoted itself to promoting "criminal" conduct abroad, Dr. Tsironis' story posed the question of whether Sweden could at the same time punish in Sweden offenses it had incited or attempted to incite. Each group that engages in armed conflict with a governmental power unquestionably commits acts that correspond to murder, manslaughter, assault and battery, unlawful deprivation of freedom, etc. Each act of support in such a conflict is sanctioned by the Swedish Penal Code that condemns for conspiracy one who "seeks to incite another . . . to commit" a criminal act.

Two lines can be discerned in Swedish legal thinking. One line claims the jurisdiction of Chapter 24 of the Penal Code. The text of the Chapter mentions "the right . . . to use force," but the rules of this chapter are not exhaustive. The authoritative commentary to the Penal Code by Justice Beckman states that the courts "have the faculty to acquit in cases that it cannot reasonably have been the intent to criminalize." There are not only the reservations expressed in the preparatory works but also "implied reservations" built into the penal provisions.[13] For example, the Minister of Justice once stated that communications abroad were not to be protected by the Swedish penal provisions against sabotage.[14] This makes it possible for the Government to engage in, notwithstanding the Penal Code, a foreign policy that calls forth acts abroad that formally collide with Swedish penal provisions.

The Rivalry between states gives birth in every country to the wish to censure the world abroad. The floods of refugees in Europe after the second world war have exercised a major impact on legal thinking in this respect. The International Refugee Organization originally refused, in conformity with its constitution, to extend help to those who had "voluntarily assisted the enemy forces since the outbreak of the second world war in their operations against the United Nations."[15] However, after acquiring additional knowledge about the fate of Balts, Croats, the men in Vlassov's Army, and others, it found that "many persons might technically have collaborated with the Germans and yet were in refugee status."[16] The

---

[13]Nils Bechman and others, Brottsbalgen jämte förklaringar, Band II: Brotten mot allmänheten och staten m.m., Stockholm 1966, p. 598.

[14]See Kungl. Proposition (1948) No. 80, p. 288; as to subsequent discussion, see Beckman *et al, supra* note 13 p. 24 sq.

[15]Constitution of the International Refugee Organization, December 15, 1946, 18 *U.N.T.S.* 3, see Annex I, Part II, point 2(–b).

[16]Holborn, The International Refugee Organization, London 1956, p. 210 sq.

United States and Great Britain initiated proceedings before the International Court of Justice in The Hague against Bulgaria, Hungary and Roumania, alleging their failure to respect, as required under their peace treaties,[17] human rights and fundamental freedoms when they socialized the country, a process involving the removal of the old social system taking place on an internal level in the conditions of a fierce opposition on the part of the classes which were losing their positions.[18] The increasing censure of socialism and its confiscatory policies was reflected in contemporary conventions.

The 1949 Geneva Conventions for the protection of the victims of war prohibits "adverse distinction founded on . . . wealth or any other similar criteria."[19] In the Convention Relating to the Status of Refugees, 1951,[20] was inserted, at the initiative of Mr. Sture Petrén[21] and as a reflection of what was intended for inclusion in the Swedish Act on Foreigners, at that time in preparation,[22] among the criteria for refugee status, persecution for reasons of membership of a particular social group. Furthermore, the convention precluded the imposition of punishment for crossing the border by illegal means. At the same time the political offense exception to extradition was formulated to protect those who had committed criminal acts in escaping from socialist countries. It was accepted that it was the totalitarian society itself that made the escape therefrom a political act,[23] and consequently a political crime

[17]See e.g. 42 *U.N.T.S.*, 3, Art. 3.

[18]Elian, *The International Court of Justice,* (L 1971), p. 134 sq.

[19]"Convention Relative to the Treatment of Civilian Persons in Time of War," Art. 3, No. 1.

[20]189 *U.N.T.S.*, 152.

[21]See Melander (note 5 supra) p. 76; Grahl-Madsen, The Status of Refugees in International Law, vol. I, (1966) p. 219.

[22]Mr. Sture Petrén was a member of "1949 års utlänningskommitté" which prepared the report (Statens Offentliga Utrednigar 1951 No. 42, signed November 21, 1951) on which the Government Bill for the new act relating to foreigners was based (subsequently passed as law in 1954). On July 2nd, 1951, Mr. Petrén, acting as a Delegate for Sweden, proposed to the Diplomatic Conference the adoption of the formula here discussed in order to achieve harmony with the formula which had then already been selected by the legal experts working on the said Swedish report.

[23]In re Kavic, Bjelanovic and Arsenijevic, BCE 78 I, 19 *I.L.R.*, 371 (1952); this judgment by the Swiss Supreme Federal Court was subsequently followed by the British in the case Regina vs. Governor of Brixton Prison ex parte Kolczynski 1 *QB*, 540 (1955).

protected under contemporary international law principles from extradition.[24]

In Sweden, which at this time openly confessed that it was pursuing the same goals as the socialistic regimes thus censured,[25] and the government of which consequently was most reluctant to face an international censure of societal developments in Sweden, the formula of the Convention on the Status of Refugees, as found in section 2 of the Act on Refugees of 1954, was rarely invoked. Instead the more nebulous expression was preferred: persecution "due to political conditions."[26] Parallel to the West European development, it was Swedish practice to give political refugee status to refugees from East Germany and Poland.[27] Since these refugees "generally . . . had not been politically active in their home countries," but were merely rejecting the totalitarian politicisation of life, they were not hampered by Swedish insistence that they refrain from political activity.[28] In addition, the Swedish government began to ignore the criminal acts that were part of the pattern of the refugees' escape from those countries.

The coup of April 21, 1967, and the transition in Sweden to the Papandreou Line reoriented the Swedish censure and generated new conditions for the treatment of refugees. According to the commission that was charged with revising the legislation on foreigners a person is considered to be a refugee under the convention if "he has left out of political reasons . . . and it may be assumed that due thereto he will be hit harder."[29] The Papandreous Line conferred

---

[24]Cf Mosler, "European Law—Does it Exist?" *Current Legal Problems*, 174 sq., (1966).

[25]A declaration to this effect was read in the Swedish Diet on March 22, 1950, by the Prime Minister Tage Erlander and the Foreign Minister Östen Undén: see the minutes in the two chambers of the Diet, Första Kammarens protokoll, (1950) No. 11, p. 13 and Andra Kammarens protokoll, (1950) No. 11, p. 11. Sweden was also particularly slow in accepting the jurisdiction of the European Court of Human Rights. While the substantive part of the European Convention for the Protection of Human Rights and Fundamental Freedoms was ratified by deposition on February 4, 1952, it was not until 1966 that Sweden accepted the jurisdiction of the Court.

[26]See Melander *supra* note 5 pp. 77, 79.

[27]See Melander *supra* note 5 p. 45; Statens Offentliga Utredningar (1972) No. 85, p. 19 sq.

[28]See Melander *supra* note 5 p. 49, of 47 sq., 70.

[29]Statens Offentliga Utredningar, (1972) No. 84, p. 141.

upon the very escape to Sweden a political element.

Sweden became a haven for an increasing number of members of opposition parties who attracted the repression of local dictatorships. Although the new direction of the censureship towards western dictatorships rivalled the older Swedish censureship directed against the totalitarian powers in the socialist camp, it appears that the established line for the treatment of refugees from the latter countries was still maintained. The implied reservations in the Swedish penal provisions were instead modified.

The other line of thought is that it is the duty of all civilized states to punish crimes committed abroad. The role of censureship is now gone. Emotional shock normally strengthens the idea of human solidarity. Celestin Jacquin's attempt on the life of Napoleon III in September 1854 thus led to the Belgian *clause d' attentat*. The Ustasja murder of King Alexander I of Yugoslavia and the French Foreign Minister Barthou on October 9, 1934 in Marseille, similarly brought into being the 1937 Convention for the Prevention and Punishment of Terrorism.

The rising tide of hijackers towards the end of the 1960's had a similar effect because the aircraft is an internationalized phenomenon. An airliner will carry passengers of many different nationalities and its fate thus affects a number of different nations. Hijackings were seen in Sweden as a technicial aviation problem that should be handled by the technical international agency, ICAO. When Dr. Tsironis arrived in Sweden in the autumn of 1969, however, the General Assembly of the United Nations authored and published resolutions calling for legislation against and prose-

---

[30]See Sulzberger, International Herald Tribune, Aug. 23, 1968; Cötebergs Handels och Sjöfartstidning, Apr. 17, 1968.

[31]Art. 58 in the RSFSR Penal Code of 1926. In 1934, jurisdiction in cases of terrorist acts was given to the military tribunals and a special procedure was established, including i.a. that the case was to be heard without the participation of the defendant or his counsel: see Berman, *Soviet Criminal Law and Procedure—The RSFSR Codes,* (Cambr. 1966), p. 29, 70 sq. Compare the interventions of Pashukanis at the Copenhagen conference for the unification of penal law, 1935: VIe Conférence internationale pour l'unification du droit pénal—Actes de la Conférence (Paris 1938), p. 375 sq.

[32]See 7 International Legislation (ed. Hudson) 862 sqq.

[33]See the Note in, *British Yearbook of International Law,* (1938), pp. 214-216.

cution of hijackers[34] and for extradition of hijackers to secure their punishment.[35]

In Sweden, traditionally sensitive to UN resolutions on fighting obnoxious regimes, could not ignore these signals. The first debate in the General Assembly took place some months after the arrival of Dr. Tsironis; before his case was finally adjudicated, the situation had been so aggravated by Operation Abu Thalaat that even the Security Council issued a statement on the matter.[36] The implied reservations to the Swedish penal provisions that had operated so well in favor of Professor Papandreou did not operate at all in favor of Dr. Tsironis.

The dramatic change in Swedish legal thinking was also accompanied by a peripety in the life of Dr. Tsironis, who fell from the privileges of a Papandreou to the miseries of the prison of Långholmen. No doubt this fall made him particularly sensitive to the contradictions in the Swedish attitude towards unlawfulness. Dr. Tsironis naturally wanted to awaken the Swedish to the existence of this contradiction. Perhaps he believed himself able to utilize the methods of Abbie Hoffman and Jerry Rubin in the Chicago conspiracy trial the same winter: to sabotage the trial so systematically and so provokingly that the trial in itself acquired a publicity value that attracted mass media and thus was likely to awaken the Americans to what was taking place. If Dr. Tsironis thought along these lines, he was not unjustified, since the Swedish press generous in its coverage of the Chicago trial.

Throughout his trials Dr. Tsironis behaved in a manner unparallelled in modern Swedish procedural history. He turned the proceedings into a farce. The trial that took place in February was dominated by his attacks on the Swedish authorities. He fired one defense counsel after the other. In April, when another trial had started, he threw himself at the judge in order to show his wrists with marks of mishandling. The prosecutors and the authorities were buried under accusations of torture and corruption: it was not Dr. Tsironis that was guilty, it was the Swedish government, the

---

[34]Resolution 2561/1969.

[35]Resolution 2645/1970.

[36]Cf Kungl. Proposition (1971) No. 92, p. 19.

prosecutor and the police. He incessantly interrupted the proceedings. He threatened to scream throughout the whole session. Eventually, he was made to wait in the Långholmen prison while the case was processed in his absence. In the Court of Appeals, in June, he was held by the prison guards during the sessions. In the hijacking judgment the Court said:[37]

> Tsironis has refused to cooperate in the proceedings, explaining among other things that he does not want to make any statements in his own case and does not want to be present at the trial. He has behaved in an extremely disturbing way before the Court and he has in no way obeyed the directives that have been given to maintain order and carry out the trial. The main hearing consequently had to take place without Tsironis being present in the courtroom; during the sessions he was placed in an adjoining room that was among the localities disposed by the Division. Day by day, Tsironis has been informed about what part of the case that was treated, and he has been given opportunity to participate in the session. He has consecutively been offered to have access to what was said during the interrogations of witnesses and aggrieved parties, but he rejected those offers. He has refused to talk to his defense counsel and he has not even made contact with the interpreter that was appointed for the case.

THE RENAISSANCE OF SWEDISH NEUTRALITY

The general public in Sweden never realized the contradiction that had so infuriated Dr. Tsironis. It required several years and a hijacking taking place in Sweden herself and involving a SAS aircraft for the Swedish Government to seriously undertake to harmonize its support of foreign rebel movements in the world with the worldwide flight against hijackings. The Terrorist Act is inclined towards a philosophy of neutrality, but in conformity with the 1971 Montreal Convention the legislation seeks to develop cooperation between the different national police forces so that the Swedish police can act upon information received from a foreign police force. The foreigner suspected then could be expelled from Sweden or his entry into Sweden could be refused.[38]

---

[37]Stockholms tingsrätt, avdelning 17, judgment DB 409 July 7, 1971.

[38]Convention for the Suppression of Unlawful Acts Against the Safety of Civil Aviation, signed at Montreal on Sep. 23, 1971 (ICAO Doc 8966) requires in Art. 12 every "Contracting State having reason to believe that one of the offenses mentioned in Article 1 will be committed" to furnish the State threatened with "any relevant information in its possession."

The many Swedish organizations that support foreign liberation movement reacted vehemently against the proposed legislation, since it would certainly threaten their activities on Swedish
territory. The authors of the bill tried to fend off their opposition
by stating that the legislation only required neutrality since it was
directed only against foreigners who used violence on Swedish territory. Eventually, the Minister in charge of the bill gave his word
that the legislation would not be used without prior special permission of the Swedish Cabinet itself except against two specified
movements: the Ustasja and Black September. Thus a terrorist
movement acting on foreign soil to change political conditions anywhere other than Sweden remained privileged in the eyes of
Swedish law. Once more we find the implied reservation in Swedish
penal provisions by which Sweden has chosen to guide its foreign
policy of constructive neutrality.

APPENDIX P

Some Treaty Provisions and Proposed Texts on the Exclusion of Certain Acts of Terrorism from the "Political Offense" Exception in Extradition

(1) The Belgian "Attentat Clause" Model.[1]

(a) *Agreement on Extradition* adopted at Caracas on July 18, 1911 by Ecuador, Peru, Colombia, Bolivia and Venezuela:[2]

"Article 4 . . . An attack on the life of a Chief of State will not be considered a political offense or an act in connection with it."

(b) *Code of Private International Law* (Bustamante Code) annexed to the Convention on Private International Law adopted at Havana on February 20, 1928:[3]

"Article 357. Homicide or murder of the head of a contracting State or of any other person who exercises authority in said State, shall not be deemed a political offense nor an act related thereto.

(c) *Convention on Extradition* adopted at Montevideo on December 26, 1933:[4]

"Article 3 . . . (e) . . . An attempt against the life or person of the Chief of State or members of his family, shall not be deemed to be a political offense . . . "

---

[1]As a result of the difference of interpretation of article 6 of the Belgium extradition law of October 1, 1833 which arose among Belgian courts following a request by France for the extradition of some French nationals accused of attempting to blow up a train carrying Napoleon III, the Belgian Parliament enacted a law on the basis of a draft submitted by the Government, adding to article 6 of the law of October 1, 1833 the following provisions: "There shall not be considered as political crime or as an act connected with such a crime an attack upon the person of the head of a foreign government or of the members of his family, when this attack takes the form of either murder, assassination or poisoning." *(Annales Parlementaires,* Chambre des Représentants, session du 18 décembre 1855, p. 312). The above clause was subsequently included in several bilateral treaties on extradition.

[2]*Tratados públicos de Venezuela,* vol II, p. 435.

[3]*Final Act, Sixth International Conference of American States,* Havana, 1928, pp. 16-88.

[4]*Final Act, Seventh International Confernce of American States,* Montevideo, 1933, pp. 155-167.

[5]Pan American Union, *Bulletin,* June 1934, vol. 68, No. 6, p. 416.

(d) *Central American Extradition Convention* adopted at Guatemala City on April 12, 1934:[5]

"Article III . . . Attempts against the life of the head of a Government or public functionaries . . . shall not be considered political crimes . . . "

(e) *Treaty on International Penal Law* adopted at Montevideo on March 19, 1940:[6]

"Article XXIII. The taking, or attempted taking, of the life of the Head of a Contracting State shall not be deemed to be a political offense, nor an act related thereto."

(f) *European Convention on Extradition* adopted at Paris on December 13, 1957:[7]

Article 3 . . . 3. The taking or attempted taking of the life of a Head of State or a member of his family shall not be deemed to be a political offense for the purposes of this Convention . . . "

(2) Texts covering activities or crimes other than those covered under the Belgian clause.

(a) *Treaty for the Extradition of Criminals and for the Protection against Anarchism,* adopted at Mexico City on January 28, 1902:[8]

Article 2 . . . There shall not be considered as political offenses acts which may be classified as pertaining to anarchism . . . "

(b) *Central American Extradition Convention* adopted at Guatemala City on April 12, 1934:[9]

Article III. . .anarchistic attacks shall not be considered as political crimes."

(c) *Resolutions on Extradition* adopted by the Institute of Institute of International Law in 1892:[10]

---

[6]*Final Act, Second South American Congress of Private International Law,* Montevideo, 1940.

[7]*European Treaty Series* No. 24.

[8]G. Martens, *Nouveau Recueil Général de Traités* (3rd ser.) p. 185.

[9]Pan American Union, *Bulletin,* June 1934, vol. 68, No. 6, p. 416.

[10]Resolutions on Extradition consisting of 26 articles were first adopted by the Institute of International Law at its Oxford session on September 9, 1880. Articles 13 and 14 of those resolutions were later revised at the Geneva session of the Institute

Article 14. Criminal acts directed against the bases of all social organization, and not only against a certain State or a certain form of government, are not considered political offenses in the application of the preceding rules."

    (d) *Model Draft of an Extradition Treaty* prepared in 1931 by a sub-commission of the International Penal and Prison Commission:[11]

"Article 6 . . . All crimes directed not against a definite State authority but against all State authority shall also be regarded as common crimes."

    (e) *Draft Convention on Extradition* adopted by the Inter-American Council of jurists in 1959:[12]

"Article 10. . . . 6. For the purposes of this article, neither genocide, nor in general, crimes against humanity, committed either in time of peace or in time of war, shall be considered political offenses."

To this provision, Argentina entered the following reservation:[13]

The delegation of Argentina understands that serious acts of terrorism are included under crimes aganinst humanity."

    (f) *Resolutions on Extradition* adopted by the Institute of International Law:[14]

"Article 13. . . . 3. So far as concerns acts committed in the course of an insurrection of a civil war by one of the parties engaged in the struggle and in the interest of its cause, they cannot give occasion to extradition unless they are acts of odious barbarity or vandalism forbidden by the laws of war, and then only when the civil war is at an end."

    (g) *Model Draft of an Extradition Treaty* prepared in 1931 by

---

on September 8, 1892. For the texts see Institut de Droit International, *Tableau Général des Résolutions* (1873-1956), publié par Hans Wheberg, Bâle 1957, Editions juridiques et sociologiques S.A., pp. 380-384. English text in Scott, Resolutions of the Institute of International Law (1916) pp. 42-45.

[11]*Recueil de Documents en matière Pénale et Pénitentiaire*, 1931, vol. 1, p. 478.

[12]*Final Act of the Fourth Meeting of the Inter-American Council of Jurists*, Santiago, Chile, 24 August-9 September 1959, OAS *Official Records* OAS/SER-C/IV.4 CIJ-43, Pan American Union, General Secretariat, Organization of American States, Washington D.C., September 1962, p. 18.

[13]*Ibid.*, p. 78.

[14]See *supra* 5, p. 19.

a sub-commission of the International Penal and Prison Commission:[15]

"Article 6. . .murder and attempted murder of other persons [than the Head of a State] shall also not be so regarded if they are committed with special barbarity or cruelty."

(h) Conclusions adopted by the Inter-American Juridical Committee in its 1959 *Study on Political Offenses:*[16]

(3) By including a clause to the effect that an offense in which the common crime element predominates is not a political offence. are not political offenses."

(3) Texts on The "Dominant Factor" Model.

Examples of this kind of approach may be found in the following instruments:

(a) *Resolutions on Extradition* adopted by the Institute of International Law:[17]

"Article 13. . .2. Nor can (extradition) be admitted for unlawful acts of a mixed character or connected with political crimes or offenses, also called relative political offenses, unless in the case of crimes of greater gravity from the point of view of morality and of the common law, such as murder, manslaughter, poisoning, mutilation, grave wounds inflicted wilfully with premeditation, attempts at crimes of that kind, outrages to property by arson, explosion or flooding, and serious thefts, especially when committed with weapons and violence."

(b) *Draft Extradition Convention* approved in 1928 by the International Law Association:[18]

"Article 7. . .Nevertheless the extradition of a person accused or convicted of a crime involving the loss of human life or grievous bodily harm . . . shall be accorded notwithstanding the political character of the crime alleged."

---

[15]See *supra* note 1.
[16]CIJ-54 Pan American Union, General Secretariat, Organizatio of American States, Washington D.C., August 1960, p. 29.
[17]See *supra* note 5 p. 19.
[18]International Law Association, *Report of the Thirty-fifth Conference* (1928), pp. 324-329.

(4) An Enforcement Model.

The Sixth International Conference for the Unification of Penal Law,[19] proposed in a resolution the following:

"Considering that most of the offenses referred to in the above articles are particularly dangerous to mankind and are liable to jeopardize good international relations,

Expresses the *voeu* that, when extradition is not granted, the offenders may be referred to an *international criminal court,* unless the State to which the request for extradition was addressed prefers to have them tried by its own courts."

Also, the Sixth International Conference adopted a text on political offenses which, under the heading *"Defintion of a political offense at the international level,"* included the following provision: "Offenses which endanger the community or create a state of terror shall not be deemed to be political."

---

[19]Held in Copenhagen August 31—September 3, 1935, *Actes de la Conference,* 1938.

CHAPTER VI

INTERNATIONAL CONTROL
OF TERRORISM

AN HISTORICAL INTRODUCTION TO INTERNATIONAL LEGAL CONTROL OF TERRORISM

Pursuant to a recommendation adopted by the First International Congress of Penal Law held at Brussels from July 26 to 29, 1926,[1] a series of International Conferences for the Unification of Penal Law was held under the auspices of the International Association of Penal Law[2] (later the International Bureau for the Unification of Penal Law).[3] The first such Conference held at Warsaw from 1 to 5 November 1927, adopted, *inter alia,* a text on International Penal Law consisting of eight articles. Under the heading "délits du droit des gens" ("offenses under international law") it included the following provision:[4]

Article 6. An offense punishable according to the laws . . . (x) shall also be committed, irrespective of the law of the place where the offense is committed or the nationality of the offended, by any person who commits abroad any of the following offenses:

(e) The deliberate use of any means capable of causing a common danger.

The question of terrorism was considered by the Third to Sixth

---

[1]First International Congress on Penal Law, Brussels, July 26-29, 1926, Actes du Congrès, 1927, Paris, Librairie des Juris-Classeurs, Editions Godde, p. 636.

[2]First International Conference for the Unification of Penal Law, Warsaw, November 1-5, 1927, *Actes de la Conférence,* 1929, Paris, Recueil Sirey, p. 1. The conferences were attended by delegations representing States and both governmental and nongovernmental international organizations.

[3]Second International Conference for the Unification of Penal Law, Rome May 21-25, 1928, *Actes de la Conférence,* 1931, Paris Librairie des Juris-Classeurs, Editions Godde, p. 1.

[4]First International Conference for the Unification of Penal Law, Warsaw, November 1-5, 1927, *op. cit.,* p. 133.

467

International Conference for the Unification of Penal Law held respectively at Brussels (June 26 to 30, 1930), Paris (December 27 to 30, 1931), Madrid (October 14 to 20, 1934) and Copenhagen (August 31 to September 3, 1935). At the Third (Brussels) International Conference, the term "terrorism" was expressly used for the first time. On the basis of a report submitted by a special rapporteur, Committee V of the Conference recommended for adoption a text on "terrorism" consisting of five articles. The Third Conference, however, owing to the lack of time, decided to refer the matter to the Fourth Conference to be held the following year. The text adopted by Committee V of the Third Conference, reads as follows:[5]

Article 1. The deliberate use of means capable of producing a common danger shall be deemed to have occurred whenever an accused person has committed an act imperilling life, physical integrity or human health or threatening to destroy substantial property, including, in particular:

(a) Arson, explosion, flooding or submersion: ignition of asphyxiating or noxious substances: destruction or damaging of signals, lamps, works or equipment intended for firefighting or life-saving;

(b) Wilful interruption of the normal operation of means of transport or communication, railways, or telegraphic, telephonic or postal services, wilful damaging of governmental or public utility water, lighting, heating or power installations;

(c) Pollution, fouling or deliberating poisoning of drinking-water or staple foods, causing or propagating contagious or epidemic diseases or diseases of animals or plants of prime importance to agriculture, forestry or stock-raising.

Article 2. It shall be a punishable offense to make deliberate use of means of producing a common danger, which shall constitute an

---

[5]Third International Conference for the Unification of Penal Law, Brussels, June 26-30, 1930, *Actes de la Conférence*, 1931, *Brussels*, Office de publicité, 36, rue Neuve. For the text see also annex I to the reports submitted by the special rapporteurs to the Sixth International Conference for the Unification of Penal Law, Copenhagen, August 31-September 3, 1935, *Actes de la Conférence*, 1938, Paris, Editions A. Pedone, p. 176.

act of terrorism chargeable against any person employing crimes against the life, liberty or physical integrity of persons or against governmental or private property for the purpose of propounding or putting into practice political or social ideas.

Article 3. The deliberate use of means capable of producing a common danger shall also be deemed to exist where it is established that an association was formed for the purpose of committing violence against persons or property.

Any persons who form or cooperate in the formation of such association, knowing the purpose for which it was formed, may be convicted under this provision.

Article 4. Crimes and offenses covered by the enumeration in articles 1 and 2 shall be proceeded against and punished, irrespective of the place where the offense is committed or the nationality of the offender, in accordance with the law in force in the country of which he is a national.

If penalties prescribed in the country where the offense is committed differ from those applicable in the country of prosecution, the lighter penalties shall be imposed.

Article 5. The courts and tribunals having jurisdiction pursuant to article 4 shall also have jurisdiction in respect of prosecutions for attempted offenses or for complicity in accordance with the law of the country of prosecution.

At the Fourth (Paris) International Conference, on the basis of reports submitted by special rapporteurs, Committee III of the Conference adopted a text on "terrorism" consisting of five articles, together with the recommendation that the consideration of offenses creating a common and general danger should be deferred until the next Conference and that an international convention should be concluded to ensure the universal repression of terrorist attacks. The text adopted by Committee III of the Fourth Conference reads as follows:[6]

Article 1. Any person who, with a view to terrorizing the popu-

---

[6]Fourth International Conference for the Unification of Penal Law, Paris, December 27-30, 1931, *Actes de la Conférence,* 1933, Paris, Recueil Sirey. For the text, see also annex II to the reports submitted by the special rapporteurs to the Sixth International Conference for the Unification of Penal Law, Copenhagen, August 31-September 3, 1935, *Actes de la Conférence,* 1938, Paris, Editions A. Pedone, p. 178.

lation, makes use against persons or property of bombs, mines, explosive or incendiary devices or products, fire-arms or other lethal or destructive devices, or who causes or attempts to cause, propagates or attempts to propagate any epidemic, animal disease or other calamity, or who interrupts or attempts to interrupt any governmental or public utility service shall be punishable by. . . , without prejudice to any heavier penalties which may be applicable.

Article 2. Any person who knowingly makes, possesses, introduces or transports an object mentioned in article 1 which is intended for the commission of the offense referred to therein shall be punishable by . . .

Article 3. Any person who, by public utterances or by writings or drawings circulated among the public or publicly displayed, incites others to commit the offense referred to in Article 1 or defends the act constituting the said offence or the persons committing it shall be punishable by. . . .

Article 4. Any person who has been a member of an association formed or combination established with a view to the commission of the offenses specified above shall be punishable by . . .

Article 5. Any persons other than the instigator who, prior to the commission of the offenses referred to in the preceding articles and prior to any prosecution, inform the public authorities thereof and disclose to them the perpetrators or who, even after prosecution has been initiated, cause the arrest of the other offenders shall be exempt from punishment.

The courts may nevertheless order . . . (preventive detention) .

At the Fifth (Madrid) International Conference, on the basis of reports submitted by special rapporteurs, the following text and resolution were adopted by the Conference:[7]

Article 1. Any person who, with a view to destroying any social organization, employs means calculated to terrorize the population,

---

[7]Fifth International Conference for the Unification of Penal Law. Madrid, October 14-20, 1935, *Actes de la Conférence,* 1935, Paris, Editions A. Pedone. For the test see also annex III to the reports submitted by the special rapporteurs to the Sixth International Conference for the Unification of Penal Law, Copenhagen, August 31-September 3, 1935, *Actes de la Conférence,* 1938. Paris, Editions A. Pedone, p. 179.

shall be punishable by. . . .

Article 2. Any person who knowingly makes, possesses, introduces or transports substances or objects intended for the commission of the offence referred to in the preceding article shall be punishable by. . .

Article 3. Any person who, by any means whatsoever, publicly incites others to commit the offense referred to in Article 1 or defends the said offense or the person committing it shall be punishable by. . . .

Article 4. Any person who has been a member of an association formed or combination established for the purpose of committing the offense referred to in Article 1 shall be punishable by. . . .

RESOLUTIONS

The Conference is of the opinion that:
(a) As regards jurisdiction, States may continue for the time being to follow the rules of territorial jurisdiction or may opt for the rule of universal jurisdiction already adopted in some legal systems.
(b) Extradition should always be allowed. In the case of States whose Constitutions prohibit the extradition of social offenders, the preceding provision does not apply.
(c) The question of offenses causing general danger should be referred to the next Conference.

Lastly, at the Sixth (Copenhagen) International Conference, on the basis of reports submitted by special rapporteurs, the Conference adopted the following text on terrorism, consisting of eight articles:[8]

Terrorism Texts

PREAMBLE: Whereas it is necessary to punish certain acts as special offenses, apart from the general incrimination of which they may already be the subject in the legislation of States, when they have endangered the community or created a state of terror

---

[8]Sixth International Conference for the Unification of Penal Law, Copenhagen, August 31-September 3, 1935, *Actes de la Conférence, 1938,* Paris, Editions A. Pedone, pp. 420-421.

calculated to cause a change in, or impediment to, the operation of the public authorities or to disturb international relations, creating in particular a threat to peace, a section or chapter entitled "Outrages endangering the community or creating a state of terror" worded as follows, shall be included in the Penal Code or in a special Act:

Article 1. Any person who, by wilful acts directed against the life, physical integrity, health or freedom of a Head of State or his or her spouse, a person exercising the prerogatives of a Head of State, Crown Princes, members of a Government, persons possessing diplomatic immunity, or members of constitutional, legislative or judiciary bodies, has endangered the community or created a state of terror calculated to cause a change in or impediment to the operation of the public authorities or to disturb international relations,

Shall be liable to . . . . (an increased penalty).

Article 2. Any person who has thus endangered the community or created a state of terror:

1. By any wilful act causing a disaster by impeding railway, maritime, river or air communications or by interrupting public services or services of public utility.

   Or causing a disaster by the use of explosive, incendiary, asphyxiating or harmful materials.

   Or causing the pollution, fouling, or poisoning of drinking water or food, or propagating or provoking contagious or epidemic diseases, epizootic or epiphytic diseases, or any other wilful act calculated to endanger human lives;

2. By wilful destruction of, or damage to, public buildings or public supplies, ways and means of transport and communication, signals, lanterns, works and apparatus used for extinguished fires and rescue operations;

   Or by destruction of or damage to hydraulic, ligting, heating or power installations belonging to public services or public utilities;

3. By the wilful use of explosives in a public place;

4. By any other wilful act which endangers human lives and the community; shall be liable to . . . (an increased penalty).

Article 3. Direct successful incitement to the commission of the offenses mentioned in the two preceding articles, as well as wilful participation in and attempts to commit such offenses, shall entail a penalty of . . .

Article 4. Any person who has organized a conspiracy with a view to the commission of any of the offenses mentioned in articles 1 and 2, or who has participated in such a conspiracy, shall be liable to a penalty of . . .

Article 5. Direct incitement, by any means of publicity, to the commission of any of the offenses mentioned in article 1 and 2 shall entail a penalty of . . .

Article 6. Any person who has manufactured, possessed, exported, imported, transported, sold, transferred or distributed materials or objects knowing that they are destined for the preparation or commission of any of the offenses mentioned in articles 1 and 2 shall be liable to a penalty of . . .

Article 7. Any person who has knowingly assisted by any means the person committing any of the offenses mentioned in articles 1 and 2 or his accomplices shall be liable to a penalty of . . .

Article 8. If the acts referred to in the preceding articles are committed in different countries, each shall be considered as a separate offense.

———— SECTION 2 ————

HISTORY OF
INTERNATIONAL TERRORISM
AND ITS LEGAL CONTROL

Bogdan Zlataric

INTRODUCTION

"THE INTENSIFICATION of terroristic activity in the past few years has made terrorism one of the most pressing present-day problems." It was with this statement that the learned jurist Anthony Sottile, of Sicilian origin (born in Catania in 1883), began his lectures at the Academy of International Law at The Hague in 1938.[1] History repeats itself, and now, 35 years after this statement was made, it can still serve as an introduction to the proceedings of this meeting.* Moreover, one could assert, and rightly so, that this problem has become, in present times, even more serious than it has ever been in the past.

The task that we have undertaken is that of surveying, in a cursory manner, the history of the development of the juridical concept of international terrorism, and that is, the apparition of the term[2] and the evolution of its juridic content, as well as the methods which have been considered to combat this scourge of humanity more effectively at an international level.

If we temporarily adopt, as a working hypothesis, the notion of terrorism, in its widest sense, as criminal acts of violence which provoke terror for the purpose of arrival at a given goal, then

---

*Ed's Note: This paper was presented at International Symposium on international terrorism and political crimes, which was held in Siracuse, Italy.

[1]*See* Recueil des Cours, 1938, T 65, p. 91.

[2]It seems that the term "terrorists" was used for the first time to indicate Robespierre and his companions in reference to his famous "Committee of Public Health" of the "Tribunal of Terror." Nevertheless, this was a regime of terror or a system of domination by terror, instituted by a particular government.

474

without doubt these acts have been perpetrated throughout history.

In most cases they have been committed for a political scope, and for this reason the history of terrorism, as a distinct juridic notion *(delictum sui generis)*, is closely tied to the history of political crime, since the two concepts serve only as general terms of classification.

In effect, in the course of the 19th century, certain forms of terrorism, despite their political motivations, have in a sense broken away from the notion of political crime *strictu sensu.* This will be the first period of our historical survey.

The second period will be dedicated to the scientific search for a juridic definition of this phenomenon.

The third period concerns the attempt to regulate terrorism at an international level (Conventions of 1937).

Lastly, the fourth period includes both the efforts carried on within the U.N. and the international regulations already established to deal with certain new forms of international terrorism, such as air piracy (Conventions of The Hague, 1971, and Montreal, 1972) and the kidnapping of diplomats (Convention of Washington 1971).

Nevertheless, given that international regulation of new forms of terrorism is a subject that will be dealt with in other reports presented at this meeting, we will limit our discussion solely to a brief survey of the first three periods mentioned above.

SEPARATION OF CERTAIN FORMS OF TERRORISM FROM THE NOTION OF POLITICAL CRIME

In the course of history, political criminals have long been treated as the worst of villains and considered as prime public enemies. This point of view has undergone a change in the course of the 19th century. An innovation has come about—perhaps the greatest yet in criminal law—consisting of a more tolerant attitude toward political crimes. Guizot, a French statesman and historian, as early as 1822, made an appeal for the abolition of the death penalty for political crimes. Since the Revolution of 1830, more liberal measures have been introduced for political crimes (alternative penalties, preferential treatment during the execution of the penalties, procedural guaranties) and in 1848 the death penalty for political crimes was completely abolished in France.

Insofar as extradition is concerned, this change in attitude is reflected in the exclusion of political criminals from those turned over to the State in which the crime was committed, and by the fact that they are given the right to political asylum in the state of refuge.

The Belgian law of 1833 was the first to open the way in this sense, by suppressing crimes against the security of the state among those for which extradition could be granted. The extradition agreements between France and Switzerland in 1832 and between France and Belgium in 1834, already contained the rule according to which extradition could not be applied to political offenses. Since then this rule has become nearly universal and appears in numerous extradition treaties, both bilateral and multilateral.

Nevertheless, this tendency toward a more liberal treatment of political crimes soon ended with the introduction in extradition treaties of the attempt clause, or the *Belge* clause, inserted in the French-Belgian Convention of 1856 for the first time, following the attempt on the life of Napoleon III. This clause was conceived in the following manner: "An attempt on the life of the head of a foreign government or members of his family will not be considered a political crime nor an act connected to such a crime when this attempt constitutes an act of murder, assassination, or poisoning." Since then the "attempt" clause has been introduced in a large number of extradition treaties and it is also found in the 1957 European Convention on extradition. This was the first form of terroristic activity to be internationally controlled, thereby facilitating its repression at least in those States which were allied by extradition treaties.[3]

Nevertheless, two thoughts come to mind concerning the clause on attempts. It may be objected, and rightly so, that this clause preserves a certain sense of aristocratic privilege in introducing the inequality of the value of human lives, which is in obvious contrast with the equalitarian tendencies of modern law. On the other hand, it may be asked whether all attempts on the life of a head of

---

[3]Marc Ancel, "Le crime politique et le droit pénal du XXᵉ siècle," in 1 *Revue d'histoire politique et constitutionnelle*, (1938) p. 89.

state deserve the qualification of a terroristic act in a negative sense. We are thinking in particular of the unsuccessful attempt on the life of Hitler which, if it had succeeded, would have saved hundreds of thousands of human lives. It would have been a case of "tyranicide," a doctrine which has been defended in the past by the great theologists and politicians of the sixteenth and seventeenth centuries.

Toward the end of the nineteenth century, following numerous anarchist attacks, many countries passed new laws introducing an extremely rigorous regime with respect to this new form of terroristic activity.[4] At an international level, anarchist plots were given a new name—that of social crimes—thereby attempting to withdraw them from the category of political crimes. The International Law Institute in particular, during its session at Geneva in 1892, voted a resolution stating that "criminal acts directed against the basis of social organization, and not solely against a given state or a given form of government" are not considered political crimes insofar as the application of the rule on extradition. Unfortunately, in the course of the twentieth century, the renewed repression of anarchist terrorism has degenerated, due to certain reactionary theories, into a brutal repression of socialist and communist doctrines as such. In effect, in qualifying a given act as a criminal offense[5] one must not consider the nature of the political doctrine behind such an act but, rather, the means by which it is carried out. Otherwise one risks falling into the odious pitfall of crimes of opinion.

Finally, along the same general lines, another clause in extradition law has had the effect of excluding certain terroristic acts from the more liberal regime adopted toward political crimes. Again, the International Law Institute during its above-mentioned session (Geneva 1892) stated that the loathful nature of the means employed, which reveal base criminality, cancels the normally political nature of certain crimes as far as extradition. Inspired by this idea, the French law of 1927, on the extradition of foreigners, stipulates in Article 5 as follows: "Insofar as concerns the actions committed

---

[4]Pella, "La répression des crimes contre la personalité de l'Etat," *Recueil des Cours,* 1930, T. 33, p. 703.

[5]*Ibid.,* p. 746.

in the course of an insurrection, or a civil war by either of the parties engaged in the conflict and in the interest of the cause, such acts can be subject to extradition only if they constitute odious barbarian acts and vandalism prohibited by the laws of war and only when the civil war has ended." The German law of 1929 regarding extradition, accords such extradition in the case of intentional crimes against the life of a person unless committed in open combat.

SCIENTIFIC SEARCH FOR A JURIDICAL DEFINITION OF TERRORISM

This part falls in the period between the two world wars and is connected particularly to activities, in the sphere of unification of penal law, which were carried out following a recommendation adopted during the 1st International Congress of Penal Law (Brussels, 1926).

The first part, as we have seen, was characterized by efforts to assure a more effective repression of certain forms of terrorism at an international level and by the suppression of the exceptions in the extradition of guilty parties. The second part, instead, is characterized by the attempts to combat terrorism more effectively by placing it among those crimes against the law of nations *(criminal juris gentium)*, thereby subjecting it to the universal principle which permits, in certain conditions, the application of national criminal law, regardless of the place in which the offense was committed and the nationality of the person responsible.

The First International Conference for the Unification of Penal Law (Warsaw 1927) in its resolution regarding the principles of international criminal law *(stricto sensu)*, placed crimes such as piracy, counterfeiting, slave trade, etc. among those against the law of nations and subjected to the universal principle of repression "the intentional use of any means capable of bringing forth a common danger." This vague definition can include certain terroristic activities. The rapporteur on this theme (Ionesco-Dolj) also briefly dealt with the nature of "social crimes" or crimes "against humanity" but the term "terrorism" does not yet appear in the proceedings of this Conference.

It was only at the IIIrd Conference for the Unification of Penal Law (Brussels, 1930) that the notion of terrorism was more accurately defined. In effect, one of the reports was entitled "international use of any means capable of causing a common danger (terrorism) ."

During the working sessions on the Unification of Panel Law the term terrorism appears for the first time. The rapporteur on this subject (Gunzburg) proposed a definition which listed the different means intentionally employed and capable of causing a common danger, while omitting the word "terrorism" from his definition. The final proposal of the Commission which dealt with this subject contained a new article (besides the definition of the rapporteur) which stipulated: "The intentional use of means capable of producing a common danger that represents an act of terrorism on the part of anyone making use of crimes against life, liberty or physical integrity of persons or directed against private or state property with the purpose of expressing or executing political or social ideas will be punished."

Hence, according to this conception, there is a precise motivation which, aside from the action described, becomes the factor constituting the criminal act of terrorism. The question was, nevertheless, deferred to the following Conference.

The IVth Conference, held in Paris in 1931, again took up the subject of terrorism and discussed it on the basis of two reports. The first rapporteur (Radulesco), who gave a strongly anti-communist tone to his report, proposed the following definition: "All offenses, preparatory acts for such offenses, as well as agreements and conspiracies aimed at imposing a political or social doctrine through violence or intimidation, will be considered acts of terrorism." In the following article there is a long list of acts capable of producing a common danger. According to the rapporteur, even counterfeiting falls among acts of terrorism if it is perpetrated with the above-indicated purpose.

The other rapporteur (Lemkin), after having set forth numerous ways in which a common danger is produced, formulated the following definition of terrorism: "Whoever, in order to express, propagate, or carry out a political or social doctrine, commits an action which causes a common danger to life, health or physical integrity, or to private property or that of the local community or the state, or causes the danger of interrupting public communications or the functioning of public utilities, will be considered a terrorist and punished by . . . "

The Commission, following the discussion, adopted the following resolution: "Whoever, for the purpose of terrorizing the population, uses against persons or property bombs, mines, incendiary or explosive devices or products, fire arms or other deadly or deleterious devices, or who provokes or attempts to provoke, spreads or attempts to spread an epidemy, a contagious disease or other disaster, or who interrupts or attempts to interrupt a public service or public utility will be punished by. . ."

The Conference approved a recommendation that "an International Convention be concluded to assure the universal represssion of terrorist attempts."

Given that the preceding formula was never favorably received at the General Assembly of the IVth Convention, the discussion was adjourned to the Vth Conference that was held in Madrid in 1934. During this Conference, on the basis of a new report (ROUX), it was decided that terrorism and crimes of common danger should be examined separately. The discussions were concentrated exclusively on the first question. Roux took up the definition of terrorism that had been proposed during the preceding conference, whereas the second rapporteur (Lemkin) broke away from the concepts of terrorism and proposed introducing among the *"crimina juris gentium,"* the act of provoking a catastrophe in the international community, the destruction of works of art and the participation in massacres or other collective atrocities committed against the defenseless or helpless general population. These offenses, according to the rapporteur, must be subject to universal repression. In the course of the discussion, terrorism was divided into political and social terrorism. The definition which was finally adopted by the Conference included only the latter and spoke of "He, who with the scope of undermining the social order, employs any means whatsoever to terrorize the population, will be punished. . ." Terrorism insofar as it is a crime against the law of nations therefore comes down to an anarchist crime.

Following a series of attempts that had taken place in the meantime having as their victims, in particular, the Romanian Minister Duca, the Austrian Chancellor Dolfuss and, in one and the same attempt, King Alexander of Yugoslavia and the French Minister Barthou, the French government directed a memorandum to the League of Nations calling for the elaboration of an international convention for the repression of crimes having political terrorism as their goal. A committee composed of 11 members worked out two drafts: one for a "Convention for the Repression of Terrorism" and the other for the Creation of an International Criminal Court.

As a result of this new situation, at the VIth International Conference for the Unification of Criminal Law, held in Copenhagen in 1935, the question of terrorism was again in the order of the day. Four reports on this subejct were presented at the Conference (Givanovitch, Gunzburg, Lemkin, Saldana). This was the first time that the USSR was represented at such a conference and one of its delegates was the famous Pachoukanis. During the discussion he set forth the official soviet position on terrorism. He first declared himself in favor of maintaining the principle of nonextradition of political criminals, calling to mind that the persons who took part in the *Commune de Paris* in 1871 were not extradited by the countries where they sought asylum. He then declared that the Communist Party in his country had always been against individual terrorism. According to him, international terrorism is distinguished above all by the fact that it provokes a threat to the peace. The text approved at the end of this Conference contained, first of all, a preamble proposing "the repression of certain acts as special offenses when they create a common danger, or a state of terror that might incite either a change in or raise an obstacle to the functioning of public bodies, or a disturbance of international relations which represents a particular threat to the peace." In the first article, terrorism is defined as "intentional acts directed against the life, physical integrity, health or freedom of a head of state or his spouse, or any person holding the prerogatives of a head of state, as well as crown princes, members of governments, people enjoying diplomatic immunity, and members of the constitutional, legislative, or judicial bodies," if the perpetrator has created "a common danger, or a state of terror that might incite a change or raise an obstacle to the functioning of public bodies or a disturbance in international relations."

Article 2 contains a limited list of other acts which create a common danger or provoke a state of terror—particularly the act of instigating a catastrophe or a calamity, that of polluting drinking water, spreading contagious diseases, destroying public utilities, the use of explosives in a public place, etc.

The following articles refer to offenses called "satellites" (instigation, attempt, conspiracy, preparatory acts, assistance).

The text of the resolution ends with a vow "that when extradition is not granted, the delinquents can be deferred to an international penal jurisdiction, unless the state concerned prefers to have them tried by its own law Courts."

Lastly, let us add that, owing to the efforts made in elaborating and clarifying the juridic concept of terrorism at a scientific level, many classifications have been made and, in particular:

a) domestic and international terrorism
b) terrorism against common law, political terrorism and social terrorism
c) direct and indirect terrorism
d) individual terrorism and governmental or state terrorism

We believe that these denominations alone give a rather clear idea of the nature of the problem and it is for this reason that we shall refrain from giving any further explanations.

ATTEMPT AT INTERNATIONAL CONTROL (CONVENTIONS OF 1937)

November 16, 1937 in the League of Nations two international Conventions were concluded in Geneva: one for the Prevention and Repression of Terrorism, the other for the Creation of an International Criminal Court. At the Diplomatic Conference 35 countries were represented. The first Convention was signed by the delegations of 24 states and the second by 13.

Nevertheless, due to the grave incidents which took place prior to the 2nd World War, the two Conventions did not obtain a sufficient number of ratifications (there were only three ratifications for the first) and consequently they never came into force.

We will limit ourselves here to a brief examination of the first convention since the possibilities of creating an international criminal jurisdiction of the type provided for in the second convention are so slight at present that a thorough discussion would hardly be profitable from a practical point of view.

Article 1 of the Convention for the Prevention and the Repression of Terrorism first of all reaffirms "the principle of international law according to which every state has the duty to refrain from any act intended to favor terroristic activities directed against another State and to prevent the acts by which such activities are carried out." Further on it is established that the contracting parties agree "to prevent and repress activities of this nature and to give one another mutual assistance." Paragraph 2 of this article is dedicated to a general definition of "acts of terrorism," intending by this term "criminal acts directed against a state and having the purpose or the characteristic of provoking terror in determined persons, groups of persons, or in the public."

Article 2 of the Convention stipulates that each of the contracting states is obligated to consider acts of terrorism in its criminal legislation when such acts are directed against another contracting state. The acts are the following:

1) intentional acts directed against life, physical integrity, health or freedom of
   a) heads of state, persons holding the preogatives of head of state, their hereditary successors or appointees
   b) the spouse of the persons listed above
   c) persons vested with public duties or responsibility, when the said act has been committed by reason of the duties or responsibilities exercised by these persons;
2) The intentional act consists in destroying or impairing property which is public or serves for public use, which belongs to or is administered by a High Contracting Party;
3) An intentional act of such a nature as to imperil human lives in creating a common danger;
4) The attempt to commit the offenses listed above;

5) The act of manufacturing, procuring, detaining or furnishing arms, ammunition, explosives or harmful substances intended for use in carrying out one of the above-listed offenses in any country whatsoever.

Articles 3 to 7 deal with the incrimination of conspiracy, instigation and assistance and with the repetition of an international offense and the private claim for damages. The regulations in Article 8 deal with extradition and, substantially sanction the principle "aut dedere, aut punire." Articles 9 and 10 confirm the principles of "personalité active" (a State has the right to try its own citizen even when he has committed a crime in another nation) and universality insofar as concerns the repression of terrorist acts. The following articles contain the clauses relating to the control of the circulation of fire arms, incrimination for questions of passports and other similar documents, the centralization of information on terroristic activity and the exchange of such information, the functioning of Rogatory Commissions, the interpretation of the Convention and the regulation of disputes on the interpretation. The last articles of the Convention contain the usual clauses of protocol and closure.

CONCLUSION

The present report is nothing more than a modest contribution aimed at facilitating the proceedings of our meeting. We have endeavored to outline in a general manner the route taken and the efforts made up to the last World War to ensure a more effective fight against terrorism, a phenomenon that has spread considerably in recent times and is today one of the most pressing problems of humanity.

This problem is extremely delicate and difficult to resolve on a political and juridic level, given the diverging philosophies, ideologies and mortals that divide the international community. The rule that the end does not justify the means is not thoroughly accepted at a theoretical level and even less respected in practice.

It is our duty as jurists to shed light on this problem and our contribution must be taken into consideration for, as stated in the well-known phrase of de Lamartine, "It is through enlightenment that the world will rise to unity."

METHODOLOGICAL OPTIONS FOR INTERNATIONAL LEGAL CONTROL OF TERRORISM

M. CHERIF BASSIOUNI

SOCIAL AND BEHAVIORAL SCIENTISTS will in time tell us more about the conditions, reasons, causes and motivations leading to terror-violence.[1] With such knowledge jurists will be better equipped to develop the type of legal controls most likely to reduce the impact of violent strategies. But any scheme for the legal regulation and control of types of behavior cannot be framed without a value-oriented goal. I shall not elaborate on this point, but it is nonetheless my position that no regulatory scheme can rest on a repressive basis because of the conflicting values reflected in the very activity sought to be regulated and controlled. Indeed, what is terrorism to some is heroism to others.[2] An international regulatory scheme must therefore be in a position to mediate between conflicting values and claims, and therefore, it must, as much as possible, remain neutral in respect to competing values, and claims. To whatever degree a regulatory scheme embodies certain values, they must be clearly identified to avoid any ambiguity. This is significant at the level of interpretation and implementation. The value-oriented goal which serves as the premise of this speaker's discussion is the attempt to minimize violence—to prevent its spill over effects to uninvolved participants and to limit its arenas. In other words: 1. reduce the impact of violence; 2. restrict its extension to potential victims

Reprinted with permission of *The Akron Law Journal* where this article list appeared in Vol. 7, p. 386-396 (1974).
[1]See Chapter I of this book.
[2]See Symposium on International Control of Terrorism, *The Globe*, Vol 11-1 (1973).

and; 3. prevent its exportation to arenas beyond those wherein a given conflict exists.

With this in mind, the threshold questions are whether to define certain manifestations of terror-violence, and how to regulate them, i.e. from a substantive or complementary legal aspect. In other words whether or not to define terrorism as international crime establishing an international enforcement machinery or not to define it but to require states to increase their collaboration in the fields of extradition and other forms of judicial co-operation in respect to certain activities. Assuming the choice is substantive control, the question then becomes how to define terrorism. The problems in defining aggression are analogous to those of defining terrorism.[3] Transcending the significant ideological implications in the elaboration of any definition, the methodology by which it is arrived at deserves consideration.

In this context there are three methodological options:

1. The elaboration of a general (generic) definition.

2. The selection of certain specific acts which are phrased in a manner stating the specific content of the behavior sought to be proscribed.

3. A mixed formula which combines a general (generic) statement and some illustrative applications phrased with specificity of content as to the proscribed conduct.

Considering that all legal systems of the world require that certain drafting principles be met it is important to ascertain those principles which are often referred to as principles of legality e.g. *ex post facto, nulla Poena sine legge, nullum crimen sine legge.*[4] Furthermore, to insure the proper application of these principles, the doctrine of analogy in interpreting penal statutes is prohibited and penal proscriptions must be construed narrowly and in accordance with the plain and common meaning of the language used. This is indispensable in order to provide notice of the prohibited conduct and thereby afford opportunity

---

[3]Bassiouni, "A Definition of Aggression in International Law," Vol. I, Bassiouni and Nanda, *A Treatise on International Criminal Law,* p. 159 (1973); also, Hazard, "Why Try Again to Define Aggression," 62 *A.J.I.L.,* 702 (1968).

[4]Bassiouni, *Criminal Law and its Processes,* (1969) p. 37.

for compliance with the legal mandate. Thus, in view of these principles, it appears that option 1 and 3 would not satisfy all these requirements and that only option 2, namely, description of specific acts with a well-defined content, could meet such standards.

A casual survey of acts deemed terroristic according to the literature on the subject would tend to indicate that these acts fall within the categories of common crimes which are prohibited in every penal legislation of the world. Indeed, there is so much agreement on such crimes as homicide, kidnapping, theft, robbery and extortion, that one can raise the issue of whether it is at all necessary to elaborate a new international crime which would encompass such conduct. The answer, however, lies in the questions of enforcement and jurisdiction rather than in regard to the substantive content of those specific crimes enumerated above.

The very fact that murder or kidnapping is deemed criminal in all legal systems is not sufficient to make it an international crime. To become so at least one of the following five elements must be present in addition to those of the common crime: 1. The act or series of acts takes place in more than one state; 2. the act or series of acts takes place wherein no state has exclusive national jurisdiction; 3. the acts affect citizens of more than one state; 4. the acts affect internationally protected persons i.e. diplomats, personnel of international organizations; and 5. the acts affect internationally protected objects such as international civil aviation and international means of communications. Thus, whenever any one of these five elements exists in conjunction with a common crime, it can become an international crime in addition to being a municipal crime wherever it occurred. Such a theory must nonetheless be codified or be the subject of a multilateral treaty. In such a case a definition of the specific acts sought to be internationally proscribed must be clearly set forth showing the elements of the common crime as well as the international elements which render it internationally cognizable.

Assuming all these requirements for international codification are met, one cannot underestimate the difficulties involved in any attempt to achieve that very codification of international crimes. The history of such efforts as the Draft Code of Offenses Against the Peace and Security of Mankind,[6] attest thereto. However, if one is encouraged by the somewhat successful treaty-making efforts in the prohibition of slavery,[7] international traffic in narcotics[8] and hijacking,[9] it is nonetheless clear that no agreement can be reached as to penalties. Such efforts in the 1971 Montreal Convention on Hijacking[10] have not proven successful, and the 1972 Amending Protocol to the 1961 Single Convention on Narcotic Drugs[11] took the approach of merely requiring signatory states to impose appropriate penalties.

Finally, the problems of enforcement and implementation which have plagued the progress of international law in general are particularly visible in this area. That is why the 1937 Convention on Terrorism saw fit to prescribe the establishment of a criminal court.[12] Since then the idea has been recommended from time to time, and the United Nations elaborated two drafts in 1951 and 1953 for the creation of an international criminal court.[13] There are, however, no more apparent signs of accept-

---

[6]This is generally the position taken by the III International Symposium on "Terrorism and Political Crimes" of the International Institute for Advanced Criminal Sciences, June, 1973. See Final Document" p. XI et Seq.

[6]9 U.N. GAOR, Supp 9 at 11-12, U.N. Doc. A/2693 (1954).

[7]See Nanda and Bassiouni, "Slavery and the Slave Trade: Steps Toward Eradication," 12 *Santa Clara L Rev,* 424 (1972).

[8]"The International Narcotics Control System: A Proposal," 46 *St. John's L Rev,* 713 (1972).

[9]Convention on offenses and certain other acts committed on board aircraft, signed at Tokyo on September 14, 1963.

Convention for the suppression of unlawful seizure of aircraft, signed at The Hague on December 16, 1970.

Convention for the suppression of unlawful acts against the safety of civil aviation, signed at Montreal on September 23, 1971.

[10]*Ibid.*

[11]Draft Convention for prevention and punishment of certain acts of international terrorism, A/C.6/L.850, September 25, 1972.

[12]Convention for the prevention and punishment of terrorism, opened for signatures at Geneva on November 16, 1937.

[13]5 U.N. GAOR Supp. 12 at 18, U.N. Doc. A/1316 (1950); 9 U.N. GAOR Supp. 12 at 23, U.N. Doc. A/2645 (1954). See, also, United Nations Secretariat, Historical Survey of the question of international criminal jurisdiction, U.N. Doc. A/CN.4/7 at 18 (1949).

ance of the idea save for the writings of scholars defending it.[14]

The contemporary approach seems to avoid the issue of an international enforcement mechanism, and consequently the trend is moving away from the elaboration of a general treaty defining an international crime of terrorism.[15] The direction seems to be the one adopted in the 1970 Hague Convention on Hijacking and 1972 Amending Protocol on Narcotics, namely to impose upon states the duty to prosecute under municipal law or to extradite. Thus, the methodological choice appears to steer away from substantive international criminal law to adjective (complementary) international criminal law. This is highlighted by the 1972 United States Proposed Draft Convention on Terrorism, that proposal embodies the value-oriented goals stated earlier in this presentation, namely the minimization of violence, its restriction to participants in a given conflict and its limitation to the arenas of these conflicts.[16] The 1972 Draft Convention was the product of Professor Moore's efforts[17] whose position seems to be that an international regulatory scheme is more likely to be accepted and succeed if it avoids the ideological implications of the conflicting values which are usually at the very base of terror-violence strategies. The United States proposal illustrates the fact that no international superstructure is contemplated, but instead that increased judicial cooperation is the desirable option to effectively control the problem.

---

[14]See Dautricourt, "The International Criminal Court" in Vol. I, Bassiouni and Nanda, *A Treatise on International Criminal Law,* (1973), p. 636, and L. Kos-Rabcewicz-Zubkowski, "The Creation of an International Criminal Court for the *Suppression of International Terrorism" infra* section 6 of this chapter.

[15]See Study prepared by the United Nations Secretariat entitled, Measures to prevent international terrorism which endangers or takes innocent human lives or jeopardizes fundamental freedoms, and study of the underlying causes of those forms of terrorism and acts of violence which lie in misery, frustration, grievance and despair and which cause some people to sacrifice human lives, including their own, in an attempt to effect radical changes, U.N. Doc. A/C.6/418, November 2, 1972.

[16]*Supra,* note 11.

[17]John Norton Moore, Professor of Law, University of Virginia, was councellor in International Law in the Department of State, 1972, and prepared this draft in this capacity.

[18]On the topic of judicial cooperation in extradition, see, e.g. Vol. II, Bassiouni and Nanda, *A Treatise on International Criminal Law* (1973).

The duty to prosecute or extradite is well established in international criminal law and has its origin in a maximum by Hugo Grotius, namely, *aut dedere aut punire*. This speaker suggests that a more appropriate *maseim is aut dedere aut iudicare*. It appears to me that the future may well see two stages of development. The first one will be in the field of adjective international criminal law,[18] and the second state of substantive international control may only come into being after the first one has been successful in the course of the customary practice of states. That second stage would be the elaboration of an international criminal code with an international supporting structure for its enforcement and implementation. That stage may prove unnecessary if the first one produces satisfactory outcomes. However since this is not likely, the second stage may prove necessary if a sufficient number of states deem it in their best interest and in the interest of preserving minimum world order to abate jealously guarded concepts of sovereignty. The exigencies of the problems may accelerate international cooperation, particularly if its dimensions continue to grow beyond the ability of existing or contemplated schemes to control it.

From this speaker's perspective, the strategies of terror-violence throughout the world are not likely to abate but on the contrary are certain to increase. The reason for this prediction is based on three factors: conventional wars appear to have outlived their historical usefulness; nuclear strategy has not developed to a point where it can be a useful instrument in attaining power outcomes; and there are no conflict resolution devices available for the settlement of disputes arising out of ideological claims and human rights violations. Nevertheless, we must not be as indiscriminate as we have been with respect to considering all forms of terror-violence as terroristic strategies requiring international controls. There are three distinctions which must be made and which arise out of common experience with the various

---

[19]For the regulation of armed conflict, see Vol. I, Bassiouni and Nanda, *A Treatise on International Criminal Law*, Part 3, p. 295-454 (1973); see, also, Yingling and Ginnane, "The Geneva Conventions of 1949" 46 *A.J.I.L.*, 393 (1952).

manifestation of terror-violence. These distinctions must be based on the motivations of the perpetrators of such acts. Namely, whether we are dealing with psychopathological cases which so far have produced the majority of hijackings; common criminals or persons acting for personal or private profit—motive as in some hijacking cases and kidnapping; and ideologically motivated persons who are part of national liberation movements or internal political opposition movements. Certainly as to participants in national liberation movements the regulation of armed conflicts and the four 1949 Geneva Conventions regulate such conducts[19] and the only weakness is the lack of enforcement machinery. As to other forms of idealogically motivated terror-violence, the ability to control that violence will be only as successful as alternative conflict resolution devices are found to channel such conflicts into a peaceful arena. The present situation leaves no alternative but a resort to terror violence to accomplish what is sometimes a legitimate end based on legitimate rights, but which find no legal or peaceful remedy for their redress.

It must also be stated that not all forms of ideologically declared terror-violence are to benefit from the mitigation if not justification advanced earlier. Some criteria must be set forth to distinguish between legitimate resort to violence and its permissible limits as a last resort and terror-violence whose only connection to a legitimizing reason is the self-proclaimed rhetoric of its perpetrators. This will be of great importance to determine whether extradition is to be granted or whether the accused can benefit from the political offense exceptions.[20]

We must also be mindful that efforts to regulate and control terror-violence cannot be only one-sided. All too often the same behavior, or behavior similar in-nature or outcome to that which is proscribed for some, and accepted when committed by others. The terror-violence of colonization cannot be condoned while the terror-violence of liberation is condemned. Similarly kidnap-

---

[20]Bassiouni, "Ideologically Motivated Offenses and the Political Offense Exception in Extradition, a Proposed Juridical Standard for an Unruly Problem," 19 *DePaul L Rev.* 217 (1970) and Section 3, Chapter V of this Book.

ping[21] and hijacking[22] cannot be deemed a crime when committed by individuals and permissible when committed by agents of a state.

In conclusion, allow me to state that however abhorrent all forms of violence are, the "terrorism" we know today is probably the beginning of a new historical cycle. If such acts of violence are to replace wars, whether conventional or in any other form, then "terrorism" is welcome because its harmful consequences are minimal in comparison to the well known consequences of war. A single bombing raid in World War II or Viet Nam caused more damage, harm and destruction than all the consequences of "terrorism" during the last quarter of the century. This is true even if the random and haphazard nature of contemporary terror-violence can be distinguished from the better aspects of regulated conventional warfare. This is not a glorification of terror-violence, nor for that matter even an apology for it, but a mere observation which reflects on the nature of our civilization. Indeed, terrorism is nothing more than a manifestation of the quality of our civilization and its elimination is in function of the thickening of its thin veneer.[23]

---

[21]Bassiouni, "Unlawful Seizures and Irregular Rendition Devices as Alternatives to Extradition," 7 *Vanderbilt Journal of Transnational Law,* 25 (1973), discussing various forms of unlawful seizures by states of persons outside their jurisdiction; Among such cases are those of Eichmann, Tsombe, Soblen, Argoud, Ahlers, and 11 Arabs seized by Israel in Lebanon in 1973 and brought to trial, discussed in Bassiouni, pp 28-33.

[22]As an example, the unlawful seizure in Lebanese air space of an Iraqi Airways plane by Israeli military aircraft, forcing it to land in Israel. See *Time* magazine, August 20, 1973, p. 28.

[23]Bassiouni, "The Human Rights Program the Veneer of Civilization Thickens," 21 *DePaul L. Rev.,* 271 (1971).

UNITED NATIONS PROPOSALS ON THE CONTROL AND REPRESSION OF TERRORISM

John F. Murphy

For purposes of this article, "United Nations" will be defined narrowly to include only the United Nations organization itself and not its specialized agencies. There will be no detailed discussion of proposals of the specialized agencies on terrorism, such as the several conventions on hijacking and other offenses against civil aviation concluded under the auspices of the International Civil Aviation Organization. Primary focus will be on the most recent proposals on terrorism: the United States Draft Convention for the Prevention and Punishment of Certain Acts of International Terrorism and its accompanying draft resolution, debate on and adoption by the 27th session of the General Assembly of Resolution 3034 (XXVII) and subsequent developments.

Another problem to be resolved at the outset of this discussion is definition of the term "terrorism." A variety of definitions of this slippery concept have been proposed, all are controversial, and a primary unfinished task for the world community is to agree upon a precise definition of the term. For purposes of this discussion the approach adopted by the United Nations Secretariat in its study on terrorism of November 2, 1972 will be followed. Only international terrorism will be considered and not the acts of governments within their own territories with respect to their own citizens. Under this approach the interests of more than one state must be involved, as, for example, when the perpetrator or the victim is a foreigner in the state where the act is done, or when the perpetrator has fled to another state. Indeed, as defined in this paper terrorism does not include the acts of governments but rather actions by individuals or groups of individuals. The victims of these terrorist acts, moreover, are innocent individuals whose lives are taken, whose bodily security is violated or whose fundamental liberties are jeopardized. Examples of such victims are passengers on a hijacked airplane, diplomats kidnaped or killed by terrorist groups and the Israeli competitors killed at the 1972 Olympics.

This approach does not denigrate the importance of understanding the underlying causes which give rise to the terrorist act. However, it proceeds on the premise that the use of some forms of violence, especially against the innocent, are illegitimate regardless of the merits of the underlying cause.

Finally, this approach distinguishes between revolutionary mass movements attempting to effect the overthrow of governments or radical changes in society and individual terrorist acts with more immediate aims committed in the name of the revolutionary mass movement. In the words of the Secretariat study these aims might include "the acquisition of funds, the liberation of prisoners, the spread of general terror, the demonstration of the impotence of Government authorities, or the provocation of ill-judged measures of repression which will alienate public opinion."

UNITED NATIONS PROPOSALS ON TERRORISM

In passing, the primary pre-United Nations effort on terrorism should be noted. The Convention for the Prevention and Punishment of Terrorism, concluded at Geneva under the auspices of the League of Nations on November 16, 1937, defined terrorism broadly to include criminal acts directed against a state and intended to create a state of terror in the minds of particular persons, or a group of persons or the general public. This proved conceptually satisfying but practically inefficacious, as only one member state of the League of Nations ratified the convention, and it never came into force.

A similarly broad approach was taken by the International Law Commission in its 1954 Draft Code of Offenses against the

Peace and Security of Mankind. The Draft Code provided as to terrorism that "the undertaking or encouragement by the authorities of a State of terrorist activity in another State, or the toleration by the authorities of a State of organized activities calculated to carry out terrorist acts in another State" is declared to be an offense against the peace and security of mankind and a crime under international law. The General Assembly, however, has on several occasions decided to defer consideration of the Draft Code until such time as greater progress has been made in arriving at a generally agreed definition of aggression.

As to the definition of aggression the Special Committee on the Question of Defining Aggression has experienced considerable difficulty in carrying out its mandate from the General Assembly. Definitions of terrorism submitted to the committee have related to actions by states in sending, organizing or supporting armed bands of terrorists who commit acts of terrorism in another state.

Similar injunctions against state support of terrorist activity in another state are to be found in the General Assembly's 1970 Declarations on Principles of International Law concerning Friendly Relations and Cooperation among States in Accordance with the Charter of the United Nations and on the Strengthening of International Security. The General Assembly and Security Council have also recently adopted resolutions expressing concern at the increase in hijackings of aircraft and calling upon states to take appropriate domestic and international measures to prevent such acts and to deal with those who commit them.

Pursuant to a mandate from the General Assembly, in 1972 the International Law Commission prepared Draft Articles on the Prevention and Punishment of Crimes against Diplomatic Agents and other Internationally Protected Persons. In its summary of debate on the problem of terrorism, the commission noted the assembly's mandate required that the scope of the draft be limited to crimes committed against diplomatic agents and other persons entitled to special protection under international law. At the same time the commission recognized that the question of crimes committed against such persons was but one facet of the problem of acts of terrorism and suggested that the Assembly might wish to consider the wider problem at an early opportunity. The Draft Articles have been circulated to member states for comments, and have been included on the provisional agenda of the 28th session of the General Assembly.

MUNICH AND THE UNITED NATIONS RESPONSE

Events in the summer and early fall of 1972 precipitated General Assembly consideration of the problem of international terrorism. In submitting the United States draft convention and resolution on terrorism on September 25, Secretary of State William Rogers referred to several of these events, including the slaughter of 26 tourists in the Lod International Airport of Israel and the firing of shots into the New York apartment of a member of the Soviet Mission to the United Nations. The primary event stimulating United States submission of the draft convention and resolution, however, was the kidnapping and killing at Munich on September 6 of eleven Israeli Olympic competitors by Arab terrorists.

Before turning to the United Nations reaction to the United States proposals and possible reasons for that reaction let us for a moment consider the primary provisions of the United States draft convention. Unlike most prior United Nations efforts regarding terrorism, the United States draft convention focuses not on state support of terrorist activity but on terrorist acts committed by individuals and their prevention and prosecution. Most important, it differs from its League of Nations predecessor in not seeking to define terrorism or to deal with all acts that might fall within the definition of terrorism. Thus under article 1 only unlawful killing, serious bodily harm or kidnapping fall within the scope of the convention. Moreover, four separate conditions must be met before the terms of the convention apply. First, the act must be committed or take effect outside the territory of a state of which the alleged offender is a national. Second, the act must be committed or take effect outside of the state against which the act is directed, unless such acts are knowingly directed against a nonnational of that state. Under this provision an armed attack in the passenger lounge of an international airport would be covered. Third, the act must not be committed either by or against a member of the armed forces of a state in the course of military hostilities. And, fourth, the act must be intended to damage the interests of or obtain concessions from a state or an international organization.

According to United States representatives, the purpose of the limited focus of the draft convention is to secure as wide an acceptance as possible of its provisions. Thus exceedingly controversial activities which arguably are terrorist in nature, such as fedayeen attacks in Israel against Israeli citizens and a wide range of activities by armed forces in Indochina and in Southern Africa, are deliberately excluded from the convention's coverage, although United States representatives have noted that the involvement of states in assisting terrorist groups or the use of force to prohibit self-determination are already prohibited under international law.

As to persons allegedly committing offenses covered by the convention, state parties would be required to establish severe penalties for covered acts and to either prosecute or extradite offenders found in their territories. The choice of whether to extradite or prosecute is left to the unfettered discretion of the state in whose territory the alleged offender is found. Accordingly, no state party would be required to return a person to a place in which it believed he might be subject to unfair treatment.

Article 4 (1) of the draft Convention provides:

> Each State Party shall take such measures as may be necessary to establish its jurisdiction over the offenses set forth in Article 1:
> (a) when the offense is committed in its territory, or
> (b) when the offense is committed by its national.

When read in conjunction with article 7, paragraphs 4 and 5, these provisions give rise to a measure of ambiguity, with the potential to create conflict between state parties. Article 7, paragraph 4, provides that "Each of the offenses shall be treated, for the purpose of extradition between State Parties as if it has been committed not only in the place in which it occurred but also in the territories of the States required to establish their jurisdiction in accordance with Article 4, paragraph 1 (b) ." Paragraph 5 of article 7 in turn provides that an extradition request from the state in which the offense is committed shall have priority over other such requests. Accordingly, in the event the state in which the offense was actually committed and the state whose national allegedly committed the offense were both to request extradition of the alleged offender, and the offense were to be treated for purposes of extradition as having been committed in both states, it is unclear whose request would enjoy priority under the convention.

It should also be noted that paragraph 2 of article 4 would require each state party to establish jurisdiction over the offenses set forth in article 1 if an alleged offender is present in its territory and the state decides not to extradite him. Thus persons committing terrorist acts covered by the convention would, in the event of widespread ratification or approval, be subject to a near universal jurisdiction.

Under article 8 of all convention, a person is guaranteed "fair treatment" at all stages of any proceedings that may be brought against him for allegedly committing any of the offenses set forth in article 1. However, no definition of fair treatment is given, and a listing of some of the fundamental elements of due process, such as a fair hearing and the right to be informed of the charges and to present a defense might add content to this vital concept.

By its terms the draft convention would yield in case of conflict to other more specialized conventions on terrorism concerning the law of armed conflict or covering attacks against diplomats or hijacking of aircraft. In the words of the United States representative to the Sixth Committee (Legal) the purpose of these provisions is to allow the draft convention "to concentrate as an urgent first step on those categories of international terrorism which present the greatest current global threat and which, ironically, have received the least attention."

Under article 16 of the draft convention disputes between

the parties arising out of the application or interpretation of the draft convention not settled by negotiation would be submitted to a conciliation commission to be established under the provisions of the article. The commission's conclusions upon the facts and questions of law would be submitted to the parties to the dispute in the form of recommendations. Apparently in the interest of securing the widest possible acceptance of the draft convention, there is no provision for reference of disputes to the International Court of Justice for binding decision, although the commission would be empowered to ask any organ that is authorized to do so to request an advisory opinion from the Court. Such an omission seems unfortunate in light of recent efforts to induce states to make greater use of the Court but perhaps required in view of the opposition of many states to binding third party adjudication.

The United States draft resolution accompanying the draft convention would, *inter alia,* have had the Assembly decide to convene a plenipotentiary conference in early 1973 with a view to adoption of such a convention, call upon all states as a matter of urgency to become parties to and implement the ICAO conventions on hijacking of and other offenses against aircraft and request ICAO to draft as an urgent matter a convention on arrangements to enforce the principles of the conventions. From the outset, however, it was apparent that the United States initiative faced substantial opposition from the Arab states, China, and a bloc of African states. In the general debate this opposition was expressed in perhaps its most extreme form by the Libyan representative, who described the United States initiative as a "ploy . . . against the legitimate struggle of the people under the yoke of colonialism and alien domination" and warned against the United Nations becoming an "instrument in local election campaigns and a pawn of international propaganda based on falsehood and deceit."

In response the United States representative admitted the necessity of studying the underlying causes of terrorism but contended that progress in eliminating such causes would by necessity come slowly and that in the meantime there was an urgent need to agree on measures to prevent and prosecute acts of international terrorism against innocent individuals. He noted that "[w]e do not hesitate in our domestic law to prohibit murder even though we have not eliminated all sources of injustice or identified all the causes which lead men to commit violent acts." As to the questions of wars of national liberation and self-determination, the United States representative quoted from Secretary of State Roger's speech to the General Assembly:

> The issue is not war—war between states, civil war, or revolutionary war. The issue is not the strivings of people to achieve self-determination and independence.
>
> Rather, it is whether millions of air travelers can continue to fly in safety each year. It is whether a person who receives a letter can open it without the fear of being blown up. It is whether diplomats can safely carry out their duties. It is whether international meetings —like the Olympic games, like this Assembly—can proceed without the everpresent threat of violence.

Finally, the United States representative warned that, should the United Nations fail to take meaningful action on international terrorism, like-minded states would agree among themselves on controls and sanctions with respect to transport and other facilities under their control, or private groups such as airline pilot associations and labor organizations would take action in their own defense. Such actions by groups of states or by private organizations he said, would be less than fully effective and might "do more harm than good to the delicately interwoven and interdependent structure of modern communication and transportation."

In an effort to reach a compromise, Italy and a number of cosponsors introduced a draft resolution which would have provided for a full study and analysis of the underlying causes of international terrorism and stressed the right of every government and all people to sovereign equality, to equal rights and to self determination. At the same time, it requested the International Law Commission to prepare a convention on international terrorism for submission to the 28th session of the General Assembly.

This compromise approach was not accepted by the great majority of the committee members, and on December 11, 1972, the Sixth Committee adopted a draft resolution submitted by Algeria and other cosponsors by a vote of 76 to 34 (U.S., with 16 abstentions. On December 18, the Assembly approved the Committee's decision by adopting Resolution 3034 (XXVII) by a roll call vote of 76 to 35 (U.S.) , with 17 abstentions. Resolution 3034 (XXVII) —while expressing *"deep concern* over increasing acts of violence which endanger or take innocent human lives or jeopardize fundamental freedoms," and inviting states to become parties to existing conventions on international terrorism and to take appropriate measures at the national level to eliminate terrorism focuses its primary attention on "finding just and peaceful solutions to the underlying causes which give rise to such acts of violence." The resolution also *"Reaffirms* the inalienable right to self-determination and independence of all peoples under the colonial and racist regimes and other forms of alien domination and upholds the legitimacy of their struggle. . . ." By way of implementation the resolution invites states to study the problem on an urgent basis and submit their observations to the Secretary-General by April 10, 1973, and decides to establish an *ad hoc* committee, to be appointed by the President of the General Assembly, to study these observations and to submit a report with recommendations for elimination of the problem to the 28th session of the Assembly. On April 26, 1973, the President of the Assembly announced he had appointed the members of the *ad hoc* committee.

EVALUATION OF UNITED NATIONS PROPOSALS

Any evaluation of United Nations proposals on terrorism should take into account the strikingly large margin by which the United States draft resolution was rejected by member states. It should also consider that the terms of Resolution 3034 (XXVII) could arguably be construed as a condonation rather than a condemnation of terrorism, at least under certain circumstances. Does the refusal of the great majority of United Nations members to adopt meaningful measures toward the prevention of individual acts of international terrorism in any way imply approval of the Munich killings, the murder of diplomats, the sending of letter bombs or the hijacking of aircraft? Viewed in its entirety, the context of the United Nations actions lends no support to such a conclusion.

In the view of this writer the timing of the United States initiative was most unfortunate and ensured its defeat. On September 6, the killing of Israeli Olympic competitors by Arab terrorists took place at Munich; on September 8, the Secretary-General, due in large part to the strong urging of the United States, requested that an international terrorism item be placed on the Assembly's agenda; and on September 25, Secretary of State Rogers introduced the United States draft convention and resolution to the Assembly. Not surprisingly, the Arab states regarded this scenario as a hostile United States-Israeli plot endangering their vital interests, and succeeded in convincing a number of states that the United States draft convention and resolution were directed against all liberation movements. Even many of those states who saw no such intent in the terms of the United States draft convention and resolution were unwilling to support proposals which the Arab states believed were directed sepcifically at them.*

True, the United States made valiant efforts to quiet these fears and objections, As we have seen, the terms of its draft convention are narrowly drawn so as to exclude from its coverage such controversial actions as fedayeen raids into Israel or Israeli response thereto. In their public statements United States representatives sought to assure member states that their draft convention and resolution were not directed toward national liberation movements or intended to affect the right to self-determination. But such reasoned responses were of no avail in the heated atmosphere engendered by the Munich killings and by the charges and countercharges passing between Israel and the Arab states.

Also, upon reflection one may perhaps view more kindly the action of the General Assembly in adopting Resolution 3034 (XXVII) . Although by this resolution the Assembly has not taken or even proposed any immediately effective measures to combat international terrorism, it has required the world community to focus its attention on this problem and on possible measures to-

*Ed's Note: Several Arab states voted favorably on that issue, notably Egypt.

ward its elimination. In accordance with the resolution, possible measures toward the elimination of international terrorism will be considered and debated by member states and by the *ad hoc* committee established by the resolution over the course of the year and will be before the Sixth Committee and the General Assembly next fall.

What, if any, meaningful measures might the Assembly adopt next fall? Some have questioned the feasibility of a convention in this area on the ground that the terrorist acts a convention might cover are already crimes under the domestic laws of most states, but these laws are often not enforced because of sympathy with the aims of the terrorists or because the terrorists work underground and cannot be apprehended. According to this view no legal measures will be passed or obeyed unless or until there exists a consensus as to what acts are to be regarded as illegitimate. It is also argued that conventions along the lines of the United States draft have little relevance to the real issues of terrorism which concern acts by or against armed forces.

In response it is contended that, although a convention will not solve all problems of terrorism, it would be a significant first step and could make a contribution toward the elimination of terrorism by denying sanctuaries to individuals who commit terrorist acts against innocent persons. As to acts of terrorism committed by or against armed forces, it is argued that these are covered by other conventions and by customary rules of international law.

There is a measure of truth in the arguments on both sides. Surely under the present atmosphere the probabilities of the General Assembly adopting a convention along the lines of the United States draft are nonexistent. However, the adoption of such a convention should be regarded not as a first step in combating international terrorism against innocent individuals, but as a later if not last step in the process. What is needed first are extended negotiations among all concerned parties as to precisely what acts of terrorism are to be regarded as illegitimate under all circumstances no matter what the underlying cause of the act may be.

A primary problem under present circumstances is that Arab

states are ambivalent about the legitimacy of actions such as the killings at Munich. Although they may deplore the loss of innocent life involved, their fervent support of the cause espoused by the terrorists, and their hatred of Israel, make them reluctant to prosecute the terrorists. Unless and until this attitude changes, no international convention on terrorism will be effective, even if adopted by many states, because a large area of sanctuary will remain.

What considerations, if any, might induce these Arab states to change their attitude? The anti-hijacking agreement concluded between Cuba and the United States on February 15, 1973 may give rise to some cause for optimism. Before and after conclusion of this agreement relations between the United States and Cuba were and have been exceedingly hostile with little prospect at this time for improvement. Nonetheless, one of the reasons for the successful conclusion of this agreement was that both states decided it was in their interest to take steps to prevent the hijacking of boats and aircraft by force in either country to escape to the other in order to protect innocent individuals from possible injury. This action was taken although each country had substantial sympathy with the underlying cause of the act, namely, the desire to escape from what each country regarded as an oppressive social system in the other. In this case the conclusion of the parties was that the end did not justify the means.

Similarly, the Arab states may eventually conclude that it is not in their interest to condone the killing of innocent civilians, the sending of letter bombs or the hijacking of aircraft in the name of the Palestinian cause. Such acts of terrorism are a two-way street, and recently the Arab states have been subjected to exploding letter bombs and murderous attacks on their diplomats. The incidence of such terrorist attacks against Arab citizens, diplomats and transportation systems may be expected to increase unless effective measures are taken against terrorism.

Assuming that a consensus may ultimately be reached on the need for such measures, might a convention along the lines of the United States draft be one of the measures adopted? On the whole the United States draft convention seems suited to the task, subject to certain revisions. Some possible revisions have been suggested briefly. Some other possible revisions will now be considered.

In view of the difficulties the world community has had in defining "terrorism" and the emotionalism engendered by United Nations debates on the subject, it might be desirable to delete any reference to terrorism from the United States draft convention. Indeed, in its present form, as we have seen, the convention contains no definition of terrorism, and the only references to the term are in its title and preambular provisions. The substantive, operative articles of the convention drop the term entirely, and refer instead to "offenses of international significance."

Deletion of any reference to terrorism might help to focus attention more sharply on the precise kinds of acts intended to be classified as international crimes by the convention and avoid diversion in United Nations debates into wide-ranging and emotional discussions of terrorism. Also to this end, reference might be made, either in the preamble or in article 1 of the convention, by way of illustration but not of limitation, to some specific examples of the kinds of acts intended to be covered by the convention. Thus, for example, there might be reference to attacks on third party diplomats, hijacking of aircraft and the sending of letter bombs.

In the same vein, the reference in the preamble of the convention to the duty of states to refrain from organizing or assisting in terrorist acts in another state might be deleted, in order to ensure that the convention would be interpreted as limited in its coverage to prevention and prosecution of *individual* acts defined thereunder as international crimes, and not directed toward alleged governmental derelictions in aiding and abetting such acts. Also, it will probably be necessary to include a provision in the convention along the lines of paragraph 3 of Resolution 3034 (XXVII) reaffirming the "inalienable right to self-determination and independence of all peoples under colonial and racist regimes and other forms of alien domination." Although from a strictly technical point of view such a provision may seem anomalous in a convention of this kind, it would appear necessary to allay the concern of some states that the convention might be cited to call into question the legitimacy of national liberation movements.

It might also be desirable to include some language in the preamble of the convention referring to other kinds of international crimes, including acts of terrorism, such as those arising out of war, and noting the importance of efforts being taken elsewhere to deal with them in order to eliminate any possible implication that the convention is based on a premise that these efforts should have a lower priority in terms of world order values than the goals set forth in the convention.

Pending conclusion of a convention along the lines of the United States draft, the United Nations might take other steps toward combating international terrorism. A first step might be adoption of a resolution urging ICAO to conclude as a matter of urgency a convention that would impose sanctions against non-signatory states that violated it.

The 28th session of the General Assembly should also consider and adopt as a matter of priority a convention along the lines of the Draft Articles on the Prevention and Punishment of Crimes against Diplomatic Agents and other Internationally Protected Persons, prepared by the International Law Commission. This would serve to broaden the protections afforded by the 1971 OAS Convention to Prevent and Punish the Acts of Terrorism Taking the Form of Crimes against Persons and Related Extortion that are of International Significance.

Lastly, the United Nations should continue and intensify its actions against other forms of terrorism, especially those committed by or against the armed forces of states. The prevention and elimination of all forms of terrorism is a matter of the highest urgency for the world community. Failure of the United Nations to perform this task with the utmost vigor would be incompatible with its primary purposes of maintaining international peace and security and "promoting and encouraging respect for human rights and for fundamental freedoms for all without distinction as to race, sex, language, or religion."

SECTION 5

CODIFICATION OF TERRORISM AS AN INTERNATIONAL CRIME

BRUCE PALMER

THERE IS A TYPE of criminal activity that transcends national boundaries, and in the suppression and punishment of which all states, members of the world community, have a communality of interest. This is the principle *aut dedere aut punire*.[1] The present demand for legal controls and possible solutions arising from the variety of terroristic activities experienced by the international community is not a new effort.[2] Such crimes indiscriminately threaten the life and property of individuals who are randomly injured. For these reasons it is advanced that terrorism also jeopardizes world public order and affects the broader interest of mankind.

Acts of terrorism are considered by many to constitute a crime of international significance while its authors and their supporters view the commission of such acts as heroic. Thus, "what is terrorism to some is heroism to others."[3] The question most often raised about terrorism is whether it is capable of definition? It is this writer's contention that "terrorism" is capable of definition if the acts encompassed within its meaning are specifically listed and de-

---

[1] The maxim of "aut dedere aut punire" is attributed to Hugo Grotius.

[2] *See* Convention for the Prevention and Punishment of Terrorism, concluded at Geneva under auspices of the League of Nations on November 16, 1937, League of Nations Document A.7. 1936 V. *See also* League of Nations, Records of the Seventh Ordinary Sessions of the Assembly. Plenary Meetings, p. 135; *see* for an exhaustive effort of the origins and actions taken to prevent terrorisms, a study prepared by the Secretariat, U.N. General Assembly, 27th Session, 6th Committee, Agenda Item 92; see A. Sottile, Le Terrorisms International, *Receuil des Cours de l'Academie de Droit International 5* (1939).

[3] Bassiouni, "Perspectives on Terrorism and Political Crimes," a 1973 Law Day Conference, April 25, 1973, The Globe vol. II-1.

fined in an objective manner, without distinctions as to the authors e.g. individuals, members of political groups, agents of a state. With this particular perspective, the difficulty in ascertaining a commonly acceptable juridical definition and hence legal solution will be avoided because it is the target which will be protected. It must be realized that there is a certain of minimum behavior that we do not want to go below, regardless of who is the perpetrator, and that certain interests of the international community must be protected. Thus, any individual acting on his own or for the benefit of a state may be held criminally accountable for the commission of the prohibited acts. Also, if an individual acts on behalf of a state, then on the basis of corporate responsibility principles, the state if found responsible is to be held equally accountable and sanctionable.

Prior to an analysis of the two different standards and criminal sanctions to be applied to the individual and to the state, it is necessary at this time to state the need and indispensibility of a supranational structure in the form of an international criminal court to handle such matters.

The decision of what type of structure is necessary to contain the crime of terrorism has been the source of great difficulty, and in the final analysis has presented itself as what the law is and what the law ought to be. If in fact we have seen the end of global warfare or the delimitation of such, then how are we to deal with these new types of activities that arise? De we draw on and look to existing law and structures that were not designed for dealing with this new type of activity we call terrorism, or do we create new laws and structures specifically designed to deal with these new activities. The latter of the two seems to be the most palatable answer, which in turn supports the idea of the creation of an International Criminal Court as the best structure and response to the type of crime we are dealing with, and accordingly all efforts must concentrate on the creation of such a tribunal.

The premise of this proposal, however, is that such a tribunal would have jurisdiction over the crime of terrorism.[4] The Interna-

---

[4] For an in depth analysis of this idea see J.Y. Dautricourt, "The International Criminal Court: The Concept of International Criminal Jurisdiction—Definition and Limitation of the Subject," in I Bassiouni and Nanda,, eds., *A Treatise on International Criminal Law,* (1973), p. 636.

tional Criminal Court shall take such measures as may be necessary to establish its judisdiction over the offense or any other act of violence committed by the alleged offender in connection with the offense. Offenders shall here be transported to the International Prison and to the custody of the International Criminal Court by the state whose territory the offender is in. The sanctions proposed are that the individual may be liable for criminal penalties while the state may be liable for reparations and damages.

In analyzing the crime of terrorism committed by the *individual* it should be noted at the outset that this author finds Article 1 of the United States Draft Convention for the Prevention and Punishment of Certain Acts of International Terrorism (see Appendix R, p. 557) and the four elements enunciated therein definitionally sufficient. (These are points a, b, c and d below.) Although I have many reservations regarding the rest of the United States Draft and the machinery enunciated therein, it appears that this article coupled with a conflict resolution scheme for interpretation purposes covers the crime of individual terrorism sufficiently. The United States Draft did not deal with the underlying causes or motivational forces of terrorism because it felt the compulsion to repress such acts immediately, which in many ways is politically naive. An *ad hoc* committee to study the problem was not established until April 26, 1973. Thus, for purposes of this framework, individual terrorism would be defined in the International Criminal Code as follows:

A person commits the crime of terrorism when that person unlawfully kills, causes serious bodily harm or kidnaps another person, attempts to commit any such act, or participates as an accomplice of a person who commits or attempts to commit any such act, if the act

(a) Is committed or takes effect outside the territory of a state of which the alleged offender is a national; and

(b) Is committed to take effect
 (i) outside the territory of the State against which the act is directed, or
 (ii) within the territory of the State against which the act is directed and the alleged offender knows or has reason to know that a person against whom the act is directed is not a national of the state; and

(c) Is committed neither by nor against a member of the armed forces of a State in the course of military hostilities; and

(d) Is intended to damage the interests of or obtain concessions from a State or an international organization.

Taken alone these elements are virtually worthless. It is envisioned here that the court must not only classify the act but determine the perpetrators motivation and the objectives sought to be attained.

The following guidelines are suggested: A classification scheme based upon the individual's motivation: the common criminal, the psychopathological offender, and the ideologically motivated offender.[5]

The *common criminal* is an individual who is socialized only in part, although he is quite reality-oriented and his awareness of social disapproval directs him towards avoidance of capture rather than toward the avoidance of society's disapproval. This individual shares socially approved goals, as the acquiring of material goods, etc., but he does not observe social prohibitions. This criminal often works with an accomplice and will have a preconceived plan.

The *psychopathological offender* is in effect an unsocialized individual. His behavior only serves to demonstrate that his values are exclusively personal. He does not relate to any society and his behavioral responses are motivated by purely idiosyncratic values. Accordingly, this offender is unable to find an accomplice who shares his values.

The third classification is that of the *ideologically motivated offender*. This participant is hypersocialized so that his values coincide with those of society; thus the individual and his society are virtually inseparable. He is reality-oriented like the common criminal but in a peculiar sense. It can be said that he has sacrificed his personality to society and if society is experiencing a fragmentation phrase, the incidence of ideologically motivated offenders can be expected to increase. A furthering of the goals of his group is totally equivalent to furthering his personal goals.

The next step in analysis of this proposed juridical standard is to ascertain the objectives sought to be attained by the participant.

---

[5]Bassiouni and Sewell, "The Psychology of Political Violence, an Attempted Definition and a Proposed Juridical Standard," paper presented to the American Society of Criminology and the Interamerican Association of Criminology, Caracas, Venezuela, November, 1972. Much of this analysis was taken from this work.

What are the strategies employed and his motivational forces?

The objectives of the common criminal engaging in an act of terrorism is usually directed toward a specific target and specific means and strategies are employed, generally economical and for self-aggrandizement. The psychopathological offender lacks identification with any group and his behavior influences political only incidentally, its essential motivation being personal not political. In contradistinction, the identification of the ideologically motivated offender with his specified group is excessive. His behavior is intrinsically political and its motivation is directed toward the destruction of institutionalized social values.

These three classifications of offenders through their terroristic acts cause major concern for international law and offend contemporary community standards by perpetrating a private wrong as a means of creating a public wrong. Therefore terroristic activities may be clearly criminal but the *motivation* may or may nor be political. It is envisioned as the duty of the International Criminal Court to decide in which category the offender falls and then to determine his motivational force. This determination requires a standard and guidelines against which the terroristic activities may be weighed.[6]

If the motivation is determined to be ideological, the offender is at this point in time given the right to establish a claim of self defense or ideological self defense. Prior to an analysis of the right of ideological self preservation, it should be noted that there are certain cases where the resort to what is called "terrorism," and the behavior incident thereto, can be exonerated. Such instances should not be limited to the refusal of the right of self determination and situations which give rise to the constant and systematic violations of the rights of man.

As the acts entailed in the four elements of the first article in the United States Draft and the crime of terrorism as defined here are in reality responses to prior oppression, then certain individuals or groups have the right of resistance to oppression as is repeated

---

[6]These classifications and analyses following were first created by Professor M. Cherif Bassiouni, 19 *DePaul L Rev*, 217 (1969). It was designed primarily for application of the political offense exception, however, it can be expanded to be equally applicable to the crime of terrorism as defined herein.

in the preamble to the Universal Declaration of Human Rights.

Since the terrorist threatens minimum world public order and the very existence of the political establishment, he is at this point given the right to establish a claim of ideological self-defense or individual self-preservation. Just as municipal law recognizes the right of the individual to defend himself against threats of physical safety and to the preservation of his property, the terrorist must offer and substantiate a claim of ideological self-defense.[7]

A substantiation of a claim of self-defense stands as exoneration of behavior which in other circumstances would be judged criminal. The offender must establish the existence and nature of the rights which have been violated; next he must establish that these rights were indeed violated; and finally, he must establish that his behavior constituted an attempt to re-establish these rights or to redress grievance occasioned by violation of these rights. The following factors and analysis were enunciated by Professor M. Cherif Bassiouni (19 DePaul L. Rev. 217, 1969)* designed primarily for the application of the political offense exception but can be expanded to be equally applicable to the crime of terrorism.

1. Factors bearing on the nature of the rights which have been violated and which violation thereupon gives rights to defend the violated rights include (a) the nature of the rights and their sources; (b) the extent to which those rights are necessary to the survival or basic values of the people possessing them; (c) the historical and traditional existence of those rights and the degree of their availability and enjoyment by the people; (d) the extent of the people's reliance upon those rights in relation to their implantation in the social psychology as necessary, indispensible, or fundamental to the way of life; (e) the duration of their abridgement and, if sporadic, its recurrence; (f) the potential or foreseeable voluntary termination of the transgression of those rights; (g) the existence and reasonable availability of remedies to the alleged transgressions. These factors can, in general, be objectively ascertained.

2. Factors bearing upon the conduct of the nation-state which was

---

[7]*Ibid.*
*See also Chapter V, Section 3.

allegedly violative of these fundamental rights include (a) the nature of the transgression, abridgment, violation, termination, subversion, or abolition of the right or rights claimed; (b) the quantitative and qualitative character of the violations; (c) the manner in which rights were violated, the extent of the violation, the means used to accomplish the violation, the duration of the violation, and the frequency of its recurrence; (d) an explicit or implicit intention to continue these violations or to terminate them within a declared or foreseeable future; (e) whether these violations were conditioned, caused, prompted, or forced by conditions of necessity such as natural catastrophe, disaster, war, or insurrection; (f) available methods and means of redress or remedy; (g) repressive actions taken against those who have claimed grievance and have pursued legal channels of remedy in the prescribed manner or who have challenged the offensive public conduct in a manner deemed lawful by the common standards of the ordinary times of that nation. These factors, too, generally lend themselves to objective inquiry.

3. Factors bearing upon the conduct of the individual who has violated the crime of terrorism and now claims ideological self-preservation include (a) exhaustion of all available remedies, local and international, saving risks of repression; (b) the explicit or implicit understanding in the ordinary reasonable man of the nation-state in question that no redress was available in the reasonably foreseeable future and that such conduct was, if not warranted, at least excusable because no other alternative existed; (c) the proportionately or commensurateness of the conduct with the nature of the rights violated in terms of their objective significance in the common understanding of the ordinary reasonable man of the nation-state in question; (d) whether the conduct was related to the original wrong in only a negative or vengeful way or whether it was also intended to terminate or redress the wrong in a positive manner; (e) whether the means used were limited to achieve these purposes and there was no violation committed which was not necessitated by the attainment of these purposes through the least harmful manner; (f) whether the assumption of any risks created would fall on the individual perpetrator and whether the

means and tactics used would not endanger innocent persons. To some extent these factors require subjective evaluation, but of a degree hardly in excess of that customarily employed in the adjudication of a claim of self-defense in common criminal proceedings.

With the classification of offenders and the proposed juridical standard of ideological self-defense, and the guidelines for its application and interpretation, the individual can be held accountable in international criminal law, impartially and in conjunction with the requirements of international due process of law.

While on the one hand this treatment of individual terrorism offers an inducement to its participants, on the other it offers deterrence by penal sanctions. Sanctions against members of a group may deter such a group. I say "may," because with indirect deterrence we only see the deterrence, and not what means deterred it. It is possible that this scheme of criminally treating individual terrorists may result in potential terrorists accepting to be bound by certain minimum standards of behavior in their acts.

As individual responsibility may be assessed for the commission of terroristic activities (as previously defined) and penal sanctions may be imposed so that the individual offender may be liable to criminal penalties assessed by the International Criminal Court, so too may the state be held accountable before this tribunal for the commission of the crime of state terrorism.

Thus we have two standards for the crime of terrorism; one applicable to individuals who may be liable for criminal penalties and the second applicable to states which may be held liable and forced to pay reparations or punitive damages.

The question then remains that if there is such a concept as institutionalized terror, then what certain acts of the state could be considered terrorism? Acts of state which could be considered terrorism are covered by the humanitarian and customary laws of armed conflict. Thus it is apparent that in this context there are two types of acts of state: first are those acts specifically prohibited by the Hague and Geneva Conventions of 1949 and the second are those other acts committed outside of these conventions.

Activities of the first category would be grave breaches of these conventions, crimes against prisoners or against civilians. These acts of states are specifically controlled in international law by these conventions.

The second category includes those acts which are not codified in or controlled by the customary or conventional laws of armed conflict. It is these acts that may be labeled as crimes of state terrorism and the commission thereof transcends national borders in that they are crimes of international significance which need be specifically prescribed under the jurisdiction of the International Criminal Court. The following are examples of states going beyond the legality of their own system.

These acts outside of The Hague and Geneva Conventions would include, but are not limited to, assassination, espionage, sabotage, and kidnapping; examples include the Eichman incident, unlawful seizure of persons whether by and through the immigration process, police cooperation or by agents of states seizing persons.

While it may be laudable to prosecute decision makers and heads of State, although it may not reach the heart of the problem, it is unlikely that this will take place. Thus the alternative would be punitive damages and reparations imposed upon the state for institutionalized terrorism. The court being a permanent tribunal, not an ad hoc tribunal established at the end of hostilities, is better able to deal with those activities falling outside of the conventions, thereby eliminating the possibility of victors' justice and providing for an impartial and neutral trial.

Why should these acts fall under immunity? It cannot be disputed that they produce the same means and results as individual terrorism. Thus, referring back to my original theme, we must define and treat terrorism regardless of its perpetrators.

There are many reasons for dealing with acts of state terrorism as proposed here. Judgment of these acts by a permanent International Criminal Court will through negative judgment stigmatize terroristic acts of states as reprehensible. World public opinion as well as local public opinion will strengthen international and internal reaction as a means of restraining such governments which would otherwise engage in such acts if they felt no other external and internal restraints.

Another reason in support of this method is that through adjudication, a remedy is provided for victimized individuals and their families. This would be handled the same way as victim compensation is handled on the municipal level, coupled with a punitive damage element as an economic deterrent.

It should also be realized that the adjudication of such claims provides finality in what would otherwise be an escalating process of reprisals and counter reprisals. It is common knowledge that the idea of imputing criminal responsibility to a state under the auspices of the International Criminal Court was not envisioned in the 1953 or 1954 United Nations Draft Statutes or In the Wingspread or Bellagio conference resolutions. The states could be held criminally responsible for institutionalized acts of terrorism is a stumbling block to the creation of the court. States should be parties to an international criminal tribunal, especially if it is given jurisdiction over terrorism. Compliance in the meantime will have to remain voluntary, but voluntary compliance is the enunciation of an important principle which will not be compulsorily complied with until the international community is ready for the implementation stage.

PROPOSED DRAFT CODE

ARTICLE I

A person commits the crime of terrorism when that person unlawfully kills, causes serious bodily harm or kidnaps another person, attempts to commit any such act, or participates as an accomplice of a person who commits or attempts to commit any such act, if the act

(a) Is committed or takes effect outside the territory of a State of which the alleged offender is a national; and

(b) Is committed or takes effect
  (i) outside the territory of the State against which the act is directed, or
  (ii) within the territory of the State against which the act is directed and the alleged offender knows or has reason to

know that a person against whom the act is directed is not a national of that State; and

(c) Is committed neither by nor against a member of the armed forces of a State in the course of military hostilities; and

(d) Is intended to damage the interests of or obtain concessions from a State or an international organization.

ARTICLE 2

The crime of terrorism shall be punishable by no less and no more than ⸻ and a fine of ⸻.

ARTICLE 3

1. The International Criminal Court shall take such measures as may be necessary to establish its jurisdiction over the offense or any other act of violence committed by the alleged offender in connection with the offense.

2. Offenders shall be transported to the International Prison and to the custody of the International Criminal Court by the state whose territory the offender is in.

ARTICLE 4

A state in which one or more of the offenses set forth in Article 1 have been committed shall, if it has reason to believe an alleged offender has fled from its territory, communicate to all other states and to Interpol, all the pertinent facts regarding the offense committed, and all available information regarding the identity of the alleged offender.

ARTICLE 5

Aircraft hijacking is an offense that will be considered a crime of terrorism. As enunciated in the Hague Convention for the suppression of unlawful seizure of aircraft, a person commits that offense when that person who on board an aircraft in flight:

1) unlawfully, by force or threat thereof, or by another form of intimidation, seizes, or exercises control of, that aircraft, or attempts to perform any such act, or

2) is an accomplice of a person who performs or attempts to perform such an act.

ARTICLE 6

For the purposes of this section, an aircraft is considered to be in flight at any time from the moment when all its external doors are closed following embarcation until the moment when any such door is opened for disembarcation. In case of a forced landing, the flight shall be deemed to continue until the competent authorities take over the responsibility for the aircraft and for persons and property on board.

ARTICLE 7

Kidnapping or any other offense against the life, the person, or the freedom of a foreign diplomatic or consular agent who enjoys inviolability under international law, or to whom the state has a duty to extend special protection, or a member of the family of such a person protected by that prerogative will be considered a crime of terrorism (see O.A.S., 3d Special Session, O.A.S./Off. Rec. /Ser. P./A.G./Doc. 68, Jan. 13, 1971, signed Rio de Janeiro September 26, 1970).

THE CREATION OF AN INTERNATIONAL CRIMINAL COURT

L. Kos-Rabcewicz Zubkowski

AN INTERNATIONAL CRIMINAL COURT IN THE TWENTIETH CENTURY

ATTEMPTS TO ESTABLISH an International Criminal Court already have a relatively long history, reflected in the abundant literature.[1] This chapter highlights the efforts that have been

[1]See in Historical Survey of the Question of International Criminal Jurisdiction. United Nations Publications. Sales No.: 1949, V. 8. Doc. A/CN.4/7/Rev. I, p. 2, 7, 8; 1-2 Revue Internationale de Droit Pénal 1964, articles by J. Graven, P.S. Romashkin, J.-B. Herzog, B.V.A. Roling, H.-H. Jescheck, A. Quintano Ripolles, G.O.W. Mueller, F.J. Klein, and D. Wilkes, J.-Y. Dautricourt and St. Glaser, Towards a Feasible International Criminal Court, ed. by J. Stone, and R.K. Woetzel, World Peace Through Law Center, Geneva, 1970: contributions by R.A. Bloom, A. Gastmann, J. Graven, R.-L. Perret, E.C. Schneider, J. Stone, Y. Takano, R.K. Woetzel, H. Wood and B.A. Wortley; Besides the Survey already mentioned, there are two reports submitted by special rapporteurs to the U.N. International Law Commission: Ricardo J. Alfaro, Doc. A/CN4/15, 1950 II Yearbook of the International Law Commission, pp. 1-18, and Emil Sandstrom, Doc. A/CN4/20, ib. pp. 18-23. The Revue internationale de droit pénal devoted its vol. 35 of 1964 to "Les projects des Nations Unies pour l'institution d'une Justice Pénale Internationale." See also F.J. Kein, and D. Wilkes, "United Nations Draft Statute for an International Criminal Court; An American Evaluation" in International Criminal Law, G.O.W. Mueller and L.M. Wise ed., 1965, pp. 566-583 and bibliography pp. 586-587. J.W. Bridge, "The Case for an International Court of Criminal Justice and the Formulation of International Criminal Law," in The International and Comparative Law Quarterly, 1964, pp. 1255-1281. G. Levasseur, The Prevention of Genocide, VIII Journal of the International Commission of Jurists, December 1967, pp. 74-82. P.M. Carjeu, Projet d'une juridiction pénale internationale, 1953, S. Glaser, Droit international pénal conventionnel, 1970. H.-H. Jescheck, Die Entwicklung des Volkerstrafrecnts nach Nurnberg, Sohw. Z. f. St.R., 72, Jahrg. 1957, 217-248. R.K. Woetzel, The Nuremberg Trials in International Law, 1962. J.A. Appleman, Military Tribunals and International Crimes, 1954. B.V.A. Roling, The United Nations and the Development of International Criminal Law. The

made towards the establishment of an international criminal court.[2]

As early at 1937 twenty-four states signed a convention for the prevention and punishment of terrorism[3] and thirteen states signed a convention for the creation of an international criminal court.[4] Those conventions, however, were never entered into force, due partly to the approaching world conflict of 1939.

Two international criminal courts were established after World War II: the International Military Tribunal for the trial of major war criminals at Nuremberg[5] and the International Military Tribunal for the Far East.[6]

In 1950 the General Assembly of the United Nations appointed a Committee on International Criminal Jurisdiction[7] which submitted a draft statute for an International Criminal Court.[8] In 1953, a new committee[9] produced a revised draft statute.[10] Developments stopped at this point because of the decision of the General Assembly to postpone this matter until after its decision on the report of the "defining of aggression."[11]

United Nations—Ten Years' Legal Progress, 1956, 61-91. G. Hoffman, *Strafrechtliche Verantwortung im Volkerrecht*, 1962. Eustathiades, "La Cour Pénale Internationale pour la Répression du Terrorisme et le Problè, e de la Responsabilité Internationale des Etats," in *Rev Gén de Droit International Public*, 1936, p. 385.

[2]L. Kos-Rabcewicz-Zubkowski, "Towards a Feasible International Criminal Court" paper submitted to the 1971 World Conference on World Peace Through Law, Belgrade, July 21-25, 1971; 5 *World Law Review*, 1972, pp. 392-398.

[3]League of Nations, c.546(1). M. 383(1), 1937, V.

[4]League of Nations, c.547(1). M 384(1), 1937, V.

[5]Trial of the Major War Criminals before the International Military Tribunal, Nuremberg, November 14, 1945—October 1, 1946, 42 volumes, published by the Secretariat, of the Tribunal, under the jurisdiction of the Allied Central Authority for Germany.

[6]S. Horowitz, "The Tokyo Trial 465 *International Conciliation*," (1950).

[7]Resolution 489 (v), December 12, 1950.

[8]Report of the Committee on International Criminal Jurisdiction on its session held from August 1 to 31, 1951, Official Records, Seventh Session, Supp. No. 11, A/2136, pp. 21-25.

[9]Resolution 687 (VII) of December 5, 1952.

[10]United Nations, Report of the 1953 Committee on International Criminal Jurisdiction, 27 July-20 August 1953. General Assembly: Ninth Session, Supplement No. 12 (A/2645), New York, 1954.

[11]Last resolution in this matter was in 1957: Resolution 1187 (XII).

WORLD PEACE THROUGH LAW CENTER

The 1971 Belgrade World Conference on World Peace Through Law, organized by the World Peace Through Law Center, chose to devote one of its ten working sessions to the subject "Towards a feasible international criminal court." Professor M. Cherif Bassiouni, DePaul University, Chicago, summed up the recommendations of the International Criminal Court Committee at that conference.

The Committee recommended that the issue of defining aggression be differentiated from the continuing work of the Committee on a Court of International Jurisdiction to facilitate its preparation of a draft statute for that court. In encouraged scholars, professional associations and other interested groups to pursue their efforts for the creation of an International Criminal Court and proposed that those charged with creating the International Criminal Court study the resolution of international conflicts of criminal jurisdiction, wherein said Court would be granted jurisdiction over special environments wherein no state can claim territorial jurisdiction and states be permitted to choose that international forum as an alternative to other available forums.[12]

These recommendations were essentially incorporated into Resolution 27 of the Belgrade World Conference. This resolution stated, *inter alia,* that consideration be given in the creation of such an International Criminal Court to:

a. the resolution of international conflicts of criminal jurisdiction;

b. granting the Court jurisdiction over special environments wherein no state can claim territorial jurisdiction; and

c. furnishing states the choice of that forum as an alternative to other forums.[13]

FOUNDATION FOR THE ESTABLISHMENT OF THE INTERNATIONAL CRIMINAL COURT

As a result of the 1971 and 1972 Wingspread-Bellagio Conferences, sponsored by the Foundation for the Establishment of

---

[12]5 *World Law Review,* 1972, p. 399.
[13]5*World Law Review,* 1972, p. 659.

an International Criminal Court and chaired by Professor Robert K. Woetzel, a Draft Convention on International Crimes and a Draft Statute for an International Criminal Court were drawn up.[14]

Draft Convention on International Crimes

The Draft Convention on International Crimes is a relatively short document of 10 articles; it lists offences to be punished under international law, whether or not they constitute crimes under national law.[15] However, any state ratifying the Convention may limit its obligations as to certain of those offences.[16]

The draft convention uses two methods in its description of crimes. It incorporates the definitions already in existence in international agreements[17] and it writes its own descriptions of other offences.[18] The first category contains the following acts specified by international agreements:

a) crimes against peace as they are defined in the Charter of the International Military Tribunal for the Trial of the Major War Criminals of 1945;

b) war crimes as they are defined in the Charter of the International Military Tribunal for the Trial of the Major War Criminals of 1945;

c) acts subject to criminal sanctions under the Geneva conventions of 1949;

d) crimes against humanity as they are defined in the Charter of the International Military Tribunal for the Trial of the Major War Criminals of 1945;

e) genocide as defined in the Convention on the Prevention and Punishment of the Crime of Genocide of 1948;

f) slavery, slave trade and related practices as provided for in the Slavery Convention of 1926, the Protocol of 1953, and the

---

[14]See Robert K. Woetzel, "The Establishment of an International Criminal Court, a Report on the First and Second International Criminal Law Conferences, and Commentary."
[15]Art. 1.
[16]Art. 3(1).
[17]Art. 3(2).
[18]Art. 3(3).

Supplementary Convention of 1956;

g) piracy as defined in the Convention on the High Seas of 1958;

h) hijacking and related offences as they are defined in the Convention for the Suppression of Unlawful Seizure of Aircraft of 1970 and the Convention for the Suppression of Unlawful Acts against the Safety of Civil Aviation of 1971;

i) international traffic in drugs and other acts subject to criminal sanctions under the Single Convention on Narcotic Drugs of 1961 and the Amending Protocol of 1972.[19]

The group of acts described in the convention includes:

a) the planning, preparation, initiation or waging of a war of aggression;

b) war crimes, being violations of the laws and customs of war committed in armed conflicts of an international or noninternational character;

c) crimes against humanity, being (i) genocide, (ii) mass murder, extermination, enslavement, deportation and other inhumane acts committed against any civilian population, (iii) persecutions on political, racial, religious or cultural grounds;

d) slavery, slave trade and related practices;

e) piracy;

f) unlawful seizure of aircraft or unlawful acts against the safety of civil aviation;

g) unlawful kidnapping for political, racial or religious reasons and taking across a national frontier a person engaged in governmental or public activities;

h) acts of violence directed against persons who enjoy protection under international law in respect of their functions or office;

i) international acts of terrorism, being criminal acts intended or calculated to create a state of terror in the minds of particular persons, or a group of persons or the general public;

j) international traffic in drugs made illicit by international law;

k) international pollution or spoliation of the environment

---

[19]Art. 3(2).

causing substantial harm to the health, safety and welfare of mankind.[20]

Complicity in or culpable failure to prevent the commission of any of these offences, as well as attempts to commit any of them, may also be among the international crimes included in ratifications.[21]

Draft Statute for an International Criminal Court

Organization of the Court

The Wingspread Draft Statute for an International Criminal Court is a detailed document. The jurisdiction of the International Criminal Court is limited to natural persons; this corresponds to the provisions of the 1953 United Nations draft.[22] Consequently states as well as other juridical persons are not envisaged as criminal defendants before the International Criminal Court. This attitude appears justified because the possibility of enforcing the sanctions against states and other judicial persons is remote.

Applicable law is described as international law, including international criminal law and, where appropriate, national law,[23] which wording reproduces article 2 of the United Nations draft.

Chapter II of the Wingspread Draft deals mainly with judges.[24] States party to the statute may nominate not more than four candidates, of whom no more than two may be from among their own nationals. This provision of the Wingspread Draft is an attempt to introduce an international aspect even in nominations, although a state is entitled to nominate one or two national candidates while abstaining from nominating others.[25] Apart from this,

---

[20]Art. 3(3).

[21]Art. 3(4).

[22]Art. 1, Draft Statute for an International Criminal Court, Report of the 1953 Committee on International Criminal Jurisdiction, General Assembly Official Records, IX, Supp. 12 (A/2645) 23-26 (1954), repr. in G.O.W. Mueller and E.M. Wise, eds. *International Criminal Law*, 1965, p.513 ss.

[23]Art. 2, Wingspread Draft.

[24]Arts. 3 to 14.

[25]Art. 4 (2).

the provisions regarding judges are similar to those of the United Nations Draft.

No significant changes to the United Nations Draft concerning the competence of the International Criminal Court were suggested by the Wingspread conference.

Instead of following articles 33 and 34 of the United Nations Draft on the Committing Chamber and the Prosecuting Attorney, the Wingspread conferees suggested other provisions concerning prosecution, the procurator, the commission of inquiry and the public defender. Article 16 of the Wingspread Draft, entitled "Subsidiary organs of the Court," states: "To aid the Court in the performance of its functions the following organs are established: 1. Procurator; 2. Public Defender; 3. Commission of Inquiry; 4. Prosecution; 5. Board of Clemency and Parole."

Procedure

The procedure suggested by the Wingspread Conference was aimed at the establishment of a pretrial fact-finding body and the elimination of frivolous complaints.

INITIATION OF PROCEEDINGS. When a complaint is handed over to one of the prosecutors, after ascertaining that sufficient facts warrant the issuance of an official complaint, he shall prepare a complaint upon the basis of which all further proceedings before the Commission of Inquiry shall be conducted.[26] A complaint, therefore, becomes "official" only when it is issued by a prosecutor. This wording seems to indicate that a prosecutor may consider that there are no "sufficient facts warranting the issuance of an official complaint" and refuse to prepare a complaint for submission to the Commission of Inquiry. No recourse against such a decision is provided by the Draft. It is suggested here that access to the Commission of Inquiry should not be barred by a prosecutor's decision. The Commission of Inquiry should act 1) either on its own initiative, or 2) upon a complaint by a prosecutor, whether on the latter's own initiative or following a complaint submitted to the Prosecution Office or 3) upon a private complaint.

---

[26]Art. 28(4), Wingspread Draft.

Besides prosecutors, the Wingspread Draft also creates a procurator who shall serve as the general administrative superior and coordinator of all prosecutors. We shall present to the Court cases that have been certified for trial by the Commission of Inquiry.[27] This official is essentially a prosecutor; the title Chief Prosecutor or Director of Prosecution would seem to be more appropriate than Procurator.

INVESTIGATION BY THE PROSECUTION. In consequence of a complaint or upon its own initiative the prosecution may initiate proceedings and conduct investigation with a view toward an exhaustive ascertainment of all the facts.[28]

OFFICIAL COMPLAINT. Upon ascertaining sufficient facts, the prosecution issues an official complaint and submits this to the Commission of Inquiry.[29] Should the prosecution reject a private complaint, it is proposed that the complainant should be free to submit his complaint directly to the Commission of Inquiry.

NOTIFICATION. Once the official complaint is issued, the prosecution shall notify all parties to the proceedings of such a complaint.[30] The private complainant whose complaint has been espoused by the prosecution should also be notified.

INQUIRY. Several Wingspread conferees felt that the purpose of the inquiry is the search for material truth. The prosecutor must participate in the inquiry as it may result in a case being referred for prosecution before the court.[31] The accused has the right to testify at the inquiry and produce evidence on his own behalf;[32] he also has the right to be represented by counsel before the Commission. In the event that the accused chooses not to designate counsel the public defender will present facts and arguments in his defense and act as his counsel.[33]

DECISIONS OF THE COMMISSION OF INQUIRY. The Commission of Inquiry evaluates the evidence;[34] it may remit the case to the

---

[27]Art. 29, Wingspread Draft.
[28]Art. 28(1), Wingspread Draft.
[29]Art. 28(4), Wingspread Draft.
[30]Art. 28(4), Wingspread Draft.
[31]Art. 28(5), Wingspread Draft.
[32]Art. 30(2), Wingspread Draft.
[33]Art. 30(3), & 31, Wingspread Draft.
[34]Art. 30(1), Wingspread Draft.

prosecution with or without specific instructions for further investigation.[35] If the evidence is complete in the opinion of the Commission it shall make one of the following decisions:

    a) dismiss the complaint;

    b) draft an indictment and certify the case for trial, taking into account in the preparation of the indictment the complaint prepared by the prosecution;

    c) make other arrangements for the disposition of the case, if the interests of international justice are served thereby and if the accused and the Prosecution accept them. The method of disposition shall be submitted to the court for final approval.[36]

COMPOSITION OF THE COMMISSION OF INQUIRY. The Wingspread Draft does not describe the composition of the Commission of Inquiry, yet this matter is important; the Commission must handle all complaints initially, whether or not any of them will be referred for trial. The United Nation Draft provides that judges shall sit in an analogous body, called the Committing Chamber.[37] It is here proposed that provisions relating to judges should apply *mutatis mutandis* to Commissioners of Inquiry.

TRIAL PROCEEDINGS. The Wingspread Draft chapter V on trial proceedings[38] makes no significant changes from those in the United Nations Draft.[39]

As to the rights of the accused, the Wingspread Draft does not reproduce the right of the accused to have reasonable expenses of his defence charged to a special fund if the Court is satisfied that he is unable to engage the services of counsel.[40] This means that under the Wingspread Draft an accused without sufficient means cannot have an attorney of his choice paid from public funds, but must rely on the Public Defender.

BOARD OF CLEMENCY AND PAROLE. The Wingspread Draft does not describe the composition and election of the Board of Clemency and Parole.[41] It is here suggested that members of the Board

---

[35]Art. 28(1)(b) Wingspread Draft.
[36]Art. 30(1)(a)(c)(d), Wingspread Draft.
[37]Art. 33, United Nations Draft.
[38]Arts. 32 to 48, Wingspread Draft.
[39]Arts. 35 to 52, United Nations Draft.
[40]Art. 38 (2)(c), United Nations Draft.
[41]Art. 48, Wingspread Draft.

of Clemency and Parole should be elected in the same manner as the judges.

REGIONALIZATION. The Wingspread Draft emerged from three short conferences and notwithstanding the high qualifications of the conferees could not be completed in detail due to the lack of time.

Several Wingspread conferees emphasized the importance of a geographically easy access to the International Criminal Court, especially to the Commission of Inquiry. Opinions were advanced that investigating magistrates should be able to act until they ascertained the necessity of bringing a complainant before the Commission of Inquiry; such magistrates should have their permanent offices in major cities of important geographical regions, e.g. one in Latin America, another in Africa, etc. However, the majority felt that the addition of a hearing before an Investigating Magistrate would result in an exceedingly cumbersome structure for the International Criminal Court. The Wingspread Draft leaves the question of the location of the Court, Commission of Inquiry, Prosecution, Public Defender and the Board of Clemency and Parole open. The states party to the Statute of the International Criminal Court shall determine the seat of the Court and the location of its subsidiary organs, provided, that the Court or its subsidiary organs sit and exercise their functions in other locations whenever this is considered desirable in the interests of the sound administration of justice.[42]

Nonexclusive Jurisdiction

The Wingspread Draft repeats the provisions of the United Nations Draft that the International Criminal Court has no exclusive jurisdiction.[43]

Attorney for the Complainant

Attorney for the complainant could be admitted as a party to the proceedings, in addition to the prosecutor. This seems especially important at the stage before the Commission of Inquiry.

---

[42]Art. 17, Wingspread Draft.
[43]Art. 49, Wingspread Draft; Art. 54, United Nations Draft.

POLITICAL CRIMES, TERRORISM AND
INTERNATIONAL ADMINISTRATION OF JUSTICE*

It is suggested here that acts of international terrorism, whether committed for political or nonpolitical reasons, should be subject to the jurisdiction of the International Criminal Court.

The Inter-American Human Rights Commission condemned in 1970 acts of political terrorism and urban and rural guerrilla warfare which cause serious damage to an individual's right to life, security, physical freedom, freedom of conscience, opinion and the right of self-defence, said rights confirmed by the American Declaration on Human Rights and Duties. The Commission declared that political or ideological motivations do not change the character of these acts as serious violation of human rights and fundamental freedoms, and cannot free their perpetrators from accountability. The subject "Terrorism with political or ideological aims as a source of violation of human rights" is included in the program of studies of the Commission.[44]

The General Assembly of the Organization of American States condemned in 1970 acts of terrorism, especially kidnapping and extortion of ransom as crimes against humanity and serious offences of general penal law.[45]

The Inter-American Convention to Prevent and Punish the Acts of Terrorism taking the Form of Crimes against Persons and Related Extortion that are of International Significance, signed at the Third Special Session of the General Assembly of the Organization of American States on February 2, 1971, refers in its preamble to the resolution of June 30, 1970.[46] The convention states that for its purposes kidnapping, murder and other assaults against the life or personal integrity of those persons to whom the state has the duty to give special protection according to inter-

---

*See Chapter V.

[44]Resolution adopted on April 16, 1970, Ninth Session, Inter-American Human Rights Commission, Organization of American States, OAS ser. L/V & /II, 23, Doc. 19, Rev. 1.

[45]Resolution of the General Asssembly of the Organization of American States of June 30, 1970, Doc. AG/RES. 4 (I-E/70), Rev. 1.

[46]Organization of American States Treaty Series, No. 37. Organization of American States Doc. OEA/Ser.A/17 (SEFP).

national law, as well as extortion in connection with those crimes shall be considered common crimes of international significance, regardless of motive.[47]

This convention does not provide for submissions to an international criminal tribunal.

The Wingspread Draft mentions only international acts of terrorism without describing the meaning of the qualification "international."[48] Criminal acts, presumably according to either international law or national law,[49] intended or calculated to create a state of terror in the minds of particular persons, or groups of persons, or the general public, are considered as acts of terrorism by the Wingspread Draft convention on international crimes. This wording resembles the definition in the 1937 League of Nations Convention for the Prevention and Punishment of Terrorism.[50] The 1937 Convention dealt with criminal acts directed against a state but included:

(1) any wilful act causing death or grievous bodily harm or loss of liberty to:
   (a) heads of states, persons exercising the prerogatives of a head of state, their hereditary or designated successors;
   (b) the wives or husbands of the above-mentioned persons;
   (c) persons charged with public functions or holding public position when the act is directed against them in their public capacity.

(2) wilful destruction of, or damage to, public property or property devoted to public purpose which belongs to or is subject to the authority of another high contracting party;

(3) any wilful act calculated to endanger the lives of members of the public;

(4) any attempt to commit an offence falling within the foregoing provisions of the present article;

(5) the manufacturing, obtaining, possessing, or supplying of arms, ammunition, explosives or harmful substances with

---

[47]Art. 2.
[48]Art. 3(3)(i), Wingspread Draft Convention of International Crimes.
[49]Art. 2, Wingspread Draft of the Statute of the International Criminal Court.
[50]Art. 1.

a view to the commission in any country whatsoever of an offence falling within the present article.[51]

Political crimes which are not "acts of terrorism" and have no international character should not be subject to an international administration of justice.

UNITED STATES DRAFT CONVENTION FOR THE PREVENTION AND PUNISHMENT OF CERTAIN ACTS OF INTERNATIONAL TERRORISM*

The 1972 United States Draft Convention for the Prevention and Punishment of certain Acts of International Terrorism[52] discussed in the Sixth Committee of the General Assembly of the United Nations does not contemplate the jurisdiction of an international criminal court. It does not exclude, however, "any criminal jurisdiction exercised in accordance with national law,"[53] and a corresponding national law may probably provide for the jurisdiction of an international criminal Court. This draft convention creates only a Conciliation Commission to which a state may refer a dispute between states party to the convention, arising out of the application or interpretation of the Convention.[54]

RATIFICATION AND RESERVATIONS

Ratification should include reservations excluding an international undertaking as to the submission of certain crimes to the International Criminal Court. It is to be hoped that states will gradually broaden their respective submissions.

The right of choice of forum, either the forum of the International Criminal Court or another forum, by a state party to the Statute of the International Criminal Court could be allowed by way of reservation.[55]

---

[51]Art. 2.

*See Appendix R.

[52]United Nations A/C. 6/L.850, 25 September 1972.

[53]Art. 4(3).

[54]Art. 16.

[55]"Resolution 27(2)(c) of the 1971 Belgrade World Conference on World Peace Through Law," 5 *World Law Review*, p. 659.

THE INTERNATIONAL CRIMINAL COURT AND THE INTERNATIONAL COURT OF JUSTICE

It does not appear practical to extend the jurisdiction of the International Court of Justice to cover international criminal cases of natural persons.

It is unlikely that a sufficient majority could be obtained in the United Nations Organization to modify the Statute of the International Court of Justice. The International Court of Justice should continue to try disputes between states.

SOME PROBLEMS REQUIRING CONSIDERATION

All present drafts fail to elaborate several important provisions. This study refers to some of the corresponding problems. Some points necessitating further consideration are here listed:

A. provisions regarding prosecution and prosecutors;

B. admissions of attorneys for the complainant;

C. election of commissioners, their qualifications, and structure of the Commission of Inquiry;

D. access to the Commission of Inquiry; it is suggested that the prosecutors refusal to submit a complaint to the Commission of Inquiry should be subject to appeal to the Commission;

E. qualifications and election of the Members of the Board of Clemency and Parole;

F. enforcement of decisions of the International Criminal Court;

G. possibility to entrust the parole and probation supervision to national authorities (see the 1964 European Convention on the Supervision of Conditionally Sentenced or Conditionally Released Offenders) ;

H. reasonable expenses of the defence to be covered from a special fund, raising the possibility that an impecunious defendant could choose his attorney and not necessarily rely on the Public Defender;

I. regional offices of the International Criminal Court and sessions of the Commission of Inquiry and the International Criminal Court in places related to the offence and the offender.

JURISDICTION

The problem of the jurisdiction of an International Criminal Court was considered in several reports submitted at the international symposium on "Terrorism and Political Crimes" organized under the auspices of the International Association of Penal Law and chaired by its Deputy Secretary General, Professor Cherif Bassiouni, DePaul University, Chicago, U.S.A., and held at the International Institute of Higher Studies in Criminal Sciences, Siracuse, Italy, June 4 to 15, 1973. Additional observations were made by other participants[56] during discussions.

Jurisdiction "Ratione Personae"

It is submitted that the International Criminal Court should try natural persons but not states. That a ruler or a government be criminally accountable should not imply the criminal responsibility of the whole population of a state. Criminal responsibility is an individual and not a collective matter, although collective criminal responsibility is not without precedent in history. Indeed a criminally responsible member of government is quite often not elected by the citizens but imposed upon them: i) by an external force due to a geopolitical situation, or ii) by an internal *coup d'état* or revolution by a minority. The population, often victimized by its government, should not bear the stigma of collective criminal responsibility resulting from the criminal action of its government or some members of the government.

Collective criminal responsibility is to a certain degree recognized by national laws as to certain crimes deemed committed by a corporate body. However, the situation of a shareholder of a corporation and that of a citizen of a state differ. A shareholder

---

[56]e.g. Judge J.Y. Dautricourt, "The International Criminal Court"; I. Bassiouni and Nauda, "A Treatise on International Criminal Law (1973), p. 636; Prof. Bart de Schutter, "Problems of Jurisdiction in the International Control and Repression of Terrorism," *supra* Chapter V, p. 377; Prof. Alan F. Sewell, "Political crime: A Psychologist's Perspective, *"supra* Chapter I, p. 11; Bruce B. Palmer, "A Proposed Codification of International Criminal Activities Deemed "Terroristic," *supra* p. 507.

may dissociate himself from the corporation simply by selling his shares. A citizen has no such easy solution at his disposal. If he cannot change his government by way of free elections, his only means of disassociating himself from it is by emigration, often as a political refugee. Those who do not choose exile and stay within their country should not be penalized for the criminal actions of the government imposed upon them.

In addition to these moral reasons, there are several technical reasons why criminal judgments against states are not practical. In the first place, it is extremely unlikely that governments will submit their states to the jurisdiction of an International Criminal Court. In addition, the sanctions that might be used against states differ entirely from those which can be applied against natural persons, the sanctions against states being limited to those of an economic or political character. The International Court of Justice constitutes a sufficient forum for cases against states. There remains the problem of corporate bodies (judicial persons). Such bodies are criminally responsible according to numerous national laws and they could be tried by an International Criminal Court.

Jurisdiction "Ratione Materiae"

While it is submitted that an International Criminal Court should be an "open court" to which various cases could be submitted, it is of interest to speculate as to what these cases might be. In the first place, the International Criminal Court should try international crimes. As present draft statutes provide for a nonexclusive jurisdiction of the International Criminal Court, the latter could be empowered to act as a court of appeal from the final judgments of national courts rendered in cases of international crimes and in certain other matters. It is submitted that such jurisdiction in appeal could comprise: (a) appeals from the final judgments of national courts in cases of international crimes;

(ii) appeals as to the determination of offences as political or common crimes;

(iii) appeals from the final decisions of national immigration appeal boards and other national bodies having jurisdiction over deportation and asylum;

(iv) appeals from the final decisions of national courts and other national bodies having jurisdiction over extradition.

The International Criminal Court could also be empowered to decide in matters of international conflicts of jurisdiction between national courts of two or more states.

International Participation in National Courts

It is submitted that international participation in trials before national courts may constitute a useful solution, intermediate between a purely national and an exclusively international jurisdiction.

(i) International judge within a national court.

This solution does not appear practical. The national laws of all countries would have to be amended to allow such participation and it is unlikely that national parliaments and/or legislative chambers of competent units of federal states would easily follow such a suggestion. Furthermore, an international judge could in any case be outvoted by national judges and/or assessors.

(ii) Subsidiary international prosecution and/or defence before national courts.

It is submitted that the International Criminal Court should be empowered to appoint international prosecutors and/or defenders to act before national courts in cases of international crimes. Such prosecutors and defenders would act in a subsidiary way in addition to national prosecutors and defenders. Their role would be to assure that all necessary evidence be submitted to the national court and be made public.

National Participation in the International Criminal Court

It has been pointed out that under certain national laws an international prosecutor has no power to obtain necessary evidence.[57] The statute of the International Criminal Court con-

---

[57]Statement by Professor Jacob Sundberg, University of Stockholm, Sweden, during the 1973 Siracuse Symposium.

*Ed's Note: see Preface.

tains provisions for the cooperation of national prosecutors and investigating magistrates with the International Criminal Court and for their subsidiary role before the International Criminal Court.

Submission to the Jurisdiction of the International Criminal Court

It is submitted that an International Criminal Court could be created as a court open to future submissions to its jurisdiction. Such submissions could be made at any time by way of:

a) multilateral conventions;
b) bilateral treaties;
c) amendments to existing international treaties;
d) special agreements;
e) unilateral declarations;
f) national legislation;
g) ad hoc submission of a case;
h) tacit recognition of the jurisdiction of the International Criminal Court in a given case.

Indeed, a state may find that the handling of a case in its national courts would cause problems, both as to the pressure of public opinion within such a state, and as to external political presures. In such circumstances the government may consider the submission of the case to an international jurisdiction a most welcome solution.

THE U.S. GOVERNMENT RESPONSE TO TERRORISM: A GLOBAL APPROACH*

LEWIS HOFFACKER

THE WORLD HAS LIVED with violence and terror since the beginning of time. But we now are experiencing new forms of international terrorism which have reached the point where innocent people far removed from the source of a dispute can be victimized. Nothing has more dramatically underscored this fact than the cruel tragedies at the Munich Olympics of 1972, the virtual epidemic of kidnapings in Latin America, and the wanton murder of two of our diplomats and a Belgian official in the Sudan.

These and other incidents bear witness to the terrible potential of a disturbed or determined person or group to terrorize the international community. Moreover, this capability for traumatic disruption of society appears to expand with the increasing technological and economic complexity of our society and with the added incentive of wide and rapid publicity.

What is terrorism? Last summer a U.N. group failed to agree on a definition of the term and became diverted by an inconclusive discussion of the causes and motives of terrorists. Such disagreement, however, should not deter us from getting on with the business at hand, which we, for our working purposes, regard as defense against violent attacks by politically or ideologically motivated parties on innocent bystanders who fall under our protective responsibility. I am talking primarily of Americans abroad and foreign officials and their families in this country. At the same time, we are concerned with terrorism throughout the world, even

---

*Reprinted with permission of the Department of State Bulletin (1974) as Ambassador Hoffacker's contribution to their goals.

though our people may not be directly involved, since this is a global phenomenon to which we are all vulnerable and which we cannot solve without global attention.

A private research organization has estimated that in the six years ending December 31, 1973, the casualty toll in all acts of international terrorism was 268 dead and 571 wounded. These victims were innocents attacked in places other than in the terrorists' homeland. The cost in measurable destruction in the same time period was said, by the same source, to be $163,000,000 plus $32,-000,000 in ransoms. It is difficult to estimate the money spent by governments, airlines, and others to finance counter-measures, but it is assumed that such figures run into the hundreds of millions of dollars. While hijacking in the United States is statistically much improved from some years ago, abroad there is a different picture: in 1969, there were 42 hijackings outside the U.S.; in 1973 10 hijacking incidents were reported, in addition to 10 attempts. We thus continue face an international problem of serious dimensions.

The U.S. Government has responded forthrightly to this serious challenge in fulfillment of its traditional responsibilities to protect its citizens and its foreign guests. In September of 1972 President Nixon established a Cabinet Committee To Combat Terrorism to consider, in his words, "the most effective means by which to prevent terrorism here and abroad." The Secretary of State chairs this Committee, which includes also the Secretaries of the Treasury, Defense, and Transportation, the Attorney General, our Ambassador to the United Nations, the Directors of the FBI and CIA and the President's Assistants on National Security and Domestic Affairs. This body is directed to coordinate interagency activity for the prevention of terrorism and, should acts of terrorism occur, to devise procedures for reacting swiftly and effectively.

Under the Cabinet Committee, a Working Group composed of personally designated senior representatives of the members of the Cabinet Committee meets regularly. It is this Group which I chair and which is in daily contact as issues arise and incidents occur. While we would prefer to be a policy planning body dealing in preventive measures, we are geared to respond to emergencies.

Over the past year and a half, this interagency group has dealt with a wide variety of matters and in my view has made us as a government more effective in responding to the continuing threat from a variety of organizations or individuals seeking to strike at us at home and abroad. This is not to say that we have solved all the problems facing us. But we are using governmentwide resources to better advantage and have at least reduced the risk to our people and our foreign guests. We must face the reality that there is no such thing as 100 percent security. But we are doing our job if we reduce risks to a practical minimum.

RESOURCES TO DETER TERRORISM

I would like to make clear at the outset that individual departments and agencies continue to manage programs dealing with terrorism under their respective mandates. The important difference is that these efforts, which individually deserve commendation, are now fully coordinated and consequently are greater deterrents to potential terrorists,

Intelligence is one of our more valuable resources in this self-defense endeavor. All security agencies have improved the quality of their intelligence relating to terrorism, and the Working Group insures that this product is fully shared and coordinated throughout the government.

Abroad, security at our embassies and consulates has been steadily improved. Last summer the President submitted to the Congress a request for $21 million for personnel and material to better our overseas security and, hopefully, reduce the risk which our official personnel suffer throughout the world. These funds are now being disbursed, based on highest priority needs at our posts abroad.

We are mindful that our mandate also covers private citizens as well as American officials. For example, we are pleased to advise American businessmen with overseas interests. Our embassies and consulates are in constant touch with American business abroad, especially in such places as Argentina, where they are particularly vulnerable. We are prepared to share with them security techniques and experiences. Although we may not agree on tactics such as the advisability of paying ransom, it is important that we stick together in tight situations such as Buenos Aires, where terrorists have taken advantage of serious internal security deficiencies to kidnap businessmen for increasingly higher ransoms. We were concerned with the Bank of America case in Beirut, where a representative of Douglas Aircraft was murdered by bank robbers posing unconvincingly as *fedayeen*.

Visa, immigration, and customs procedures have been tightened. The regulation allowing a foreigner to transit the United States without a visa has been suspended except for passengers with immediate onward reservations to a point outside the United States. This suspension applies to every traveler on a nondiscriminatory basis and closes a loophole through which 600,000 visitors per year formerly passed.

In several categories of visa applicants which have been particularly susceptible to terrorist penetration, deeper screening of applications has shown some useful results.

In the fall of 1972 Congress approved a public law aimed at increasing protection for foreign official and their immediate families in this country through the creation of Federal criminal offenses for various acts directed at them and at other official guests. Under this legislation the FBI has investgative jurisdiction concurrent with that already held by local law enforcement authorities. This expanded legal coverage of our foreign guests will, hopefully, add a further deterrent to those who might be tempted to molest them. There has been one conviction under this law, and several other cases are now before Federal courts or are expected to be submitted soon.

For some time the Postal Service has alerted post offices and other likely targets of letter-bomb activity. Many hundreds of such devices have been circulating internationally. Some have been intercepted in this country by alert customs and postal employees, with one injury sustained by a postal clerk in the process. Unfortunately a letter bomb exploded in the British Embassy last September, maiming a secretary and illustrating dramatically that international terrorists can probably penetrate our security screen.

Hijacking within the United States has fallen off significantly since the beginning of last year. This happy trend is not just a stroke of luck. Aside from the rigorous airport security program now underway, a principal factor in this favorable evolution is the bilateral agreement with Cuba whereby hijackers are denied asylum in that country. Other countries, with or without our encouragement, have taken similar steps to close their doors to individuals who look for refuge from prosecution after a hijacking. Let us recall, at the same time, that the domestic variety of hijacker in the United States is usually different from those who operate abroad, often with special ruthlessness, under the control of terrorist organizations.

U.S. INTERNATIONAL INITIATIVES

The United States has been busy internationally. We have been in the forefront of those who have sought tightly international air security.

We have pressed for three important multilateral conventions dealing with hijacking: the 1963 Tokyo Convention, which in effect requires countries to return a plane and passengers if it has been hijacked; the 1970 Hague Convention, which says that countries should either extradite or prosecute the skyjackers; and the 1971 Montreal Convention, requiring that any kind of sabotage of aviation such as blowing up planes on the ground be dealt with by prosecution or extradition of the offenders. We had modest expectations as we sent a delegation to two conferences in Rome last summer in the hope that the international community would advance a step forward in tightening controls on skyjacker and aerial saboteurs.

Despite our disappointment over the meager results in Rome, we are confident that there remains a sufficient sense of international responsibility and national self-interest to make possible other steps to discourage those who would threaten international air travelers. For one thing, we are seeing a steady stream of accessions to the aforementioned convention by countries representing all ideologies. This in itself should have a good deterrent effect.

In Interpol [International Criminal Police Organization], in the Organization of American States, and in other appropriate forums, we achieve what is feasible in the way of multilateral discouragement of the international terrorist. Simultaneously we maintain quiet liaison with individual governments which share our abhorrence of terrorism. We are pleased to assist others when they suffer hijackings by providing communications and other services even though the affected plane may not be over or in our country.

At the United Nations in 1972 we sought to prohibit the export of violence to innocent persons who are many countries, sometimes continents, removed from the scene of a conflict.* This approach became bogged down in debate over what some countries called justifiable, as opposed to illegal, violence even against innocent parties. Accordingly, for the time being we have narrowed our objectives to more specific categories of offenses which, because of grave and inhuman effect on innocent individuals or because of their serious interference with the vital machinery of international life, should be condemned by states of every ideology and alignment. We therefore supported in the last General Assembly a convention for protection of diplomats. The Assembly agreed in December to this measure, which requires that persons who attack or kidnap diplomats or officials of foreign governments or international organizations be extradited or prosecuted.†

DEALING WITH CRISIS SITUATIONS

If in spite of all our efforts, an act of terrorism should occur, we are prepared to deal with it as swiftly and effectively as possible. Within the State Department, task forces can be assembled on short notice to manage such critical events as the Southern Airways hijacking, the seizure of American diplomats in Haiti, the murder of two of our officers in the Sudan, the kidnaping of our consul general in Guadalajara, the hijacking last summer of the Japanese airliner out of Amsterdam, the attack on emigrant Jews in Austria last fall, various incidents at Rome and Athens airports, and the recent terrorism in Karachi and Singapore harbors and in Kuwait.

Such task forces are composed of selected specialists who can call on the full resources of the U.S. Government to rescue, or at least to monitor, the beleaguered parties. The State Department

*Ed's Note: see Appendix R, p. 557 and John Murphy, *supra* p. 493.

†Ed's Note: see Appendix N, p. 333 and James Murphy, *supra* p. 285.

Operations Center, which is the site of such task forces, is in instant contact with the White House, Pentagon, CIA, and other agencies concerned, as well as with foreign governments and overseas posts. By swift and intelligent action in such circumstances we, hopefully, can overcome the terrorists by one means or another.

FIRMNESS IN RESPONSE TO TERRORISM

Tactics vary in each crisis situation, but one consistent factor should be understood by all parties concerned: the U.S. Government will not pay ransom to kidnapers. We urge other governments and individuals to adopt the same position, to resist other forms of blackmail, and to apprehend the criminal attackers.

I hasten to underline the importance which we attach to human life. We do not glibly sacrifice hostages for the sake of this admittedly firm policy. We believe that firmness in response to terrorists' threats, if applied with the best diplomacy we can muster, can save lives in the long run and probably in the short run as well.

We have had more terrorist experiences than we had anticipated in the past five years, during which period 25 of our officials abroad who normally enjoy diplomatic protection were kidnaped. Ten of these individuals were murdered and 12 wounded. When we Foreign Service people elected to follow this career, we appreciated that there were risks different in type and intensity from those to which we are exposed in this country. Abroad we experience increased threats of subversion, kidnaping, blackmail, civil disturbances, and politically motivated violence, including assassination.

In my 23 years' Foreign Service experience, mostly abroad in the Middle East and Africa, I have not seen any of our people behave cowardly in a dangerous situation. We have learned to take reasonable precautions. We do not want to live in fortresses or armed camps. We use ingenuity to reduce risks. Most importantly, we must remind the host government of its undoubted responsibility for protecting foreigners within its territory. I recall, for example, when I was once put under house arrest by an angry Minister, I reminded him and his government that that government continued to be responsible for my personal security and would face dire consequences if anything happened to me. I am glad to report that my consular colleagues rallied round me and after a week I was able to resume my normal movements.

It would be unfair to assign labels to countries as to their hawk-like or dovelike qualities in facing up to the terrorist challenge. Each country naturally performs in the light of its own interests, which may vary from case to case. Some are more cautious than others to avoid provoking militants who engage in terrorism. Even countries friendly to us are understandably selfish about their sovereign right to decide what is best in a terrorist confrontation; e.g. whether or not to yield to demands for ransom, release of prisoners, et cetera. Moreover, we in the United States have not found ourselves in excruciating circumstances such as some countries like Haiti or Mexico have undergone with foreign diplomats held in their territory under terrorists' guns.

The U.S. approach to counterterrorism is based on the principle derived from our liberal heritage, as well as from the U.N. Declaration of Human Rights, which affirms that every human being has a right to life, liberty, and "security of person." Yet the violence of international terrorism violates that principle. The issue is not war. The issue is not the strivings of people to achieve selfdetermination and independence. Rather the issue is—and here I quote from former Secretary of State Rogers before the U.N. General Assembly:[1]

> (The issue is) whether millions of air travelers can continue to fly in safety each year. It is whether a person who receives a letter can open it without fear of being blown up. It is whether diplomats can safely carry out their duties. It is whether international meetings—like the Olympic games, like this Assembly—can proceed without the ever-present threat of violence.
>
> In short, the issue is whether the vulnerable lines of international communication—the airways and the mails, diplomatic discourse and international meetings—can continue, without disruption, to bring nations and peoples together. All who have a stake in this have a stake in decisive action to suppress these demented acts of terrorism.
>
> We are all aware that, aside from the psychotic and the purely felonious, many criminal acts of terrorism derive from political origins.

---

[1]For Secretary Rogers' statement before the U.N. General Assembly on Sept. 25, 1972, see *Bulletin,* Oct. 16, 1972, p. 425.

We all recognize that issues such as self-determination must continue to be addressed seriously by the international community. But political passion, however deeply held, cannot be a justification for criminal violence against innocent persons.[2]

The United States has attempted to show leadership in stimulating a global preoccupation with this apparently growing international threat. We have not achieved all that we have sought in international cooperation. Our multilateral, bilateral, and unilateral efforts must continue because the outlook is not as promising as it might be. There seems to be increased collaboration among terrorist groups of different nationalities. Such groups seem to be moving farther and farther afield, including toward North America. There is, moreover, evidence of ample financial sources for some terrorist groups not only from ransoms collected but also from governments which, for one reason or another, are sympathetic toward certain terrorist groups. And last but not least, there seems to be no shortage of politico-economic-social frustrations to spawn terrorists on all continents.

Accordingly, we must increase our vigilance, our expertise, and our determination in the face of what may be an expanding threat to our personnel and other interests abroad, as well as on the home front. In fact, this global epidemic still threatens the very fabric of international order.

We as a government must be cool and tough—and I might add, sensitive—in responding to these vicious attacks against our citizens and other interests. As we seek to defend ourselves against this viciousness, we are not unmindful of the motivation inspiring the frustrated political terrorist who feels he has no other way to deal with his grievances than by terrorist action. As ways are found to convince him to reason otherwise, he must be made to understand now that it is unprofitable for him to attack innocent bystanders.

In the meantime also, we as a government have a continuing obligation to safeguard the most fundamental right of all—the right of life. There is no reason why protection of this right and of our citizens need necessarily conflict with other human rights such as self-determination and individual liberty.

---

[2]Ibid.

APPENDIX Q

Convention for the Prevention and Punishment of Terrorism,
Opened for Signature at Geneva on November 16, 1937[1]

. . .

Being desirous of making more effective the prevention and punishment of terrorism of an international character,

. . .

Who, having communicated their full powers, which were found in good and due form, have agreed upon the following provisions:

Article 1.-1. The High Contracting Parties, reaffirming the principle of international law in virtue of which it is the duty of every State to refrain from any act designed to encourage terrorist activities directed against another State and to prevent the acts in which such activities take shape, undertake as hereinafter provided to prevent and punish activities of this nature and to collaborate for this purpose.

2. In the present Convention, the expression "act of terrorism" means criminal acts directed against a State and intended or calculated to create a state of terror in the minds of particular persons, or a group of persons or the general public.

Article 2. Each of the High Contracting Parties shall, if this has not already been done, make the following acts committed on his own territory criminal offenses if they are directed against another High Contracting Party and if they constitute acts of terrorism within the meaning of Article 1:

(1) Any willful act causing death or grievous bodily harm or loss of liberty to:

(a) Heads of State, persons exercising the prerogatives of

---

[1]Not entered into force; ratified by India on January 1, 1941; signed by Albania, Argentine Republic, Belgium, India, Bulgaria, Cuba, Dominican Republic, Egypt, Ecuador, Spain, Estonia, France, Greece, Haiti, Monaco, Norway, Netherlands, Peru, Romania, Czechoslovakia, Turkey, Union of Soviet Socialist Republics, Venezuela and Yugoslavia.

the head of the State, their hereditary or designated
successors;

(b) The wives or husbands of the above-mentioned persons;

(c) Persons charged with public functions or holding public position when the act is directed against them in
their public capacity.

(2) Willful destruction of, or damage to, public property or
property devoted to a public purpose belonging to or subject to the authority of another High Contracting Party.

(3) Any willful calculated to endanger the lives of members of
the public.

(4) Any attempt to commit an offense falling within the foregoing provisions of the present article.

(5) The manufacture, obtaining, possession, or supplying of
arms, ammunition, explosives or harmful substances with a
view to the commission in any country whatsoever of an offense falling within the present article.

Article 3. Each of the High Contracting Parties shall make the
following acts criminal offenses when they are committed on his
own territory with a view to an act of terrorism falling within
Article 2 and directed against another High Contracting Party,
whatever the country in which the act of terrorism is to be carried
out:

(1) Conspiracy to commit any such act;

(2) Any incitement to any such act, if successful;

(3) Direct public incitement to any act mentioned under heads
(1), (2) or (3) of Article 2, whether the incitement be
successful or not;

(4) Willful participation in any such act;

(5) Assistance, knowingly given, towards the commission of any
such act.

Article 4. Each of the offences mentioned in Article 3 shall be
treated by the law as a distinct offence in all cases where this is
necessary in order to prevent an offender escaping punishment.

Article 5. Subject to any special provisions of national law for
the protection of the persons mentioned under head (1) of Article
2, or of the property mentioned under head (2) of Article 2, each

High Contracting Party shall provide the same punishment for the acts set out in Articles 2 and 3, whether they be directed against that or another High Contracting Party.

Article 6.-1. In countries where the principle of the international recognition of previous convictions is accepted, foreign convictions for any of the offenses mentioned in Articles 2 and 3 will, within the conditions prescribed by domestic law, be taken into account for the purpose of establishing habitual criminality.

2. Such convictions will, further, in the case of High Contracting Parties whose law recognizes foreign convictions, be taken into account, with or without special proceedings, for the purpose of imposing, in the manner, provided by that law, incapacities, disqualifications or interdictions whether in the sphere of public or of private law.

Article 7. In so far as *parties civiles* are admitted under the domestic law, foreign *parties civiles,* including, in proper cases, a High Contracting Party shall be entitled to all rights allowed to nationals by the law of the country in which the case is tried.

Article 8.-1. Without prejudice to the provisions of paragraph 4 below, the offenses set out in Articles 2 and 3 shall be deemed to be included as extradition crimes in any extradition treaty which has been, or may hereafter be, concluded between any of the High Contracting Parties.

2. The High Contracting Parties who do not make extradition conditional on the existence of a treaty shall henceforward, without prejudice to the provisions of paragraph 4 below and subject to reciprocity, recognize the offenses set out in Articles 2 and 3 as extradition crimes as between themselves.

3. For the purpose of the present article, any offence specified in Articles 2 and 3, if committed in the territory of the High Contracting Party against whom it is directed, shall also be deemed to be an extradition crime.

4. The obligation to grant extradition under the present article shall be subject to any conditions and limitations recognized by the law or the practice of the country to which application is made.

Article 9.-1. When the principle of the extradition of nationals is not recognized by a High Contracting Party, nationals who have returned to the territory of their own country after the commission abroad of an offence mentioned in Article 2 or 3 shall be prosecuted and punished in the same manner as if the offense had been committed on that territory, even in a case where the offender has acquired his nationality after the commission of the offense.

2. The provisions of the present article shall not apply if, in similar circumstances, the extradition of a foreigner cannot be granted.

Article 10. Foreigners who are on the territory of a High Contracting Party and who have committed abroad any of the offenses set out in Articles 2 and 3 shall be prosecuted and punished as though the offense had been committed in the territory of that High Contracting Party, if the following conditions are fulfilled —namely, that:

(a) Extradition has been demanded and could not be granted for a reason not connected with the offense itself.

(b) The law of the country of refuge recognizes the jurisdiction of its own courts in respect of offenses committed abroad by foreigners;

(c) The foreigner is a national of a country which recognizes the jurisdiction of its own courts in respect of offenses committed abroad by foreigners.

Article 11.-1. The provisions of Articles 9 and 10 shall also apply to offenses referred to in Article 2 and 3 which have been committed in the territory of the High Contracting Party against whom they were directed.

2. As regards the application of Articles 9 and 10, the High Contracting Parties do not understake to pass a sentence exceeding the maximum sentence provided by the law of the country where the offense was committed.

Article 12. Each High Contracting Party shall take on his own territory and within the limits of his own law and administrative organization the measures which he considers appropriate for the effective prevention of all activities contrary to the purpose of the present Convention.

Article 13.-1. Without prejudice to the provisions of head (5) of Article 2, the carrying, possession and distribution of fire-arms, other than smooth-bore sporting-guns, and of ammunition shall be subjected to regulation. It shall be a punishable offense to transfer, sell or distribute such arms or munitions to any person who does not hold such license or make such declaration as may be required by domestic legislation concerning the possession and carrying of such articles; this shall apply also to the transfer, sale or distribution of explosives.

2. Manufacturers of fire-arms, other than smooth-bore sporting guns, shall be required to mark each arm with a serial number or other distinctive mark permitting it to be identified; both manufacturers and retailers shall be obliged to keep a register of the names and addresses of purchasers.

Article 14.-1. The following acts shall be punishable:

(a) Any fraudulent manufacture or alteration of passports or other equivalent documents;

(b) Bringing into the country, obtaining or being in possession of such forged or falsified documents knowing them to be forged or falsified;

(c) Obtaining such documents by means of false declarations or documents;

(d) Wilfully using any such documents which are forged or falsified or were made out for a person other than the bearer.

2. The willful issue of passports, other equivalent documents, or visas by competent officials to persons known not to have the right thereto under the laws or regulations applicable, with the object of assisting any activity contrary to the purpose of the present Convention, shall also be punishable.

3. The provisions of the present article shall apply irrespective of the national or foreign character of the document.

Article 15.1. Results of the investigation of offenses mentioned in Articles 2 and 3 and (where there may be a connection between the offense and preparations for an act of terrorism) in Article 14 shall in each country, subject to the provisions of its law, be centralized in an appropriate service.

2. Such service shall be in close contact:

(a) With the police authorities of the country;

(b) With the corresponding services in other countries.

3. It shall furthermore bring together all information calculated to facilitate the prevention and punishment of the offenses mentioned in Article 2 and 3 and (where there may be a connection between the offense and preparations for an act of terrorism) in Article 14; it shall, as far as possible, keep in close contact with the judicial authorities of the country.

Article 16. Each service; so far as it considers it desirable to do so, shall notify to the services of the other countries, giving all necessary particulars:

(a) Any act mentioned in Artices 2 and 3, even if it has not been carried into effect, such notification to be accompanied by descriptions, copies and photographs;

(b) Any search for, any prosecution, arrest, conviction or expulsion of persons guilty of offenses dealt with in the present Convention, the movements of such persons and any pertinent information with regard to them, as well as their description, finger-prints and photographs;

(c) Discovery of documents, arms, appliances or other objects connected with offences mentioned in Articles 2, 3, 13 and 14.

Article 17.-1. The High Contracting Parties shall be bound to execute letters of request relating to offenses referred to in the present Convention in accordance with their domestic law and practice and any international conventions concluded or to be concluded by them.

2. The transmission of letters of request shall be effected:

(a) By direct communication between the judicial authorities;

(b) By direct correspondence between the Ministers of Justice of the two countries;

(c) By direct correspondence between the authority of the country making the request and the Minister of Justice of the country to which the request is made;

(d) Through the diplomatic or consular representative of the country making the request in the country to which the request is made; this representative shall send the letters of request, either directly or through the Minister for Foreign Affairs, to the competent judicial authority or to the authority indicated by the Government of the country to which the request is made and shall receive the papers constituting the execution of the letters of request from this authority either directly or through the Minister for Foreign Affairs.

3. In cases (a) and (d), a copy of the letters of request shall always be sent simultaneously to the Minister of Justice of the country to which application is made.

4. Unless otherwise agreed, the letters of request shall be drawn up in the language of the authority making the request, provided always that the country to which the request is made may require a translation in its own language, certified correct by the authority making the request.

5. Each High Contracting Party shall notify to each of the other High Contracting Parties the method or methods of transmission mentioned above which he will recognize for the letters of request of the latter High Contracting Party.

6. Until such notification is made by a High Contracting Party, his existing procedure in regard to letters of request shall remain in force.

7. Execution of letters of request shall not rise to a claim for reimbursement of charges or expenses of any nature whatever other than expenses of experts.

8. Nothing in the present article shall be construed as an undertaking on the part of the High Contracting Parties to adopt in criminal matters any form or methods of proof contrary to their laws.

Article 18. The participation of a High Contracting Party in the present Convention shall not be interpreted as affecting that Party's attitude on the general question of the limits of criminal jurisdiction as a question of international law.

Article 19. The present Convention does not affect the principle that, provided the offender is not allowed to escape punishment owing to an omission in the criminal law, the characterization of the various offenses dealt with in the present Convention, the imposition of sentences, the methods of prosecution and trial, and the rules as to mitigating circumstances, pardon and amnesty are determined in each country by the provisions of domestic law.

Article 20.-1. If any dispute should arise between the High Contracting Parties relating to the interpretation or application of the present Convention, and if such dispute has not been satisfactorily solved by diplomatic means, it shall be settled in conformity with the provisions in force between the parties concerning the settlement of international disputes.

2. If such provisions should not exist between the parties to the dispute, the parties shall refer the dispute to an arbitral or judicial procedure. If no agreement is reached on the choice of another court, the parties shall refer the dispute to the Permanent Court of International Justice, if they are all parties to the Protocol of December 16, 1920, relating to the Statute of that Court; and if they are not all parties to that Protocol, they shall refer the dispute to a court of arbitration constituted in accordance with the Convention of The Hague of October 18, 1907, for the Pacific Settlement of International Disputes.

3. The above provisions of the present article shall not prevent High Contracting Parties, if they are Members of the League of Nations, from bringing the dispute before the Council or the Assembly of the League if the Covenant gives them the power to do so.

Article 21-1. The present Convention, of which the French and English texts shall be both authentic, shall bear today's date. Until May 31, 1938, it shall be open for signature on behalf of any Member of the League of Nations and on behalf of any nonmember State represented at the Conference which drew up the present Convention or to which a copy thereof is communicated for this purpose by the Council of the League of Nations.

2. The present Convention shall be ratified. The instruments of ratification shall be transmitted to the Secretary-General of the League of Nations to be deposited in the archives of the League; the Secretary-General shall notify their deposit to all the Members of the League and to the nonmember States mentioned in the preceding paragraph.

Article 22.-1. After June 1, 1938, the present Convention shall be open to accession by any Member of the League of Nations, and any of the nonmember States referred to in Article 21, on whose behalf the Convention has not been signed.

2. The instruments of accession shall be transmitted to the Secretary-General of the League of Nations to be deposited in the archives of the League; the Secretary-General shall notify their receipt to all the Members of the League and to the nonmember States referred to in Article 21.

Article 23.-1. Any Member of the League of Nations or non-member States whose signature of the Convention has not yet been the second paragraph of Article 21, or to accede to the Convention under Article 22, but desires to be allowed to make reservations with regard to the application of the Convention, may so inform the Secretary-General of the League of Nations, who shall forth-with communicate such reservations to all the Members of the League and nonmember States on whose behalf ratifications or ac-cessions have been deposited and inquire whether they have any objection thereto. Should the reservation be formulated within three years from the entry into force of the Convention, the same inquiry shall be addressed to Members of the League and non-member States whose signature of the Convention has not yet been followed by ratification. If within six months from the date of the Secretary-General's communication, no objection to the reservation has been made, it shall be treated as accepted by the High Contract-ing Parties.

2. In the event of any objection being received, the Secretary-General of the League of Nations shall inform the Government which desired to make the reservation and request it to inform him whether it is prepared to ratify or accede without the reservation or whether it prefers to abstain from ratification or accession.

Article 24. Ratification of, or accession to, the present Conven-tion by any High Conracting Party implies an assurance by him that his legislation and his administrative organization enable him to give effect to the provisions of the present Convention.

Article 25.-1. Any High Contracting Party may declare, at the time of signature, ratification or accession, that, in accepting the present Convention, he is not assuming any obligation in respect of all or any of his colonies, protectorates, oversea territories, territories under his suzerainty or territories in respect of which a mandate has been entrusted to him; the present Convention shall, in that case, not be applicable to the territories named in such declaration.

2. Any High Contracting Party may subsequently notify the Secretary-General of the League of Nations that he desires the present Convention to apply to all or any of the territories in respect of which the declaration provided for in the preceding paragraph has been made. In making such notification, the High Contracting Party concerned may state that the application of the Convention to any of such territories shall be subject to any reservations which have been accepted in respect of that High Contracting Party under Article 23. The Convention shall then apply, with any such reservations, to all the territories named in such notification ninety days after the receipt thereof by the Secretary-General of the League of Nations. Should it be desired as regards any such territories to make reservations other than those already made under Article 23 by the High Contracting Party concerned, the procedure set out in that Article shall be followed.

3. Any High Contracting Party may at any time declare that he desires the present Convention to cease to apply to all or any of his colonies, protectorates, oversea territories, territories under his suzerainty or territories in respect of which a mandate has been entrusted to him. The Convention shall, in that case, cease to apply to the territories named in such declaration one year after the receipt of this declaration by the Secretary-General of the League of Nations.

4. The Secretary-General of the League of Nations shall communicate to all the Members of the League of Nations and to the non-members referred to in Article 21 the declarations and notifications received in virtue of the present Article.

Article 26.-1. The present Convention shall, in accordance with the provisions of Article 18 of the Covenant, be registered by the Secretary-General of the League of Nations on the ninetieth day after the receipt by the Secretary-General of the third instrument of ratification or accession.

2. The Convention shall come into force on the date of such registration.

Article 27. Each ratification or accession taking place after the deposit of the third instrument of ratification or accession shall take effect on the ninetieth day following the date on which the instrument of ratification or accession is received by the Secretary-General of the League of Nations.

Article 28. A request for the revision of the present Convention may be made at any time by any High Contracting Party by means of a notification to the Secretary-General of the League of Nations. Such notification shall be communicated by the Secretary-General to all the other High Contracting Parties and, if it is supported by at least a third of those Parties, the High Contracting Parties undertake to hold a conference for the revision of the Convention.

Article 29. The present Convention may be denounced on behalf of any High Contracting Party by a notification in writing addressed to the Secretary-General of the League of Nations, who shall inform all the Members of the League and the non-member States referred to in Article 21. Such denunciation shall take effect one year after the date of its receipt by the Secretary-General of the League of Nations, and shall be operative only in respect of the High Contracting Party on whose behalf it was made.

APPENDIX R

Measures to Prevent International Terrorism Which Endangers or Takes Innocent Human Lives or Jeopardizes Fundamental Freedoms and Study of the Underlying Causes of Those Forms of Terrorism and Acts of Violence Which Lie in Misery, Frustration, Grievance and Despair and Which Cause Some People to Sacrifice Human Lives, Including Their Own, in an Attempt to Effect Radical Changes*

UNITED STATES DRAFT CONVENTION FOR THE PREVENTION AND PUNISHMENT OF CERTAIN ACTS OF INTERNATIONAL TERRORISM

The States Parties to this Convention,

Recalling United Nations General Assembly resolution 2625 (XXV), proclaiming principles of international law concerning friendly relations and cooperation among States in accordance with the Charter of the United Nations,

Considering that this resolution provides that every State has the duty to refrain from organizing, instigating, assisting or participating in terrorist acts in another State or acquiescing in organized activities within its territory directed towards the commission of such acts,

Considering the common danger posed by the spread of terrorist acts across national boundaries,

Considering that civilians must be protected from terrorist acts,

Affirming that effective measures to control international terrorism are urgently needed and require international as well as national action,

Have agreed as follows:

Article 1

1. Any person who unlawfully kills, causes serious bodily harm or kidnaps another person, attempts to commit any such act, or par-

*A/C.6/L.850, September 25, 1972.

557

ticipates as an accomplice of a person who commits or attempts to commit any such act, commits an offence of international significance if the act

(a) Is committed or takes effect outside the territory of a State of which the alleged offender is a national; and

(b) Is committed or takes effect
   (i) Outside the territory of the State against the act is directed, or
   (ii) Within the territory of the State against which the act is directed and the alleged offender knows or has reason to know that a person against whom the act is directed is not a national of that State; and

(c) Is committed neither by nor against a member of the armed forces of a State in the course of military hostilities; and

(d) Is intended to damage the interests of or obtain concessions from a State or an international organization.

2. For the purposes of this Convention:
   (a) An "international organization" means an international intergovernmental organization;
   (b) An "alleged offender" means a person as to whom there are grounds to believe that he has committed one or more of the offenses of international significance set forth in this article;
   (c) The "territory" of a State includes all territory under the jurisdiction or administration of the State.

Article 2

Each State Party undertakes to make the offenses set forth in article 1 punishable by severe penalties.

Article 3

A State Party in whose territory an alleged offender is found shall, if it does not extradite him, submit, without exception whatsoever and without undue delay, the case to its competent authorities for the purpose of prosecution, through proceedings in accordance with the laws of that State.

Article 4

1. Each State Party shall take such measures as may be necessary to establish its jurisdiction over the offenses set forth in article 1:

    (a) When the offense is committed in its territory; or

    (b) When the offense is committed by its national.

2. Each State Party shall likewise take such measures as may be necessary to establish its jurisdiction over the offenses set forth in article 1 in the case where an alleged offender is present in its territory and the State does not extradite him to any of the States mentioned in paragraph 1 of this article.

3. This Convention does not exclude any criminal jurisdiction exercised in accordance with national law.

Article 5

A State Party in which one or more of the offences set forth in article 1 have been committed shall, if it has reason to believe an alleged offender has fled from its territory, communicate to all other States Parties all the pertinet facts regarding the offence committed and all available information regarding the identity of the alleged offender.

Article 6

1. The State Party in whose territory an alleged offender is found shall take appropriate measures under its internal law so as to ensure his presence for prosecution or extradition. Such measures shall be immediately notified to the States mentioned in article 4, paragraph 1, and all other interested States.

2. Any person regarding whom the measures referred to in pararaph 1 of this article are being taken shall be entitled to communicate immediately with the nearest appropriate representative of the State of which he is a national and to be visited by a representative of that State.

Article 7

1. To the extent that the offenses set forth in article 1 are not listed as extraditable offenses in any extradition treaty existing be-

tween States Parties they shall be deemed to have been included as such therein. State Parties undertake to include those offenses as extraditable offenses in every future extradition treaty to be concluded between them.

2. If a State Party which makes extradition conditional on the existence of a treaty receives a request for extradition from another State Party with which it has no extradition treaty, it may, if it decides to extradite, consider the present articles as the legal basis for extradition in respect of the offenses. Extradition shall be subject to the provisions of the law of the requested State.

3. States Parties which do not make extradition conditional upon the existence of a treaty shall recognize the offences as extraditable offenses between themselves subject to the provisions of the law of the requested State.

4. Each of the offenses shall be treated, for the purpose of extradition between States Parties as if it has been committed not only in the place in which it occurred but also in the territories of the States required to establish their jurisdiction in accordance with article 4, paragraph 1 (b).

5. An extradition request from the State in which the offenses were committed shall have priority over other such requests if received by the State Party in whose territory the alleged offender has been found within 30 days after the communication required under paragraph 1 of article 6 has been made.

Article 8

Any person regarding whom proceedings are being carried out in connection with any of the offenses set forth in article 1 shall be guaranteed fair treatment at all stages of the proceedings.

Article 9

The statutory limitation as to the time within which prosecution may be instituted for the offenses set forth in article 1 shall be, in each State Party, that fixed for the most serious crimes under its internal law.

Article 10

1. States Parties shall, in accordance with international and national law, endeavor to take all practicable measures for the purpose of preventing the offences set forth in article 1.

2. Any State Party having reason to believe that one of the offence set forth in article 1 may be committed shall, in accordance with its national law, furnish any relevant information in its possession to those States which it believes would be the State mentioned in article 4, paragraph 1, if any such offense were committed.

Article 11

1. States Parties shall afford one another the greatest measure of assistance in connection with criminal proceedings brought in respect of the offenses set forth in article 1, including the supply of all evidence at their disposal necessary for the proceedings.

2. The provisions of paragraph 1 of this article shall not affect obligations concerning mutual assistance embodied in any other treaty.

Article 12

States Parties shall consult together for the purpose of considering and implementing such other cooperative measures as may seem useful for carrying out the purposes of this Convention.

Article 13

In any case in which one or more of the Geneva Conventions of August 12, 1949, or any other convention concerning the law of armed conflicts is applicable, such conventions shall, if in conflict with any provisions of this Convention, take precedence. In particular:

(a) Nothing in this Convention shall make an offense of any act which is permissible under the Geneva Convention Relative to the Protection of Civilian Persons in Time of War or any other international law applicable in armed conflicts; and

(b) Nothing in this Convention shall deprive any person of prisoner of war status if entitled to such status under the

Geneva Convention Relative to the Treatment of Prisoners of War or any other applicable convention concerning respect for human rights in armed conflicts.

Article 14

In any case in which the Convention on offenses and Certain Other Acts Committed on Board Aircraft, the Convention for the Suppression of Unlawful Seizure of Aircraft, the Convention for the Suppression of Unlawful Acts Against the Safety of Civil Aviation, the Convention to Prevent and Punish the Acts of Terrorism Taking the Form of Crimes Against Persons and Related Extortion that are of International Significance, or any other convention which has or may be concluded concerning the protection of civil aviation, diplomatic agents and other internationally protected persons, is applicable, such convention shall, if in conflict with any provision of this Convention, take precedence.

Article 15

Nothing in this Convention shall derogate from any obligations of the Parties under the United Nations Charter.

Article 16

1. Any dispute between the Parties arising out of the application or interpretation of the present articles that is not settled through negotiation may be brought by any State Party to the dispute before a Conciliation Commission to be constituted in accordance with the provisions of this article by the giving of written notice to the other State or States Party to the dispute and to the Secretary-General of the United Nations.

2. A Conciliation Commission will be composed of three members. One member shall be appointed by each party to the dispute. If there is more than one party on either side of the dispute they shall jointly appoint a member of the Conciliation Commission. These two appointments shall be made within two months of the written notice referred to in paragraph 1. The third member, the Chairman, shall be chosen by the other two members.

3. If either side has failed to appoint its members within the

time-limit referred to in paragraph 2, the Secretary-General of the United Nations shall appoint such member within a further period of two months. If no agreement is reached on the choice of the Chairman within five months of the written notice referred to in paragraph 1, the Secretary-General shall within the further period of one month appoint as the Chairman a qualified jurist who is not a national of any State Party to the dispute.

4. Any vacancy shall be filled in the same manner as the original appointment was made.

5. The Commission shall establish its own rules of procedure and shall reach its decisions and recommendations by a majority vote. It shall be competent to ask any organ that is authorized by or in accordance with the Charter of the United Nations to request an advisory opinion from the International Court of Justice to make such a request regarding the interpretation or application of the present articles.

6. If the Commission is unable to obtain an agreement among the parties on a settlement of the dispute within six months of its initial meeting, it shall prepare as soon as possible a report of its proceedings and transmit it to the parties and to the depositary. The report shall include the Commission's conclusions upon the facts and questions of law and the recommendations it has submitted to the parties in order to facilitate a settlement of the dispute. The six months time-limit may be extended by decision of the Commission.

7. This article is without prejudice to provisions concerning the settlement of disputes contained in international agreements in force between States.

APPENDIX S

Excerpts From The
Report of the *Ad Hoc* Committee on International Terrorism*

ANNEX
DRAFT PROPOSALS AND SUGGESTIONS SUBMITTED
TO THE THREE SUB-COMMITTEES OF THE WHOLE
SUB-COMMITTEE OF THE WHOLE ON THE
DEFINITION OF INTERNATIONAL TERRORISM

1. Draft Proposal Submitted by the Non-Aligned Group in the
Ad Hoc Committee (Algeria, Congo, Democratic Yemen, Guinea,
India, Mauritania, Nigeria, Syrian Arab Republic, Tunisia,
United Republic of Tanzania, Yeman, Yugoslavia, Zaire
and Zambia

The acts of international terrorism for the purposes of carrying out the mandate of the *Ad Hoc* Committee on International Terrorism entrusted to it by General Assembly resolution 3034 (XXVII), include:

(1) Acts of violence and other repressive acts by colonial, racist and alien régimes against peoples struggling for their liberation, for their legitimate right to self-determination, independence and other human rights and fundamental freedoms;

(2) Tolerating or assisting by a State the organizations of the remnants of fascists or mercenary groups whose terrorist activity is directed against other sovereign countries;

(3) Acts of violence committed by individuals or groups of individuals which endanger or take innocent human lives or jeopardize fundamental freedoms. This should not affect the inalienable right to self-determination and independence of all peoples under colonial and racist régimes and other forms of alien domination and the legitimacy of their struggle, in par-

*G.A.O.R. Supp. No. 28 (Algo 28) (xxviii) (1973).

564

ticular the struggle of national liberation movements, in accordance with the purposes and principles of the Charter and the relevant resolutions of the organs of the United Nations;

(4) Acts of violence committed by individuals or groups of individuals for private gain, the effects of which are not confined to one State.

2. Draft Proposal Submitted by France

A heinous act of barbarism committed in the territory of a third State by a foreigner against a person possessing a nationality other than that of the offender for the purpose of exerting pressure in a conflict not strictly internal in nature.

3. Contribution of Greece to the Search for a Description of the So-called "International Terrorism" Problem

1. This is a serious and dangerous problem, manifested in reprehensible and particularly inadmissible acts which evoke revulsion in the conscience of mankind (however noble may be, in the case in question, the cause in furtherance of which the said acts were attempted or committed).

2. The fact that this problem is tending to become more widespread has, in the final analysis, a detrimental effect on the normal and friendly development of international relations. It must therefore be prevented and, where possible, eliminated by the application at the international level of appropriate judicial measures approved by the international community, and of the general principle of law *aut dedere aut judicare*.

3. The (constant, continuing, recognized and legitima) struggle of the people in its own territory aimed at:

(a) The achievement of its self-determination and independence;

(b) Its liberation from a foreign occupation which exploits it, oppresses it and deprives it of its sovereignty;

(c) Its liberation from the colonial yoke;

(d) The elimination of all forms of social, racial or other discrimination of which it is the principal victim;

(e) Defence against any form of aggression or attack (whether direct or indirect) against its territory, by violent means, and the prevention of any foreign instigated subversive activity directed against the integrity and sovereignty of its country is not included in this context and can never be interpreted or considered as forming part of it.

4. Any other violent act of a criminal nature by an individual or group of individuals against any innocent person or group of persons, irrespective of the nationality of the author or authors, which is committed in the territory of a third State with the aim of exercising pressure in any dispute, or with the aim of obtaining personal gain or emotional satisfaction, shall be deemed to be an "act of international terrorism" and condemned as such by the conscience of mankind.

4. Draft Proposal Submitted by Haiti

Any threat or act of violence committed by a person or group of persons on foreign territory or in any other place under international jurisdiction against any person with a view to achieving a political objective.

5. Draft Proposal Submitted by Iran

Possible list of acts of terrorism to be considered:

(1) Acts of violence and of terrorism directed against peoples struggling for their right to self-determination or for national identity;

(2) Acts of mercenary groups whose terrorist activities are directed against other sovereign countries;

(3) Act of violence committed by individuals or groups of individuals which endanger or take innocent human lives or endanger fundamental freedoms;

(4) Acts of violence directed against persons who ought to enjoy special protection from the States in which they are performing their functions.

6. Submission of Nigeria

The Nigerian delegation is of the opinion that acts such as the recent Portuguese massacre, the kidnapping of diplomats attending a cocktail party and their subsequent murder, hijacking of aircrafts or even the holding at bay innocent tourists in a hotel lobby with the muzzles of sub-machine guns pointing at them— all constitute some forms of international terrorism. These acts do *not* include the activities, within their own countries, of those peoples struggling to liberate themselves from foreign oppression and exploitation.

7. Draft Proposal Submitted by Venezuela

Any threat or act of violence which endangers or takes innocent human lives, or jeopardizes fundamental freedoms, committed by an individual or group of individuals on foreign territory, on the high seas or on board an aircraft in flight in the air space superjacent to the open or free seas for the purpose of instilling terror and designed to achieve a political goal.

Inhuman repressive measures carried out by colonial or racist régimes, and all measures conducive to the exercise of alien domination, in denying peoples their legitimate right to self-determination and independence and other human rights and fundamental freedoms, shall also be deemed to be acts of international terrorism.

Serious bodily harm, murder, the taking of hostages, kidnapping, the sending of letter-bombs and damage to objects and property, when committed in foreign territory, or by or against foreigners, for the purpose of instilling terror with a view to achieving a political objective, shall also be deemed to be acts of international terrorism, since they constitute offences against social morality and violations of the dignity of the human person.

B. SUB-COMMITTEE OF THE WHOLE ON THE UNDERLYING CAUSES OF INTERNATIONAL TERRORISM

Suggestion Submitted by Algeria

Since terrorism is an extreme form of violence, its causes are those which provoke the use of violence. Violence becomes terrorism when situations which lead to violence are exacerbated.

I. *Individual Terrorism*

The motivation of "individual terrorism" is a subject for study in sociology, psychology, genetics and other contemporary human sciences.

Its study is not within the terms of reference of the *Ad Hoc* Committee.

II. *Political Terrorism*

A. *State terrorism*

1. It takes the form of mass imprisonments, the use of torture, the massacre of whole groups, widespread reprisals, the bombing of a civilian population, the use of defoliants, the destruction of the economic structures of a country, etc.

2. States resort to violence and terrorism:

(a) When they want to break the will of a people in order to impose direct rule, to subject them to a policy or to use their territory and resources for purposes contrary to that people's interests;

(b) When they practice a policy of expansionism and egemony.

3. These factors are present in many situations affecting the international community, including:

(a) The maintenance of colonial domination;

(b) Foreign occupation of a territory whose population is forced to leave it;

(c) Application of a policy of racial discrimination and *apartheid;*

(d) "Punitive" aggression of a State against another country;

(e) Foreign intervention in the policy of a country;

(f) Foreign exploitation of the natural resources of a country;

(g) Systematic destruction by a foreign Power of a country, its population, its flora and fauna, its means of transport, its economic structures, etc.;

(h) Use of armed force by a State against another State in circumstances other than those laid down in international law defining a state of war.

B. *Terrorism directed against States*

1. A social group (or a population) resorts to terrorism and

violence against a State:

(a) When their rights are flouted;

(b) When they are victims of political, social or economic injustice;

(c) When all legal remedies for obtaining justice are of no avail.

2. The violence is then used against the State in question:

(a) On the territory occupied by the social group (or population) ;

(b) On the territory of the State against which the violence is directed;

(c) Against any other country which provides assistance to the State in question in its harmful action against the social group (or population) .

3. The situations which give rise to violent action against a State include:

(a) Subjecting a people to colonial domination;

(b) Expelling a population from its own territory;

(c) Applying a policy of racial discrimination and *apartheid;*

(d) Foreign intervention in the policy of a country;

(e) Foreign exploitation of the resources of a country;

(f) Foreign aggression against a country;

(g) Indifference of the foreign community towards the injustice being visited upon a population;

(h) Powerlessness of international organizations to restore the legitimate rights of a population.

C. SUB-COMMITTEE OF THE WHOLE ON THE MEASURES FOR THE PREVENTION OF INTERNATIONAL TERRORISM

1. Draft Proposal Submitted by the Non-Aligned Group in the *Ad Hoc* Committee (Alberia, Congo, Democratic Yemen, Guinea, India, Mauritania, Nigeria, Syrian Arab Republic, Tunisia, United Republic of Tanzania, Yemen, Yugoslavia, Zaire and Zambia)

The following measures against international terrorism could be recommended:

(a) The definitive elimination of situations of colonial domination;

(b) Intensification of the campaign against racial discrimination and *apartheid;*

(c) The settlement of situations of foreign occupation and restoration of their territory to populations who have been expelled from them;

(d) Prohibition of all material, military, financial, economic, diplomatic and other aid to any State which practises a policy of colonialism, racial discrimination or territorial usurpation;

(e) Application of the provisions of Chapter VII of the United Nations Charter to those colonialist, racist and alien régimes which contravene international law or which refuse to implement the resolutions of international organizations and of the Security Council in particular;

(f) The strengthening of international organizations and of their efforts to secure effective application of the principles of the Charter in international relations;

(g) Representation in international organizations, as full members, of peoples under colonial domination or whose territory is under foreign occupation;

(h) Condemnation of the continuation of repressive and terrorist acts by colonial racist and alien régimes in denying peoples their legitimate right to self-determination and independence and other human rights and fundamental freedoms, and of all acts of violence which endanger or take innocent human lives;

(i) Taking all appropriate measures by States at the national level for the speedy and final elimination of international terrorism;

(j) Close cooperation between States in order to prevent acts of international terrorism;

(k) Strict implementation of provisions of the Declaration on Principles of International Law concerning Friendly Relations and Cooperation among States in accordance with the Charter of the United Nations;

(l) Cooperation in elaboration of the new international legal instruments relating to certain aspects of international terrorism not covered by the existing international conventions;

(m) When people engage in violent action against colonialist, racist and alien régimes as part of a struggle to regain its legitimate rights or to redress an injustice of which it is the victim, the international community, when it has recognized the validity of these objectives, cannot take repressive measures against any action which it ought, on the contrary, to encourage, support and defend;

(n) When individuals engage in violent action but their motivation is not of the nature described above, such action should be considered by the international community as coming under the ordinary law of each State concerned.

2. Contribution Submitted by Greece*

Indicative and nonexhaustive list of acts of violence which endanger or take innocent human lives and other reprehensible acts perpetrated in the territory of a third State, in the air space or on the high seas with the object of exerting pressure in a foreign political conflict or for personal profit or emotional satisfaction

1. The hijacking of a civil aircraft or a commercial vessel of any kind.

2. Any act or attempted act endangering the security of a civil aircraft or commercial vessel, the crew thereof and any passengers who may be on board.

3. The damaging or premeditated destruction of foreign property in the air, on the sea or on the ground.

4. The use or threat of force, which engenders fear, terror and panic, this jeopardizing human dignity and the fundamental freedoms of innocent persons.

5. The taking of innocent hostages.

6. The kidnapping and unlawful restraint of persons entitled to international protection and of serving diplomats.

7. The infliction of serious bodily harm on, and the murder

---

*This contribution should be considered in the light of the contribution submitted by Greece to the Sub-Committee of the Whole on the definition of international terrorism.

of, all categories of the aforementioned persons.

8. The premeditated use of explosives and letter-bombs.

9. The premeditated setting on fire of cultural centres, industrial installations, commercial and professional buildings and of official or private residences.

10. Any act of sabotage directed against public installations.

3. Submission of Nigeria

1. The draft convention submitted by the United States should be further elaborated to take into consideration:

(a) State terrorism;

(b) The adequacy of municipal laws to deal with such crimes enumerated in article 1 of the draft convention;

(c) Criminal acts the purposes of which *do not* lie in frustration, injustice, racism, occupation and foreign domination;

(d) The draft should contain an exemption clause to cover liberation movements within their territories.

2. The Nigerian delegation, for the time being, thinks that the proposals put forward by the United Kingdom, with some amendments, would meet its views, as embodied in its submissions to the Secretary-General. The Nigerian delegation would find it difficult to accept items 1 and 2 of the United Kingdom proposals without some modifications which would exclude all activities done in aid of or by liberation movements within their territories. It also notices the word "suppression" in item 7 of the United Kingdom proposal. The Nigerian delegation would prefer the word "prevention."

4. Draft Proposal Submitted by the United Kingdom of Great Britain and Northern Ireland

The *Ad Hoc* Committee on International Terrorism recommends to the General Assembly that the General Assembly should:

1. Condemn all acts of violence which endanger or take innocent human lives;

2. Recall the duty of States to refrain from organizing, insti-

gating, assisting or participating in acts of civil strife or terrorist acts in another State or acquiescing in organized activities within its territory directed towards the commission of such acts;

3. Urge States to strengthen and make more effective their existing national measures to combat international terrorism;

4. Encourage States to cooperate more closely with one another in order to strengthen and make more effective their existing national measures to combat international terrorism;

5. Encourage other organs of the United Nations system concerned with aspects of the problem of international terrorism to intensify their efforts towards a solution of that problem;

6. Invite States to become parties to the existing international conventions which relate to various aspects of the problem of international terrorism;

7. Elaborate and adopt as a matter of priority an international convention for the suppression of certain acts of international terrorism, based, *inter alia,* on the principle that a State should either extradite the offender or submit his case for prosecution and on relevant conventions and draft conventions already adopted or in the course of elaboration within the United Nations system.

5. Working Paper Submitted by the United States of America

DRAFT CONVENTION FOR THE PREVENTION AND PUNISHMENT OF CERTAIN ACTS OF INTERNATIONAL TERRORISM*

The States Parties to this Convention,

Recalling General Assembly resolution 2625 (XXV) of October 24, 1970, proclaiming principles of international law concerning friendly relations and cooperation among States in accordance with the Charter of the United Nations,

Considering that this resolution provides that every State has the duty to refrain from organizing, instigating, assisting or participating in terrorist acts in another State or acquiescing in organized activities within its territory directed towards the commission of such acts,

*See *supra* Appendix R, p. 557.

Considering the common danger posed by the spread of terrorist acts across national boundaries,

Considering that civilians must be protected from terrorist acts,

Affirming that effective measures to control international terrorism are urgently needed and require international as well as national action,

Have agreed as follows:

Article 1

1. Any person who unlawfully kills, causes serious bodily harm or kidnaps another person, attempts to commit any such act, or participates as an accomplice of a person who commits or attempts to commit any such act, commits an offence of international significance if the act

(a) Is committed or takes effect outside the territory of a State of which the alleged offender is a national;

(b) Is committed or takes effect

  (i) Outside the territory of the State against which the act is directed, or

  (ii) Within the territory of the State against which the act is directed and the alleged offender knows or has reason to know that a person against whom the act is directed is not a national of that State;

(c) Is committed neither by nor against a member of the armed forces of a State in the course of military hostilities;

(d) Is intended to damage the interests of or obtain concessions from a State or an international organization.

2. For the purposes of this Convention:

(a) An "international organization" means an international intergovernmental organization;

(b) An "alleged offender" means a person as to whom there are grounds to believe that he has committed one or more of the offenses of international significance set forth in this article;

(c) The "territory" of a State includes all territory under the jurisdiction or administration of the State.

Article 2

Each State Party undertakes to make the offences set forth in article 1 punishable by severe penalties.

Article 3

A State Party in whose territory an alleged offender is found shall, if it does not extradite him, submit, without exception whatsoever and without undue delay, the case to its competent authorities for the purpose of prosecution, through proceedings in accordance with the laws of that State.

Article 4

1. Each State Party shall take such measures as may be necessary to establish its jurisdiction over the offenses set forth in article 1:

(a) When the offense is committed in its territory; or

(b) When the offense is committed by its national.

2. Each State Party shall likewise take such measures as may be necessary to establish its jurisdiction over the offenses set forth in article 1 in the case where an alleged offender is present in its territory and the State does not extradite him to any of the States mentioned in paragraph 1 of this article.

3. This Convention does not exclude any criminal jurisdiction exercised in accordance with national law.

Article 5

A State Party in which one or more of the offenses set forth in article I have been committed shall, if it has reason to believe an alleged offender has fled from its territory, communicate to all other States Parties all the pertinent facts regarding the offense committed and all available information regarding the identity of the alleged offender.

Article 6

1. The State Party in whose terrritory an alleged offender is found shall take appropriate measures under its internal law so as to ensure his presence for prosecution or extradition. Such measures shall be immediately notified to the States mentioned in article 4, paragraph 1, and all other interested States.

2. Any person regarding whom the measures referred to in paragraph 1 of this article are being taken shall be entitled to communicate immediately with the nearest appropriate representative of the State of which he is a national and to be visited by a representative of that State.

Article 7

1. To the extent that the offenses set forth in article 1 are not listed as extraditable offenses in any extradition treaty existing between States Parties they shall be deemed to have been included as such therein. States Parties undertake to include those offenses as extraditable offenses in every future extradition treaty to be concluded between them.

2. If a State Party which makes extradition conditional on the existence of a treaty receives a request for extradition from another State Party with which it has no extradition treaty, it may, if it decides to extradite, consider the present articles as the legal basis for extradition in respect of the offenses. Extradition shall be subject to the provisions of the law of the requested State.

3. States Parties which do not make extradition conditional upon the existence of a treaty shall recognize the offenses as extraditable offenses between themselves subject to the provisions of the law of the requested State.

4. Each of the offenses shall be treated, for the purpose of extradition between States Parties as if it has been committed not only in the place in which it occurred but also in the territories of the States required to establish their jurisdiction in accordance with article 4, paragraph 1 (b).

5. An extradition request from the State in which the offenses were committed shall have priority over other such requests if received by the State Party in whose territory the alleged offender has been found within 30 days after the communication required under paragraph 1 of article 6 has been made.

Article 8

Any person regarding whom proceedings are being carried out in connection with any of the offenses set forth in article 1 shall be guaranteed fair treatment at all stages of the proceedings.

Article 9

The statutory limitation as to the time within which prosecution may be instituted for the offenses set forth in article 1 shall be, in each State Party, that fixed for the most serious crimes under its internal law.

Article 10

1. States Parties shall, in accordance with international and national law, endeavor to take all practicable measures for the purpose of preventing the offenses set forth in article 1.

2. Any State Party having reason to believe that one of the offenses set forth in article 1 may be committed shall, in accordance with its national law, furnish any relevant information in its possession to those States which it believes would be the States mentioned in article 4, paragraph 1, if any such offense were committed.

Article 11

1. States Parties shall afford one another the greatest measure of assistance in connection with criminal proceedings brought in respect of the offenses set forth in article 1, including the supply of all evidence at their disposal necessary for the proceedings.

2. The provisions of paragraph 1 of this article shall not affect obligations concerning mutual assistance embodied in any other treaty.

Article 12

States Parties shall consult together for the purpose of considering and implementing such other cooperative measures as may seem useful for carrying out the purposes of this Convention.

Article 13

In any case in which one or more of the Geneva Convention of August 12, 1949, or any other convention concerning the law of armed conflicts is applicable, such convention shall, if in conflict with any provision of this Convention, take precedence. In particular:

(a) Nothing in this Convention shall make an offense of any act which is permissible under the Geneva Convention Relative to the Protection of Civilian Persons in Time of War or any other international law applicable in armed conflicts;

(b) Nothing in this Convention shall deprive any person of prisoner of war status if entitled to such status under the Geneva Convention Relative to the Treatment of Prisoners of War or any other applicable convention concerning respect for human rights in armed conflicts.

Article 14

In any case in which the Convention on Offences and Certain Other Acts Committed on Board Aircraft, the Convention for the Suppression of Unlawful Seizure of Aircraft, the Convention for the Suppression of Unlawful Acts Against the Safety of Civil Aviation, the Convention to Prevent and Punish the Acts of Terrorism Taking the Form of Crimes Against Persons and Related Extortion that are of International Significance, or any other convention which has or may be concluded concerning the protection of civil aviation, diplomatic agents and other internationally protected persons, is applicable, such convention shall, if in conflict with any provision of this Convention, take precedence.

Article 15

Nothing in this Convention shall derogate from any obligations of the Parties under the United Nations Charter.

Article 16

1. Any dispute between the Parties arising out of the application or interpretation of the present articles that is not settled through negotiation may be brought by any State Party to the dispute before a Conciliation Commission to be constituted in accordance with the provisions of this article by the giving of written notice to the other State or States Party to the dispute and to the Secretary-General of the United Nations.

2. Conciliation Commission will be composed of their members. One member shall be appointed by each party to the dispute.

If there is more than one party on either side of the dispute they shall jointly appoint a member of the Conciliation Commission. These two appointments shall be made within two months of the written notice referred to in paragraph 1. The third member, the Chairman, shall be chosen by the other two members.

3. If either side has failed to appoint its members within the time-limit referred to in paragraph 2, the Secretary-General of the United Nations shall appoint such members within a further period of two months. If no agreement is reached on the choice of the Chairman within five months of the written notice referred to in paragraph 1, the Secretary-General shall within the further period of one month appoint as the Chairman a qualified jurist who is not a national of any State Party to the dispute.

4. Any vacancy shall be filled in the same manner as the original appointment was made.

5. The Commission shall establish its own rules of procedure and shall reach its decisions and recommendations by a majority vote. It shall be competent to ask any organ that is authorized by or in accordance with the Charter of the United Nations to request an advisory opinion from the International Court of Justice to make such a request regarding the interpretation or application of the present articles.

6. If the Commission is unable to obtain an agreement among the parties on a settlement of the dispute within six months of its initial meeting, it shall prepare as soon as possible a report of its proceedings and transmit it to the parties and to the depositary. The report shall include the Commission's conclusions upon the facts and questions of law and the recommendations it has submitted to the parties in order to facilitate a settlement of the dispute. The six-months time-limit may be extended by decision of the Commission.

7. This article is without prejudice to provisions concerning the settlement of disputes contained in international agreements in force between States.

6. Draft Proposals Submitted by Uruguay

(a) *Draft resolution*
The General Assembly,

Considering the increase in terrorist acts, the seriousness of which is a source of concern to the international community, since they generate a climate of violence which may affect security and peace,

Bearing in mind especially international terrorist activity aimed at the kidnapping and assassination of persons, the taking of hostages, and the extortion connected with such acts,

Recognizing the disapproval expressed by States Members of the United Nations of resort to such ruthless acts which take a toll of innocent lives and violate the essential rights of the human person,

Convinced that the political and ideological pretexts involved to justify these crimes in no way diminish their cruelty or irrationality or the infamous means employed,

Bearing in mind the acts of terrorism which are committed to repress the legitimate struggle of liberation movements in defense of their inalienable rights,

Recognizing that the cooperation of States is essential in order to prevent and eliminate international terrorism and its causes, through both the adoption of internal legal measures and the fulfilment of obligations under the Charter of the United Nations and the relevant resolutions of the Organization and its organs.

Convinced that the proliferation of acts of international terrorism calls for prompt and effective measures to counteract this scourge,

Recalling resolutions 380 (V) of November 17, 1950, 2131 (XX) of December 22, 1965, 2225 (XXI) of December 19, 1966 and 2625 (XXV) of October 24, 1970, all of which concern friendly relations and cooperation among States in accordance with the Charter of the United Nations and international law,

1. *Strongly condemns* acts of terrorism which take a toll of innocent lives and in particular the assassination and kidnapping of persons, the taking of hostages and the extortion connected with such crimes, as crimes against humanity;

2. *Condemns* the use of terrorist methods employed by States to combat peoples under colonial and alien domination and their liberation movements;

3. *Reaffirms* the principle of international law that every State has the duty to refrain from acts designed to encourage terrorist activities directed against another State, and to prevent acts by which they may be manifested, by undertaking, in the conditions set forth below, to prevent and punish activities of this kind and to lend each other mutual assistance;

4. *Reaffirms* the principle of nonintervention, according to which no State shall organize, assist, foment, finance, incite or tolerate subversive, terrorist or armed activities directed towards the violent overthrow of the régime of another State, or interfere in civil strife in another State;

5. *Invites* Member States to sign and ratify international instruments relevant to this problem;

6. *Recommends* that the International Law Commission should continue its work in the light of the concrete recommendations received from the *Ad Hoc* Committee on International Terrorism by preparing new international norms capable of combating international terrorism, and submit them to the General Assembly for consideration at its twenty-ninth session.

(b) *Draft decision*
The Ad Hoc Committee on International Terrorism
Decides

1. To submit the above draft resolution to the General Assembly for consideration at its next session.

2. To recommend the General Assembly, in accordance with resolution 2926 (XXVII) of November 28, 1972, to prepare and approve, at its next session, the convention on the prevention and punishment of crimes against diplomatic agents and other internationally protected persons.

3. Further to recommend the General Assembly, in the light of the reports of this Committee, to request the International Law Commission to continue its work by preparing new international norms capable of combating international terrorism and submit them to it for consideration of its twenty-ninth session.

SELECTED BIBLIOGRAPHY

James Murphy

THE FOLLOWING BIBLIOGRAPHY is by no means meant to be an authoritative list of available material on the subjects listed. Rather its purpose is to function as a guide sufficient to serve as an introduction to terrorism and its related problems.

HIJACKING, KIDNAPPING, AND OTHER TERRORIST ACTIVITIES

Anti-soviet zionist terrorism in the U.S. 23 *Current Digest of the Soviet Press,* 1971 6-8, Feb., 1971.

Arab terrorism, 36 *Jewish Frontier* 13-16, Jan., 1969.

Arey, J. A.: *The Sky Pirates.* New York, Scribner, 1972.

Bartos, M.: International terrorism, 23 *Review of International Affairs,* 25-26, April 20, 1972.

Baumann, C. E.: *The Diplomatic Kidnappings: A Revolutionary Tactic of Urban Terrorism.* The Hague Martinus Miyhoff 1973.

Beaton, L.: Crisis in Quebec. *Round Table, 241*:147-152, Jan., 1971.

Brownlie, I.: Interrogation in depth: the compton and parker reports. 35 *Modern Law Review.* 501-7. Sept., 1972.

Burki, S.J.: Social and economic detriments of political violence: a case study of the punjab. 25 *Middle East Journal.* 465-480, Aug. 1971.

Callanan, E. F.: Terror in Venezuela, 1960-1964, 49 *Military Review,* 49-56, Feb., 1969.

Calvert, P.: The diminishing returns of political violence. 56 *New Middle East,* 25-27, May, 1973.

Chaliand, G.: *La Resistance Palestinienne.* Paris, Le Seuil, 1970.

Cohen, G.: *Woman of Violence: Memoirs of a Young Terrorist* (1943-1948). New York, Stanford U. Pr, 1966.

Dallin, A.: *Political Terror In Communist Systems.* Stanford, Jordan, 1970.

Davis, M.: *Jews Fight Too!* New York, Jordan, 1945.

deGramont, A.: How one pleasant, scholarly young man from Brazil became a kidnapping, gun-toting, bombing revolutionary. New York Times Magazine, Nov. 15, 1970.

Eayrs, J.: *Diplomacy and Its Discontents.* Toronto, of Toronto Pr, 1971.

Ferreira, J. C.: *Carlos Marighella.* Havana, Tricontinental 1970.

Fisher, E. M., and Bassiouni, M. C.: *Storm Over the Arab World.* Chicago, Follett, 1972.

Frank, G.: *The Deed: The Assassination In Cairo During World War II of Lord Moyne.* New York, S & S, 1963.

Friedmann, W.: Terrorist and subsersive activities 50 *A.J.I.L.* 475-513, July, 1956.

Friedrich, C. J.: Uses of Terror, 19 Problems of Communism. Nov., 1970, pp. 46-48.

Gann, L. H.: *Guerrillas in History. Stanford,* Hoover Inst, 1971.

Gaucher, R.: *Les Terroristes.* Paris, 1965.

Gerassi, F. (ed.): *Venceremos!* New York, S & S, 1968.

Grivas, G.: *Guerrilla Warfare and EOKA's Struggle.* London, Longman's Ltd., 1964.

Guevara, E.: *Guerrilla Warfare,* New York, Random, 1961.

Hempstone, S.: *Rebels, Mercenaries, and Dividends: The Katanga Story.* New York, Praeger, 1962.

Horowitz, J., de Castro, and Gerassi (eds.): *Latin American Radicalism.* New York, Vintage, 1969.

Hosmer, S. T.: *Viet Cong Repression and Its Implications for the Future.* Lexington, Lexington, 1970.

Horrell, M.: *Terrorism In Southern Africa.* Johannesburg, South African Institute of Race Relations, 1968.

Human rights and Uganda's expulsion of its Asian minority. Demerm *Journal of International Law and Politics,* Spring, 1973, pp. 107-115.

Katz, S.: *Days of Fire—The Secret History of the Irgun Zvai Leumi.* Garden City, Doubleday, 1968.

Khan, M. A.: *Guerrilla Warfare: Its Past, Present and Future.* Karachi, Rangrut, 1960.

Kidnapping Incidents. Bulletin of the International Commission of Jurists, Dec., 1967, pp. 24-33.

Kuriyama, Y.: Terrorism At Tel Aviv airport and a "new left" group in Japan. 13 *Asian Survey,* 336-346, Mar., 1973.

Lawrence, T. E.: *Seven Pillars of Wisdom, A Triumph.* Garden City, Doubleday, 1935.

Lowry, D.: Ill-treatment, brutality, and torture: some thoughts upon the "treatment" of Irish political prisoners. 22 *DePaul Law Review,* 553-581, Spring, 1973.

Mallin, J. (ed.) : *Terror and Urban Guerrillas.* Coral Gables, U of Miami Pr, 1971.

———: Terrorism as a political weapon, 22 *Air Univ. Review,* 45-52, Aug., 1971.

Mardor, M.: *Haganah.* New York, New American Library, 1964.

Marighella, C.: *Minimanual of the Urban Guerrilla.* Havana, Tricontinental 1970.

Means, J.: Political kidnappings and terrorism. *North Am Review, 5.* Winter, 1970.

Meron, T.: Some legal aspects of Arab terrorists claim to privileged combatancy. 40 *Nordisk Tidsakrift for International Ret,* 47-85, 1970.

Moore B.: *Terror and Progress, USSR.* Cambridge, Harvard U Pr, *40:* 1954.

Moss, R.: International terrorism and western societies. 28 *Int'l. Journal,* 418-430, Summer, 1973.

———: *The War For The Cities.* New York, Coward, 1972.

Nekhlek, E. A.: Anatomy of violence: theoretical reflections on palestinian resistance 25 *Middle East Journal,* 180-200, Spring, 1971.

Paret, P., and Shy, J.: *Guerrillas in the 1960's.* New York, Prager, 1962.

Payne, R.: *Zero: The Story of Terrorism.* New York, U. D.y Co., 1950.

Radovanovic, L.: *The Problem of International Terrorism,* 23 *Review of Int'l. Affairs,* 5-20, Oct., 1972.

Rose, T. (ed.): *Violence In America.* New York, Random, 1969.

Russell, C. A., and Hildner, R. E.: Urban insurgency in Latin America: its implications for the future. 22 *Air University Review,* 54-64, Sept.-Oct., 1971.

Saldana, I.: *Le Terrorisme.* 13 *Revue International de droit Penal,* 26-37, 1936.

Schloesing, E.: La Repression Internationale du Terrorisme. 841 *Revue Politque et Parlementaire* 50-61, April, 1973.

Schwarzenberger, G.: Terrorists, Hijackers, Guerrilleros, and Mercenaries. *Current Legal Problems, 24:*257-282, 1971.

Shaffer, H. B.: *Political Terrorism, Editorial Research Reports.* Washington, Congr Quarterly 1970, Vol 1.

Shubber, S.: Aircraft hijacking under The Hague convention 1970—a new regime? 22 *International and Comp. Law Q.,* 687-726, Oct., 1973.

Sperber, M.: Violence from below. *Survey, 18:*189-204, Summer, 1972.

Sponsler, T. H.: International kidnapping. 5 *International Lawyer,* 25-52, 1970.

Standing, P. D.: *Guerrilla Leaders of the World.* London, Cassell, 1913.

Stechel, I.: Terrorist kidnapping of diplomatic personnel. 5 *Cornell J. of Int'l. Law,* 189-217 (1972).

Szabo, M. O.: Political Armies: A historical perspective *Denver J. Int'l. L. & Pol.;* 2, 1972.

Task force on kidnapping. 23 *External Affairs,* 6-11, Jan., 1971.

Taulbee, J. L.: Retaliation and irregular warfare in contemporary international law. 7 *Int'l. Lawyer,* 195-204, Jan., 1973.

Walter, E. V.: *Terror and Resistance: A Study of Political Violence.* New York, Oxford U Pr, 1969.

Wilson, R. D.: *Cordon and Search With the 6th Airborne Division in Palestine.* Aldershot, Gale, 1949.

WARS OF NATIONAL LIBERATION, INSURRECTIONS, REBELLIONS, CIVIL WAR AND COUNTER MEASURES

Abd-el-Krim: *Memoiren: Mein Krieg Gegen Spanien und Frankreich*. Dresden, Reissner, 1927.

Action, L.: *Lectures on the French Revolution (1910)*. New York, Noonday, FS & G, 1959.

Ali, T.: *The New Revolutionaries*. New York, Morrow, 1969.

Bailey, T. A.: *A Diplomatic History of the American People*. New York, Appleton, 1964.

Barnett, D. L., and Harvey, R.: *The Revolution In Angola*. Indianapolis, Bobbs Merrill, 1972.

Bassiouni, M. C.: *The Law of Dissent and Riots*. Springfield, Thomas, 1972.

Bauer, Y.: *From Diplomacy to Resistance: A History of Jewish Palestine 1939-1945*. Philadelphia, Jewish Pubn, 1970.

Bell, J.: *The Secret Army: The IRA, 1916-1970*. New York, John Day Co., 1971.

Bennett, R.: *The Black and Tans*. London, Houghton Mifflin, 1959.

Bloomfield, J.: *Evolution or Revolution? The U.N. and the Problem of Peaceful Territorial Change*. New York, Oxford U Pr, 1957.

Bourguiba, H.: *Introduction To the History of the Nationalist Movement*. Tunis, Ministry of Cultural Affairs. 1969.

von Clausewitz, K.: *On War*. London, Trench, Trubner & Co., Ltd, 1940.

Coogan, T. P.: *The IRA*. New York, Praeger, 1970.

Crozier, B.: *The Rebels: A Study In Postwar Insurrection*. New York, Beacon Pr., 1960.

Debray, Regis: *Revolution In the Revolution?* New York, Mr Pr, 1968.

Dixon, C. A., and Heilbrunn, D.: *Communist Guerrilla Warfare*. New York, Praeger, 1954.

Dougherty, J. E.: The Aswan decision in perspective. 74 *Pol. Science Q.*, 21-45, 1959.

Douglas, W. O.: *Points of Rebellion*. New York, Vintage, 1970.

Downton, J. V.: *Rebel Leadership*. New York, Free Pr, 1973.

Duncan, P.: *South Africa's Rule of Violence*. London, Methuen, 1964.

Falls, C. B.: *The Art of War: From the Age of Napoleon to the Present Day*. London, Oxford U Pr, 1961.

Fanon, F.: *Toward the African Revolution*. New York, Monthly Rev. 1967.

Feit, R.: *Urban Revolt In South Africa*. Evanston, Northwestern U Pr, 1971.

Feldman, H.: *Revolution In Pakistan*. London, Oxford U Pr, 1967.

Galula, D.: *Counterinsurgency Warfare: Theory and Practice*. New York, Praeger, 1964.

Gaspard, J.: The end of the Libyan revolution: what next? *The New Middle East, 24:* June, 1970.

————: The Sudan revolution: why it happened. 11 *The New Middle East,* Aug., 1969.

Gibson, R.: *African Liberation Movements.* London, Oxford U Pr, 1972.

Gillespie, J.: *Algeria: Rebellion and Revolution.* New York, Praeger, 1961.

Gott, R.: *Guerrilla Movements in Latin America.* London, Helson, 1970.

Griffith, J. B.: *Mao Tse-Tung: On Guerrilla Warfare.* New York, Praeger, 1961.

Grundy, K. W.: *Guerrilla Struggle in Africa.* New York, Grossman, 1971.

Hammarskjold Forum: Expansion of the Viet Nam war into Cambodia—the legal issues. 45 *New York U. Law Review,* June, 1970.

Haskins, J.: *Revolutionaries: Agents of Change.* Philadelphia, Lippincott, 1971.

Hennessy, M. N.: *The Congo: A Brief History and Appraisal.* London, Pall Mall, 1961.

Huberman, L., and Sweezy, P. M. (eds.): *Regis Debray and the Latin American Revolution.* New York, Monthly Rev, 1968.

Hurewitz, J. C.: *Middle East Politics: The Military Dimension.* New York, Praeger, 1969.

Jackson, G.: *The Spanish Civil War: Domestic Crisis or International Conspiracy.* Boston, Heath, 1967.

———— (ed.): *The Spanish Civil War.* Chicago, Quadrangle, 1970.

James, C. L. R.: *The Black Jacobins: Toussaint L'Overture and the San Domingo Revolution.* New York, Vintage, 1963.

Kosut, H. (ed.): *Cyprus, 1946-1948.* New York, Facts on File, 1970.

Lenin, V. I.: *State and Revolution.* New York, Vanguard, 1932.

McCuen, J. J.: *The Art of Counter-Revolutionary War.* Harrisburg, Stackpole, 1966.

Marcuse, H.: *Counterrevolution and Revolt.* Boston, Beacon Pr, 1972.

Marek, F.: *Philosophy of World Revolution.* New York, Int Publ Co., 1969.

May, E. R.: *Imperial Democracy.* New York, Harcourt, Brace & World, 1961.

Meyer, K. E., and Szulc, T.: *The Cuban Invasion: The Chronicle of a Disaster.* New York, Praeger. 1962.

Mirsky, G.: Israeli aggression and Arab unity. 28 *New Times,* July 12, 1967.

Molnar, T. S.: *The Counter Revolution.* New York, Funk & W., 1969.

Myers, J. J.: *The Revolutionists.* New York, Washington Sq Pr, 1971.

Naegelen, M. F.: *La Revolution Assassinee, Hongre, October-November, 1956.* Paris, 1966.

Nelson, T. J.: *The Right of Revolution.* Boston, Beacon Pr. 1968.

Neumann, S.: The structure and strategy of revolution: 1848 and 1948. *Journal of Politics,* August, 1949.

Nighewonger, W. A.: *Rural Pacification In Viet Nam.* New York, Praeger, 1966.

Nkrumah, K.: *Handbook of Revolutionary Warfare.* London, Panaf Books Ltd. 1969.

O'Ballance, E.: *The Algerian Insurrection, 1954-1962*. Hamden, Shoestring, 1967.

——: *The Arab-Israeli War, 1948*. New York, Praeger, 1951.

——: *The Kurdish Revolt, 1961-1970*. Hamden, Archon. Shoe String.

——: *The Indo-China War 1945-1954: A Study in Guerrilla Warfare*. London, Faber and Faber, 1964.

O'Sullivan, P. M.: *Patriot Graves: Resistance in Ireland*. Chicago, Follett, 1972.

Palmer, R. R.: *The Age of Democratic Revolution: A Political History of Europe and America, 1760-1800. The Struggle*. Princeton, Princeton U Pr, 1964.

Peterson, R. W. (ed.): *South Africa & Apartheid*. New York, Facts of Life, 1971.

Pike, D.: Vietcong: *The Organization and Techniques of the National Liberation Front of South Vietnam*. New York, Center for International Studies, 1966.

Puzzo, D. A.: *Spain and the Great Powers, 1936-1941*. New York, Columbia U Pr. 1962.

Ransom, H. R.: *Central Intelligence and National Security*. New York, Harvard U Pr, 1958.

Robertson, D. W.: Debate among American International lawyers about the Vietnam War. 46 *Texas Law Review*, July, 1968.

Roy, J.: *The War In Algeria*. New York, Grove, 1961.

Safran, N.: *From War to War*. New York, Pegasus. 1969.

Schmidt, D. A.: *Yemen: The Unknown War*. London, Bodley Head, 1968.

Schwab, P. (ed.): *Biafra*. New York, Facts on File, 1971.

Schwab, P., and Frangos, G. D. (eds.): *Greece Under the Junta*. New York, Facts on File, 1970.

Sharabi, H.: *Nationalism and Revolution In the Arab World*. Princeton, Van Nostrand, 1966.

——: *Palestine and Israel: The Lethal Dilemma*. New York, Pegasus, 1969.

Simoniza, N. A.: On the character of the National Liberation Revolution. *Narody Azii i Afriki, 6:* 1966.

Sobel, L. A. (ed.): *South Vietnam: U.S.—Communist Confrontation In Southeast Asia*. New York, Facts on File, 1969.

South Vietnamese Refugees: Powers of insurgency. 7 *Journal of Law & Economics*, June, 1972.

Spanier, J. W.: *World Politics In An Age of Revolution*. New York, Praeger, 1967.

Special Operations Research Office. Case Studies In Insurgency and Revolutionary Warfare. 4 Vols. Washington, American University, 1963-4.

Stewart, A. T. Q.: *The Ulster Crisis*. London, Faber and Faber, 1967.

Tanham, G. K.: *Communist Revolutionary Warfare: From the Vietminh to the Viet Cong*. New York, Praeger, 1967.

Thomas, H.: *The Spanish Civil War.* London, Exre & Spottiswoode, Ltd, 1961.

Thompson, R.: *No Exit From Vietnam.* New York, McKay, 1969.

Valeriano, N. D., and Bohannan, C. T. R.: *Counter-Guerrilla Operations: The Phillipine Experience.* New York, Prager, 1962.

Van den Berghe, P. L.: *South Africa: A Study In Conflict.* Middletown, Wesleyan U Pr, 1965.

Waines, D.: *The Unholy War: Israel and Palestine, 1897-1971.* Wilmette, Meding U Pr, International, 1971.

Wolf, E. R.: *Peasant Wars of the Twentieth Century.* New York, Harper, 1969.

Woods, J.: *New Theories of Revolution: A Commentary On the Views of Frantz Fanon, Regis Debray, and Herbert Marcuse.* New York, International Publishers, 1972.

EXTRADITION, EXTRATERRITORIALITY, ASYLUM, AND JURISDICTION

Agrawala, S. K.: *International Law, Indian Courts and Legislation.* Bombay, M U Tripathi, 1965.

Ahluwalia, K.: *The Legal Status, Privileges and Immunities of the United Nations and Certain Other International Organizations.* The Hague, Martinus nijhoff, 1964.

Amerasinghe, C. F.: *State Responsibility For Injury To Aliens.* Oxford, Oxford U Pr, 1967.

Bassiouni, M. C.: *Criminal Law and Its Processes.* Springfield, Thomas, 1970.

——: Ideologically motivated offenses and the political offense exceptions in extradition—a proposed judicial standard for an unruly problem. 19 *DePaul L. R.* 217-259, Winter, 1969.

——: International extradition: an American experience and a proposed formula. *Revue Internationale De Droit Penal,* 3-4, 1968.

——: International extradition in the American practice and world public order. 36 *Tennessee L. R.,* 1969.

——:Self-determination and the Palestinians, 1971 Proc of the Am Society of Int'l L., 65 *A.J.I.L.* 1971.

Bassiouni, M. C., and Nanda, V. P.: *A Treatise On International Criminal Law. Jurisdiction and Cooperation.* Springfield, Thomas, 1973, Vol. II.

Blix, H.: *The Rights of Diplomatic Missions and Consulates to Communicate With Authorities of the Host Country.* Sweden, Almquist & Wiksell, 1964.

Cardozo, M. H.: When extradition fails, is abduction and solution. 55 *A.J.I.L.,* 127-135, 1961.

Collins, E.: *International Law In A Changing World.* New York, Random House, 1970.

Delaume, G. R.: Jurisdiction over crimes committed abroad: French and

American law. *George Washington L.R.* 173-196 (1952).

Evans, A. E.: Reflections upon the political offense in international practice. 57 *A.J.I.L.*, 1963.

Friedmann, W., Lissitzyn, O.J., and Pugh, R. C.: *Cases and Materials On International Law.* St. Paul, West, 1969.

Garcia-Mora, M. R.: Crimes against humanity and the principle of non-extradition of political offenders, *Michigan Law Review, 62:*927-960, 1964.

———: Criminal jurisdiction over foreigners for treason and offenses against the safety of the state committed upon foreign territory, 19 *U of Pittsburg L.R.*, 567-590, 1958.

Garcia-Mora, M. R.: *International Law and Asylum As a Human Right.* Washington, Pub Aff Pr, 1956.

———: *International Responsibility For Hostile Acts of Private Persons Against Foreign States.* The Hague, Martinus Nijhoff, 1962.

———: The nature of political offenses: a knotty problem of extradition law, 48 *Virginia L.R.*, 1226-1257, 1962.

———: The present status of political offenses in the law of extradition and asylum, 14 *U. of Pittsburg L.R.*, 371-396, 1953.

Gutteridge, J. A. C.: The notion of political offenses and the law of extradition, 31 *Brit. Y.B. Int'l.*, 1954.

Hill, C.: Sanctions constraining diplomatic representatives to abide by the local law, 25 *A.J.I.L.*, 1931.

Hirsch, A. I. and Fuller, D. O.: Aircraft piracy and extradition, 16 *N.Y. Law Forum,* 1970.

Jenks, C. W.: *International Immunities.* New York, Oceana, 1961.

Joseph, C.: *Nationality and Diplomatic Protection.* Leyden, A.W. Sijth Off, 1969.

Lauterpacht, H.: Allegiance, diplomatic protection and criminal jurisdiction over aliens. *Q Cambridge L.J.*, 330-348, 1946.

———: Revolutionary activities by private persons against foreign states, 22 *A.J.I.L.*, 1928.

Leigh, G. I. F.: Nationality and diplomatic protection, 20 *Int'l. and Comp. L. Q.*, 453-475, July, 1971.

Michaels, D. B.: *International Privileges and Immunities.* The Hague, Martinus Nijhoff, 1971.

Naijar, M. G. K.: The right of asylum in international law: its status and prospects, 17 *St. Louis L.J.*, 17-46, Fall, 1972.

Nanda, V. P.: Self-determination in international law, 66 *A.J.I.L.*, 1972.

Rafuse, R. W.: *The Extradition of Nationals.* Urbana, U of Ill Pr, 1939.

Ronning, C. N.: *Diplomatic Asylum.* The Hague, Martinu Nijhoff, 1965.

Sareen, C. L.: *Bid For Freedom: USSR v. Tarasov.* Engelwood Cliffs, P-H,: 1966.

Shearer, I. A.: *Extradition In International Law.* Manchester, Manchester U Pr, 1971.

Sponsler, T. H.: Universality principle of jurisdiction and the threatened trials of American airmen, 15 *Loyola L.R.*, 1968-1969.

Staal, R.: The protective principle in extraterritorial civil jurisdiction. *U. of Minnesota L.R.*, 428-433, 1961.

Stewart, I.: *Consular Privileges and Immunities.* New York, Ams Pr, 1968.

Van Panhuys: In the borderland between the art of state doctrine and questions of jurisdictional immunities, 13 *Int'l. & Comp. L. Q.*, 1964.

Von Glahn, G.: *Law Among Nations.* Toronto, MacMillan, *13:* 1970.

Wilson, C. E.: *Diplomatic Privileges and Immunities.* Tucson, U. of Ariz Pr, 1967.

Wood, J. R., and Serres, J.: *Diplomatic Ceremonial and Protocol.* New York, Columbia U Pr, 1970.

INTERNATIONAL CONTROL AND REGULATION OF TERRORISM

Books and Periodicals, General

Antiskyjacking System: A matter of search—or seizure. *48 Notre Dame Lawyer,* 1261-80, June, 1973.

Bassiouni, M. C. (ed.) : International criminal law. *2 Law In American Society,* No. 3, Oct., 1973.

—— (ed.): *The Law of Dissent and Riots.* Springfield, 1971.

Bassiouni, M. C., and Nanda, V. P., (eds.): *A Treatise On International Criminal Law:—Crimes and Punishment.* Springfield, Thomas, 1973, Vol. 1.

Brach, R. S.: The inter-American convention on the kidnapping of diplomats. *10 Columbia J of Transnational L,* 392-412, Fall, 1971.

Cahier, P., and Lee, L. T.: *Vienna Convention On Diplomatic and Consular Relations.* New York, Canegie Endow, 1969.

Dunn, F. S.: *The Protection of Nationals: A Study In the Application of International Law.* Baltimore, Johns Hopkins, 1932.

Evans, A. E.: Aircraft hijacking: what is being done. *67 A.J.I.L.,* 641-671, Oct., 1973.

Ferencz, B. B.: War crimes law and the Vietnam war. *17 Am U.L.R.,* June, 1968.

Franklin, W. M.: *Protection of Foreign Interests.* New York, Greenwood, 1969.

Garcia-Mora, M. R.: The crimes against peace. *34 Fordham L. R.,* 1-22, 1965.

Gottlieb, G. A.: International assistance to civilian populations in armed conflicts. *N.Y.U. J of Int'l L and Politics,* Winter, 1971.

Hewitt, W. E.: Respect for human rights in armed conflicts. *4 N.Y.U. J. of Int'l. L. & Pol.,* Sp., 1971.

Loy, F. E.: Some international approaches to dealing with hijacking of aircraft. *4 Int'l. Lawyer,* April, 1970.

McDougal, M., and Lasswell, H.: The identification and appraisal of diverse systems of public order. *53 A.J.I.L.,* 1959.

Pella, V. V.: La Repression Du Terrorisme et La Creation d'une Cour Internationale, 5-6 Nouvelle Revue De Droit International Prive 785-810 (5); 120-138 (6) (1939).

Potter, P. B.: Offenses against the peace and security of mankind. *46 A.J.I.L.,* 1952.

Przetacynik, F.: Special protection of diplomatic agents *50 Revue De Droit International, De Sciences Diplomatiques et Politiques,* 270-289, Oct.-Dec., 1972.

Schloesing, E.: La Repression Internationale Du Terrorisme. *841 Revue Politique et Parlementaire,* 50-61, April, 1973.

Searching For Hijackers: Constitutionality, Costs and Alternatives. *40 U. of Chicago L.R.,* Winter, 1973.

Skyjacking: Problems and potential solutions—a symposium. *18 Villanova L.R.,* 985-1085, June, 1973.

Stevenson, J. R.: International law and the export of terrorism. *Record of the Assoc of the Bar of the City of N.Y.,* 716-730, 1972.

Symposium: *Introductional Control of Terrorism. A. Kron L. R.,* 1974.

Symposium on Hijacking. *37 Journal of Air Law,* Spring, 1971.

Taylor, T.: *Neuremberg and Vietnam: An American Tragedy.* New York, Quadrangle, 1970.

Taulbee, J. L.: Retaliation and irregular warfare in contemporary international law. *7 Int'l. Lawyer,* 195-204, Jan., 1973.

Thomas, C. S., and Kirby, M. J.: Convention for the suppression of unlawful acts against the safety of civil aviation. *22 Int'l. and Comp. L.Q.,* June, 1973.

Tiewul, S. A.: Terrorism: A step towards international control. *14 Harvard International Law Journal,* 585-595, Summer, 1973.

Tran Tam: Terrorisme et le Droit Penal International Contemporian *45 Revue De Droit International De Sciences Diplomatiques et Politiques,* 11-25, Jan.-Mar., 1967.

Van Panhuys, A. F.: Aircraft hijacking and international law, *9 Columbia J. of Transnational,* Spring 1970.

Volpe, J. A. and Stewart, J. T.: Aircraft hijacking: some domestic and international responses, *59 Kentucky L.J.* 1970-1971.

Wohl, J.: Responses to terrorism: self defense or reprisal? *12 Int'l Problems* 28-34, June, 1973.

Zivic, J.: The nonaligned and the problem of international terrorism, *24 Review of International Affairs,* Jan., 1973.

SELECTED INTERNATIONAL CONVENTIONS, AGREEMENTS, AND DOCUMENTS ON TERRORISM

Convention For the Suppression of Unlawful Acts Against the Safety of Civil Aviation, Montreal, Sept. 23, 1971. U.N.–A/C. 6/418 Annex 4–Nov. 2, 1972.

Convention For the Suppression of the Unlawful Zeizure of Aircraft, The Hague, Dec. 16, 1970. U.N.–A/C. 6/418 Annex 3–Nov. 2, 1972.

Convention on Offenses and Certain Other Acts Committed on Board Aircraft, Tokyo, Sept. 14, 1963. U.N.–A/C. 6/418 Annex 2–Nov. 2, 1972.

ICAO, The Use of Sanctions to Assure Members Comply with Anti Skyjacking and Conventions, A U.S. Proposal, 1970. L.C. Working Draft N, No. 776, Oct. 9, 1970.

International Law Commission, Draft Articles On the Prevention and Punishment of Crimes Against Diplomatic Agents and Other Internationally Protected Persons, 11 *Int'l Legal Materials—Curr Documents*, Sept., 1972.

I.L.C. Question of the Protection and Inviolability of Diplomatic Agents and Other Persons Entitled to Special Protection Under International Law, 11 *Int'l Legal Materials—Curr Doc*, May, 1972.

League of Nations, Convention for the Creation of An International Criminal Court. Geneva, Nov. 16, 1937.

League of Nations, Convention For the Prevention and Punishment of Terrorism, Geneva November 16, 1937, U.N.–A/C. 6/418 Annex 1–Nov. 2, 1972.

Organization of American States, Convention to Prevent and Punish the Acts of Terrorism Taking the Form of Crimes Against Persons and Related Extortion That Are of International Significance, Washington, Feb. 2, 1971, U.N.–A/C. 6/418 Annex 5–Nov. 2, 1972.

U.N. Analytical Study Prepared By the Secretary-General of Observations of States Submitted In Accordance With General Assembly Resolution 3034 (xxvii), A/Ac. 160/2, June, 1973.

U.N. Causes and Preventions of International Terrorism, A Study. A/C. 6/418/Corr 1/Add 1/, Nov. 2, 1972.

U.N. Comments of Member States On the Question of the Protection and Inviolability of Diplomatic Agents and Other Persons Entitled to Special Protection Under International Law, A/8710/Add. 1, 1972.

U.N. Draft Code of Offenses Against the Peace and Security of Mankind A/2693, 6AOR, 9, Sess. Suppl. 9, Paris, 1954.

U.N. Draft Resolution On Terrorism Submitted by the U.S., A/C. 6/L. 850, Sept. 25, 1972.

U.N. The General Assembly Resolution on Terrorism: The Final Text and Member Votes, A/Res/3034 (XXVII), Dec. 18, 1972.

U.N. Legal Committee's Chairman Reports On Consultations With The Members. A/C. 6/L. 866/Con 1, Nov. 9, 1972.

U.N. Legal Committee report On the Terrorism Issue. A/8069, Dec. 16, 1972.

U.N. Observations of States Submitted In Accordance With General Assembly Resolution 3034 (XXVII), A/Ac. 160/1/add. 1, June, 1973.

U.N. Precedents In the Aborted League of Nations 1937 Treaty Outlawing Terrorism, A/C. 6/418 Annex 1, Nov. 2, 1972.

U.N. A Select Bibliography on Aerial Piracy. List No. 6, Nov. 20, 1972.

U.N. A Select Bibliography on International Terrorism, List No. 5/Rev.1, Oct. 25, 1972.

U.N. State Responsibility to Deter, Prevent or Suppress Skyjacking Activities In Their Territory, 1970. A/Res/2645 (XXV), Nov. 25, 1970.

U.N. Vienna Convention On Diplomatic Relations—Official Records, A/Conf. 20/14/add 1, 1962.

BEHAVIORAL ASPECTS OF TERRORISM, AND PROPAGANDA

Arendt, H.: *On Revolutions.* New York, Viking Pr, 1965.

——: Reflections on violence. *23 J of Int'l Affairs,* 1-35, 1969.

——: Reflections on violence *23 J of Int'l Affairs,* 1-35, 1969.

Bell, J.: *The Myth of the Guerrilla.* New York, Knopf, 1971.

Bienen, H.: *Violence and Social Change.* Chicago, U of Chicago Pr, 1968.

Blanchard, W. H.: *Rousseau and the Spirit of Revolt.* Ann Arbor, U of Michigan Pr, 1967.

Boelcke, W. A. (ed.): The Secret Conferences of Dr. Goebbels; The Nazi Propaganda War 1939-43. New York, Dutton, 1970.

Burke, E.: *Reflections On the Revolution In France.* London, Dent, 1910.

Calvert, P.: *A Study of Revolution.* Oxford, Clarendon Pr. 1970.

Center For Research In Social Systems. Human Factors Considerations of Undergrounds In Insurgencies. Washington, American U. 1966.

Chakhotin, S.: *The Rape of the Masses.* New York, Haskell, 1971.

Coblentz, S. A.: *The Militant Dissenters.* South Brunswick, Barnes, 1970.

Cobo, J.: The Roots of "Violencia," New Times 25-27, Aug. 5, 1970.

Davies, J. C.: *When Men Revolt and Why.* New York, Free Pr. 1971.

Dies, M.: *Martin Dies' Story.* New York, Bookmailer, 1963.

Ellul, J.: *Propaganda: The Formation of Man's Attitude.* New York, Knopf, 1965.

Fanon, F.: *The Wretched of the Earth.* New York, Grove, 1963.

Fay, B.: *The Revolutionary Spirit In France and America.* New York, George Allen & Unwin, Ltd., 1927.

Friedrich, C. J.: *The Pathology of Politics: Violence, Betrayal, Corruption, Secrecy and Propaganda.* New York, Harper & Row, 1972.

Gurr, T. R.: *Why Men Rebel.* Princeton, Princeton U Pr, 1970.

Havighurst, C. C. (ed.): *International Control of Propaganda.* Dobbs Ferry, Oceana, 1967.

Hobsbawm, E. J.: *Primitive Rebels: Studies In Archaic Forms of Social Movements In the 19th and 20th Centuries.* New York, Praeger, 1959.

Lasswell, H. D., and Cleveland, H. (eds.): *The Ethics of Power.* New York, Harper & Brothers, 1962.

Lasswell, H. D., and Lerner, D. (eds.): *World Revolutionary Elites: Studies In Coercive Ideological Movements.* Cambridge, MIT Pr., 1965.

Lasswell, H. D.: *World Revolutionary Propaganda.* Freeport, 1939 Books For Libraries Pr. 1939.

Leiden, C., and Schmitt, K. M. (eds.): *The Politics of Violence.* Englewood Cliffs, P.H., 1968.

Lenin, V. I.: *State and Revolution (1918).* New York, Intl Pub Co, 1932.

Lerner, D. (ed.): *Propaganda In War and Crisis.* New York, Arno, 1972.

Martin, L. J.: *International Propaganda: Its Legal and Diplomatic.* Gloucester, P. Smith, 1969.

Marx, K.: *Revolution and Counter-Revolution.* New York, New York Tribune, 1851.

Murty, B. S.: *Propaganda and World Public Order: The Legal Regulation of the Ideological Instrument of Coercion.* New Haven, Yale U Pr, 1968.

Nomad, M.: *Aspects of Revolt.* New York, Bookman Associated, 1959.

Oppenheimer, M.: *The Urban Guerrilla.* Chicago, Quadrangle, 1969.

Qualter, T. H.: *Propaganda and Psychological Warfare.* New York, Random House, 1962.

Said, A. A., and Collier, D. M.: *Revolutionism.* Boston, Allyn, 1971.

Whitaker, N. G.: *Propaganda and International Relations.* San Francisco, Chandler Pub, 1960.

Wolfenstein, E. V.: *The Revolutionary Personality.* Princeton, Princeton U. U. Pr, 1967.

INTERNATIONAL TERRORISM AND POLITICAL CRIMES

(With 38 Contributors)

Terrorism is a strategy of terror-violence which relies on psychological impact to attain political objectives. Individuals as well as states resort to such means to attain their political goals. Such acts of terror-violence occur almost everywhere in the world with increasing frequency.

The very word is value-laden. Indeed, what is terrorism to some is heroism to others. One objective of this book is to sort out the meanings of the word as to different conflicts and objects. The multidisciplinary approach of this book covers the causes of terrorism and its application: Wars of National Liberation and their regulation are described; individual acts of terror-violence are considered as they most frequently occur in hijacking and kidnapping. A chapter on jurisdiction and extradition stresses the need for stronger cooperation between states. The concluding chapter examines alternative means for international legal controls and outlines proposed plans.

INTERNATIONAL TERRORISM AND POLITICAL CRIMES is the first book published to cover the subject so entirely. Representing over twenty-two countries, many contributors are world renowned experts who have assembled at the International Institute of Advanced Criminal Sciences in Siracuse, Italy, for a two-week study of all facets of this worldwide phenomenon of terrorism and political crimes. U.S. experts have also contributed significantly to this book.

CHARLES C THOMAS • PUBLISHER • SPRINGFIELD • ILLINOIS

INTERNATIONAL

TERRORISM
AND
POLITICAL
CRIMES

Edited by

M. CHERIF BASSIOUNI

LL.B., J.D., LL.M., J.S.D.

Professor of Law
De Paul University
Chicago, Illinois

CHARLES C THOMAS • PUBLISHER • SPRINGFIELD • ILLINOIS